Competing Motivations in Grammar and Usage

Competing Motivations in Grammar and Usage

Edited by
BRIAN MACWHINNEY,
ANDREJ MALCHUKOV, AND
EDITH MORAVCSIK

OXFORD
UNIVERSITY PRESS

OXFORD
UNIVERSITY PRESS

Great Clarendon Street, Oxford OX2 6DP
United Kingdom

Oxford University Press is a department of the University of Oxford.
It furthers the University's objective of excellence in research, scholarship,
and education by publishing worldwide. Oxford is a registered trade mark of
Oxford University Press in the UK and in certain other countries

First Edition published in 2014
Impression: 2

Published in the United States of America by Oxford University Press
198 Madison Avenue, New York, NY 10016, United States of America

British Library Cataloguing in Publication Data
Data available

Library of Congress Control Number: 2014930786

ISBN 978–0–19–870984–8

As printed and bound by
CPI Group (UK) Ltd, Croydon CR0 4YY

Contents

Preface

The chapters in this book form a subset of the papers given at the conference on competing motivations held on November 23–25, 2010 at the Max Planck Institute for Evolutionary Anthropology in Leipzig. We are very grateful for the stimulating, friendly, and comfortable setting that the MPI provided for the meeting. Special thanks are offered to Bernard Comrie, Head of MPI's Department of Linguistics, for his hospitality and support, to Claudia Bavero, who took care of the local arrangements, and to the many volunteers who helped the conference run smoothly.

We are grateful to John Davey, Editor in the Humanities and Social Sciences Department of Oxford University Press, to our in-house Editor Julia Steer, Production Editor Kate Gilks, and our proofreader Michael Janes for their conscientious and friendly assistance, and to the two anonymous reviewers at OUP for their very thorough and insightful comments.

The book has been a team effort: each contributor has provided comments on at least one chapter; we much appreciate all their work. Our special thanks go to Wolfgang U. Dressler, John A. Hawkins, and Fritz Newmeyer, who were instrumental in the formation of the basic concept of the volume.

Flanked by a brief introduction and a concluding chapter, the studies are grouped into three parts: syntax (grammatical relations and word order), morphosyntax, and general issues. Within each part, topically germane papers are next to each other. There are numerous other conceptual connections among the studies but these are too complex to be reflected in a linear arrangement; some of these connections are taken up in the introduction and especially in the concluding chapter.

Brian MacWhinney
Andrej Malchukov
Edith Moravcsik

Notes on contributors

SHANLEY ALLEN is Professor of Psycholinguistics and Language Development at the University of Kaiserslautern (Germany). She has published extensively on the acquisition of argument realization, the acquisition of morphosyntax and narrative by Inuktitut-speaking children, the coordination of speech and gesture in motion events across typologically different languages, and code mixing in bilingual preschool children. She is a series editor of the *Trends in Language Acquisition Research* (TILAR) book series, and is on the Editorial Board of *Bilingualism: Language and Cognition, International Journal of Language Sciences*, and *Journal of Child Language*.

MIRA ARIEL is Professor of Linguistics at Tel Aviv University. Her main research areas are the semantics/pragmatics interface, grammaticization, and reference, which she examines from a discourse point of view, based on corpus data. She is the author of *Accessing NP Antecedents* (Routledge, 1990), *Pragmatics and Grammar* (Cambridge University Press, 2008), *Defining Pragmatics* (Cambridge University Press, 2010) and numerous articles on key issues in pragmatics (types of meanings, reference, givenness marking, scalar quantifiers, and more).

INA BORNKESSEL-SCHLESEWSKY is Professor of Cognitive Neuroscience at the University of South Australia in Adelaide, and Professor of Neurolinguistics at the University of Marburg, Germany. Previously, she was head of the Research Group Neurotypology at the Max Planck Institute for Human Cognitive and Brain Sciences in Leipzig, Germany. She is the author of articles in a range of linguistic, psychological, and neuroscientific journals, including *Psychological Review, Brain Research Reviews, Neuroimage, Cognition*, and *Lingua* and co-author, together with Matthias Schlesewsky, of *Processing Syntax and Morphology: A Neurocognitive Perspective* (Oxford University Press, 2009). Her current research is focused on the development of a neurobiologically and crosslinguistically plausible model of language.

ANGEL CHAN is Assistant Professor at the Department of Chinese and Bilingual Studies of the Hong Kong Polytechnic University. She studies child first and second language acquisition in crosslinguistic and multi-lingual contexts, so far involving Cantonese, Mandarin, Dong, English, and German. Her interests also include cognitive linguistic, typological-functional and processing approaches to the study of language acquisition and child language impairments, clinical linguistics, and the development of speech and language assessment tools in a Chinese context.

SONIA CRISTOFARO is Associate Professor of Linguistics at the University of Pavia, Italy. Her research interests focus on typology and historical linguistics. Her publications include two books: *Subordination* (Oxford University Press, 2003) and *Aspetti sintattici e semantici delle frasi completive in greco antico* (La Nuova Italia, 1996), as well as several scholarly articles published in international journals and volumes.

HELEN DE HOOP is Professor of Theoretical Linguistics at the Radboud University Nijmegen, and the principal investigator of the research group "Grammar and Cognition" at the Centre for Language Studies (CLS) in Nijmegen. This research team pursues both theoretical and applied (experimental) work in syntax, semantics, and pragmatics, focusing on the roles of the speaker and the hearer in communication. Helen de Hoop obtained her PhD degree in Linguistics at the University of Groningen in 1992. In the late 1990s, she was one of the initiators of the Optimality Theoretic approach to semantics. She has co-authored several publications in which Optimality Theory is applied to phenomena in the domain of case, word order, and animacy.

WOLFGANG U. DRESSLER was born in Vienna in 1939 and studied linguistics and classical philology in Vienna, Rome, and Paris, taught at UCLA, OSU, Stanford, Montreal, Pisa, was Professor of Linguistics and department head at the University of Vienna (1971–2008), and is now head of the Working group "Comparative Psycholinguistics" at the Dept. of Linguistics of Vienna University and deputy head of the Institute for Corpus Linguistics and Text Technology of the Austrian Academy of Sciences. Member of several academies and Dr.h.c. of Paris-Sorbonne and Athens, honorary member of the LSA, he has worked on diachrony, text linguistics, pragmatics, phonology, morphology, aphasia, and first language acquisition.

JOHN W. DU BOIS (PhD UC Berkeley, 1981) is Professor of Linguistics at the University of California, Santa Barbara. A specialist in functional linguistics, sociocultural linguistics, and discourse, his work centers on the connection between discourse and grammar. The author of *Competing Motivations* (1985), he has long been interested in how conflicting functional demands result in complex competitions that drive the emergence of grammar as a complex adaptive system, yielding the dramatic typological diversity of the world's languages. Publications include *The Discourse Basis of Ergativity* (1987), *Discourse and Grammar* (2003), *The Stance Triangle* (2007), and *Preferred Argument Structure* (Benjamins, 2003).

ELAINE J. FRANCIS is an Associate Professor in the Department of English and in the Linguistics Program at Purdue University. Her research focuses on the nature of grammatical categories from synchronic and diachronic perspectives, and on the syntactic, semantic, discourse-pragmatic, and psycholinguistic factors that underlie the grammar and usage of complex sentence structures. She is the co-editor, with Laura A. Michaelis, of *Mismatch: Form–Function Incongruity and the Architecture of Grammar* (CSLI, 2003). Her work has appeared in journals such as *Cognitive Linguistics, Journal of Linguistics, Journal of Psycholinguistic Research, Language Sciences,* and *Natural Language and Linguistic Theory.*

JOHN HAIMAN has been teaching general linguistics at Macalester College, Minnesota since 1989. He has done fieldwork on Hua (New Guinea) and Cambodian, and is the author of *Natural Syntax* (1988), *Talk is Cheap* (1998), and other books.

MARTIN HASPELMATH is Senior Scientist at the Max Planck Institute for Evolutionary Anthropology and Honorary Professor at the University of Leipzig. He received his PhD from the Freie Universität Berlin and also spent time in Vienna, Cologne, Buffalo, Moscow, Bamberg, and Pavia in his earlier career. His research interests are primarily in the area of broadly comparative and diachronic morphosyntax (*Indefinite Pronouns*, 1997; *From Space to Time*, 1997; *Understanding Morphology*, 2002) and in language contact (*Loanwords in the World's Languages*, co-edited with Uri Tadmor, 2009). He is one of the editors of Oxford University Press's *World Atlas of Language Structures* (2005) and of the recent *Atlas of Pidgin and Creole Language Structures* (2013).

JOHN A. HAWKINS is Professor of Linguistics at the University of California Davis and Emeritus Professor of English and Applied Linguistics at Cambridge University. He has held previous positions at the University of Southern California, the Max-Planck-Institute for Psycholinguistics in Nijmegen, and the University of Essex, and visiting appointments at institutions including UC Berkeley, the Free University of Berlin, and the Max-Planck-Institute for Evolutionary Anthropology in Leipzig. He has broad interests in the language sciences and has published widely on language typology and universals, efficiency and complexity in language, psycholinguistics, the Germanic language family, and language change.

BERND HEINE is Emeritus Professor at the Institute of African Studies (Institut für Afrikanistik), University of Cologne. He has held visiting professorships in Europe, Eastern Asia (Japan, Korea, China), Australia, Africa (Kenya, South Africa), North America (University of New Mexico, Dartmouth College), and South America (Brazil). His 33 books include *Possession*: *Cognitive Sources, Forces, and Grammaticalization* (Cambridge University Press, 1997); *Auxiliaries: Cognitive Forces and Grammaticalization* (Oxford University Press, 1993); *Cognitive Foundations of Grammar* (Oxford University Press, 1997); with Derek Nurse, *African Languages: An Introduction* (Cambridge University Press, 2000); *A Linguistic Geography of Africa* (Cambridge University Press, 2008); with Tania Kuteva, *World Lexicon of Grammaticalization* (Cambridge University Press, 2002); *Language Contact and Grammatical Change* (Cambridge University Press, 2005); *The Changing Languages of Europe* (Oxford University Press, 2006), and *The Evolution of Grammar* (Oxford University Press, 2007); and with Heiko Narrog as co-editor, *The Oxford Handbook of Linguistic Analysis* (Oxford University Press, 2011).

JOHANNES HELMBRECHT holds a chair in General and Comparative Linguistics at the University of Regensburg, Germany. Major fields of research are East-Caucasian languages spoken in Dagestan and Siouan languages, in particular Hoocąk (Winnebago) still spoken in Wisconsin, USA. During the last few years, he has published several articles on descriptive and typological aspects of Hoocąk and is currently working on a corpus-based grammatical description. Other more theoretical fields of research are the typology and grammaticalization of personal pronouns—in particular politeness distinctions in personal pronouns—and more recently the morphosyntactic coding of proper names in the languages of the world. In addition, Johannes Helmbrecht is involved in the emerging field of language documentation and the study of endangered languages.

MARY HUGHES is currently a Lecturer in Linguistics and Language Acquisition at Boston University. She completed her PhD in 2011 in Applied Linguistics at Boston University. Her dissertation research focused on the interaction of syntactic and discourse-pragmatic effects in the acquisition of reference in an attempt to shed light on the early development of referential choice in dyadic conversation and to determine the extent to which the early acquisition of reference involves rudimentary aspects of Theory of Mind. Her research interests include the integration of competence-based and usage-based linguistic approaches in order to show the range of factors at work in L1 acquisition. As well as presenting her work at international conferences, she has also published findings from her dissertation in current issues of the *Journal of Pragmatics* and *Lingua*. Her other research interests include second language acquisition, multilingualism, and minority language revitalization, with special regard to the acquisition of Irish Gaelic.

GUNTER KALTENBÖCK is Senior Lecturer in the English Department of the University of Vienna. He holds an MA from the University of London and a PhD and postdoctoral thesis (*Habilitation*) from the University of Vienna. He has published numerous book chapters and articles in international journals mainly on cognitive-functional grammar and corpus linguistics, a book on *It-extraposition and non-extraposition in English* with Braumüller and has co-edited three volumes, such as *New Approaches to Hedging* with Emerald.

KATHARINA KORECKY-KRÖLL is a postdoctoral university assistant at the Department of Linguistics of the University of Vienna. Her main research interests are early first and second language acquisition and morphological processing in older children and adults. She has been investigating longitudinal spontaneous speech corpora of young monolingual German-speaking children since 1999, with a focus on noun and adjective morphology. Since 2005, she has also been involved in several online processing experiments. Since 2012, she has been working on the INPUT project that investigates the acquisition of German by monolingual German-speaking children and by bilingual children who have Turkish as their family language and who acquire German in kindergarten.

GRZEGORZ KRAJEWSKI did his PhD on the development of grammar at the University of Manchester in 2008. Between 2004 and 2011, he worked in the Max Planck Child Study Centre and then as a Research Associate in the School of Psychological Sciences at Manchester. In 2012 he moved to Warsaw, Poland, where he works in the Faculty of Psychology at the University of Warsaw and at the Educational Research Institute.

MONIQUE LAMERS is a researcher at the Department of Language and Communication, VU University Amsterdam, The Netherlands. She studied Speech and Language Pathology in Nijmegen (Radboud University Nijmegen, The Netherlands) and Neurolinguistics in Brussels (Vrije Universiteit, Belgium). She carried out her PhD research in Groningen (Rijks Universiteit Groningen, The Netherlands) where she defended her thesis *Sentence processing: using syntactic, semantic and thematic information* in 2001. From 2000 to 2009 she was a postdoctoral researcher in Magdeburg (Germany) and Nijmegen. Making use of temporal (neuroimaging) tools, such as the registration of event related brain potentials (ERPs), she investigated the role of case marking, animacy, and word order in language comprehension and production. In 2009 she received a research grant from the VU University Amsterdam for the project "In search of the referent" to investigate anaphor resolution in written discourse using eye movement registration. In her current position, she combines different techniques to investigate written and spoken language understanding and production in typical and atypical populations including hearing impaired children and adults, and children with Specific Language Impairment or dyslexia.

GARY LIBBEN is Professor (Applied Linguistics and Psychology) and Vice-President Research at Brock University. His research focuses on laboratory investigations of the representation and processing of multimorphemic words in the mind. In this research, he has probed questions of the underlying psychological nature of morphology and morphological ability as well as the ways in which morphological processing varies across populations and languages. Gary Libben is a Fellow of the Royal Society of Canada, former President of the Canadian Linguistics Association, and co-founder (with Gonia Jarema) of the journal *The Mental Lexicon*. He was founding director of the University of Alberta's Centre for Comparative Psycholinguistics and director of *Words in the Mind, Words in the Brain*, a Major Collaborative Research Initiative Project funded by the Social Sciences and Humanities Research Council of Canada.

ELENA LIEVEN's principal areas of research involve usage-based approaches to language development; the emergence and construction of grammar; the relationship between input characteristics and the process of language development; and variation in children's communicative environments, crosslinguistically and cross-culturally. She is Director of the Max Planck Child Study Centre at the University of Manchester and Honorary Senior Scientist at the Max Planck Institute for Evolutionary Anthropology, Leipzig. She was Editor of the *Journal of Child Language* from 1996 to 2005 and President of the International Association for the Study of Child Language from 2008 to 2011.

BRIAN MACWHINNEY is Professor of Psychology, Computational Linguistics, and Modern Languages at Carnegie Mellon University. He has developed a model of first and second language processing and acquisition based on competition between item-based patterns. In 1984, he and Catherine Snow co-founded the CHILDES (Child Language Data Exchange System) Project for the computational study of child language transcript data. He is now extending this system to six additional research areas in the form of the TalkBank Project. MacWhinney's recent work includes studies of online learning of second language vocabulary and grammar, neural network modeling of lexical development, fMRI studies of children with focal brain lesions, and ERP studies of between-language competition. He is also exploring the role of grammatical constructions in the marking of perspective shifting and the construction of mental models in scientific reasoning.

ANDREJ L. MALCHUKOV is a Senior Researcher at the St.-Petersburg Institute for Linguistic Research (Russian Academy of Sciences), currently affiliated as a Visiting Professor to the University of Mainz. Apart from descriptive work on Siberian (in particular, Tungusic) languages, his main research interests lie in the domain of language typology. He has published extensively on the issues of morphosyntactic typology; in particular, he edited *The Oxford Handbook of Case* (together with Andrew Spencer; Oxford University Press, 2009), *Studies in Ditransitive Constructions: A Comparative Handbook* (together with Bernard Comrie and Martin Haspelmath; Mouton de Gruyter, 2010), and *Impersonal Constructions: A Cross-linguistic Perspective* (together with Anna Siewierska; John Benjamins, 2011).

LAURA A. MICHAELIS is a Professor of Linguistics and a Faculty Fellow in the Institute of Cognitive Science at the University of Colorado Boulder. Her research specializations include the interface between discourse pragmatics and constructions, (formalized) Construction Grammar, aspectual meaning, nonstandard syntax, and lexical semantics. She is the author of *Aspectual Grammar and Past-Time Reference* (Routledge; 1998) and *Beyond Alternations: A Constructional Model of the German Applicative Construction* (CSLI; 2001, co-authored with Josef Ruppenhofer). Her work has appeared in the journals *Language*, *Linguistics and Philosophy*, *Journal of Semantics*, and *Studies in Language*, among other outlets. She is currently at work on a book under contract to Oxford University Press, entitled *Syntactic Innovation and Construction Grammar*.

BRITTA MONDORF is Professor of English Linguistics at Mainz University, Germany. She has published in the areas of Grammatical Variation and Cognitive Complexity, Functional Grammar, Historical Linguistics, and Language and Gender. Her current research interests include (de)transitivizing strategies, Support Strategies and the role of language processing in variation and change, morphosyntactic British–American contrast and epistemic grounding in women's and men's use of subordinate clauses.

EDITH MORAVCSIK, a native of Hungary, has worked at various American and European universities including the University of Wisconsin-Milwaukee, where she taught for 33 years. In addition to three textbooks—two on syntax and syntactic theories and one on language typology—she has published articles on language typology and universals, on Hungarian grammar, and on conflict resolution. She has also co-edited a number of books.

FREDERICK J. NEWMEYER is Professor Emeritus at the University of Washington and Adjunct Professor at the University of British Columbia and Simon Fraser University. He is the author of seven books, the editor of eight others, and has published over a hundred articles. Newmeyer is Past President of the Linguistic Society of America and a Fellow of the American Association for the Advancement of Science. His primary linguistic interests are syntax and the history of the field.

CLAIRE NOBLE is a research associate at the Max Planck Child Study Centre in Manchester. Her research focuses on how children learn their first language, specifically how children learn the combinatory rules or grammar of their language.

MARTIN PFEIFFER is a researcher at the German Department at the University of Freiburg. Martin Pfeiffer studied German Linguistics, Cognitive Science, and Romance Philology at the

Universities of Freiburg and Tours. From 2009 to 2012, he held a doctoral scholarship at the Hermann Paul School of Linguistics Basel-Freiburg and in 2010 a DAAD scholarship for a stay as a visiting scholar at the Department of Linguistics at the University of California, Santa Barbara. In 2013, he was a researcher at the Freiburg Institute for Advanced Studies (FRIAS). His research interests include interactional linguistics, conversation analysis, and dialectology.

CAROLINE ROWLAND is Professor of Developmental Psychology at the University of Liverpool. Her research focuses on how children acquire language, with a particular interest in grammar and in assessing how the child's environment promotes and shapes language growth. She is a series editor for the Trends in Language Acquisition (TiLAR) book series and an associate editor for the *Journal of Child Language*.

MATTHIAS SCHLESEWSKY is Professor of General Linguistics at the Johannes Gutenberg-University in Mainz, Germany. He has published widely in the domains of psycholinguistics and neurolinguistics, with a particular focus on word order and the syntax–semantics interface. He is co-editor, with Gisbert Fanselow, Caroline Féry, and Ralf Vogel of *Gradience in Grammar: Generative Perspectives* (Oxford University Press, 2006), and co-author, with Ina Bornkessel-Schlesewsky, of *Processing Syntax and Morphology: A Neurocognitive Perspective* (Oxford University Press, 2009). His current research is focused on the development of a neurobiologically and crosslinguistically plausible model of language.

JAN STRUNK studied linguistics in Bochum and Stanford and is currently a doctoral student with Nikolaus P. Himmelmann in Cologne working on relative clause extraposition in German. He also participates in the DoBeS project "The relative frequencies of nouns, pronouns, and verbs cross-linguistically" at the University of Amsterdam and in the project AUVIS at the University of Cologne. Additional interests include syntactic alternations, corpus linguistics, experimental syntax, sentence boundary detection, and using computational linguistic methods in language documentation and typology.

List of figures and tables

Figures

Tables

List of abbreviations

Except as indicated by asterisks, all terms come from the Leipzig Glossing Rules at http://www.eva.mpg.de/lingua/resources/glossing-rules.php.

1/2/3	first, second, third person
*1sA	first person singular agent marking
*1INC	first person inclusive
*2SG	second person singular
*2SG.HON	(e.g. *vous*)
*A	actor
A	Agent
ABL	ablative
ABS	absolutive
ACC	accusative
ADJ	adjective
ADV	adverb(ial)
ANTIP	antipassive
*AP	adjectival phrase
APPL	applicative
ART	article
AUX	auxiliary
BEN	benefactive
*C	common
CAUS	causative
*CF	counterfactual
*CL	class marker
CLF	classifier
*COLL	collective
COM	comitative
COMP	complementizer
COMPL	completive
*CON	connective
COP	copula
*CSL	cislocative
DAT	dative
DECL	declarative

*DEERG	deergative (detransitivizer)
DEM	demonstrative
DET	determiner
*DIM	diminutive
DIST	distal
DISTR	distributive
*DL	dual
*DP	noun (determiner) phrase
DU	dual
*EMPH	emphasis
*EP	epenthetic vowel
ERG	ergative
EXCL	exclusive
F	feminine
*FAM	familiar
FOC	focus
FUT	future
GEN	genitive
*H	hearer
*HAB	habitual
*HHON	super-honorific
*HON	honorific
*HPL	human plural prefix
*IC	immediate constituent
*IMM	immediate
IMP	imperative
*IMPERS	impersonal
IMPF	imperfect
INCL	inclusive
IND	indicative
*INDEF	indefinite
INF	infinitive
*INSTR	instrumental
INTR	intransitive
IPFV	imperfective
IRR	irrealis
LOC	locative
*LOG	logophoric

M	masculine
*MID	middle (voice)
*MO	motion
*N	noun, nominal expression
NEG	negative
*NFUT	non-future
NMLZ	nominalizer
NOM	nominative
*NONHUM	non-human
*NONPL	non-plural
*NP	noun phrase
*NPST	non-past
*O	object
OBJ	object
OBL	oblique
P	Patient
*PART	participle
PASS	passive
PFV	perfective
PL	plural
*PNCT	punctual
POS	possessive
POSS	possessor
*PP	past perfective
*PP	prepositional phrase
*PRES	present
PRF	perfect
PROG	progressive
PROH	prohibitive
PROX	proximal/proximate
PST	past
*PTCL	particle
*PTCPL	participle
PURP	purposive
Q	question
*R	Recipient
*RC	relative clause
RECP	recipient, reciprocal

REFL	reflexive, reflexive pronoun
REL	relativizer
RES	resultative
*RR	reflexive/reciprocal
*S	speaker
*S	subject
*SEC	secundative
*SENT	sentential
*SFP	sentence final particle
SG	singular
*SRC	source
*SUBJ	subject
*T	second person familiar pronoun (2FAM)
*T	Theme
*TERM	term
TOP	topic
*TP	topic persistence
TR	transitive
U	undergoer
*V	second person polite pronoun (2HON)
*VE	vegetable
VOC	vocative
*VP	verb phrase

1

Introduction

EDITH MORAVCSIK

This volume presents twenty-one studies on competing motivations in language. To our knowledge, this is the first book specifically devoted to the topic. Since the concept of competing motivations is a fundamental issue in all areas of linguistics, we invited contributions from several fields and of various theoretical persuasions. As a result, the chapters vary broadly by general topic such as synchronic grammar, usage, acquisition, and diachrony and extend over many subtopics, for example argument structure, relative clauses, disjunction, and pronouns. They also differ in the theoretical framework assumed—Optimality Theory, the Competition Model, and various approaches to Functional Grammar—and whether they describe competitions within individual languages or across languages.

Below, first the general issue of the analytic framework of competing motivations is presented including an example. Next, a cursory outlook on past research is given followed by brief summaries of the studies in the book.[1]

1.1 Basic issues

In analyzing language, linguists have proposed various generalizations to account for facts about individual languages and about crosslinguistic patterns. Some of these statements are specific to separate constructions and thus their effects are **independent** of each other. For example, rules of relativization in English and terminal devoicing in German apply to distinct sets of data and therefore do not interact.

In other cases, the predictions made by two or more generalizations apply to the same set of data and they **converge**: they make the same predictions. An example is the recent evolution of the indefinite article in Basque. The Basque numeral *bat* 'one' has been attested since the end of the eighteenth century as a marker of specificity. While the process of 'one' evolving into an indefinite article is a well-known instance

[1] I am grateful to Joan Bybee and the two reviewers of Oxford University Press for their critical comments on a previous version of this introduction. Very special thanks are due to Brian MacWhinney and Andrej Malchukov: much of this introduction closely follows their suggestions. Many thanks also to Johannes Helmbrecht, who called my attention to Simon Dik's article of 1986, and to Mira Ariel and Wolfgang U. Dressler for their criticism of a draft of this introduction.

of grammaticalization, Heine and Kuteva suggest (2006: 132–3) that the process in Basque is likely to have been precipitated by contact with languages that had indefinite articles. In this case, spontaneous grammaticalization and language contact converge in fostering the evolution of the indefinite article. Either grammaticalization by itself or language contact by itself may have been at work; or perhaps, as Heine and Kuteva propose, the two have acted together—a case of multi-causality.

A third scenario also involves two generalizations that make predictions about the same construction but here the predictions are **in conflict** rather than convergent. Take the distribution of gender in English personal pronouns. The third-person singular pronoun differentiates gender (*he, she, it*); what might we predict for the third-person plural pronoun? Paradigmatic Uniformity—an instance of analogy—would call for gender in the third-person plural as well. However, Economy bars against it: gender differentiation in the plural is less useful than in the singular. Of the two tendencies, Economy prevails: English has a single undifferentiated third-person plural pronoun (*they*). French, however, makes a different choice: both the singular and the plural third-person pronouns have gender (*il, elle; ils, elles*). In this case, Paradigmatic Uniformity appears to trump Economy rather than the other way around. For an overview of the ways in which principles can relate to each other, see Dressler, Libben, and Korecky-Kröll (this volume).

This simple example shows that generalizations may make conflicting predictions: they may compete; and that the resulting conflicts may be resolved in more than one way. Given the possibility of competitions among generalizations, dubbed motivations below, the following questions arise.

1. What motivations compete?
2. Competition in synchrony:
   - In what domains of grammar (syntax, morphology, etc.) are hypotheses of competing motivations useful analytic tools?
   - Are such hypotheses useful both for accounting for single-language grammars and for variation across languages?
3. Competition in processes:
   - Are competing motivations detectable in diachronic change?
   - Are competing motivations detectable in language use (production and comprehension)?
   - Are competing motivations detectable in first- and second-language acquisition?
4. Resolving competitions: How are competitions resolved in various grammatical domains and in various processes? There is a limited set of logical possibilities (cf. Moravcsik 2010):
   - SEPARATION: each motivation applies to a different token of the construction (this is labeled Variation in Malchukov (this volume))
   - COMPROMISE: each motivation applies to the same construction but with one or both modified so as to eliminate the conflict (labeled "divide the spoils" in Bates and MacWhinney 1982)

- OVERRIDE: only one motivation applies (labeled "winner take all" in Bates and MacWhinney 1982)
- DEADLOCK: neither motivation applies and thus there is no output reflecting the effect of either motivation (labeled Blocking in Malchukov (this volume))
5. Explaining competing motivations
    - Why are competing motivations and their resolutions distributed over grammatical domains, processes, and languages the way they are?
    - Why are there competing motivations in language to begin with?

The chapters of this volume discuss many of these issues. Several studies posit competing motivations in synchronic grammars internal to individual languages, including ways in which speakers choose from among alternative constructions (Lamers and de Hoop, Francis and Michaelis, Strunk, Ariel, Mondorf, Haiman, Helmbrecht). Other studies document competing motivations as evidenced in cross-linguistic variation (Malchukov, Haspelmath). A number of chapters address the competition among syntactic, pragmatic, and semantic factors during the online production and comprehension of grammatical dependencies (Bornkessel-Schlesewsky and Schlesewsky, Pfeiffer, Kaltenböck and Heine), in language acquisition (Rowland, Noble, and Chan, Hughes and Allen, Krajewski and Lieven), and in language change (Cristofaro, Newmeyer); others (Dressler, Libben, and Korecky, Du Bois, Hawkins, and MacWhinney) cover multiple topics. All four types of resolutions are documented in the case studies: Separation (e.g. Mondorf), Compromise (e.g. Helmbrecht), Override (e.g. Kaltenböck and Heine), and Deadlock (e.g. Malchukov). Answers to the why-questions about the nature, distribution, and the very existence of competing motivations are sought in conflicting high-level desiderata in human behavior, such as the speaker's needs versus the listener's demands, faithfulness to code versus economy, and, ultimately, in the various conflicting factors embedded in the multiple timeframes that underlie the functioning of complex objects in the world.

1.2 Past research

The five issues listed above have been part of linguistic analysis for a long time, whether explicitly or implicitly. An early pronouncement by Georg von der Gabelentz (1901: 181–5) identifies two conflicting desiderata in grammar: *Bequemlichkeit*, referring to the comfort of the speaker, and *Deutlichkeit*: clarity, which favors the addressee. More recently, the rule-ordering debates of the 1970s and 1980s about which rules take precedence over which other rules in a derivation may also be construed as a search for resolutions of competing motivations (Koutsoudas, Sanders, and Noll 1974; Anderson 1979).

The idea that competition is a fundamental force in shaping grammars has been repeatedly articulated. From data taken from several languages, Haiman (1983) illustrates the role of Iconicity and Economy: the two may be in harmony supporting the same output or they may be in conflict, and particular principles of iconicity itself may also compete. Du Bois suggested that "it is largely the need to consistently resolve the competition between diverse external motivations that leads in the first place to the existence—as a fixed structure—of grammar itself" (Du Bois 1985: 360). Similarly, Simon Dik proposed that a natural language "can be seen as one of a set of possible solutions to a complex problem: the achievement of inter-human communication.... There is thus continuous competition between different functional prerequisites; the actual synchronic design of a language is a compromise solution, a precarious balance in efficacy with respect to different functional prerequisites" (Dik 1986: 18, 21–2).

The influential frameworks of Natural Phonology and Natural Morphology were first put forth by Wolfgang U. Dressler and his colleagues (Dressler 1984, 1986, 1995; Dressler et al. 1987). With the notion of conflict being a central issue in these theories, they formed the basis of the subsequent development of Optimality Theory.

Relevant research has been pursued in different frameworks: in the functional-typological tradition (Haiman 1983, 1985; Du Bois 1985, 1987b; Dik 1986; Dressler 1995; Kirby 1997; Croft 2003; Francis and Michaelis 2003; Corbett 2006: 238–63), in Optimality Theory (Prince and Smolensky 1993, 2004b), and in the Competition Model of language acquisition (Bates and MacWhinney 1982, 1987, 1989; MacWhinney 2012). For competition in the framework of Distributed Morphology, see Bobaljik (2012: 137 *et passim*).

A study in child language acquisition that formulates two conflicting principles and states the conditions under which one or the other applies is presented in a classic statement of the Competition Model (Bates and MacWhinney 1987: esp. 172–3). The authors note that children identify arguments of transitive sentences—what is the agent, what is the patient—differently in different languages, such as in English and Italian. In English, children of two years of age and above tend to identify arguments by word order rather than animacy. In Italian, however, children of the same age group tend to identify arguments by animacy rather than word order. The explanation is based on the crucial constructs of cue validity (a function of the frequency of a construction in a language) and cue reliability (how frequently is a particular choice the right one). The English children tend to identify arguments by word order rather than animacy because word order has higher cue validity and cue reliability than animacy in the ambient language, whereas in Italian, animacy is the dominant cue. Thus, the nature of crosslinguistically variable performance in acquisition is proposed to be dependent on the nature of crosslinguistically variable language input. This type of resolution is labeled Separation in Section 1.1 of this chapter and Variation in Malchukov (this volume): each alternative scenario occurs in a separate context.

More recently, there have been efforts to integrate functional-typological and psycholinguistic work—an area where Hawkins's oeuvre (e.g. 2004, 2009b) stands out as a prime bridge-building effort. There has also been work on unifying Optimality Theory's view with that of the functional-typological approach and with the Competition Model of language acquisition (Haspelmath 1999b; Aissen 2003; de Hoop and Lamers 2006; de Hoop and Malchukov 2008; Malchukov 2011; MacWhinney 2012).

What the various approaches all have in common is the recognition that language patterns are underlain by multiple causes and that the various factors may be in conflict. The approaches also differ in some ways. Given that Optimality Theory has been an influential framework, it is worth comparing it with other approaches. For the purposes of laying out the similarities and differences between Optimality Theory and other frameworks, Andrej Malchukov (personal communication) has brought to my attention the example of weather verbs, such as 'to rain', as discussed by Grimshaw and Samek-Lodovici (1998). Some languages like Italian use bare verbs (e.g. *Piove*), others like English use a dummy subject (*It is raining*). Working within the framework of Optimality Theory, Grimshaw and Samek-Lodovici analyze this variation by positing the variable ranking of two general constraints: Full-Int (which states that lexical items must contribute to the interpretation of a structure and thus penalizes dummy arguments), and SUBJect or EPP (Extended Projection Principle, which, roughly speaking, requires subjects in all sentences).

- If EPP or SUBJect ≫ Full-Int (i.e. if EPP or SUBJect is the dominating constraint), then the English pattern results with a dummy subject.
- If Full-Int ≫ EPP or SUBJect (i.e. if Full-Int is the dominating constraint), then the Italian impersonal pattern results.

This analysis is consistent with both the functional-typological approach and the Competition Model. One difference is that the Competition Model focuses on comprehension rather than production as the others do. Additional differences have to do with the factors that are assumed to compete and with the resolutions. As far as the competing principles as concerned: first, in OT's classic version, constraints are absolute while in the functional-typological approach and in the Competition Model, they are probabilistic. Second, constraints in OT are taken to be universal whereas in the other two approaches, there is no such commitment. Third, in the functional-typological approach and in the Competition Model, the source of the constraints is explicitly tied to processing, whereas OT accounts generally do not explore usage-based reasons behind the constraints.

Regarding types of resolutions: OT is best suited to handle cases of Override (or "Winner take all" (Bates and MacWhinney 1982)): where one principle trumps the other (as embodied in the principle of strict domination: a higher-ranked constraint strictly dominates a lower-ranked one). However, as noted in Section 1.1, there are also other kinds of resolutions to competitions. For example, **both** principles may apply to different constructions in a language or across languages (Separation, labeled Variation in Malchukov (this volume)); or Deadlock, labeled Blocking in Malchukov (this volume), where **neither** principle applies and thus the construction is blocked. Examples of both Separation (Variation) and Deadlock (Blocking) are given in Malchukov (this volume). Of the two conflicting motivations Malchukov posits to account for various alignment patterns—Harmony and Bias—each overrides the other in distinct contexts in some cases, while in other instances, the clash results in no output: the construction is blocked. Outside this volume, the lack of multiple wh-questions in Irish is cited as the result of a conflict in Ackema and Neeleman (1998: 479–82). On how languages resort to a passive (or antipassive) construction in order to make up for an active construction that is blocked due to a conflict of two principles, see Malchukov (2006b: 349–50), and Mithun (2005, 2007). Since languages do find ways of expressing meanings even if one type of expression is blocked, Deadlock holds only with respect to a specific construction type. Once the possibility of additional expressions is taken into account, the data configuration is best analyzed as Override. In the light of the possibility of alternative expressions of the intended meaning, Brian MacWhinney suggests (personal communication) that the term Evasion may be more appropriate than Blocking or Deadlock.

Representing Separation and Deadlock in OT is less straightforward than accounts of Override. Cases of Separation have been discussed in OT in connection to (pseudo-)optionality, which is known to be problematic for classical OT approaches. The solutions proposed range from assuming a constraint 'tie' (two constraints being unranked relative to each other), or by viewing the outcome of competition as dependent on further constraints. Malchukov suggests (personal communication) that the tie between two constraints may be handled by the alternative ranking of the constraints for different constructions (e.g. for agreement and case morphology). Deadlock in turn, he suggests, may be described in OT either as 'zero output' represented as optimal, or by an optimal candidate incurring a faithfulness violation, or else as being spurious under proper extension of the candidate set. For further discussion, see Ackema and Neeleman (1998) and Baković and Keer (2001).

For detailed illustrations of OT's account of competing motivations, see Malchukov (this volume) Section 2.4 and Lamers and de Hoop (this volume). For comparisons of other approaches, see Bornkessel-Schlesewsky and Schlesewsky (this volume), Section 7.7, where the authors' Argument Dependency Model is compared with MacWhinney's Competition Model. For additional references on the history of research on competing motivations, see Haiman (2010) and the chapters by Du Bois, Haiman, and MacWhinney (this volume).

1.3 Overview of the book

The studies are presented in three parts followed by a concluding chapter. The first and second parts provide case studies of competing motivations in syntax and morphology; the third part and the concluding chapter focus on general issues.

The first part, titled "Competition in Syntax: Grammatical Relations and Word Order," is the largest, consisting of nine chapters. The syntactic patterns central to the discussions have to do with grammatical relations: alignment patterns and argument interpretation as related to word order and case marking. The ordering of relative clauses is discussed in two of the chapters and one study is about the interpretation of disjunctions. The domains in which competition is demonstrated include synchronic grammar, language use—both production and comprehension— and child language acquisition. Some of the chapters posit competing motivations to explain patterns of single languages while others address crosslinguistic variation.

Andrej Malchukov's chapter titled "Resolving alignment conflicts: A competing motivations approach" raises the issue of crosslinguistic variation and convergence in alignment patterns. The cases considered are monotransitive sentences (accusative vs. ergative alignment) and ditransitive constructions (indirective vs. secundative alignment). Malchukov argues that crosslinguistic variation in this domain can be explained by the interaction of two general factors: Harmony embodying the analogical tendency to match the coding and syntactic behavior of noun phrases, and Bias calling for alignment preferences dictated by functional properties of individual constructions. He shows that the interaction between these two factors explains both the frequent crosslinguistic recurrence of those patterns where both motivations prefer the same alignment, and crosslinguistic variation, which is the result of the two motivations being in conflict. As outputs of competitions, the chapter provides examples of both Separation (labeled here Variation) and Deadlock (labeled Blocking).

The next five chapters by Lamers and de Hoop, Hawkins, Francis and Michaelis, Strunk, and Bornkessel-Schlesewsky and Schlesewsky explore competing factors in language use and their relationship to grammar. Just as Malchukov (this volume), **Monique J. A. Lamers** and **Helen de Hoop** also adopt Optimality Theory's basic approach in the chapter "Animate object fronting in Dutch: A production study." They note that in Dutch, there is a preference to start a sentence with an animate noun phrase. At the same time, as in many other languages, there is also a strong tendency to start a sentence with the grammatical subject. These two tendencies—Animate First and Subject First—coincide when the subject is animate, as is usually the case. If, however, the subject is inanimate while the object is animate, they compete. The authors report on a sentence production study of two classes of psych verbs with animate objects. They found that object fronting is more frequent with unaccusative psych verbs such as "please" than with causative psych verbs, e.g. "convince." They argue that this pattern results from a grammatical difference between the two types of verbs: causative verbs allow for passivization but unaccusative verbs do not. Thus, with unaccusative psych verbs, Animate First can be satisfied only by fronting the animate object. The presence of both fronted and unfronted animate objects illustrates Separation as a resolution.

In his chapter "Patterns in competing motivations and the interaction of principles," **John A. Hawkins** sees conflicting desiderata in grammars as direct reflexes of competitions that arise in language use. The chapter examines empirical patterns in language performance and in the distribution of grammatical variants across languages and uses them to shed light on how multiple principles work together. Some data from second-language acquisition are also briefly considered. Three types of general patterns are observed. The first set illustrates a Degree of Preference generalization for individual principles. The second set illustrates Cooperation, whereby the more principles there are that define a collective preference for a common set of outputs, the greater is the preference for and size of that output. The third set involves Competition: when there is competition between two principles, the relative strength of their outputs will be in proportion to the degree of preference for their respective outputs; where preference is defined in terms of the overall ease and efficiency of structures.

Further examples of Separation are provided in the two studies on relative clause extraposition. In the chapter titled "Why move? How weight and discourse factors combine to predict relative clause extraposition in English," **Elaine J. Francis and Laura A. Michaelis** take up relative clause extraposition (RCE) in English—that is, sentences where a subject-modifying relative clause appears after the verb phrase, as in *Some research has been conducted that supports the existing theory*. Previous studies have revealed that both grammatical weight and discourse factors induce speakers to resort to RCE. However, this study is the first to examine the details of the interaction between the two. A quantitative analysis of RCE and comparable non-RCE tokens in the International Corpus of English–Great Britain shows the effect of weight: there is a strong preference for RCE when the relative clause is at least five times longer than the verb phrase, and a strong preference for canonical order when the relative clause is the same length or shorter than the verb phrase. For those tokens with length ratios falling between these limits, choice of structure depends primarily on discourse factors.

The same language-internal grammatical variation is taken up in **Jan Strunk**'s chapter ("A statistical model of competing motivations affecting relative clause extraposition in German"). Strunk observes that relative clause extraposition has been studied by both generativists and functionalists. Whereas generativists have concentrated on structural and semantic factors, such as syntactic locality, definiteness, and restrictiveness, functionalists have investigated surface-oriented factors: the length of the relative clause and the distance between it and its antecedent. Most studies, however, have only looked at individual factors separately and did not try to construct an integrated model. Based on a statistical study of relative clause extraposition in German, the author concludes that the decision whether to extrapose a relative clause cannot be attributed to only one factor and that multiple motivations have to be taken into account. He also reports on an acceptability study showing that constraints against extraposition can sometimes be overridden by increasing the antecedent's salience and the predictability of the relative clause.

The neurobiological roots of argument interpretation in language use are investigated in "Competition in argument interpretation: Evidence from the neurobiology of language" by **Ina Bornkessel-Schlesewsky** and **Matthias Schlesewsky**. The chapter presents an approach to competition in incremental argument interpretation based on the extended Argument Dependency Model developed by the authors. They argue that in the course of real-time language comprehension, each potential argument (i.e. every "nouny" constituent in a sentence) competes for interpretation as one of three cardinal categories: actor, subject, and topic. These cardinal categories serve to anchor arguments in the current event (actor), the upcoming discourse (subject), and the preceding discourse (topic). The authors outline a neurobiological processing architecture based on the theory of Cardinal Categories and on additional assumptions about information processing in the human brain. They discuss existing evidence supporting this approach as well as some testable new predictions and compare their approach to the Competition Model.

Besides competition in grammar and in the process of language use, competing principles are documented in another process as well: child language acquisition. The remaining three chapters of Part 1 address this topic.

In "Competition all the way down: How children learn word order cues to sentence meaning," **Caroline F. Rowland, Claire Noble,** and **Angel Chan** note that most work on competing cues in language acquisition has focused on what happens when cues compete within a certain construction. There has been less work on what happens when constructions themselves compete. In studying children's acquisition of English, Welsh, and Cantonese, they show that rather than acquiring alternative constructions separately (e.g. each of the two bitransitive structures in English, with shifted and unshifted datives) children generalize across synonymous structures. As a result, the alternative constructions compete in the child's mind and the existence of such synonymous sets delays acquisition.

In their chapter "Competing constraints in children's omission of subjects? The interaction between verb finiteness and referent accessibility," **Mary E. Hughes** and **Shanley E. M. Allen**'s initial observation is that children acquiring a first language omit sentential subjects more frequently than adults. The posited motivation for these non-target-like omissions differs across theoretical accounts: nativists claim that subjects are omitted when the accompanying verb is non-finite, while usage-based theorists claim that subjects are omitted when referents are accessible. According to the authors, these two motivations interact rather than compete. In spontaneous speech data from monolingual English-speaking children and their caregivers, the authors find that subjects are more likely to be omitted when their referents are accessible in both finite and non-finite contexts, and that subjects are more likely to be omitted in non-finite contexts whether the referents are or are not maximally accessible. This finding underlines the need for an integrated analysis of acquisition phenomena combining motivations identified in nativist and usage-based analyses.

In "Competing cues in early syntactic development," **Grzegorz Krajewski** and **Elena Lieven** review a number of studies exploring young children's development of grammar within Bates and MacWhinney's Competition Model framework. They focus on studies investigating children's ability to comprehend a simple transitive sentence, that is, their ability to identify its subject and object, and in particular on the role that word order and case marking play in this process in different languages. The results suggest that children can initially process sentences that follow a prototypical pattern of their language and as such provide a number of redundant cues, and that the process of pulling apart individual cues is slow and gradual. The ability to use cues productively with novel items is delayed and sentences with competing cues remain particularly difficult for a long time. The authors discuss the implications these results have for our understanding of early grammatical development.

The five chapters of the second part of the volume—"Competition in Morphosyntax and the Lexicon"—broaden the study of competing motivations in grammar, usage, and acquisition by focusing on the morphological correlates of syntax.

"Conflicting vs. convergent vs. interdependent motivations in morphology" by **Wolfgang U. Dressler, Gary Libben,** and **Katharina Korecky-Kröll** is a comprehensive, semiotically- and typologically-based study of competing motivations in morphology. The authors discuss examples of competing motivations in morphology itself (affix order and markedness vs. frequency) as well as in its interface with the lexicon, with discourse, and with phonology. They also identify competing motivations in first-language acquisition and in the results of experiments on the acquisition and processing of actual, potential, and illegal German plurals. The chapter concludes with a general discussion of how the study of conflict resolutions in language can lead to the advancement of knowledge in linguistics and psycho-linguistics.

Martin Haspelmath's chapter ("On system pressure competing with economic motivation") starts out with the observation that grammatical marking is typically economical, that is, the more frequent member of a grammatical opposition tends to be coded by zero, while the rarer member is coded overtly. This is evidenced in person marking, argument coding and adnominal possessive marking. But, he says, if frequency as a motivating factor had no competition, we would expect a lot more variation than we actually find because different lexemes show different frequencies. Given that grammatical coding is fairly uniform within word classes, a second force, identified as System Pressure (or analogy: the tendency for words to behave like other similar words), is posited as a powerful competing motivation which leads languages to adopt uniform patterns at the expense of Economy.

The remaining three chapters in Part II are concerned with competing motivations in language use: the conditions under which speakers make choices in how to express themselves. In **Britta Mondorf**'s chapter, "Apparently competing motivations in morphosyntactic variation," the competing factors are the analytic and synthetic means of expressing comparison. The solution is a division of labor, or Separation, as labeled in Section 1.1: each factor prevails in a given context. Analyticity is resorted to if explicitness is required because of an increased processing effort; syntheticity in turn is preferred in easy-to-process environments. The chapter raises the possibility that a corresponding claim might hold for other synthetic–analytic contrasts, such as Spanish future alternation (e.g. *comeré* vs. *voy a comer*) or English genitive alternation (e.g. *the topic's relevance* vs. *the relevance of the topic*).

The next chapter addresses the frequent mismatch between the flow of normal communication and the temporary needs of the speaker. The solution is labeled Compromise in Section 1.1. Based on German data, which he then compares with English evidence, **Martin Pfeiffer** analyzes self-repair ("Formal vs. functional motivations for the structure of self-repair in German"). In recent years, he says, comparative studies in Interactional Linguistics have shown that the syntactic organization of self-repair is influenced by the different morphosyntactic characteristics of the respective languages. However, it is yet largely unknown to what extent functional motivations compete with formal motivations in determining the syntax of self-repair. By focusing on the influence of the cognitive and interactional needs of speakers and hearers on the structure of self-repair, the chapter shows that the on-line need of self-repair and the pressure to stick to the language code are in conflict and lays out the specifics of how the structure of the resulting self-repairs is influenced by the morphosyntax of the language.

Mondorf's and Pfeiffer's chapters deal with competing motivations in speech production. **John Haiman** ("Six competing motives for repetition") notes that while most discussions of competing motivations have implicitly adopted the point of view of the speaker: "Given that I want to say M, in what form should I express it?," one may also take the point of view of the hearer and ask the question: "Given a specific linguistic structure, specifically a repetition of a form F, what (competing) meanings could lie behind that repetition, and how can I, as the hearer, tell which one was intended?" Haiman suggests that within a text, repetition may serve as an icon of amplitude in the broadest sense, a partially unintended index of staginess, or simply as an ornament. Intertextually in turn, a speaker may repeat another speaker in order to pretend that he is that other speaker, or to voice his agreement with the other speaker, or to mock him. These options may be distinguished from each other by the use of disambiguating "diacritics"—minor signs that are added to clarify what was intended. These motivations and the clarifying diacritics are documented for Cambodian.

The six studies of the third part of the book, titled "General Issues and the Extension of the Approach," broaden the scope of discussion even further by probing into the basic why-questions.

John W. Du Bois's study ("Motivating competitions") is a general overview of motivations, competitions, and resolutions. It is about the motivations that shape the organization of grammar, the competitions that arise between these motivations, and the resolution of these competitions through the systematic and systematizing processes of grammaticization. The author proposes that it is in the real-time decision-making of verbalization and interpretation that competitions first arise and where they must be resolved. Competing motivations are pervasive and powerful in language and thus play a critical role in answering the fundamental question that underlies all of the chapters of this volume: why are grammars as they are? The chapter explores how competitions between functional units relate to speakers' strategies for achieving their communicative goals and explores how competition and motivation interact to produce competing motivations, with important consequences for the adaptive emergence of grammar.

As demonstrated in many studies, competing motivations can be identified in synchronic structure. However, the concept of competition is a dynamic one: it is a process that must take place in real time. The question is: which are the processes that form the source of the competition that are detected in synchronic grammars in frozen form? Candidate processes are historical change, language use, and language acquisition. Since the immediate process that lies behind synchronic structure is historical change, we might search for competitions of motivations in diachrony. Is historical change the source of competing motivations in grammar?

In "Competing motivation models and diachrony: What evidence for what motivations?," **Sonia Cristofaro** argues that this is mostly not the case. As she explains, competing motivation models are usually established on synchronic grounds. If the use of different constructions within the same grammatical domain is associated with different functional factors, then the competition between these factors is assumed to motivate the distribution of the various constructions, independently of how the constructions actually originated in individual languages. The chapter discusses several diachronic processes involved in the development of patterns that have been accounted for in terms of competing motivations, such as the development of different alignment systems and that of overt as opposed to zero marking for number. These processes challenge the relevant competing motivations models because they provide no evidence for the principles postulated in these models and their competitions.

Nonetheless, where the genesis of structures does not reflect the synchronically detectable competitions, the survival and propagation of these structures may. Cristofaro notes that, in the course of acquisition and use, the mind's construal of language structures may be governed by principles other than those that brought them about in history and these principles in turn may show competition. As stated by Newmeyer (this volume), "the forces...that bring a construction into a language are not necessarily the same ones that keep it there." This is also Malchukov's position (2010: esp. 155–9), according to which use and acquisition act as filters on the evolution of structures. Forces such as economy or iconicity that are traceable in synchronic structure may be the result of these filters that shape "good design."

This takes us to the immediate source of competing motivations. The term "competition" requires a process and historical change is indeed a process, but the term "motivation" cannot directly apply to historical change since it implies individuals who are motivated and who make (largely unintended) choices among the motivations. Thus, the ultimate locus of competing motivations must be **individual minds**: the mind of the language learner and the mind of the language user, which then trigger communal effects resulting in language change (cf. Blevins 2004). Real-time speech and acquisition are the arenas where motivations compete. The source of the motivations is argued by MacWhinney (this volume) to be the variety of timeframes operative in speech production and speech comprehension.

Frederick J. Newmeyer's chapter ("Where do motivations compete?") is devoted to the very issue of the locus of competing functional motivations. He identifies two positions on this issue, which he calls "direct competition" and "indirect competition." According to the concept of direct competition, there is direct synchronic linkage between properties of particular grammars and functional motivations for those properties. According to the alternative, there is no direct linkage. Several arguments lead Newmeyer to the conclusion that the notion of indirect competition is the correct one. In a nutshell, while it is possible to pinpoint parsing ease, iconicity, etc. as motivating factors for overall grammatical structure, there is no hope of identifying parsing or iconicity as motivators for particular structures or rules in particular languages.

In his chapter titled "Politeness distinctions in pronouns: A case study on competing motivations," **Johannes Helmbrecht** argues for the historical and psychological roots of the competitions apparent in synchronic structure. He notes that the great majority of the languages of Europe display politeness distinctions in personal pronouns, such as French *tu* (2SG) and *vous* (2SG.HON). The goal of the study is to present a functional analysis of the emergence and diffusion of politeness distinctions in personal pronouns in Europe through a competing motivations approach. It is shown that the social or pragmatic functions—politeness and prestige—are in conflict with the cognitive/psychological factor of economy. It is argued that the different degrees of grammatical integration (grammaticalization) of the polite pronouns into the pronominal paradigm of the respective languages may be explained by this conflict, not in terms of a winning and a losing factor but in terms of a compromise between the factors involved.

Mira Ariel ("*Or* constructions: Monosemy vs. polysemy") shows that codes and inferences compete in language and that the competition manifests itself both at the level of the language system and in real-time interactions. The author examines various disjunctive interpretations and finds a number of competing alternatives for expressing them. First, the disjunctive idea may be expressed by a polysemous construction, for example, [X *or* Y], the specific interpretation of which (e.g. exclusive, inclusive, etc.) is derived through context-driven inferences. Second, monosemous constructions may be used, which directly encode the specific inter-pretation. The author's hypothesis is that the dearth of contextual clues favors monosemy; polysemy in turn serves the addressee's interest only if the context allows him to make inferences in interpreting what he has heard. The presence of both monosemous and polysemous expressions is an instance of Separation: both code and inference prevail under different conditions.

A study about spur-of-the-moment changes that the speaker makes in speech is presented in **Gunther Kaltenböck** and **Bernd Heine**'s "Sentence grammar vs. thetical grammar: Two competing domains." The authors highlight a competition between two purposes of the speaker: to proceed with the intended message and to respond to temporary needs that arise from the communicative situation. The authors define two separate systems labeled Sentence Grammar and Thetic Gram-mar, each suited to one of the two goals. Thetic interpolations may be of several types, such as instructions like *could you please turn off the slide projector*, or explanatory notes, such as *I use the word advisedly*. The study defines the main characteristics of the two systems and demonstrates how the two compete in the construction of utterances.

The proposal that the competition of motivation takes place in language use and language acquisition identifies the stages where competitions happen. This still leaves the question of the mechanism behind the conflicts. **Brian MacWhinney**'s compre-hensive study "Competition across time," which concludes the volume, argues that, like other biological systems, language emerges as a product of competing motiva-tions that interact at the moment of speaking. The different motivations are each linked to a different timeframe involved in the processing of language, in memory, in social interaction, and in interaction with the environment. The different motiva-tions need to mesh at the moment of speaking and they ultimately produce long-term impacts on individual speakers and on language communities.

Many of the chapters in this volume find their place in the theory of timeframe integration. For example, MacWhinney analyzes some of the competitions as between "rote and combination"—that is, whether forms are stored as wholes or are created on the spot by the combination of stored elements. Mondorf shows that, of synthetic and analytic comparatives—for example *nicer* versus *more beautiful*—synthetic ones are preferred if the adjective is short and frequent. MacWhinney explains this by the fact that synthetic forms are stored in memory by rote and can be retrieved more quickly than the analytic ones that must be assembled. Of the two timeframes, the easier one is preferred. The crosslinguistically widely recurrent pattern of derivational affixes standing on the inner side of inflectional ones discussed in Dressler, Libben, and Koreczky-Kröll is also explained by the difference between the amounts of time that rote and combination require: derived forms are stored as wholes by rote and thus quick retrieval has priority over the combinatory act required for adding inflections.

MacWhinney's sweeping perspective on competing motivations provides the reader not only with ways of integrating many of the insights presented in the chapters in this volume; it also takes us beyond language by highlighting the pervasive presence of competition both in social systems and in nature. The study of competing motivations in language is revealed as part of the fundamental issue of conflict resolution in the world.

Part I

Competition in Syntax: Grammatical Relations and Word Order

2

Resolving alignment conflicts: A competing motivations approach

ANDREJ MALCHUKOV

2.1 Introduction

2.1.1 *Alignment hierarchies: some proposals*

As is well-known, issues of syntactic alignment have figured prominently in the recent typological literature.[1] Alignment is conventionally defined by the coding of arguments in a transitive construction, transitive subject/Agent (A) and transitive object/Patient (P), as compared to coding of intransitive subject (S) (see Figure 2.1, representing accusative, ergative, and neutral alignment). Early studies aimed at categorizing languages *in toto* into accusative, ergative, etc., yet as early as in the 1970s linguists became aware that such categorization is misleading since ergative or accusative alignment more often than not does not apply across the board in a particular language. An early influential paper by Anderson (1976) highlighted the fact that morphological ergativity does not need to (and in fact rarely does) correlate with syntactic ergativity. Moreover, a number of researchers (Heath 1976; Comrie 1978; Moravcsik 1978; Dixon 1979), apparently independently, came to the conclusion that syntactic constructions do not behave in a uniform way either, but show certain alignment preferences. For example, Dixon (1979, 1994) observed that imperatives universally show accusative alignment, Comrie (1981/1989) noted that resultatives exhibit ergative alignment, and Moravcsik (1978) observed the same for verbal plurality. A consequence of such an approach is that each construction may have its own alignment preference. This position squares well with the approach of Construction Grammar (Goldberg 1995), which associates specific functional (semantic) properties with individual constructions, even though alignment preferences have not been systematically investigated in this framework (see, however, Croft's 2001 Radical Construction Grammar). It is also in line with the approach of

[1] Acknowledgments. I am grateful to Denis Creissels, Martin Haspelmath, Brian MacWhinney, Edith Moravcsik, and Fritz Newmeyer for insightful comments on an earlier draft of this paper. The usual disclaimers apply.

Role and Reference Grammar (RRG; Van Valin 2005 passim), which introduced the notion of a Privileged Syntactic Argument (PSA) to capture alignment patterns (cf. Dixon's 1979 'pivot'). A PSA may be the same across different constructions, approximating the role of subject (controller of verb agreement, pivot/gap in conjunction reduction, pivot/deleted argument in imperative formation, etc.), but importantly, this is not necessary: in principle, each construction can have its own PSA. This raises the question whether it is possible to predict the PSA for particular constructions across languages. Since the PSA is understood in RRG in terms of (macro)role neutralization, this question translates into the question of alignment preferences in different constructions. This question has been vigorously pursued in typological literature, but the results so far are mixed.

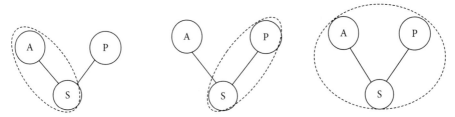

FIGURE 2.1 Basic types of monotransitive alignment: accusative, ergative, and neutral

Indeed, there do seem to be crosslinguistically consistent patterns in alignment preferences. One of the early findings, which has been replicated on different samples, is that coding may show an alignment mismatch with respect to head- vs. dependent-marking. In particular, coding mismatches in ergative languages have shown that agreement exhibits a stronger preference for accusative alignment as compared to case.

Thus, we find languages (like Warlpiri) with ergative case marking (A vs. S=P) that have accusative-style agreement (A=S vs. P), but not an opposite pattern (see Haspelmath 2005b and Siewierska 2004, following up on earlier observations by Comrie 1981, 1989; Croft 1990; Dixon 1994).

(1)   Preferences in coding:

   case   >   agreement

      accusative alignment

This pattern is conceivable given that case marking is more sensitive to role properties, while agreement is more sensitive to prominence (therefore, favoring A/S neutralization). The ultimate explanation for this hierarchy may be in part diachronic (as is well-known, agreement arises from cliticization of pronouns, which tend to be 'prominent', i.e. animate and/or definite; Givón 1984: 364–5; Siewierska 2004: 262–72), and partially due to the inventory size of these markers (agreement rarely extends beyond subject and object agreement, while case systems often feature larger inventories).

Encouraged by this result, a number of typologists have suggested alignment hierarchies, which would allow extending such observations (henceforth called **alignment preferences**) to further syntactic patterns. One proposal due to Croft (2001: 155; cf. Croft 1991; Kazenin 1994) is represented in the form of the Subject Construction Hierarchy (constructions on the right are assumed to have a stronger accusative preference, operating in terms of the 'subject' notion (A=S)).

(2)   Subject Construction Hierarchy

Case > Agreement > Relativization > Control > Conjunction reduction

———————————————————————————————➤ accusative (A/S)
                                                      preference

The claim embodied in this hierarchy is interesting, since it predicts that if a construction to the left on the hierarchy (e.g. case) has an accusative pattern in some language, a construction to the right on the hierarchy (e.g. relative clause construction) should show an accusative pattern as well (e.g. the same relativization strategy is used for A and S arguments). Similar proposals have been made by other authors, although various authors differ with respect to the range of constructions considered, and there does not seem to be a general consensus on the exact shape of the extended alignment hierarchy. Different authors also differ on whether these preferences are seen as absolute universals. For example, Dixon (1994) and Manning (1996) suggest that imperatives and control constructions always operate on an accusative basis. Yet, as will be clear from the following discussion, such hierarchies are better viewed as implicational statistical universals, rather than absolute universals.

2.1.2 *Problematic cases*

Although alignment hierarchies enjoy a certain popularity in the typological literature, their validity has not gone unchallenged. A number of counterexamples to the purported alignment universals have been recently reviewed by Bickel (2011), who notes that many universal claims have been falsified by the data from individual languages. For example, against the background of claims that control constructions are universally accusatively aligned (with an A/S controllee), he notes that in Belhare (Kiranti), control constructions operate on an ergative basis (the controllee must bear the {S,O}-relation).[2]

(3)   Belhare (Bickel 2011: 422–3)
       a.   *Khoŋ-ma   nui-ka.*
                play-INF   may.NPST-2
                'You may play.'
       b. *Lu-ma   nui-ka.*
            tell-INF   may.NPST-2SG
            '(They/someone) may tell you.', not 'You may tell someone.'

---

[2] See Bickel (2011) for evidence that it is a control rather than a 'raising' construction.

Note that in (3b), the omitted argument that is coreferential to the matrix S argument is the object (P) rather than the transitive subject (A). This goes against the general tendency for control constructions to target the subject NP (A,S). This is not an isolated case: as Bickel's overview makes clear, there are counterexamples to most proposals of universal alignment preferences and universal rankings between individual constructions on the extended alignment hierarchy. Generally, Bickel opts for a more conservative bottom-up approach to the study of alignment preferences, emphasizing a need for more groundwork on documenting alignment preferences for individual constructions across larger samples. While more empirical work in this field is clearly desirable, it seems equally important to make progress on the theoretical issues to elucidate functional motivations behind individual preferences. In the present article I follow this latter thread, trying to show how both expected patterns as well as counterexamples can be accounted for within a competing motivations approach.

2.1.3 *Accounting for alignment patterns: a competing motivations approach*

In the present chapter I apply a competing motivations approach as developed in the 1980s by Du Bois (1985), Haiman (1985b), and Croft (1990), among others, to the domain of alignment conflicts (cf. also the conceptually similar approach in psycholinguistics known as the Competition Model; Bates and MacWhinney 1987). This approach is similar and compatible with functional Optimality Theoretic approaches (e.g. Bresnan and Aissen 2002; Aissen 2003); indeed the latter can be seen as formalization of the former (cf. de Hoop and Malchukov 2008). While there remain a number of important open questions about functional approaches in general, and functional Optimality Theoretic approaches in particular, that deserve further discussion (see Newmeyer 2005, this volume, for the discussion of direct vs. indirect competition in grammar), I will largely disregard them in the present chapter (see the conclusions section though for a brief comment). Rather I will concentrate on developing a general competing motivations model which can account for the crosslinguistic variation in syntactic alignment, and which, importantly, eschews stipulation. In particular, I propose to account for both recurrent patterns and exceptions through interaction of two different factors (functional constraints).

- **Harmony**: syntactic behavior follows coding.
- **Bias**: syntactic behavior is determined by functional (semantic and pragmatic) properties of the construction in question.

Importantly, both types of constraints are independently motivated ("grounded") rather than stipulated. Harmony is basically driven by analogy: arguments which show similar coding will show a similar syntactic behavior.[3] Motivating ("ground-

---

[3] Martin Haspelmath (p.c.) raises an interesting question, whether a connection between coding and behavior is one way or bidirectional. (A partially related question, raised by Fritz Newmeyer, is whether Harmony and Bias constraints, as conceived in this chapter, are independent of each other). Now, if we conceive Harmony as analogical pressure from the basic clause type (declarative indicative main clause) on other clause types (e.g. imperative clauses) then the direction is arguably unidirectional. Note that the Bias constraints we discuss here are concerned with non-basic clause types (imperatives, nominalizations,

ing") Bias constraints is more challenging, as it should ultimately be derived from the semantic analysis of individual constructions. While such a task will not be attempted in the present chapter, Bias constraints for individual constructions have been long acknowledged in the literature and seem to be largely uncontroversial. Within a competing motivations model, Harmony and Bias are conceived as (potentially) conflicting constraints, whose interaction determines crosslinguistic variation in alignment patterns. Note that on the competing motivations approach Harmony and Bias may either strengthen each other (converge on the same pattern) or conflict. In the former case, the pattern is predicted to be more consistent crosslinguistically, in the latter case, more crosslinguistic variation is expected (see Malchukov 2010 for a proposal relating frequency of patterns to the way constraints interact).

In the remainder of this chapter, the competing motivations approach will be applied to the domain of monotransitive constructions in §2.2, and to the domain of ditransitive constructions in §2.3. The latter section draws heavily on joint work with Martin Haspelmath and Bernard Comrie (see Malchukov, Haspelmath, and Comrie 2010). §2.4 shows how the competing motivations approach can be formalized in Optimality Theory. Finally, §2.5 summarizes the main conclusions and mentions some questions for further research.

2.2 Alignment conflicts in the monotransitive domain

2.2.1 *Introductory remarks*

As noted above, it is generally acknowledged in the typological literature that constructions may display alignment preferences. Table 2.1 contains an incomplete list of constructions which have been suggested to have an accusative or an ergative bias (Comrie 1978, 1981; Moravcsik 1978; Dixon 1979, 1994; Van Valin 1981a; Keenan 1984; Givón 1984; Kibrik 1985; Croft 1990; Manning 1996; Lazard 1998).

TABLE 2.1. **Alignment preferences in monotransitive domain**

Alignment	**Accusative**	**Ergative**
Preferred by operations	imperatives	nominalization
	control constructions	resultatives
	(antecedent of) reflexives	verbal plurality
	(control of) switch reference	possessor ascension

constructions involving incorporation, etc.), and we have not considered here potential Biases associated with the basic construction. As an example of the latter one can mention preferential alignment of the most prominent argument of a transitive clause (the one that is highest on the animacy/definiteness scales) with the subject. This Bias can account for the fact that experiencer object constructions (of the 'please'-type) can be eventually reanalyzed as experiencer subject constructions (of the 'like'-type); Cole et al. 1990; Haspelmath 2001; Malchukov 2008b. This type of competition is, however, different insofar as Bias constraints that are responsible for reanalysis compete not with Harmony constraints but rather with 'faithfulness' constraints grounded in the semantics (argument structure) of the verb in its original sense.

In what follows we will apply the competing motivations approach to some constructions that attracted more attention in the literature such as imperative formation, control constructions, and nominalizations. No exhaustive treatment will be attempted here, as the purpose of the chapter is primarily methodological: to demonstrate the typological feasibility of the proposed competing motivations approach. In particular, it will be shown that there will be more crosslinguistic variation if Bias and Harmony constraints are in conflict. The discussion of biases in imperative formation in §2.2.2 is somewhat more detailed, since it also serves for exposition of the proposed analysis.

2.2.2 *Alignment in imperative formation*

Let us start from the probably best known proposal, due to Dixon (1979, 1994), that imperatives universally show accusative alignment.[4] It is uncontroversial that the accusative (or active–stative) Bias of imperative constructions is determined by the semantics of the construction: the addressee must be a controlling subject (A or S) (Dixon 1994: 131–3; cf. Manning 1996).[5] My approach, on the other hand, while acknowledging the accusative Bias of imperative formation, predicts that the alignment pattern depends on the alignment type of the language. In particular, it predicts that imperative formation should show an accusative pattern in languages with accusative alignment, since both Harmony and Bias prefer this pattern, while in ergative languages, the outcome will be more variegated, since the two factors are in conflict.

Thus, the general prediction of our approach for **accusative languages** is that rules of imperative formation treat A and S argument alike. These rules can, of course, vary across languages, yet this does not affect alignment as such, insofar as both A and S are treated alike by a syntactic rule. One syntactic rule, familiar from many languages is that both A and S addressees are omitted (cf. _ *Come in!* _ *Read the book aloud!*). The phenomenon of A/S deletion in imperatives is very common crosslinguistically and well documented in the typological literature (Xrakovskij 2001; Aikhenvald 2010a). In some languages which feature both subject and object agreement, subject-agreement markers may be omitted as well, while object agreement is not affected. This is the case in Ainu where A/S agreement affixes are omitted, while O-agreement markers are expectedly retained:

(4)   Ainu (Tamura 2000: 54, 241):
    a. *E-nu.*
       IMP.PTCL.PL-hear
       'You hear (him).'

---

[4] Maybe, more correctly, it should be formulated as a dispreference for ergative alignment, as some authors prefer to speak of an active–stative preference of imperatives (cf. Donohue 2008).

[5] Dixon (1994: 101) also mentions languages like Sumerian and Päri, where only imperatives show accusative alignment in contrast to other moods with ergative alignment, as evidence for the accusative preference. See also Malchukov and de Hoop 2011 for a recent discussion of TAM-based splits from an Optimality-Theoretic perspective.

b. *Nu   yan!*
   hear   IMP.PTCL.PL
   'Listen (you PL)!'

c. *En-erampokiwen   wa   en-kore!*
   1SG.O-pity   CON   1SG.O-give
   'Pity me!'

The consistency of imperative formation in accusative languages is predicted as here accusative Bias does not conflict with Harmony (coding properties).

On the other hand, **ergative languages**, show more variation in imperative formation. Some ergative languages (like Dyirbal and Yidiny; Dixon 1994) treat A and S alike insofar as second person S/A addressees are deleted (an accusative behavior). Since Dyirbal shows "deep" (syntactic) ergativity in syntax elsewhere, Dixon takes this as evidence that all languages, including ergative ones, show accusative alignment in imperative formation. Yet, this statement needs some qualification. Thus, it should be noted that Dyirbal and Yidiny (like many other Australian languages) show an NP-split ergativity to the effect that (1st and 2nd person) pronouns actually show an accusative pattern, in contrast to other nominals. Given that the rule of imperative formation crucially refers to second person pronouns, a similar behavior may also be attributed to the coding pattern (this point is taken up in §2.4). More importantly, some ergative languages, among them many Caucasian languages, demonstrably retain the ergative pattern both in case (insofar as the addressee is overt) and agreement.[6] This is illustrated in example (5) for Khwarshi (a Nakh-Daghestanian language):

(5)   Khwarshi (Khalilova 2009, and p.c.),
      a. (*Mižo*)   *m-ok'-o!*
         2.PL.ABS   HPL-go-IMP
         'You (plural) go!'

      b. (*Miže*)   *l-i-yo!*
         2PL.ERG   IV-do-IMP
         'You do (it)!'

Note that in Khwarshi the absolutive S aligns with the absolutive P, insofar as it is retained in imperatives, and more importantly triggers absolutive agreement on the verb in the same way it does in the indicative construction (as manifested in the

---

[6] In fairness, Dixon (1994) is aware of similar cases but does not regard them as evidence against the universal S/A alignment in imperatives. He writes (1994: 133): "Such languages simply have a grammatical constraint (that there must be S/O cross-referencing, or that there must be an A pronominal clitic) which overrides the universal tendency to omit specification of A or S from an imperative when it is second person. They are in no way exceptions to the universal." Yet, it seems to me that despite the claim to the contrary, his wording also suggests that similar treatment of A and S (with respect to omission, etc.) is better viewed as a violable constraint than as a universal. If, on the other hand, Dixon's claim is more narrow and refers to the rule of omission of imperative addressee exclusively, it is largely consistent with the present approach, which is more concerned with the potential impact of the Bias constraints on the overall coding pattern. Yet, some languages (like Shipibo-Konibo discussed in Section 2.2) might be problematic for universality of the accusative pattern of addressee omission as well.

choice of the prefixal gender/class markers, conventionally indicated by numbers (e.g. 'IV' in (5b)) except for the human plural prefix in ('HPL' in 5a)). The same is true for another Northeast Caucasian language, Chechen (Z. Molochieva, p.c.). Also in Abkhaz (Hewitt 1979), a West Caucasian language, the ergative agreement marker is lost with a second person singular A, while the absolutive agreement is retained (for both P and S arguments). The second person plural A-agreement marker is retained, though, as illustrated by the contrast between (6a) and (6b):

(6) Abkhaz (Hewitt 1979: 113)
    a. *Də-šə!*
        him/her-kill.IMP
        'Kill him!' (singular addressee)
    b. *Də-š°-šə!*
        him/her-2A.PL-kill.IMP
        'Kill him!' (plural addressee)

Thus, deletion of the addressee marker in the second person singular imperatives in Abkhaz proceeds on the ergative basis, in accordance with Harmony. Coast Tsimshian (Smalgyax) (Mulder 1994) is similar insofar as deletion of person agreement also proceeds on an ergative basis: A-agreement is deleted, while S-agreement is retained:

(7) Smalgyax (Mulder 1994: 117–18)
    a. *Lümoom-i!*
        help-1SG
        'Help me!'
    b. *Liimi-sm!*
        sing-2PL
        '(You) sing!'

Thus, while in Dyirbal the ergative pattern is realigned to accusative due to the accusative Bias of imperatives, in other cases considered above in (5)–(7), Harmony prevails. In some other languages realignment in imperative formation is partial. In Shipibo-Konibo (Valenzuela 2003), the ergative A cannot be expressed in an imperative construction at all, while the absolutive S is optional (absolutive P is regularly retained):

(8) Shipibo-Konibo (Valenzuela 2003: 398)
    a. *(*Mi-n)   piti   pe-wé!*
        (2-ERG)   fish   eat-IMP
        'Eat fish!'
    b. *(Mi-a)   katan-we!*
        (2-ABS)   go.do-IMP
        '(You) go!'

A still different outcome is attested for languages that restrict imperatives to S arguments. In Kuikúro (Franchetto 1990) a transitive verb in the imperative form is detransitivized (through the use of the "deergative" marker) and triggers absolutive agreement (compare the imperative construction in (9b) with the indicative in (9a)):

(9)   Kuikúro (Franchetto 1990: 414)
    a. *Kága   egé-lâ   kupehé-ni.*
       fish   eat-PNCT   1INC.ERG-PL
       'We all eat fish.'

    b. *E-g-egé-ke*   *kága!*
       2ABS-DEERG-eat-IMP   fish
       'Eat fish!'

The latter two types can be seen as a compromise between two conflicting patterns: either S may alternatively align with either A or P, or else the conflict between the two factors leads to **blocking** of a transitive imperative construction altogether.

    Thus, languages with ergative coding vary with respect to the imperative formation. Some languages retain their ergative features (like Khwarshi), while others show realignment, shedding their ergative characteristics. Some outcomes are more complex, and may be seen as a kind of a compromise between two conflicting constraints. We will have more to say about constraint interaction in §2.4, where this interaction is formalized in Optimality Theory.

2.2.3 *Alignment in control constructions*

Like imperatives, control constructions (also called equi-constructions) are often assumed to have an accusative bias (Dixon 1979, 1994; Kazenin 1994; Manning 1996; Croft 2001): It is the A/S argument that is gapped in the subordinate clause (cf. *I tried _ to be on time*; *I tried _ to finish the paper*). The explanation for this preference is usually the same as for the accusative alignment in imperative formation: the omitted argument should be a controlling/volitional agent/subject. Dixon (1994) and Manning (1996: 18) argue that control structures are universally accusatively aligned, referring to ergative languages such as Mam, Chukchi, Tagalog, and Inuit Eskimo, which omit an A/S controllee in control constructions.

    Yet, again, the situation is less clear-cut than suggested by these authors. Like imperatives, control constructions can be shown to be unproblematic in accusative languages, but show less consistency in ergative languages. In accusative languages, to the best of my knowledge, the gapped argument is always an A/S. In ergative languages, however, variation is attested. While some languages like Tongan (Anderson 1976) follow an accusative pattern in control constructions, other languages like Belhare (as illustrated in (3) above) rather follow an ergative pattern. Yet another possibility is that a control construction is **blocked** with transitives altogether, as in Yucatec Maya, where the controllee is restricted to the intransitive subject (S):

(10)   Yucatec Mayan (Verhoeven 2007, cited in Bickel 2011)
     a. *In=k'áat   bin   Cancun.*
       1SG.A-wish   go   C.
       'I want to go to Cancun.'

When the subordinate verb is transitive, the infinitive in a control pattern is impossible, and a finite form must be used instead:

>   b. *In=k'áat   in=kan   Màaya.*
>   1SG.A-wish   1SG.A-learn[-3SG.O]   M.
>   'I want to learn Maya.'

Thus, the variation in control constructions across ergative languages is similar to the variation we have seen earlier for the imperative formation. The pattern in Tongan is attributed to the accusative Bias, the pattern in Belhare to Harmony, while blocking illustrates a third outcome of the constraint conflict. Yet another resolution of the constraint conflict is attested in Tindi (Daghestanian), where either the ergative or the absolutive NP can be the controllee (Kibrik 1985).

(11)   Tindi (Kibrik 1985, adopted from Van Valin 2001: 57)
>   a. *Wacuła   [jaći   hēła]   q'očā   hik̲'i.*
>   brother.DAT   sister.ABS   see   want   not
>   'Brother doesn't want to see sister.'   Omitted NP = subject

>   b. *Jaćuła   [waći   L'eła]   q'očā   hik̲'i.*
>   sister.DAT   brother.ERG   beat   want   not
>   'Sister_i doesn't want brother to beat __i.'   Omitted NP = direct object

The two latter options (neither A and P, or both A and P are controllees) can again be seen as a compromise in resolving a conflict between the accusative Bias and the Harmony with ergative coding.

   The role of structural factors (our Harmony) for ergative languages has been recognized by Primus (1999: 91), who suggests that "ergativity of syntactic rules is an epiphenomenon of ergative morphological coding". Yet, as we will see shortly this conclusion needs to be generalized, as Harmony is operative both in ergative and accusative languages (ergative vs. accusative Harmony). Moreover, Bias constraints are not homogeneous either: while certain constructions (like imperatives and control constructions considered above) have an accusative Bias, some other constructions (like nominalizations) have an ergative Bias (see Section 2.2.4).

2.2.4 *Alignment in nominalizations*

The constructions considered so far (imperatives, control constructions) have an accusative Bias. One of the constructions which has been reported to have an ergative Bias is nominalization. As is well-known, one of the crosslinguistically common patterns with action nominals is the pattern with S/P genitivized and A either omitted or expressed by an oblique (Comrie 1976). In the literature such cases have been referred to as "passive nominalizations" (for languages that use the same expression for the counterpart of the A as for the agent of passives; Comrie and Thompson 1985), or "ergative-possessive nominalizations" (Koptjevskaja-Tamm 1993). The familiar examples from Russian as well as English counterparts illustrate:

(12) Russian
    a. *prixod   otc-a*
       arrival   father-GEN

    a′. *the arrival of the father*

    b. *čtenie   knig-i   učenikami*
       reading book-GEN   schoolchildren.INSTR

    b′. *the reading of the book by schoolchildren*

Koptjevskaja-Tamm (1993) contrasts ergative-possessive (ERG-POS) nominaliza-tions of the type exemplified above with other basic types of nominalizations: 'sentential' (SENT; both A and P retain sentential form), 'double possessive' (POS-POS: both A and P appear in the genitive/possessive form), and possessive-accusa-tive (POS-ACC: the A is expressed as a possessor, P retains its accusative marking). As illustrated above, ERG-POS nominalizations are also frequent in accusative languages, where Harmony would otherwise predict an accusative pattern. Predic-tably, the ERG-POS pattern is common in ergative languages as well. Thus, in Niuean nominalizations S and P are represented by a possessive form, while A retains ergative marking:

(13) Niuean (Seiter 1980: 120)
    e   *[katofa   haaku   e*   *lautolu]*
    ABS   [choose   my   ERG   they]
    'my being chosen by them to speak'

The same pattern has been reported for many other ergative languages, including Tongan and Samoan (see Koptjevskaja-Tamm 1993 for further references). Espe-cially instructive are the data from ergative languages like Eskimo that restrict genitivization to S/P arguments, but need antipassivization to genitivize an A (Fortescue 1984; Manning 1996):

(14) Greenlandic Eskimo (Fortescue 1984: 46)
    a. *anguti-p   tuqun-nir-a*
       man-REL   kill-NMLZ-his
       'the killing of the man (by somebody)'

    b. *Ikinngum-mi-nik   tuqut-si-nir-a   tusar-para.*
       friend-REFL.POS-INSTR   kill-ANTIP-NMLZ-his   hear-IND.1SG->3SG
       'I heard of his killing his friend.'

Note that in (14) the nominalized verb must take the antipassive marker in order to encode an A as a possessor (as manifested in the possessive agreement). The predominance of the ergative-possessive nominalization in ergative languages can be attributed to the joint effect of Harmony and Bias.

    In accusative languages, however, the ERG-POS pattern is in competition with the POS-ACC pattern, where the A and S arguments genitivize and the P argument retains its sentential marking. As is clear from the literature (Koptjevskaja-Tamm 1993; Malchukov 2004) this pattern is widespread crosslinguistically, in particular it is a prevailing strategy in Altaic languages. Here is one example from Even (Tungusic):

(15)   Even (Malchukov 2004, and fieldnotes)
        [*Hin   buju-m   ma-ča-vu-s]   ehem   har.*
        your   reindeer-ACC kill-NMLZ-ACC-2SG.POS NEG.NFUT.1SG know
        'I didn't know that you killed the (wild) reindeer.'

In (15), the object retains its accusative case, while the embedded subject is cross-referenced by a possessive agreement marker on the participle and appears in the possessive form if pronominal (there is no corresponding genitive case form for nouns in Even).

Importantly, there is no regular corresponding POS-ABS pattern (A/S > POS, P=Abs) attested for ergative languages (Koptjevskaja-Tamm 1993). This distribution, illustrated in Table 2.2, is predicted by the interaction of Bias and Harmony:

TABLE 2.2. **Alignment preferences in nominalizations**

	Harmony	Bias
Accusative	POS-ACC	ERG-POS
Ergative	ERG-POS	ERG-POS

The motivation for the ergative bias of nominalization is not totally clear. Dik (1997) suggests that S and P are privileged candidates for possessive encoding, since these two arguments are most commonly found with nominalizations while the expression of A is infrequent. Ultimately, this can probably be attributed to the fact that A is mostly given, and therefore preferentially absent (cf. Du Bois 1987b on the discourse basis of ergativity). An alternative explanation appeals to affectedness (or related aspectual notions of telicity and incrementality) as an explanatory factor behind the ergative Bias of nominalizations (see Levin and Rappaport Hovav 2005: 97–8 for references and discussion).[7]

2.2.4 Conclusions

Let us summarize the essentials of our approach to the resolution of alignment conflicts in the monotransitive domain:

- certain constructions may have functionally determined Biases;
- when these Biases conform to the coding alignment (Harmony), more cross-linguistic consistency is found;

---

[7] As observed by Brian MacWhinney (p.c), an explanation in terms of affectedness seems to be preferable, since it pertains more specifically to nominalizations, while a discourse-based explanation applies more generally. Yet the exact nature of the connection of affectedness and nominalization still needs to be established. Denis Creissels (p.c.) suggested that this connection may be of diachronic nature: action nominalizations frequently derived from result nominalizations.

- when these Biases conflict with the coding alignment (Harmony), more cross-linguistic variation is found.

In the following section, we will see that the same factors are operating in the domain of ditransitive constructions.

2.3 Alignment conflicts in the ditransitive domain

2.3.1 *Introducing ditransitive alignment*

There has recently been a rise of interest in the typology of ditransitive construc-tions, featuring Agent (A), Theme (T), and Recipient (R) arguments (see Malchukov, Haspelmath, and Comrie 2010 for an overview). Haspelmath (2005a, 2005b), build-ing on the earlier literature (cf. Comrie 1982; Blansitt 1984; Dryer 1986; Siewierska 2004), suggested to define ditransitive alignment in terms of encoding of T (Theme) and R (Recipient) with respect to monotransitive P (Patient). In terms of Haspel-math (2005b; cf. Malchukov, Haspelmath, and Comrie 2010), the basic ditransitive alignment types are indirective (T = P vs. R, as in German (16)), secundative (T vs. P = R, as in Eskimo in (17)), and neutral (T = P = R, as in the English Double Object Construction in (18)):

(16) German
    a. (monotransitive) *Ich*   *aß*   *den*   *Apfel.*
                    I.NOM   ate   the.ACC   apple
                    'I ate the apple.'
    b. (ditransitive) *Ich*   *gab*   *dem*   *Kind*   *den*   *Apfel.*
                  I.NOM   gave   the.DAT   child   the.ACC   apple
                  'I gave the child the apple.'

(17) West Greenlandic (Fortescue 1984: 193, 88)
    a. (monotransitive) *Piita-p*   *takurnarta.q*   *tuqup-paa?*
                    Peter-ERG.SG   stranger.ABS.SG   kill-INT.3SG->3SG
                    'Did Peter kill the stranger?'
    b. (ditransitive) *(Uuma)*   *Niisi*   *aningaasa-nik*   *tuni-vaa.*
                  (that.ERG)   Nisi   money-INSTR.PL   give-ind.3sg->3SG
                  'He gave Nisi money.'

(18) a. (monotransitive) *I read a book.*
    b. (ditransitive) *I gave him a book.*

Schematically, ditransitive alignment can be represented in a way similar to mono-transitive alignment (Haspelmath 2005a, 2005b; cf. Siewierska 2004: Dryer 2007; Malchukov, Haspelmath, and Comrie 2010) (Figure 2.2).

Again as in the case of monotransitive alignment, certain alignment preferences have been noted with respect to dependent marking (case/preposition marking or 'flagging', in terms of Haspelmath) and head marking (agreement, or 'indexing' in terms of Haspelmath). In particular, both Haspelmath (2005b) and Siewierska

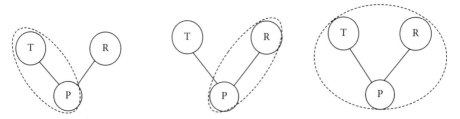

FIGURE 2.2 Basic types of ditransitive alignment: indirective, secundative, and neutral

(2004), working with different samples, showed that flagging exhibits an indirective Bias, while indexing has a secundative Bias.

As in the case of monotransitive alignment, we can further inquire whether other syntactic constructions show alignment preferences. This is the question addressed by Malchukov, Haspelmath, Comrie (2010), who probe into alignment preferences of a number of constructions (passivization; antipassivization; relativization; constituent question formation; reflexivization; reciprocalization; nominalization; incorporation; inverse marking). The question they address is which of the ditransitive objects (T, R) behaves like P with respect to these constructions ("transformations"). In what follows I will selectively consider some constructions which display alignment preferences with the goal of demonstrating how crosslinguistic variation can be explained in a competing motivations approach.

2.3.2 *Ditransitive alignment: antipassives*

While there is no single ditransitive alignment preference associated with different types of passive constructions (Malchukov, Haspelmath, and Comrie 2010),[8] antipassive constructions have a pronounced indirective bias. This is true irrespective of the antipassive type (a deleting antipassive, which prohibits expression of P altogether, or a demoting antipassive, which demotes the P to an oblique). This indirective Bias is understandable, since T provides a better candidate than R for being an incremental theme measuring out an event, so it should be targeted by an antipassive to cancel the entailment that the incremental theme is totally affected (cf. Polinsky 2005 on the semantic function of antipassives). This explanation pertains more directly to demoting antipassives where the direct argument alternates with an oblique, for deleting antipassives the explanation in terms of animacy mentioned in connection with incorporation also seems to apply (see 2.3.3).

The indirective Bias can be demonstrated by considering the application of the antipassive to ditransitive constructions with different alignments. If the construction is indirective, T is targeted (deleted or demoted) in the antipassive. This is illustrated below for the indirective ditransitive pattern in Dyirbal in (19a), contrasted with the antipassive pattern in (19b):

---

[8] Malchukov, Haspelmath, and Comrie (2010) observe that passives with an agentive phrase have secundative Bias, while agentless passives have rather an indirective Bias. Alternatively agentless passives may be viewed as distinct voice categories (anticausatives, resultatives; cf. Siewierska 2005).

(19)   Dyirbal (Dixon 1972: 102, 91)

   a. *Balam*   *miraɲ*   *baŋgul*   *yaṛaŋgu*
      DET.NOM   bean.NOM   DET.ERG   man.ERG
      budin   *bagun*   *ḍugumbilgu.*
      take.PRES/PAST   DET.DAT   woman.DAT
      'The man is taking beans to the woman.'

   b. *Bayi*   *wugal-ɲaɲu*   *bagum*   *ḍiga-gu.*
      he.ABS   give-ANTIP   DET.DAT   cigarette-DAT
      'He is giving out cigarettes.'

In (19b), the T is "demoted" to an oblique (dative) argument, while the recipient (unexpressed here) remains unaffected. Thus, the alignment of antipassives is indirective in Dyirbal. Yet such a language does not provide evidence for an indirective Bias, as this may be due to Harmony as well.

   Evidence for the indirective Bias of antipassives can be found in languages which have secundative or neutral alignment. Thus, Ainu has an "indefinite object prefix" *i-* used as a kind of antipassive; cf. *ku* "drink" vs. *i-ku* "drink (liquor)" (Bugaeva 2010). Ainu features a double object construction with secundative indexing, but the "indefinite object marker" relates to (indefiniteness) of the Theme.

(20)   Ainu (Bugaeva 2010)
      A=i=ko-i-puni   *wa*   *ipe=an.*
      IMPERS=LOG.OBJ=to.APPL-ANTIP-offer   and   eat=LOG.SBJ
      'They served me (food) and I ate.'

In some other languages featuring a secundative construction, both R and T can be deleted. This is the case in Ojibwe:

(21)   Ojibwe (Rhodes 2010: 643)
      (a) ditransitive
          N-gii=miiN-aa.
          1PERS-PAST=give -3OBJ
          'I gave it to him.'
      (b) notional ditransitive with antipassive of both objects
          N-gii= mii-gwe.
          1PERS-PAST=give-INDEF
          'I made a donation.'

Still another outcome of alignment conflicts can be blocking: in some languages with a secundative ditransitive construction, an antipassive cannot be derived from ditransitives. This is the case in Tzotzil (Aissen 1987: 292), and, with a few exceptions, in Halkomelem (Gerdts 2010). In Halkomelem, which features a secundative construction with both basic and derived (applicative) ditransitives, the beneficiary cannot be targeted by the antipassive.

(22) Halkomelem (Gerdts 2010: 584)

    a. *Neṁ   ʔə č   θəy-əłc-t   kwθə-nə   məṅə ʔə   kwθə   snəxwəł-s?*
       go   Q 2SG fix-BEN-TR DET-1SG.POS child OBL DET canoe-3POS
       'Are you going to fix his canoe for your son?'

    b. * *Neṁ   ʔə   č   θəy-əłc-əm   ʔə   kwθə-nə   məṅə*
       go   Q   2SG fix-BEN-MID OBL DET-1SG.POS child
       ʔə   kwθə   snəxwəł-s?
       OBL   DET   canoe-3POS
       'Are you going to fix his canoe for your son?'

In all these cases where indirective Bias conflicts with the secundative coding, the Bias either wins, or their conflict is resolved in variation or blocking. Sometimes, however, Harmony wins. In Chamorro (Cooreman 1987), antipassivization of R arguments is possible for some ditransitive verbs (although most ditransitive verbs do not allow this):

(23) Chamorro (Cooreman 1987: 122)

    a. *Ha-offresi   hao   si   Juan   ni   salape'.*
       ERG.3SG-offer ABS.2SG the Juan OBL money
       'Juan offered you the money.'

    b. *Man-offresi si   Juan   nu   hagu   ni   salape'.*
       ANTIP-offer the Juan OBL EMPH.2SG OBL money
       'Juan offered the money to you.'

On the other hand, we don't readily find languages where coding in a ditransitive construction is indirective, while antipassive operates on a secundative basis (targeting R and P arguments).

Thus, the scenarios of resolution of conflicts between Bias and Harmony constraints in the ditransitive domain are the same as the ones observed for the monotransitive domain. For the case of conflict between secundative Harmony and indirective Bias of antipassives, either Harmony wins (as in Chamorro), or Bias wins (as in Ainu), or else alignment conflict is resolved in blocking (as in Halkomelem) or variation (as in Ojibwe).

2.3.3 *Ditransitive alignment: incorporation*

Another construction which has an indirective Bias is incorporation: It is T that incorporates rather than R. We therefore find more variation in languages with secundative alignment. In some cases Harmony overrides Bias, resulting in R incorporation. Thus, in Ojibwa, R-incorporation yields what Rhodes (1990) calls a "pseudo-transitive" construction with a sole secondary object:

(24) Ojibwe (Rhodes 2010: 646)

    (a) unincorporated
       Miin-an   o-gii=asham-aa-an   o-niijaanis-an.
       blueberry-PL   3ERG=PAST-feed-3OBJ-OBV   3POS-child-OBV
       'She fed her children blueberries.'

(b) incorporated
   Miin-an   *o-gii=asham-aawaso-n-an.*
   blueberry-PL   3ERG-PAST=feed-child-N-INAN.PL
   'She fed her children blueberries.'

Other secundative languages, however, display an opposite pattern: only T can be incorporated. This is the case in nominal compounding/incorporation found with gerundives in Yoruba (Atoyebi, Haspelmath, and Malchukov 2010: 162): only T can be incorporated, as predicted by the Bias constraints:

(25) Yoruba (Atoyebi et al. 2010)
   a. *Bọ́lá*   *fún*   *tálákà*   *ní*   *oúnjẹ.*
      Bola   give   poor   SEC   food
      'Bola gave food to the poor.'

   b. *oúnjẹ*   *fífún*
      food   giving
      'giving of food'

   c. **tálákà*   *fífún*   *(ní oúnjẹ)*
      poor   giving   (of food)

Also in Tukang Besi (Donohue 1999), benefactives/applied objects (primary objects with derived ditransitives) cannot be incorporated:

(26) Tukang Besi (Donohue 1999: 168)
   * *No-sai-ako-wowine.*
   3R-make-APPL-woman
   'He makes (them) for woman.'

Thus, in both Yoruba and Tukang Besi, Bias constraints prevent an R argument from incorporation. The motivation for resistance of R to incorporation probably resides in animacy/prominence: animate arguments tend to resist incorporation. Mithun (1984: 863) suggests that this is due to the fact that incorporation usually targets backgrounded arguments, while animate arguments tend to be foregrounded. The same factor has been implicated in restrictions on idiom formation (Nunberg, Sag, and Wasow 1994; Levin and Rappaport Hovav 2005: 182–3).

2.3.4 *Ditransitive alignment: reciprocal formation*

The two constructions considered so far reveal an indirective Bias. Some other constructions, however, demonstrably have a secundative Bias. This is perhaps most pronounced for reciprocal constructions, which regularly feature a secundative pattern with an A cross-coreferential to R ("give to each other"), rather that an indirective pattern with an A cross-coreferential to T ("give each other (to somebody"). The reason for this Bias is obvious: R, like A, is usually animate, while T is usually inanimate.

Thus, verbal reciprocals usually have secundative alignment with ditransitives (Nedjalkov's (2007a) "indirect diathesis"; A=R reciprocals). This is illustrated for

Even (Tungusic) below, where a reciprocal construction from a monotransitive clause (in 27b) is contrasted with a reciprocal construction from a ditransitive clause (in 28b):

(27)   Even (Malchukov 1995, and own fieldnotes)
    a. *Bej   hurke-m   čor-ra-n.*
       man   youth-ACC   hit-NFUT-3SG
       'The man hit the youth.'

    b. *Hurke-r   čor-mat-ta.*
       youth-PL   hit-RECP-NFUT.3PL
       'The youths are hitting each other.'

(28)   a. *Bej   nimek-tu   d'eple-v   bö-gre-n.*
       man   neighbor-DAT   food-ACC   give-HAB-NFUT.3SG
       'The man gave food to the neighbor.'

    b. *Nimeke-l   d'eple-v   bö-met-kere-r.*
       neighbor-PL   food-ACC   give-RECP-HAB-NFUT.3PL
       'The neighbors used to give food to each other.'

As extensively documented in Nedjalkov (2007a), similar patterns of reciprocals with "indirect diathesis" are common crosslinguistically. As illustrated for Even, they are common in languages with indirective ditransitives, where the secundative Bias conflicts with indirective Harmony. Expectedly, indirect diathesis also prevails in languages with a neutral ditransitive coding pattern. Thus, in Jóola Banjal, only A-R coreference is possible in reciprocals derived from the double object construction.

(29)   Jóola Banjal (Bassène 2010: 200)
    a. *Gu-tteg-or-e   su-mmok.*
       3PL-bit-RECP-TAM   CL4-punch
       'They punched each other.'

    b. *Gu-boɲ-or-boɲ-or   si-letar.*
       3PL-send-RECP-send-RECP   CL4-letter
       'They sent letters to each other.'

In other languages, however, Harmony overrides Bias. Consider Sahaptin (Rude 1997b), which features two different constructions, indirective (with T taking the "object case") and secundative (with R taking the "object case"), the choice being determined by the animacy hierarchy. In particular, when the theme is inanimate, the alignment will be indirective, but with an animate theme[9] both indirective and secundative patterns are an option.

(30)   Sahaptin (Rude 1997b: 335)
    a. *Pa-ní-ya   tílaaki-na   miyuux-mí-yaw.*
       3PL.NOM-give-PST   woman-OBJ   chief-GEN-ALL
       'They gave the woman to the chief.'

---

[9] When the theme is animate and pronominal, only a double object construction is possible.

b. *Pa-ní-ya*   *tílaaki*   *miyúux-na.*
   3PL.NOM-give-PST   woman   chief-OBJ
   'They gave the woman to the chief.'

In accordance with alignment of coding, the reciprocal marks A/T cross-coreference in the indirective construction (31a), and A/R cross-coreference in the secundative construction (31b).

(31)   Sahaptin (Rude 1997b: 336)

     a. *Pápa-ni-ya=taš*   *miyuux-mí-yaw.*
       RECP-gave=we   chief-GEN-ALL
       'We gave each other to the chief.'

     b. *Pápa-ni-ya=taš*   *xaxáykw.*
       RECP-gave=we   money
       'We gave each other money.'

Thus, alignment of the reciprocal construction in Sahaptin largely follows Harmony: alignment in reciprocal formation is indirective in the indirective construction and secundative in the secundative construction. Thus, here as well as in other cases, either factor can win the competition, or the competition is resolved in some other way.

2.3.5 Conclusions: ditransitive alignment

As in the monotransitive domain, the ditransitive alignment is determined by interaction of Harmony and Bias constraints. Table 2.3 (from Malchukov, Haspelmath, and Comrie 2010: 47) summarizes the Bias constraints:[10]

TABLE 2.3. **Alignment preferences in ditransitive domain**

Alignment	**Indirective**	**Secundative**
Preferred by operations	incorporation (and idiom formation) nominalization antipassivization	reciprocalization passivization direct-inverse marking

The mode of the interaction is the same as we have already found for the monotransitive domain: if the Harmony and Bias constraints conspire (converge on the same pattern), more crosslinguistic consistency is observed; if Harmony and Bias constraints conflict, there is more crosslinguistic variation.

---

[10] Recall, however, the cautionary remark in footnote 8: secundative Bias, reflecting the higher prominence/topicality of the recipient argument (cf. Givón 1984: 367–8) is detectable only for passives allowing an agentive phrase. A standard example illustrating the secundative Bias is preferential passivization of the Recipient in the Double Object Construction in English (cf. *John was given a book* and ??*The book was given John*). See Malchukov, Haspelmath, and Comrie 2010 for more discussion.

2.4 Discussion: modeling constraint competition in Optimality Theory

I now show how the competing motivations approach can be modeled in Optimality Theory (Prince and Smolensky 2004b), taking imperative formation for the mono-transitive domain and antipassive formation for the ditransitive domain as representative examples. In Optimality Theory (OT) the two factors considered, Bias and Harmony, are conceptualized as two general constraints, the interaction of which will determine the resultant pattern. The Bias constraints can be conceived as a family of faithfulness constraints (as long as they are rooted in the semantic input), but can also be viewed as markedness constraints, where (local) markedness pertains to naturalness of certain feature combinations. Harmony constraints, requiring matching of behavior to coding are, by contrast, form-based and can be conceived as a particular case of constraints on Output–Output Correspondences (which is a standard way of modeling analogical effects in OT). Under standard assumptions of the theory, the strongest (higher ranking) constraint determines the outcome of the competition. The competition of the constraints is conventionally visualized through the use of tableaux, where competing patterns in rows are evaluated by constraints (shown in columns). The optimal candidate is the one which does not violate a higher ranking constraint (constraint violation is indicated by *, the optimal candidate by ☞).

Let us look first at imperatives from an OT perspective. Imperatives in **accusative-coding** languages show consistently accusative pattern irrespective of the imperative strategy, and the strength of the two constraints. This is illustrated in Table 2.4. This table (as well as Table 2.7 below) is generalized across languages: it applies cross-linguistically, no particular ranking of constraints is assumed. Table 2.4 is also generalized with respect to alignment representation: it glosses over the way in which alignment is manifested (in case, agreement, etc.), rather representing two alignment patterns themselves as a short-cut for candidates. As shown by Table 2.4, in accusative languages, the pattern with accusative alignment (A addressee behaving like an S addressee) will be the winning pattern irrespective of the ranking of the two constraints, as it is preferred both by Harmony and Bias.

TABLE 2.4. **Imperative formation in accusative languages**

Imperative pattern	Bias	(Accusative) Harmony
☞ S = A		
S = P	*	*

Imperatives in ergative languages are expected to show more variation depending on the strength of the two constraints.

TABLE 2.5. **Imperative formation in ergative languages: Bias wins**

Imperative pattern	Bias	(Ergative) Harmony
☞ S = A		*
S = P	*!	

TABLE 2.6. **Imperative formation in ergative languages: Harmony wins**

Imperative pattern	(Ergative) Harmony	Bias
S = A	*!	
☞ S = P		*

If Bias is stronger (higher ranked) than Harmony (Bias ≫ Harmony, as in Table 2.5), the imperative will show accusative alignment (as is the case in Dyirbal, on Dixon's analysis[11]). If Harmony is stronger than Bias (Harmony ≫ Bias, as in Table 2.6), the imperative pattern will be ergative. As we have seen earlier in Khwarshi (see (5)), the coding of participants in the imperative construction shows the same ergative features (in head-, as well as dependent-marking) as attested elsewhere (in indicative constructions).

In some other languages, the outcome can be more complex: as we saw earlier, the conflict can be resolved in a "compromise" resulting in blocking (cf. (9) from Kuikúro), or partial realignment (cf. (8) from Shipibo-Konibo). These other outcomes might need more machinery that the simple "asymmetric" scenarios, when one constraint outranks another, but in principle, OT provides tools to account for such cases. For the blocking scenario, the set of candidates must be extended to include derived patterns (e.g., the "deergative"/antipassive pattern in Kuikúro in (9)). The assumption is that an extra (markedness) constraint against a derived pattern disqualifies the other candidates in cases when Bias and Harmony constraints conflict, but being low ranked, it will not interfere in the competition in a case when no violation of Bias and Harmony constraints is incurred. For the case of partial realignment, one must assume different Harmony ranking for dependent- vs. head-marking: the Harmony constraints for head-marking are ranked higher, capturing the fact that verbal morphology is more entrenched and more resistant to rules of syntax.

The resolution of alignment conflicts in the ditransitive domain is represented in the same way, as illustrated below for antipassive formation (see Table 2.7 and Tables 2.8 and 2.9). As noted earlier, antipassives show a strong indirective Bias, hence their interaction with Harmony constraints lead to different predictions in languages with different ditransitive alignments. In indirective constructions, both Bias and Harmony

---

[11] Dixon (1994: 133–4) notes though an alternative pattern when imperative formation for transitive verbs is mediated through an antipassive.

constraints favor deletion/demotion of a T argument. This is true under any ranking of Bias and Harmony constraints. Since both constraints converge on the same pattern, no crosslinguistic variation is attested: if a language with indirective coding has an antipassive, it is the T that is antipassivized (deleted/demoted).

TABLE 2.7. **Antipassive formation in indirective constructions/languages**

	Bias	(Indirective) Harmony
☞ T-antipassive		
R-antipassive	*	*

The situation is different when an antipassive operates in a secundative-coding construction. In this situation Bias will favor T-demotion/deletion, but Harmony will favor R-demotion/deletion. Here we are dealing with crosslinguistic variation. If Bias wins (Bias ≫ Harmony), antipassivization targets T, rather than the primary object (as, e.g., in (20) from Ainu; see Table 2.8).

TABLE 2.8. **Antipassive formation in secundative constructions/languages: Bias wins**

	Bias	(Secundative) Harmony
☞ T-antipassive		*
R-antipassive	*!	

If Harmony wins (Harmony ≫ Bias): antipassivization targets R (the primary object), violating the indirective Bias (as, e.g., in Chamorro; see (23) and Table 2.9).

TABLE 2.9. **Antipassive formation in secundative constructions/languages: Harmony wins**

	(Secundative) Harmony	Bias
T-antipassive	*!	
☞ R-antipassive		*

Again, some cases represent more complex scenarios of conflict resolution than standard "asymmetric" scenarios. A conflict between Bias and Harmony constraints can either lead to **Blocking** (neither T nor R is antipassivized, as in Halkomelem; cf. (22)), or it can lead to **Variation** (both R and T antipassivize, as in Ojibwe; cf. (21)). Blocking will be represented by extending the list of candidates and constraints, while variation could be routinely represented as a constraint tie (or through methods of stochastic OT for cases when one option is significantly more frequent than another).

Since Harmony and Bias constraints are of a different nature (Bias constraints are purely functional, and can be argued to be a kind of faithfulness constraint, while Harmony constraints are form-based), it is clear that these constraints cannot be ranked intrinsically; rather, their different ranking will give variation across languages ('factorial typology'). Yet, we can provisionally mention some patterns which might determine the constraint ranking for particular cases. First, Bias constraints might be of different strength for particular constructions. Thus, Malchukov, Haspelmath, and Comrie (2010) observe that the secundative Bias is more pronounced for reciprocal as compared to reflexive constructions. Second, the strength of the Harmony constraints tends to be weaker in cases when the coding pattern is inconsistent (split). Thus, it seems symptomatic that Dyirbal which follows Bias at the cost of Harmony in imperative formation (see §2.2.2) is not consistently ergative in coding but like many other Australian languages displays split ergativity. While the majority pattern of nominals is ergative, the minority pattern involving first and second person pronouns follows an accusative pattern. Since the imperative formation rule crucially implicates (the deletion of) second person pronominal subjects, the role of Harmony is equivocal. Looking beyond imperative formation, we may note that when a general rule conflicts with a narrow rule (majority pattern with the minor pattern implicated in the rule), both rules could be relevant, and the outcome is more difficult to predict.[12]

2.5 Concluding remarks

We have considered the outcome of alignment conflicts in the monotransitive and ditransitive domain. We have shown that both recurrent patterns as well as counter-examples can be explained through the interaction of two general factors, Harmony embodying the analogical tendency for coding/behavior matching, and Bias embodying intrinsic alignment preferences dictated by functional properties of individual constructions. When the two factors converge on the same candidate, a crosslinguistically consistent pattern emerges, but when the two constraints are in conflict, we observe crosslinguistic variation. In case of a conflict there are several different scenarios to be considered. First, there are asymmetric scenarios (formalized by strict domination in OT), when the dominating constraint wins (in OT terms, a higher ranking constraint determines the competition). There are also more complex scenarios of conflict resolution, involving variation and blocking. It is satisfying that these scenarios fit nicely into the typology of syntactic conflicts outlined by Moravcsik (2010), as well as a typology of morphological conflicts discussed in Malchukov (2009, 2011).

---

[12] There is èvidence that in case of coding splits both a majority pattern and a minority pattern (insofar as it is relevant for a specific rule) could be important. Thus, in Dyirbal the rule of conjunction reduction operates on an ergative basis both for nouns and pronouns, following the majority pattern (Dixon 1994: 15). In Yidiny, by contrast, conjunction reduction operates on an ergative basis for nouns and on an accusative basis for pronouns, in both cases in accordance with the coding pattern (Dixon 1994: 175). In the former case the majority pattern is implicated by the Harmony constraints, in the latter case the minor pattern is implicated.

Of course, there remain a number of open questions that could not be addressed in this chapter. Thus, more work should be done on providing independent evidence for individual Bias constraints, as well as more theoretical consideration being given to the question of how these Biases can be represented in a model of grammar. A further controversial issue is to what extent the Bias constraints manifested by different constructions can be weighted with respect to each other, and if it is possible to rank them on an extended hierarchy along the lines of Croft (2001). It goes without saying that this can be done in a principled way only to the extent that the same factor is implicated in different Bias constraints, which is not obvious at this stage.[13] More should also be said about Harmony constraints, especially in case of coding splits, leading to different analogical pressures. Yet, it seems that already in the present form the competing motivations approach can go a long way in explaining both recurrent and exceptional patterns in syntactic alignment in terms of two very general and independently motivated constraints.

It may be appropriate to conclude this chapter by addressing a thorny question of whether competing motivations operate in synchrony or, rather, in diachrony (as suggested by Cristofaro, this volume, and Newmeyer, this volume), and a related question of the 'cognitive reality' of competing motivations. My position (as also articulated in Malchukov 2010) is that functional explanations, as advocated by practitioners of the Competing Motivations approach, are not in competition but rather are complementary to diachronic explanations, which explain the rise of a particular language structure by relating it to its historical source. On this view, functional factors are responsible for the stability and spread of constructions, while a diachronic approach provides an explanation why a certain structure arises in the first place (this process may be partially driven by different factors; see Cristofaro, this volume). Furthermore, as long as proposed motivations are externally motivated ("grounded", in terms of Optimality Theory), they are also assumed to be present synchronically and manifest themselves in language processing and language use. For the case at hand, recall that the proposed Harmony and Bias constraints are conceived as specific instantiations of cognitive constraints underlying analogy (Harmony) or functional fitness (Bias), which are also known to operate elsewhere (Haspelmath, this volume, for example, describes analogical effects in terms of "system pressure," and Dressler et al., this volume, discuss functional fitness in terms of markedness). Now, both analogical pressures (as manifested in Harmony) and functional fitness/markedness of certain structures (as manifested in Biases) are well established factors in psycholinguistic research. Analogical effects have been repeatedly demonstrated in priming studies, while markedness effects have been discussed in connection to frequency (they manifest themselves, or, on some accounts, are

---

[13]   Recall that different factors have been implicated in different Bias constraints, including agentivity (imperatives, control constructions), prominence/animacy (reciprocals, incorporation), and possibly affectedness/event structure (antipassives). Levin and Rappaport Hovav (2005: 164–75) review conflicting claims in the literature concerning the shape of the argument hierarchy and show that controversies are largely due to the fact that some hierarchies are designed to reflect the position of arguments in the event structure, while others reflect prominence relations between arguments.

derived from frequency of particular property clusters), and also in relation to the status of prototypical or cardinal categories (see Bornkessel-Schlesewsky and Schlesewsky, this volume, on cardinal categories as "attractors" in cognitive space). Of course, the task of firmly establishing the nature and psycholinguistic mechanisms behind individual constraints (e.g. behind individual Bias constraints) is beyond the scope of this study and can only be achieved through a concerted effort of a linguistic and psycholinguistic community.

3

Animate object fronting in Dutch: A production study

MONIQUE J. A. LAMERS AND HELEN DE HOOP

3.1 Introduction

Subject-before-object is by far the most common word order in the languages of the world (cf. Greenberg 1966b: 76–7; Hawkins 1983: 1; Tomlin 1986: 22; Comrie 1989: 87–8), and one of the principles Tomlin (1986) suggests to explain this general preference is the principle he calls *Animated-first*. Because subjects are mostly animate noun phrases (or because animate noun phrases are often subjects), *Animated-first* predicts subjects occur in clause-initial position. Psycholinguistic research has revealed that in many languages animacy, independently of grammatical function, influences preferred word order in the sense that speakers prefer to start with an animate noun phrase and hearers are better at recalling sentences that start with an animate noun phrase (a.o., Bock and Warren 1985; McDonald et al. 1993; Ferreira 1994; Prat-Sala and Branigan 2000; Christianson and Ferreira 2005; Branigan et al. 2008; Bornkessel-Schlesewsky and Schlesewsky 2009b). In general, this preference is explained in terms of prominence in different hierarchies possibly affecting the conceptual accessibility (see also Primus 1999; van Bergen 2011; Lamers 2012).

Corpus research (Bouma 2008: 87–102) shows that about 70% of the main clauses in Dutch start with their grammatical subject. Fronted objects are generally con-sidered to be grammatical in Dutch, but some types of objects are difficult to front, while others front more easily or even preferably. Bouma (2008: 111–12) finds that the difference between demonstrative pronouns and personal pronouns is dramatic in the case of objects. Personal pronominal objects have a less than 1% chance of appearing sentence-initially, while demonstrative pronominal objects topicalize more often than not (that is, in 60%). In other words, a construction like (1) taken from the spoken Dutch Corpus CGN (Bouma 2008: 115) is extremely rare, while utterances like (2) and (3), also found in the CGN (Bouma 2008: 280, 99) are very common and may sound even more natural than their counterparts in subject-before-object word order:

(1) *Jou   moest   ik hebben*
     you   must.PAST I   have
     'You, I was looking for.'

(2) *Dat zegt ie   altijd*
     that says he.REDUCED always
     'That's what he always says.'

(3) *Dat hoort u   mij niet zeggen*
     that hear   you me   not   say
     'You didn't/won't hear me say that.'

Note that across languages most transitive sentences come with an animate subject (Comrie 1989). When the subject is animate and the object is inanimate, as indeed is the case in most transitive sentences in Dutch (van Tiel and Lamers 2007), object fronting would violate two important tendencies in Dutch: the tendency to start a sentence with a subject and the tendency to start a sentence with an animate noun phrase. We formulate these tendencies in terms of two violable, in principle independent, and potentially conflicting constraints in an Optimality Theoretic fashion, called SUBJECT FIRST and ANIMATE FIRST (see de Hoop and Lamers 2006; de Swart 2007; Bouma 2008; van Bergen 2011 for similar proposals).

(4) SUBJECT FIRST: Start a clause with the subject.

(5) ANIMATE FIRST: Start a clause with an animate noun phrase.

Although these tendencies are notoriously present in Dutch, both can be violated, as can be seen from the existence of utterances such as (2)–(3) above. Those utterances start with a noun phrase which not only has the grammatical function of object, but which is inanimate as well, hence both constraints are violated. We assume that other factors may overrule the constraints in (4) and (5), such that the optimal result can be an utterance with an inanimate object preceding an animate subject, as in the examples (2) and (3). According to Bouma (2008), one important predictor for object fronting in Dutch is the type of noun phrase. Because in (2) and (3) the object is a demonstrative pronoun and the subject is a personal pronoun, the probability that the object in these utterances appears in clause-initial position is higher than that it remains in situ. The type of noun phrase (demonstrative pronoun, personal pronoun) in relation to its grammatical function thus clearly overrules the influence of other factors such as animacy. That is why sentences like (2) and (3) are very common in Dutch, even though the fronted object is inanimate, while constructions like (1) are extremely rare, despite the animacy of the fronted object.

Since for this chapter we are mainly interested in the interplay between animacy, grammatical function and word order, we will only take into account sentences with full noun phrases where one argument (the subject or the object) is animate, while the other is inanimate. In order to determine the role of animacy on object fronting in Dutch, we will focus on the competition between the two preferences formulated above. We take these preferences to be two violable, potentially conflicting constraints in an Optimality Theoretic sense (cf. Blutner et al. 2006; Smolensky and Legendre; 2006) and we will examine verb classes with different types of selectional (animacy) restrictions (cf. Lamers 2001).

In most transitive clauses the two constraints SUBJECT FIRST and ANIMATE FIRST go hand in hand, because usually the subject of a transitive verb is animate whereas its object is inanimate (Comrie 1989; van Tiel and Lamers 2007; see also Lamers and van Tiel 2012). However, for certain classes of psych verbs, the situation is different. Psych verbs such as *convince* and *disgust* in English select an animate object, while the subject can be inanimate. If this is the case, and a sentence contains one animate and one inanimate noun phrase, the two constraints SUBJECT FIRST and ANIMATE FIRST are necessarily in conflict. Dependent on the relative strengths of the two constraints, we might expect object fronting to occur more often with these types of verbs than with most transitive verbs, such as agentive verbs which usually have an animate subject, and experiencer-subject verbs which never have an inanimate subject.

In this chapter we present the results of a production experiment that was carried out using three types of verbs in connection with animate and inanimate noun phrases (DPs). In this experiment, besides a strong preference for subject-initial sentences, a clear ANIMATE FIRST effect is found. Although this ANIMATE FIRST preference is less strong than the SUBJECT FIRST preference, it does play an important role in language production. We analyzed the results and came to the conclusion that object fronting can be viewed as the resolution of a conflict between ANIMATE FIRST and SUBJECT FIRST.

Whereas both types of psych verbs select an animate object, we find increased object fronting only for one type of psych verbs. Interestingly, two rating studies by Lamers (2001: 141–67; 2007) showed a similar difference between the two classes of psych verbs. In these studies ease of comprehensibility was rated for subject- and object-initial clauses with agentive/experiencer-subject verbs, causative psych verbs, and unaccusative psych verbs. Besides an overall subject-first preference, object-initial clauses were rated as easiest to comprehend if an unaccusative psych verb was used. In other words, unaccusative psych verbs allow object-initial clauses to a greater extent than the other type, the causative psych verbs. This difference corroborates the findings of our production experiment. We will argue that the key to the puzzle lies in a syntactic difference between the two types of psych verbs; causative psych verbs allow for passivization while unaccusative psych verbs do not. This characteristic provides the speaker with the possibility to satisfy not only the ANIMATE FIRST, but also the stronger SUBJECT FIRST constraint. Of course, in order to do so, the speaker has to produce a passive construction which is more costly than producing an active sentence (Levelt 1989: 260–5; Bock, Loebell, and Morey 1992). Following Malchukov (2006b), we assume that fulfilling the higher ranked constraints SUBJECT FIRST and ANIMATE FIRST happens at the cost of violating a lower ranked constraint, one that penalizes the use of passive voice. Because passivization is no option for unaccusative psych verbs, a speaker who wishes to satisfy ANIMATE FIRST has no choice but to front the object, thereby violating SUBJECT FIRST. This explains not only the results of our production experiment but also the difference found in Lamers' (2001, 2007) earlier rating studies.

3.2 Animacy selected by different types of verbs

As we have briefly discussed above, whether the two constraints, SUBJECT FIRST and ANIMATE FIRST, can both be satisfied by a speaker or not depends on the animacy of the arguments as well as the selectional restrictions of the verb. To investigate the possible interplay between selectional restrictions and animacy on the one hand, and how these two factors relate to the constraints SUBJECT FIRST and ANIMATE FIRST on the other hand, we will discuss argument linearization of three different classes of verbs in Dutch, basically following Lamers' (2001: 15–35) distinction in verb classes. The first class of verbs contains verbs which normally require their subjects to be animate. Thematically these subjects can be either Agents, such as the subject of *bijten* "bite," or Experiencers such as the subject of *bewonderen* "admire." We will follow Lamers (2001) and name all of these verbs *agentive verbs*, that is, both the Agent-Patient as well as the Experiencer-Theme verbs. The other two classes of verbs are usually called *psych verbs*, and following again Lamers (2001), within this group we distinguish between the *causative psych verbs* (of which the subject gets the thematic role of Stimulus or Cause, whereas the object has the thematic role of Experiencer) and the *unaccusative psych verbs* (whose subject and object get the thematic roles of Theme and Experiencer, respectively) (cf. Lamers 2001: 15–35; also Grimshaw 1990: 35–42). An example of a causative psych verb in Dutch is *overtuigen* "convince" and an example of a unaccusative psych verb in Dutch is *bevallen* "please," or *piacere* "please" in Italian (Belletti and Rizzi 1988; Hoekstra 1984: 123– 56; Levin and Rappaport Hovav 2005: 158–66). Note that the characteristics of the verb *please* in English are different. Dowty (1991) analyzes *please* as a causative psych verb in English, while Belletti and Rizzi (1988) as well as Grimshaw (1990: 29–30) consider it to be unaccusative. In English, passivization is less restricted than in Dutch and the object of *please* can become the subject in a passive sentence. Since Experiencers are necessarily animate, both classes of psych verbs require their object to be animate. However, the two classes differ in the thematic role of the subject: the subject of causative psych verbs is more 'agent-like' than the subject of an unaccusative psych verb. The two classes of verbs can be distinguished in Dutch on the basis of a syntactic test. Whereas causative psych verbs allow passivization, unaccusative psych verbs do not:

(6) a. *De foto   overtuigde   de journalist*
        the photo   convinced   the reporter
        'The photo convinced the reporter.'

    b. *De journalist   werd   door   de foto   overtuigd*
        the reporter   became   by   the photo   convinced
        'The reporter became convinced by the photo.'

(7)   a. *De foto   beviel   de journalist*
          the photo   pleased   the reporter
          'The photo pleased the reporter.'

     b. **De journalist   werd   door   de foto   bevallen*
          the reporter   became   by   the photo   pleased

Unaccusative psych verbs are comparable with German psych verbs that assign dative instead of accusative case to their objects. These sentences with dative case objects cannot passivize, nor is an impersonal passive possible (Zaenen 1993). Note, however, that in Dutch there is no difference in morphological case marking of the objects of the two classes of psych verbs as there is no morphological difference between accusative and dative case in Dutch. For a more detailed discussion of the possible differences in underlying structure of causative psych verbs and unaccusative verbs, see den Besten (1989: 245–52). So, whereas causative psych verbs can passivise in Dutch (cf. (6b)), unaccusative psych verbs cannot (cf. (7b)). This cannot be related to a difference in the type of object, since both types of objects have the thematic role of Experiencer and thus have to be animate, while there is neither a difference in morphological case (unlike in German). Hence, the difference seems to be related to the different thematic roles of the subjects of these two types of verbs. The subject of a causative psych verb has more Proto-Agent properties than the subject of an unaccusative psych verb, which is a Theme (cf. Primus 1999, 2012; see also Lamers 2012). Passive formation is crosslinguistically characterized as demotion of the Agent. As a consequence, the Stimulus subject gets demoted in a passive construction, while the Theme subject of an unaccusative psych verb cannot.

In order to investigate the influence of animacy on word order in Dutch, we will thus investigate three types of verbs: (i) agentive verbs that select an animate subject and can passivize; (ii) causative psych verbs that select an animate object and can passivize; (iii) unaccusative psych verbs that select an animate object and cannot passivize.

3.3 A production experiment with different types of verbs

In our experiment we followed a similar procedure to the one used by Ferreira (1994). In a series of production experiments Ferreira (1994) asked participants to form an English sentence using the words in a prompt consisting of two DPs and a verb. The DPs either differed in animacy, or were both animate. Besides this, Ferreira used two different verb groups that differed in selectional restriction. One group consisted of agentive verbs (both Agent-Patient and Experiencer-Theme verbs, e.g., *avoid, upset*) choosing an animate subject as the subject of the sentence. The other group of verbs consisted of the causative psych verbs (e.g., *depress*). The results showed that in English more passive sentences are produced when the two nouns differ in animacy, thus indicating a direct effect of animacy.

English differs from Dutch in that, given an animate and an inanimate argument, the use of a passive construction is not the only way to promote the animate argument in a sentence with a causative psych verb. It is also possible to front the object to clause-initial position. Moreover, in the case of unaccusative psych verbs object fronting is the only possibility to start the sentence with the animate argument, because these verbs do not passivize. Hence, in our study we not only tested agentive and causative psych verbs (as Ferreira 1994 did for English), but we also tested unaccusative psych verbs, the same ones as used by Lamers (2001, 2007) in ease of comprehensibility ratings. In accordance with the findings of Ferreira (1994), we expect to find more passive sentences with causative psych verbs than with agentive verbs. For unaccusative psych verbs we expect more object fronting as sentences with unaccusative psych verbs lack a passive counterpart. With regard to causative psych verbs, we expect object fronting to be less likely to occur than passivization, because the latter allows satisfaction of both ANIMATE FIRST and SUBJECT FIRST. Thus, the highest number of object-before-subject sentences is expected with unaccusative psych verbs. However, given the strong effect of SUBJECT FIRST in Dutch, a high number of subject-before-object sentences is expected for each verb type. Because in subject-before-object sentences with agentive verbs, both ANIMATE FIRST and SUBJECT FIRST are satisfied, we expect the frequency of subject-initial sentences with agentive verbs to be the highest.

3.3.1 *Methods*

In this production study participants had to make a sentence using a verb in combination with two specific arguments presented in a stimulus/prompt on a list. Participants were told to carefully read the instructions which included three examples. They were instructed to write down a sentence on the line below the stimulus, using all three words presented in the stimulus. In Figure 3.1 an example of such a stimulus is provided. It was stressed that participants should make one sentence for each stimulus on the list. Additionally, it was emphasized that they were free to form their own sentences using the three words in the stimulus. This was different from the instruction that was given in the study by Ferreira (1994). In her study, participants were instructed to use no other content words than the words given in the prompt. Although such an instruction might limit the variation in produced sentence construction, which is an advantage for analyzing the data, it might also instantiate the construction of shorter and less natural sentences. As a consequence, this might discourage the forming of passive constructions which are longer and more complex. In order to allow natural language production as much as possible, we did not restrict the participants' use of additional content words. Therefore, the example sentences could be different from sentences the participants would have constructed using the three words in the each of the example stimuli. An additional problem that became apparent in the pilot study was that participants could be tempted to use some of the verbs with a reflexive pronoun, as illustrated with the verb *ergeren* "annoy" in (8b):

(8) a. *De   rotzooi   ergert   de   buurman*
       the   mess   annoys   the   neighbour
       'The mess is annoying the neighbour.'

b. *De   buurman   ergert   zich   aan   de   rotzooi*
   the   neighbour annoys   REFL   at   the   mess
   'The neighbour is annoyed by the mess.'

Therefore, in one of the examples such a verb form was used, pointing out that this type of construction was not allowed. It took participants approximately 20 minutes to fill out the questionnaire.

| *Gebruik:* | *bewonderen* | *de kleur* | *de schilder* |
| *Use:* | *admire* | *the colour* | *the painter* |

FIGURE 3.1 Example of a stimulus

3.3.2 *Material*

We selected eighteen verbs (six of each verb type) from Lamers' (2001) rating study. These were combined with six pairs of animate and inanimate definite DPs in such a way that each combination occurred in a stimulus with one item of each verb type. This way each animate–inanimate DP pair was combined with three different verbs. Stimuli were distributed over two lists. In a stimulus the verb preceded the two DPs. The animate DP preceded the inanimate DP in half the stimuli and vice versa. The order was equally distributed over verb types and lists in such a way that if one order was used on a given list, the order was different on the other list. Repetitions of DP combinations were kept as far apart as possible by dividing each list in three different blocks. No verbs were repeated on a single list.

3.3.3 *Participants*

Thirty native speakers of Dutch (10 male, 20 female; mean age 63,5 years) participated.

3.3.4 *Results*

The sentences produced by the participants were categorized per verb type in four different categories: (I) subject-initial active constructions, (II) subject-initial (pseudo)passive constructions, (III) object-initial active constructions, and (IV) other constructions.

Data were analyzed for word order and animacy, because of the difference in selectional restrictions of the verbs. The categorization as indicated above was used for word order. Sentences were categorized by the animacy of the subject and object for animacy. Subject-first sentences (category I) were classified as animate-first sentences for agentive verbs, as were the passive constructions with causative psych verbs (category II), and the object-initial sentences with both types of psych verbs (category III). Inanimate-first sentences were passive constructions and object-initial sentences with agentive verbs (categories II and III), and subject-first sentences with causative and unaccusative psych verbs (category I). An overview of the categories is given in Table 3.1.

TABLE 3.1. **Overview of categories of produced sentences and the animacy and syntactic function of the first DP**

Verb type	Category I SO Active	Category II Passive	Category III OS Active
Agentive	Animate subject	Inanimate subject	Inanimate object
Causative "psych"	Inanimate subject	Animate subject	Animate object
Unaccusative "psych"	Inanimate subject		Animate object

Loglinear analyses were used.[1] The level for significance used was 0.01 ($α ≤ 0.01$; $z > 2.33$) to account for the repeated measures design.[2] The significance level was adjusted for the pairwise comparisons to the number of comparisons ($α ≤ 0.0033$; $z > 2.72$).[3] For the analyses on syntactic word order the independent variables were Verb Type with possible levels of agentive verb, causative psych verb, unaccusative psych verb, and Structure with the possible levels being the produced constructions, or a combination of these constructions (category I, II, III, IV). For the conceptual word order analysis, Structure has the levels animate-first, inanimate-first, and other. All analyses were initially run including Presentation Word Order as an independent factor as well. The analyses reported in this chapter did not include this factor as no significant effect of Presentation Word Order was found in the initial analyses. Only significant effects are reported.

As expected, most constructions produced in this experiment were subject-initial sentences (category I and II). With agentive verbs 95% of the sentences were subject-initial with 79% using active voice and 16% passive. Stimuli with causative psych verbs resulted also mainly in subject-initial constructions with 60% active and 27% passive constructions. The number of subject-initial constructions was lowest for stimuli with unaccusative psych verbs with 61% active constructions. There were no object-initial constructions with agentive verbs. The number of object-initial structures was highest for unaccusative psych verbs (24%). Object-initial sentences were hardly produced if a causative psych verb had to be used (2%). An overview of the results is given in Table 3.2 and Figure 3.2.

---

[1] A loglinear analysis was chosen because it is the most suitable analysis to predict the expected cell frequencies in a multiway contingency table of categorical data. A reported main effect indicates that the factor influences the dependent variable (i.e. frequencies of the structures, or the frequencies of animacy word order). An interaction points out that there is an interplay between the two independent factors on the dependent variable.

[2] This way we reduced the probability of incorrectly rejecting the H_o hypothesis (Type I error) because of violations of assumptions of the loglinear analysis using a repeated measure design (see Field 2010).

[3] Because multiple comparisons increase the probability of committing a type I error we reduced the level of significance according the Bonferroni correction (Field 2010).

TABLE 3.2. **Percentage of produced sentences per category and verb type**

Verb type	Category I SO Active (%)	Category II Passive (%)	Category III OS Active (%)	Category IV Other (%)
Agentive	79	16	0	6
Causative "psych"	60	27	2	11
Unaccusative "psych"	61		24	14

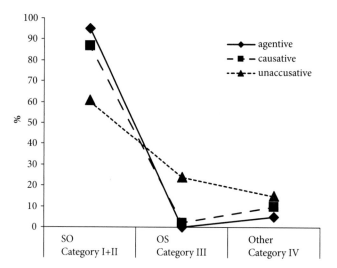

FIGURE 3.2 Percentage of produced subject-initial and object-initial sentences for each verb type

Statistical analyses, including Verb Type (agentive, causative psych, unaccusative psych) and Structure (subject-initial (categories I + II), Object-initial (category III), other (category IV)) as dependent variables showed an interaction of Verb Type and Structure ($z = 2.63$). Pairwise comparisons showed significant differences between agentive and unaccusative psych verbs ($z = 4.22$), as well as between causative and unaccusative psych verbs ($z = 5.18$). The comparison between agentive verbs and causative psych verbs revealed a main effect ($z = 9.14$). This is illustrated in Figure 3.2. However, the analysis in which the subject-initial structure was split between active constructions (category I) and passive constructions (category II) and, hence, Structure as an independent variable included all four categories (I, II, III, IV), and with Verb Type being agentive verb and causative psych verb showed an interaction of Verb Type and Construction as well ($z = 2.63$) (see also Figure 3.3).[4]

---

[4] Unaccusative psych verbs as a level of Verb Type was not included since it is not possible to form a passive construction with this verb type.

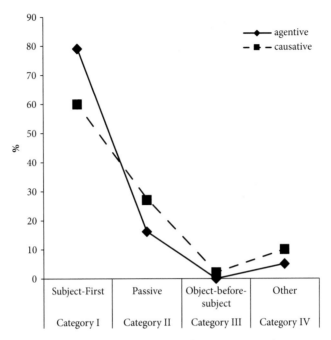

FIGURE 3.3 Percentage of produced sentences in the four categories with agentive and causative psych verbs

Table 3.3 shows that the highest incidence of sentences with an animate DP preceding the inanimate DP is found for stimuli with agentive verbs (79%). Less than one-third of the stimuli with verbs in which animate-initial and subject-initial cannot go hand in hand in active constructions resulted in an animate-first sentence (29% for causative psych verbs and 24% for unaccusative psych verbs). Statistical analysis showed an interaction of Verb Type and Construction (z = 8.97). Pairwise comparisons revealed differences between agentive verbs and causative psych verbs (z = 7.26), as well as between agentive verbs and unaccusative psych verbs (z = 8.48). There was a main effect between the two types of psych verbs (z = 10.38).

TABLE 3.3. Percentage of produced animate-first and inanimate-first sentences per verb type

Verb type	Animate-first (%)	Inanimate-first (%)	Other (%)
Agentive verbs	79	16	6
Causative "psych" verbs	29	60	11
Unaccusative "psych" verbs	24	61	14

In summary, as we expected, following the differences in strength of the two preferences, for each verb type more subject-initial than object-initial sentences were produced. Stimuli with agentive verbs resulted in the highest percentage of active subject-initial sentences, in accordance with the fact that these sentences satisfy both ANIMATE FIRST and SUBJECT FIRST. With agentive verbs no object fronting with the inanimate object preceding the animate subject was produced. Stimuli with causative psych verbs resulted in a relatively high number of passive constructions with an animate sentence-initial subject, again satisfying both ANIMATE FIRST and SUBJECT FIRST. As predicted, object fronting occurred only with animate objects, by which the participants satisfied ANIMATE FIRST but violated SUBJECT FIRST. Moreover, although object fronting is generally rare due to the strength of SUBJECT FIRST, object-before-subject sentences with unaccusative psych verbs (leading to satisfaction of ANIMATE FIRST) were almost as frequent as passive sentences with causative psych verbs (leading to satisfaction of both ANIMATE FIRST and SUBJECT FIRST).

3.3.5 *Discussion*

As we expected on the basis of a preference to start a sentence with an animate noun phrase (ANIMATE FIRST), object fronting of a full noun phrase occurs more often when the object is necessarily animate. There is clearly an overall preference to produce subject-initial active sentences. Besides that, the results show a striking difference between the two classes of psych verbs that require an animate object: more passive constructions are produced for causative psych verbs. Passives in the case of psych verbs allow the speaker to start with the subject as well as with an animate DP. Since unaccusative psych verbs cannot be used in passives, speakers must choose whether they start with the subject (SUBJECT FIRST), *or* with the animate DP (ANIMATE FIRST). In the latter case they front the object, that is, they produce an object-before-subject sentence. We claim that the difference in passivization possibilities between the two types of verbs explains the increase in production of object fronting in the case of unaccusative psych verbs. At the same time, this difference between the two types of verbs can explain the increase in comprehensibility rating of object-before-subject sentences with unaccusative psych verbs (Lamers 2001, 2007).

De Swart (2007) put forward an explanation for word order variation. He suggests that the speaker takes the hearer's perspective into account when calculating the optimal form. In such an asymmetric model of bidirectional optimization, object fronting is only possible in case the grammatical functions remain recoverable (de Swart 2007; see also Malchukov 2006b). This would explain a higher acceptability of object fronting in the case of psych verbs, since a difference in animacy between the two DPs facilitates the interpretation of the animate DP as the object even when it is in initial position. After all, with the object being the Experiencer, it is the animate DP that has to be the object. However, object fronting in the case of causative psych verbs was rated to be more difficult to understand than in the case of unaccusative psych verbs (Lamers 2001, 2007). This can be explained in the light of our findings in the production experiment: because a speaker does not have the possibility to produce an alternative (passive) form, fronting the animate object becomes the only way to satisfy ANIMATE FIRST. This leads to an increase in the production of object-before-subject sentences and it also explains the increase in the acceptability of object-before-subject in Lamers' (2001, 2007) rating studies.

3.4 Conclusion

We examined the phenomenon of object fronting in Dutch sentence production. We conducted a production experiment and found that, next to the preference to produce subject-initial sentences, object fronting is relatively frequent in cases of unaccusative psych verbs, while causative psych verbs give rise to the use of more passive sentences. Because a speaker cannot use a passive construction in the case of an unaccusative psych verb (as these verbs do not allow passivization), fronting the animate object is the only way for a speaker to satisfy the preference to start the sentence with an animate noun phrase. This then leads to an increase in the production of object fronting in an experimental setting. In addition, the order in which the object precedes the subject is also understood more easily with unaccusative verbs than with the other two types of verbs (that is, object-before-subject is rated higher on a scale of comprehensibility when the verb is an unaccusative psych verb), as reported in Lamers (2001, 2007).

Acknowledgments

We thank Geertje van Bergen, Lotte Hogeweg, Sander Lestrade, Kees de Schepper, and Peter de Swart for constructive discussions of the ideas presented in this chapter. We are grateful for valuable comments provided by the editors of this volume, Brian MacWhinney, Edith Moravcsik, and Andrej Malchukov, and by two anonymous reviewers. A special word of thanks goes to Vera van Mulken and Thijs Trompenaars for their help in the final editing stage. The Netherlands Organisation of Scientific Research (NWO) is gratefully acknowledged for financial support.

4

Patterns in competing motivations and the interaction of principles

JOHN A. HAWKINS

4.1 Introduction

This chapter investigates the ways in which different linguistic principles cooperate and compete, as seen in data from language performance and in the distribution of grammatical variants across languages. Some data from (second) language learning will also be briefly considered. I shall point to three general patterns in these data that shed light on how principles interact and work together to define possible vs. impossible, and preferred vs. less preferred outputs, in performance, in grammars, and in learning stages.

My purpose in drawing attention to these patterns is *not* primarily to try and better understand what the exact principles are in these respective areas. Progress on that front is already being made in the various subdisciplines of linguistics and psycholinguistics. Rather my goal is to clarify *how* principles work together and *why* some should be stronger than others and should win more of the competitions. It is the logic of this interaction that is, I submit, currently mysterious, largely stipulated, and that has been, at best, anecdotally observed in the literature and not explained. I have a general hypothesis to offer, which appears to account for my data and for data sets discussed in other chapters in this volume and which may merit further testing. Ultimately we want to know how and why different principles reinforce one another in the ways they do, and how and why they compete as they do.

I will argue that the patterns of cooperation and competition, even in grammars, make a lot of sense when viewed from the perspective of language use, specifically when viewed from the kinds of efficiency and ease of processing considerations that I have defined in Hawkins (2004, 2009a, 2014). Just as efficiency and ease of processing can be argued to structure the basic principles of performance and of grammar, so too the interaction between principles, the manner of their cooperation, and their relative strength or weakness in competition seem to be determined by these same general forces of efficiency and ease that structure the principles themselves.

4.2 Pattern One: Degree of preference

(1) PATTERN ONE: Each principle P applies to predict a set of outputs {P}, as opposed to a competing set {P′} possibly empty, in proportion to the degree of preference defined by P for {P} over {P′} within a theory of processing ease and efficiency.

4.2.1 *Performance*

There are degrees of syntactic complexity and weight that impact word order selections in languages with choices in different languages. Extensive data have been discussed in Hawkins (2004, 2009a, 2014) and are claimed to follow from a principle of Minimize Domains:

(2) MINIMIZE DOMAINS (MiD)
The human processor prefers to minimize the connected sequences of linguistic forms and their conventionally associated syntactic and semantic properties in which relations of combination and/or dependency are processed. The degree of this preference is proportional to the number of relations whose domains can be minimized in competing sequences or structures, and to the extent of the minimization difference in each domain.

Some linear orderings reduce the number of words needed to recognize and construct the phrases of a sentence and their combinatorial relations, compared with other ordering possibilities, making phrase structure processing faster. This is exemplified in (3).

(3) a. The man [$_{VP}$ waited [$_{PP_1}$ for his son] [$_{PP_2}$ in the cold but not unpleasant wind]]
                                  1   2   3   4   5

     b. The man [$_{VP}$ waited [$_{PP_2}$ in the cold but not unpleasant wind] [$_{PP_1}$ for his son]]
                              1   2   3   4   5   6   7   8   9

The three items, V, PP1, PP2 can be recognized and constructed on the basis of five words in (3a), that is, in the string proceeding from the verb *waited* to the second preposition *in*, compared with nine in (3b), that is, in the string from *waited* to the second preposition *for*, assuming that (head) categories such as P immediately project to mother nodes like PP, enabling the parser to construct them online. Sentence (3a) involves a shorter domain for recognizing the VP Phrasal Combination Domain (PCD) with a high IC-to-word ratio of $3/5 = 60\%$. Sentence (3b) involves a longer domain with a lower $3/9 = 33\%$ ratio.

Minimize Domains predicts that PCDs should be as short as possible and IC-to-word ratios as high as possible, and the degree of this preference should be proportional to the minimization difference between competing orderings. For a head-initial language like English this amounts to a preference for short before long constituents, in proportion to their relative weight and complexity. For a head-final language like Japanese, domains for phrase structure processing are shortened by positioning long before short phrases.

(4) PHRASAL COMBINATION DOMAIN (PCD)
The PCD for a mother node M and its I(mmediate) C(onstituent)s consists of the smallest string of terminal elements (plus all M-dominated non-terminals over the terminals) on the basis of which the processor can construct M and its ICs.

Structures like (3) have been examined (Hawkins 2000) in which the two PPs are permutable with truth-conditional equivalence (i.e. the speaker had a choice). Only 15% (58/394) had long before short. Among those with at least a one-word weight difference, 82% had short before long, and there was a gradual reduction in the long before short orders the bigger the weight difference, as predicted by MiD (PPS = shorter PP, PPL = longer PP) and in accordance with Pattern One (1):

(5) n = 323   PPL > PPS by 1 word   by 2–4   by 5–6   by 7+
     [V PPS PPL]   60% (58)   86% (108)   94% (31)   99% (68)
     [V PPL PPS]   40% (38)   14% (17)   6% (2)   1% (1)

I consider further aspects of these post-verbal PP ordering data in 4.3.1 and 4.4.1 below.

4.2.2 *Grammars*

The effects of MiD can be seen in the conventionalized constituent orders of grammars in crosslinguistic samples, in accordance with the following principle proposed in Hawkins (2004: 3):

PERFORMANCE–GRAMMAR CORRESPONDENCE HYPOTHESIS (PGCH)
Grammars have conventionalized syntactic structures in proportion to their degree of preference in performance, as evidenced by patterns of selection in corpora and by ease of processing in psycholinguistic experiments.

4.2.2.1 *Greenberg's correlations*   The adjacency of lexical heads and of other phrasal constructing categories provides optimal domains for phrase structure processing and is massively preferred in crosslinguistic samples. The data in (6a) and (6b) show a strong correlation between verb-initial order in VP and prepositions before NP, that is, with V and P adjacent, and between verb-final order and postpositions after NP, again with V and P adjacent (in phrases corresponding to [***drove** [**to** the cinema]]* and *[[the cinema **to**] **drove**]]* respectively). Examples (6c) and (6d) with non-adjacent V and P (i.e. [***drove** [the cinema **to**]]* and [[**to** the cinema] **drove**] respectively) are both infrequent. Examples (6a) and (6b) involve the most minimal domains for phrase structure processing: the adjacent V and P permit construction of VP and attachment of two immediate constituents to it, V and PP, resulting in optimal IC-to-word ratios. Examples (6c) and (6d) involve longer domains for VP construction and attachment of these ICs to it, and lower ratios, since V and P are separated by NP. These data are taken from Matthew Dryer's sample, measuring languages rather than 'genera' and are ultimately inspired by the correlations first pointed out by Greenberg (1966) (see Dryer 1992; Hawkins 1994: 257 for further details).

(6) a. $[_{VP}$ V $[_{PP}$ P NP]] = 161 (41%)   b. $[[$NP P $_{PP}]$ V $_{VP}]$ = 204 (52%)
        IC-to-word: 2/2 = 100%   IC-to-word: 2/2 = 100%

    c. $[_{VP}$ V [NP P $_{PP}]]$ = 18 (5%)   d. $[[_{PP}$ P NP] V $_{VP}]$ = 6 (2%)
        IC-to-word: 2/4 = 50%   IC-to-word: 2/4 = 50%

       MiD-preferred (6a)+(6b) = 365/389 (94%)

The data of (7) (from Hawkins 1983) show a similar correlation between prepositions and nouns preceding possessive (/genitive) phrases and between postpositions and nouns following (in phrases corresponding to [**with** [**friends** *of my father*]] and [[*my father of* **friends**] **with**] respectively). The adjacent heads, P and N, in (7a) and (7b) have minimal domains for the construction of PP and attachment of its immediate constituents, P and NP, and optimal IC-to-word ratios, and are crosslinguistically highly preferred compared with the non-adjacent heads in (7c) and (7d).

(7) a. $[_{PP}$ P $[_{NP}$ N Possp]] = 134 (40%) b. $[[$Possp N $_{NP}]$ P $_{PP}]$ = 177 (53%)
    c. $[_{PP}$ P [Possp N $_{NP}]]$ = 14 (4%)   d. $[[_{NP}$ N Possp] P $_{PP}]$ = 11 (3%)

4.2.2.2 *Center-embedding hierarchies*   Constituents that intervene between otherwise adjacent heads are permitted in grammars, it seems, in proportion to their weight. For example, a single word adjective can intervene between P and N in English and many other languages ([**under** [*yellow* **books**]]) whereas an adjective phrase cannot ([**under** [yellow with age **books**]]). That is, $[_{PP}$ P $[_{NP}$ Adj N]] is more tolerated than $[_{PP}$ P $[_{NP}$ AdjP N]]

   More generally, the more complex a center-embedded constituent (Rel > Possp > Adj) and the longer the PCD for its containing phrase, the fewer languages there are (cf. Hawkins 2004: 128–31). For the environment $[_{PP}$ P $[_{NP}$ __ N]] we have the following center-embedding hierarchy in the sample of Hawkins (1983), in accordance with MiD and Pattern One (1):

(8) Prepositional lgs: AdjN   32% NAdj   68%
                      PosspN 12% NPossp 88%
                      RelN   1% NRel   99%

4.3 Pattern Two: Cooperation

(9) PATTERN TWO: The more principles there are that define a collective preference for a common set of outputs {P}, as opposed to a proper subset or complement set {P′} motivated by fewer principles, the greater will be the preference for and size of {P}.

4.3.1 *Performance*

Performance data illustrating Pattern Two come from the stronger preference in English for post-verbal prepositional phrases and particles adjacent to a verb when that adjacency is supported both by syntactic weight and by lexical-semantic dependencies with the verb, rather than by just one of these principles alone.

Recall that a PCD ((4) above) is a domain for the processing of a syntactic relation of phrasal combination or sisterhood between constituents. Some of these sisters may contract additional relations of a semantic or lexical nature, whose processing requires a 'lexical domain' sufficient to recognize the lexical combination in question and assign the appropriate syntactic and semantic properties to it (Hawkins 2004: 117). Entailment tests are used in Lohse, Hawkins, and Wasow (2004) and Hawkins (2004) as evidence for this lexical listing of verb-particle and verb-preposition combinations. For example, *John lifted the child up* entails both "John lifted the child" and "the child WENT up." *John washed the dishes up* does not entail "the dishes WENT up," but it does entail "John washed the dishes" (Lohse, Hawkins, and Wasow 2004). These tests provide evidence for both lexical listing and for lexical domains of processing in addition to syntactic domains such as PCDs.

The dependency of a particle (*wash X up*) has a significant and consistent effect on its preferred adjacency to the verb compared with independent particles (*lift X up*): NPs that intervene and split verbs and particles creating larger PCDs are systematically less tolerated when the particles are also dependent and lexical-semantic processing prefers a smaller distance between them, supporting Pattern Two. This is shown in the data given in Lohse, Hawkins, and Wasow. (2004: 248, Figure 2) in which dependent particles are systematically more adjacent to the verb for all lengths of intervening NP compared with independent particles.

Similarly, the preposition *on* in *John counted on his father* cannot be processed independently of *counted*, nor can *counted* be processed independently of *on*. This sentence does not entail "John counted," removing the PP, nor does it entail "John did something on his father," removing the verb and replacing it with a general Pro-Verb (Hawkins 2000, 2004). *John played on the playground* is different: it entails "John played" and "John did something on the playground."

V-PP combinations such as *count on his father* show a similar stronger adjacency to V to the verb-particle combinations classified as dependent by the entailment tests. There is cooperation and reinforcement in the principles favoring adjacency between V and a dependent PP when two prepositional phrases follow a verb (see (5) above). Specifically in the data of Hawkins (2000) 82% (265/323) had the syntactically preferred short PP adjacent to V preceding a longer one, that is, their PCDs were minimal while 73% (151/206) had a lexically interdependent PP adjacent to V, that is, their lexical processing domains were minimal. For PPs that were *both* shorter *and* lexically dependent, however, the adjacency rate to V was 96%, which was (statistically) significantly higher than for each factor alone, thereby supporting Pattern Two (see Section 4.4.1 for further data and discussion on post-verbal PPs).

Notice that for the purpose of this quantification, a PP was considered lexically dependent on V if the dependency went in at least one direction, from V to P or vice versa. See Hawkins (2000) for a detailed discussion and exemplification of the combinatorial possibilities and their impact on adjacency. See Lohse, Hawkins, and Wasow (2004) for a similar discussion of verb-particle dependency types and their adjacency effects.

4.3.2 *Grammars*

A grammatical example for Pattern Two comes from certain basic word order types that are supported by three vs. two vs. just one preference principle, with correlating quantities of grammars. For example, Hawkins (2008) examines the basic word orders for Oblique (X) phrases relative to a Verb and (Direct) Object in the data of Dryer and Gensler (2005: 342–5) (WALS map 84), for example (*Mary*) *opened the door with the key*. Oblique NPs are PPs such as *with the key* and also NPs with non-argument oblique cases—typically cases other than Nominative/Accusative/Dative and Absolutive/Ergative/Dative in the relevant languages. Hawkins (2008) finds three preference patterns in the language quantities which he explains in terms of the principles of Hawkins (2004). These preferences are shown in the three columns of (10). A plus sign in the row alongside each basic word order, VOX, XVO, etc., indicates that the preference in question is satisfied in that basic order, a minus sign indicates that it is not.

(10)

	V & O ADJACENCY	O & X ON SAME SIDE	O BEFORE X
VOX	+	+	+
XVO	+	−	−
VXO	−	+	−
XOV	+	+	−
OXV	−	+	+
OVX	+	−	+

VOX languages conform to all three patterns. The OV language types, on the other hand, each conform to only two, while the other VO competitors (XVO and VXO) conform to at most one. Correlating with this are the quantities of grammars shown in (11). The more principles a grammatical type exemplifies, therefore, the more such grammars there are, which supports Pattern Two.

(11)   VOX   >   XOV/OXV/OVX   >   XVO/VXO
                3   2   1
     Lgs: 189   45/23/37   3/0

Notice that it is not being claimed here that these three principles are equally strong, merely that they have a mutually reinforcing and additive effect. Some indication of what their relative strengths are can be seen in the quantitative data of Dryer and Gensler (2005) and in the numbers of grammars that conform to each, as summarized in Hawkins (2008). Hawkins also gives a detailed discussion of what the plausible advantages are for each of these preferences, in terms of processing ease and efficiency. For further discussion of relative strength, see the next section.

4.4 Pattern Three: A competition hypothesis

(12)   PATTERN THREE: When there is competition between two principles A and B, where each predicts a (partially) different set of outputs in the competing structures to which both apply, {A} versus {B}, then each continues to apply

(a) in proportion to its intrinsic degree of preference, as in Pattern One;
(b) each may be reinforced by supporting principles, as in Pattern Two; but
(c) the relative strength of A over B will be in proportion to the relative degree
of preference defined for {A} > {B} within a theory of processing ease and
efficiency.

According to Pattern Three the relative strength of principles under competition,
even in grammars, reflects the overall processing ease and efficiency advantages for
the set {A} versus {B}, taking into account the intrinsic strength of each and
reinforcement from supporting principles if any. But what is it precisely about all
of the recorded examples in the literature (and in this volume) of one principle being
stronger than another that actually makes them so? The general hypothesis I wish to
advance here is that, just as the principles themselves (Minimize Domains, etc.) are
ultimately explained by ease of processing and efficiency, so too is their **relative**
strength when they are opposed to one another. In other words, the outputs {A}
defined by A are preferred over {B} defined by B, because the {A} structures are
easier or more efficient to process when they are in conflict.

The devil lies in the detail when making a proposal like this. But the details will
vary considerably from example to example, in syntax, in phonology and morphology, in the interaction between syntax and lexical semantics, between syntax and
pragmatics, and so on. I do not have a fully worked out theory at this point. What I
do have is a general hypothesis for structuring the way in which we think about these
interactions and for the tests we can conduct in order to refine the hypothesis. The
patterns in the data to be summarized in this section are, I believe, revealing and
worthy of discussion in this context.

4.4.1 *Performance*

Notice first that even when there is competition, the degrees of preference defined by
single principles (Pattern One) and cooperation and reinforcement among principles (Pattern Two) continue to assert themselves where relevant, as specified in (a)
and (b) respectively in (12). Consider (12a), for example. In the post-verbal English
data of (5) comprising two PPs, if one of them is a PP that is lexically dependent on
V (Pd) (e.g. *count [on his father] [in his youth]*), that is V-Pd-Pi, and prefers
adjacency to V for lexical processing, it will nonetheless be postposed to the right
of a lexically independent PP (Pi), in proportion to its heaviness, for example *count
[in his youth] [on his much-adored and generous father]*. Syntactic weight continues
to assert itself gradiently, even when opposed by a lexical adjacency principle for a
V-Pd pair (see Hawkins 2000). This is shown in the data of (13) in which a heavy
dependent Pd like *on his . . . father* is postposed and separated from V in proportion
to its increasing weight relative to an independent Pi like *in his youth*.

(13)		Pd = Pi	Pd > Pi by 1 word	by 2–4	by 5+
	[V Pd Pi]	83% (24)	74% (17)	33% (6)	7% (2)
	[V Pi Pd]	17% (5)	26% (6)	67% (12)	93% (28)

Wiechmann and Lohmann (2012) investigate these post-verbal PPs of English further, testing Hawkins' patterns and using a larger and more controlled database (over three times more data points), which lead them to revise some of my earlier conclusions. Their findings are directly relevant to all of (a), (b), and (c) in Pattern Three (12). First of all, they show that although syntactic weight applies to more structures to define an ordering preference between PPs, when the two actually compete (see (12c)) it is the lexical-semantic dependencies that exert a stronger preference for adjacency with V than syntactic domain minimization (i.e. short before long). The lexical-semantic factor is 1.7 times stronger than the syntactic one in these conflicts. They arise whenever a semantically dependent phrase is longer than an independent one, for example *dwelling* [*for a few moments*] [*on what the police have done or have not done*] (V-Pi-Pd), to take an example from their data. An arrangement minimizing the domain for lexical-semantic processing was favored over one minimizing the domain for syntactic processing significantly more often in these cases of conflict. This result also replicates the experimental findings conducted on the use of these structures by older and younger adults in Marblestone (2007). Again there was a preference for short lexical-semantic domains of processing over short syntactic ones in cases of conflict.

The explanation that suggests itself for this is that the online processing disadvantages of not assigning meanings immediately online to words like *count* and *on* or *dwell* and *on* are more severe than delays in syntactic phrasal processing through weight. That is to say, in this structure the disadvantages for lexical-semantic processing are stronger and priority is given to their more rapid resolution. This general efficiency consideration motivates their relative strength, in accordance with (12c).

Wiechmann and Lohmann (2012) formulate this idea in terms of a model of language production like Levelt's (1989), whereby conceptual-semantic planning is prior to constituent assembly. According to this view the combination *count on his father* is part of an early planning phase verbalizing the central proposition. Independent PPs like the time adjunct *in his youth* may be planned either later than this or simultaneously with it, resulting in less adjacency overall and in later production. Whether this is the best explanation or not will need to await the analysis of head-final languages, in which adjunct phrases often precede arguments and semantically dependent phrases (see Hawkins 2014, and also (10) above). In the interim I suggest that the greater priority for positioning semantically interdependent words together follows from processing ease and efficiency since meanings are assigned sooner to words in online processing that way.

The general principle that I would invoke here is Maximize Online Processing in Hawkins (2004). Within the set of linguistic properties that are assigned to forms in online processing, semantic properties are the most important ones for communication. Hence, whatever the best formalization of this insight turns out to be, I would argue that the relative strength of conflicting principles follows from general principles of processing ease and efficiency in language use.

Wiechmann and Lohmann (2012) provide further quantitative and statistical data of relevance to (12). In addition to measuring lexical-semantic dependency domains and phrasal constituency domains for post-verbal PP structures, they examine two further factors which have been argued in the literature to affect post-verbal orderings and which are tested in Hawkins (2000). The first is the Manner > Place > Time (MPT) generalization (cf. Quirk et al. 1985), and the second is information structure, specifically the Given before New principle. Both of these are shown to be weak predictors, compared to lexical-semantic dependencies and syntax, but they are not insignificant, as Hawkins had argued. MPT raises the accuracy of ordering predictions (compared to the combined lexical-semantic and syntactic preferences), that is, it raises the "classification accuracy", from 74.6% to 76.8%. Adding information status raises it further from 76.8% to 78.7%. What is interesting about these small increases is that they show the effect of reinforcing principles amidst competition, that is, they show the effect of (b) in (12). When additional factors such as MPT and Given before New are at play, they also contribute to the overall ordering prediction for PPs and they reinforce each other, therefore, and help to offset a competing principle.

Why should information status be among the weakest predictors? Specifically, why should pragmatic principles such as Given before New be so much less powerful than both phrasal syntax and lexical-semantic dependencies in these unconventionalized orderings of PPs? Not only Wiechmann and Lohmann, but also Wasow (2002), Kizach (2010), and Hawkins (1994) have all argued that syntactic processing preferences are stronger in these cases and trump pragmatic ones most of the time in data sets that systematically control for both.

A possible answer is this. Notice first that pragmatic meanings differ from lexical-semantic dependencies in that one word does not need access to another in order for the processor to assign a basic meaning to it. Second, the set of structures that involve different weights between categories and on which MiD defines a preference for shorter PCDs far exceeds the set which are differentiated pragmatically (either by Given before New or by New before Given) and for which a pragmatic theory defines a preference. Every syntactic category (V, Adj, etc.) in every phrase, and on every occasion of use is subject to a MiD ordering preference. Pragmatic differences in information structure, on the other hand, affect a much smaller number of clauses in a language, namely those containing at least two NPs that differ in the pragmatic values in question. Hence, even in the competing structures containing two NPs, the syntactic processing advantages continue to apply both to the NPs and their ordering and to all the other categories and phrases in the clauses that contain them, making the overall advantages of following MiD more extensive than the advantages afforded by information structure ordering. Third, there is also a certain indeterminacy in the pragmatics literature over whether Given before New or New before Given is actually the preferred ordering for discourse processing (see Hawkins (1994) for detailed discussion and critique and a discussion of Japanese), which makes it less clear what the overall benefits of different pragmatic orders are for processing ease and efficiency. Given items have the advantage of recent activation, but they delay new and newsworthy information.

The descriptive and explanatory details of these pragmatic principles of ordering require further investigation. What is emerging from controlled data sets, however, is that pragmatic principles are weaker than lexical-semantic and syntactic ones. The general hypothesis I propose for this is that they have much less impact on overall processing ease and efficiency, for the kinds of reasons enumerated here, and hence they win fewer of the conflicts in the competition sets {A} and {B}, though they do have a small reinforcing effect when they support stronger principles.

The chapter by Francis and Michaelis (this volume) on relative clause extraposition in English is also relevant here since it shows that grammatical weight is a stronger determinant of extraposition than various discourse factors, which operate only in "those tokens that [fall] within a relatively narrow range of length ratios—those that might be considered neutral with respect to RCE". Similarly Strunk (this volume) finds grammatical weight in German (relative clause length and extraposition distance) to be a stronger determinant of relative clause extraposition than the discourse factor of definiteness vs. indefiniteness. It appears that the efficiency of extraposition in both languages is determined primarily by considerations of syntactic processing and by the weights of different phrases that need to be attached together, and that discourse factors add significant and independent, but nonetheless weaker, motivations. The syntax, and related processes of semantic interpretation, are stronger than discourse factors in these conflicts, plausibly because they have a bigger effect on the overall processing ease and efficiency of the structures containing them, in accordance with (12c). It remains to be seen whether the cooperation and competition between the other factors that Strunk (this volume) finds statistical evidence for in his German corpus data can be linked to considerations of overall efficiency and processing ease, in the manner of (12b) and (12c).

4.4.2 *Grammars*

In relative clause constructions we see a competition between a Filler before Gap (or Filler before Subcategorizer) processing preference (Fodor 1978; Hawkins 1999, 2004) and MiD's word order preferences (see (2)). The head noun is the Filler in a relative clause construction (*the book*i *that John read O*i) and NRel order is preferred in all languages by the Filler before Gap preference, which is ultimately derived from Maximize On-line Processing in Hawkins (2004, 2009), whereas MiD (2) prefers NRel in VO languages and RelN in OV. This is shown in (14).

(14)	Minimize Domains	Fillers before Gaps
VO & NRel	+	+
VO & RelN	−	−
OV & RelN	+	−
OV & NRel	−	+

Empirically, Fillers before Gaps is the stronger principle in this competition within OV languages in the WALS data of Dryer (2005), as shown in (15):

(15) (Dryer 2005, WALS)	Rel-Noun	Noun-Rel or Mixed/Correlative/Other
Rigid SOV {O, X} V	50% (17)	50% (17)
Non-rigid SOV OVX	0% (0)	100% (17)

Only one third of OV languages (17/51) in WALS have the MiD-preferred RelN, all of them rigid OV languages whose containing head-final phrases (VP, etc.) define the strongest overall preference for head-finality in NPs, see Hawkins (2004). Two thirds of OV languages (34/51) have NRel with the head noun Filler before its Gap, therefore, either as the only strategy or in combination with some other one.

Why should this be? I hypothesize here that the processing disadvantages of Gaps before Fillers are quantifiably very severe (through garden paths/misassignments and unassignments online, Hawkins 2004: 205–10; Fodor 1978), and outweigh the MiD disadvantages of head ordering inconsistencies with NRel in SOV (e.g. Persian and German), which can in any case be readily relieved by Extraposition from NP and other postposing transformations. In other words, considerations of processing ease and efficiency favor Fillers before Gaps over Minimize Domains in the competition sets {A} and {B} that arise in OV languages in (14), in accordance with (12c).

As an example of a semantically-based ordering principle trumping one based on morphological form, consider Primus's (1999) hierarchies for Case and Theta roles:

(16)   Theta: Ag [Erg] > Pat [Abs]
         Case: Abs [Pat] > Erg [Ag]

Primus shows that these and other hierarchies underlying NP ordering are preferably linearized from left to right, for example Agent before Patient, which in Ergative languages creates competition between the Theta hierarchy and the Case hierarchy that prefers Absolutive [Patient] before Ergative [Agent]. The great majority of Ergative languages favor the Theta hierarchy, which then results in Agent before Patient ordering having greater "cue strength" in these languages in the sense of MacWhinney's (1987, this volume) Competition Model. A minority favor Absolutive before Ergative basic order, giving this alternative greater cue strength in relevant languages, and these have often been misanalyzed, Primus argues, as OSV languages (Dyirbal, Hurrian, Siuslaw, Kabardian, Fasu) or OVS (Apalai, Arecuna, Bacairi, Macushi, Hianacoto, Hishkaryana, Panare, Wayana, Asurini, Oiampi, Teribe, Pari, Jur Luo, Mangarayi).

Agent and Patient are semantic notions and their preferred relative ordering is argued by Primus to have online processing advantages that trump those of the purely formal case morphology hierarchy, that is, Absolutive before Ergative. A Patient is thematically and conceptually dependent on an Agent for bringing about the action described in an event, and it is preferable for event construal to have the Agent presented first. The conflicting preference, I suggest in Hawkins (2014), may be motivated by a variant of the "memory cost" explanation that Gibson (1998) proposed for Nominative before Accusative in languages with these cases, namely: an Accusative predicts a following Nominative, whereas an initial Nominative does not necessarily predict an Accusative (since Nominatives are most often the subjects of intransitive verbs). Similarly, an Ergative predicts a following Absolutive, adding to online working memory load. The reverse Absolutive before Ergative reduces this. The fact that the great majority of ergative languages position the Ergative first shows that the ordering preference based on thematic roles is the stronger principle. And this in turn, I would suggest following Primus, is because the overall efficiency of processing is improved when asymmetric semantic dependencies are reflected in online processing orders, in accordance with (12c).

The interesting competitions discussed in Mondorf's (this volume) chapter involving for example synthetic and analytic comparatives, *fuller* vs. *more full*, etc., can also be profitably linked to the competition hypothesis in (12c). It is the overall ease and efficiency of the structure in question that determines the selection of the one or the other and their development in the history of English, with the synthetic occurring in easier to process environments and the analytic in harder ones. The respective grammatical operations and processing counterparts that underlie the two forms are therefore selected in different environments based on an overall cost–benefit analysis, whereby the more explicit form eases harder processing, and the less explicit one occurs efficiently in easier processing environments.

Finally in this section I note that the competition hypothesis defined in (12) provides general support for Newmeyer's (this volume) theory of "Indirect Competition" regarding external functions and their grammaticalization. He writes: "There is no direct linkage between competing external functions and grammatical properties. The influence of the former on the latter is played out in language use and acquisition and (therefore) language change and manifests itself in the crosslinguistic distribution of grammatical elements." The relative degrees of preference defined in (12c) are indeed reflected in performance and acquisition, and the quantities of structural selections that are visible in the performance of languages with for example word order freedom are reflected in the correlating numbers of grammars with fixed orders (Hawkins 1994, 2004, 2014). The conflicts and their resolution cannot be seen directly in individual grammars, many of which have suppressed the competing alternative altogether through conventionalization, but only indirectly, as Newmeyer points out.

4.5 Cooperation and competition in learning

The kinds of patterns of cooperation and competition exemplified for performance data and grammars in preceding sections can also be seen in data from second language learning. Hawkins and Filipović (2012) and Filipović and Hawkins (2013) have formulated a number of general principles of SLA and have illustrated their interaction in some detail, within the context of their multi-factor "CASP" model (short for Complex Adaptive System Principles of SLA). In the present chapter I refer the reader to these publications and draw attention only to general patterns of interaction that are reminiscent of those considered above.

One SLA principle proposed by Hawkins and Filipović (2012) is (17):

(17)   MAXIMIZE FREQUENTLY OCCURRING PROPERTIES (MaF)
       Properties of the L2 are learned in proportion to their frequency of occurrence (as measured, for example, in the British National Corpus): more frequent exposure of a property to the learner facilitates its learning and reduces learning effort.

For example, new construction types in the Cambridge Learner Corpus of English L2, as defined by different subcategorization frames for verbs, appear to be learned at successive proficiency stages in direct proportion to their frequency in the input, as reflected in native English corpora such as the BNC (cf. Hawkins and Filipović 2012: 86–90). This accords well with the notion of "cue strength" and "cue validity" for particular grammatical features in a language and their order of acquisition as proposed in MacWhinney (1987, 2005), see also Krajewski and Lieven (this volume) and MacWhinney (this volume).

Another interacting principle is (18):

(18)   MAXIMIZE POSITIVE TRANSFER (MaPT)
        Properties of the L1 which are also present in the L2 are learned more easily and with less learning effort, and are readily transferred, on account of pre-existing knowledge in L1.

When linguistic properties are shared between L1 and L2, the result is, in general, earlier L2 acquisition, more of the relevant properties learned, and fewer errors.

When learning is supported by both (17) and (18), then these principles reinforce each other, in accordance with Pattern Two (9). L2 learning takes place earlier and is more productive and error-free than learning supported by one or the other principle alone. In short, the size of the set {P} of structures successfully acquired at each acquisition stage is greater when more principles facilitate learning.

This can be illustrated by the grammar and usage of definite and indefinite articles in English and the manner in which they are learned by speakers of different languages. Learning should be, and is, easier when L1 has the same or similar grammar and usage as L2 English. Hawkins and Buttery (2009, 2010) and Hawkins and Filipović (2012) give data involving Missing Determiner errors in the Cambridge Learner Corpus, that is, errors such as *I spoke to President* instead of *I spoke to the President*, with a missing "the", and *I have car* instead of *I have a car*, with missing "a".

For first languages like French, German, and Spanish that have definite and indefinite articles (albeit with certain typologically fairly minor contrasts to English) the error rates at all acquisition stages are very low, typically less than 5%, and improvements through greater exposure to the L2 are relatively small. For first languages like Turkish, Japanese, Korean, and Russian that lack an article system, error rates range from 20% to 40% at earlier acquisition stages and there is a significant improvement, that is a decline in error rates, with increasing proficiency at later stages.

Definite and indefinite articles are among the most frequent words of English, so both MaF (17) and MaPT (18) work together to predict the earlier and relatively error-free data of French, German, and Spanish learners. The learning data of Turkish, Japanese, Korean, and Russian speakers are much less successful and error-free since they are supported by only one principle, namely frequency in the input (MaF), in accordance with Pattern Two. Conversely, when certain structures or meanings are shared between L1 and L2 but are infrequent in the input then positive transfer asserts itself less, since only MaPT (18) is operative. For example,

Kellerman (1983) has argued that less frequent, more complex and non-core lexical meanings of verbs like *break* are not initially transferred from L1 Dutch to L2 English, even when the two languages share these semantic extensions from their core lexical meanings.

In general, frequency in the input (MaF (17)) appears to be one of the strongest principles and predictors of relative speed of L2 learning and it can often override other factors such as MaPT (18). In Hawkins and Filipović (2012) we show how less frequent and more complex meanings of lexical verbs are regularly NOT initially transferred into L2 English, as in Kellerman's Dutch examples, even when they are shared between the two languages. Why this relative strength in learning principles?

I suggest it has to do with the ease and efficiency of learning, in a way that is reminiscent of the ease and efficiency in processing that was invoked to explain the relative strength of principles in 4.4. Frequency metrics can impose a ranking on all the structures and meaning assignments to words and phrases in an L2, and frequency in the input for each such property is a general facilitator of learning in proportion to the ranking of that property on the metric. The set of L2 properties that is actually shared with any given L1, by contrast, is much smaller than the total set of L2 properties that figure in the frequency metric. Hence frequency in the input is always going to be a reliable guide and aid to learning, for a much larger set of structures than the potential (positive) transfer sets of overlapping structures. Learning that is based on MaF and sensitive to L2 input will outweigh the benefits of MaPT in cases of conflict, therefore, especially in the initial stages of learning when many shared properties are infrequently occurring and when there is insufficient evidence for their existence in the L2. Gradually as frequency in the input increases, MaPT can provide a reinforcing boost to the acquisition of less frequent structures, when they are shared between L1 and L2.

Another example of competition in learning can be seen in negative transfers, that is, in the errorful transfer of an L1 property into an L2, and in certain principles that oppose such transfers, often with powerful effect. An example of such a conflict is that between the Permit Negative Transfer principle and Communicative Blocking of Negative Transfer in Hawkins and Filipović (2012):

(19)   PERMIT NEGATIVE TRANSFER (PNT)
       Properties of the L1 which are not present in the L2 can be transferred, resulting in errors, in order to achieve an expressive power and communicative efficiency in L2 comparable to that in L1, while minimizing learning effort and/or processing effort (see Hawkins and Filipović 2012 and Filipović and Hawkins 2013 for general principles of L2 learning).

(20)   COMMUNICATIVE BLOCKING OF NEGATIVE TRANSFER (CBN)
       The transfer of negative properties from L1 to L2 is filtered in proportion to communicative efficiency: the more an L1 property impedes efficient communication in L2, the less negative transfer there is.

This conflict can be exemplified with data involving basic word orders in English and Japanese. These two languages have equally simple and productive, but mirror-image, word order patterns, head-initial vs. head-final: e.g. [*went* [*to* [*the cinema*]]] vs. [[[*the cinema*] *to*] *went*], see Greenberg (1966b), Hawkins (1983, 1994, 2004), Dryer (1992), and Section 4.2.2. It turns out that the negative transfer of head-final orders into L2 English by Japanese learners does not occur in the data of Hawkins and Filipović (2012) and is blocked, we argue, by its communicative inefficiency: speakers importing Japanese word orders into English (e.g. *John the cinema to went!*) would simply not be understood! In other words, (20) trumps (19). However Spanish-style head-initial variants of English word order that do not impact efficient communication *are* negatively transferred into English L2 (e.g. *I read yesterday the book*).

Because Japanese is a head-final language, the contrast with the mirror-image word order patterns of English is considerable and transferring "head-final" patterns into a "head-initial" language such as English, and vice versa, would significantly impair communication. This is why it is imperative for Japanese learners of English, and for English learners of Japanese, to acquire basic word order in their L2s early. On the other hand, speakers of L1 languages with flexible SVO like Spanish do not have the same incentive, because even when they transfer from their L1s into a fundamentally similar head-initial English L2, communication is not significantly impaired. We have here an efficiency of usage explanation for the relative strength of one principle over another. Learners want to communicate successfully with other speakers of the L2, native and otherwise. The demands of efficient communication impose a ranking on certain principles in learning and usage, and it is this that explains their relative strength.

4.6 Conclusions

I have defined three general patterns in this chapter that can be seen when multiple principles cooperate and compete in data from performance and grammars: (1), (9), and (12). My basic hypothesis, derived from these patterns, is that the strength of principles, and especially their relative strength in competition, reflects the processing ease and efficiency of the competing data sets {A} vs. {B} etc. predicted by different principles. One principle A will be stronger than another B in proportion to the greater processing ease and efficiency of {A} over {B}, according to some independently motivated theory of ease and efficiency of the kind I have defined in Hawkins (2004, 2009, 2014). The patterned preferences in the data can come from a single principle (Section 4.2), from cumulative preferences from mutually reinforcing principles (Section 4.3), and from the relative strength of both cooperating and competing principles (Section 4.4). By examining the interaction of principles from the same explanatory perspective that I have proposed for the principles themselves (in terms of the Performance–Grammar Correspondence Hypothesis in 4.2.2), the patterns of interaction begin to make sense. In this perspective processing ease and efficiency are paramount.

I then suggested in 4.5 that the same interaction logic applies to second language acquisition data, with strength and relative strength of the learning principles being determined by ease and efficiency of learning and also, I would add, of learning to process as well. MacWhinney (1987, 2005) has proposed a very similar way of looking at acquisition in his Competition Model (see Hawkins and Filipović 2012 for a detailed literature review of first and second language acquisition in relation to the learning principles proposed here).

There are many details in the principles invoked in the present chapter that need further definition and research, and there are many details of their interaction that await further specification. But I believe that this general way of looking at cooperation and competition may be helpful in better understanding other examples in the literature and in this volume, in suggesting further areas to test, and in shedding light on why principles interact in the ways they do, in these different areas of the language sciences.

In a nutshell, think of the interaction between principles in terms of ease and efficiency of use, and ease and efficiency of learning. If you believe, as I do, that ease and efficiency shape all of performance, grammar, and learning and their respective principles, then it makes sense that the way principles interact with one another, and their relative strengths in conflict, should also be determined by ease and efficiency as well. That is the basic idea I propose.

Acknowledgments

This chapter has benefited from the comments of three anonymous reviewers and from those of the volume editors, which are all gratefully acknowledged. The research reported here was supported financially by research funds received from the University of California Davis 2007–10, and by funds paid from the University of Cambridge to UC Davis for teaching buyouts 2008–10. These funds are gratefully acknowledged, as is the financial support received from Cambridge Assessment in 2009–10 for completion of the 2012 Cambridge University Press book *Criterial Features in L2 English* by Hawkins and Filipović, cited in Section 4.5.

5

Why move? How weight and discourse factors combine to predict relative clause extraposition in English

ELAINE J. FRANCIS AND LAURA A. MICHAELIS

5.1 Introduction

In this chapter, we examine a well-known constituent-order option of English, relative clause extraposition (RCE), and ask whether it subserves sentence processing, information packaging, or both. In RCE from subject NP position (referred to by Ross 1967 as Extraposition from NP), a subject-modifying relative clause occurs following the VP, as in the example from the International Corpus of English–Great Britain (henceforth ICE-GB) in (1a),[1] rather than adjacent to its head noun, as in the corresponding non-RCE sentence (1b).

(1)   a. <u>Further research</u> has been conducted on this <u>that indicates this criticism may not be just.</u>   (ICE-GB)

    b. <u>Further research that indicates this criticism may not be just</u> has been conducted on this.

The alternative sentences in (1a–b) seem to express exactly the same meaning. Structurally, however, (1a) is more complex because there is a discontinuous dependency between the subject NP and the relative clause. Most syntactic accounts of RCE have avoided positing an actual discontinuous constituent, instead licensing RCE through rightward movement (Ross 1967; Baltin 1981), leftward movement (Kayne 1994), adjunction and co-indexing (Culicover and Rochemont 1990) or

---

[1] The International Corpus of English Great Britain (Nelson, Wallis, and Aarts 2002) includes about one million words of British English in a variety of genres of both speech and writing. All example sentences culled from the corpus will be indicated with the abbreviation ICE-GB in parentheses, as in (1a). This is also the corpus that we used for the empirical study described in Section 5.2.

percolation of a list-valued EXTRA feature (Kay and Sag 2012). Nevertheless, this kind of dependency relation strains rule-to-rule semantic composition, while also requiring greater processing effort in word-by-word reading (Levy et al. 2012). Further, unlike many other constructions featuring non-canonical word order, like wh-movement and topicalization, RCE has no obvious functional motivation.

Given the added complexity of RCE, and its apparent lack of semantico-pragmatic effect, one can reasonably ask why speakers use the construction. The literature has provided two main answers. The first answer, provided by the majority of the studies, is that RCE is used to place presentational focus on the denotatum of the subject NP, and thus has a function similar to that of the presentational *there*-construction (PTC):

(2)   There exists further research on this that indicates this criticism may not be just.

The general consensus is that RCE is used to highlight new, contrastive, or important information conveyed by the subject NP while backgrounding the information contained in the main-clause predicate (Huck and Na 1990; Kuno and Takami 2004; Rochemont and Culicover 1990; Takami 1999). Both the RCE sentence (1a) and the PTC sentence (2) assert that research findings of a particular type exist, rather than that research of this type was conducted.

Such a discourse-based approach has been used to explain some of the formal properties that are typically, but not categorically, associated with RCE. For example, the subject of an RCE sentence is typically an indefinite NP, reflecting the focal status of the NP's referent. However, focal status does not require indefiniteness; an RCE token may, for example, contain a definite subject NP interpreted as a contrastive focus (Huck and Na 1990). In (3), the speaker has already introduced two guys, and is contrasting the guy from Treno's with the guy from a different restaurant:

(3)   The guy just came in that I met at TRENO's yesterday. (Huck and Na 1990: 54)

Similarly, RCE tokens typically contain a presentative matrix predicate. Following Levy et al. (2012: 17), we define a presentative predicate as one containing an intransitive head verb of existence or appearance; such predicates are typically used to introduce the referent of the subject NP into a scene (e.g. *came in* in (3) above). However, Rochemont and Culicover (1990: 65–8) point out that it is possible to use a non-presentative verb in an RCE predication, provided that the predicate is "directly c-construable,"—already in the discourse (Rochemont 1986: 174). For example, the verb *scream* can be used when the property of screaming is already evoked in the discourse, as in (4):

(4)   Suddenly there was the sound of lions growling. Several women screamed. Then a man screamed who was standing at the very edge of the crowd.
                                               (Rochemont and Culicover 1990: 65)

In short, these discourse-based theories predict that definiteness and predicate type may vary across different RCE sentences, while the subject NP should consistently represent a focal argument.

While these predictions are plausible, empirical support for them has mostly been provided by constructed examples (as in (3)–(4) above) rather than analysis of actual language use. One exception is Francis (2010), who did not investigate discourse status, but did look at corpus frequencies for different predicate types and found that although RCE occurred with presentative verbs more frequently than with transitive or non-presentative intransitive verbs, RCE was most commonly used with passive verbs (as in (1a) above). Arguing that passive verbs are semantically similar to presentative verbs (as intransitive predicates which select a Theme argument) and just as felicitous in presentational contexts, Francis (2010: 63) concluded that the prevalence of passive predicates is compatible with theories that posit a presentational function for RCE.

The second functional rationale for the existence of RCE involves grammatical weight. Arnold et al. (2000), Wasow (2002), and Hawkins (2004), among others, have shown that shifting heavy (i.e. long and/or syntactically complex) constituents to the end of a clause can facilitate language production and comprehension. In production, heavy constituents may be difficult to formulate. Therefore, postponing them offers speakers more time to finish formulating the sentence while they produce the shorter, easier phrases (Arnold et al. 2000: 32). In comprehension, shifting heavy constituents to the end allows listeners to reduce the storage and integration costs associated with non-local dependencies (Gibson 1998; Hawkins 2004). For example, although RCE always increases the distance between the head noun and its relative-clause modifier, a long relative clause in a non-RCE sentence increases the distance between the subject NP and its predicate. Hawkins' (2004) theory of domain minimization, which quantifies the notion of integration distance in terms of the amount of material that must be processed in order to construct a given mother node—say, S—from its immediate constituents, thus predicts a greater overall processing cost for the non-RCE sentence (5b) as compared with the RCE sentence (5a). This is because the relative clause which separates the subject from the predicate in (5b) is much longer than the VP which separates the head noun from the relative clause in (5a).

(5) a. Certain conditions existed which cannot be applied to all other countries at all times.   (ICE-GB)

   b. Certain conditions which cannot be applied to all other countries at all times existed.

Consistent with these predictions, Francis (2010) found significant effects of grammatical weight in both production and comprehension. An analysis of RCE and non-RCE tokens in the ICE-GB corpus showed that RCE was strongly preferred over canonical (non-RCE) order when the relative clause was at least five times longer (in words) than the main-clause VP, whereas RCE occurred only rarely when the VP was the same length or longer than the relative clause. In addition, a full-sentence reading-time task showed that RCE sentences were read significantly faster than non-RCE sentences when the relative clause was long, but that there was no difference in reading time with short relative clauses.[2]

---

[2] The latter result is somewhat at odds with the reading time results of Levy et al. (2012), in which RCE sentences were processed more slowly than non-RCE sentences in the absence of facilitating cues. However, the Levy et al. study had a different task (word-by-word reading) and did not include any weight manipulation.

As these studies have shown, both discourse factors and grammatical weight appear to play a role in speakers' use of RCE. However, no previous studies have examined both factors simultaneously. Thus, it is not known to what extent discourse factors are independent of weight, nor is it known which factors have the strongest influence over speakers' choice of structure. To address these questions, we conducted a quantitative analysis of naturally occurring tokens of RCE and non-RCE from the International Corpus of English–Great Britain (ICE-GB). Our findings confirmed that RCE is in fact typically associated with presentational contexts, and that grammatical weight and certain discourse-related factors independently influence speakers' choice of structure.

Although this study is the first of its kind to examine RCE in English, it aligns with several other recent studies of constituent-order alternations in English, including the ditransitive alternation (Bresnan and Ford 2010), particle shift (Gries 2003a; Lohse, Hawkins, and Wasow 2004), genitive placement (Rosenbach 2005), heavy NP shift (Arnold et al. 2000), and object fronting in Dutch (Lamers and de Hoop, this volume)—as well as the closely-related RCE construction in German (Strunk, this volume). These studies have all shown that constituent-order alternations tend to be conditioned by multiple interacting factors, including grammatical weight, information structure, animacy, lexical bias, and structural priming.

The remainder of this chapter is organized as follows. Section 5.2 describes the methods and quantitative results of a corpus analysis of RCE and non-RCE tokens in the ICE-GB corpus. Section 5.3 presents a qualitative analysis of exceptional cases from the corpus. Finally, Section 5.4 briefly outlines some implications of the current study for linguistic theory.

5.2 Corpus study

ICE-GB (Nelson et al. 2002) includes about one million words of British English, culled from a variety of spoken and written genres; it is parsed and tagged to facilitate identification of syntactic structures. The current analysis is based on a subset of sentences from the ICE-GB, which were originally collected for Francis (2010). Using Francis' (2010) original coding for phrase length and predicate type, the current analysis provides additional coding for several discourse-related categories. The remainder of this section describes the coding scheme, hypotheses and quantitative results.

5.2.1 *Coding scheme*

This analysis includes 345 sentences with a lexical subject NP modified by a finite relative clause—the total number of such sentences found in the ICE-GB corpus. These were collected as a subset of the 391 sentences from Francis (2010), excluding the forty-six tokens with pronominally headed relative clauses. Pronominally headed relative clauses were excluded from the present analysis because they are known to have somewhat different information-structure properties from lexically headed RCs, and we wanted to eliminate variation due to the activation status of the nominal-head denotatum (Gundel, Hedberg, and Zacharski 1993; Michaelis and H. Francis 2007). These sentences were originally extracted from the corpus using tree-fragment searches to identify the non-RCE tokens and function searches (specifically, "floating post-nominal modifier") in combination with manual checking to identify the RCE tokens. Grammatical weight was coded according to the original measurements in Francis (2010): VP length (in words), RC length (in words), and VP-to-RC length ratio (VP length divided by RC length).[3] VP-to-RC length ratio was used as a measure of relative length, in accordance with previous corpus and experimental studies that have found relative length to be a more significant predictor of word-order choice than absolute length (Hawkins 1994; Wasow and Arnold 2003; Stallings and MacDonald 2011). Length difference (VP length minus RC length) was calculated as an additional measure of relative length, to determine which measure made the more accurate predictions. We used the predicate-type coding from Francis (2010). Specifically, we distinguished between passive or presentative predicates and other predicate types. All morphologically passive verbs (consisting of *be* + past participle) were counted in the passive category. Following Rochemont and Culicover (1990: 66), who claim that only presentative predicates are felicitous with PTC (whereas RCE allows a wider range of predicates), we operationally defined presentative predicates as those active intransitive verbs that remain felicitous when the sentence is converted from an RCE or non-RCE sentence, as in (6a–b), to a PTC sentence, as in (6c):

(6)   a. Certain conditions <u>existed</u> which cannot be applied to all other countries at all times.   (ICE-GB)

   b. Certain conditions which cannot be applied to all other countries at all times <u>existed</u>.

   c. There <u>existed</u> certain conditions which cannot be applied to all other countries at all times.

As Ward and Birner (1996: 469–71) show based on 428 corpus examples, PTC sentences appear to require a post-verbal NP denoting a discourse-new entity. Because we wanted our presentative category to be independent from definiteness and discourse status of the subject NP referent, we also counted a predicate as presentative if it became felicitous in a PTC context when the NP was changed from definite to indefinite.

In addition, we coded each sentence for definiteness of the main-clause subject NP, discourse status of the main-clause subject NP, and discourse status of the main-clause VP. Subject NPs with a definite article (*the*), demonstrative determiner (*this, that, these, those*), strong quantifier (*all, both, each, every, most*), or possessive determiner (*our, your, his,* etc.) were classified as definite, while subject NPs with an indefinite article (*a, an*), weak quantifier (*some, many, few,*

---

[3] For the purposes of statistical analysis, VP-to-RC length ratio is coded as a proportion. For example, for a ratio of 1:5, where the RC is five times longer than the VP, this was coded as 0.2.

no, several, one, cardinal numbers), or no determiner (e.g. *people*) were classified as indefinite, based on Carlson's (1977) claim that bare nouns are intrinsically non-quantificational. Classifications of discourse status were based on the preceding twenty lines of text. Following Michaelis and H. Francis (2007) and Gregory and Michaelis (2001), we used three categories to label information status: given (prior mention), superset mention, and new (no prior mention). Subject NPs with a prior mention of the same referent within the preceding twenty lines were classified as given. Subject NPs with a prior mention of the category including the referent but no prior mention of the referent itself were classified as superset mention (Michaelis and H. Francis 2007: 28). For example, for the sentence *The point that Paula made was well justified*, the subject NP would be classified as a superset mention if there were a prior mention of a point made by another speaker, or if the general idea of making a point had been brought up. Subject NPs with no prior mention of the referent or of the category including the referent were classified as new. Predicate VPs were coded in a similar manner. Predicate VPs with a prior mention of the exact same event/situation within the preceding twenty lines of text were classified as given. Predicate VPs with a prior mention of the type of event/situation (but not the exact event/situation) were classified as superset mention. For example, for the sentence *The organ which you hear is over 100 years old*, the predicate VP would be classified as superset mention if there were a previous discussion of something else (not this particular organ) being over 100 years old. Predicate VPs with no prior mention of the exact event/situation or of the type of event/situation denoted by the predicate were classified as new.

Two independent raters classified every item for the discourse status of the subject NP and the predicate VP. A third rater then independently rated all of the items for which the first two raters disagreed, and for those cases, the category selected by two out of the three raters was used for the analysis. Overall, the first two raters agreed for 69% of the subjects and 89% of the predicates.

5.2.2 *Discourse-related properties of RCE and non-RCE tokens*

Although the main goal of this study is to determine whether and how grammatical weight and several discourse-related factors influence the speaker's choice of structure, we first briefly compare and contrast the respective discourse profiles of RCE and non-RCE clauses in order to verify whether our corpus data are in line with previous claims from the discourse literature. Owing to limitations of space, we include only descriptive statistics here.

As shown in Figure 5.1 and Table 5.1, RCE tokens had predominantly indefinite subject NPs, with passive or presentative predicates. Non-RCE tokens differed from RCE tokens in having predominantly definite subject NPs and fewer passive and presentative predicates. Further analysis revealed that non-RCE tokens occurred predominantly with transitive and copular predicates.

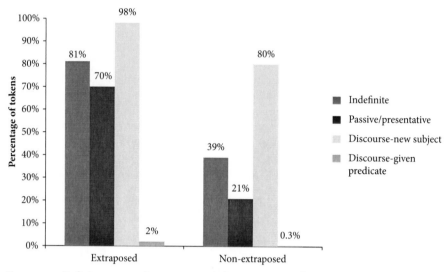

FIGURE 5.1 Definiteness, predicate type, and discourse status for RCE tokens ($n = 53$) and non-RCE tokens ($n = 292$)

TABLE 5.1. Proportions and counts for RCE and non-RCE tokens with respect to definiteness and predicate type

	Definiteness			Predicate type	
	% of RCE tokens	% of Non-RCE tokens		% of RCE tokens	% of Non-RCE tokens
Definite	19 ($n = 10$)	61 ($n = 178$)	Passive/presentative	70 ($n = 37$)	21 ($n = 61$)
Indefinite	81 ($n = 43$)	39 ($n = 114$)	Other predicate	30 ($n = 16$)	79 ($n = 231$)
Total	100 ($n = 53$)	100 ($n = 292$)	Total	100 ($n = 53$)	100 ($n = 292$)

As shown in Figure 5.1 and Table 5.2, RCE and non-RCE tokens differed relatively little with regard to discourse status: tokens of both kinds typically contained discourse-new subjects and discourse-new predicates.[4] However, there were some differences. Non-RCE tokens more frequently contained discourse-given subject NPs than did RCE tokens (19.9% vs. 1.9%). This finding is consistent with the traditional analysis of RCE as a presentational construction and with the analysis of non-RCE subjects as topics. However, it is notable that both RCE tokens and non-

---

[4] In Figure 5.1, superset mention tokens are included in the discourse-new category. In Table 5.2, superset-mention tokens are counted separately.

RCE tokens occurred predominantly with discourse-new subject NPs. This tendency is not predicted by previous accounts of RCE, but is in line with a corpus study by Michaelis and H. Francis (2007), which found that subject NPs headed by a lexical (common) noun were typically discourse-new, despite expressing a sentence topic and containing a definite determiner. The authors proposed that sentences with a lexically headed subject NP typically serve a dual role of both introducing a new topic and commenting on it.

TABLE 5.2. **Proportions and counts for discourse status of subject and predicate for RCE tokens ($n = 53$) and non-RCE tokens ($n = 291$)***

	Subject accessibility		Predicate accessibility	
	% of RCE tokens	% of non-RCE tokens	% of RCE tokens	% of non-RCE tokens
Given	1.9 ($n = 1$)	19.9 ($n = 58$)	1.9 ($n = 1$)	0.3 ($n = 1$)
Superset mention	49.1 ($n = 26$)	29.6 ($n = 86$)	18.9 ($n = 10$)	3.1 ($n = 9$)
No prior mention	49.1 ($n = 26$)	50.5 ($n = 147$)	79.2 ($n = 42$)	96.6 ($n = 281$)
Total	100 ($n = 53$)	100 ($n = 291$)	100 ($n = 53$)	100 ($n = 291$)

* One of the 292 non-RCE tokens was not analyzed for discourse status due to inadequate context.

RCE and non-RCE tokens did not differ in their dispreference for discourse-given predicates. However, breaking down the discourse-new category into "superset mention" and "no prior mention" reveals an interesting difference. Predicates of RCE tokens appear more frequently than predicates of non-RCE tokens in the superset mention category (18.9% vs. 3.1%), as shown in Table 5.2. Thus, although predicates of RCE sentences were almost never discourse-given, predicates in RCE tokens are more frequently accessible from the context.

In summary, the descriptive findings reported in this section appear to support a presentational analysis of RCE, as put forth in previous studies of extraposition (Huck and Na 1990; Rochemont and Culicover 1990; Kuno and Takami 2004). RCE tokens typically had indefinite, discourse-new subjects and passive or presentative predicates. In contrast, non-RCE tokens typically had definite, discourse-new subjects and transitive or copular predicates. The major unexpected finding was that the predicates of RCE tokens were almost never discourse-given. However, predicates of RCE tokens did occur in the superset mention category more often than predicates of non-RCE tokens. In fact, the lack of discourse-given predicates in our RCE data may be less surprising than it appears, if we view RCE predicates through the lens of informativeness rather than discourse status. Perhaps what distinguishes RCE predicates from those in canonical predications is that the latter have relatively bleached semantics (e.g. denoting superordinate-level events or states), rather than "being in the presupposition" (see Takami 1999: 27ff). We leave information-based labeling of predicates to a future effort.

5.2.3 *Discourse and weight-based factors as independent predictors of RCE usage*

In this section, we report findings related to the primary aim of this study—to determine the relative influence of grammatical weight and discourse factors on speakers' choice of RCE as against a non-RCE structure. Although we will consider some of the same factors as in the previous section, we will begin to characterize these factors as *predictors* of structural choices. That is, definiteness and predicate type are among the independent variables that we will use to predict the value of the dependent variable, extraposition status (RCE or non-RCE). This analysis is based on a binary logistic regression model. By entering all of the factors into a logistic regression model, we were able to determine whether each factor contributed independently to the predictive power of the model. In addition, the logistic regression model allowed us to test for interactions and to determine the relative strength of each factor.

Based on the descriptive results reported in the previous section, in which only two tokens had a discourse-given predicate, we framed our hypothesis regarding predicate accessibility with reference to the "superset mention" category. To the discourse-based factors considered in the previous section we added the factor *length ratio* (a measure of grammatical weight). Our hypotheses were as follows:

1. Probability of RCE should be highest for tokens with the lowest VP-to-RC length ratio, and should decrease as this ratio increases (Francis 2010).
2. Probability of RCE should be higher for tokens with a passive or presentative predicate than for tokens with other predicate types (Francis 2010).
3. Probability of RCE should be higher for tokens with an indefinite subject NP than for tokens with a definite subject NP (Huck and Na 1990).
4. Probability of RCE should be higher for tokens with a superset-mention predicate than for tokens with a discourse-new (no prior mention) predicate (Rochemont and Culicover 1990).
5. Probability of RCE should be higher for tokens with a discourse-new subject (superset mention or no prior mention) than for tokens with a discourse-given subject (Rochemont and Culicover 1990).

We had no specific predictions regarding the relative strengths of the different factors, and no specific predictions regarding statistical interactions.

Before reporting the results of the logistic regression analysis, we will first provide some basic descriptive statistics showing the trends in the data (Figures 5.2–5.6). In the discussion that follows, extraposition status will be expressed in terms of the percentage of all tokens from a particular category which had RCE word order.

Overall, canonical (non-RCE) word order was used much more frequently than RCE, with RCE used in only 15% of all tokens (53 of 345). However, frequency of RCE increased to 54% (31 of 57) for items that both had an indefinite subject NP and a passive or presentative predicate (Figure 5.2), while frequency remained at 15% or less for items belonging to the other three definiteness/predicate type combinations.

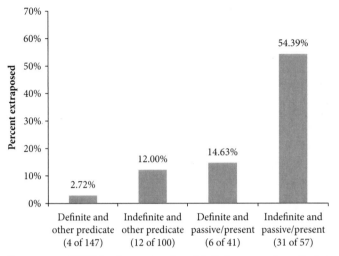

FIGURE 5.2 Percentage of RCE for four categories of definiteness and predicate type

The incidence of RCE also differed according to discourse status. As shown in Figure 5.3, RCE occurred very rarely in items with a given subject NP (1 of 59 tokens), but occurred more frequently in items with a superset-mention predicate (10 of 19 tokens). Consistent with the previous literature, the former trend suggests a dispreference for RCE outside of presentational contexts, while the latter trend suggests a slight preference for RCE when the main-clause predicate is relatively accessible. As discussed in 5.2.2, there were only two tokens with discourse-given predicates in the entire sample. Thus, the apparently high rate of RCE shown in Figure 5.3 (50%) represents one out of two tokens, and therefore does not indicate any identifiable trend.

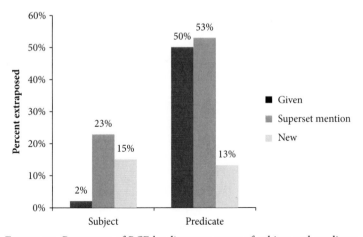

FIGURE 5.3 Percentage of RCE by discourse status of subject and predicate

As in Francis (2010), dramatic differences in the incidence of RCE were found for different ratios of VP to RC length. As shown in Figure 5.4, the incidence of RCE was highest for length ratios of 0.2 (or 1:5) and lower (tokens for which the RC was at least five times longer than the VP), at 91%, and decreased as this ratio increased. For length ratios of 1.0 (or 5:5) and higher (tokens for which the RC was the same length or shorter than the VP), RCE occurred in only 2% of tokens.

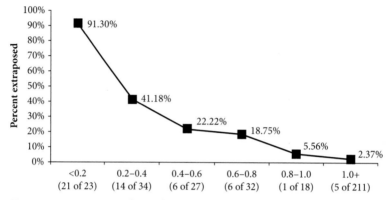

FIGURE 5.4 Percentage of RCE for increasing ratios of VP length to RC length

Crucially, the effect of length ratio differed for items of different definiteness statuses and predicate types, as shown in Figures 5.5–5.6. For tokens with a definite subject NP (Figure 5.5), RCE was preferred over non-RCE order only when the VP-to-RC length ratio was less than 0.2, or 1:5 (i.e. when the RC was at least five times longer than the VP). The same was true for items belonging to the "other" predicate type: 67% of tokens with length ratios of 0.2 or less were instances of RCE, but this immediately dropped to 29% for ratios between 0.2 and 0.4 (or 1:5 and 2:5) and less than 1% for items of length ratios greater than 0.6 (or 3:5). However, for tokens with an indefinite subject NP and a passive/presentative predicate, RCE was strongly preferred for items with length ratios up to 0.8, or 4:5 (Figure 5.6). This pattern suggests that grammatical weight plays the strongest role in predicting extraposition status for ratios less than 0.2, or 1:5 (where extraposition is usually preferred) and for ratios greater than 0.8, or 4:5 (where extraposition rarely ever occurs). For ratios between 0.2 and 0.8 (1:5 and 4:5), extraposition status appears to depend more on definiteness and predicate type than on grammatical weight.

These descriptive data suggest that length ratio, definiteness, and predicate type are important predictors of extraposition status, with possible interactions between definiteness and predicate type (Figure 5.2) and between definiteness and length ratio (Figures 5.5–5.6). Effects of subject accessibility (dispreference for RCE with given subjects) and predicate accessibility (preference for RCE with superset mention predicates) are also apparent (Figure 5.3).

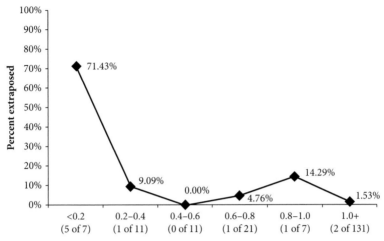

FIGURE 5.5 Percentage of RCE for increasing ratios of VP length to RC length, definite tokens only

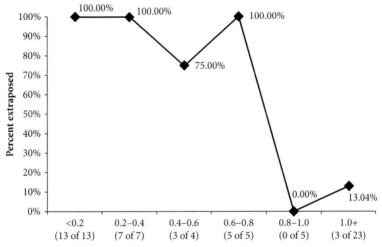

FIGURE 5.6 Percentage of RCE for increasing ratios of VP length to RC length, indefinite and passive/presentative tokens only

To test which factors were statistically significant, we used a binary logistic regression model with stepwise selection (cf. Diessel 2008), calculated using the PROC LOGISTIC function in SAS. The dependent variable was extraposition status (RCE = 1, non-RCE = 0). The primary indicator chosen for determining the predictive power of the model and of each of the independent variables was the area under the Receiver Operating Characteristic (ROC) curve, where 0.5 indicates that the model predictions were at chance and 1.0 indicates that the model was 100% accurate (Zou, O'Malley, and Mauri 2007). To find the best measure of grammatical weight for predicting these data, alternative measures of grammatical weight were first tested one by one in a logistic regression model with no other independent variables: VP-to-RC length ratio (VP length divided by RC length), VP length alone, RC length alone, and length difference (RC length minus VP length). The area under the ROC curve was highest (at 0.91) for length ratio, and therefore length ratio was used as the measure for grammatical weight in the full model. The other independent variables included in the full model were as follows: definiteness (indefinite = 1, definite = 0), predicate type (passive/presentative = 1, other predicate type = 0), subject accessibility (given = 1, other = 0), predicate accessibility (superset mention = 1, other = 0), and all possible interactions. Note that "superset mention" was chosen as the relevant measure for predicate accessibility, because of the paucity of examples of discourse-given predicates (only two) in the corpus sample.

Statistics for the significant factors are summarized in Table 5.3, following Diessel (2008: 482). Four of the five independent variables were found to be significant predictors of extraposition status at an alpha level of $p < 0.05$: length ratio, predicate type, definiteness, and predicate accessibility.[5] In addition, there were significant interactions between length ratio and definiteness and between predicate type and definiteness. These main effects and interactions are indicated by the Wald χ^2 values and associated p-values in Table 5.3. Subject accessibility (givenness of the subject) was not a significant factor. The regression coefficients in Table 5.3 indicate whether RCE is more or less likely given a particular value of an independent variable. The positive regression coefficients for definiteness, predicate type, and predicate accessibility show that indefinite subject NPs, passive or presentative predicates, and superset mention predicates each increase the likelihood of RCE. The negative value for length ratio (a continuous variable) shows that higher length ratios are associated with a *lower* likelihood for RCE (see Figure 5.4). As shown by the ROC curve values, length ratio was the strongest predictor of extraposition status, followed by predicate type, definiteness, and predicate accessibility. The overall prediction accuracy of the model, as indicated by the area under the ROC curve after inclusion of all the independent variables, was 0.9613 out of 1.0. Thus, the model was highly accurate for predicting extraposition status on this dataset.

TABLE 5.3. **Statistically significant factors from logistic regression analysis ($n = 345$)**

Independent variable	Wald χ^2	p-value	Regression coefficient	Area under ROC curve when added first
Length ratio	$\chi^2 = 7.207$	$p = 0.007$	−2.562	0.918
Predicate type	$\chi^2 = 2.736$	$p = 0.098$	1.218	0.745
Definiteness	$\chi^2 = 8.246$	$p = 0.004$	3.062	0.711
Predicate accessibility	$\chi^2 = 5.012$	$p = 0.025$	1.869	0.579
Interaction: predicate type * Definiteness	$\chi^2 = 6.276$	$p = 0.012$	3.529	0.748
Interaction: length ratio * Definiteness	$\chi^2 = 7.030$	$p = 0.008$	−5.639	0.425

[5] As shown in Table 5.3, the *p*-value for predicate type of 0.098 was not significant due to the inclusion of the interaction between predicate type and definiteness in the model. When interactions are excluded, predicate type becomes highly significant at $p < 0.0001$.

In summary, the statistically significant effects from the logistic regression analysis are consistent with our hypotheses, and also fill in details for which we had no clear predictions. Significant effects for length ratio, predicate type, definiteness, and predicate accessibility were as predicted in hypotheses (1–4) above. Subject accessibility (hypothesis 5) was not a statistically significant predictor of RCE, but numerically, the trend was in the expected direction: RCE occurred less often with given subject NPs than with new subject NPs. Interactions between predicate type and definiteness and between length ratio and definiteness, as illustrated in Figures 5.3, 5.5, and 5.6, were also found to be significant. In terms of relative strength, grammatical weight (length ratio) was the most reliable predictor of extraposition status, followed by predicate type, definiteness, and predicate accessibility.

5.3 Qualitative analysis of exceptional cases

The trends reported in the quantitative analysis were in the direction that previous studies of extraposition would lead us to expect. However, previous studies have relied on features or properties assumed to occur *consistently* in RCE tokens, and have not considered the independent effect of grammatical weight. If we see the formal and discourse-pragmatic features identified with RCE (discourse-new subject, presentative verb, heavy relative clause) as properties of an RCE *prototype*, what do we learn from examining "outliers"—exceptional cases in our corpus data?

Exceptional cases were defined as RCE items that lacked some of the theoretically significant features predicted by previous discourse-based analyses of RCE. We retrieved exceptional cases by using an SAS script to identify all RCE tokens that were incorrectly predicted by the logistic regression model. Subsequently, all of the other RCE cases were examined manually to identify any additional exceptions. A total of 16 out of 53 RCE items were identified as "false negatives"—RCE tokens that were predicted by the model to have a non-RCE structure. An additional three items were then identified manually as exceptional, based on their apparent discourse function.

Of the sixteen RCE items that the model failed to predict, at least six were theoretically unproblematic. In (7a–b), for example, all of the discourse and morphological features appropriate for RCE were present; for example, both *changes* in (7a) and *some friends* in (7b) denote discourse-new entities. The model likely failed in these cases because of the relatively high VP-to-RC length ratio, which would have favored non-RCE structure, and which indeed makes these sentences sound rather awkward.

(7) a. This is because <u>changes</u> were made to the standard rate contributions paid by employees <u>that do not affect the married woman's reduced rate contributions.</u>   (written)

 b. We've got <u>some friends</u> coming to supper <u>whose daughter's there</u> so I can question tomorrow so I can question her about it.   (spoken)

More common among the exceptions were sentences that appeared to have topical subjects and focal predicates, as is more typical of non-RCE sentences. In each of the examples in (8a–c), the definite subject NP appears to denote a sentence topic, with focal stress falling somewhere on the predicate. Note, in addition, that (8a–b) exceptionally have copular predicates.

(8)   a.   A: <u>The one you did last time</u> was for my wife actually, <u>which was F name</u>.
            B: That probably explains why I can't find it under H.   (spoken)

      b.   As you can imagine <u>the first few days</u> will be a bit hectic, <u>during which time I will be ringing you, and every client personally to invite you into my office</u>.   (written)

      c.   In aeolian environments <u>the sand</u> is blown until it accumulates, <u>which can take on various features e.g. barchans, etc.</u>   (written)

The examples in (8) allow a non-restrictive interpretation of the relative clause, in which it expresses a distinct assertion from that of the matrix predicate. Accordingly, (8a–b) appear equivalent to (9a–b).

(9)   a.   A: The one you did last time was for my wife actually. It was F name.
            B: That probably explains why I can't find it under H.

      b.   As you can imagine the first few days will be a bit hectic. During this time I will be ringing you, and every client personally to invite you into my office.

If the RCE construction allows only restrictive relative clauses, as is commonly assumed in the syntactic literature (see Baltin 2006), (8a–b) can perhaps be treated as something other than RCE. It is worth noting, however, that our corpus sample gave us no clear grounds for eliminating non-restrictive relative clauses: both (intuitively) restrictive and non-restrictive clauses modified a common noun and were introduced by a *wh* relative pronoun. Therefore, it appears problematic to exclude items like (8a–b) from analysis based on suppositions about the discourse function of relative clauses within RCE.

We will close with a final illustration of the challenges inherent in describing RCE function in (potentially) disfluent spoken English, where RCE may serve as a form of self-repair. In (10a), the subject NP, *the best singer*, is definite and has a discourse-active, topical referent, and the predicate *is this Olaf Bergh*, appears to be focal. In addition, the relative clause is introduced by the complementizer *that*, preventing a non-restrictive reading, and the VP-to-RC length ratio of 4:3 is one that should disfavor RCE.

(10) a.   <u>The best singer</u> is this Olaf Bergh <u>that I've seen</u>.   (spoken)
      b.   ?<u>The singer</u> is this Olaf Bergh <u>that I like best</u>.   (constructed example)

At least out of context, (10a) seems to us to be only marginally acceptable. What might be happening here? In (10a), the speaker seems to add the restrictive relative clause *that I've seen* as an afterthought, in order to qualify the claim made in the previous statement. As Wasow, Jaeger, and Orr (2011) observe, relative clauses are a common means of restricting the reference set over which a superlative applies, making a relative clause a natural choice of structure for such a qualifying statement. Consistent with this possibility, (10a) seems more felicitous than the constructed (10b), in which the subject contains no superlative and the relative clause is not used as a qualification. Thus, the sentence-final relative clause in (10a) appears to be a conventional self-repair, while that in (10b) is not. Support for this conjecture comes from a study of RCE comprehension by Levy et al. (2012), in which reading times were found to be faster for those RCE sentences in which the NP set up a strong expectation for a following relative clause (e.g. *only those executives . . .*), while RCE sentences were read more slowly than non-RCE sentences under weak-expectation conditions (e.g. *the executives . . .*).

In this section, we have discussed several cases of RCE from the corpus that appear to be problematic for current theories of RCE. Especially challenging are those tokens of RCE containing a topical subject and a focal predicate. Such cases call for an approach that acknowledges both the effect of grammatical weight and the range of discourse functions extraposition may perform.

5.4 General discussion and conclusions

The current study reveals a complex interplay among several different factors contributing to speakers' and writers' choice of RCE as against non-RCE word order in English. Overall, there was a strong preference for RCE when the relative clause was at least five times longer than the VP (length ratio less than 0.2), and a strong preference for canonical order when the relative clause was the same length or shorter than the VP (length ratio 0.8 or higher). For those items with length ratios falling in the middle range (between 0.2 and 0.8), choice of structure appeared to depend primarily on the definiteness of the subject NP and on the type of predicate occurring in the main clause. Items with an indefinite subject NP and a passive or presentative main verb were much more likely to contain RCE than were items with other combinations of features. The accessibility of the predicate also had a small but significant effect: RCE was more likely with superset-mention predicates than with new (no prior mention) predicates. In short, it appears that length ratio sets soft limits on RCE based on ease of processing, while discourse-related factors regulate choice of structure within these limits.

More generally, this pattern of results appears to reflect a strategy by which speakers/writers resolved potential conflict between grammatical weight and discourse factors by giving preference to each under different conditions: grammatical weight was given priority in almost all cases, while discourse factors were given priority only for those tokens that fell within a relatively narrow range of length ratios—those that might be considered neutral with respect to RCE. However, exceptional cases discussed in Section 5.3 show that this tradeoff was not always straightforward. For example, the sentences in (8a–b) show that occasionally, information-packaging considerations prevailed in licensing an RCE clause even when the length ratio favored a non-RCE structure. Future studies are needed to refine the conditions under which discourse factors may prevail over grammatical weight.

The results of the current study also have suggestive parallels with a corpus study by Jan Strunk on relative clause extraposition in German (Strunk, this volume). Similar to the current study, but on a larger scale (1,300 tokens from the Tübingen Treebank of Written German), Strunk's study investigated a number of factors that independently contribute to writers' choice of extraposed or non-extraposed order in German. Unlike the current study, Strunk's study was not restricted to subject-modifying relative clauses but also included various kinds of complement-modifying relative clauses. Perhaps for this reason, in combination with language-specific differences, RCE was much more common in the German corpus. However, the results of the two studies are strikingly similar. As in the current study, factors related to grammatical weight (extraposition distance and relative clause length) were among the strongest predictors of extraposition. And as in the current study, discourse-related factors including definiteness and position of the relative clause antecedent (head noun) within the sentence were significant predictors of extraposition status, independent of grammatical weight. Like the English RCE option, the German RCE option was more likely to be chosen when the predication contained an indefinite antecedent than when it contained a definite antecedent. More generally, both studies suggest that speakers and writers are simultaneously sensitive to several different kinds of factors when making structural choices in language production, thus supporting the general approach of several recent studies of word-order alternations (Arnold et al. 2000; Bresnan and Ford 2010; Gries 2003a; Lohse, Hawkins, and Wasow 2004; Rosenbach 2005).

In addition to highlighting the interacting factors at play in the selection of an extraposed structure, the current study also calls into question common theoretical assumptions regarding the discourse function of RCE in English. Although a majority of tokens in the corpus were compatible with the predominant view of RCE as a presentational construction (Section 5.2.2), a significant minority of RCE tokens (about 20%) appeared to have topical subjects and focal predicates (Section 5.3). In contrast to previous analyses of RCE, which propose certain invariant use conditions (e.g. Rochemont and Culicover's claim that predicates of RCE sentences *must* be directly or indirectly c-construable), our results point toward a revised theoretical approach that allows for more flexibility in the way that extraposition is licensed. It is important to note that while length ratios favoring RCE (i.e. a short VP and long relative clause) can help explain a subset of these exceptional cases, other cases, including (8a) and (10a) above, cannot be explained in terms of a simple tradeoff between discourse factors and weight. For (8a) and (10a), both the length ratios and the discourse properties should have favored a non-RCE structure. Thus, if only one discourse function were available for this construction, these cases would be difficult to accommodate. To capture the range of functions served by RCE, one could take a procedural approach, in which possible output forms are evaluated by means of ranked constraints, as in Optimality Theory (e.g. Bresnan, Deo, and Sharma 2007), or a declarative approach, in which construct types with shared formal, semantic, or use conditions (e.g. various RCE construct types) are organized in a type hierarchy, as in classic Construction Grammar (e.g. Fillmore 1999), Head-Driven Phrase Structure Grammar (e.g. Malouf 2003), and Sign-Based Construction

Grammar (e.g. Sag 2010). While a theoretical account is beyond the scope of this short chapter, we tend to favor some version of the latter approach, in which non-prototypical construct types inherit basic properties from the prototypical one while lacking one or more of the properties that characterize the prototypical case. Cases like (8a–b) and (10a) could then be viewed as instantiations of a minor type that inherits the syntactic properties of the basic RCE type, while having a distinct discourse profile.

The need for a more flexible mapping between syntactic form and discourse function relates to a more general issue in research on non-canonical constituent order. Despite the recent trend toward multi-factorial studies of the kind reported here and in Strunk's chapter, many studies of non-canonical constituent order still assume a relatively narrow domain of explanation (e.g. syntax, semantics, and/or discourse information structure), based on a few selected examples. As we hope to have shown here, however, multi-factorial studies examining naturally occurring language have much to contribute to theories of how non-canonical constituent-order patterns are used and represented.

Acknowledgments

We gratefully acknowledge the help of our research assistants Maryana Bendus, Corinne Feight, and Sunny Park, as well as our statistics consultants, Kenny Wakeland and Gayla Olbricht. We also thank colleagues and students who commented on earlier versions of this work, especially Jill Duffield, Roger Levy, Jack Hawkins, Brian MacWhinney, Edith Moravcsik, Jan Strunk, Tom Wasow, and two anonymous reviewers. This research was jointly funded by the Department of English and the Linguistics Program at Purdue University and the Department of Linguistics at the University of Colorado Boulder.

6

A statistical model of competing motivations affecting relative clause extraposition in German

JAN STRUNK

6.1 Introduction

6.1.1 *Relative clause extraposition*

Relative clauses in English, German, and other languages can either appear adjacent to the antecedent that they modify, that is, *integrated* into the noun phrase of their head noun as in (1), or in *extraposed* position at the right edge of the matrix clause as in (2). It is usually assumed that the integrated and extraposed variants are semantically equivalent (cf. e.g. Kiss 2005: 285).[1]

(1) Ich habe [DP alle diesbezüglichen Threads [RC die ich finden
    I   have   all relevant   threads   that I   find
    konnte]] gelesen.
    could   read
    'I have read all relevant threads that I could find.'
    (<www.rcforum.de/ftopic6950.html>, slightly abbreviated, accessed 11 March 2007)

(2) Ich habe [DP alle Bücher t] gelesen, [RC die ich finden konnte.]
    I   have   all books   read   that I   find could
    'I have read all books that I could find.'
    (<www.wer-weiss-was.de/theme46/article2357606.html>, accessed 11 March 2007)

---

[1] I would like to thank all participants in the experiment that I report on in this article and Lena Normann for helping me recruit participants. I would also like to thank the audience at the Conference on Competing Motivations, Elaine Francis, Jack Hawkins, Katja Keßelmeier, Tibor Kiss, Brian MacWhinney, Andrej Malchukov, Laura Michaelis, Edith Moravcsik, and three anonymous reviewers for very helpful comments. Finally, I am grateful to Ruhr-Universität Bochum, Germany, for financial support.

The integrated position is usually considered canonical, whereas the extraposed position is traditionally regarded as the derived variant with marked word order (cf. Baltin 2006: 237). The reason for this is that the extraposed variant violates one of the main assumptions of modern syntax, namely, that parts of an utterance that belong together semantically also occur next to each other and form a constituent, as already formulated by Behaghel:

Das oberste Gesetz ist dieses, daß das geistig eng Zusammengehörige auch eng zusammengestellt wird. (Behaghel 1932: 4)

(The supreme law is this, that things belonging closely together in mind are also placed close to each other.) (translation by JS)

This basic principle is a motivation not to extrapose a relative clause since the integrated position enables a straightforward syntax–semantics mapping and compositional interpretation. Of course, there thus also have to be factors that motivate extraposition and that compete with this principle, otherwise all relative clauses would always be realized in integrated position. Before discussing six factors allegedly favoring or disfavoring extraposition that feature prominently in the functionalist and generative literature in Section 6.2, I provide a brief overview of the corpus of German relative clauses that forms the data set used in the statistical investigation described in the following sections.

6.1.2 *A corpus of German relative clauses*

I created my corpus of German relative clauses by extracting all sentences containing a relative clause from the second release of the Tübingen Treebank of Written German (TüBa-D/Z) (Telljohann et al. 2005).[2] This treebank contains articles from the German newspaper *taz* and comprises 22,091 sentences and 381,525 tokens in all. In order to keep my corpus up-to-date and to benefit from corrections in the annotation, I have meanwhile updated the sentence ids and primary annotation to the sixth version of TüBa-D/Z. The treebank is annotated with part-of-speech tags and morphosyntactic information, relatively shallow phrase-structure trees (including maximal projections and topological fields), and grammatical functions. The position of a relative clause can be determined automatically on the basis of the tree structures, additional secondary edges, and the functional annotation (cf. Strunk 2010). On top of the primary annotation, I have added a secondary annotation layer that models the structure of relative constructions and is enriched with various features partly derived automatically from the existing annotation and partly annotated by hand (cf. Strunk 2010), including the position of the relative clause, its restrictiveness, various lengths and distances, and the definiteness and level of embedding of the antecedent.

---

[2] <http://www.sfs.uni-tuebingen.de/de/ascl/ressourcen/corpora/tueba-dz.html> accessed February 13, 2014.

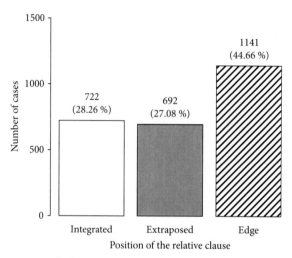

FIGURE 6.1 Linearization of relative clauses in the corpus (TüBa-D/Z)

The corpus contains 2,593 sentences with at least one relative clause and a total of 2,777 relative clauses, 222 of which were excluded from this study because they were not contained in a complete matrix clause. Thus, 2,555 relative clauses were considered for this study. Figure 6.1 provides an overview of the distribution of the different linearization possibilities in this corpus. A total of 722 relative clauses (28.26%) occurred in integrated position; 692 relative clauses (27.08%) were clearly extraposed. These numbers already show that the marked word order of the extraposed variant is not reflected in a substantially lower frequency of occurrence (in contrast to English, cf. Francis and Michaelis, this volume). Thus, there have to be some strong motivations favoring extraposition. The shaded bar in Figure 6.1 labeled *edge* represents all 1,141 relative clauses (44.66%) which could not easily be classified as extraposed or integrated because antecedent and relative clause occurred adjacent to each other at the right edge of the matrix clause so that there was no (potentially) intervening material that the relative clause could have been extraposed over. Since the possibility of string vacuous extraposition cannot be ruled out *a priori*, these cases were excluded from the analysis and not counted as integrated (cf. Shannon 1992; Uszkoreit et al. 1998). The following statistical analyses are based on the 1,414 clearly integrated and clearly extraposed cases.

6.2 Competing motivations affecting extraposition

Relative clause extraposition has been investigated both from a generative and from a functionalist and psycholinguistic perspective. In the next sections, I will discuss in detail six factors hypothesized to influence the likelihood or possibility of extraposition. Section 6.2.1 discusses the three most prominent factors from the functionalist and psycholinguistic literature: the length of the relative clause, the (hypothetical) extraposition distance, and the existence of (potentially) intervening noun phrases.

Section 6.2.2 examines the principal factors from the generative literature: syntactic locality, the definiteness of the antecedent, and the restrictiveness of the relative clause. For every factor, I provide a brief discussion of the literature and a bar chart that gives an impression of the influence the factor seems to have on the likelihood of extraposition when investigated in isolation. I also often give an authentic counterexample to show that a constraint should not be regarded as categorical or as the only relevant factor. Of course, there are a lot more potentially relevant factors than the six I discuss in detail. In Section 6.2.3, I present a multivariate model of extraposition that also includes many additional factors. It is, however, difficult to provide a lot of details on these additional factors within the limits of this chapter. My dissertation (Strunk forthcoming) contains a much more in-depth discussion of the individual factors and the multivariate model. This volume, in fact, contains another, very interesting article on relative clause extraposition in English by Francis and Michaelis, which to some extent enables a crosslinguistic comparison of the factors influencing extraposition in German and English.

6.2.1 *Factors proposed in the functionalist literature*

6.2.1.1 *Length of the relative clause*   A classic functionalist word-order principle is the principle of end weight, going back at least to Behaghel (1909). A modern formulation is given by Wasow (2002): "Phrases are presented in order of increasing weight." Since relative clauses are heavy both in a categorical sense because they are finite clauses and in a measurable sense because they are usually quite long, this principle provides a motivation for extraposing them to the end of the matrix clause. Hawkins' word-order theory (1994, 2004) also predicts that extraposition becomes more likely with increasing length of the relative clause. This prediction has been confirmed on another German corpus by Uszkoreit et al. (1998) and in a corpus study and an experiment on English by Francis (2010).

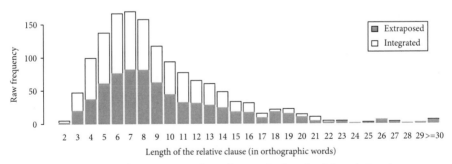

FIGURE 6.2 Likelihood of extraposition depending on the length of the relative clause

Figure 6.2 displays the absolute frequency of integrated and extraposed relative clauses conditioned on the length of the relative clause in words. As Figure 6.2 shows, Hawkins' prediction is confirmed also for this corpus: there is a significant, though relatively weak positive correlation between the length of a relative clause and the likelihood that it will be extraposed ($r_{pb} = 0.13$, $t = 5.02$, df = 1412, $p < 0.001$)

(cf. also Francis and Michaelis, this volume, for English). This tendency, however, does not mean that short relative clauses never get extraposed, as example (3) demonstrates.

(3)   ...als   sie   endlich   selbst   über   [DP die   Musik *t*] erzählen   darf,
      when   she   finally   herself   about   the   music   tell   may
      [RC die   sie   macht.]
          that   she   makes

   '...when she finally is allowed to speak herself about the music that she makes.'
   (TüBa-D/Z, abbreviated version of sentence 280)

6.2.1.2 *Linear distance between antecedent and relative clause*   Another reason to extrapose relative clauses according to Hawkins (1994, 2004) is that, especially in a verb-final language like German, dependencies between a final verb and its arguments and modifiers preceding it can be significantly shortened by evacuating the relative clause from the matrix clause. However, extraposition also incurs a penalty because it lengthens the dependency between antecedent and relative clause. According to Hawkins (2004: 142–6), the likelihood of extraposition should therefore decrease with increasing distance between the antecedent and the extraposed position of the relative clause. This prediction was confirmed in corpus studies by Uszkoreit et al. (1998) for German and by Francis (2010) for English as well as in experimental studies for German (Uszkoreit et al. 1998; Konieczny 2000) and for English (Francis 2010). Linear distance also plays a role in psycholinguistic theories of parsing complexity such as Gibson (1998, 2000).

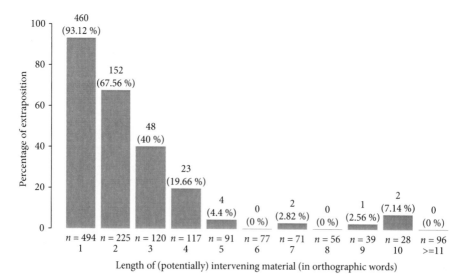

FIGURE 6.3 Likelihood of extraposition depending on the (hypothetical) distance between antecedent and relative clause

As can be seen in Figure 6.3, my corpus data also confirm Hawkins' prediction: The likelihood of extraposition decreases almost linearly as the length of the (potentially) intervening material increases from one to five words. A correlation test using the point-biserial correlation coefficient shows that there is a strong negative correlation between the (hypothetical) distance between antecedent and relative clause and the likelihood of relative clause extraposition (r_{pb} = −0.63, t = 30.26, df = 1412, p < 0.001) (cf. also Francis and Michaelis, this volume, for English). There are, however, a few exceptional cases of long-distance extraposition in my corpus; cf. example (4). These will be discussed further in Section 6.3, where I present an experimental investigation on how increasing the salience of the antecedent can facilitate extraposition over a longer distance.

(4) Wie   kann   [$_{DP}$ einer t]   sich   derart   empören   über   den
      how   can   someone   himself   such   revolt   about   the
      Wortbruch   bei   den   Großflächen-Plakaten,   [$_{RC}$ dessen   Partei
      breach-of-promise   with   the   large-billboards   whose   party
      selbst   Großflächen-Plakate   in Auftrag gegeben   und   geklebt   hat]?
      itself   large-billboards   ordered   and   posted   has
      'How can somebody revolt in such a way against the breach of promise in the matter
      of large billboards, whose party has itself ordered and posted large billboards?'
      (TüBa-D/Z, sentence 347)

6.2.1.3 *Intervening noun phrases*   Gibson (1998, 2000) defines dependency locality in terms of the number of discourse referents that intervene between two dependents. Extraposition should become harder and less likely with an increasing number of intervening discourse referents (operationalized here as DPs) (cf. also Shannon 1992).

As Figure 6.4 shows, the existence of (potentially) intervening DPs between antecedent and relative clause seems to be a strong motivation against extraposition: Whereas 81.12% of relative clauses are extraposed if no intervening DP exists, the likelihood of extraposition drops to 21.36% with one (potentially) intervening DP and to about 2% with more than one (potentially) intervening DP. There is a strong negative correlation between the number of (potentially) intervening DPs and the likelihood of extraposition (r_{pb} = −0.58, t = 26.54, df = 1412, p < 0.001). Moreover, in many of the sixty-nine examples in the corpus with extraposition over an intervening DP, the intervening DP does not have specific reference or is part of a support verb construction, as *auf den Punkt bringen* ("to bring to the point/to sum up") in example (5), and thus may not really count as an intervening discourse referent.

(5) Mit   diesem   treffenden   Satz   bringt   der   13jährige   Kevin
      with   this   accurate   sentence   brings   the   13-year-old   Kevin
      [$_{DP}$ die   Lage t]   auf   [$_{DP}$ den   Punkt,]   [$_{RC}$ in   der   sich
          the   situation   to   the   point,   in   which   themselves
      sein   Klassenkamerad   Max   und   er   befinden ...]
      his   classmate   Max   and   he   find   ...
      'With this accurate sentence, the 13-year-old Kevin sums up the situation in which he and his classmate Max find themselves.'
                                      (TüBa-D/Z, abbreviated version of sentence 7164)

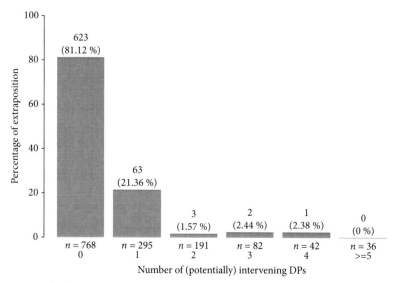

Figure 6.4 Likelihood of extraposition depending on the number of DPs (potentially) intervening between antecedent and relative clause

6.2.2 *Factors proposed in the generative literature*

6.2.2.1 *Syntactic locality*   Generative theories of syntactic locality claim that extraposition is not only clause-bounded (as established by Ross 1967) but that relative clauses cannot be extraposed from antecedents embedded arbitrarily deeply inside the matrix clause, either. Chomsky's (1973) subjacency principle predicts that a relative clause cannot be extraposed out of a DP that is embedded in another DP (since DPs have a special status as cyclic categories). Baltin (2006: 241) is even more restrictive: "An extraposed phrase is adjoined to the first maximal projection that dominates the phrase in which it originates." Müller (2004) and Kiss (2005), however, present both authentic and constructed German counterexamples to these predictions. Strunk and Snider (2013) likewise argue against the assumption of categorical subclausal locality constraints but also provide experimental evidence for a gradual, noncategorical influence of syntactic locality on the acceptability of extraposition in English and German.

As the embedding of antecedents can be automatically determined in the tree-bank, the predictions of theories of syntactic locality can easily be tested. The left panel of Figure 6.5 shows that the likelihood of extraposition decreases monotonically with a deeper embedding of the antecedent (measured in maximal projections), but the correlation is only marginally significant ($r_{pb} = -0.05$, $t = 1.89$, df $= 1412$, $p = 0.06$) and the decrease very gradual: from 49.89% extraposition with no embedding to 49.06% at one level of embedding, to 46.43% at level two, to 39.39% at level three, and to 16.67% with antecedents embedded four levels deep. There are no examples of extraposition from antecedents embedded more deeply than four levels.

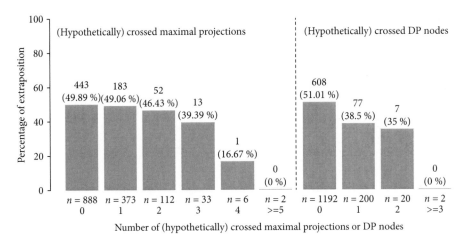

FIGURE 6.5 Likelihood of extraposition depending on the depth of embedding of the antecedent

The right panel of Figure 6.5 shows that the negative correlation between the number of (hypothetically) crossed DP nodes and the likelihood of extraposition is somewhat stronger (r_{pb} = −0.10, t = 3.71, df = 1412, p < 0.001): The percentage of extraposition drops from 51.01% if no DP is or would be crossed to 38.50% with antecedents dominated by one DP and to 35.00% if two DP nodes are or would be crossed. One example that clearly violates the different versions of subjacency by Chomsky (1973) and Baltin (2006) is given in (6).

(6) Und dann sollte   ich [DP Augenzeuge [DP der   Zerstörung [DP einer
     and then   should I   eye-witness   the.GEN destruction   a.GEN
     Stadt *t*]]] werden, [RC die   mir   am   Herzen   lag]   —   Sarajevo.
     city   become   that me   at.the   heart   lay   —   Sarajevo
     'And then I was about to become an eye-witness of the destruction of a city that
     was dear to my heart—Sarajevo.'   (TüBa-D/Z, sentence 16391)

6.2.2.2 *Definiteness of the antecedent*   Some authors also claim that definite noun phrases cannot be modified by an extraposed relative clause (cf. e.g. Kayne 1994; Baltin 2006). Guéron and May (1984) propose a theory in which relative clause extraposition is mediated by quantifier raising. Fox and Nissenbaum (1999) is a more recent incarnation of this idea. Since only quantified noun phrases undergo quantifier raising, extraposition from a definite antecedent is predicted to be ungrammatical. In addition, it has also been proposed that extraposition is associated in one way or another with focus (Shannon 1992; Rochemont and Culicover 1997; Takami 1999), which is likely also correlated with indefinite antecedents.

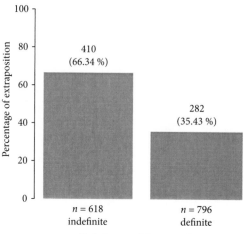

FIGURE 6.6 Likelihood of extraposition depending on the antecedent's definiteness

Figure 6.6 shows that there is a strong correlation between the definiteness of the antecedent and the likelihood of extraposition ($\chi^2 = 133.07$, df = 1, $p < 0.001$, Cramér's V = 0.31) (cf. also Francis and Michaelis, this volume, for English). A categorical constraint against extraposition from definite DPs is, however, clearly unjustified: In my corpus, 35.43% of relative clauses with a definite antecedent are extraposed (example (3) is one such counterexample) versus 66.34% with an indefinite antecedent.

6.2.2.3 *Restrictiveness of the relative clause*   Ziv (1973) and Ziv and Cole (1974) claim that extraposition of appositive relative clauses is ungrammatical. Figure 6.7 shows that this is not true in my corpus.[3] Extraposition of nonrestrictive relative clauses is significantly but not dramatically less likely (37.20%) than extraposition of restrictive relative clauses (54.30%) ($\chi^2 = 38.50$, df = 1, $p < 0.001$, Cramér's V = 0.17). Positing a categorical constraint is again clearly not justified; cf. example (7).

(7) Immerhin hatte er bis dahin [$_{DP}$ alle Entlassungsaktionen *t*] überstanden,
     after all   had   he till then   all   layoffs   survived
     [$_{RC}$ bei denen seit 1990 mehr als 2.100 Leute gehen mußten.]
         in   which since 1990 more than 2,100 people go   must
     'After all, he had survived all layoffs till then, in which more than 2,100 people
     had had to leave since 1990.'   (TüBa-D/Z, sentence 2667)

---

[3] I excluded 84 relative clauses from the diagram and the χ^2 test in Section 6.2.2.3 that I could not confidently classify as clearly restrictive or clearly nonrestrictive.

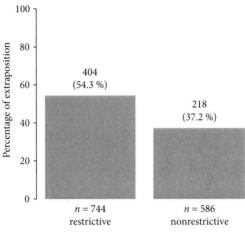

FIGURE 6.7 Likelihood of extraposition depending on the restrictiveness of the relative clause

6.2.3 *A multivariate model of relative clause extraposition*

In the preceding section, I have discussed six factors potentially relevant to relative clause extraposition that have been proposed in the literature: the length of the relative clause, the (hypothetical) distance between antecedent and relative clause, the number of (potentially) intervening DPs, the depth of embedding of the antecedent (syntactic locality), its definiteness, and the restrictiveness of the relative clause. The bivariate analyses have shown that all six seem to have an influence on the likelihood of extraposition when looked at in isolation. It is unclear, however, whether they model different aspects of extraposition and are all required in a good model of extraposition or whether they simply correlate with each other and are therefore redundant. Moreover, there may be additional motivating factors that should be taken into account.

In this section, I fit a binary logistic regression model to the corpus data, using R (R Development Core Team 2013), that includes a larger number of potentially relevant factors in addition to the six discussed in Sections 6.2.1 and 6.2.2 in order to predict the likelihood of extraposition. Building such a multivariate model makes it possible to test which factors are required to account for the corpus data and which of them are most important. The list in (8) contains all the different factors that I included in the model, grouped by the different parts of the relative construction. The six factors discussed in Sections 6.2.1 and 6.2.2 are printed in small capitals. I hope that most of the factor names are self-explanatory.

(8)　**Antecedent:** cataphoric + contains apposition + contains coordination + contains focus particle + contains superlative + DEFINITENESS + DEPTH OF EMBEDDING + gender + grammatical function + length + number + number of modifiers + pronominal + topological field + type of determiner;
　　Relative clause: complex (contains subordinate clause) + coordinated + LENGTH + RESTRICTIVENESS;

TABLE 6.1. **Coefficients of the logistic regression model of relative clause extraposition that are significantly different from zero (omitting the intercept)**

Factor	Coefficient	Std. Error	z Value	p Value
Accusative object antecedent	1.0709	0.3910	2.739	0.0062
Cataphoric demonstrative	2.4238	1.0141	2.390	0.0168
Definite antecedent	−1.7753	0.6486	−2.737	0.0062
Possessive determiner	2.7241	1.4198	1.919	0.0550
Universal determiner	−2.8026	0.7969	−3.517	0.0004
Antecedent in nachfeld	−2.6778	1.2555	−2.133	0.0329
Antecedent in vorfeld	−3.6973	0.5263	−7.025	<0.0001
Pronominal antecedent	1.9567	0.7908	2.474	0.0134
Nonrestrictive relative clause	−0.6130	0.3302	−1.857	0.0634
Complex relative clause	2.4332	0.7923	3.071	0.0021
Coordinated relative clause	−4.3384	1.6809	−2.581	0.0099
Length of relative clause	0.1908	0.0401	4.758	<0.0001
Adverbial relative pronoun	2.2248	1.1877	1.873	0.0610
Nachfeld already occupied	−3.8211	0.7318	−5.222	<0.0001
(hyp.) extraposition distance	−0.7760	0.1251	−6.206	<0.0001
(pot.) intervening DP	−1.1574	0.4029	−2.873	0.0041
(pot.) intervening adverbial	−0.8096	0.3868	−2.093	0.0364
(pot.) intervening negation	−2.7853	0.7499	−3.714	0.0002

Relative pronoun: depth of embedding + grammatical function + pronominal form (*d-* or *w-*);

Extracted phrase inside relative clause: length;

Matrix clause: copular construction + (HYPOTHETICAL) DISTANCE BETWEEN ANTECEDENT AND RELATIVE CLAUSE + length + nachfeld already occupied + passive + (potentially) intervening adverbial + (POTENTIALLY) INTERVENING DP + (potentially) intervening negation + (potentially) intervening superlative + (potentially) intervening universal.

The factor *cataphoric* indicates whether the antecedent contains a special cataphoric form of the demonstrative with -*jen(ig)*- (cf. Section 6.3). *Topological field* contains information about where in the topological structure of the German clause the antecedent is located. The factor *pronominal form* indicates whether the relative pronoun is from the demonstrative (*d-*) or the *wh*-paradigm (*w-*). Last but not least, *nachfeld already occupied* specifies whether the position of extraposed elements at the end of the matrix clause (nachfeld) is already occupied, for example, by another subordinate clause.[4]

---

[4] All factors were derived automatically from the annotation of the treebank except for the *restrictiveness* and *complexity* of the relative clause, the *(hypothetical) distance between antecedent and relative clause*, the presence of a *(potentially) intervening adverbial / negation / superlative*, or *universal*, the presence of a *(potentially) intervening DP*, and the factor *nachfeld already occupied*, which were annotated manually. All factors were checked manually.

Table 6.1 provides the coefficients of the factors obtained by fitting this model to the corpus data. Because of space constraints, I have only listed factors and factor levels whose coefficients were significantly different from zero and omitted all others. A positive coefficient indicates that a factor favors extraposition, a negative one that it favors integration of the relative clause.

The mean error rate of the complete model on the corpus (tested using ten-fold crossvalidation) is 7.86% (vs. a baseline of 48.76%). It is thus able to predict whether a relative clause will be extraposed with impressive accuracy.

For each factor, I also tested whether it should be kept in the model or could be dropped from it without losing significant explanatory power. I fit a reduced model keeping only the factors for which a log-likelihood ratio test yielded at least a marginally significant result (p < 0.1); cf. the model in (9).

(9) **Antecedent:** cataphoric + DEFINITENESS + grammatical function + pronominal + topological field + type of determiner;
Relative clause: complex (contains subordinate clause) + coordinated + LENGTH + RESTRICTIVENESS;
Matrix clause: (HYPOTHETICAL) DISTANCE BETWEEN ANTECEDENT AND RELATIVE CLAUSE + nachfeld already occupied + (potentially) intervening adverbial + (POTENTIALLY) INTERVENING DP + (potentially) intervening negation.

This reduced model yields a slightly improved mean error rate of 7.14%. It makes significantly better predictions than a model including only the six factors discussed in Sections 6.2.1 and 6.2.2 (error rate 11.83%) ($t = 6.34$, df = 9, $p < 0.001$), which in turn has a significantly lower error rate than a model including only the three functionalist factors (Section 6.2.1) (mean error rate 13.13%) ($t = 3.04$, df = 9, $p = 0.01$). Further omitting the factor *(potentially) intervening DP*, which results in a model similar to Hawkins' (1994, 2004) word-order theory, does not further degrade performance (mean error rate 13.13%). Both the model incorporating the three functionalist factors from Section 6.2.1 and Hawkins' model yield significantly lower error rates than a model including only the three generative factors discussed in Section 6.2.2 (mean error rate 34.05%) ($t = 15.89$, df = 9, $p < 0.001$). However, the fact that the model including the three functionalist as well as the three generative factors outperforms the model including only functionalist factors shows that the generative factors from Section 6.2.2 are useful for predicting extraposition.

Four of the six factors discussed in Sections 6.2.1 and 6.2.2, namely, the *definiteness of the antecedent*, the *(hypothetical) distance between antecedent and relative clause*, the *existence of a (potentially) intervening DP*, and the *length of the relative clause*, are indeed significant predictors of extraposition and influence the likelihood of extraposition in the predicted direction. Extraposition from definite antecedents is less likely than from indefinite antecedents (cf. Baltin 2006). A higher extraposition *distance* makes extraposition less likely, as predicted by Hawkins (1994, 2004); so does the existence of an intervening DP. In accordance with the principle of end weight, a growing length of the relative clause leads to a higher likelihood of extraposition. The *restrictiveness of the relative clause* (Ziv 1973; Ziv and Cole 1974), in contrast, seems to be less important to account for the corpus data.

Nonrestrictive relative clauses are only marginally less likely to be extraposed. *The depth of embedding of the antecedent* (syntactic locality), emphasized by generative accounts (Baltin 2006), is not required in the model (χ^2 = 0.32, df = 1, p = 0.57), even though Strunk and Snider (2013) were able to detect an effect of subclausal syntactic locality on the acceptability of extraposition in systematic experiments.

Interestingly, several factors relating to the intervening material between antecedent and relative clause are justified even within one model. The presence of a *(potentially) intervening DP* has a significant negative effect on the likelihood of extraposition in addition to the general negative effect of an increasing *(hypothetical) distance between antecedent and relative clause*. With an extraposition distance of two words, for example, the likelihood of extraposition is 71.65% if there is no (potentially) intervening DP but only 29.17% if there is a one (χ^2 = 17.43, df = 1, p < 0.001, Cramér's V = 0.28). The existence of a *(potentially) intervening adverbial* or *negator* also reduces the likelihood of extraposition (cf. Shannon 1992; Takami 1999). Finally, relative clauses modifying an antecedent located in the vorfeld before the finite verb in a V2 clause are extraposed much less frequently than relative clauses whose antecedent is located in the middle of the matrix clause (Shannon 1992).

The weight of the relative clause is similarly represented by several statistically significant factors. Complex relative clauses (containing a subordinate clause) have a higher likelihood of extraposition than simplex relative clauses, over and above the more general positive effect of a growing length of the relative clause. Coordinated relative clauses, in contrast, are not extraposed more often than simplex relative clauses, even though they are of course longer on average. This fact results in a negative coefficient for the factor *coordinated relative clause* in Table 6.1. These findings suggest that the structural complexity of the relative clause is also relevant to relative clause extraposition in addition to its length in words, which would be in accordance with assumptions in the generative literature (e.g. Ross 1967).

The weight and internal structure of the antecedent, in contrast, seem to be irrelevant to relative clause extraposition, as are its gender and number. Those features of the antecedent that are useful for predicting relative clause extraposition largely seem to have to do with reference, namely, *definiteness*, *pronominality*, and the specific *type of determiner* used. As already discussed, extraposition from definite antecedents is less likely than extraposition from indefinite antecedents. Moreover, extraposition from pronominal antecedents is more likely than extraposition from nonpronominal antecedents.[5] The positive coefficient of *possessive determiner* in Table 6.1 is a result of the fact that possessive determiners disfavor extraposition less strongly than other definite determiners. Conversely, the negative coefficient of *universal determiner* is due to the fact that the likelihood of extraposition from universally quantified antecedents is lower than extraposition from other indefinite antecedents. One possible generalization might be that a more restricted, fixed reference and an obligatory identifiability of the antecedent is detrimental to relative clause extraposition, especially if the relative clause is required to identify the

---

[5] Most pronominal antecedents involve demonstrative or indefinite pronouns.

referent of the antecedent and to justify using a definite determiner. Delaying the relative clause by extraposition is probably especially problematic if the antecedent is in a topic position, like the vorfeld or the beginning of the mittelfeld (further to the left in the matrix clause) (as also suggested by Hawkins, personal communication). Relative clause extraposition is thus probably not only connected to the referential properties of the antecedent but also to the information structure of the matrix clause and focus in particular (cf. Shannon 1992; Takami 1999).[6] The presence of a special *cataphoric* demonstrative in the antecedent (cf. Section 6.3), finally, also encourages relative clause extraposition (in comparison to ordinary demonstratives).

An interesting observation is that no factors relating to the internal structure or internal features of the antecedent, on the one hand, and the relative pronoun and the extracted phrase inside the relative clause, on the other hand, play an important role for extraposition. This finding may perhaps be evidence for the locality of syntactic processing in that only the antecedent and the relative clause as a whole, constituting the two parts of the relative construction, as well as the (potentially) intervening material determine the linearization of the relative clause, while the internal syntax of the antecedent and of the relative clause is largely irrelevant.

On the one hand, the model is a strong confirmation of the word-order theory of Hawkins (1994, 2004): The factors *distance between antecedent and relative clause* and *length of the relative clause* emphasized by Hawkins are indeed two of the most important factors. The strong negative effects of the *definiteness of the antecedent* and of the *vorfeld* position, on the other hand, also point to the importance of the referential properties of the antecedent and of the information structure of the matrix clause (as proposed by Shannon 1992 and Takami 1999, among others). The model shows that the effect of the *definiteness of the antecedent* cannot simply be explained as arising from a correlation with the *(hypothetical) distance between antecedent and relative* (as suggested by Hawkins, personal communication). *Definiteness* does correlate with *distance* in my corpus (r_{pb} = 0.23, t = 8.95, df = 1384, p < 0.001) in that definite antecedents tend to occur earlier in the matrix clause than indefinite antecedents, but if one looks, for example, only at cases with a restrictive relative clause of six to nine words and a (hypothetical) extraposition distance of one or two words, extraposition from definite antecedents is still significantly less likely (78.08%) than extraposition from indefinite antecedents (90.65%) (χ^2 = 5.55, df = 1, p < 0.018, Cramér's V = 0.18). My results are thus very similar overall to those of Francis and Michaelis (this volume) for English in that both distance/weight and definiteness have an impact on the likelihood of relative clause extraposition and cannot be reduced to one another. In addition, the strong negative effect of an *occupied nachfeld position* on extraposition suggests that the globally optimal structure of the matrix clause also has to be taken into account in the linearization decision. Finally, the grammatical function of the antecedent also seems to be relevant in that extraposition is especially likely from accusative objects (cf. Shannon 1992), although it is as yet unclear why exactly this is the case. To

---

[6] The presence of a *focus particle* or of a *superlative* adjective in the antecedent did, however, not come out as significant predictors in my model (contra Shannon 1992).

conclude, extraposition of relative clauses is subject to multiple competing motivations which have to be taken into account at the same time in order to explain extraposition and to predict it with high accuracy.

6.3 Salience of the antecedent and exceptions to constraints on extraposition

6.3.1 *Motivation*

The statistical model derived from the corpus data shows that there are some strong soft constraints against extraposition. As claimed by Hawkins (1994, 2004), a growing *(hypothetical) distance between antecedent and relative clause* makes extraposition more and more unlikely. However, as Figure 6.3 shows, one can find exceptional examples like those in (4) and (10) with extraposition over quite a long distance. The antecedent in such examples is frequently pronominal and focused and often contains an emphatic cataphoric demonstrative with *-jen-* ("that"/"those"); cf. example (10). I call such demonstratives emphatic because they are usually stressed and cataphoric because forms of *derjenige* ("that one"), as in (10), have a signaling function in that they are nearly always followed by a relative clause (cf. Strunk forthcoming).

(10) [$_{DP}$ Nur derjenige *t*] kann eine Anrechnung einer Maßnahme bei
         only DEM   can   a   consideration a.GEN measure   during
      künftigen Eingriffen in Natur und Landschaft verlangen (Ökokonto),
      future   interference in nature and landscape   demand   eco-account
      [$_{RC}$ der   ...]
           who ...
      'Only he can demand the consideration of a measure during future interference with nature or landscape (eco-account) who...'
                                    (Natur und Recht, Vol. 28, No. 7, July 2006, 471–2(2))

The factor *cataphoric*, recording the presence of such a demonstrative in the antecedent, has in fact been a significant predictor in the statistical corpus analysis in Section 6.2.3. However, since my corpus only contains 40 examples with a cataphoric demonstrative, I also carried out a systematic acceptability experiment to test whether making the antecedent more salient by marking it with a cataphoric demonstrative with *-jen-* and thereby also signaling an upcoming relative clause can compensate for violations of a strong soft constraint against extraposition, in this case long extraposition over an intervening prepositional phrase (as claimed, for example, by Lehmann 1984: 204).

   The following experiment investigates two questions: First, does a longer distance between the antecedent and the extraposed relative clause lead to reduced acceptability compared to extraposition over a shorter distance? And second, does marking the antecedent with a cataphoric demonstrative to make it more salient and to signal an upcoming relative clause compensate for this negative effect of an increased distance?

6.3.2 *Experimental method*

I carried out an acceptability study as a web experiment using WebExp2.[7] Participants read a sentence on screen and judged it on a scale from 1 (acceptable) to 8 (unacceptable). I use the mean z-normalized acceptability rating of the different conditions as the dependent variable in my analysis. Twenty-four native speakers of German recruited by myself and a student of mine, who were not linguists, participated in the experiment. They were not paid but could participate in a prize draw.

6.3.3 *Experimental design*

The experiment was a 2 × 2 factorial design crossing the factor *distance between antecedent and relative clause*, which could be either *short* or *long*, and the factor *determiner of the antecedent*, which could be either the (definite) *art(icle)* or the cataphoric *dem(onstrative)* with *-jenige*. In the long condition, there was an additional PP intervening between antecedent and relative clause. Because of the gender marking on the relative pronoun, the attachment of the relative clause was always unambiguously to the object (the intended antecedent) and not to the DP in the intervening PP. The four experimental conditions are listed in (11) with a combined English translation in (12).

(11) • **short-art:** Jens hat [DP **die** Musikerin *t*] ausgelacht,
      [RC die das einfache Stück nicht spielen konnte.]
    • **long-art:** Jens hat [DP **die** Musikerin *t*] **nach dem Konzert** ausgelacht,
      [RC die das einfache Stück nicht spielen konnte.]
    • **short-dem:** Jens hat [DP **diejenige** Musikerin *t*] ausgelacht,
      [RC die das einfache Stück nicht spielen konnte.]
    • **long-dem:** Jens hat [DP **diejenige** Musikerin *t*] **nach dem Konzert** ausgelacht,
      [RC die das einfache Stück nicht spielen konnte.]

(12) Jens has laughed at the/that musician (after the concert) who couldn't play the easy piece.

6.3.4 *Predictions*

The increased distance between antecedent and relative clause in the *long* condition should lead to a lower acceptability of *long-art* compared to *short-art*. This follows from the word-order theory by Hawkins (1994, 2004), Behaghel's first law (1909), and the psycholinguistic theory by Gibson (1998, 2000) and is also suggested by the corpus evidence presented in Section 6.2. Based on individual examples of long extraposition (often with a cataphoric demonstrative), I predict that *long-dem* should be judged as more acceptable on average than *long-art*, that is, that the cataphoric demonstrative can alleviate the acceptability penalty incurred by long extraposition (cf. Levy et al. 2012, who have found that increasing the predictability of the relative clause alleviates the processing load incurred by extraposition in English). In order to be able to detect this effect, *short-dem* should ideally not be

---

[7] <http://www.webexp.info/> accessed February 13, 2014.

judged as more acceptable than *short-art*. I suspect that this will be the case because forms of *derjenige* ("that one") are often considered somewhat marked and formal.

6.3.5 *Results*

Figure 6.8 shows the results of the experiment. The acceptability scale has been turned around so that higher values indicate a higher average acceptability. As predicted, there is an interaction between *distance* and *determiner* in that *art* is judged as more acceptable than *dem* in the *short* condition but it is the other way round in the *long* condition.

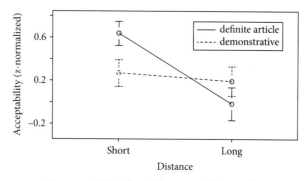

FIGURE 6.8 Results of the acceptability study

I fit a linear mixed-effects model including random effects for subjects and items to the experimental results. Model comparison using log-likelihood ratio tests indicates that *distance* (χ^2 = 29.67, df = 1, p < 0.001) and crucially also the interaction between *distance* and *determiner* (χ^2 = 19.97, df = 1, p < 0.001), and therefore also the main effect of *determiner*, are required in the model. Table 6.2 provides the coefficients of the fixed effects in the model. They have the predicted direction: A longer distance leads to significantly lower acceptability, but using a *demonstrative* instead of a definite *article* significantly reduces this penalty in the *long* condition. Post-hoc *t*-tests confirm the negative effect of long extraposition on acceptability within the definite *art(icle)* condition (t = 6.90, df = 218.46, p < 0.001). They also indicate that whereas *short-art* is judged as significantly more acceptable than *short-dem* (t = 4.38, df = 234.89, p < 0.001), *long-art* is judged as significantly worse than *long-dem* (t = −2.05, df = 235.63, p = 0.04).[8] The difference between *short-dem* and *long-dem* is not significant (t = 0.79, df = 236.01, p = 0.43).

The results of the experiment show that the constraint against long extraposition can not only be detected in actual linearization choices in corpus data (cf. Section 6.2) but is also reflected in a robust negative effect of an increased distance on the acceptability of extraposition. The analysis of the experimental results also yielded a significant interaction between *distance* and *determiner* such that marking with

---

[8] In addition to this web experiment, I also ran a parallel study with Linger (<http://tedlab.mit.edu/~dr/Linger/> accessed February 13, 2014) using a smaller acceptability scale from 1 to 6. The results were very similar but the post-hoc test comparing *long-art* and *long-dem* was non-significant.

TABLE 6.2. **Fixed effects in the analysis of the experiment (omitting the intercept)**

Factor	Coefficient	Std. Error	*t* Value	*p* Value
Long distance	−0.3629	0.0642	−5.653	<0.0001
Demonstrative	−0.7911	0.0642	−1.232	0.2044
Long distance and demonstrative	0.5787	0.1284	4.507	<0.0001

a demonstrative can alleviate the negative effect of a longer distance on the acceptability of extraposition. The prediction that making the antecedent more salient by using an emphatic demonstrative and making the upcoming relative clause more predictable by using a special cataphoric form can partly compensate for violations of strong constraints against extraposition, such as an increased extraposition distance, is thus confirmed. Whether using an emphatic cataphoric demonstrative has a compensatory effect beyond the acceptability of extraposition that also extends to online measures of processing difficulty (cf. Levy et al. 2012), that is, whether it facilitates the processing of long-distance extraposition during production and/or reception will have to be tested in further experiments.

6.4 Conclusion

The corpus analysis has shown that relative clause extraposition is governed by several competing motivations that cannot be reduced to one another, despite the existence of correlations between some factors. The processing considerations proposed by Hawkins (1994, 2004), involving the distance of extraposition and the length of the relative clause, are indeed the most important factors influencing the likelihood of extraposition (cf. also Francis and Michaelis, this volume, for English).[9] However, there are additional motivations that influence the likelihood of extraposition. One, perhaps also subsumable under processing considerations, is the desire to optimize the global structure of the matrix clause by avoiding multiple extraposition. Another group of factors concerns the reference of the antecedent: definiteness, pronominality, and the specific type of determiner used. The relevance of the antecedent's definiteness and of its position in the topological structure of the matrix clause as well as of the presence of a (potentially) intervening DP, adverbial, or negator may perhaps be due to the oft-claimed connection between information structure and extraposition (cf. Shannon 1992; Rochemont and Culicover 1997; Takami 1999; Francis and Michaelis, this volume). Finally, the restrictiveness of the relative clause and the grammatical function of the antecedent also have an impact on the likelihood of extraposition. In contrast, the relevance of syntactic locality, emphasized in the generative literature, could not be corroborated in the corpus study (but see Strunk and Snider 2013 for an experimental confirmation of locality effects on extraposition).

---

[9] An interesting question is to what degree these motivations play out online in production and reception and to what degree they are fossilized in grammar (cf. Hawkins 2004: 3).

Exceptional corpus examples and the results of my experiment show that even strong constraints can be violated under special circumstances. Increasing the salience of the antecedent and the predictability of the relative clause by using a special cataphoric demonstrative in the antecedent, for example, makes long extra-position more acceptable. An interesting question in this regard is the relationship between statistical and theoretical models since a factor may need to outrank all others in an optimality-theoretic model, for example, to allow for exceptional cases but may only have marginal influence in a statistical model because of the rarity of such exceptions. I therefore conclude that it is important to look at exceptional cases in order to learn something about the interaction of different motivations and the existence of special strategies and constructions to compensate for the violation of strong constraints and also to conduct systematic experimental studies in order to examine individual motivations and their interactions more closely.

7

Competition in argument interpretation: Evidence from the neurobiology of language

INA BORNKESSEL-SCHLESEWSKY AND
MATTHIAS SCHLESEWSKY

7.1 Introduction

Language is marvellously complex. Though readily apparent with regard to any individual language, this perhaps becomes even clearer when the languages of the world are considered in all their diversity. To some extent, complexity can be viewed as the result of "competing motivations", that is, pressures which serve to shape language(s) in particular ways and which may conflict. Consequently, languages manifest multiple alternative architectural solutions to a similar problem: speaker–hearer communication.

A source of complexity and competition that is often disregarded is that language is processed in real time: we never produce or perceive language in complete utterances, but rather as a continuing stream that unfolds over time. This places demands on linguistic analysis that are not readily apparent in theoretical approaches. Local ambiguities are a case in point: while a feminine noun phrase (NP) in German (e.g. *die Winzerin*, "the (female) winemaker") theoretically displays a nominative/accusative syncretism and its usage in a given sentence can be described as nominative or accusative depending on the sentence context (e.g. NOM: *Die Winzerin verjagte den Feldhasen*, "The winemaker chased away the hare"; ACC: *Die Winzerin erschreckte der Feldhase*, "The hare startled the wine-maker"), the same NP is locally ambiguous between the two readings as a sentence unfolds in real time (*Die Winzerin*..., "[The winemaker]:NOM/ACC..."). At this point, the human language comprehension system is faced with multiple competing analyses.

One might posit that a potential solution to the "ambiguity problem" and the concomitant increase in competition could be to wait until enough information is available for ambiguity resolution. In the above examples, this would entail waiting until the second NP is encountered. However, psycholinguists agree that this type of "wait-and-see" strategy does not correspond to the human language processing system's behaviour. Rather, sentences are processed *incrementally*, that is, each new incoming input element is integrated with the previous input and interpreted as deeply as possible (Marslen-Wilson 1973; Crocker 1994; Stabler 1994; for a cross-linguistic review, see Bornkessel-Schlesewsky and Schlesewsky 2009a).

In addition to incremental interpretation, a second source of competition in language processing results from the neurobiological basis of language, that is, the fact that language is a product of the human brain. While the notion of "language centres" in the brain has been very persistent, it is now generally accepted that language is processed by a widely distributed neural network (see Price 2010). Moreover, the flow of information from "input" (i.e. primary sensory regions) to "output" (i.e. regions responsible for the planning and execution of actions appropriate to the current input) proceeds in multiple parallel pathways (Mishkin et al. 1983, for the visual; Rauschecker 1998, for the auditory system). Thus, competition arises between alternative pathways and in the interaction between spatially distributed information sources.

The "competition problem" in language is thus clearly multiplied when language is considered from a real-time, neurobiological perspective. Here, we put forward a proposal regarding the most potent sources of this competition in the domain of argument processing and outline a potential solution for how competition is resolved. While we view competition as a basic property of the neural language architecture, we argue that "competing motivations" in the typical linguistic sense (i.e. multiple principles or functional pressures that compete) do not form part of this architecture. Rather, the assumption that different motivations compete emerges from the application of domain-general control mechanisms in the frontal cortex.

7.2 Actor as a cardinal category of argument processing

The astounding diversity of the world's languages not only raises intriguing questions regarding sources of competing motivations. In language processing, it can even lead one to ask whether crosslinguistically applicable processing strategies are possible at all (cf. Evans and Levinson 2009). In the following, we argue that—from the perspective of real time comprehension—this question can be answered in the affirmative. Specifically, evidence from typologically different languages supports a crosslinguistically applicable "actor" category and comprehension strategies based on this category. We posit that actor can be viewed as a cardinal category of language, that is, a category that provides an optimal and neurobiologically plausible solution to the demands of real-time information processing. In the following, we first review the evidence for the actor category before going on to describe architectural characteristics of cardinal categories as attractors.

Over the past years, we have conducted neurophysiological studies of sentence processing in a wide range of languages, including Chechen, English, Finnish, German, Hindi, Icelandic, Italian, Japanese, Mandarin Chinese, Russian, Tamil, and Turkish. Across these very different languages, we have found evidence for a strategy of incremental interpretation that we have termed the "actor identification strategy" (AIS; 1). (Note that this strategy forms a central part of a more comprehensive neurocognitive model of language comprehension, the extended Argument Dependency Model, eADM: Bornkessel 2002; Schlesewsky and Bornkessel 2004; Bornkessel and Schlesewsky 2006; Bornkessel-Schlesewsky and Schlesewsky 2008, 2009b, 2013a, 2013b).

(1)   Actor Identification Strategy (AIS) (Bornkessel-Schlesewsky and Schlesewsky 2013b: 248)
      The processing system attempts to identify the actor role—i.e. the participant primarily responsible for the state of affairs under discussion—as quickly and unambiguously as possible.
      Corollaries:
      a. The processing system prefers actor-initial orders.
      b. (Potential) arguments compete for the actor role.

Actor is a prototype concept, with a number of characteristics (see 2).

(2)   Properties characterizing the actor prototype (Primus 2006: 55)
      a. ctrl(x,s)   x controls the situation s denoted by the predicate
      b. exp(x,y)   x is sentient of y
      c. phys(x,y), phys(x)   x physically contacts or moves y; x moves or is active
      d. poss(x,y)   x possesses y

In the basic predicates in (2), x is the actor and y is the undergoer (i.e. the participant more strongly affected by the event). Crucially, the involvement of the y-participant in the event depends on the type of involvement of the x-participant, that is, a y-participant is controlled via the presence of a controller, moved via the presence of a mover, experienced via the presence of an experiencer etc. (see Primus 2006). There is thus a fundamental asymmetry between the actor and undergoer in that only the actor is associated with prototypical properties, while the undergoer is not (i.e. its properties depend on those of the actor).[1] Consequently (see Primus 2006), the sole argument of an intransitive verb is never categorized as an undergoer. The actor-centered view advocated here thus groups together S and A arguments (for the relevance of this observation for language processing and its relation to language typology and language change, see Bornkessel-Schlesewsky et al. 2008a; Wang et al. 2009).

   Crucially for language comprehension, the actor properties in (2) correlate closely with (semantic and morphosyntactic) prominence features which can be used to identify actor arguments during processing (see 3).

---

[1] In accordance with this observation, there has been some debate in language typology as to whether a prototypical transitive construction involves an inanimate or an animate undergoer (Hopper and Thompson 1980; DeLancey 1981; Comrie 1989). By contrast, there is a general consensus regarding the status of prototypical actors.

(3) Prominence features correlating with actor (Primus 1999; Bornkessel-Schlesewsky and Schlesewsky 2009b, 2013b): a prototypical actor will bear all these features, less prototypical actors only subsets

+animate (vs. −animate)

+human (vs. −human)

+definite (vs. −definite)

+1st person, "self" (vs. other)

+nominative (vs. −nominative) (in nominative-accusative languages)

+1st (argument) position (vs. other positions)

We have argued extensively elsewhere (e.g. Schlesewsky and Bornkessel 2004; Bornkessel and Schlesewsky 2006; Bornkessel-Schlesewsky and Schlesewsky 2009b) that the language comprehension system uses the prominence features in (3) to deduce which argument is the actor in the current sentence. Arguments thus compete for the actor role in accordance with their prominence (i.e. their combined ranking on the prominence scales in 3; for a computationally more precise formulation, see Alday et al. 2014). Since it proceeds via prominence information, this competition can take place in the absence of verb information.

Evidence for actor-initiality—AIS corollary 1—stems from electrophysiological studies in typologically varied languages, including Turkish (Demiral, Schlesewsky, and Bornkessel-Schlesewsky 2008), Chinese (Wang et al. 2009) and Hindi (Choudhary et al. 2010). Beyond earlier findings of a "subject-first" preference in European languages (e.g. Frazier 1987; de Vincenzi 1991; Schriefers, Friederici, and Kühn 1995; Bader and Meng 1999; Schlesewsky et al. 2000; Bornkessel et al. 2004; Penolazzi et al. 2005), the findings from non-European languages rule out interpretations based on structural simplicity, frequency, or a functional advantage for subjecthood (see Wang et al. 2009, for a summary). The finding of an actor-first preference even in a (split-)ergative language (Hindi) suggests that this interpretive preference may be able to override morphosyntactic criteria. The actor-first preference is illustrated in example (4) from Turkish (Demiral, Schlesewsky, and Bornkessel-Schlesewsky 2008), which involves an argument that is locally ambiguous between actor and undergoer. At the clause-final verb, the sentences are disambiguated towards an undergoer-initial reading and this engendered a reanalysis effect in event-related brain potential (ERP) measures (for an introduction to the ERP methodology directed at a linguistic audience, see Bornkessel-Schlesewsky and Schlesewsky 2009a) in comparison to similar sentences with an initial NP unambiguously marked for accusative (Turkish marks specific undergoers with accusative, e.g. Erguvanlı 1984). This effect occurred for both animate (4a) and inanimate (4b) initial arguments, thus suggesting that the language comprehension system initially analyzes the first argument as an actor even when it is inanimate and when an undergoer-initial analysis is information-structurally neutral and highly frequent (as in Turkish because of the high propensity for subject drop).

(4) An actor-first preference for both animate and inanimate arguments in Turkish (Demiral, Schlesewsky, and Bornkessel-Schlesewsky 2008)

   (a) Dün   adam   gördüm.
        yesterday man   see-PST-1sg
        'I saw (a) man yesterday.'

   (b) Dün   taş   gördüm.
        yesterday stone see-PST-1sg
        'I saw (a) stone yesterday.'

Competition for actorhood (AIS corollary 2) manifests itself in a similarly ubiquitous way. First, there is consistent evidence for actor atypicality effects: when an argument that is unambiguously the actor in a transitive (two participant) relation is non-prototypical (inanimate), this engenders a crosslinguistically comparable neurophysiological reaction, namely a centro-parietal negativity with a peak latency of approximately 400 ms post critical word onset ("N400"; for a comprehensive review of the crosslinguistic results, see Bornkessel-Schlesewsky and Schlesewsky 2009, and Table 7.1). This effect is illustrated in example (5).

(5) Effect of actor atypicality in Mandarin Chinese (Philipp et al. 2008)

   a. 王子被挑战者刺死了。
     prince BEI <u>contender</u> stab-PFV
     'The prince was stabbed by the contender.'

   b. 王子被绳子勒死了。
     prince BEI <u>cord</u> strangle-PFV
     'The prince was strangled by the cord.'

In the sentences in (5), the coverb *bèi* (often described as a passive marker) makes clear that the first noun is the undergoer and the second the actor. Once the second noun is reached, it engenders an N400 when it is inanimate and thereby a non-prototypical actor (5b) in comparison to when it is animate (5a). (Note that the effect observed here is not dependent on the *bèi*-construction, see Philipp et al. 2008).

Strikingly, the actor atypicality effect is independent of how strong an interpretive cue animacy is in the language under consideration: English (Weckerly and Kutas 1999) and Chinese (Philipp et al. 2008) show qualitatively similar ERP responses though animacy is a strong interpretive cue only in the latter (Li, Bates, and MacWhinney 1993). The effect is also independent of whether animacy is morphosyntactically relevant: German (Frisch and Schlesewsky 2001; Roehm et al. 2004) and Tamil (Muralikrishnan, Schlesewsky, and Bornkessel-Schlesewsky 2008) both show a similar effect, though animacy is relevant to a case marking rule (differential object marking) only in Tamil. The effect is qualitatively similar in all cases, thus supporting the assumption of a crosslinguistically applicable processing strategy that is—qualitatively—independent of language-specific properties.[2]

---

[2] This indicates that the human language processing system does not distinguish the different types of actor properties in (3) depending on whether they are "grammatically relevant" in a given language. For further neurobiological evidence see Bornkessel et al. (2005), Grewe et al. (2005, 2006) and, for an overview, Bornkessel-Schlesewsky and Schlesewsky (2009b).

TABLE 7.1. **Summary of the most pertinent neurophysiological results supporting the eADM's actor interpretation strategy**

Phenomenon	Type of effect	Languages	References
Actor atypicality effect			
– inanimate actor following undergoer	N400	English, German, Mandarin Chinese, Tamil	Weckerly and Kutas (1999), Roehm et al. (2004), Philipp et al. (2008), Muralikrishnan et al. (2008)
– psych-verb disambiguates to actor without physical causation or movement	N400	German, Turkish	Bornkessel (2002), Demiral (2007) (see also Bornkessel-Schlesewsky and Schlesewsky 2009c)
Actor non-initiality effect			
– initial argument disambiguated towards non-actor reading at a later point	N400 (+late positivity)	German, Hindi, Mandarin Chinese	e.g. Bornkessel et al. (2004), Haupt et al. (2008); Choudhary et al. (2010); Wang et al. (2009)
	early positivity	Turkish	Demiral et al. (2008)
	late positivity	Italian	Penolazzi et al. (2005)

Interestingly, actor prototypicality effects are typically not found when an argument could be the sole argument in an intransitive relation (S). In addition, non-actor arguments (undergoers) do not appear to be subject to comparable prototypicality effects. (For a full discussion, see Bornkessel-Schlesewsky and Schlesewsky 2009b and Table 7.1). These observations provide converging support for the notion of *competition for the actor role*, explaining why actor prototypicality effects are not generally observed when the argument under consideration could be the only argument (since there is no competitor under these circumstances; Bornkessel-Schlesewsky and Schlesewsky 2009c), and why prototypicality effects are observed for actors but not other arguments (since competition is for actor only; Bornkessel-Schlesewsky and Schlesewsky 2009b).

Why should the actor category play such an important role in language understanding? Bornkessel-Schlesewsky and Schlesewsky (2013b: 250) propose that linguistic actorhood may be based upon a "stable, language-independent category, possibly rooted in the human ability to understand goal-directed action". The fact that humans are attuned to this category could be due to basic evolutionary demands: "Agents are a class of objects possessing sets of causal properties that distinguish them from other physical objects" and "as a result of evolution, we have become adapted to track these sets of properties and to efficiently learn to interpret the behaviour of these objects in specific ways" (Leslie 1995: 122). Thus, by tracking (potential) actors, that is, those entities potentially suited to bringing about changes in the environment, we can interpret the world around us and make predictions about upcoming events (see also Frith and Frith 2010). This assumption is also in line with the finding that the human attention system appears attuned towards monitoring humans and non-human animals as opposed to other categories (for evidence, see New, Cosmides, and Tooby, 2007).

In summary, the actor role is a strong candidate for a crosslinguistically applicable category of language which serves to structure incremental comprehension in a way that optimizes our interaction with the world around us (i.e. provides a fast identification of participants potentially or actually responsible for the initiation of events). We have argued that competition for the actor role is the basic mechanism by which actor identification takes place. In the following, we introduce attractor networks as a neurobiologically plausible means of modeling the actor category and cardinal linguistic categories in general.

7.3 Modeling cardinal categories as attractors

If competition for the actor role is a possible language processing universal, this raises questions regarding its neural and cognitive basis. We propose that the actor role may be a candidate for a cognitive and neural *attractor category*. In cognitive terms, an attractor can be envisaged as a stable, language-independent category (see also Evans and Levinson 2009), which, for actor, may be based on the self as an acting agent (Haggard 2008), thus rendering the first person the basic agent prototype (Tomasello 2003a; Dahl 2008). In neural terms, these notions could potentially be modeled by means of attractor networks (e.g. Deco, Rolls, and Romo 2009).

Broadly speaking, attractors are stable states within a dynamical system, which are "attractive" because of their low energy states: "A useful analogy of the system's trajectory through state space is a particle that moves on an energy landscape with valleys, corresponding to attractors or stable fixed points, and hills, corresponding to unstable, repellent fixed points" (Deco et al. 2013: 199).

Attractor networks have been employed to model a range of neuroscientific phenomena, but we focus on their use in the computational neuroscience of decision-making, because we consider this domain most directly relevant to the classification question under consideration (i.e. whether an argument is classified as a topic or not, an actor or not, etc.). This perspective is in line with the view that there are general brain mechanisms for decision making, irrespective of whether the decision comprises a perceptual classification ("perceptual decision-making") or a more complex value-based choice (e.g. Heekeren et al. 2004; Basten et al. 2010). In an attractor network, decisions can be modeled via attractor states in a neural network which are associated with (stable) high firing rates. Which state "wins" during decision-making is determined by the current input and the initial stochastic firing behavior of the network. This is illustrated schematically in Figure 7.1b, while Figure 7.1a illustrates the transition from a spontaneous stable network state with a low firing rate to a decision state with a high firing rate.

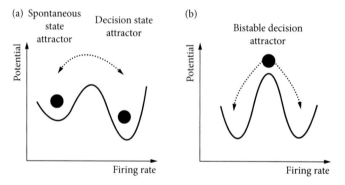

FIGURE 7.1 (a) Schematic illustration of how a neural attractor network may change from a spontaneous state attractor with a low firing rate to a decision (categorization) state attractor with a high firing rate; (b) Schematic illustration of different attractor states in a neural attractor network. Crucially, the attractor state that is reached and, hence, the decision/categorization undertaken depends both on the input and initial stochastic firing pattern of the network. Hence, the behavior of an attractor network is nondeterministic

Source: Adapted from Deco et al. (2009), Bornkessel-Schlesewsky and Schlesewsky (2013b).

Decision states in Figure 7.1 can also be viewed as states that allow for a categorization (e.g. of an entity as an actor). Possibly, then, an attractor network for actor categorization exists independently of language and, resulting from the general human ability to recognize goal-directed action and to differentiate self from other, it is universal. Stable firing patterns inherent to this network will be based on sets of input features that co-occur in domain-general actor recognition. The linguistic actor category overlaps to a certain degree with these general features (e.g. via the features +human, +animate and +1st person), thus leading to a propensity for actor recognition via the general attractor network. With regard to more language-specific features (e.g. case marking), the system will learn that these correlate with the remaining actor features such that, in the mature system, they also push the network towards the actor recognition attractor state.[3]

In summary, the assumption that actor is a cognitive and neural attractor category accounts for its importance in language comprehension. It is also compatible with the crosslinguistic variation described above: to produce an attractor state within the network, the overlap between a linguistic actor and acting agents in general will necessarily be conditioned by language-specific properties, for example the strength of a particular cue for actorhood. In addition, attractors have the advantage that they naturally allow for exceptions: they are stable, but not irreversible states in a nondeterministic system. Thus, in contrast to traditional linguistic universals, they provide a possible explanation for why some patterns occur frequently in the languages of the world though not being exceptionless.

From the perspective of competition in language and, specifically, language comprehension, attractors provide a computationally and biologically plausible means of resolving competition for a particular category. Thus, whether an attractor state is reached depends in part on the degree of evidence for the attractor category that the input provides (see Alday, Schlesewsky, and Bornkessel-Schlesewsky 2014). Assuming that every argument (more generally: every "nouny" thing in the input) aspires to occupy the attractor, the question becomes whether, once a new argument is encountered, it bears enough evidence to displace a previous candidate from the attractor state. This will be "easier" or "more difficult" depending on the degree of evidence for the actor role associated with the previous competitor and, thereby, its volatility as an occupant of the attractor state.

7.4 The three dimensions of argument processing (competition and interference)

The preceding sections have been primarily concerned with single sentences. However, language clearly does not consist only of isolated sentences in succession, but rather involves discourses of interrelated utterances. We propose that this crucial property of language can be captured and integrated with a sentence-internal perspective by means of the assumption that incremental argument processing takes place in three dimensions: what relation it bears to the prior discourse (the past), what role it plays in the current utterance (the present), and how important it will be for the upcoming discourse (the future). These three dimensions are

---

[3] In this context, one might ask whether the actor category emerges as a result of the interplay between general cognitive properties and the properties of the language being learnt, as has been proposed for categorization in other domains (e.g. Bowerman and Choi 2001; Choi 2006). In the strongest case, this would imply changes in the language-independent actor prototype depending on one's native language (cf. Fausey et al. 2010).

independent of one another in the sense that they cannot be derived from common principles or from one another, but there are correlations between them. The dimensions can be modeled in terms of three attractor basins—aboutness, prominence, and persistence—and their associated cardinal categories (CCs): topic, actor, subject (privileged syntactic argument).[4] We envisage the relationship between the attractor states and the CCs as follows: actor is a convenient shorthand for "the most prominent (potent to act) argument"; the same holds for topic and subject (i.e. topic: the argument with the highest degree of aboutness; subject: the argument with the highest degree of persistence). As described above, the actor in the argument is primarily responsible for the state of affairs in the current utterance, based on its prominence and that of its co-arguments. In addition, we propose that the subject plays a central role in determining argument persistence, that is, it sets up an expectation as to how central the argument will be in forthcoming utterances. In the default case, the most persistent argument in sentence *n* will then be the argument which sentence *n+1* is about (the topic); however, a topic shift may also occur (when the persistence-based expectation is not met), hence motivating topic (aboutness) as an independent category. In this way, all three categories have a similar function (namely to focus attention on one particular argument), but they differ with regard to the temporal dimension within which this focusing takes place.

Another crucial property of the CCs is that they do not have opposing categories. For example, an argument that is not a subject is simply a non-subject rather than a distinct category with its own characteristic features (e.g. object). As an analogy, consider the physical definition of rest as zero movement: rest is not the opposition of movement, but its absence. Likewise, without a better candidate for a particular CC, every argument has the potential to take on that CC's role. As a natural consequence, competition for each CC emerges whenever an utterance contains more than one argument.

In terms of the attractor networks introduced in Section 7.3, we assume that, within the language processing system itself, the attractor states aboutness, prominence, and persistence can be modeled as single decision attractor states (cf. Figure 7.1a).[5] Thus, in this type of system, there is always only a single attractor category and no opposing category. We propose that the impression of a binary opposition between the attractor categories and an opposing category (e.g. topic–non-topic (focus or comment), actor–undergoer, subject–object) does *not* result from linguistic processing per se (i.e. the linguistic attractor network), but rather from a more general cognitive processing system for binary decision-making (cf. Figure 7.1b). In other words, we claim that the familiar category of grammatical object, for example, is not one that results from processing within a linguistic attractor network, but rather from a language-external need to categorize linguistic elements as part of

---

[4] The term "privileged syntactic argument" (PSA) is taken from Role and Reference Grammar (RRG; Van Valin 2005). PSA differs from the traditional notion of "subject" in that it is language and construction-specific. In the following, we will use "subject" in the sense of PSA.

[5] Note that firing rate is not to be confused with processing complexity of any sort; even the attractor with the higher firing rate corresponds to a low energy state.

an evaluative decision-making process (i.e. "object" is the outcome of categorizing an argument as "non-subject"). We envisage this as a mechanism of frontal cortex (see Section 7.6): the locus, in our view, of domain general processes of evaluation, integration, and cognitive control as opposed to linguistic processing per se (Bornkessel-Schlesewsky, Grewe, and Schlesewsky 2012; Bornkessel-Schlesewsky and Schlesewsky 2013).

It is important to add that the attractor-based perspective is not only neurophysiologically plausible, but can also explain phenomena of language diversity and language change. For example, grammaticalization can be characterized as evolving within a state space including stable fixed points (attractors or repellers) (Bisang 1996; Dahl 2004; Malchukov 2010). Attractors not only serve to explain the trajectories of language change, but also help to demarcate the boundaries between different linguistic areas (i.e. geographical regions containing particular linguistic features or phenomena as opposed to others). Evans and Levinson (2009) have further suggested that the attractor notion could provide a solution to the problem that universals of language are not absolute—there are virtually always exceptions—and may thus be better characterized in statistical terms (i.e. as frequent as opposed to infrequent patterns, see Dryer 1998; Bickel 2007, 2010).

7.5 Linking the present to future and past: Motivating the subject and topic categories

We argued above that the three CCs can be viewed as devices to direct the attention of a hearer/reader towards particular referents. For actor, a possible function of this attentional orienting was discussed in Section 7.2 in terms of what is likely to be an evolutionarily motivated monitoring of potential event instigators. What, then, might be the function of the other two CCs, subject and topic?

For subject, there is good evidence from language production that attentional cueing correlates with subject choice (see Myachykov et al. 2011, for a review). For example, in Tomlin's "fish film" paradigm (Tomlin 1995, 1997), participants view two fish swimming towards one another, which are identical in all attributes except color. One fish subsequently eats the other and participants are asked to describe the event (e.g. "The red fish ate the blue fish"). Before the event unfolds, one of the two fish is cued by means of an arrow. Studies using this paradigm have shown that participants have a high tendency to code the cued participant as the grammatical subject, irrespective of its semantic role: when the cued fish is the actor, English speakers will use an active sentence to describe the event; if the cued fish is the undergoer, they will tend to use a passive sentence. Similar results have been found using static pictures depicting spatial relationships between referents (Forrest 1996) and implicit cueing of a referent's location prior to presentation (Gleitman et al. 2007). Tomlin proposes the following functional principle for English: "At the time of utterance formulation, the speaker codes the referent currently in **focal attention** as the **syntactic subject** of the utterance" (Tomlin 1995: 527, original emphasis). This motivates competition for the subject category, which we interpret as a correlate of argument persistence in discourse (see below).

The generalizability of the fish film results to other languages depends, at least to some degree, on the coding options afforded by the language, for example the availability of passive or word order variations. For example, speakers of Russian—in which passive is less preferred/frequent than in English—tend to produce a higher proportion of object-initial structures for cued undergoers (Myachykov and Tomlin 2008). This suggests that the results from English are not only driven by the close connection between attentional cueing and grammatical subject, but perhaps also by the desire to realize the cued participant as the "starting point" (cf. DeLancey 1981). However, further findings from Malagasy, a VOS language, support the subject-based rather than the linear order-based view, since speakers consistently realized cued participants as (sentence-final) subject arguments (Rasolofo 2006). From the data across languages, Myachykov et al. (2011: 104) conclude: "Overall, the existing reports using different languages suggest the existence of a mapping mechanism which uses both linear-ordering and grammatical-role routes from visual salience to structural choice, possibly with a larger weight on the grammatical-role route".

Do these findings carry over to language comprehension? In other words, assuming the same design principles as for actor (competition and attractorhood), what is the function of the CC subject in comprehension? We can formulate a possible hypothesis (see Section 7.6) based on Givónian-style text counts in a range of languages (Givón 1983a, 1994a). Endeavoring to operationalize the notion of topicality, Givón defined two measures: referential distance (RD) and topic persistence (TP). RD is an anaphoric relation and measures the "gap between the previous occurrence in the discourse of a referent/topic and its current occurrence in a clause" (Givón 1983b: 13) in terms of the number of intervening clauses. TP is a cataphoric relation which measures how often a referent occurs in the subsequent discourse (expressed either in terms of decay, that is, the number of consecutive clauses in which the referent appears, or the overall number of subsequent appearances in a set number of clauses). Crucially, persistence is particularly high for subjects (Givón 1983b), including non-actor arguments in passive and inverse constructions (Givón 1994b). Thus, persistence is more strongly related to subjecthood than to actorhood. Combining these observations with the attentional cueing results from production, we can view the subject category as a means of orienting attention towards a particular referent in language comprehension (cf. Gildea 2012, for a similar proposal).

(6) Subject as an attentional orienting device (SAOD)
     In language comprehension, grammatical subjects serve to orient the hearer's attention towards the subject referent in upcoming discourse. Subjecthood serves as a cue for the cataphoric importance of a referent (persistence) in the continuing information transfer between speaker and hearer.

The SAOD principle suggests how the actor and subject CCs may be related. For production, Gildea (2012) proposes that arguments that are good potential actors (i.e. animate entities) are very likely to be coded as subject because of our high degree of reflexive attentional orienting towards animates (cf. Section 7.2). Thus, in many cases, actor and subject will converge. However, there may be circumstances under which attention needs to be oriented towards a non-actor and this can be achieved by coding the non-actor argument in question as a subject (e.g. by means of a passive or inverse). As noted by Thompson (1994: 53) in a discussion of TP in Koyukon (Athabaskan, Alaska): "there is no suppression of the agent in inverse clauses, but … an increase in the topicality of the non-agent".

Initial support for these claims stems from neuroimaging studies that have compared active and passive sentences. Since passives involve coding a non-actor as subject, this should increase the strength of the orienting cue due to deviation from the default. Indeed, functional magnetic resonance imaging (fMRI) studies in Japanese (Yokoyama et al. 2006, 2007; Hirotani et al. 2011) reported increased activation for passive vs. active sentences in a fronto-parietal network which is neuroanatomically similar to the orienting networks identified in the context of nonlinguistic tasks (Corbetta and Shulman 2002; Petersen and Posner 2012). These findings are fully compatible with the view that subject choice serves to orient the hearer's attention towards a particular referent during comprehension.

Finally, let us turn to the third proposed CC: topic. Topics can be viewed as a mirror image of subjects in the sense defined above, namely as anaphoric rather than cataphoric discourse devices. In other words: topics serve to anchor a current clause with regard to the previous discourse and thus show a low (Givónian) RD value. A topic therefore often corresponds to the subject of the previous sentence (in accordance with the high persistence of the subject) and "topic continuity" in discourse will thus often reduce to subject continuity. The independent, and thereby more important, function of the topic as a CC comes into play when the subject chain is broken and an argument that was not previously a subject is realized as the topic. Under these circumstances, attentional reorienting is required.

This proposal is supported by initial experimental evidence. In an ERP study on Mandarin Chinese, Hung and Schumacher (2012) examined question–answer pairs such as (7) and (8):

(7)   Example stimuli from Hung and Schumacher (2012); SOV target sentence
   a. Topic-continuity context
      张三　　　怎么　　了？
      Zhangsan zenme   le
      Zhangsan what   ASP
      'What about Zhangsan?'

   a'. Topic-shift context
      李四　怎么　　　了？
      Lisi   zenme   le
      Lisi   what   ASP
      'What about Lisi?'

   a''. Neutral ("novel topic") context
      怎么　　了？
      Zenme   le
      what   ASP
      'What happened?'

   b. SOV target sentence

张三	李四	殴打	了。
Zhangsan	Lisi	ouda	le
Zhangsan	Lisi	beat	ASP

   'Lisi beat Zhangsan.'

(8) Example stimuli from Hung and Schumacher (2012); SVO target sentence

   a. Topic-continuity context

李四	怎么	了?
Lisi	zenme	le
Lisi	what	ASP

   'What about Lisi?'

  a′. Topic-shift context

张三	怎么	了?
Zhangsan	zenme	le
Zhangsan	what	ASP

   'What about Zhangsan?'

  a″. Neutral ("novel topic") context

怎么	了?
Zenme	le
what	ASP

   'What happened?'

   b. SVO target sentence

李四	殴打	了	张三。
Lisi	ouda	le	Zhangsan
Lisi	beat	ASP	Zhangsan

   'Lisi beat Zhangsan.'

At the initial NP in the target sentence (7/8b), Hung and Schumacher observed several differences between the three conditions: a graded P200 (novel > shift > continuity); a graded N400 (shift > novel > continuity) and a late positivity for topic shift versus the other conditions. These results provide converging support for the present proposal. P200 effects have been linked to attentional orienting such that targets following invalid or neutral cues engender more pronounced P200s (Golob, Pratt, and Starr 2002; Luck and Hillyard 1994). This is compatible with Hung and Schumacher's results, since topic continuity can be equated with a valid cue, topic shift with an invalid cue (the context should lead the listener to expect a different topic in the target sentence) and the novel topic (i.e. neutral context) case with a neutral cue. The N400 pattern, by contrast, appears to mirror the degree of competition for the topic category. Here, the novel topic can be viewed as the control, since in this condition there is no topic as yet (this is the first NP in the discourse). The topic continuity condition shows a reduced N400 effect because of the match with the cataphoric predictability of the topic based on the question. Finally, the topic shift condition leads to increased competition for topic, namely between the predicted and the newly established topic, thereby eliciting an increased N400. Thus, the topic shift condition shows an analogous electrophysiological response to that for a predicted, but atypical actor (see Section 7.2) or the required reanalysis of which argument is the subject (Haupt et al. 2008): competition for a CC is reflected in an increased N400 effect.

In summary, together with the discussion of the actor category (Section 7.2), the findings discussed in this section suggest that the notion of three CCs processed via common mechanisms (competition for an attractor state) provides a promising and neurobiologically motivated account of competing motivations in language comprehension. The assumption of common mechanisms can derive the parallels in the neurophysiological responses to the different CCs. Moreover, the CC/attractor perspective sheds new light on the function of competition during comprehension: individual CCs become particularly important when there is a lack of convergence between them (e.g. when actor competition converges on a different argument than subject competition). Under these circumstances, the attentional (re-)orientation brought about by the attractor basins is maximized.

7.6 Cardinal categories in (real) time and (neural) space: A neurobiological perspective

We will conclude the chapter by providing a brief outline of a neurobiological framework for modeling competition between CCs, based on the latest version of the eADM (Bornkessel-Schlesewsky and Schlesewsky 2013a). As already noted, it is well established that information processing in the human brain proceeds via parallel streams (e.g. Ungerleider and Mishkin 1982, for the visual; Rauschecker 1998, for the auditory system) and there is widespread agreement that this also applies to language (Scott and Wise 2004; Hickok and Poeppel 2004, 2007; Saur et al. 2008; Friederici 2009; Ueno et al. 2011; Rauschecker and Scott 2009). The present approach is concerned with how the CCs motivated above might be implemented within a neural architecture of this type. The basic architecture of the model is illustrated in Figure 7.2.

As is apparent from Figure 7.2, the model assumes a distinction between a dorsal processing pathway (DoP), which connects auditory cortex to frontal cortex via posterior temporal and parietal cortex, and a ventral pathway (VeP), which connects auditory cortex to a somewhat more anterior portion of inferior frontal cortex via the anterior temporal lobe (for the underlying structural connectivity, see e.g. Catani, Jones, and ffytche 2005; Glasser and Rilling 2008). It posits that the basic functional difference between the two pathways is that the DoP performs time-dependent computations (i.e. establishes relations between elements for which the order in which they occur is relevant), while the VeP performs time-independent processing (i.e. subserves the identification and unification of successively more complex conceptual units, with ordering irrelevant). In accordance with the focus of the present chapter, we restrict the following discussion to the DoP, since this is the pathway deemed responsible for the processing of the three CCs. For a detailed discussion of the VeP, see Bornkessel-Schlesewsky and Schlesewsky (2013a).

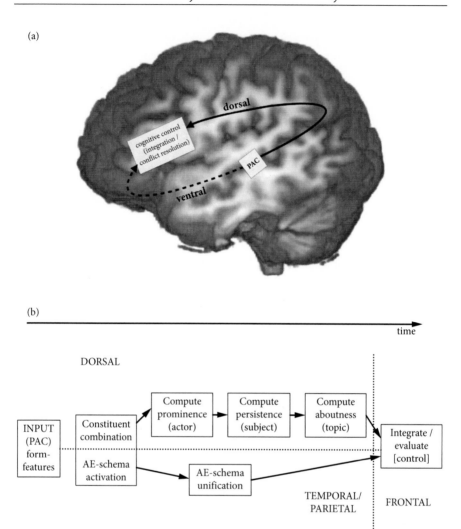

Figure 7.2 Schematic depiction of the processing framework proposed here. (a) Approximate neural location of the dorsal (solid line) and ventral (dashed line) pathways; note that both pathways include feed-forward and feed-back connections, though the dominant direction-ality of information flow is assumed to be as indicated by the arrows (i.e. from primary auditory cortex, PAC, to frontal cortex). (b) Functional characteristics of information proces-sing in the dorsal and ventral streams

Within the DoP, processing begins with auditory segmentation (not shown in Figure 7.2), proceeds to constituent combination and subsequently to CC computa-tion. We will have little to say about syntactic structuring here, except that we assume a surface-based syntax that encodes linear order and hierarchical structure but does not involve movement. Linear order is a particularly important prerequisite for the next processing step, computation of the CC actor, since an argument's position in a sentence is one important cue to actorhood. As is apparent from Figure 7.2a, we assume that CC computation is hierarchically ordered, with subject computation (compute persistence) dependent on actor computation (compute prominence) and topic computation (compute aboutness) dependent on subject computation. This ordering follows functionally from the considerations discussed in Section 7.5 regarding the relationship and dependencies between CCs. It is also in accordance with two neurobiological design principles of the model, termed "hierarchical processing" and "time–space correspondence", respectively (Bornkessel-Schlesewsky and Schlesewsky 2013a), see (9) and (10).

(9)   Hierarchical processing as a basic property of brain function
    Basic research on the visual (e.g. Felleman and Van Essen 1991) and auditory systems (Rauschecker 1998) indicates that information processing in the brain takes place in a hierarchical manner. In spatial terms this essentially means that the farther away from a primary sensory (input) region an area is, the more complex the processing that it performs, with complexity referring to an increasing need to consider multiple information sources (see Rauschecker and Scott 2009).

(10)   Time–space correspondence
    Neurobiological models of language should be compatible with information about functional neuroanatomy as well as temporal aspects of processing. Thus, stages of information processing posited in one of the two domains should also be applicable in the other.

This overall architecture has important consequences for competition both within and across CCs. On the one hand, there is competition between arguments for each CC in the manner outlined above based on the attractor notion. (Note in this context that the "nodes" for CC computation within the architecture in Figure 7.2 are assumed to provide an interface to more broadly distributed attractor networks including language-independent regions. Thus, the figure is not intended to imply that CC computation is performed exclusively within the regions shown.) On the other hand, hierarchical organization implies that the influence of the CCs on one another is not symmetrical. Rather, a CC that is earlier in the hierarchy will exert a stronger influence on a CC that is later in the hierarchy than the other way around (e.g. actor competition may have an effect on subject competition, but the reverse effect is predicted to be weaker). The assumption of an asymmetric relationship rather than a completely unidirectional information flow is based on the observation that information flow within the human brain is never unidirectional, that is, there is always feedback. However, we assume that there is a dominant directionality of information flow, namely from primary sensory cortices to frontal cortex (which determines the "output" in the sense of action planning and execution).

7.7 Relation to the Competition Model

Many readers will be wondering how the approach outlined here relates to the Competition Model (CM; e.g. Bates et al. 1982; MacWhinney, Bates, and Kliegl 1984; MacWhinney and Bates 1989; Bates, Devescovi, and Wulfeck 2001). Indeed, there are a number of similarities between the two proposals.

The CM envisages sentence comprehension as a direct form-to-function mapping based on a variety of interacting information types ("cues"; e.g. word order, animacy). The relative importance of a cue is language specific and determined via "cue validity": a cue that is highly valid exerts the strongest influence on interpretation. Cue validity is determined by the combination of "cue applicability" (high when a cue is always available) and "cue reliability" (high when a cue is always unambiguous and never misleading). The interpretation of a sentence (e.g. which argument is identified as actor) results from a competition between cues. As all cues interact directly and only differ in their language-specific weighting, the CM was the first proponent of an "interface"-type sentence processing architecture in the sense that cues from different domains (e.g. semantic cues such as animacy and morphosyntactic cues such as case marking) interact directly. It also posits actor, subject, and topic categories as defining different representational levels in language comprehension (Bates and MacWhinney 1982).

Perhaps the most pronounced difference between the eADM and the CM is that the eADM aims to model the neurobiology of language comprehension, while the CM is a cognitive model. An architectural distinction arising from this difference concerns temporal organization of processing: while the eADM assumes a cascade of information processing at each input item, the CM's architecture involves interacting constraints as in a connectionist model. The eADM's motivation for positing a cascaded architecture stems from the notion of hierarchical processing as a key neurobiological principle. An important consequence of hierarchical organization is that the CCs discussed here (actor, subject, topic) must be ordered relative to one another. Thus, they interact only in a directed (asymmetric) manner, while there is no principled reason to order them within the CM. Indeed, it appears much more in keeping with the CM's philosophy to view them as parallel and interactive. This means that the CCs can induce competing motivations within the CM: for example, both actors and topics are preferentially realized as subjects ("perspectives") in this model (MacWhinney 1977, 1987), thereby leading to potential competition between the principles "Realize the most agent-like argument as the subject" and "Realize the most topical argument as the subject". In the eADM, by contrast, the CCs do not induce competing motivations. Rather, they are three hierarchically ordered categories, with the identification of an argument as one particular CC depending, in part, on the processing of the previous CCs.

Somewhat more fine-grained differences are apparent at the level of the CCs themselves. As is apparent from the preceding discussion, the status of the subject CC differs between the CM and the eADM: while it is defined as perspective in the former, it is viewed as an attention-orienting device in the latter. An interesting topic for future research is that these two viewpoints may converge, that is, that the perspective adopted by the speaker also leads to a higher degree of persistence for the referent whose perspective was adopted (namely the sentence subject). A second point of divergence concerns the role of the first person, which is viewed as essential in defining perspective in the CM, but as fundamental for the actor role in the eADM. This leads to diverging predictions when privileged syntactic argument and actor do not align, for example in ergative languages and constructions such as passives. While the eADM predicts that changes in the first-person perspective (e.g. due to cultural differences; Markus and Kitayama 1991) should affect processing of the actor category in such situations, the CM should predict effects on the processing of perspective and hence the subject category. Finally, a third difference is due to the eADM's assumption that CCs do not have an opposing category and that, therefore, every argument remains a competitor for a particular CC until a better competitor is encountered. In the CM, by contrast, cues can block arguments as candidates for a particular role: for example accusative case blocks candidacy for the actor role in Hungarian (MacWhinney and Pléh 1997). In the eADM, an initial accusative in Hungarian would be analyzed as an actor candidate, albeit a very poor one.

In summary, the eADM is comparable to the CM with regard to the assumption of cue-based form-to-function mappings and the two models are in good agreement with regard to the CCs underlying language processing. They differ with regard to their scope in that the CM is a cognitive model and the eADM aspires to neurobiological plausibility. As outlined above, this leads to architectural differences between the models, specifically to the assumption of cascaded, hierarchical processing within the eADM but not the CM. Possibly, the CM could be viewed as a model of the output of the two processing streams posited in the eADM, mirroring the result of their integration in frontal cortex. Finally, though the two models agree on the three CCs, they define them in somewhat different ways. The degree to which these differing definitions might converge or whether their divergence is supported by empirical evidence will need to be examined more closely in future research.

7.8 Summary and conclusions

Based on an updated version of the extended Argument Dependency Model, we have provided an overview of a new, neurobiologically, and crosslinguistically motivated perspective on three cardinal categories (CCs) of argument interpretation: actor (compute prominence), subject (compute persistence), and topic (compute aboutness). We have argued that CCs can be modeled in terms of attractor networks, which provide an architecture for competition that is both neurobiologically plausible and compatible with a high degree of crosslinguistic diversity. Furthermore, the CCs can be integrated straightforwardly into a neuroanatomically grounded information processing system, which leads to new predictions regarding language processing and language structures.

Acknowledgments

Parts of the research reported here were supported by the LOEWE programme (funded by the German state of Hesse) as part of the project "The building blocks of language." We would like to thank Spike Gildea and Steve Small for very helpful and inspiring discussions. We are also grateful to Luming Wang for transliterating examples (7) and (8).

8

Competition all the way down: How children learn word order cues to sentence meaning

CAROLINE F. ROWLAND, CLAIRE NOBLE, AND ANGEL CHAN

8.1 Introduction

A central task in language acquisition is working out how the individual words in a sentence combine to convey meaning. For example, English uses word order to assign meaning, which means that the order of words in the sentence *the dog bit the man* tells us that the dog is the biter (or agent) and the man is the one who is bitten (or patient of the action). However, languages such as Turkish assign meaning using case marking. Thus, the same sentence in Turkish could also mean that the **man** (agent) bit the **dog** (patient) depending on how the nouns are marked for case.

The child's task is complicated by the fact that multiple, sometimes competing, cues to meaning are present in a sentence. However, the child's problem works to the researcher's advantage; we can study how children weight different cues when they compete, and thus test different theories about what cognitive mechanisms are co-opted into the language acquisition process, and how such mechanisms process the input. For example, if we find that children rely on the cues that are the most frequent and salient in their language, we would want to build theories around a mechanism that prioritizes frequently occurring patterns. Alternatively, if children preferentially pay attention to particular cues regardless of their frequency or salience in the input, we would want to build some particular sensitivity to these cues into the learning mechanism.

Most work on competing cues has focused on what happens when cues compete within a construction (i.e. within a particular sentence structure; see e.g. Bates et al. 1984; Bates and MacWhinney 1989). There has been far less work on what happens when constructions themselves compete. The aim of the present chapter is to explore how the acquisition mechanism behaves when constructions compete, with the goal of adding to our knowledge of how the language learning mechanism works. We present three experimental studies, all of which focus on the acquisition of the syntactic function of word order as a marker of the Theme–Recipient relation in ditransitives.

8.1.1 *Competing constructions in language acquisition*

There is a large literature on what happens when cues compete, much of it framed within a Competition Model framework, which suggests that "decisions in sentence interpretation are made by evaluating the relative weights of the cues present in the stimulus" (Bates et al. 1984: 344). For example, Bates et al. (1984) report that English adults and children will choose word order over animacy cues when interpreting transitive sentences with conflicting cues (e.g. *the chair pushed the tiger*) but that Italians will choose to interpret the sentence according to the animacy cues. Both decisions are consistent with the most reliable cues in the English and Italian language (see also Chan, Lieven, and Tomasello 2009; Dittmar et al. 2008; Ibbotson and Tomasello 2009).

However, this work has focused only on competition between cues within a sentence. Far fewer studies look at what happens when there is competition between structures—in other words, how the language acquisition mechanism behaves when there are two syntactic options to convey the same semantic information at the level of the argument structure construction. For example, English allows dative alternation—there are two ditransitive structures that express similar meaning but use different word orders to do so (as do about 6% of the world's languages; Siewierska, 1998). One of these structures—the prepositional dative—uses the word order Donor-Verb-**Theme-Recipient**. So in *the boy gave the book to the girl*, the Theme role (the object transferred) occupies the first post-verbal position, followed by the Recipient (who receives the object). The other structure—the double object dative (e.g. *the boy gave the girl the book*)—requires the speaker/listener to assign the roles in the opposite order—Donor-Verb-**Recipient-Theme**—the Recipient (who receives the object) occupies the first post-verbal position and the Theme comes afterwards. In order to identify the semantic roles in the two datives correctly, English children have to learn two diametrically opposed (post-verbal) word orders, differentiated by the presence or absence of the preposition *to*.[1]

Assessing the effect of such competing constructions is important for distinguishing between two different models of acquisition. On the one hand is the idea that children are initially reluctant to move away from the instances they hear to impose more abstract generalizations on the language (see e.g. Tomasello 2000). On this model, acquisition starts with children building up a store of lexically-constrained schemas, many of which are centered around particular verbs. For example, the child might learn the double object dative schemas *giver-give-givee-object.given* and *sender-send-sendee-object.sent*. These schemas are at first isolated, in the sense that the

---

[1] There are subtle pragmatic and functional differences between the meanings of the two datives, which means that they are not wholly equivalent (Pinker 1989; Haspelmath 2007a; Bresnan and Nikitina 2008; Rappaport Hovav 2008). However, it is very unlikely that young children are aware of these distinctions, especially since children incorrectly overgeneralize verbs into both constructions (Bowerman 1988).

children have not yet generalized across them to extract semantic or syntactic commonalities across givers and senders, or across objects given and objects sent. Generalization, based on both syntactic and semantic commonalities, only occurs once a sufficiently large store of lexically-based schemas has been acquired. The generalization process links lexically-specific schemas together to build more abstract constructions (e.g. *pronoun-Ving-pronoun-NP*) which themselves are linked to other constructions until higher first-order constructions such as the double object dative (*NP-V-NP-NP*) are acquired.

According to this theory, the more instances of schemas a child hears, and the more often she hears them, the earlier in acquisition she will extract the commonalities necessary to generalize across them and link them together. Thus, input frequency is an important predictor of acquisition. In English, the double object dative is substantially more frequent than the prepositional dative in children's input. Studies based on analyses of speech to children in naturalistic conversations have reported that about two-thirds of all dative utterances in speech to children are double object datives (Campbell and Tomasello 2001; Snyder and Stromswold 1997). We confirmed this by performing our own counts of dative use in the ICE-GB corpus (Greenbaum 1996) and in the speech of two 3-year-old UK children (Billy and Helen; Theakston and Rowland 2009). Between 65% (Billy) and 89% (ICE-GB) of all dative utterances were double object datives, confirming that the double object dative is substantially more frequent. We also checked the figures for verb types (i.e. the number of different verbs that occur in the two datives) because the ability to generalize across lexically-specific frames requires that the child hears the structure not only frequently but with a number of different verbs. There were twelve different verbs in double object datives in the sample of Billy's input and fourteen in prepositional datives (the figures for Helen are 15 and 9 respectively; for ICE-GB; 44 and 52). In sum, not only is the double object dative more frequent, but it is also heard with the wide range of different verb types that is required for generalization.

This theory also predicts that there will be no competition between the two dative forms at the initial stages of development. Within the theory, links between first order constructions such as the double object and prepositional datives are only made later in acquisition, on the basis of second order structure mapping. Since the first order constructions must logically be learnt first, generalization within a construction (necessary to create the first order construction) must precede generalization across constructions (necessary to link first order constructions together). In other words, it is only "older children [who] can, by a process of second order structure mapping, construct some higher order constructions such as the Subject-Predicate constructions" (Tomasello 2000: 242). As a result, the theory predicts very little competition between the two dative constructions at first, with the speed of acquisition of each dependent simply on the frequency with which it occurs in children's input. Since the double object dative is more frequent than the prepositional dative, the theory predicts that the double object dative will be acquired first.

An alternative theory proposes that children generalize more widely across constructions in acquisition from early on, especially across constructions that share salient syntactic or semantic properties. This idea that constructions influence the acquisition of other constructions has been proposed both for language learning (Abbot-Smith and Behrens 2006; Morris, Cottrell, and Elman 2000; Ruhland, Winjnen, and van Geert 1995) and for non-linguistic tasks (Rehder 2001). On this view, the presence of two constructions in the input that denote similar meanings but are expressed using different syntactic structures might be expected to *hinder* acquisition. This is because the learner is receiving conflicting information about what semantic role should be assigned to a noun, given the meaning of the construction, the noun's position in the sentence, and its surface form. For example, the two English dative constructions occur with relatively high frequency in the child's input but require a different ordering of the Theme and Recipient roles. This might be expected to hinder children's ability to learn these word order constraints and to assign Theme and Recipient roles correctly. This would be a competing constructions account, which could be seen as an extension of Bates and MacWhinney's (1989) Competition Model.

One illustration of how this type of construction-general learning might work is presented by Chang (Chang 2002; Chang, Dell, and Bock 2006). Their dual-route connectionist model contained built-in pre-linguistic architectural constraints: both a meaning system (for encoding concepts and semantic roles) and a sequencing system (a simple recurrent network that learned to predict the next word in a sentence). The model was then exposed to sentences with real verbs in a learning phase, in which it gradually developed knowledge of the meaning constraints of each syntactic construction as the outcome of increasing experience with specific sentence-message pairs. Importantly, the model did not discriminate between constructions. Instead, it built up a store of cross-verb and cross-construction information about what role was most likely to be assigned to a noun, given both its position in the sentence and its surface form. Thus, it was capable of generalizing from the start across constructions on the basis of commonalities in either form or meaning.

If children are generalizing across constructions in this way, competition between semantically similar forms should hinder acquisition. In fact, there is already some evidence to support this idea from German. Abbot-Smith and Behrens (2006) reported that the child's acquisition of the *werden-future* construction was delayed because of the prior acquisition of the semantically similar (but structurally different) *präsens-future* construction. Thus, we predict that the similarity in meaning between the two dative constructions, both of which occur with relatively high frequency in the child's input, should hinder children's ability to learn the different word order constraints of these constructions. This is particularly likely to be the case for the dative because the pragmatic and functional features that might help children distinguish between them are subtle and probably opaque to young children (Malchukov, Haspelmath, and Comrie 2010). We suggest that, on this model, children would be predicted not only to acquire the datives relatively late but also to acquire the two datives simultaneously, once they have learnt how to distinguish between them.

The aim of our first study was, then, to test these two different ideas of how children's linguistic knowledge may be represented by assessing at what age English children learn to assign the thematic roles of Theme and Recipient in prepositional and double object datives.

8.2 Study 1: English prepositional and double object datives

In Study 1, we assessed whether English 3- and 4-year-old children can use word order cues to assign Theme and Recipient roles correctly in prepositional and double object datives (analogous to the work on the transitive by Gertner, Fisher, and Eisengart 2006).

It is important to note that three previous studies have reported that English children can interpret both prepositional and double object datives by the age of 3 years (Conwell and Demuth 2007; Shimpi et al. 2007; Thothathiri and Snedeker 2008). However, the stimuli in all of these studies contained familiar verbs and/or animacy contrasts between the Theme (e.g. a ball) and the Recipient (e.g. a bird) roles. In other words, the tasks provided the children with correlated non-structural, as well as structural, cues to meaning. Children parsing sentences with familiar verbs have a number of advantages over those parsing sentences with novel verbs, including familiarity with typical semantic roles and potential referents, frequency of exposure to particular form–meaning mappings and the availability of well-established mappings between word and world knowledge (Bowerman 1983; Gropen et al. 1989; Snyder and Stromswold, 1997; Campbell and Tomasello 2001; Shimpi et al. 2007; Thothathiri and Snedeker, 2008). Similarly, the presence of animacy contrasts can guide children's sentence interpretation strategies, particularly of the double object dative (Cook 1976; Roeper et al. 1981; Osgood and Zehler 1981). As a result, we still do not know at what age children, like adults, can interpret the double object and prepositional datives on the basis of structural cues alone. In the present study we used novel verbs to ensure that we are tapping into knowledge that is independent of specific lexical verbs and we ensured that all characters were animate to ensure that the children could not use animacy cues to parse the sentences.

Eighty English-speaking children took part; thirty-nine 3-year-olds (mean age = 3;8, range = 2;11 to 4;3) and forty-one 4-year-olds (mean age = 4;9, range = 4;4 to 5;4). We used a forced choice comprehension task in which children had to choose which of the two actions corresponded to a sentence being spoken by a toy rabbit. The children saw two videos of transfer actions side by side and listened as the rabbit "asked" them to point to a particular picture (e.g. *point to where I'm bilking the frog to the teddy*). Training trials were used to familiarize the children with the procedure and the task. The children easily learnt what to do after only one or two training trials.

The procedure, including details of training, is illustrated in Figure 8.1. There were four test trials using four novel verbs (*glorping, bilking, jemming, meeping*). For each test trial, the child saw two video animations side by side and heard a toy rabbit speak a pre-recorded sentence—either a double object or prepositional dative sentence. All the animations depicted prototypical transfer actions—the transfer of an object from a Donor to a Recipient—with animal participants (e.g. a rabbit, a frog, and a duck). The transferred animal was always portrayed as smaller than the Donor and Recipient animals and it never expressed any self-generated movement in order to ensure that it was unambiguously capable of being possessed by the Recipient.

The Recipient always actively received the object animal (e.g. picked it up from the conveyer belt). For each test trial, one animation was assigned as the Target and one as the Foil event. Importantly, the Foil animation depicted a transfer event taking place between the same characters as depicted in the Target animation, but with the Theme and Recipient roles reversed. For example, if the Target animation showed a rabbit catapulting a frog (Theme) to a duck (Recipient), the Foil showed a rabbit sending a duck (Theme) to a frog (Recipient) across the screen on a conveyer belt.[2] This meant that the child's knowledge of the word order constraints of the dative constructions was crucial in determining their ability to point to the correct screen.

Trial	Visual stimuli	Audio stimulus
Character identification		Where's the/can you point to the … duck/teddy/frog/rabbit.
Training (4 different items; one example given here)		I'm the rabbit. I'm gonna be bilked. I'm being bilked. Point to where I'm being bilked
Test (4 different items; one example given here)		I'm gonna glorp the frog to the duck. I'm glorping the frog to the duck. Point to where I'm glorping the frog to the duck.

FIGURE 8.1 Example procedure for prepositional dative condition

There were two conditions, both with novel verbs—a prepositional dative condition (e.g. *I'm glorping the frog to the duck*) and a double object dative condition (e.g. *I'm glorping the duck the frog*). The audio stimuli were set up to be spoken by the toy rabbit, which enabled us to present the test sentence with a first person pronoun subject (*I'm . . .*). This helped engage the children in the task as well as shortening the length of the sentence, thus reducing working memory load. The children heard three sentences for each trial. In order to reduce the length of each testing session for each child, we used a between-subjects design, so children heard either double object or prepositional dative sentences.

---

[2] Pilot data demonstrated that children have difficulty identifying the salient differences between the two visual scenes if the actions on both screens are the same. Using different actions in the two scenes ensures that we do not underestimate children's linguistic knowledge.

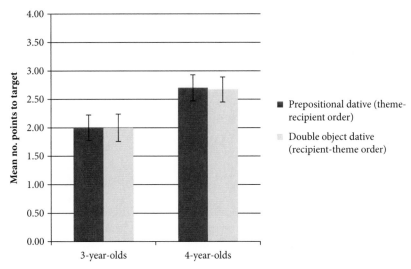

FIGURE 8.2 Mean number of correct points to target screen by age group: English children (maximum score = 4, error bars show standard error)

Figure 8.2 illustrates the mean number of times the children pointed to the video showing the correct target action, broken down by age group and dative type. Since all children completed all four test trials, the total possible score was four, with chance performance indicated by a score of two (50%). A simple linear regression was applied to the data, since regression is robust with respect to missing data and unbalanced cells and allows us to use Age in months (35–64 months) as a continuous variable. Dative type was the fixed effect (Prepositional/Double object dative; coded as a dummy variable). To map the dependent measure (number of points to target) into the range of the real numbers, the figures were transformed with the empirical logit (log(points to the target + 0.5)/(points to the foil +0.5)) (Agresti 2002). Age in months was centered in order to reduce multicolinearity (Neter, Wasserman, and Kutner 1985).

Only Age in months significantly predicted performance; $\beta = 0.05$ (SE = 0.02), $t = 2.27$, $p = .03$. There were no other main effects or interactions. Most notable is the fact that there was no interaction between Dative type and Age in months; $\beta = 0.004$ (SE = 0.03), $t = 0.14$, $p = .89$. In other words, although the children produced more correct points to the target screen with development, there was no difference in their performance with double object and prepositional datives at any age.

One-sample t-tests were then used to investigate whether the children were able to interpret both structures successfully at above chance levels (chance = 2). For this analysis, the children were divided into the two age groups; 3-year-olds and 4-year-olds. The 3-year-olds could not interpret either structure correctly (prepositional dative: M = 2.00, SD = 0.77, $t = 0.00$, df = 20, $p = 1.00$; double object dative: M = 2.00, SD = 1.03, $t = 0.00$ df = 17, $p = 1.00$). The 4-year-olds, however, interpreted both structures correctly (prepositional dative; $M = 2.70$, $SD = 1.26$, $t = 2.48$, $df = 19$, $p = .02$; double object dative; $M = 2.67$, $SD = 0.97$, $t = 3.16$, $df = 20$, $p = .005$).

The results suggest that 4-year-old, but not 3-year-old, English children have acquired the ability to use structural cues to interpret prepositional and double object datives, and that they acquire both datives at approximately the same time. However, we were worried by the possibility that our use of definite determiner noun phrases in the audio stimuli (e.g.... *blicking **the** teddy **the** frog*) may have depressed performance with the double object dative. This is because it is difficult to parse identically marked noun phrases that are presented in sequence (Gordon, Hendrick, and Johnson 2001). This is not a factor that could have affected the children's interpretation of prepositional datives, as the Recipient and Theme noun phrases are separated by a preposition, but it may have applied to the double object condition.

Thus, we repeated the double object condition of Study 1 using sentences in which the post-verbal nouns were marked distinctively and canonically—the Theme with a determiner noun phrase (*the teddy*) and the Recipient with a proper noun (e.g. *Frog*; see Rowland and Noble 2011, for evidence that this solves the problem in an analogous task). Thirty-three English-speaking children took part; fourteen 3-year-olds (mean age = 3;7, range = 2;5 to 4;1) and nineteen 4-year-olds (age = 4;5, range = 4;2 to 4;10). The materials and procedure were identical to those for the double object condition of the original study except that the Recipient was marked with a proper noun and the Theme with a determiner + noun phrase. In other words, the children heard *I'm verbing NOUN the NOUN* (e.g. *I'm blicking Teddy the frog*). The results showed that the modification made no difference to the children's ability to interpret the sentences. The 3-year-olds were not able to identify the Theme and Recipient roles at above chance levels ($M = 2.14$, $SD = 0.86$; $p = .55$). The 4-year-olds, however, were, once again, successful at the task ($M = 2.42$, $SD = 0.90$; $t = 2.04$, $df = 18$, $p < .057$).[3]

In sum, 4-, but not 3-, year-old, English children have acquired the ability to use structural word order cues to interpret double object and prepositional datives. There was no indication that the children acquired the more frequent double object dative construction first. This is contrary to what we would predict according to a conservative learner theory that sees children as conservative generalizers, with little cross-construction generalization (Tomasello 2000). Instead, the results support a competing constructions account, which suggests that English children acquire the ability to interpret the word order cues of both datives at the same time, as predicted by the competing constructions account.

8.3 Study 2: Welsh prepositional datives

An alternative explanation for the results reported in the Section 8.2 is that it is simply difficult to learn the word order constraints of complex structures like the

---

[3] In fact, the 4-year-olds in Study 2 were slightly less successful at interpreting double object datives than the 4-year-olds in Study 1, although the difference was not significant ($t = 0.74$, $df = 39$, $p = .46$).

ditransitive, which requires the child to process three semantic roles. This may be a particularly difficult task in studies like ours, which strip out all the non-structural cues to meaning (e.g. animacy). Thus, it is possible that children do not acquire these structures until age 4 years even in languages in which there are no competing constructions.

To assess this explanation we compared our English data with data from a language that does not allow dative alternation—Welsh (Primus 1998). Like English, Welsh ditransitives refer to transfer events involving three semantic roles—Agent (or Donor), Theme and Recipient, and syntactically involve three grammatical functions (Subject, Direct Object, Indirect Object). Like the English prepositional dative, the Welsh prepositional dative has Theme-Recipient word order and requires a prepositional dative marker (*to* in English, *i* in Welsh) before the Recipient noun (see (1)). However, unlike English, there is no competing double object dative structure.

(1) *Y   bachgen rhoddodd y   llyfr   i'r   Ferch*
     the   boy   give.PAST the book   to.the girl
     'The boy gave the book to the girl.'

This enables us to assess whether the absence of a competing form in Welsh leads to earlier acquisition than in English. If Welsh children acquire the prepositional dative at the same time as English children, we might attribute late acquisition simply to the fact that it is difficult to learn the word order marking in structures with three participant roles. If Welsh children acquire the dative earlier, however, the findings would be consistent with our hypothesis that the acquisition of the correct word order in English is delayed because of the presence of two competing constructions.

Another aim of the Welsh study was to look at what happens when word order cues compete with the position of the preposition. It is possible that it is the position of the preposition, not word order, that is central to children's ability to interpret prepositional datives; children may simply assign the Recipient role to the noun following the preposition, without any consideration of the order of the nouns. If this were the case, children would be predicted to assign the Recipient role to the noun after the preposition, no matter what the order of the nouns (e.g. *I glorped **to the teddy** the frog*).

In Welsh, it is possible to use a reversed Recipient-Theme word order in marked contexts that require heavy focal stress on the Recipient or when the Theme NP is heavy/long (see Primus 1998). Here, the word order is similar to the English double object dative but the grammar requires a prepositional marker in front of the Recipient, overtly marking the Recipient role (2).

(2) *Y   bachgen rhoddodd i'r   ferch y   Llyfr*
     the   boy   give.PAST to.the girl   the book
     'The boy gave to the girl the book.'

The use of this reversed order dative is rare in informal spoken Welsh but the fact that it exists and, most importantly, can be correctly interpreted by Welsh adult speakers, means that we can use it to investigate the role of the preposition in children's acquisition of the dative. If Welsh children are paying attention to the position of the preposition in semantic role assignment (as Welsh adults are), they should assign the Recipient role to the noun following the preposition, whatever its position in the sentence (as Welsh adults do). However, if children are parsing the sentences on the basis of word order, and ignoring the position of the preposition, they will misinterpret the (rarely attested) reversed order datives and assign the Theme roles to the first post-verbal noun.

The method of Study 2 was identical to that of Study 1, except that the audio stimuli were recorded in Welsh by a Welsh native speaker. We also created new 'Welsh-sounding' novel verbs (*rhidon, dasgru, llemu, orioni*). To ensure that the only cues within the Welsh audio were word order and the preposition, we used sentences in which the nouns were marked with definite articles. In Welsh, direct object nouns undergo soft mutation (in which the first consonant of the word changes) when the object immediately follows the subject and is indefinite (and, thus, carries no article because there is no indefinite article in Welsh). Thus, mutation is a potential cue to objecthood (Gathercole, Laporte, and Thomas 2005; Thomas and Gathercole 2007). Since feminine nouns, such as *cat (cath)*, for example, are also subject to soft mutation after the definite article '*r*, we only used masculine nouns.

Sixty-five Welsh-speaking children took part; thirty-four 3-year-olds (mean age = 3;8, range = 2;11 to 4;3) and twenty-nine 4-year-olds (mean age = 4;9, range = 4;4 to 5;4). All were native speakers of Welsh with no recorded language or learning difficulties. It is impossible to recruit Welsh-speaking children who have had no contact with English but we minimized the influence of English by recruiting only children who spoke Welsh as the home language and who were attending Welsh speaking nurseries or schools.

Figure 8.3 illustrates the data from the Welsh children, alongside the data from the English children from Study 1. We ran a simple linear regression with Age in months (35–64 months) and Dative type (coded as a dummy variable) as fixed effects, and the empirical logit of points to target as the dependent measure. Age in months was again centered. The model showed that, unlike in English, there was a significant effect of dative type in Welsh; $\beta = 1.31$ (SE = 0.25), $t = 5.29$, $p < .001$. There was also a near-significant interaction between age and dative type: $\beta = 0.07$ (SE = 0.04), $t = 1.91$, $p = .06$, again unlike English, indicating that the standard and reversed order datives followed different developmental paths in Welsh. There were no other significant effects.

One-sample t-tests established when the Welsh children were able to interpret both structures at above chance levels (chance = 2). The Welsh 3-year-olds (mean age = 3;8) were already able to interpret the standard Theme-Recipient prepositional datives (M = 2.63, SD = 0.90, $t = 3.08$, df = 16, $p = .007$), an effect that remained in the 4-year-old age group (M = 3.27, SD = 0.96, $t = 45.10$, df = 14, $p < .001$). However, neither age group was able to interpret the reversed Recipient-Theme order datives correctly. The 3-year-old Welsh children were at chance levels (M = 1.76, SD = 1.15, $t = 0.85$, df = 16, $p = .41$) and the 4-year-olds performed significantly below chance (M = 1.43, SD = 0.76, $t = 2.83$, df = 13, $p = .01$). In other words, the Welsh 4-year-olds

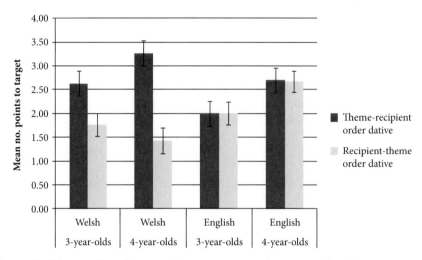

FIGURE 8.3 Mean number of correct points to target screen by age group (maximum score = 4) for Welsh children, with English children from Study 1 for comparison (error bars illustrate standard error)

were interpreting reversed order Recipient-Theme datives as if they were standard prepositional Theme-Recipient datives.

In sum, the results of Study 2 suggest that children can acquire the word order marking of the prepositional dative by age 3 as long as there are no competing constructions in their input. Thus, the delayed acquisition of the word order constraints of the two datives in English cannot be attributed to the complexity of the structures.

Also, the Welsh children were not able to interpret the reversed order dative even at age 4. In fact, the Welsh 4-year-olds misinterpreted reversed order datives as if they were standard prepositional datives. In other words, the Welsh children were not interpreting datives simply by paying attention to the presence of the prepositional dative marker but were using the most frequent word order cues of their language to assign semantic roles.

These data are consistent with the competing constructions model. In Welsh, the lack of a competition construction means the prepositional dative is acquired earlier than in English. In English, in order to learn to interpret the two structures correctly, the children must learn to distinguish between them. This may require substantial exposure to both structures and may rely on the children learning the significance of the position of the preposition with respect to the two nouns. This, as the Welsh data attest, may be late acquired.

8.4 Study 3: Cantonese *bei2* ditransitives

The aim of Study 3 was to investigate what happens when there is no dative alternation (as in English), but when children hear different combinations of Verb, Theme, and Recipient ordering.

In Cantonese, when adults express a transfer event with the word *give* (*bei2*) in pragmatically neutral contexts, they use a double object ditransitive construction, in which the Theme is expressed first, followed by the Recipient as in (3). The word order of the two objects is identical to that of the English prepositional dative, but it is not necessary to have a dative marker, like the prepositional dative marker *to* in English, between the Theme and the Recipient.[4]

(3) *Ngo5 bei2 jat1 bun2 syu1 lei5 laa1*
     I   give one CLF   book you SFP
    'I give you a book.'

In Cantonese, there is also a serial verb dative construction used with other transfer verbs (e.g. *take*, see example (4)), with the verb *bei2* (*give*) functioning as a dative marker before the recipient. This serial verb dative construction is similar to the English prepositional dative, in terms of surface form [Verb-Theme-Dative.marker-Recipient].

(4) *Ngo5 lo2   bun2 syu1 bei2 keoi5*
     I   take CLF   book give 3.SG
    'I take a book for him/her.'

Unlike English, there is not a subset of verbs in Cantonese that can occur in both the serial verb [Verb-Theme-*bei2*-Recipient] schema and the double object [Verb-Recipient-Theme] construction involving the same thematic roles (Donor, Theme, Recipient/Beneficiary). Thus, there is no dative alternation between the serial verb construction and its double object counterpart in Cantonese.

However, although the canonical word order is *bei2* (*give*)-Theme-Recipient in pragmatically neutral contexts, Cantonese children are also exposed to different, possibly competing, word orders. In pragmatically marked contexts and when the Theme NP is long/heavy, the reversed order (*bei2*-Recipient-Theme) can be used. Alternatively, speakers can use the serial verb construction (*bei2*-Theme-*bei2*-Recipient), which is also the construction used with other transfer verbs (e.g. *take*, see example (4)). It is also possible to displace the Theme role (in topic, right-dislocated, and relative clause constructions, for example), which results in the Recipient coming after the verb (see (5) for an example of a Theme in topicalized position).

(5) *Lei1 bun2 syu1 ngo5 bei2 lei5 aa1*
    DET CLF   book I   give you SFP
    'This book, I give you.'

---

[4] Tang (1998) calls this the "inverted" double object construction, on the basis that the usual order in double object datives is that used in English and Mandarin double object datives—Recipient before Theme.

Finally, widespread argument ellipsis means that children rarely hear both Theme and Recipient roles expressed together in the same utterance. In fact, Chan (2010) reported that only about 30% of *bei2* ditransitives in monolingual Cantonese children's input contain both Theme and Recipient in the canonical Theme-Recipient order. Much of the time (48% of *bei2* datives) the Theme role is omitted because it is easily retrievable from prior discourse or context, so Cantonese children hear only the verb and the Recipient noun phrase (*bei2*-Recipient). Thus, although there is no competition from dative alternation (as in English), there are still competing structures in the input as a result of frequent ellipsis, use of a serial verb construction, or displacement of the Theme argument. This means that sometimes the first postverbal argument after *bei2(give)* is the Theme but sometime it is the Recipient.[5]

If our competing constructions model is correct, these competing structures in the input will delay acquisition of the canonical Theme-Recipient word order marking with *bei2* (*give*) ditransitives. In Study 3, we investigated whether the presence of competing word order structures in the input would delay acquisition of word order marking of the Cantonese *bei2* (*give*) ditransitive. We tested sixty-four 3-year-olds (mean 3;5, range 3;2 to 3;10) using our forced-choice pointing task. One group of children heard full, two noun canonical *bei2* ditransitives (e.g. *I-bei2(give)-monkey-rabbit*). If the children had knowledge of the word order marking of Cantonese, we expected them to assign the Theme role to the first noun and the Recipient role to the second (interpreting the sentence correctly as *I give the monkey to the rabbit*). Another group heard elliptical utterances (*I-bei2(give)-monkey*), in which only one noun was expressed. This condition tested whether children would follow the most frequently heard interpretation of such sentences in their language and assign the Recipient role to the noun (interpreting the sentence as *I give the rabbit to the monkey*). We also tested the children's ability to interpret unambiguously marked serial verb dative constructions (both with real verbs like *sung3* [*give* as a present] and novel verbs like *tam1*) for comparison and to ensure that any problems could not be attributed to task difficulty.[6]

The method was very similar to that of Studies 1 and 2 except for three modifications that we introduced after piloting; we created new animations with animals that were designed to be familiar to Cantonese children, the children first saw the two animations individually before seeing them concurrently, and there were eight items per condition not four (see Figure 8.4 for an example of the stimuli).

---

[5] There might also be competition from ditransitives with *teach* verbs which take Recipient-Theme order in Cantonese. The presence of *teach* verb constructions does not provide Cantonese with a ditransitive alternation like English but a lexical split: "A split is the situation where different verbs use different constructions, while an alternation is the situation where one and the same verb can occur with different constructions with roughly the same meaning" (Malchukov, Haspelmath, and Comrie 2010). However, it is possible that lexical splits may act as competing constructions in acquisition.

[6] It was not possible to use all novel verbs because in contemporary Cantonese the [Verb-Noun-Noun] double object configuration is only natural/grammatical with the verb *bei2* among dative verbs which depict physical transfer events of tangible entities, or with *teach* verbs, but these verbs and their argument roles are hard to depict clearly in the visual pointing paradigm, and impossible to depict without non-structural animacy cues.

Target transfer scene   Foil transfer scene

FIGURE 8.4 Example test trial for Cantonese study (original videos were in color; the audio for this trial translates as *Point and let me see: which picture is I give* (bei2) *monkey rabbit?*)

Figure 8.5 illustrates the mean number of correct points to the target screen, demonstrating how often the children correctly interpreted the full ditransitives (*bei2*-Noun-Noun) and the serial verb construction (Verb-Noun-*bei2*-Noun), and how often they interpreted the elliptical (*bei2*-Noun) sentences as expressing the Theme. The children were above chance with the (unambiguous) serial verb constructions with real and novel verbs ($t = 6.39$, df = 31, $p < .001$). Thus, we know that the task is not too difficult for them. However, the children were at chance for both the full two-noun construction (*bei2*-Noun-Noun; $t = 1.16$, df = 15, $p = .26$) and for the elliptical construction (*bei2*-Noun; $t = 10.85$, df = 15, $p = .41$).

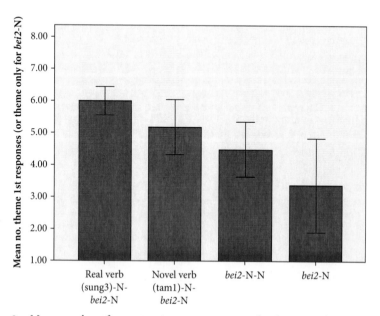

FIGURE 8.5 Mean number of correct points to target screen by dative condition (maximum score = 8, error bars illustrate standard error)

In other words, they were equally likely to assign the Recipient role to the first (or only) noun as they were to assign the Theme role. When we repeated the study on a control sample of adults, however, they interpreted all the sentences in the predicted direction (*bei2*-Theme-Recipient for the full ditransitives and *bei2*-Recipient for the elliptical utterances). In sum, though there is no competition from dative alternation in Cantonese, the competing word order structures in the input meant that, like English 3-year-olds, the Cantonese 3-year-olds had not yet acquired the word order marking constraints of *bei2* ditransitives.

8.5 Discussion

The conclusion we draw from these studies is that there is competition between constructions as well as competition between cues in language acquisition. The English data tell us that the existence of two constructions expressing similar meanings with different word orders delays acquisition. The Cantonese data tell us that competition does not necessarily come from a dative alternation; delayed acquisition also occurs when there are other competing word order structures in the input. The ease with which Welsh 3- and 4-year-olds passed the task with prepositional datives tells us that these delays cannot be attributed to the difficulty of the task or to the fact that ditransitives require children to process three separate participant roles. In fact, the 4-year-old Welsh children's knowledge of prepositional datives was so robust that they used the canonical word order of their language even when it conflicted with another, salient cue to meaning in reversed order datives: the position of the preposition.

These results suggest that children may be generalizing across constructions from early on, constructing both verb- and construction-general representations. They, thus, count against a conservative learner account that predicts that a significant amount of learning must take place before generalization across constructions can take place (e.g. the strongest version of the verb-island hypothesis, Tomasello 1992). On this model, links between first order constructions such as the double object and prepositional dative are only made later on in acquisition, on the basis of second order structure mapping. Since the first order constructions must logically be learnt first, generalization within a construction must precede generalization across constructions. Thus, the theory predicts that there will be little competition between the two dative forms at the initial stages of development so that the order of acquisition will correlate with the relative frequency of the constructions in the input. This prediction was not supported by our data.

Instead the data suggest that children generalize more widely across both verbs and constructions from early on, especially across constructions that share salient syntactic or semantic properties. These data are compatible with a competing constructions account that suggests that the presence of two constructions that denote similar meanings but are expressed using different syntactic structures will hinder acquisition. This is because the learner is receiving conflicting information about what semantic role should be assigned to a noun, given the meaning of the construction, the noun's position in the sentence and its surface form.

This idea that children quickly generalize across specific instances in acquisition is neither new nor controversial. As Bates and MacWhinney (1989) argue, there is an impressive body of evidence showing that children can pick up quite abstract cues in their language very quickly—a process that must involve generalization. There is also evidence that such cues are quite specific to the language being learnt, suggesting that the process is one of rapid learning rather than resulting from innate predispositions (e.g. Bates et al. 1984 demonstrated that English children rely on word order but Italian children on animacy when the two cues conflict). What we are suggesting, however, is an extension to the Competition Model, whereby such generalizations can take place across constructions as easily as they take place within constructions, whenever there are salient similarities to form the basis of the generalization.

This idea is also consistent with other models of similarity-based generalization. For example, in structural alignment models of similarity matching in non-linguistic domains (see Gentner 1983, 1989), the process of analogy required for generalization is facilitated when the instances being compared are similar on **any** dimension. In language acquisition, cross-situational (and thus cross-constructional) similarity matching is highly likely to play a role in the acquisition of the meaning of novel words and, may in fact, be required in order for the child to converge on the correct meaning (Childers and Paik 2009). We simply extend this mechanism to the acquisition of form–meaning mappings. In other words, we suggest that the language acquisition mechanism can generalize across specific instances both within and across construction boundaries from early on because it is sensitive to similarities in structure and meaning wherever they occur.

The final question to address is how to reconcile our results, which show that children generalize both within and across constructions, with the large body of work demonstrating that children's early productions are lexically specific (see e.g. Pine, Lieven, and Rowland 1998; Theakston et al. 2005). In the literature, there has traditionally been a dichotomy between those who argue for lexically specific learning and those who argue that children are generalizing across specific instances, extracting verb- and construction-general information about the regularities of their language from early on. We suggest that these are not mutually exclusive. Children are undoubtedly building up their knowledge of the language from the specific utterances they hear. As a result, children will learn those lexically specific patterns that occur with high frequency (e.g. *where's X going*), they will use these patterns in their production (see Pine, Lieven, and Rowland 1998) and they will be faster (Bannard and Matthews 2008) and more accurate (Rowland 2007) at using them. However, this does not prevent the learner from generalizing across them on the basis of shared commonalities in form and meaning, extracting relevant cues such as word order cues and applying them across construction boundaries. In other words, at any one point in developmental time, children's knowledge is the product both of the learning of lexically specific patterns and of generalizations across these patterns in an attempt to extract commonalities in form and meaning.

We conclude by proposing two characteristics that future models of the acquisition mechanism must exhibit. First, models must be capable of both cross-verb and cross-structural generalizations on the basis of structural and semantic similarities.

For example, models must be capable of building up a store of information about what semantic role is most likely to be assigned to a noun, given both its position in the sentence and its surface form. Second, the model must also incorporate a mechanism that allows for earlier and easier identification of sentences containing correlated cues to meaning and for delayed acquisition when cues compete. It must, thus, make predictions about what cues will be available to children at different stages of development, as well as how these cues might interact throughout development. It will also be important to make crosslinguistic comparisons in order to identify what factors influence competition (e.g. Hungarian children may acquire negation earlier than German children because of the large number of negative constructions and forms in German[7]). Models with these characteristics will allow us to test predictions about how the child's developing knowledge across different syntactic structures might interact, as well as allowing us to make predictions about when similarities across structures and meanings will help, and when they will hinder, acquisition.

[7] We thank one of the editors for this suggestion.

Competing motivations in children's omission of subjects? The interaction between verb finiteness and referent accessibility

MARY E. HUGHES AND SHANLEY E. M. ALLEN

9.1 Introduction

Over the last fifty years since child language development has become a focus of scientific study, research and reasoning in the field has largely been divided along theoretical lines (Tomasello 2000; Crain and Pietroski 2002; Pullum and Scholz 2002; MacWhinney 2004; Valian 2009). Nativist accounts claim that children have adult-like grammatical competence from the outset as a result of innate linguistic knowledge. They highlight the central role of formal structures in language development, and acknowledge little relevance of interaction or external input other than to trigger innate linguistic knowledge and provide lexical items for the language at hand (Crain and Thornton 1998). In contrast, emergentist and usage-based accounts assume no innate knowledge specific to language. They rather emphasize the crucial role of external input in language development since they hold that language is learned through interactive cues from caregivers, distributional patterns in the input, frequency information, and the like (Tomasello 2003a). Research from each theoretical perspective has largely been pursued in isolation from the others, with the implicit assumption that other perspectives are wrong, irrelevant, or uninteresting as a suitable explanation of the issues at hand. In other words, discussion in the field has largely been framed as a theory-based competition between explanations or motivations for particular phenomena in language development. Each theory champions one motivation to explain a particular phenomenon, and any inter-theory discussion focuses on which one account provides the best explanation of the data. A similar pattern is found in the literature on explanations for phenomena in linguistic structure, as discussed in other chapters in this volume (see Strunk, this volume, on relative clause extraposition, and Pfeiffer, this volume, on self-repair).

Only in the last fifteen to twenty years have language development researchers seriously attempted to evaluate theoretical positions in the light of each other rather than simply ignoring or dismissing other positions (Russell 2004; Ambridge and Lieven 2011; Dressler, Libben, and Korecky-Kröll, this volume; Krajewski and Lieven, this volume). In ideal cases, the focus has moved from assuming that theories *compete* with each other to instead exploring areas where theories might *complement* each other—such that one theory explains subset A of the data while another theory explains subset B—or even *interact* with each other—such that factors relevant to two theories are not independent from each other but rather are both necessary to explain the full set of data. As a result, understanding has advanced considerably in certain areas of language development including how children identify syntactic categories, acquire basic word order, retreat from overgeneralization errors, and acquire complex syntactic constructions like passives and relative clauses. For other key phenomena in language development, however, much progress remains to be made.

The present chapter focuses on one such phenomenon: the early non-target-like omission of sentential subjects. This issue has been central to argumentation in several competing theories of language development for over thirty years (e.g. Bloom 1970; Hyams 1986; Clancy 1993), but little thorough attempt has yet been made to determine whether the explanations posited for it by different theories indeed compete, or whether they might be complementary or even interact (though see Valian 1991). In this chapter, we compare explanations for early non-target-like subject omission from the two theories most current in the literature—nativists claim that subjects are omitted when their accompanying verb is non-finite, while usage-based theorists claim that subjects are omitted when their referents are accessible in discourse. Through analysis of spontaneous speech data from monolingual English-speaking children and their caregivers, we demonstrate that these two motivations interact, rather than compete as commonly claimed in the literature.

9.1.1 *Early non-target-like subject omission*

It has been widely observed that young children (up to about 3;6) acquiring a first language omit subjects more frequently than adults, thereby producing utterances that are either ungrammatical or highly marked by the norms of the target language as shown in (1).

(1)   *Ø fall down* [cf. The grape fell down] (Thomas 2;5)
    (telling his mother about a grape that fell on the floor)

This over-omission occurs both in languages like English and German where the target requires overt subjects (e.g. Bloom 1990; Hyams and Wexler 1993) and in languages like Italian and Inuktitut where the target does not require overt subjects (e.g. Valian 1991; Valian and Eisenberg 1996; Skarabela and Allen 2002). However, here we focus on the former language type, specifically on English.

A veritable cottage industry of research in the last 30 years has investigated why young children omit subjects in languages where adults do not. Explanations have been put forward from three main theoretical accounts. According to the *nativist account*, the child grammar differs from the adult grammar in some crucial way such that subject omission is permitted as a grammatical option for the child (see review in Hyams 2011). The *cognitivist account* claims that subject omission results from processing or production limitations due to the child's limited cognitive capacity (e.g. L. Bloom 1970; P. Bloom 1990; Valian 1991; Gerken 1991). From the perspective of the *usage-based account* rooted in discourse-pragmatics, children are sensitive to interlocutor knowledge and omit subjects when they think the referent is already known to the interlocutor (see review in Allen, Skarabela, and Hughes 2008). We focus here on the nativist and usage-based accounts since they are the most salient in the current literature.

Most research on early non-target-like subject omission in English has been from the nativist perspective, which posits that the locus of subject omission lies in the grammar rather than in other aspects of the linguistic system. Research has thus focused on ways in which the child grammar differs from the adult target grammar such that subject omission is permitted for the child but not for the adult. The two currently accepted hypotheses, "underspecification" (Hyams 1996; Wexler 1998) and "truncation" (Rizzi 1993/1994, 2005), both propose child grammars that allow children optionally to produce non-finite verbs in contexts where adults would produce finite verbs—the so-called "root infinitive" stage. (Note that this is different from "infinitive" forms which are correctly produced in the adult target without number, person, or tense marking.) An example of a root infinitive is shown in (2) (Brown 1973).

(2)   *Papa have it* [cf. Papa has it] (Eve 1;6)

These non-finite verbs are missing the number, tense, and agreement features that are required in the equivalent adult target utterance. Because the number, tense, and agreement features are what trigger production of subjects under the nativist account, children assume that the subject can be omitted. Indeed, numerous studies have found that subjects are omitted much more frequently in non-finite clauses than in finite clauses in child English (e.g. Sano and Hyams 1994; Bromberg and Wexler 1995; Wexler 1998; see summary of crosslinguistic results in Guasti 2002: 163). Researchers from the grammatical perspective have thus concluded that the frequent lack of finiteness provides a nearly complete explanation for early subject omission in English. Little attention is given to the omitted subjects of finite verbs that do not fit within this explanation.

Detailed research on child subject omission from the usage-based perspective began some twenty years ago with Clancy (1993), and has emphasized children's discourse-pragmatic sensitivity to the complexities of information flow as the locus of early subject omission. Numerous studies have shown that adults choose whether and in what form (e.g. pronoun, demonstrative, lexical NP) to realize subjects in their speech depending on their belief about the cognitive accessibility of the referent (e.g. Givón 1983a; Bock and Warren 1985; Gundel, Hedberg, and Zacharski 1993; Ariel 2001). A variety of discourse factors feed into determining accessibility. For example, a subject is considered accessible and thus is often omitted when its referent has just been mentioned, is present in the physical context, and/or is the current focus of attention of the speaker and hearer. Both experimental and spontaneous speech studies have revealed that English-speaking children are sensitive to the same discourse-pragmatic factors as adults, and omit subjects in contexts where the referent is cognitively accessible (Campbell, Brooks, and Tomasello 2000; Serratrice, Sorace, and Paoli 2004; Hughes and Allen 2006, 2013; Guerriero, Oshima-Takane, and Kuriyama 2006; Matthews et al. 2006; Graf 2010; see summary of crosslinguistic results in Allen, Skarabela, and Hughes 2008). Thus, researchers from the usage-based perspective have concluded that the cognitive accessibility of the referent provides a solid explanation for early subject omission in English.

9.1.2 *Research questions*

As just discussed, nativist and usage-based accounts make very different claims about the motivation for children's early non-target-like omission of subjects and are usually considered orthogonal. To our knowledge, no previous studies from the usage-based perspective have investigated any possible complementarity or interaction with the nativist perspective apart from occasionally acknowledging that the grammar controls whether or not subject can be omitted in principle (Serratrice and Sorace 2003). The few studies from the nativist perspective that have investigated a possible role for discourse-pragmatics in explaining subject omission have been limited by a lack of detail or depth in their analysis of the data. Hamann and Plunkett (1998) explored the effect of only one feature of discourse-pragmatics—whether a subject is newly introduced to discourse or already previously introduced. And the oft-cited study by Hyams and Wexler (1993) is based on data for which it is simply assumed that all omitted subjects and pronominal subjects in the data are fully accessible to the listener, rather than on data where each subject is actually coded for referent accessibility. In a review of previous research on subject omission from the nativist perspective, Hyams (2011) acknowledges a potential role for discourse-pragmatic factors in affecting subject omission, but limits this possible effect to subjects of finite verbs without substantiating her assumption with data. She states: "I will assume that the missing subjects in non-finite clauses are licensed by whatever mechanisms license PRO in infinitival contexts in adult grammars" and "I will restrict my discussion [of discourse-pragmatic explanations] to null subjects in finite clauses" (Hyams (2011: 24). She, as well as Wexler and his colleagues (Bromberg and Wexler 1995; Wexler 1998), consider "topic drop" (very similar in practice to the discourse-pragmatic notion of cognitive accessibility) a likely candidate for explaining subject omission, but only in the 10% or so of cases of subject omission in finite contexts.

In the present study, then, we investigate the possible complementarity or interaction of these two "competing motivations" for early non-target-like subject omission in English—non-finiteness from the nativist account and discourse-pragmatic accessibility from the usage-based account. We evaluate Hyams's (2011) assertion that the two motivations are *complementary*—that the nativist account (i.e. non-finiteness) explains the bulk of subject omissions and the usage-based account (i.e. accessibility) plays a role only for a small subset of omissions—and test it against the possibility that the two theories rather crucially *interact* such that both non-finiteness and accessibility are essential for explaining the full range of data. We do so using a set of naturalistic spontaneous speech data from English-speaking children aged 2 and 3 years (i.e. early and late in the subject omission stage), coded for both finiteness and accessibility.

The *nativist account* makes two predictions relevant to our study. First, no effect of discourse-pragmatics will be evident for subject omission in non-finite contexts (Prediction N1). Second, the asymmetry of more subject omission in non-finite than finite contexts will not be explainable by a discourse-pragmatic account (Prediction N2). The *usage-based perspective* also makes two predictions relevant to our study. First, accessible subjects will be realized in the same way regardless of whether they appear in finite or non-finite contexts (Prediction U1). Second, there will be no relationship between referent accessibility and finiteness (Prediction U2).

If the *competing theories* approach is correct, then both the predictions from one perspective will be met and neither of the predictions from the other perspective.

If the *complementary theories* approach is correct under the scenario proposed by Hyams (2011), then both the predictions from the nativist perspective will be met (i.e. N1 and N2), and neither of the predictions from the usage-based perspective will be met (i.e. neither U1 nor U2). Further, accessibility will be shown to play a role in explaining subject omissions in finite contexts.

If the *interacting theories* approach is correct, then none of the four predictions will be met because *both* non-finiteness and accessibility will play a crucial role in explaining patterns for *all* of the data. We would then expect effects of accessibility in each of non-finite and finite contexts, and we would expect discourse-pragmatic explanations for the finite/non-finite asymmetry; for example, that non-finite verbs attract subjects with low information content or that accessible referents attract non-finite verb forms.

9.2 Methodology

9.2.1 *Participants*

Data for this study were taken from The Manchester-Max Planck Dense Database (Lieven et al. 2003; Lieven, Salomo, and Tomasello 2009). Participants were four monolingual English-speaking children: Annie, Thomas,[1] Eleanor, and Fraser. All the children lived with their families in a large metropolitan area in England and came from middle-class backgrounds. The children's language was recorded while interacting with their mother and/or a familiar researcher during such everyday activities as playing with toys and having snacks.

---

[1] Thomas is sometimes referred to as *Brian*, which was the Max Planck pseudonym for the child.

9.2.2 *Data*

For this study, we used only the videotaped portion of the Dense Database corpus. Videotapes were collected one hour per week for six weeks at ages 2;0–2;1, and again at 3;0–3;1 (seven weeks were available for Annie at the younger age, and only three weeks at the older age). Thomas was also videotaped once per week from 2;1 to 3;0. All utterances spoken by and to the child were transcribed by research assistants in CHAT format (MacWhinney (2000); see Lieven et al. (2003) for further details about the method of recording and transcription). The transcripts and videotapes were kindly made available to us by Elena Lieven.

Previous studies have shown that both frequency of subject omission and sensitivity to accessibility features change over time (e.g. Valian 1991; Serratrice 2005; Matthews et al. 2006). Therefore, we analyzed utterances separately at the two available time points to assess development. Time 1 for three of the children comprised data from 2;0 to 2;1. One child, Thomas, had a somewhat lower mean length of utterance (MLU) than the other three children during these earliest recordings. Since we also had later recordings for him, we used a slightly later set of data for his Time 1—from 2;4 to 2;7—so that the linguistic level of all four children would be as comparable as possible.[2] Time 2 for all four children comprised data from 3;0 to 3;1, by which point the children all had a similar linguistic level as measured by MLU.

We then determined which subjects from the available data to include in our coding and analysis. Only fully intelligible utterances containing a verb were selected for coding. Because a crucial part of our study is determining the effect of discourse-pragmatics on subject omission, we excluded from analysis all utterances in contexts where the omission or overtness of the subject is fixed and thus cannot vary depending on the accessibility of the referent for that subject. This comprised four types of contexts (see Hughes and Allen 2013 for a detailed explanation): all imperative utterances (where subjects are uniformly prohibited), all utterances containing first and second person subjects (where subjects are considered accessible by definition), all utterances containing subjects that are explicitly contrasted with an alternative referent (e.g. using stress or tone of voice—where subjects cannot be omitted by definition), and all utterances containing subjects that themselves are the referent of or the answer to a question (where subjects cannot be omitted by definition).

The final data set for analysis, then, comprised all fully intelligible and non-imperative utterances that included a verb and a third-person subject context that was not explicitly contrasted or queried. The age ranges, MLUs, and number of utterances analyzed for each child is given in Table 9.1.

---

[2] Lieven, Salomo, and Tomasello (2009) analyzed the T1 data from all four children and mention the same problem. They took the approach of analyzing Thomas's data at four different time points—one at the same age as the other children and then three later ages, one to match the MLU of each of the other children at 2;0.

TABLE 9.1. **Age, mean length of utterance in words, and number of third-person subject contexts produced by four children at Time 1 and Time 2**

		Annie	Thomas	Eleanor	Fraser
Time 1	Age	2;0.4–2;1.22	2;4.17–2; 7.1	2;0.4–2;1.8	2;0.1–2;1.10
	Sessions	7×1 hour	6×1 hour	6×1 hour	6×1 hour
	MLU	2.15 to 2.45	1.88 to 2.22	1.68 to 2.17	1.35 to 1.74
	N of subject contexts (765)	352	154	81	178
Time 2	Age	3;0.4–3;0.18	3;0.1–3;1.27	3;0.0–3;1.15	3;0.0–3;1.11
	Sessions	3×1 hour	6×1hour	6×1 hour	6×1 hour
	MLU	3.12 to 3.42	2.5 to 3.11	2.17 to 2.49	2.25 to 2.65
	N of subject contexts (1010)	185	259	249	317

These utterances were coded for both discourse-pragmatic and grammatical information, including the finiteness of the verb. In order to test intercoder reliability, 9% of the data was blind-coded by two research assistants. These two coders achieved an average agreement of 85%. Moreover, every file was coded by one research assistant, and then subsequently checked by a second research assistant. All files were then reviewed by the first author in order to resolve any intercoder differences.

9.2.3 *Accessibility coding*

All third-person subjects that fit the above criteria were coded for accessibility. Six accessibility features were selected for analysis, based on those previously investigated in child language studies (Allen et al. 2008): ANIMACY, PHYSICAL PRESENCE, CONTEXTUAL DISAMBIGUATION, PRIOR MENTION, LINGUISTIC DISAMBIGUATION, and JOINT ATTENTION. Each feature was given a binary value based on how accessible the referent of that subject was in the discourse context (Clancy 1993; Allen 2000; Ariel 2001; Skarabela 2007).[3] The value *accessible* indicates that the referent can be easily identified in the discourse context on the basis of the feature being coded, while the value *inaccessible* indicates that the referent is *not* easily identified in the discourse context on the basis of the feature being coded. The values for each feature are summarized in Table 9.2.

To illustrate the application of this coding, consider the subject of the child utterance in the interaction in (3). At the time of this utterance, the mother and child are playing with multiple blocks on the table. The mother is looking at and touching the block in question (Block B), and the child is also looking at it.

---

[3] In reality, these features are not necessarily binary; instead, they may be more gradient in nature. However, as it has been the practice in the literature to treat these features as binary in order to simplify the analysis and to allow for statistical analysis based on these values, the current study maintains the use of binary values.

TABLE 9.2. **Accessible and inaccessible values for each accessibility feature**

Accessibility feature	Accessible value	Inaccessible value
ANIMACY (AN)	Animate	Inanimate
CONTEXTUAL DISAMBIGUATION (CD)	Only referent in physical context	Multiple referents in physical context
PHYSICAL PRESENCE (PP)	Physically present	Physically absent
PRIOR MENTION (PM)	Given: mentioned within preceding 5 utterances	New: not mentioned within preceding 5 utterances
LINGUISTIC DISAMBIGUATION (LD)	No other possible referents in preceding 5 utterances	Other possible referents in preceding 5 utterances
JOINT ATTENTION (JA)	Referent focus of attention for child and interlocutor	Referent *not* focus of attention for child and interlocutor

(3) MOT: *That block fell down.* [referring to Block A]
    MOT: *Where does this block go?* [referring to Block B]
    CHI: *Ø go there.* [referring to Block B] (Annie 2;0)

The subject in the final utterance was coded *accessible* for three features: PHYSICAL PRESENCE, PRIOR MENTION, and JOINT ATTENTION. It was coded *inaccessible* for the other three features.

Following the method outlined in Hughes (2011), we then calculated an INACCESSIBILITY SCORE for each subject. Each feature coded as *accessible* counted as "0" while each feature coded as *inaccessible* counted as "1." The possible values for the INACCESSIBILITY SCORE in this study range from 0 (meaning that the argument was *accessible* for all six features) to 6 (meaning that the argument was *inaccessible* for all six features).[4] For the subject under scrutiny in example (1), three of the six features were coded as *inaccessible* so its INACCESSIBILITY SCORE is 3. As shown in Hughes (2011), a high INACCESSIBILITY SCORE predicts that a subject is more likely to be realized using an overt lexical form.

9.2.4 *Referential form coding*

All subjects in the data were coded as one of four possible referential forms: lexical noun phrase (4a), demonstrative (4b), pronoun (4c), and omitted (4d).

(4) a. ***Boy*** *go.* (Thomas 2;7)
    b. ***This*** *go round here.* (Fraser 2;0)
    c. ***It*** *goes there.* (Annie 2;0)
    d. ***Ø*** *want chips.* (Eleanor 2;0)

---

[4] It is most likely the case that each feature does not contribute equally to subject choice, but for the purposes of this discussion, the features will be summed without regard to the possible variation in the weight of each feature's contribution.

9.2.5 Verb finiteness coding

All verbs associated with the subjects under study were coded for finiteness. Limiting the analysis to third person subjects meant that the finiteness of the verb was relatively easy to establish. However, because English does not have a true infinitival form that differs morphologically from other verbal forms, it was necessary to establish specific criteria to determine the status of non-finite verb forms. In sum, only correctly conjugated main verbs or correctly conjugated forms of the auxiliaries *be, have,* and *do* were considered finite. The detailed possibilities for FINITE third-person verbs are listed in (5).

(5) a. Regular and irregular verbs in the present tense where the agreement marker -*s* was produced or the correct form of the verb was produced—e.g. *He wants to park* (Annie, 3;0)
   b. Present and past progressives for which the auxiliary verb *be* was produced and correctly conjugated—e.g. *My torch is shining* (Thomas, 2;11)
   c. Present perfect and present perfect progressive verbs for which the auxiliary verb *have* was produced and correctly conjugated—e.g. *Helga has fall over* (Annie, 2;0)
   d. Present and past passive verbs for which the auxiliary verb *be* was produced and correctly conjugated—e.g. *She was sting by a bee* (Fraser, 3;0)
   e. Present and past verbs for which *do*-support was required, was provided, and was correctly conjugated—e.g. *Where does it go?* (Annie, 2;1)
   f. Correctly conjugated tensed verbs produced with the auxiliary verb *be* and the main verb *go* with a future interpretation—e.g. *This is going to be very hot* (Annie, 3;0)
   g. Present and past tense copular verbs correctly conjugated for third person[5]—e.g. *He's in the car* (Fraser, 2;1)

The possibilities for NON-FINITE third-person verbs are listed in (6):

(6) a. Regular and irregular verbs in the present tense for which the agreement marker -*s* was missing—e.g. *He don't like to go in* (Fraser, 3;0)
   b. Present and past progressive verbs for which the auxiliary verb *be* was missing—e.g. *The pig going now* (Eleanor, 3;1)
   c. Present perfect verbs for which the auxiliary verb *have* was missing—e.g. *She been crying* (Annie, 3;1)
   d. Passive verbs for which the auxiliary was omitted—e.g. *What that called?* (Eleanor, 2;1)
   e. Verbs which require *do*-support for which the auxiliary *do* was missing—e.g. *No go in there* (Fraser, 2;6)
   f. Verbs that were produced with the auxiliary verb *be* and the main verb *go* with a future interpretation, for which the auxiliary was missing—e.g. *Big elephant going a kiss Mitra* (Thomas, 2;10)
   g. Constructions where modals are missing—e.g. *Thomas put it on* [meaning: Thomas can or will put it on] (Thomas, 2;7)

---

[5] Utterances with missing copulas were not included in the data set because they do not contain a verb.

Finally, the verb forms listed in (7) were excluded from the analysis because, although they show tense, they do not overtly show agreement in adult English:

(7) a. Modal verbs for which the verb form remains constant in all persons—e.g. *She can stay there* (Annie 3;0)

   b. Past and future forms in the simple, progressive, and perfect forms for which the verb form remains constant in all persons—e.g. *That will be good* (Fraser 2;1)

9.2.6 *Hypotheses and data analysis*

Our analysis of the data comprised four steps. First, we assessed subject form in relation to finiteness by determining the proportion of each of the four subject forms in finite vs. non-finite verbal contexts. Based on previous studies, we expected to find more omitted subjects in non-finite clauses and more of the three other forms in finite clauses. Second, we assessed subject form in relation to discourse-pragmatics by determining the proportion of each of the four subject forms for accessible vs. inaccessible referents. Again based on previous studies, we expected to find more omitted subjects for accessible referents and fewer omitted subjects for inaccessible referents. We also expected to find more lexical noun phrases for inaccessible referents, and pronouns and demonstratives used more for subjects of intermediate accessibility. All of these expectations were confirmed in our data.

Once we established that our data replicated previous findings from each of the grammatical and discourse-pragmatic perspectives, we then assessed whether there was an interaction between the two accounts. In the third analysis, we investigated whether subjects of non-finite verbs were more likely to be highly accessible than subjects of finite verbs. The nativist perspective would predict that accessibility has no effect on which verbs end up being finite or non-finite (Prediction N2); it is only after finiteness is determined that accessibility might play a role in subject omission, and then only for subjects of finite verbs (i.e. if a *complementarity* account is assumed). The usage-based perspective would also predict that accessibility has no effect on which verbs end up being finite or non-finite, but rather that accessibility affects subject realization independently from finiteness (Predictions U1 and U2).

In the fourth analysis, we determined whether accessible referents were realized differently in non-finite vs. finite verbal contexts. Based on claims from the nativist perspective, we would expect that the realization of subjects would not be affected by accessibility in non-finite contexts (Prediction N1), but might be affected by accessibility in finite contexts (i.e. if a *complementarity* account is assumed). In contrast, the usage-based perspective would predict that effects of accessibility should be found equally in non-finite and finite contexts (Predictions U1 and U2).

9.3 Results

As expected on the basis of many previous studies of subject omission in English child language, the children in the present study omitted many subjects at Time 1

(27%) and relatively fewer at Time 2 (4%), χ^2 = 185.471, *p* < .0001. Regardless, enough subjects were omitted at each age to allow us to continue with our analyses. In the following sections, we present the results from the four stages of the analysis as just described.

9.3.1 *Effect of finiteness*

Our first goal was to determine whether our data set mirrors findings in the literature that subjects are omitted more frequently in non-finite than in finite clauses. Figure 9.1 shows the distribution of the four argument forms in the context of verb finiteness at Time 1 and Time 2. Chi-square results show that the children at both ages omit significantly more subjects in the context of non-finite verbs than in the context of finite verbs: Time 1, 49% non-finite vs. 12% finite, χ^2 = 127.292, *p* < .0001; Time 2, 25% non-finite vs. 1% finite, χ^2 = 145.969, *p* < .0001. Thus, our data are consistent with previous findings in the literature from the nativist perspective.

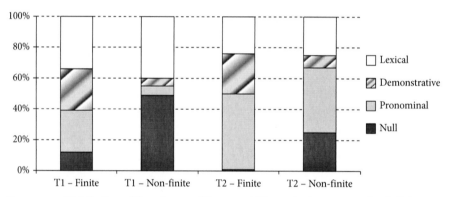

FIGURE 9.1 Distribution of four forms at Time 1 and Time 2 in the context of verb finiteness T1 total *n* finite = 458; T1 total *n* non-finite = 307; T2 total *n* finite = 893; T2 total *n* non-finite = 117

Hyams and Wexler (1993) suggested that omitted subjects are really omitted pronouns and not omitted demonstratives or lexical NPs. If this were the case, we would expect that the number of pronouns plus omissions taken together would be the same in finite and non-finite contexts at both Time 1 and 2. However, this is not the case. There is a significantly higher number of pronouns plus omissions in non-finite than finite contexts at both time points: Time 1, non-finite 55% vs. finite 39%, χ^2 = 16.900, *p* < .0001; Time 2, non-finite 67% vs. finite 50%, χ^2 = 10.834, *p* < .001. When pronouns are analyzed alone, however, there is a significant difference in the number of pronouns in finite vs. non-finite contexts only at Time 1: Time 1, non-finite 55% vs. finite 27%, χ^2 = 56.368, *p* < .0001; Time 2: non-finite 42% vs. finite 6%, χ^2 = 2.195, *p* = .138.

Significantly more demonstratives occur in finite as opposed to non-finite contexts at both time points: Time 1, non-finite 5% vs. finite 27%, χ^2 = 58.757, *p* < .0001;

Time 2: non-finite 8% vs. finite 26%, $\chi^2 = 18.688$, $p < .0001$. However, there is no difference in the number of lexical NPs occurring in finite vs. non-finite contexts at either time point: Time 1: non-finite 40% vs. finite 34%, $\chi^2 = 3.638$, $p = .056$; Time 2: non-finite 25% vs. finite 24%, $\chi^2 = 0.205$, $p = .651$.

These results suggest that, while there is obviously a strong relationship between subject omission and non-finite contexts, other factors are also at play.

9.3.2 *Effect of accessibility*

Next we determine whether subjects are omitted more frequently for referents that are highly accessible, as predicted by the usage-based account. Figure 9.2 shows the children's use of the four different argument forms in the light of the accessibility of the subject's referent, at Time 1 and Time 2. Recall that an INACCESSIBILITY SCORE of 0 denotes a referent that is maximally accessible, while an INACCESSIBILITY SCORE of 6 denotes a referent that is maximally inaccessible. The effect of accessibility is particularly visible at Time 1: subjects are omitted much more when the referent is accessible than when it is not. To test this statistically, we performed a χ^2 analysis comparing the number of omissions for the most accessible subjects (INACCESSIBILITY SCORE 0–1) vs. the least accessible subjects (INACCESSIBILITY SCORE 5–6). The difference is significant: $\chi^2 = 18.069$, $p < .0001$. The same analysis at Time 2 was not significant ($\chi^2 = 1.274$, $p = .259$) because the children omitted very few subjects. Our data are consistent with expectations from the usage-based perspective.

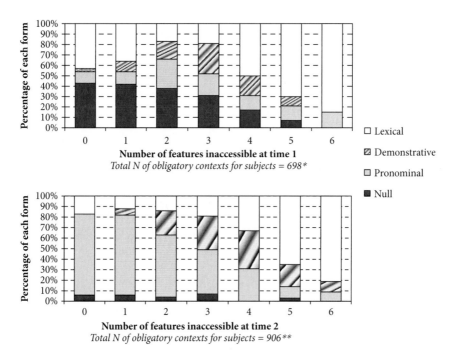

FIGURE 9.2 Effect of accessibility on subject realization at Time 1 and Time 2
*67 missing values for joint attention; **104 missing values for joint attention

9.3.3 *Occurrence of finiteness with accessible vs. inaccessible referents*

In the third analysis, we determine whether there is a relationship between finiteness and accessibility. Figures 9.3 (Time 1) and 9.4 (Time 2) feature the same accessibility categories as in Figure 9.2. However, rather than showing the form in which subjects were realized for each category as in Figure 9.2, Figures 9.3 and 9.4 show the finiteness of the clause in which the subjects were realized. If there is no relationship between finiteness and accessibility, we would expect no difference between the proportion of finite vs. non-finite clauses associated with highly accessible vs. highly inaccessible referents. If there is a relationship, we would expect more non-finite than finite clauses associated with highly accessible referents and, conversely, more finite than non-finite clauses associated with highly inaccessible referents.

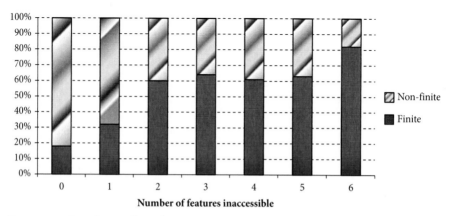

FIGURE 9.3 Cumulative effect of accessibility for six features by percent of finite and non-finite verb contexts at Time 1
Total *n* of subjects = 698; 67 subjects excluded due to missing values for JA; total *n* for each category: 0 = 28, 1 = 50, 2 = 157, 3 = 198, 4 = 158, 5 = 73, 6 = 34

The pattern is very clear at Time 1. Non-finite clauses occur more frequently with highly accessible referents, and finite clauses occur increasingly as referents become less accessible. To test this statistically, we performed a χ^2 analysis comparing the number of uses of finite clauses with the most accessible subjects (INACCESSIBILITY SCORE 0–1) vs. the least accessible subjects (INACCESSIBILITY SCORE 5–6). The difference is highly significant: $\chi^2 = 32.214$, $p < .0001$. We conclude that accessibility and verb finiteness are strongly related at Time 1.

At Time 2, however, this pattern does not hold because most of the children's utterances consist of finite rather than non-finite clauses. A comparison of the number of occurrences of finite clauses with the most accessible subjects (INACCESSIBILITY SCORE 0–1) vs. the least accessible subjects (INACCESSIBILITY SCORE 5–6) revealed that there was not a significant difference ($\chi^2 = 0.488$, $p = .485$). Therefore, a relationship between accessibility and finiteness is only visible at Time 1. This relationship is not expected from either the nativist or the usage-based account

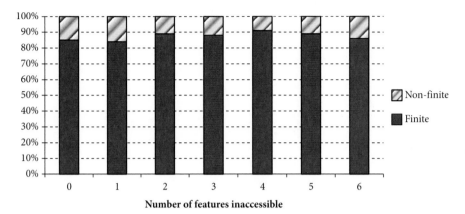

FIGURE 9.4 Cumulative effect of accessibility for six features by percent of finite and non-finite verb contexts at Time 2
Total *n* of subjects = 906; 104 subjects excluded due to missing values for JA; total *n* for each category: 0 = 69, 1 = 121, 2 = 222, 3 = 242, 4 = 169, 5 = 62, 6 = 21

(i.e. it contradicts Predictions N1, N2, U1, and U2). It strongly supports the claim that both finiteness and accessibility play a role in early subject omission, and that neither can offer a full explanation on its own.

9.3.4 *Realization of accessible referents in finite and non-finite contexts*

Finally, we investigated the relationship between accessibility and finiteness in a slightly different way by determining whether accessible referents were realized differently in finite and non-finite verbal contexts. If there is no relationship, we expect no clear pattern of accessibility affecting subject realization for the subjects of non-finite clauses, because finiteness alone would determine whether subjects are omitted or overt. If there is a relationship, we expect the same pattern of effect of accessibility found in Figure 9.2 to appear separately for each of finite verb contexts and non-finite verb contexts.

Figure 9.5 shows the cumulative effect of accessibility for Time 1, with subjects categorized separately by finite and non-finite contexts. As referents become more inaccessible, the children tend to use fewer omitted subjects across both finite and non-finite verbal contexts. They also use more lexical forms as inaccessibility increases. To test this statistically, we performed a χ^2 analysis comparing the number of omissions for the most accessible subjects (INACCESSIBILITY SCORE 0–1) vs. the least accessible subjects (INACCESSIBILITY SCORE 5–6), separately for each of the finite contexts and non-finite contexts. The difference is significant for both contexts—finite: $\chi^2 = 10.274, p < .01$; non-finite: $\chi^2 = 13.518, p < .001$. Nonetheless, it is also clear that a greater proportion of omitted subjects realize accessible referents in non-finite contexts, in comparison with a greater proportion of pronouns realizing accessible referents in finite contexts.

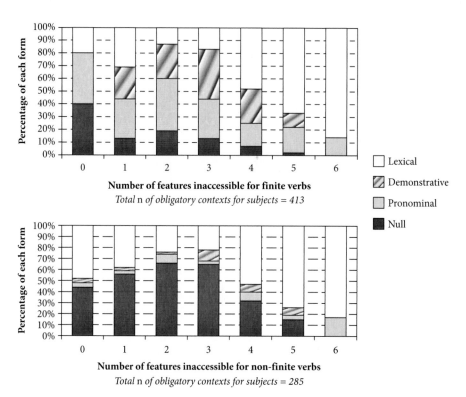

FIGURE 9.5 Cumulative effect of accessibility for six features distributed across four forms for children at Time 1 in the context of verb finiteness

Although there is a similar pattern evident at Time 2 (Figure 9.6) demonstrating the same cline of accessibility, the children are now generally using pronouns for accessible referents instead of omitting subjects in both finite and non-finite contexts. Therefore, it is not surprising that a χ^2 analysis comparing the number of omissions for the most accessible subjects (INACCESSIBILITY SCORE 0–1) vs. the least accessible subjects (INACCESSIBILITY SCORE 5–6), separately for each of the finite contexts and non-finite contexts, shows no significant difference for either context: finite, $\chi^2 = 0.915$, $p = .339$; non-finite, $\chi^2 = 0.732$, $p = .392$. However, if omissions and pronouns are combined into a single category and compared to the two other overt forms (i.e. demonstratives and lexical NPs), a χ^2 analysis now reveals a significant difference—finite: $\chi^2 = 111.426$, $p < .0001$; non-finite: $\chi^2 = 6.713$, $p < .01$. The somewhat more jagged pattern for non-finite contexts at Time 2 is due to the relatively smaller amount of data in this group (only 109 subjects).

Overall, a relationship between accessibility and finiteness is clear at Time 1 and somewhat less so at Time 2. This relationship is not expected from either the nativist or the usage-based perspectives (i.e. it contradicts Predictions N1, N2, U1, and U2). This finding provides additional support for the claim that finiteness and accessibility interact in providing an explanation for early subject omission.

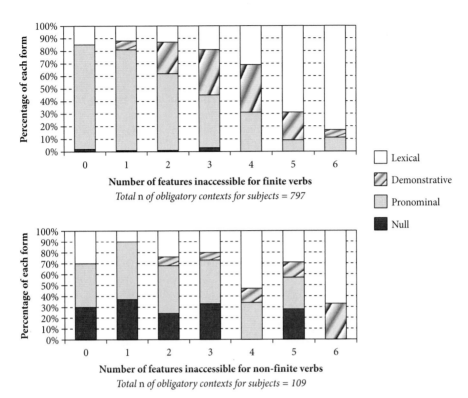

FIGURE 9.6 Cumulative effect of accessibility for six features distributed across four forms for children at Time 2 in the context of verb finiteness

9.4 Discussion and conclusions

In this chapter, we explored whether two apparently competing explanations for early non-target-like subject omission in English, as posited by two different theories, can rather be seen as interacting. We tested the predominant nativist motivation—verb finiteness—and the predominant usage-based motivation—referent accessibility—in a set of data from four English-speaking children aged 2 to 3 years. As expected, our findings for the individual explanations replicated those of many previous studies: significantly more subjects were omitted in the context of non-finite verbs, and significantly more subjects were omitted when their referents were highly accessible to the interlocutor. However, we also found a clear interaction between finiteness and accessibility of a sort that would not be predicted by either perspective. The nativist account predicts that accessibility will have no influence on subject omission in non-finite contexts (Prediction N1) but may play a role in finite contexts (i.e. if we assume *complementarity* between the two perspectives). However, we found that a subject is more likely to be omitted when its referent is accessible than when it is inaccessible *both in finite and non-finite contexts.* The usage-based account predicts that finiteness should have no influence on subject omission at all (Prediction U2). However, we found that a subject is more likely to be omitted in a non-finite context than in a finite context *both when it is maximally accessible and when it is maximally inaccessible.* This means that both accessibility and finiteness play a crucial role in subject omission. These factors should not be seen as *competing* with each other for which one can provide the "true" explanation. Rather, they are each an important part of the story and must be treated in tandem.

It is also striking that accessible subjects occur more in non-finite contexts and inaccessible subjects occur more in finite contexts, regardless of the form in which the subjects appear. We consider here two possible explanations for this pattern in the data. One explanation is that verbal agreement inflections—found in finite but not non-finite verbs—help to track reference in discourse in the same way that more overt referential forms do. If this is the case, then high accessibility of a referent in the discourse context would more often result in the child omitting the inflection, whereas low accessibility of a referent would more often result in using an overt verbal inflection.[6] A study of Inuktitut child data by Skarabela and Allen (2004) found results consistent with this hypothesis: verbal inflections were omitted significantly more often when the referent in question was jointly attended to by the child and the interlocutor than when it was not. However, this study took into account only one feature of accessibility and was conducted in a language with very different typology from English. This hypothesis remains to be tested empirically in data from English.

Another possible explanation is that some additional factor plays a mediating role—for example, that some property of non-finite verbs particularly attracts accessible subjects, which in turn tend to be omitted because of discourse-pragmatics. Further exploration of the event semantics of non-finite vs. finite clauses, as in studies by Hyams and her colleagues, may provide further insight here (e.g. Hoekstra and Hyams 1998; Hyams 2012). For example, children may omit tense and agreement markers with clauses of certain event types, and these particular event types may also tend to be expressed with accessible subjects. Then both finiteness and accessibility would be caused by a third variable, event type, which in turn would indirectly lead to omission of both tense/agreement and subjects. At any rate, the idea that a particular factor central to one theory is an indirect cause of subject omission mediated by a factor central to another theory is a new way of thinking about explaining subject omission.

Because our study used data from two points in development, it is relevant to mention developmental patterns. The most salient patterns are those already well-known and extensively discussed in the literature: the proportion of omitted subjects and the proportion of non-finite clauses both decrease significantly between 2;0 and 3;0 and disappear soon afterwards (Valian 1991; Wexler 1998; Freudenthal et al. 2007; Hyams 2011). We also find a decrease in the strength of the relationship

---

[6] We thank an anonymous reviewer for this suggestion.

between accessibility, finiteness, and subject omission between Time 1 and Time 2. For instance, we found a relationship between accessibility and subject omission at Time 1 but not at Time 2 (Section 9.3.2), and we found a difference in the proportion of finite vs. non-finite clauses associated with highly accessible vs. highly inaccessible referents at Time 1 but not at Time 2 (Sections 9.3.3 and 9.3.4). However, these results at Time 2 almost certainly occur because there are simply so few omitted subjects and non-finite verbs at Time 2 that there is not enough data to show any effects. We believe that there is no change in children's sensitivity to the strength of these relationships over time; the relationships are just no longer relevant in the same way.

We turn finally to the roles played by each of the two theories in explaining children's omitted subjects. As noted earlier, some nativist researchers have suggested a complementary role for the usage-based perspective alongside a main role for a nativist explanation. One clear statement to this effect is in Hyams (2011):

the grammar...allows the occurrence of a null element...under certain structural conditions of licensing and identification. But the syntax does not legislate when a particular subject will be omitted. This is a function of the information structure (IS) of the sentence....Conversely, discourse conditions alone cannot sanction missing arguments. (Hyams 2011: 40)

However, our study shows that this *complementarity* explanation does not go far enough. First, as found in many previous studies, subjects are not only omitted in the grammatically licensed context of non-finite verbs; they are regularly omitted in finite contexts as well. In our study, 27% of omitted subjects at Time 1 and 24% at Time 2 are in finite contexts, which are not licensed locations for subject omission in the current grammatical accounts. Second, our results indicate that finiteness and accessibility crucially interact with each other. Accessibility influences subject omission similarly in both the non-finite context that is grammatically licensed for subject omission and in the finite context that is not grammatically licensed for subject omission. And finiteness influences subject omission similarly both when the referent of the subject is accessible and when it is not. Finally, our results show that accessibility may mediate the effect of finiteness, or vice versa, such that the effect of one accessibility feature is indirect rather than direct.

In sum, the findings in this chapter show that there is a rich *interaction* between nativist and usage-based accounts of language acquisition. This is very different from a *competition* approach that focuses on trying to prove which one account is the best, and also from a *complementarity* approach that allows a small role for one theory to explain a small subset of data not explainable by another (more preferable) theory. We take the position that, at least in the data we explored here, both theories are essential for an understanding of the patterns in the full set of data. By taking a more holistic perspective of looking at the patterns predicted and revealed by the different theoretical accounts together, we come to a deeper understanding of the intricate interplay between the various factors relevant to language development. This study reveals that this interaction between theoretical perspectives is a rich area of research that will increase a general understanding of the language acquisition process and the connection between grammatical and cognitive development. We hope that this study will provide a model for further similar studies and serve as a step towards the larger goal of establishing a unified theory of language development.

Acknowledgments

We thank Elena Lieven and Jeannine Goh for providing us with transcripts and videotapes from the Manchester-Max Planck Dense Database. This research was funded by National Science Foundation grant BCS-0346841 to S. Allen.

10

Competing cues in early syntactic development

GRZEGORZ KRAJEWSKI AND ELENA LIEVEN

10.1 Introduction

The idea that there are a number of factors that compete in children's language learning has a long history in the field. A wide range of factors may affect the course of this learning, ranging from what the child wants to say through the cognitive complexity of some aspects of language (modality, for instance) as well as more specifically linguistic features such as the grammar of the language being learned. Leaving aside whatever they bring from biological endowment and their social and cognitive development in infancy, children have to learn language from what they hear. In the debates between nativists and emergentists, the precise role of this input language is of major importance. Nativist linguists emphasize the role of the language in allowing the child to arrive at the correct setting of various parameters and, with a few recent exceptions (e.g. Legate and Yang 2007), tend to downplay the role of frequency in the input (e.g. Roeper 2010). Emergentists, on the other hand, have long argued that the relative frequencies of different forms in the input are central to not only the speed of language learning but also its trajectory (for recent discussions see: Ambridge 2010; Lieven 2010).

In this chapter, we present recent developments within the Cue Competition Model (Bates and MacWhinney 1989), a particularly fruitful and prominent theory within the emergentist tradition, and we focus on children's learning of the active transitive construction. This encodes a fundamental pattern of human experience and is the first construction for which children have to learn to identify the participants of an event and decide which is the subject and which the object of the verb or, in a prototypical active causative, which is the agent of the action and which the patient. Depending on the language and what information is being conveyed, different cues to agent and patient will be available and these will differ in their relative strength. The question is when and how children come to recognize these cues and their relative importance. Many studies, both naturalistic and experimental, have been used to investigate how children learn the construction and the cues available in the input that may guide this learning: here we concentrate on the experimental approach.

10.2 Learning the transitive construction

For many years, child language researchers have been preoccupied with what might be called the speed of acquisition problem, or—in other words—how early or late children show evidence of using abstract grammar. Since emergentists emphasize the role of linguistic input more strongly than nativists, it was assumed that the former would predict that children become fully productive later than the latter: if language acquisition means learning from input rather than being just a maturation process with input acting only as a trigger, it should take more time. Hence, the 1990s and early 2000s witnessed a boom in studies of the English transitive, with various researchers using a number of different methodologies trying to pin down when exactly children start to understand and/or use the transitive construction. In one strand of such studies, Tomasello and colleagues (e.g. Akhtar and Tomasello 1997; Tomasello and Brooks 1998; Brooks and Tomasello 1999) taught children nonce verbs and elicited their use in the transitive construction, showing that only children above or around the age of three showed productivity. Akhtar (1999) used the so-called "weird word order" method, in which novel verbs were presented in ungrammatical sentences of English: SOV or VSO. When children were prompted to use these verbs themselves, the majority of children at 4;4 spontaneously reverted to the prototypical SVO, but only 4 (out of 12) children did so at 3;6, and one at 2;8, suggesting the gradual nature of the learning process. A second strand of experiments uses the "preferential looking" method (in which children simultaneously see two scenes only one of which corresponds to an utterance they hear, with length of looking time measured). These show that children as young as 21 months are sensitive to word order (e.g. Naigles 1990; Fisher 2002).

This speed of acquisition debate has been extremely fruitful, producing many interesting results and refining our understanding of grammatical development. On the one hand, emergentists have been forced to reconsider the strong claim of late abstraction (cf. Dąbrowska and Tomasello 2008). On the other hand, it has become clear that even if sensitive enough measures show evidence of some abstract knowledge early in development, this knowledge strengthens and becomes entrenched gradually with growing experience. However, an exclusive focus on speed of acquisition will not take us much further and, in fact, it is not entirely clear whether the issue of early vs. late abstraction can differentiate the two theoretical approaches. It would be extremely difficult, if not impossible, to come up with some independent predictions as to how quickly children should acquire a given structure for this to be regarded as dependent on innate syntactic knowledge or how late for this to be argued to be solely due to input. Thus, in recent years, attention has somewhat shifted towards another aspect of the hypothesized role of input: if children rely on what they hear, the properties of the ambient language should affect the learning, with different languages shaping development differently.

In fact, such studies were already being conducted back in the 1980s. In one of the first and perhaps the most prominent study of this kind, Slobin and Bever (1982; but see also Weist 1983; MacWhinney, Pléh, and Bates 1985; Sokolov 1988) tested children aged between 2;0 and 4;4 in an act-out task with familiar verbs. The basic format of these experiments is to ask participants to identify the agent and patient in transitive sentences with two nouns and a verb. Some of Slobin and Bever's sentences were grammatical and some ungrammatical; what was tested was the influence of word order, case marking, and agreement marking. The children were learning four different languages, which differed in the availability of word order and inflectional morphology to mark agent–patient relations. Thus, English words are strictly ordered and weakly inflected; Italian is weakly ordered and weakly inflectional; Serbo-Croatian is weakly ordered but with rich and complex morphology, and Turkish only minimally depends on word order for marking syntactic roles but, unlike Serbo-Croatian, has a highly regular, analytic, inflectional system. Slobin and Bever found that children are highly sensitive to these contrasting properties of their languages. In Turkish, as opposed to the other languages, children did not pay much attention to word order but were quick to learn to rely on case marking. In Serbo-Croatian, on the other hand, younger children depended on word order heavily, even in the presence of a conflicting case marking cue. It might be said that before they fully mastered the inflectional system, with all its syncretisms and allomorphs, it was not a reliable cue for them, despite being highly available. Interestingly, all children found it easiest to comprehend sentences that followed the prototypical pattern of their input language, and had difficulties in the comprehension of sentences which departed from it.

In 1989 Bates and MacWhinney produced a synthesis of these experiments and others in their Cue Competition Model which has been a central theoretical and methodological tool for the study of linguistic cues ever since (Bates and MacWhinney 1989). A cue is defined as any linguistic property that systematically co-occurs with a given function (e.g. word order or case marking are cues to the role assignment in a transitive sentence). The Competition Model codifies the dimensions along which cues to argument structure can differ. Of central importance are measures of "cue availability" and "cue reliability." Cue availability tells us how often a given linguistic marker is present when a given function is present. For instance, is nominative-accusative marking always present on the subject and object of a transitive? Cue reliability tells us how consistent a cue is in marking a given function, that is, how often the function is present when the linguistic marker is present. For instance, if the form of the nominative case-marker is the same as that for another case, then it is less reliable in marking the nominative. Together, these measures determine the validity or strength of a cue and the Competition Model provides a means to quantify this predicted strength.

Two other factors need mentioning, both escaping an easy quantification of availability and reliability and yet both important in accounting for developmental changes. One is "cue cost"—a measure of how difficult or demanding it is to process a cue. For instance, children might start using agreement as a cue later than would otherwise be predicted by cue reliability and availability because of its high demands (the need to coordinate inflections across words) relative to children's processing capacities (Bates and MacWhinney 1989 illustrate this with experimental results from Italian; see also MacWhinney 1997). Also, in some accounts local marking (e.g. case marking) is thought to have lower cost than global marking (e.g. word order, see Slobin 1982). The second factor, perhaps especially crucial from the developmental perspective, is the phonological "detectability of a cue." MacWhinney, Pléh, and Bates (1985) discuss its importance with the example of a short, and hard to hear, accusative ending in Hungarian, which proves very difficult for young children. Thus only when they are able to detect a particular form, involving the ability to hear and segment it (cf. Peters 1985, 1997), can children learn to use it as a cue. At that point the model predicts that the availability of the cue will become the main predictor. Later, as children learn more intricacies of the system, reliability will take over as the decisive factor (Sokolov 1988) and this is not yet the end of the developmental change: for adults "conflict validity," that is, its reliability, as calculated over only those instances when the cue competes with another one becomes the most powerful performance predictor (McDonald 1987, 1989; see also MacWhinney 1997).

It is also interesting to note that in its account of sentence comprehension the Competition Model does not differentiate between traditional syntactic features, like word order, agreement, and case marking on the one hand, and properties that traditionally lie beyond the scope of syntax, and certainly beyond the supposedly innate part of language knowledge: animacy, intonation, etc. The latter may serve as cues to argument structure just as well, with differences between different cues being merely quantitative. This is important, since any nativist account of language by definition proposes a sharp distinction between what is innate and universal—the core of language knowledge, and everything else—the periphery. If differences are indeed quantitative only, and the evidence cited above, as well as the studies discussed in the remainder of the paper, strongly suggest it is, then we have another important empirical argument supporting the emergentist approach to language development.

One problem with these earlier studies is that they were all conducted using familiar verbs. This means that the results might have been affected by what children already knew about these verbs, reflecting prior learning rather than any abstract knowledge of the transitive construction. This is particularly problematic if one wants to argue for input-driven learning where the fully productive knowledge of a construction should only follow the ability to use it with familiar items. More recently there has been a series of experiments exploring children's production and comprehension of the construction using novel verbs.

10.3 Recent studies

10.3.1 *Across languages*

Using an act-out task, Chan, Lieven, and Tomasello (2009) tested English, German, and Cantonese-speaking children aged 2;6, 3;6, and 4;6 on three types of active transitives with novel verbs: sentences in which the agent was animate and the patient inanimate (AVI), the most frequent type in the child-directed speech (CDS) of all three languages; sentences in which both agent and patient were animate (AVA); and, finally, sentences in which there was an inanimate agent and an animate patient (IVA). Even the youngest group in all three languages was able to choose the first noun as agent when hearing the AVI sentences, but all were at chance in the other two conditions. Across sentence types, children made significantly fewer first-noun-as-agent choices when the animacy contrast was neutralized (AVI vs. AVA) or introduced to conflict with word order (AVA vs. IVA). Cantonese children did this at all three ages; German children at ages 2;6 and 3;6; and English children at 2;6. Chan, Lieven, and Tomasello (2009) suggested that these results are directly related to the relative frequency of SVO active transitives and to the frequency of argument omission. As discussed in more detail Section 10.3.2.1, 20% of active transitives in German have OVS word order, which results in greater cue conflict in word order for German than for English. The Cantonese results can be explained by the very high rate of argument drop (of both subjects and objects) which is true both of the adult language and of CDS. This results in Cantonese children having even less evidence for SVO word order than children learning German. Children learning English with its more consistent SVO word order and low level of argument drop show the earliest dependence on word order when presented with AVA or IVA sentences.

Thus, what children hear in the input is critically important to interpreting the level of abstraction in their linguistic representations and how this develops. But, as the Competition Model attempts to quantify, it is not only the frequency of a particular form but also its salience and how reliable the mapping is of the form to the particular function. We now turn to within-language experiments that highlight this issue.

10.3.2 *Within languages: word order and case marking*

10.3.2.1 *German*   In Study 3 of Dittmar, Abbot-Smith, Lieven, and Tomasello (2008) German-speaking children aged 2;7, 4;10, and 7;3 were presented with active transitives containing novel verbs in three different conditions: SVO word order and case marking as redundant cues in coalition (e.g. *Der-*$_{NOM}$ *Hund wieft den-*$_{ACC}$ *Löwen-*$_{ACC}$ "The dog is wiefing the lion"); SVO word-order as a sole cue with no overt case marking, because both nouns were either of neuter or feminine gender (e.g. *Die Katze wieft die Ziege* "The cat is wiefing the goat"); and case marking in competition with reversed OVS word order (e.g. *Den-*$_{ACC}$ *Bären-*$_{ACC}$ *wieft der-*$_{NOM}$ *Tiger* "The bear-$_{PATIENT}$ is wiefing the tiger-$_{AGENT}$"). The results showed that the youngest group could only point to the picture with the matching agent and patient when they were presented with sentences that were both in SVO order and had case marking on the two NPs. They were at chance on sentences with case marking but OVS word order and also with sentences in which case marking was not available. The 5-year-olds chose the first noun as agent in these non-case-marked SVO sentences but still failed to reliably interpret the case-marked sentences with OVS word order. Only the group of 7-year-olds managed to interpret these latter sentences correctly.

Thus the youngest children could only understand the sentences if both cues were present and worked together, which suggests that they had a prototype or gestalt (Ibbotson and Tomasello 2009). This is similar to Chan, Lieven, and Tomasello's (2009) findings for the youngest group who could only interpret the sentences that were most frequent and prototypical in their input, that is, sentences with an animate subject and inanimate object, and is in line with earlier findings of Slobin and Bever (1982).[1] Sentences with only one cue (word order) were correctly interpreted by older children, but only the oldest group could deal with sentences in which the two cues were in competition. Thus only the 7-year-old children were aware that case marking was more reliable as a cue, and were consequently able to disregard word order.

Although the Competition Model predicts that cue reliability outweighs cue availability only later in development, these results ran counter to the initial predictions that Dittmar et al. (2008) made on the basis of the Competition Model, because sentences with OVS word order occur about 20% of the time in German CDS making word order not fully reliable, while case marking, when available, is always reliable. Depending on precisely which sentences are counted, Dittmar et al. calculated that case marking had a validity of 86% but this contrasts with a validity of 68% for word order. However, this does depend on how the cues are actually counted. The figure of 20% for OVS word order was calculated using only active transitives with two NPs and a verb. Dittmar et al. point out that if children are registering the position of the noun in relation to the verb, then fragments (i.e. clauses with one NP missing; for instance, "die Frau schubst") should be entered into the count, and this would then give word order a greater reliability than case marking. In addition, the figure for the reliability of case marking depends on counting at the level of the abstract category. In fact, however, Dittmar et al. found that 76% of the argument NPs in the OVS sentences of the German CDS corpus contained either first- or second-person pronouns (e.g. *Ich, mich, Du, dich*). Thus young children might have learned to map these words to agent and patient roles without having a fully abstract representation of case. Even for English, a language that lacks case marking except on some pronouns, Ibbotson, Theakston, Lieven, and Tomasello (2010) have shown that children just under 3;0 can interpret passive sentences with novel verbs provided they contain two case-marked pronouns (e.g. *She is being tammed by him*). Thus, again, children seem to be relying on more low-scope generalizations than a fully abstract representation of case.

---

[1] Providing a precise definition of a prototype would secure a whole new paper on its own. Here, whenever we refer to prototypes or prototypical constructions, we simply mean constructions which, both in terms of their meaning and formal characteristics, are most typical instantiations of a given concept (e.g. transitivity). Of course, this notion of prototype is not unrelated to frequency (see also Hopper and Thompson 1980; Næss 2007). What is important is that such a prototypical instance will exhibit a range of formal characteristics providing redundant cues to its meaning, and that children seem to grasp those prototypical instances as unanalyzed *gestalts*, rather than as collections of individual cues.

Children's difficulty with OVS word order in German may arise because this is highly marked and normally used in a discourse context in which a contrast is being made with a preceding statement. Indeed German adults might well show slower reaction times in processing such sentences, particularly if they are presented with neutral intonation. Following this up by looking at "extra-grammatical" cues, a study by Grünloh, Lieven, and Tomasello (2011) showed that if these sentences were presented to 5-year-olds with stress on the first NP, children did better at interpreting them and even more so when the sentences were presented in the discourse context in which they are normally used. Thus German children are used to hearing OVS word order in utterances with extremely frequent case-marked pronouns and contrastive stress. If they hear something similar in the experiment, even with a novel verb, they do much better, than if they hear sentences in which these cues are presented separately.

10.3.2.2 *Polish*   Despite the fact that case marking in adult German is the crucial, most reliable cue, it was only the 7-year-olds in Dittmar et al. (2008) who managed to use case marking as an independent cue. One possibility is that this is due to the complexity of German case marking. There are different case-markers for different gender classes and it may take some time before children integrate them and realize that different markers may mark the same case but for different nouns (see also Pelham (2011) on how complexity, and, more precisely, ambiguity contained in the system, affects children's learning of English pronouns and German articles). However, at least at first sight, German case marking is considerably less complex than a system like that of Polish, which has seven cases and two numbers (singular and plural), with several endings marking most combinations of these two categories. The correct choice of ending depends on gender (feminine, masculine, and neuter, with masculine further divided into human, animate, and inanimate) and, within gender classes, partially on semantic and phonological factors. If the complexity of the system indeed slows down the acquisition of the ability to use case marking as a cue to sentence structure, it should take Polish children even more time to master it than it does German children. A recent study using a similar method (Krajewski, Lieven, and Tomasello, in preparation) examined the development of Polish children's reliance on case marking. We present this study in detail in order to give the reader a fuller idea of what is involved in these types of experiments.

As in the Dittmar et al. (2008) study, this was a pointing task in which children were presented with two animations side by side on a computer screen. The animations showed the same action and the same two participants but in opposite roles of agent and patient. At the same time, a transitive sentence was played twice, referring to one of the animations and the child was asked to point to the correct picture. There were three conditions: the coalition condition, with SVO word order and overt case marking (NOM(-a) Verb ACC(-ę)); the word order only condition (NOM/ACC (Ø) Verb NOM/ACC(Ø)); and the conflict condition with OVS word-order and overt case marking (ACC(-ę) Verb NOM(-a)). Two novel verbs were used with four masculine and eight feminine inanimate nouns. In the masculine inanimate class the NOM–ACC distinction is neutralized, which allowed us to create the word order only condition. To control subjective levels of animacy, nouns referring to small and manipulable objects that could not move on their own (so no cars or trains, etc.) were used. There were four different nouns in each condition in fixed pairs and each pair was used with both verbs resulting in four items per condition and the total of twelve items for each child. The children tested fell into three age groups: eighteen 2-and-a-half-year-olds (2;7–3;1); twenty-five 4-year-olds (4;2–4;11); and twenty-one 8-year-olds (7;6–8;4).

The experiment had three phases. First, there was a warm-up in which the children were familiarized with the task and the nouns. Second, the novel verbs were each modeled nine times, in two different forms (present and gerund) with various participants in both roles and without revealing any cues. Finally, there was the test phase. For each item, there were two animations showing a given pair of objects involved in a particular action. Each was first shown separately on one side of the screen and then both appeared simultaneously accompanied by a pre-recorded utterance repeated twice. All utterances were recorded by the same female voice with the same intonation contour; the repetition was achieved mechanically, that is, by duplicating the same recording. Thus, all the children received exactly the same stimuli and different conditions did not involve any intonational changes. Children were asked to point to the animation that matched the sentence produced by the computer.

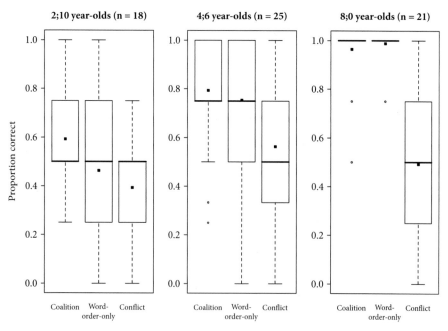

FIGURE 10.1 Distributions of proportions of correct responses (bold line: median, solid square: mean)

There were four test items in each condition and Figure 10.1 presents the results in terms of proportions of correct responses to them. In the youngest group, the coalition condition was significantly easier than both the conflict condition and the word-order-only condition. In the middle group, both the coalition and the word-order-only conditions became significantly easier than the conflict condition, with the oldest group performing at ceiling in the former two but remaining at the chance level in the conflict condition. While there was a significant improvement with age for the coalition and word-order-only conditions, children's performance in the conflict condition did not change.

These results partly replicate the Dittmar et al. (2008) study: the youngest children can only do the condition in which both cues agree while the middle group can rely on word order alone to choose the first noun as agent. Finally, the conflict condition is by far the most difficult and remains so even for the oldest group. This latter finding confirms our prediction: complexity of the whole system, of which a given cue is part, seems crucial. We have already proposed that German children's difficulty with resolving the conflict between case marking and word order might stem from the fact that a number of markers serve the same role and some of them serve a number of different roles. If this interpretation is correct, it should not be surprising that Polish children find relying on case marking even more difficult, given that the number of markers, as well as syncretisms and allomorphs among them, is even greater in Polish case inflections. A similar pattern was reported by Slobin and Bever (1982) for Serbo-Croatian and Turkish, although in their studies children were tested on real verbs and thus showed adult-like behavior earlier. Interestingly, the current finding stands in opposition to Weist (1983), who showed that 2;6-year-olds rely on case marking with familiar verbs. Both facts highlight the difference between the knowledge of cues as they work with familiar items and the ability to use them fully productively and suggest that lexically specific knowledge precedes the emergence of abstract productive generalizations.

Nevertheless, it might seem surprising that even 8-year-old children could not follow the case marking cues, particularly in the light of existing evidence of Polish children's knowledge of case inflections. The literature, however, offers a complex picture and suggests that this knowledge might develop only gradually, with different aspects being mastered at different times. It thus seems quite likely that the ability to productively use inflections as syntactic cues guiding sentence comprehension comes late in development. We will elaborate on this in the following paragraphs.

10.3.2.3 *Development of case marking in Polish*   It has been a well-known fact that Polish children start using case inflections in their spontaneous speech early and with few errors (e.g. Smoczyńska 1985). However, Krajewski, Lieven, and Theakston (2012) show that this spontaneous use is highly conservative and lexically restricted. In a densely sampled database of one child aged 2;0–2;1, the child and the mother were compared on the same nouns and the same endings and with the same number of utterances (see also Aguado-Orea 2004), making this a particularly stringent test. If the child had an adult-like knowledge of inflections, there seems to be no reason why she should not be equally as productive as the adult, *given the same nouns and the same inflections.* However, despite using virtually all the possible endings almost without any errors, the child's use of the inflections was highly restricted lexically and contextually (i.e. both in terms of stems and co-occurring lexical items). Furthermore, experimental studies (Krajewski et al. 2011) show that children find it very difficult to use inflections productively with novel nouns, especially if they were presented to them in forms other than the nominative. On the other hand, Dąbrowska and Tomasello (2008) found some challenging evidence pointing to an early abstract knowledge of case categories. In their experiment, children were taught a novel verb that took an object in the instrumental case. Nouns used in the training were all familiar but only of one gender, that is, they all took the same instrumental ending. At test, the children were asked to complete sentences with the same novel verb but with familiar nouns of another gender, requiring a different instrumental ending. Even 2½-year-olds were able to do so at rates significantly greater than chance, showing that they knew that the two instrumental endings "belonged together," that is, they had *some* abstract knowledge of the instrumental.

So, if 2½-year-olds have an abstract category of the instrumental, how is it possible that 8-year-olds cannot use the nominative and accusative (far more frequent cases than the instrumental) to identify agent and patient of a simple transitive sentence? At least a partial answer lies in the difference between the ability to link two allomorphs and the ability to use case information in a broader clausal context. What Dąbrowska and Tomasello (2008) showed was that children become aware of co-occurrences of inflectional forms quite early, that is, they can (i) group together instrumental endings as those which appear in certain contexts, and similarly (ii) they can group masculine and feminine endings as those which appear with certain nouns, and (iii) they can detect the co-occurrence pattern of (i) and (ii). In the context of the debate on early vs. late abstraction of syntactic categories, this might seem surprising, but it is less so when the evidence of young children's pattern detection skills is taken into account. In an artificial language study, which bears some striking similarities to the Dąbrowska and Tomasello experiment, Gerken, Wilson, and Lewis (2005) exposed 17-month-old American infants to a simplified part of the Russian noun inflection system and showed their ability to form an entirely abstract and arbitrary category of gender based solely on distributional cues. Further, the discrepancy between the productive use of case marking and the ability to use it as a cue at sentence level was shown for German children by Wittek and Tomasello (2005). In their studies, children were not able to use the transitive construction productively despite being productive with the required nominative and accusative case marking, the central and highly reliable cues for the transitive.

All this does not mean that the Polish 8-years-olds' poor performance with competing cues should be played down. We do not yet have figures for the number of OVS sentences in Polish CDS with clear nominative-accusative case marking which, if it is lower than the German figures of 22%, may be another important part of the explanation. It should also be noted that for nouns in the feminine gender, the nominative vs. accusative contrast may be difficult to perceive since only the word-final vowel matters (*-a* in NOM vs. *-ę* in ACC) and this may have affected comprehension in the pointing task, particularly when there is only case marking to rely on. In other words, the cue detectability of these feminine endings is almost certainly low (cf. MacWhinney, Pléh, and Bates 1985, on Hungarian).[2] Thus, there is clearly a need for further research to clarify these issues. It would also be interesting to explore systematically how using different methods affects the findings. This approach proved very insightful in the case of the English studies discussed earlier in the chapter and we already have act-out data (Chan, Lieven, and Tomasello 2009) and pointing data (Dittmar et al. 2008) in German (see also Smolík 2011 for work on word order and case marking in Czech).

10.4 Discussion

10.4.1 *The elusive status of cues*

The Competition Model paradigm has already proven very helpful, providing many interesting insights into our understanding of young children's knowledge of sentential structure. We now have strong evidence that the input children experience shapes that knowledge and, moreover, we know that extra-syntactic factors, like semantics and prosody, play important roles as well. We know that the ability to comprehend sentences with familiar items does not extend automatically to novel items, that is, does not mean an adult-like competence. At the same time, the recent studies in this framework pose two interesting challenges for future research. One is the already mentioned issue of how to calculate cue measures. How do we decide which frequencies to take into account? Is it a particular ending we should focus on? And, if so, should we include in the calculations the same ending marking a different category? Or maybe we should include all the allomorphs marking a given category? Or some of them?[3] Similarly, when calculating word order measures, should we consider the position of noun in relation to verb or the relative position of two noun phrases? Clearly, this is not just a methodological question, as the right answer depends on what exactly constitutes a cue for a child and what is a cue depends in turn on the child's current linguistic representations. Since the latter are likely to change in time, pinning down cues at different stages of development seems of paramount importance since it would help us form a detailed picture of what exactly is happening during language development. It might be tempting to calculate a number of alternative measures to see which one best predicts children's performance but of course this runs the risk of circularity. Critics might point out that various frequency measures are calculated and then the ones that better fit the data are selected (see Ambridge 2010; Lieven 2010). Thus, there is a clear need for independently based predictions.

---

[2] There were also some differences in the design of the Polish and German studies, which make the direct comparison somewhat problematic.

[3] Of course, these issues are not confined to developmental research but are of great concern in discussion of how to define productivity in general (e.g. Plag 1999). Nonetheless, they appear particularly complex with respect to language development. For example, results of Krajewski et al. (2011) suggest that it is frequency of a particular transition between forms rather than frequency of an individual form that matters.

Modeling might provide a potentially useful approach to this problem because it is necessary to make explicit the factors assumed to be involved and it allows testing the prediction that this will change with time. Modeling compels one to be precise about what cues and what weightings one is proposing. Other experimental data might be informative too: for example, results of Dąbrowska and Tomasello (2008) suggest collapsing two instrumental allomorphs if one were interested in their cue strength for 2½-year-old children. On the other hand, if children are aware of the co-occurrence of peripheral instrumental endings, they should acquire a similar knowledge for nominative and accusative markers even earlier. Yet neither German nor Polish children seem to use them as cues until quite late, which leads us to the challenge discussed in the next section: the early status of cues.

10.4.2 *From cues to constructions or from constructions to cues?*

The other, even more interesting, issue concerns the psychological status of cues and the Competition Model in general. We know that the model provides excellent means of quantifying various aspects of a linguistic system, the end-state for children's language development, and as such enables generating precise predictions for their performance on various tasks, but does it properly describe the very process of development? It assumes that children, once they are able to detect them, start counting the occurrences of cues and calculating their patterns of co-occurrence, but is this really how children come to grips with grammatical constructions? We know that even very young children are able to detect complex co-occurrence patterns in artificial languages (e.g. Saffran, Aslin, and Newport, 1996; Gerken, Wilson, and Lewis 2005) and studies like Dąbrowska and Tomasello (2008) prove that this ability works for real languages too. However, what these studies show is the ability to detect regularities in (co-)occurrences of *forms*, whereas learning a language is all about *linking* form with meaning (function). Cues, as defined within the Competition Model, are, after all, co-occurrences of form and meaning and, when it comes to mapping the two, it seems that children start with whole constructions as form–meaning pairings (Tomasello 2003a; Goldberg 2006) and single cues to form–meaning mapping do not play a big role at first. The results of the studies presented here suggest that children start with prototypical instances, amalgams of cues, and only subsequently single out individual cues. And only after identifying individual cues, perhaps based on their detectability and availability, can they take in the relative reliability of those cues. This might explain the puzzling lag between the time when children start showing evidence of productive and seemingly abstract knowledge of complex linguistic patterns and the time when they start using them as cues to form–meaning mapping.[4]

---

[4] It is worth noting in this context the striking difference between children and adult second language learners, with the latter not only being readily able to analyze individual cues but in fact finding it beneficial to focus on individual cues at a time when learning (Kempe and MacWhinney 1998; Matessa and Anderson 2000).

This finding is particularly interesting as it is in line with other research showing that language development might be proceeding in both a "bottom-up" *and* a "top-down" direction. There is good evidence suggesting that children (i) store whole sequences of words (Bannard and Matthews 2008; Matthews and Bannard 2010), and (ii) actually learn grammar by forming open slots in such initially unanalyzed chunks and, by proceeding in this way, gradually abstract more and more productive patterns (e.g. Lieven et al. 2003; Bannard, Lieven, and Tomasello 2009; Lieven, Salomo, and Tomasello 2009). Moreover, such frequent chunks make it easier for children to correctly use the morphology of their constituting elements: for instance, children are more likely to produce a correct irregular form *teeth* as part of the frequent phrase *brush your teeth* than outside such a context (Arnon 2011; Arnon and Clark 2011). Also, Study 3 of Krajewski, Lieven, and Theakston (2012) showed that the child's use of inflections was restricted contextually. In a series of nonce word elicitation experiments, in which children heard a noun in one case form and had to use it in another one, children never provided (incorrect) forms of other cases, however they made gender overgeneralizations and their performance depended on the constructions involved (Krajewski 2008; Krajewski et al. 2011). These findings suggest that early knowledge about inflections is both construction-specific and quite general in terms of case categories. Children seem to know which case is required in a given construction before they know for certain which allomorph marking for that case should be used with a particular noun. In other words, they learn different cases with respect to particular constructions in which they are used (rather than across the board) but, at the same time, they develop some abstract understanding of a given case as a category, which can be marked using a number of different endings. The exact differences between these endings are learned last. Thus, development proceeds top-down: from a construction as a whole to exact details of particular endings. As in the *Brush your teeth* example, constructions serve as cues for their parts, rather than the other way around.

An important issue to consider is other competing motivations that might play a role. It is crucial not to treat the linguistic system as if it were divorced from pragmatic and cognitive factors. An obvious example is what the child actually wants to talk about. Thus, Theakston et al. (2005) show that children's omission of BE-auxiliaries with particular subjects is predicted by the relative frequencies of specific subject-auxiliary strings in the input but *only* for third-person subjects and not for first- or second-person singular subjects. This is almost certainly because children want to talk about themselves while caretakers use the second person more frequently than the first person. Cognitive and/or pragmatic complexity is also clearly involved. In a study of the development of six children's auxiliaries, Lieven (2008) found correlations between the frequency with which these auxiliaries appeared in the caretaker's speech and their order of emergence in the children. However, there were some relatively frequent auxiliaries in the input that were late to appear in the children, for instance conditionals such as "could" and "should," presumably because of the complexity of their semantics and the pragmatic contexts of their use.

10.5 Summary and conclusions

In this chapter, we have reviewed a number of studies investigating the development of the simple transitive construction within the framework provided by the Competition Model (Bates and MacWhinney 1989). We have argued that the choice of this particular model, with its emphasis on the role of language input, might help reinforce the emergentist position in the all-too-old and heated argument with nativists. The results provide several important insights, some of which confirm earlier predictions while others present interesting challenges. First, children's performance indeed depends on the language they hear and this reliance on input exhibits itself not only in the gradualness of learning, but also in different routes to the adult-like end state. Second, when learning from input, children pay attention to semantics and prosody as well as to syntactic elements. This suggests that there may be no principled distinction between "core" syntax and what is extra-grammatical or on the "periphery" at least in the early learning of grammar. Third, children at first can only understand sentences that follow the prototypical pattern of their language, suggesting that their initial representations may resemble "gestalts" of several redundant cues, and only with time do they become able to respond to individual cues when these are presented independently. These findings corroborate the results of experiments conducted back in the 1980s. However, it is only recent studies that have used novel linguistic items, thus eliminating the impact of lexically specific knowledge and focusing on true grammatical productivity. It is therefore important to notice that, fourthly, abstract knowledge lags considerably behind the ability to use familiar lexical items as demonstrated by the earlier studies. This further supports the gradual and piecemeal character of language learning.

At the same time, though, children's poor performance with sentences containing competing cues lasted for a surprisingly long time. On the one hand, the Competition Model does predict that such conflicting cues should be particularly difficult for young children. On the other hand, given the very high reliability of case marking in both German and Polish, one might expect that children would follow it as a cue to sentence meaning earlier than at the age of 7 or 8. This later than expected full reliance on case marking might at first seem puzzling in the light of existing evidence showing that in both languages, despite the complexities of their case systems, children acquire some abstract knowledge of, and the ability to use, case marking productively much earlier. This can partly be explained by the fact that such complexities make it difficult to estimate cue validity (both for children and experimenters!). We suggest however that this is also because the two abilities are qualitatively different and their development proceeds, to some degree, separately. The ability to use even a complex system 'locally' can be accounted for by the statistical learning of co-occurrence patterns, whereas the ability to use such local marking as a cue to broader clausal meaning requires form–meaning mapping. The former in a way follows a bottom-up route: from lexically bound to gradually more productive use of markers, to classifying several different markers as belonging to the same abstract category. Form–meaning mapping, it seems, at least to some extent proceeds top-down: from prototypical gestalts to individual cues, from whole chunks to their constituting elements.

Reviving the Competition Model testing paradigm has decidedly advanced our understanding but there is a long way to go. We are still far from having a full picture of varying developmental paths and factors that might shape them. We need to employ more refined methods of generating predictions and more diverse methods of testing children. Fruitful areas for further research are, first, to extend these types of experiments to languages that show further important contrasts in the syntax of the transitive to those already studied. Secondly, extending preferential looking studies to online measures such as eye-tracking would help to identify the ways in which children move from implicit to explicit knowledge of the grammar of their languages. Finally, the use of modeling to explore the ways in which different cues compete and/or collaborate in different languages would also be an important step forward. Rather than continue with what has become a somewhat sterile debate between nativists and emergentists, the task now is to build a psychologically realistic and typologically informed theory of the ways in which cues to meaning interact in children's developing ability to use all aspects of the language they are learning to a full extent.

Part II

Competition in Morphosyntax and the Lexicon

11

Conflicting vs. convergent vs. interdependent motivations in morphology

WOLFGANG U. DRESSLER, GARY LIBBEN,
AND KATHARINA KORECKY-KRÖLL

11.1 Introduction

By "motivations" we mean the language users' motivations as modeled by linguists within a given framework. These motivations are most forceful in language acquisition and language change (cf. also Newmeyer, MacWhinney and Cristofaro, all in this volume). "Competing motivations" (cf. Haiman 2011, Moravcsik, this volume) may have different meanings. We want to briefly discuss four of them.

11.1.1 *Conflicting motivations*

Competition may mean conflicting motivations either within the same theoretical approach or between different theoretical approaches. The latter represents prototypical rivalry between motivations that exclude each other, if properly formulated. This is the classical case of the scientific ideal of monocausality, which is much easier to establish in "hard" sciences than in "soft" human sciences to which linguistics belongs in spite of all efforts to the contrary. Ideally one or more of the competing motivation hypotheses can be falsified, whereas one hypothesis survives falsification attempts. But if the contrast between two motivations is firmly embedded within two opposing full-fledged theories, then falsification of a whole theory is impossible. Here the main epistemological problem is the weight of decisive criteria. However the main problem from the perspective of the sociology of science is ideological aversion against other theoretical approaches than one's own and one's own ideology providing protective shields.

Within the same theoretical approach conflicting motivations are foreseen in preference theories (as in Dressler's naturalness approach, see Section 11.2.1 and Dressler 2002) and in Optimality Theory (OT) with its violable constraints (see, e.g.,

Bresnan and Aissen 2002, de Hoop and Malchukov 2008). At least functional and substance-based OT approaches are comparable to preference approaches. For both, the main problem is how to weight conflicting motivations, in order to obtain explanatory resolutions of the conflicts (discussed further in Sections 11.2.1, 11.2.3–5).

11.1.2 *Convergent motivations*

Convergent motivations are best conceived of as mutually independent motivations that combine or conspire in determining or promoting a certain result. Here the main problems lie in establishing multicausality, the mutual independence of motivations and in weighting the relative importance of each motivation. In social sciences multicausality is the rule in motivating phenomena. An example from political history would be the distinction between different causes of the outbreak of the First World War and its motivation by the assassination of Archduke Franz Ferdinand and its consequences. In diachronic linguistics a recurrent instance is the loaning of foreign words, which presupposes language contact, the attractiveness and fittingness of a foreign word felt by the loaners and a lacuna identified in the receiving language (discussed further in Section 11.2).

11.1.3 *Interdependent motivations*

Interdependent motivations are the most problematic ones to identify and classify. The ideal is to subordinate one motivation under another one, for example when subordinating a linguistic principle under a semiotic one, for instance the preference for affixation (as in *girl+s*) over modification (as in *foot* → *feet*) to a semiotic preference for iconicity (see Section 11.2). Here we must avoid the danger of undue reductionism. Clear criteria must be established, for example for differentiating the reduction of phonology to phonetics from establishing a phonetic basis for a phonological generalization (e.g. for consonant assimilation). Whenever general correlations are found, one should try to transform them into implications. And whenever symmetric, reciprocal implications are established, one should try to subordinate such implications under a higher level motivation. But when asymmetric implications are found, then there may exist either a superordinate motivating principle or what is implied may simply be more basic (cf. also Moravcsik, this volume).

11.1.4 *Sufficient vs. partial motivations*

An orthogonal dichotomy is the difference between sufficient and only partial motivations, where the boundaries are often difficult to draw. Ultimately we have to ask whether non-reductionist motivations are only partial motivations (because complete motivations can be considered to be reductionist, such as the reduction of phonology to phonetics) or whether partial motivations are rather a symptom of explanatory insufficiency, that is, of incapacity of providing a satisfactory explanation.

11.2 Competing motivations in grammar, lexicon, and discourse

11.2.1 *Natural Morphology*

This paper's theoretical approach is Natural Morphology (cf. Dziubalska-Kołaczyk and Weckwerth 2002) with its deductive hierarchy of subordinated motivations starting with extra-linguistic (semiotic and cognitive) bases as the highest level, then at the next, subordinated level of universal morphological preferences (sub-theory of universal markedness), next the level of typological adequacy, to the lowest level of language-specific system adequacy (cf. Dressler 2006; Kilani-Schoch and Dressler 2005). Each lower level specifies and filters the preferences of the respective higher levels. The universal preferences are isolated from each other (on the level of universal markedness theory), but coordinated at the subsequent lower levels, which includes type- and system-specific different resolutions of conflicts (cf. Malchukov, this volume). This does not exclude that generalizations of a higher level may be reweighted as less weighty than generalizations of a lower hierarchical level due to conflicts between preferences. The relative force of each conflicting motivation is relevant (this can lead to Moravcsik's (this volume) three types of adjustment, override, and blocking).

For example, the universal preference for a biunique relation between form and meaning, which is highly weighted (and thus not reweighted) in agglutinating languages (with the effect of adding up separate biunique suffixes of, for example, first number and then case) is reweighted at the lower level of typological adequacy in inflecting-fusional languages with the benefit of having just one cumulative inflectional suffix, for example, which signals simultaneously number and case, as in the Dat.Pl. Turk. *ev+ler+e* vs. AGk. *oík+ois* 'to the houses'.

Note that marked equals "less natural than" (dispreferred) and unmarked "more natural than" (preferred) in universal markedness theory (parameterized for each parameter separately, e.g. for degree of iconicity), but equals "less adequate vs. more adequate" in the lower levels of type and system adequacy.

11.2.2 *Indexicality and affix order*

Affix order, a topic which is relevant for many morphological models, is referred within Natural Morphology to the semiotic principle of indexicality which favors adjacency (cf. Kilani-Schoch and Dressler 2005: 57–66). Cognitively, indexicality is basically a spatial concept of closeness or even contiguity between a signatum and its signans. This is directly applicable to syntagmatic, endophoric indexicality in language. Thus for Peirce (1994: II.369) an index is a sign (= signans) "which like a pronoun demonstrative or relative, forces the attention to the particular object intended (= signatum) without describing it," that is, a demonstrative pronoun is an exophoric index pointing to an outside referent without naming it, whereas a relative pronoun is an endophoric, that is, intratextual index referring to an antecedent without naming or rephrasing it.

Both on the motivating extra-linguistic level and on the linguistic level, there is a preference for adjacency of signans and signatum. Already the ancient Stoics postulated smoke to be a signans for the signatum fire, but only if they are close to each other. In Givón's (1995: 51) model of functional linguistics, this is the cognitive motivation for his proximity principle. Also Bybee's (1985) Relevance Principle follows a similar indexicality approach.

To this level of universal preferences, the level of typological adequacy is subordinated. For example when we think of the order of suffixes, then plural and case suffixes are separated in the ideal construct of the agglutinating type of language, whereas number and case are cumulatively expressed in the ideal construct of the inflecting-fusional type (cf. Skalička 1979; Dressler 2006), which limits the applicability of the adjacency principle. The subordinated lowest level of language-specific system adequacy regulates which suffixes exist and how they can be combined (cf. Manova 2011).

This hierarchization of motivations can be used for explaining Greenberg's (1966b) generalization that derivational affixes tend to be positioned between lexical roots/ stems and inflectional affixes. Dressler (1989) extended this generalization to the preferential right-bound order: root/stem–prototypical derivation–non-prototypical derivation–non-prototypical (= inherent) inflection–prototypical (= contextual) inflection. This preferential order represents a derived universal preference, where two higher-order motivations combine: first the just explicated indexicality preference, second the motivations by the different main linguistic functions of derivational and inflectional morphology. These decisively different main functions are the lexical function of derivational morphology, that is, the function of providing the lexicon with morphosemantic and morphotactic motivation of derived words plus providing it with new words, vs. the syntactic function of inflection. In prototypical (= contextual) inflection, for example case, suffixation is governed by syntax, it provides syntactic constructions with appropriate inflectional markers. Therefore, due to the indexical adjacency principle, case suffixes are best posited on the periphery of a word form in order to be closest to the word-external world of syntactic constructions and to be first parsed after syntactic parsing, morphological parsing starting at the periphery of a word form. For a similar reason, attributive demonstratives are best placed at the periphery of a noun phrase (cf. Cysouw 2010).

Whereas case is obligatorily governed by the syntactic construction, number on nouns as a representative of non-prototypical (= inherent) inflection is not governed by syntactic constructions but may itself govern syntactic agreement as its controller. Therefore, due to indexicality, a plural suffix should be posited at the periphery, but not as much as a case suffix. This then motivates the typical order of case suffixes after a plural suffix, as in the German partially quasi-agglutinating dative plural *den Kind+er+n* 'to the children,' where the dative-plural suffix follows the plural suffix.

The motivating lexical function of (especially prototypical) derivation favors lexicalization. It tends to reduce morphosemantic transparency and leads to storage as a whole, in contrast to inflection, which is seldom lexicalized or morphosemantically opaque. This combines in turn with the (equally semiotically based) word base preference of morphological rules, that is, that the base of a morphological rule is preferentially an existing word (cf. Dressler 1988), which derived actual words are, whereas inflectional forms are not. The combination of the two motivations also motivates that inflectional suffixation follows derivational suffixation rather than the inverse order. This is a second chain of motivation for the Greenbergian generalization.

What remains to be deduced is the order of prototypical derivation before non-prototypical derivation. Let us exemplify this with word-class changing derivation as representative of prototypical derivation and with alteratives, that is, diminutives, augmentatives, or pejoratives, as representatives of non-prototypical derivation. Italian examples (Merlini Barbaresi 2004: 271) for this preferential order are *fasc-ist-one* 'fasc-ist-AUGMENTATIVE' (= super-fascist) with the order of agentive and augmentative (the agent noun *fasc+ista* being characterized by internal morphosemantic opacity) or *rischi+os+etto* 'somewhat risk-y' with the order quali-tative-adjective-forming and diminutive suffix (both combinations being morpho-semantically transparent). In actual utterances both alterative (= diminutive, augmentative) suffixes are likely to have a pragmatic rather than a semantic mean-ing, that is, their use is governed by the outside of the utterance level and not by word-internal lexical motivations as with prototypical derivation, and this pragmatic domination from outside the lexical level can be roughly compared with outside determination by syntactic government. This again motivates indexically a more peripheral position of alterative suffixes than of word-class changing suffixes. Nearly all exceptions to this order have a prototypical derivational suffix attached in a morphosemantically transparent way to a morphosemantically opaque diminutive or other alterative, for example *pan+in+eria* 'sandwich shop': *pan+ino* is thoroughly lexicalized as 'sandwich' and does not simply denote a small bread. And the internal, that is, non-peripheral, diminutive can never have any pragmatic meaning imposed by, or referring to, the speech situation or the speech act.

Thus we have a cline of decreasing lexicalization from the center towards the periphery, from prototypical derivation towards prototypical inflection, and an opposing cline of decreasing influence of the sentence or utterance level from the periphery towards the center.

Exceptions to the four-member order prototypical derivational suffix–non-proto-typical derivational suffix–non-prototypical inflectional suffix–prototypical inflec-tional suffix are restricted to adjacent reordering; distant reordering is disallowed. A case in point is the order of a plural suffix preceding a diminutive suffix, thus the reordering of non-prototypical derivational and non-prototypical inflectional suf-fixes, as in G. *Kind+er+chen/lein* 'child-PLU-DIM,' double pluralization in the Dutch correspondent *kind+er+tje+s*, cf. Yiddish *kind+er+lex*.

Thus we have two chains of motivation for the Greenbergian scale, depending on the syntactic function of inflection and on the lexical function of derivation. How can we weight them? Here we should not content ourselves with the pitfall of an ideological solution of the problem by deriving the priority of a motivation from assigning either to the lexicon or to syntax the central position in a grammatical model. An empirical solution is to look for crucial cases, where only one of the two chains of motivations can be predominant.

Another possibility is to look for a higher-order generalization which would reduce two principles to a single one, a typical move towards unifying complementary

principles, which also holds for some of Moravcsik's (2010) examples. This unification can be found in the assumption of a scalar continuum between lexicon and
grammar as largely assumed in grammaticalization studies and in Natural Morphology as well. This scalar continuum mirrors the gradually decreasing influence from a
word-internal attractor and from a word-external attractor which is either syntactic
or pragmatic at the utterance level.

11.2.3 *Compounds in an interface between grammar and discourse*

After considering the interface between lexicon and grammar we now move to the
interface between grammar and discourse, namely conflicting and convergent motivations relating morphology to text linguistics. In a corpus-linguistic study (Dressler
and Mörth 2012), based on the Austrian Academy Corpus of the Institute for Corpus
Linguistics and Text Technology of the Austrian Academy of Sciences, we established, as expected, a clear tendency towards cataphorical reference of nominal
compounding in titles or subtitles of texts to nouns and phrases in the following
text, in contrast to the disfavored inverse relationship. Thus a title with one opaque
and transparent compound *Die Kehr+seite der Valuta+besserung* 'The drawback/
disadvantage of the currency improvement' cross-refers cataphorically with its
second transparent compound to several non-compounds in the following text:
Besserung der/unserer Valuta 'improvement of the/our currency' (three times), *ist
die Valuta nicht besser geworden* 'the currency did not get better.' Such cases are
frequent in our corpus, whereas the inverse occurs only twice, for example: title *Die
Freiheit der Meere* 'The freedom of the seas,' in the following text: *das Problem der
Meeres+freiheit* 'the problem of the sea-freedom.'

This asymmetry is, at first sight, in blaring contradiction to the universal indexical
preference for anaphoric over cataphoric indexicality, a preference which is due to
temporal backward (= anaphoric) indexicality establishing more reliable sign relations than temporal forward (= cataphoric) indexicality. Cognitively, we can refer
more safely to facts in the past than in the future.

Reliability of signs is a semiotic preference established by Morris (1971), which is
also the basis of the preference for biuniqueness and, as here, of the preference for
anaphoric over cataphoric signs. This preference is overturned in text titles by a
motivated markedness reversal: titles or subtitles need not be reliable names of a
text, they are fundamentally cataphoric with respect to the following text and
should create expectation and tension in the reader (Dressler 2000: 766–7; Baicchi
2004). There is a norm for titles to be short, a historical development since over-
long baroque titles. The property of textual condensation justifies the use of
compounds in titles, because compounds exhibit morphosemantic and morphotactic condensation in comparison with quasi-synonymous phrases. This makes
them adequate for the use as cataphoric as well as anaphoric indexical signs. This
convergence of motivations overrides, in the case of titles, the conflicting derived
preference for short anaphoric compounds to follow longer phrases or sentences as
antecedents.

11.2.4 *Markedness vs. frequency*

Our next case is one of conflicting motivations derived from two conflicting models, one of markedness-based motivations (cf. Section 11.2.2–11.2.3), another one of frequency-based motivations as in Bybee (2010) and Tomasello (2003a), cf. Haspelmath (this volume). This necessitates a defense against Haspelmath's (2006) attack on the concept of markedness and its identification as an epiphenomenon (if that) of frequency. In this context, Haspelmath (2006: 31–2, 40, 42–4, 46, 58–60, 62) also proposes deriving preferences of Natural Morphology from frequency distributions and regularities of language change. In contrast, in Natural Morphology, the direction of motivation is inverse for morphology: frequency of use is derived from preferences (Mayerthaler 1981; Haspelmath 2006: 32, 43, 46), unless in certain cases of markedness reversal (Mayerthaler 1981: 48ff, cf. Haspelmath 2006: 44). We start with two specific cases, before going into generalities.

On three occasions Haspelmath (2006: 32, 44, 59, and repeated in Haspelmath, this volume) cites Welsh *plu+en* 'feather,' *plu* 'feathers' as counter-evidence against markedness and iconicity argumentations which posit a plural form to be preferentially longer than its singular. But *-en* is a derivational singulative suffix and it can be inflectionally pluralized with the most productive Welsh plural suffix in *pluenn+au*. This is quite productive in closely cognate Breton, for example collective *koumoul* 'clouds,' derivational singulative *koumoul+enn* 'single cloud,' plural *koumoul+enn+où* 'single, distributed clouds' (often called plurative or distributive, cf. Corbett 2000) with the most productive Breton plural suffix *-où* (cf. Trépos 1957). Thus this is completely compatible with a markedness reversal and with an explanation by iconicity, without appealing to a frequency-induced markedness reversal.

In addition, Haspelmath's (2006: 44) explanation for the relationship (markedness reversal) between Latin suffixed third-person singular imperative *lauda+to* and zero-marked second-person singular *lauda* 'praise!' is frequentist. But the deeper reason is that in general, according to Benveniste (1966) the third person is the unmarked non-person, independent of how frequently each of the three persons are used, whereas the imperative serves primarily to address directive speech acts to a single person. This justifies zero marking irrespective of whether in written texts polite forms in the second-person plural or third-person (singular or plural) are frequent or not. In other words, the general unmarkedness of the third person, and the markedness reversal in orders and other directive speech acts is based on universal pragmatics.

For Haspelmath (2006: 48) the basic and ultimate explanatory factor is text frequency. Without denying the importance of frequency in many circumstances, we contend that Haspelmath's radical and generalized postulate is flawed in two respects. The explanatory consequence of higher text frequency correctly argued by Haspelmath is greater processing ease. And here comes the first objection. What has more impact on processing ease than frequency is age of acquisition. Now the explanatory link between earlier age of acquisition and greater processing ease may be, under certain circumstances, greater cumulative frequency of use during life-time (Bonin et al. 2004). But cumulative frequency during life-time is a far cry from text frequency in written corpora.

The second objection we would like to call the tooth-brush objection. There was a time in foreign-language teaching when text frequency was assigned the pre-eminent role in planning teaching materials. But then came the objection of the tooth-brush: English *tooth-brush* and its equivalents in other languages have a rather low text frequency, nevertheless these words must be taught early for pragmatic needs. One does not even orally produce the word *tooth-brush* frequently, but one thinks of it with regular frequency and such thoughts are generally verbally shaped in silent inner language. Thus we may generalize: the text frequency of either written or oral texts cannot be the source of frequency effects: the real source is frequency of verbal thinking. And such frequency cannot be established by counting occurrences in corpora but only by judicious rating experiments (this argument also holds against the "functional frequency principle" of Du Bois, Section 16.2, this volume).

A final defense of Natural Morphology against Haspelmath's attack on marked-ness refers to the lowest hierarchical level in motivation chains: language specific system adequacy. Wurzel (1984) calls it also normalcy and this sounds like type or even token frequency, as Haspelmath (2006: 60) correctly remarks. But in Dressler's (1997a, 2003) version of system adequacy, normalcy has been replaced with produc-tivity. The most productive rules of a given category need not be those with the highest type frequency, as the debate about German plural formation has clearly shown (cf. Wegener 2002): German -s suffixation is one of the most, if not the most, productive plural formation rule, although it has much less type frequency than -en and -e plural formation. Moreover, according to Haspelmath's argumentation on zero marking, German zero plurals should be the most frequent plurals among German plurals, but they are not and they are only slightly productive, and in substandard colloquial speech non-iconic zero plurals are increasingly replaced by more iconic -en and -s plurals, such as in *die Mädchen+s* 'the girl-s,' *die Hebel+n* 'the lever-s.' The reverse change from the earlier plural *die Token+s* to the recent zero-plural variant *die Token* (Sg. *der Token*) is a sign of total morphological integration of the English loan-word *token* (cf. Wegener 2002). Productivity is particularly considered in Section 11.3.6.

11.2.5 *Morphonotactics*

Markedness vs. frequency is also a general topic in the field of morphonotactics, the subfield of phonotactics determined by morphological operations, as proposed by Dressler and Dziubalska-Kołaczyk (2006). Phonological markedness predictions are derived from Dziubalska Kołaczyk's (2009) net auditory distance principle: its basis is that a two-consonant cluster is the less marked, the more the two consonants differ in degree of sonority and articulatory position, and voicedness. Thus in word-initial double consonant clusters the net auditory distance between the two con-sonants should be greater than or equal to the net auditory distance between the second consonant and the following vowel.

Less marked consonant clusters are predicted to have a wider crosslinguistic distribution, that is, to recur with higher type frequency than corresponding marked clusters. However, in a conflict between morphotactics and phonotactics, morphological operations may introduce marked phonotactic clusters which are illegal in monomorphemic words, such as in English *roof+s*, *club+s* or by vowel deletion in Polish adjective formation: *lew* 'lion' vs. derived adjective *lw+i*, cf. *len* 'linen' vs. *lni +any*, *mech* 'moss' vs. *mch+owy*, *wieś* 'village' vs. *wsi+owy*. Here the morphologically derived initial consonant clusters are purely morphonotactic clusters.

So far, within phonotactics, type frequency is generally derived from degree of phonotactic markedness. But lexical type frequency comes in as an autonomous factor in the classification of clusters as exclusively morphonotactic vs. strong-default morphonotactic vs. weak-default morphonotactic. A German example of a merely morphonotactic cluster is word-final [xst], as in *du lach+st* 'you laugh,' a strong default cluster can be exemplified by the word-final cluster [pst], as in type-frequent second-person singular forms of the pattern *du leb+st* 'you live' vs. rare monomorphemic occurrences (as in *Papst* 'pope'), a weak default by the cluster [kst], as in *du hack+st* 'you hack' vs. relatively frequent monomorphemic cases such as *Text* 'text.'

11.3 Competing motivations in psycholinguistic research on morphology

11.3.1 *Introduction*

This psycholinguistic part of our contribution focuses on first language acquisition. The data come mainly from an international typological cooperation on first language acquisition of eighteen languages (cf. Bittner et al. 2003; Savickiene and Dressler 2007; Stephany and Voeikova 2009), that is, from the Crosslinguistic Project on Pre- and Protomorphology in Language Acquisition, and related acquisitional studies, including processing studies done by the present authors.

11.3.2 *Acquisition of phonotactics and morphonotactics*

Let us first briefly stay with our last topic: phonotactics and morphonotactics (Section 11.2.5). Phonotactic markedness has been shown to largely predict the order of acquisition of Polish and English consonant clusters (cf. Zydorowicz 2009). But what about the relationship between comparable morphonotactic clusters in morphologically complex words, that is, across morpheme boundaries (as in *sack +s*), and phonotactic clusters within morpheme boundaries (as in *six*)? Here an additional combining motivation intervenes: typically developing children acquiring English, Polish, Lithuanian, and (partially) German have been shown to fare better with morphonotactic clusters because these clusters help them to acquire morphology, that is, the interface between morphology and phonology is helpful as a bootstrapping device (cf. Weissenborn and Höhle 2000). However children with specific language impairment (SLI) fare worse with morphonotactic clusters than with phonotactic ones, demonstrated for English by Marshall and van der Lely (2006) and Marshall et al. (2007) and in our as yet unpublished work on German and Lithuanian, because this interface is difficult for children suffering from Grammatical SLI. Thus, typically developing children appear to acquire word-final morphonotactic clusters earlier, as in German /max+t/ 'make-s,' /drYk+t/ 'press+es,' /li:p+st/ 'you love' than in /axt/ 'eight,' /nakt/ 'naked,' /o:pst/ 'fruits.'

11.3.3 *Acquisition of diminutives*

The next acquisitional question is why inflection emerges earlier than derivation in first language acquisition (including affixes of equal length, i.e. word length does not play any role). This can be answered by two combined motivations: first, there is more syntactic motivation for the emergence of inflection than of derivation, but a second motivation comes from processing: peripheral morphemes are easier to segment and identify than medial morphemes ("bathtub effect," cf. Aitchison 2003: 138), which favors the acquisition of inflection over the acquisition of derivation. And if we go back to our previous discussion of affix order, then we must also make predictions for inherent (non-prototypical) vs. contextual (prototypical) inflection. In agglutinating languages case morphemes (contextual inflection) are positioned regularly after separate plural morphemes (inherent inflection). And, as predicted, the first oblique case morpheme is acquired earlier than the plural morpheme in Turkish, Hungarian, and Finnish (Stephany and Voeikova 2009).

But there is a motivated exception, in the sense of Moravcsik's (2010) exception to a prototype or to Corbett's (2007) canonical cases: the early emergence of diminutives as representatives of non-prototypical derivation (Savickiene and Dressler 2007), that is, the early appearance of a recurrent use of different diminutivized noun lemmas as opposed to other types of derived or complex words (lexemes): what is the main motivation for this exceptional early emergence of a derivational category? Is it the pragmatic importance of diminutives in child-directed speech (especially in caretakers' speech to small children up to the age of about 3 years)? Or is it the fact that inflection of diminutives is usually more productive and transparent than of the average of the simplex bases of diminutives? For example, the plural inflection of Italian *ami[k]o* 'friend,' PL *ami[č]i* is unproductive and opaque, whereas the plural inflection of its diminutive *ami[k]+etto*, PL *ami[k]+etti* is both productive and transparent. And these two factors have motivated at least the Italian, Hungarian, and Lithuanian children of our project to prefer diminutives to their simplex bases when these bases inflected in a less productive and transparent way than their diminutives.

Token frequency of diminutives, as a fourth motivating factor, highlighted by Tomasello (2003a) and other Leipzig-based scholars, but still a matter of controversy in acquisition studies (cf. Gülzow and Gagarina 2007), plays a role insofar as (a low threshold of) a critical mass of diminutives must occur in child-directed speech for children to take them up. This critical mass is lacking in the caretaker's input in languages such as French and Turkish, and therefore the small number of French-learning and Turkish children in our project do not produce diminutives at all or only in very few isolated, rote-learnt specimens.

Next, the token frequency of children's input has a clear impact on token frequency of diminutives in their output. Therefore, Dutch-learning children produce many more diminutives than German-learning children. And among our Viennese children, the girl who receives twice as many diminutive tokens in her input than the boy, produces also about twice as many diminutives as the boy. However, as far as the chronology of the emergence of diminutives is concerned, diminutives emerge as early in German as in much diminutive-richer Dutch, etc. (more in Savickiene and Dressler 2007).

Therefore we can weight the four motivating factors that we discussed for the acquisition of diminutives in the following way: a rather low threshold of token frequency in children's input is a necessary precondition, but early emergence and the acquisition of diminutives is due to their pragmatic meaning in mother–child interaction independent of frequency. This is also supported by the fact that the meanings of diminutives in early childhood are, as far as we can ascertain, only pragmatic, whereas the semantic meaning of smallness is expressed by adjectives such as *small, little*. The third and fourth factors of productivity and transparency influence only the relative chronology of acquisition and frequency of use of competing diminutive suffixes within the same language, but the early emergence of diminutives as such depends neither on productivity, nor on transparency or high frequency, but on pragmatics: further evidence comes from the acquisition of augmentatives, which share a primarily pragmatic and a secondarily (opposed) semantic meaning with diminutives. Since the pragmatics of augmentatives is much less important for the world of young children, they are acquired at least one year later than diminutives (cf. Savickiene and Dressler 2007).

This leads us to the general motivating forces of richness vs. complexity of inflectional morphology (cf. Dressler 2003) in their impact on acquisition. Here we may summarize that inflectional richness, as measured by a great number of inflectional categories and of productive patterns expressing them, apparently stimulates the child to devote more effort to acquire them (cf. Laaha and Gillis 2007; Xanthos et al. 2011; Ravid et al. 2008; Austin 2010), whereas this is dubious for additional complexity effected by unproductive patterns.

11.3.4 *German compounds*

Various online and offline processing studies by the authors and their associates (Dressler et al. 2001; Libben et al. 2002) have established the importance of productivity and morphotactic transparency for production and perception of German compounds. The same motivating forces can explain the order of emergence of German compound types: first compounds with mere concatenation (e.g. *Polizei +auto* 'police car') and then compounds with productive -n interfixation after first-member-final schwa (e.g. *Straße+n+bahn* 'tram') are the first compound types acquired (Dressler et al. 2010).

11.3.5 *Blind alley developments*

However, in the course of acquisition of nominal compounds, the Viennese boy Jan has a phase where he tends to omit this -n-interfix after final -e (schwa) and simultaneously adds an -e-interfix to consonant-final first elements (e.g. *Hase +mama* 'hare mother,' *Bank+e+sache-n* 'bank things') in a sort of output-oriented conspiracy. Such developments represent a short-term blind-alley development that children construct in deviation from adult targets and have to give up very soon (cf. Dressler et al. 2012). Such blind alleys provide the most forceful support for our constructivist approach to language acquisition. This approach (cf. Dressler and Karpf 1995) assumes that children acquire language by constructing themselves patterns by self-organizing processes (autopoiesis).

But how are such deviating child constructions motivated or constrained? Is it possible that "anything goes"?

The most spectacular cases of blind-alley construction within our project have occurred in the course of development of the Greek boy Christos in his attempts to acquire the Greek subjunctive introduced by the particle *na* (Christofidou and Kappa 1998). In a first blind alley he omitted the particle and lengthened the root vowel of the verb, although Modern Greek has no distinctive vowel length; in a second attempt he replaced the particle by a reduplicative syllable, although Modern Greek lacks reduplication as a grammatical operation. Thus he replaced the 3.SG. subjunctive of 'to cut' [na 'kopsi] from indicative ['kovi] first with ['ko:pi], then with [ko'kopsi], two operations which Natural Morphology can partially motivate. Both vowel lengthening and reduplication are iconic means of signalling marked categories, and in Modern Greek the subjunctive is a marked category in opposition to the unmarked verb category of indicative. Coincidentally, Ancient Greek (albeit in a formally slightly different way) has also used vowel lengthening for marking the subjunctive and reduplication for marking the marked tenses perfect and aorist. Thus Christos has reinvented two natural Ancient Greek techniques widespread in the languages of the world.

Such blind alley developments and their constraints present a challenge to both nativist and usage-based models, because they can be neither explained by grammatical universals of Universal Grammar (UG) nor by imitation of the adult input: in the case of Christos' two blind alleys in his attempt to acquire the Greek subjunctive, there is simply no concrete model in the input, and in the case of Jan's blind alley in acquiring German compounds he moved away from the adult target in a wrong direction which had no productive outcome. A special article on blind alleys in the longitudinal data of our crosslinguistic project is in preparation.

11.3.6 *Potential vs. illegal plurals in acquisition and processing*

Here we report on the results of joint work on the acquisition of German plurals, based on a plural well-formedness judgment test in the form of an online processing test of 114 6- to 10-year-old children compared with forty adults and with spontaneous longitudinal child corpora (cf. Korecky-Kröll et al. 2012). The test stimuli excluded the most productive -*s* and -*en* plural formation and the unproductive -*er* suffixation, but consisted of moderately productive and unproductive -*e* and zero plurals with and without umlaut. In the stimulus word list we excluded as far as possible plurals with high token frequency and words which did not appear in the inputs of our child–mother corpora.

The morphology-theoretical basis for establishing the stimulus list was our graded productivity model (Libben et al. 2002; Dressler 2003; Laaha et al. 2006). As a first step we graded productivity according to whether a plural pattern (or rule) applies to loan words, especially if these contain unfitting properties that must be changed. For example, French inanimate masculine nouns ending in an *e* muet have been and still are integrated into German as feminines in *e*-schwa obligatorily having an -*n* plural, thus French *le bel étage* lit. 'the beautiful floor' > German *die Belletage*, PL. *die Belletage+n* (with femininization even in the assumed French orthography, i.e. after fem. *belle* with a geminate). A much less important sign of productivity is diachronic change from an unproductive or even productive pattern into a new productive pattern. Thus German *der General*, loaned from French *le général* had first an -*s* plural: *die General+s*, then it changed to an -*e* plural without umlaut: *General+e*, but in 1866 at the battle of Königgrätz Prussian *General+e* defeated Austrian and Saxon *Generäl+e*, and later this -*e* plural with umlaut *Generäl+e* became the only plural of *General*. Thus -*e* plurals with and without umlaut of masculine and neuter nouns are at least moderately productive.

In a second step we established whether a productive pattern competes in a given context with another productive pattern or not. Non-competing patterns are more productive than competing ones, because they are more reliable, therefore also easier for children to apply (cf. Bates and MacWhinney 1987). Thus the -*n* plural is completely productive after final schwa, whereas the competing -*s* plus -*e* plurals with and without umlaut are three competing patterns for masculine nouns ending in a consonant and are therefore less productive.

If a productive rule forms in the right context a non-existing plural, then these plurals are potential (e.g. nowadays *General+e, General+s*), whereas a conceivable plural *die *Belletage+s* is illegal. Other cases of illegality are the never occurring patterns of an -*s* or -*(e)n* plural with umlaut.

Our stimulus inventory then consisted of one-third each of actual, potential (but non-existing), and illegal plurals. The fifty-eight stimulus sets (thus 174 stimuli) fell into five supersets: Superset 1 consisted of productive actual masculine -*e* plurals, potential -*e* plurals with umlaut, and illegal -*en* plurals with umlaut, for example *Buss +e* vs. *Büss+e* vs. *Büss+en* 'bus-es.' Superset 2 consisted of unproductive actual feminine -*e* plurals with umlaut (e.g. *Bräut+e* 'bride-s' from *Braut*), potential -*en* plurals and illegal -*e* plurals without umlaut. Superset 3 consisted of productive actual masculine -*e* plurals with umlaut (e.g. *Küss+e* 'kiss-es'), potential plurals without umlaut, and illegal -*en* plurals. Superset 4 consisted of productive actual zero plurals of masculines (e.g. *Anker* 'anchor-s'), unproductive zero plurals with umlaut, and illegal -*s* plurals with umlaut. Superset 5 consisted of unproductive zero plurals with umlaut (e.g. *Äpfel* 'apple-s'), potential plurals without umlaut, and again illegal -*s* plurals with umlaut. Clearly, in the same way as productivity, potentiality and illegality are matters of degree, just as previous experiments with adults had shown (e.g. Spina and Dressler 2002).

We measured both the accuracy and latency and our results are illustrated in Figure 11.1.

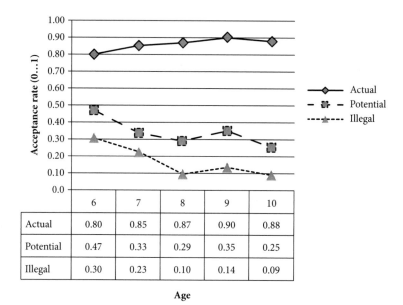

	6	7	8	9	10
Actual	0.80	0.85	0.87	0.90	0.88
Potential	0.47	0.33	0.29	0.35	0.25
Illegal	0.30	0.23	0.10	0.14	0.09

Age

FIGURE 11.1 Acceptance rates for actual, potential, and illegal plural forms across the five age groups

Source: from Korecky-Kröll et al. (2012: 45) from *Morphology* (Verlag Springer).

As shown in Figure 11.1, acceptance rates for actual words were all at the 80% level and above, whereas acceptance rates for potential and illegal words were all below 50%. For all age groups, actual plural forms were accepted significantly more often than incorrect potential and illegal forms, while incorrect but potential plural forms were accepted significantly more often than incorrect illegal plural forms. The acceptance of actual forms increasingly approaches but does not reach a 100% ceiling, in contrast to adults as well as to much younger children in spontaneous longitudinal corpora: This difference in success rates between spontaneous and test data is due to the greater language awareness needed in test performance and due to test artifacts. As expected, the acceptance of incorrect forms decreased with age (significance: $p = .0008$ for actual, $p = .0014$ for non-existing forms).

A regression analysis of response times to potential vs. illegal forms resulted in significant facilitating effects of age and plural frequency. In addition, potentiality had a significant effect ($t = 4.61$), that is, it took children significantly longer to reject potential plurals than illegal plurals. (Supersets 2 and 3 are rejected significantly faster than Superset 1. Supersets 4 and 5 do not differ from Superset 1, which is on the intercept.)

The major results of our study are: the token frequency of actual plural forms played a significant role in children's acceptance rates and response times, but this was not the case for adults who know the difference between existing and non-existing plurals much more than children. As expected, the degree of productivity also played a significant role, but in addition another influential factor emerged as a conflicting motivation in this judgment test: both actual and potential -*e* plurals with umlaut (which originated diachronically by morphologization of a phonological process) were judged better than corresponding -*e* plurals without umlaut (cf. Korecky-Kröll et al. 2012). This fits Dressler's (1985) assumption that stem vowel umlaut preceding the plural suffix is synchronically a useful redundant co-signal of plural formation, and this property made plurals sound better to the child and adult test participants.

A competing model that has made interesting alternative theoretical hypotheses on the German plurals which we tested, and that has also made interesting predictions on their acquisition is Köpcke's (1998, cf. Bittner and Köpcke 2001) schema model. Among actual plurals, he assigns to -*en* and -*s* plurals, which we excluded from our investigation, the highest cue validity (cf. Bates and MacWhinney 1987), because there are many more plurals than singulars that end in either -*en* or -*s*. To -*e* plurals (with or without umlaut) he assigns rather low cue validity and to zero plurals (with or without umlaut) the lowest degree. This may account for children's higher acceptance rates of Supersets 2 and 3 than of Supersets 4 and 5, but it cannot account for the slightness of these differences or for the much lower acceptance rates of Superset 1. Nor can Köpcke's model explain why reaction times for the zero-suffix of Supersets 4 and 5 are nearly as fast as for the suffixed Superset 3 and much faster than for the other suffixes in Supersets 2 and 1. It is unclear whether the predictions of this schema model should also hold for potential plurals. If this were so, then it would not account for the differences in acceptance rates of the different supersets.

Köpcke (1998: 309) assigns medium cue validity to umlaut, the relatively highest one to labiopalatal umlauts. But when we counted such umlauted plurals and structurally similar singular base words in the input of our children, we found that, in the inputs, singulars of the type *Büchse* 'box' and *Körper* 'body' greatly outnumber similar plurals of the type *Füchs+e* 'fox-es' (SG. *Fuchs*) and *Öfen* 'oven-s' (SG. *Ofen*). As a consequence, there is in children's input no increase whatsoever of cue validity through umlaut. Köpcke (1998: 308) also correctly assigns low degrees of salience, type frequency, and iconicity to umlaut. But all this does not explain why umlauted masculine -*e* plurals are preferred to non-umlauted ones.

Thus, in this case of conflicting motivations between two different models, the results of our tests and the analysis of spontaneous longitudinal data supported our approach. As to frequency accounts, the motivations proposed by Natural Morphology combine with frequency motivations, but neither of the two motivation types can completely replace the others. And this holds for all cases discussed in this chapter.

11.4 Conclusion

The issue of competing motivations is central to argumentation in linguistics and to the understanding of the results of empirical investigations. The reason for this is that competing motivations address the central matter of any scholarly endeavour— why does something happen? As we have demonstrated in the taxonomy offered in the initial sections of this paper, this too is often not as straightforward as it may seem. In the case of competing motivations, there is often an underlying assumption that there is a single reason "why" something happens. Therefore, if there is more than one candidate motivation, we assume that one of them must be wrong, and the task is thus to determine which one.

This situation is quite different from one in which we begin with the assumption that many factors contribute to a particular phenomenon. Here there are many reasons "why." Our task, then, is to try to understand the relative importance of each factor. This, of course, assumes that such factors are independent. But very often they are not. So, in the case of non-independent factors, an added challenge is to understand how they interact. Finally, there is another issue to consider: It is very difficult to point to aspects of language use that can be fully explained by one or more putative factors or motivations. This is easily seen in the results of experiments in which statistically significant results obtain, but, on closer inspection, the experimental factors investigated account for a relatively small proportion of the variance. These can be seen as cases of partial motivation. The key question is to what extent they are indicative of explanatory insufficiency.

In the examples provided of real instances of competing motivations in our research, it is indeed the case that the different types enumerated above represent much more than a logical taxonomy of possibilities. Rather they represent key differences in the way that we can resolve conflict among motivations in order to advance understanding. Moravcsik's dictum "conflict resolution may be the central goal of theory building" (2010: 662) clearly also holds for our approach, as it has held for Natural Phonology from its very beginnings in 1969.

12

On system pressure competing with economic motivation

MARTIN HASPELMATH

12.1 Introduction

In this chapter, I highlight and discuss a type of competition between two motivating factors that has not played a significant role in linguistic research so far: the competition between frequency-based form minimization (= "economic motivation," Haiman 1983) and the tendency of grammatical coding to target entire classes of items (= "system pressure"):

(1) two motivating principles in competition
   a. frequency-based form minimization ("economy")
      More frequent forms tend to be shorter than rarer forms.

   b. class-based grammatical coding ("system pressure")
      Rules of grammar generally target large classes of items, rather than individual expressions or small classes.

For example, it has long been well-known (since Greenberg 1966a; Croft 1990) that singulars are shorter than plurals, and often zero, because singulars are more frequent than plurals. But while this is true in general (e.g. English *book* is almost twice as frequent as *books* in corpora), not all nouns have the same frequency distribution; for example, English *eyes* is about three times as frequent as *eye*, yet it has a longer form with an additional suffix *-s*. The case of *eye/eyes* is thus unexpected from an economy point of view. Evidently, what is going on here is that *eye/eye-s* conforms to the majority pattern *book/books*, that is, system pressure wins over economy.

In a number of ways, frequency-based form minimization is a clearer concept than system pressure: Economy has long been known to work at the lexical level (Zipf 1935), and in the domain of grammar, too, economic motivation has been shown to be a very important motivating factor. The basic principle is very simple: Concepts that are used very frequently are expressed by short forms because they are highly predictable, and the more predictable an aspect of a message is, the less coding effort one needs to get it across to the hearer. The predictions are clear and easy to test, because one can simply count the occurrences and inspect the length of the forms. Moreover, the economy-based explanation of grammatical patterns is highly general and need not appeal to specific properties of grammatical organization, or even to specific properties of a subclass of rational beings or higher cognition: Economical behavior seems to be characteristic of all types of life, and of all systems that have limited resources.

But in this chapter I argue that one should not overlook another factor, which is specifically cognitive and specifically linguistic: The tendency of human language users to organize linguistic forms into systems, where classes of forms behave similarly. This factor has long been known to linguists by the name of "system pressure," and fundamentally, "analogy" refers to the same tendency to treat forms like other similar forms. In recent decades, functionally oriented linguists have tended to focus on processing or usage over system. They have preferred item-specific analyses and have tended to emphasize the heterogeneity of lexical classes. And indeed, if language learning is item-specific (Tomasello 2003a) and lexical storage involves exemplars (Pierrehumbert 2001), one would not expect much homogeneity. System pressure is a factor that is not often highlighted these days (but see Blevins and Blevins 2009), and the insight of structuralism that languages tend to be coherent systems has not found a comfortable place in functional linguistics and competing motivations accounts.

So in this chapter, I will argue that language structures are optimized both for processing or usage (economic motivation) and for systematicity (system pressure), and that these can be thought of as competing factors. I begin with a general discussion of form minimization in language (Section 12.2), illustrating it with the classical cases (and some less well-known cases) of economic motivation. The main observations are in Sections 12.3–12.4, where I show that economic motivation by itself cannot explain the tendency for entire lexeme classes or subclasses to behave alike. In Section 12.5 I highlight some logically possible systems that are not attested, before concluding with some brief remarks in Section 12.6.

12.2 Frequency-based form minimization ("economy")

Form is generally minimized in languages when it is not required for comprehension, and this may happen for a variety of reasons: A meaning may be inferrable from the pragmatic context (e.g. a continuing topic may be expected and hence zero-coded), it may be predictable from the grammatical context (e.g. the future tense need not be expressed overtly in a conditional protasis), or it may be predictable from the fact that the meaning occurs significantly more often than a contrasting meaning. The latter case, frequency-based form minimization, is probably the most important economy effect that shapes grammatical systems. Since Greenberg (1966a) and Croft (1990), this economy effect has been widely known, and has often been discussed under the heading of *markedness* (see Haspelmath 2006 for reasons to avoid this term). Economically motivated contrasts are pervasive in grammar, not only in classical inflectional categories like number and tense, but also in syntax, such as possessive constructions and purpose clauses. Table 12.1 gives a representative set of examples of frequency-based economic motivation, where one category is systematically more frequent and hence shorter (typically zero) across languages, while the other category is less frequent and hence longer. For many of these cases, the explanation of the form asymmetries in terms of frequency asymmetries is not widely recognized yet, but I refer the reader to the works mentioned in the second column of Table 12.1 for further discussion and justification (see also Haspelmath 2008a, 2008b.)

TABLE 12.1. **Frequency-based grammatical zero-overt contrasts**

Domain	Contrasting categories	Examples (Zero/short form—Overt/long form)
Number:	singular/plural (Table 12.3)	English *book-Ø—book-s*
Tense:	present/future	Spanish *cant-Ø-a* 'sings'—*cant-ar-á* 'will sing'
Subject person:	third/second (Table 12.4–12.5)	Polish *ma-Ø* 'he has'—*ma-sz* 'you have'
Argument role:	subject (nominative)/object (accusative) (Table 12.6)	Hungarian *János-Ø* (nominative)—*János-t* (accusative)
Predicate:	action predicate (verb)/property predicate (adjective) (Croft 1991)	English *she Ø know-s—she **is** tall*
Possession:	inalienable/alienable (Section 12.4)	Lango *wì Ø rwòt* [head king]—*gwôkk **à** lócə* [dog of man]
Causation:	noncausative/causative (Haspelmath et al. 2014)	Turkish *öl-Ø-dü* 'died'—*öl-**dür**-dü* 'killed'
Anaphora:	disjoint/reflexive (Haspelmath 2008c)	*Pat saw her-Ø—Pat saw her-**self**.*
Verb orientation:	introverted/extroverted (Haiman 1983; Haspelmath 2008c)	Russian *ona moet-**sja*** 'she washes'—*ona vidit **sebja*** 'she sees herself'
Purpose clauses:	motion verbs/nonmotion verbs (Schmidtke-Bode 2009)	French *je rentre Ø travailler* 'I get back in order to work'—*je travaille **pour** gagner de l'argent* 'I work in order to earn money'
Person and role:	canonical person-role association/non-canonical person-role association (Haspelmath 2004a)	French *il me Ø le présentera* 'he'll present him to me'—*il me présentera **à lui*** 'he'll present me to him'

Two points should be highlighted in connection with my claim that all these phenomena involve form minimization due to frequency: First, the minimization effect is not due to entrenchment or routinization, as was claimed repeatedly by Joan Bybee (Bybee 2001, 2006; see also Croft 2008), for example:

The explanation for [the reducing effect of high token frequency] is that the articulatory representation of words and sequences of words is made up of neuromotor routines. When sequences of neuromotor routines are repeated, their execution becomes more fluent. This increased fluency is the result of the establishment of a new routine, as when a group of words comes to be processed as a single unit.... In the new routine articulatory gestures reduce and overlap as the routine is repeated. (Bybee 2006: 714–15)

Bybee portrays the process of reduction as exclusively speaker-based, and predictability plays no role in her account. However, while routinization and entrenchment is certainly a prerequisite for shortening, it is not a sufficient condition. This can easily be seen from the fact that highly entrenched and routinized forms are not reduced when they are not predictable: For example, even though speakers say their names very often, they do not reduce them when they tell someone their name for the first time, because in this situation, the form of the name is not predictable. Routinization does lead to fluency, of course (so when we say our names, we do not insert hesitation pauses), but fluency by itself does not lead to reduction. Speakers always have the hearers' needs in mind and reduce their utterances only when parts of them are highly predictable. Moreover, in the majority of cases, contrasts such as those exemplified in Table 12.1 do not arise from differential reduction (with more frequent forms being reduced more than the less frequent forms), but from differential spread of a newly grammaticalized, longer form. For example, after a pidginized form of English in Melanesia lost the number contrast (*house* 'house' or 'houses'), this contrast was reconstituted using *all* as a new overt plural marker. In present-day Tok Pisin, the plural marker *ol* is used widely, and the contrast *haus* 'house' vs. *ol haus* 'houses' again shows economical coding. But this did not arise by any kind of reduction; instead, the singular did not develop a new number marker to begin with (and there never was a system of the kind *wan haus* 'house' vs. *ol haus* 'houses'). The rise of economical coding patterns is discussed in some detail in Haspelmath (2008b).

Second, the minimization effect is not due to iconicity (some kind of "markedness matching," with "marked forms" expressing "marked meanings"), but to economic motivation. This can easily be seen from the fact that "markedness values" may be reversed in special cases ("markedness reversal"), and this happens precisely when the category that is usually more frequent happens to be rarer in a special context. For example, with some nouns the plural form is actually more frequent than the singular form, and it is precisely in such cases that some languages also have longer singulars ("singulatives"), as in the Welsh example *plu-en* 'feather' vs. *plu* 'feathers.' And in one mood, the imperative, the second person is more frequent than the third person, so here many languages have longer third-person forms than second person forms. More examples are given in Table 12.2 (see Haspelmath 2008a for discussion).

TABLE 12.2. Frequency reversals in special cases

Number:	**singular**/plural	Welsh *plu-en* 'feather'—*plu-Ø* 'feathers'
Subject person:	**third**/second	Hungarian imperative: *él-j-en* 'let him live'—*él-j-Ø* 'live! (2SG.IMPV)'
Argument role:	**subject** (ergative)/object (absolutive)	Mangarrayi **na**-*ḷandi* (ergative) 'tree'— *ḷandi* (absolutive) (only inanimates)
Causation:	**noncausative**/causative	German *öffnet **sich*** 'opens (INTR)'—*öffnet* 'opens (TR)'
Anaphora:	**disjoint**/reflexive	*Pat saw **her**—Pat washed Ø.*

These examples cannot be explained on the basis of markedness or iconicity, but they follow directly from frequency-based form minimization.

12.3 Frequencies differ across lexemes

While on the whole the frequency differences in the contrasts in Table 12.1 are robust, the frequency differences are not uniform. In most cases, there are some contexts that do not conform to the general pattern of the category, and often these contexts are particular lexemes.

For example, in the category of **number** (singular/plural), the singular is more frequent when we look at the entire class of nouns of English, but with some nouns such as *feather/feathers*, the plural is more frequent. (That this may have an effect on the coding that was observed by Tiersma 1982.) Table 12.3 shows some illustrative frequency figures.

TABLE 12.3. English (British National Corpus of English)

	SG		PL	Percentage of SG forms
person	24671	*persons*	4034	86
house	49295	*houses*	9840	83
hare	488	*hares*	136	78
bear	1182	*bears*	611	65
feather	487	*feathers*	810	38
(All SG)	3,234,943	(all PL)	1,526,202	68

In the category of **person**, the third person is more frequent when we look at all verbs of Russian, but with some verbs such as *xotet'* 'want,' *čuvstvovat'* 'feel', and *nadejat'sja* 'hope,' the first person is more frequent. Table 12.4 shows some illustrative frequency figures.

TABLE 12.4. **Russian (National Corpus of Russian)**

3SG		1SG		Verb gloss	Percentage of 3SG forms
rabotaet	11,698	*rabotaju*	2,375	'work'	83
spit	5,165	*splju*	1,444	'sleep'	78
p'et	3,231	*p'ju*	1,681	'drink'	66
xočet	24,081	*xoču*	31,811	'want'	43
čuvstvuet	5,270	*čuvstvuju*	7,108	'feel'	43
nadeetsja	1,566	*nadejus'*	7,858	'hope'	17
All 3SG	3,909,539	All 1SG	1,315,469		75

The situation in English is completely parallel, as is shown in Table 12.5.

TABLE 12.5. **English (British National Corpus of English)**

3SG		1SG		Percentage of 3SG forms
works	6176	*I work*	489	93
sleeps	243	*I sleep*	71	77
drinks	182	*I drink*	70	72
wants	8,729	*I want*	9,283	48
feels	3,189	*I feel*	4,110	44
hopes	1,797	*I hope*	5,404	25

In the category of **argument role**, the subject role is more frequent than the object role when we look at all nouns. As a result, in languages with nominative-accusative case-marking, the nominative tends to be zero and the accusative overtly coded. However, there are some nouns (in fact many nouns, such as *tree*, *car*, and *money* in Table 12.6) which occur more often in object function than in subject function.

Although we have seen here only examples from English and Russian, we can assume that very similar figures will be found in all languages, because there is no reason to suspect that the frequency distributions have to do with language-particular structural properties. Rather, it seems clear that the speakers' pragmatic needs are responsible for these differences: Speakers more often have occasion to talk about multiple feathers than about a single feather, because feathers normally occur together in large numbers. When speakers talk about experiences (desires, feelings, and hopes), they more often talk about themselves, because only their own experiences are directly accessible to them, or because their own experiences are more interesting to them. And finally, nouns denoting people occur more often as subjects because people tend to be agents and inanimate objects patients. Thus, where an observed frequency asymmetry has an obvious universal pragmatic motivation, getting frequency data from a broader and more balanced sample of languages and texts is not high priority.

TABLE 12.6. **English (ICE-GB)**

	Subject	Object	Percentage in subject role
friend	115	13	90
boy	14	2	88
people	801	180	82
president	18	4	82
husband	24	7	77
teacher	9	3	75
woman	37	15	71
sister	11	6	65
daughter	17	10	63
house	56	43	57
dog	10	8	56
sky	3	3	50
tree	9	10	47
car	39	47	45
book	41	63	39
money	28	125	18
All nouns	27,345	22,147	55

12.4 Class-based grammatical coding ("system pressure")

Despite the fact that the actual frequencies show continuous differences, as seen in Tables 12.3–12.6, the patterns of economical coding that languages exhibit affect grammatical classes. Let us look at four different representative cases.

12.4.1 *Number marking*

In English and many other languages, plural marking is used for all nouns, not just those that occur more frequently in the singular. Languages like Welsh, where some nouns show the reverse pattern, are quite rare. Thus, in most languages the economic motivation asserts itself at the level of the lexeme class as a whole, not at the level of the individual lexeme. The coding *feather-s* for the more frequent form (contrasting with *feather-Ø*, the rarer form) is not economical at all, and is actually anti-economical. In this case and similar cases, we are evidently dealing with system pressure beating economy. The English system is more regular than the Welsh system, and can be thought of as showing analogical extension of the plural-marking pattern from the normal nouns to the nouns with frequently occurring plurals. Thus, system pressure here is a motivating factor that competes with economy. In English-type languages, system pressure wins and overt plurals are used even with "feather"-type nouns. In Welsh-type languages, economy wins and those nouns that have more frequent plurals have overtly marked singulars instead. Welsh is thus easier to process, but shows less system uniformity (making it more difficult to acquire).

12.4.2 *Verbal person-marking*

With person-marking on verbs, the power of system pressure seems to be even stronger than in the case of number marking. I am not aware of a language in which different verbs show different person-marking patterns: zero marking of the third person with standard verbs like "work," "drink," but zero marking of the first person and overt marking of the third with experiential verbs like "want," "feel," "hope." From the point of view of economy, one would expect to find such differential treatment of verbs, but all languages that I know of rank system pressure higher than economy in this domain.

12.4.3 *Argument coding*

In the domain of argument coding, the situation is the opposite: Not very many languages have a system pressure effect that is so strong that all noun phrases, regardless of the animacy of the referent, get accusative marking. An example of this relatively rare type is Hungarian, which has accusative marking on every noun or pronoun (e.g. *király-t* [king-ACC], *lov-at* [horse-ACC], and also *ház-at* [house-ACC], *kez-et* [hand-ACC], *semmi-t* [nothing-ACC]).

In the older Indo-European languages, accusative marking is very widespread, too, but sometimes it does not show a clear economy pattern because the nominative is overtly coded as well (e.g. Latin *Marcu-s* [Mark-NOM], *Marcu-m* [Mark-ACC], and nouns of the neuter gender do not show an accusative case that is distinct from the nominative (e.g. Greek *déndro-n* [tree-NOM/ACC]). The nouns of neuter gender are generally inanimate, so here we see a limited animacy effect: Inanimate nouns are less likely to get overt coding for the accusative than animate nouns. This is a very widespread tendency, known by the label of "differential object marking," which hides the fact that "undifferentiated object marking" of the Hungarian type seems to be much less common. That system pressure rarely obliterates economy effects with object marking in nouns may be due to the fact that full-NP subjects (as opposed to subjects expressed by a bound person form or by zero) are not much more frequent than objects: In Table 12.6, we see that only 55% of all non-oblique nouns in the English ICE-GB corpus have the subject role, while 45% have the object role.

Thus, there is a tendency in languages to treat the members of a lexeme class alike, even if this makes the system less efficient from a processing point of view. With lexemes of very high frequency, languages sometimes tolerate radical irregularity, but the great majority of lexemes in most languages inflect according to some general pattern.

This does not have to be the pattern of an entire word class, but it can be a subclass. For example, in Russian only nouns of the animate lexeme subclass show an overt accusative case that contrasts with zero in the nominative singular (this zero/overt alternation is not the only possibility; some inflection classes have overt markers for both cases, and others have zero for both, but these are irrelevant here). But again, the actual frequency figures show a fairly continuous picture. Some nouns have overwhelmingly more subject than object uses, while others show many more object than subject uses, as we saw in Table 12.6 and similarly for Russian in Table 12.7 (but note that the accusative case in Russian cannot be directly compared with the direct-object function in English, because accusative case also occurs after several prepositions).

TABLE 12.7. **Russian (National Corpus of Russian)**

	Nominative	Accusative	Percentage in nominative case
sestra 'sister'	8974	2647	77
kot 'cat'	4068	1479	73
mal'čik 'boy'	17883	6722	73
otec 'father'	49004	30667	62
cerkov' 'church'	13511	13467	50
derevo 'tree'	5749	5694	50
den'gi 'money'	45018	45582	50
lošad' 'horse'	9762	9754	50
mašina 'car'	19149	22717	46

In Russian, system pressure maps this continuous picture onto two discrete classes, animate nouns (with zero nominative singular) and inanimate nouns. In other languages, the cut-off point is different. Thus, in English it is only personal pronouns that have a nominative-accusative distinction (*he* vs. *him*, etc.), and other languages have yet other divisions of the continuum (see, e.g., Croft 2003: 168).

12.4.4 *Adnominal possession: alienable vs. inalienable*

In adnominal possessive constructions, quite a few languages (but none of the major languages of Europe and East Asia) show a contrast between kinship terms and/or body part terms on the one hand and other nouns on the other. The examples from Malinke in (2) are fairly typical.

(2) Malinke (Creissels 2009: 119)
    a. *mùsú Ø búlù*
       woman Ø arm
       'the woman's arm'
    b. *kě yé 'dèregê*
       man of suit
       'the man's suit'

In most cases where there is such a contrast, the alienable possessive construction has overt marking, while the inalienable construction has zero marking. Again, the pattern is economically motivated: With kinship and body-part terms, the presence of a possessor is very frequent, so it is highly expected, and therefore the coding of the possessive relationship is relatively redundant.

To give an idea of the frequencies with which a range of nouns occur as possessed nouns in a possessive construction, consider the exemplary English nouns in Table 12.8 (this takes into account only cases where the possessor is a preceding NP with genitive *'s*).

TABLE 12.8. **English possessed nouns (British National Corpus of English)**

Body-part terms	Total	Possessed	Percentage of possessed
skin	347	72	21
wrist	49	17	35
leg	527	191	36
ear	222	91	41
legs	522	255	49
head	1699	868	51
hair	1154	624	54
ears	207	114	55
hands	970	545	56
fingers	351	210	60
nose	372	235	63
		mean possessed	46

Kinship terms	Total	Possessed	Percentage of possessed
aunt	111	44	40
son	733	351	48
mother	1892	1107	59
father	1473	888	60
sister	636	402	63
wife	1107	710	64
daughter	555	358	65
brother	762	518	68
husband	818	605	74
grandmother	88	69	78
		mean possessed	49

Alienable nouns	Total	Possessed	Percentage of possessed
tree	511	13	3
health	1601	109	7
work	6226	577	9
bed	1845	160	9
money	6598	671	10
book	2271	272	12
job	3960	584	15
car	3925	617	16
house	4768	1059	22
bedroom	678	199	29
		mean possessed	15

Again, there is a continuum of different frequencies, but we see that the mean possessed frequencies of the body-part terms and the kinship terms is much higher than the mean frequencies of the "alienable nouns" (i.e. diverse non-kinship and non-body-part words). But system pressure typically leads languages to assign nouns to fairly homogeneous lexeme subclasses, that is, a class of "alienable nouns" and a class of "inalienable nouns." The latter are mostly restricted to the semantically homogeneous classes of body-part terms and kinship terms.

What is noteworthy in this example is that, at least in English, kinship terms and body-part terms do not occur more frequently with a possessor than without a possessor. The average possessed frequency of the body-part terms in Table 12.8 is 46%, which is quite far from a clear majority. However, what matters is not the relation between possessed and unpossessed occurrences of nouns, but the relation between the proportions of possessed occurrences of different types of nouns. When a kinship term occurs, it is about as likely to be possessed as to be unpossessed, but its likelihood to be possessed is much higher than the likelihood of an alienable noun to be possessed.

12.5 The power of system pressure: Some unattested systems

Word length correlates with frequency in a way that matches the continuity of frequency relatively directly. On the whole, the less frequent a word is, the more segments and the more syllables it has. Words do not normally fall into clearly delimited length classes.

The effect of frequency-based minimization on grammatical patterns is different: Here usually sets of lexemes behave uniformly, regardless of the frequencies of the individual items.

So we do not find languages where each word behaves differently. Although it would be easy to imagine and probably learnable, a language with a different plural form for each noun is not attested. Such a language would have the advantage that the length of the plural marker could be closely attuned to the frequency of the plural form. From the perspective of processing optimization, this would be optimal. But the system pressure prevents such languages from coming into being.

We also do not find languages with a substantial number of different lexeme classes, each covering a certain range of the frequency scale, and each with a different length of the grammatical marker. A hypothetical language of this kind (using pseudo-English forms) is shown in the last column of Table 12.9.

TABLE 12.9. **An unattested system**

English	SG	PL	Percentage of singular	Hypothetical language
house	49295	9840	83	*house-Ø/house-ssss*
hare	488	136	78	*hare-Ø/hare-sss*
bear	1182	611	66	*bear-Ø/bear-ss*
window	9936	8506	54	*window-Ø/window-s*
feather	487	810	38	*feather-one/feather-Ø*
parent	3706	15956	19	*parent-oneone/parent-Ø*

The plural of *house* is much rarer, relatively speaking, than the plural of *bear* or *window*, so it would be efficient to have shorter plural markers with the latter than with the former. But a language where more than three different markers with different lengths are found seems to be unattested. Earlier in Table 12.1 we saw one example from the domain of grammar where the relevant contrast is not between a zero form and an overt form, but between a short form and a long form: Russian reflexives with introverted verbs (*moet-sja* 'she washes Ø') vs. Russian reflexives with extroverted verbs (*vidit sebja* 'sees herself'). This is not very common, but it is occasionally found. (The English contrast, between zero in *she washes Ø* and an overt reflexive is *she sees herself,* is less unusual.) But more than two or three different levels, as in Table 12.9, would go against the demands of system pressure.

12.6 Concluding remarks

We have thus seen that economic motivation, even though it explains many of the observed marking asymmetries in grammar, is far from explaining everything. In addition to processing optimization, we also have to assume a kind of system optimization that is less easy to characterize and to delimit. While it is no longer puzzling that in language after language, the more frequent grammatical categories are zero-coded, we do not really know why language systems tend to treat whole lexeme classes alike or divide lexemes into very few (often just two) major subclasses.

When there are subclasses, the divisions are typically along semantic–syntactic lines: Animate vs. inanimate (or human vs. non-human), body part vs. artifact, intransitive vs. transitive verb, stative vs. dynamic, and so on. These major semantic–syntactic divisions recur in different languages, so there seems to be something very natural about them, but we do not know what it is.

Another question that needs further attention in the future is what it is that motivates system pressure. One obvious answer is that while form minimization makes language use more efficient, systematicity makes language easier to acquire. The fact that different inflectional classes present considerable difficulty to second language learners indicates that at least adult language acquisition is made easier by systematicity. But for small children, systems such as the hypothetical system in Table 12.9 may not pose a significantly greater challenge than the English system, even though it may take a little longer to acquire. Another, related factor is memory. A reviewer notes:

Generalizations make acquisition easier as well as reducing the burden on memorization. Thus, ultimately, it is a kind of economizing tendency, just as producing shorter forms for predictable meanings is a matter of economy.

One may see it this way, but it should be noted that memory limitations seem to be much less severe than the articulatory and time constraints on processing. We can easily learn multiple languages, so our memory capacity seems to far exceed the needs of storing a single language. Thus, the precise cognitive factors favoring systematicity over economy in so many cases will have to be the subject of future research.

13

Apparently competing motivations in morphosyntactic variation

BRITTA MONDORF

13.1 Introduction

Competing motivations in language systems are not easily accommodated into linguistic theory-building (cf. also Mondorf 2010). Traditional grammatical theory had, for a long time, relegated language variation to the realm of performance, thereby declaring it out of bounds for linguistic theory-building. And even in sociolinguistics, the cradle of linguistic variability, research on morphological or syntactic variation, as opposed to phonological or lexical variation, was occasionally impaired by erroneous assumptions concerning an alleged *uniformity of syntax*, which was regarded as "the marker of cohesion in society" by Hudson (1980: 44, 47). By contrast, functional approaches, which seek to explain language form in terms of its function, have tried to accommodate the true extent of grammatical variation, welcoming it as an instructive challenge for linguistic theory-building.

Several volumes explicitly dedicated to grammatical variation (cf. Chambers et al. 2003; Rohdenburg and Mondorf 2003; Kortmann et al. 2004; Dufter et al. 2009; Peters et al. 2009; Rohdenburg and Schlüter 2009; Maguire and McMahon 2011) provide ample evidence for the view that grammatical variation is much more pervasive than formerly expected. This also means that any theory that seeks to reach descriptive adequacy and predictive power needs to come to grips with the internal and external factors that shape and design grammar. The number and diversity of factors constraining grammatical variation can sharpen our eye for uncovering underlying cognitive principles and generalizations. These can neither be dealt with by strictly modular models nor by models assuming a top-down processing in which phonology does not influence grammar. The former fail to account for the observation that languages system-internally trade syntax against morphology (as shown, for instance, in Rosenbach 2002; Vosberg 2006; Mondorf 2009a), while the latter, in assuming a top-down processing that first determines grammatical structure and then arranges pronunciation, have been contradicted by findings showing that prosodic requirements govern morphological variation (cf.

Schlüter 2005). Similarly, typological approaches and historical linguistics addressing issues of syntheticity vs. analyticity call for integrating additional parameters from all language levels to arrive at a meaningful definition of syntheticity and a more accurate account of typological change (cf. Haspelmath 2009 and Nübling 2010 and the references therein). Thus, it is not surprising that recent conceptions of grammar emphasize the relevance of linguistic variation on all levels of language analysis, as reflected in the frameworks of *Cognitive Grammar* or *Construction Grammar*.

The present chapter brings together a range of studies that lend themselves to an explanation in terms of competing motivations in the form of *Analytic Support* (i.e. the tendency to resort to analytic rather than synthetic variants in cognitively demanding environments). It thus bridges the gap between traditionally descriptive variation linguistics and approaches based on typological and psycholinguistic principles, with the primary concern to explain competing motivations governing the choice between functionally equivalent morphological and syntactic structures.

More specifically, this chapter argues that at least some synthetic–analytic contrasts lend themselves to an explanation in terms of competing motivations governed by processing demands. Comparative alternation is a showcase of morphosyntactic variation,[1] where language users have the choice between a synthetic form (e.g. *fuller*) and an analytic variant (*more full*). What looks like competing motivations with two variants competing for the same functional domain at first glance appears to be an emergent division of labour between synthetic and analytic means of expressing comparison. Analyticity is resorted to if explicitness is required because of an increased processing effort. On the other hand, syntheticity is preferred in easy-to-process environments. The option to mitigate cognitive complexity provides the underlying motivation for the retention of morphosyntactic variation patterns.[2]

This chapter sets out to show that the findings emanating from research on comparatives can be extended to other synthetic–analytic contrasts displaying similar conflict resolution patterns (e.g. future alternation in Spanish and English, genitive alternation in English or mood alternation in English). After all, if the theoretical frameworks lending explanatory power to comparative alternation can justly claim universality, they need to be extendable to other synthetic–analytic contrasts as well. The parallels between English, Spanish, and German synthetic–analytic contrasts can be related to Evans and Levinson (2009: 429), stating that universal tendencies

---

[1] In contrast to Guerrero Medina (2011), the term morphosyntactic alternation is here taken to refer to variation involving a morphological and a syntactic variant, rather than covering the variation between either two morphological variants (which is more appropriately termed morphological variation) or two syntactic variants (i.e. syntactic variation).

[2] A vital and controversial issue that—to my knowledge—has not yet been solved, is whether analyticity/explicitness is apt to reduce processing costs in production or in comprehension. It has occasionally been assumed that syntheticity is speaker-friendly by primarily catering for the needs of the speaker/writer (input-economical), while analyticity mainly benefits the listener/reader (output-economical) (cf. Szmrecsanyi 2009: 322). Pending further psycholinguistic research the present chapter is deliberately non-committal in deciding whether analytic forms are preferred in order to decrease processing costs for the speaker/writer, for the hearer/reader, or for both. A possible experimental design would have to place some processing burden on speakers and see if their ratio of analytic forms increases.

are better explained as stable engineering solutions satisfying multiple design constraints, reflecting both cultural-historical factors and the constraints of human cognition. (Evans and Levinson 2009: 429)

Emphasizing the relevance of human cognition as the underlying force for cross-linguistic similarities and restrictions on variability, the present chapter suggests that apparently competing motivations in synthetic–analytic contrasts come to be resolved in the form of a finely-tuned division of labor in line with general processing principles. In accordance with Wasow and Arnold's (2003: 148) claim that "at least some categorical constraints are simply the limiting cases of more general statistical tendencies," we find that the synthetic vs. the analytic forms of comparative alternation are merely the extremes on a finely-graded scale ranging from 0% analytic formation to 100% analytic formation (Figure 13.1).

FIGURE 13.1 Synthetic–analytic scale for individual adjectives

Thus, we are faced with a high degree of variability raising the following question: Why does a language like English retain variation over centuries in its diachronic development rather than promoting one variant to the detriment of the other, thus creating a system in which form–meaning consistency is optimized?

The findings emanating from research on synthetic–analytic contrasts will be related to theoretical frameworks and generalizations that hold some potential for explaining morphosyntactic variation, such as:

- The Principle of Uniformity and Transparency (Wurzel 1987)
- The Competition Model (Bates and MacWhinney 1987)
- Theories of processing efficiency (Hawkins 1994)
- The Complexity Principle (Rohdenburg 1996)

as well as to type "C Contextualizing the two statements" of Moravcsik's (this volume) fourfold typology of conflict resolution:

This chapter is structured as follows: Section 13.2 draws on previous research on morphosyntactic alternation in order to pursue the question of which linguistic environments favor analytic variants over synthetic ones. Theoretical frameworks implying that analytic variants are easier to process than synthetic ones will be presented in Section 13.3, where it will be argued that analytic forms are apt to mitigate the cognitive complexity of their linguistic environments. This poses the intricate problem of delimiting and operationalizing syntheticity and analyticity dealt with in Section 13.4. The chapter closes with a conclusion showing that what appear to be competing motivations at first sight turns out to be a functionally motivated division of labor with analytic variants being resorted to in cognitively demanding situations.

13.2 In which linguistic environments do language users favor analytic variants over synthetic ones?

In a book-length study investigating the factors determining the choice between the *more*-variant (e.g. *more full*) and the *-er*-variant (e.g. *fuller*) I have shown that the analytic comparative variant tends to be resorted to in cognitively complex environments, that is, environments which exert an extra processing load, while the *-er*-variant is more prone to occur in easy-to-process environments (cf. Mondorf 2009a).[3] This distribution is well in line with the Complexity Principle stating that:

In the case of more or less explicit grammatical option(s) the more explicit one(s) tend to be chosen in cognitively complex environments. (Rohdenburg 1996: 151)

Thus, the more explicit variant (*more full*) is shown to be preferred in cognitively complex environments, a finding subsumed under the heading of *more*-support. We can now derive the notion of Analytic Support:

in cognitively complex environments that require an increased processing load, language users tend to compensate for the increased processing load by resorting to the analytic (*more*) rather than the synthetic (*-er*) variant. (Mondorf 2009a: 8)

This can be summarized as follows:

high processing load ⇒ higher ratio of *more*
low processing load ⇒ higher ratio of *-er*

The claim that the more explicit variant is preferred in cognitively complex environments requires defining two concepts. The first concerns the classification of the *more*-variant as more explicit than the *-er*-variant and the second concerns the notion of cognitive complexity.

The classification of *more* as the explicit variant is made on morphological and phonological grounds: Morphologically, *more* is a free form, while the *-er*-variant is bound. Phonologically *more* is able to receive stress, while *-er* is not.

Criteria for cognitive complexity are more difficult to formulate, partly because cognitive complexity can arise on all levels of linguistic analysis: morphology, syntax,

---

[3] Note that what is at stake here are relative frequencies. If analytic variants are claimed to be preferred in hard-to-process environments, this does not imply that their ratio is higher than that for synthetic variants, i.e. that they are the majority variant, but that their ratio is higher than it would be in easier-to-process environments.

semantics, lexicon, phonology, etc. Figure 13.2 presents an overview of twenty-six determinants that have been shown to affect comparative alternation (cf. Mondorf 2009a):

- Syntactic complexity, for instance, correlates with constituent structure viewed in terms of both length and hierarchical ordering. Consequently, claims concerning syntactic complexity need to draw on constituent structure and dependency relations. For instance, the presence of a prepositional complement can render the adjective phrase harder to process (e.g. *proud of him*). We will return to this issue in Section 13.4.6.
- By contrast, phonological complexity can arise from phonotactic principles, e.g. through the occurrence of certain consonant clusters (e.g. in words like *strict, apt*), which are typologically dispreferred in the world's languages, or through violations of rhythmic alternation patterns, etc.
- Semantic complexity can result from different accessibilities of, e.g., concrete vs. abstract concepts (described in more detail in Section 13.4.3).

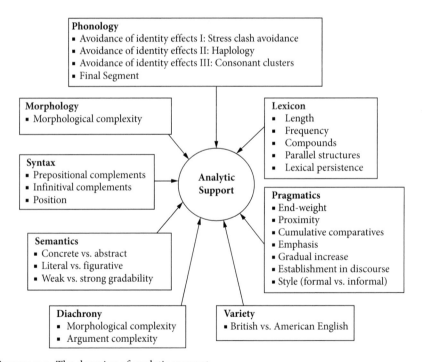

FIGURE 13.2 The domains of analytic support

Note: Figure 13.1 presents an overview of 24 factors investigated in Mondorf (2009a: 197), with the factors "style" and "lexical persistence" being supplemented here in accordance with findings reported by Mondorf (2009b: 100–5) and Szmrecsanyi (2005).

Source: Based on Mondorf (2009a: 197).

Thus, the defining features of cognitive complexity need to be developed separately for each level. This does not mean that we cannot grasp the common denominator of complexity across language levels. It just means that our measures for complexity need to adapt to these levels. Consequently, one of the problems we face when trying to define cognitive complexity is that we require a concept that is wide enough to encompass very diverse language levels (phonology, morphology, syntax, semantics, pragmatics, etc.) but at the same time narrow enough to include those—and only those—parameters that can be grasped in terms of complexity. The criteria to be discussed in the present chapter are, however, sufficiently well-established throughout the literature to permit their analysis in terms of cognitive complexity. While Figure 13.2 forms the basis for the present analysis by displaying complexity factors influencing comparative alternation as one well-researched case of synthetic–analytic contrasts, the present chapter sets out to relate these and additional complexity parameters to other synthetic–analytic contrasts, such as for example:

1. English comparative alternation: *fuller* vs. **more full**
2. English genitive alternation: *the topic's relevance* vs. *the relevance **of** the topic*
3. English future tense alternation: *will* vs. *going to*
4. English mood alternation: *if he agree-Ø* (subjunctive) or *if he agrees* (indicative) vs. *if he **should** agree* (modal periphrasis)
5. Spanish future tense alternation: *comeré* vs. **voy** *a comer*
6. German past tense alternation: Sie brauch**te**...vs. Sie **hat**...gebraucht.

It is furthermore assumed that entities that are cognitively complex are harder to process than cognitively simpler entities. This implies that delayed reaction times, higher ratios of speech errors and lower scores in serial recall tasks can be expected to correlate with compensatory use of more explicit variants. Pending psycholinguistic experiments, some of these corpus-based correlations still await independent validation. However, the in-depth analyses of the synthetic–analytic alternations covered here are characterized by a whole range of findings pointing in the same direction. Additionally, psycholinguistic evidence for the processing load of the complexity parameters presented will be adduced wherever available.

13.3 Why are analytic variants easier to process?

According to the *Principle of Uniformity and Transparency* postulated by Wurzel (1987), a high degree of form–function mapping should favor the processing of a linguistic unit, since fewer options need to be retained in working memory. Applied to morphosyntactic variation, this principle would mean that the sheer existence of a synthetic next to an analytic variant in a language should impede the processing of, for example, comparatives in English.[4] As regards the individual variants, one could argue that the *more*-variant is "better" in terms of form–function mapping, since it

---

[4] For the crucial question of determining in which cases -*er* and *more* can be conceived of as functionally equivalent, readers are referred to Mondorf (2009a: 11–13).

helps to disentangle a complex lexeme consisting of a base plus inflectional suffix by assigning each function a separate form.

The *Competition Model* by Bates and MacWhinney (1987) states that linguistic items which form reliable cues facilitate processing, while less reliable cues exert a higher processing load. A reliable cue is one that is closely linked with a specific function. Trying to apply the Competition Model to comparative alternation, we would have to find out how reliable the individual variants are as cues for the respective grammatical structure. For instance, the analytic variant *more* does not uniquely single out a degree phrase, since it can also function as quantifier:

(1)   The Americans have **more** heavy armour on the streets of Port-au-Prince than originally envisioned. [*Times* 1994]

More is not a perfect cue for comparative formation. But neither is the synthetic variant *-er*, since it has a homonymic morph which serves as agentivity marker, though not on ADJs but on nouns (cf. Köpcke 1998: 300; MacWhinney et al. 1985: 184):

(2)   paint**er**, writ**er**

If applicable at all, MacWhinney and Bates' (1985) Competition Model would predict that the analytic variant is a better cue, because *more* is closely tied to the expression of comparative degree (with the numerically small exception of quantifier uses), while the suffix *-er* is highly pervasive in other functions. However, the parameters for measuring cue applicability cannot easily be operationalized for comparative alternation: Though *more* as a quantifier is rarer and hence it is a more reliable cue for indicating comparatives, agentive *-er* attaches only to verbs, so that ambiguity would not arise at all with *-er*, which in turn might make it more reliable after all. *More* can precede adjectives in its quantifier and degree marker functions as in (1) above, which would make it potentially more ambiguous than *-er*.

Psycholinguistic research on morphologically complex words has revealed that their accessibility in the mental lexicon is constrained by an entire network of frequency-related factors. While earlier approaches have assumed that either the whole-word route is used (i.e. *fuller* would be directly accessed as one word) or the decomposed route (i.e. the components *full* + *er* would be stored and assembled on the spot), recent findings based on eye tracking suggest dual or even multiple route models which make use of all possible cues available in processing morphologically complex words (cf. Kuperman et al. 2008: 3–6; Plag 2003: 176). Comparatives offer the choice between a morphologically simple form (*more full*) and a morphologically complex one (*fuller*). However, the applicability of multiple route models to both comparative variants should not easily be discarded. After all, *more full* could also take the dual route, even though it is not morphologically complex. In the face of ample research on family size effects and other frequency-related parameters for both morphologically simple and complex words (cf. Schreuder and Baayen 1997; Hay 2001) as well as findings on the gradience of lexical fusion in adjectival compounds (*wider-spread* vs *more wide-spread* in Mondorf 2009a: 44f), we would be well-advised not to rule out the possibility that such frequency-related parameters also affect the combined processing of two separate lexemes, such as *more full*.

Another theoretical approach that can be applied to comparative alternation is Hawkins' (2003) *Theory of Processing Efficiency* which states that

language users have a choice between less form processing . . . but more dependent processing on the one hand, and more form processing (explicit marking) with less dependent processing on the other. One can speculate that the working memory demands of dependent processing across large domains exceed the processing cost of additional form (and meaning) processing through explicit marking. (Hawkins 2003: 200)

Language users thus weigh the pros and cons of the explicit *more*-variant as opposed to the more dependent *-er* variant. Note that Hawkins' (1994, 2003) approach does not conceive of working memory as capacity-constrained but rather as efficiency-based. This means that opting for *-er*, which entails more dependent processing, would not exceed the available processing capacity. It merely adds processing effort that can be avoided by choosing the more explicit analytic variant. On the other hand, when processing demands are low, we can easily afford to use the *-er* variant.

13.4 Establishing the notion of Analytic Support

One advantage of the *more*-variant that is not directly related to its analyticity but rather to ordering preferences of elements within phrases is highlighted by Hawkins' (1994) Principle of Mother Node Construction, which states that early recognition of phrase structure facilitates processing.

in the left to right parsing of a sentence a word that can uniquely determine or classify a phrase will immediately be used to construct a representation of that phrase. (Hawkins 1994: 60ff)

Early recognition can help the working memory by option-cutting. Retaining fewer options in the working memory minimizes processing effort. Extending the principle to comparative alternation, the *more*-variant would provide a relatively (though not completely) safe signal that a degree phrase (DegP) follows (Figure 13.3).

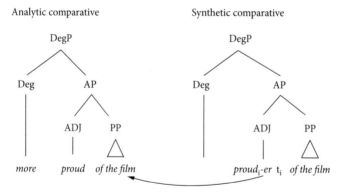

Figure 13.3 Phrase structure of analytic and synthetic comparatives

Early recognition of phrase structure is thus assumed to maximize processing speed and minimize processing effort.

13.4.1 *How can we define and measure analyticity?*

Analytic Support, however, is not restricted to ordering advantages. Other cases of morphosyntactic variation and synthetic–analytic contrasts can also be observed to display a pattern in which an analytic variant is comparatively preferred in cognitively complex environments.

When operationalizing the best-known definition of analyticity by Greenberg (1954: 192), who divides the number of morphemes by the number of words (Syntheticity = morphemes/words), we obtain the syntheticity values shown in Table 13.1:[5] Thus, *fuller* is taken to consist of two morphemes or one word. Dividing the number of morphemes (2) by the number of words (1), according to Greenberg's formula, we obtain a syntheticity index of 2. The analytic variant *more full*, however, consists of two morphemes and two words, which renders a syntheticity index of 1.

TABLE 13.1. **Categorization of synthetic–analytic contrasts based on Greenberg's parameters including controversial cases**

	Synthetic	◄───────────►	Analytic
English comparative alternation	full|er[a] $2/1 = 2$		**more** full $2/2 = 1$
English genitive alternation	the topic|'s relevance $4/2 = 2$		the relevance **of** the topic $5/5 = 1$
English future alternation		**BE** go|ing to go$5/4 = 1.25$	**will** go $2/2 = 1$
Spanish future alternation	comer|é $2/1 = 2$		**IR a** comer $3/3 = 1$
German mood alternation	bliebe $3/1 = 3$	würde bleiben $4/2 = 2$	

Note: A vertical line within a word indicates a morpheme boundary (|).

However, syntheticity values are less clear-cut as soon as we start acknowledging all grammatical properties encoded in the variants. For this reason several studies, such as Schwegler (1990: 48), Szmrecsanyi (2009) and Haspelmath (2009) set up different syntheticity or agglutination parameters. Nübling (2010: 3) provides a thorough discussion of the problems involved in measuring syntheticity and she convincingly argues for a whole range of parameters that need to enter the classification, among them syntagmatic parameters (such as concord), paradigmatic parameters (such as the number and similarity of available allomorphs) and even the frequency of a grammatical construction as a whole. As an example, consider the English *BE going to* future, which would at first sight be classified as analytic. In the

---

[5] In Greenberg's (1954) typology, languages in the range 1–1.99 are classified as analytic, 2–2.99 synthetic.

Greenbergian system, the syntheticity value of 1.25 is, however, more synthetic than that for *will* (1.0). This somewhat puzzling decision derives from the morphologically complex word *go|ing*, while the fact that BE needs to minimally display person and number agreement with the subject is not represented at all in the formula. Similarly, *will* raises the issue of how to account for the fact that it is highly idiosyncratic by not overtly inflecting for person and number, given that syncretism is one of the factors that a syntheticity index needs to account for according to Nübling (2010: 20). This also relates to the question of how a syntheticity value should deal with zero morphemes, portmanteau morphs, etc. And finally, *will* could be classified as more synthetic than *going to* on phonological and morphological grounds. It can be reduced to a single phoneme /l/ and it can be attached to a free morpheme (*I'll*, *he'll*, etc.), while *going to* has more phonological substance and more morphological autonomy.[6]

Similarly, for the Spanish future alternation we would have to acknowledge the fact that the verb (*comer|é* 'will eat') is inflected for person and number in the same fashion as the forms of *ir* 'to go' in *voy a comer, vas a comer*, etc.

Another type of variation pattern involves a zero option in competition with explicit marking (cf. Rohdenburg 2009; Eitelmann 2012). Assuming a wider conception of syntheticity and analyticity, even these variables could be included on this cline, though the Greenbergian measure would rank the more explicit variant as more synthetic.

(3)   As I approach the flats I don't try to hide **myself.**
      At school I used to read, mostly, and hide Ø in the shed at dinnertime ... (BNC)
      (cf. Eitelmann 2012)

	Synthetic ←——————————————→	Analytic
English Reflexive Alternation oneself		Ø
2/1=2		0/0 = 1[7]

Drawing on Schwegler (1990: 48), Nübling (2010: 6) argues that measures of syntheticity need to incorporate a whole range of parameters as well as syntactic, semantic morphological, and phonological interdependencies. Morphological and phonological syntheticity parameters indicate whether individual units can be separated, fused, moved, or stand in isolation, whether they are obligatory, as well as their structural and semantic transparency (cf. Nübling 2010: 6). For instance, semantic syntheticity can be illustrated for particle verbs.

(4)   Sie sollten ihren Familienstand **angeben.**
      Sie **gaben** ihren Familienstand **an.**

---

[6] I am indebted to Matthias Eitelmann (p.c.) for calling my attention to this aspect.

[7] Mathematically any division by zero renders the result 1. Whether this procedure is meaningful for computing syntheticity in languages remains doubtful.

The particle can be attached to the verb or detached from it—the semantic connection between both elements remains.

What is more, syntheticity need not only reflect syntagmatic dependencies but also paradigmatic relations. A large number of allomorphs raises syntheticity, because each allomorph needs to be selected according to its conditioning entity, be it phonologically, morphologically, or lexically conditioned (cf. also Wurzel 1996).

Additionally, stem alternations in German affect only a subset of lexical items (e.g. strong verbs) while the vast majority of verbs does not display this feature. Thus, any appropriate measure would have to quantify the relevance of stem alternation (cf. Haspelmath 2009).

As Nübling (2010: 20) points out, these and other parameters that are required for the assessment of syntheticity are neglected in the Greenbergian measure. If we acknowledge the number and multifariousness of the factors that enter into a realistic syntheticity measure, it becomes obvious that the determinants of syntheticity are no less complex than the processing-based determinants of grammatical variation—presumably because both concepts rely on the number of conditioning factors and their interdependencies that become crucial to processing.

The following sections illustrate the operation of Analytic Support on different levels of linguistic analysis for comparative alternation and other synthetic–analytic contrasts.

13.4.2 *Analytic Support with new rather than given information*

Genitive alternation is among the variation phenomena that can be arranged along a synthetic–analytic cline:

	Synthetic ←——————————→ Analytic	
English genitive alternation	the topic's relevance	the relevance of the topic

In-depth studies of the factors constraining the choice of genitive variants have, for instance, revealed that certain complexity factors trigger a higher ratio of *of*-genitives (cf. Rosenbach 2003: 392), so that we can similarly deduce the following correlation:

high processing load⇒higher ratio of *of*
low processing load ⇒higher ratio of -*'s*

Rosenbach (2003: 392) shows that possessors that express new information score significantly higher on *of*-genitives than those expressing given information (cf. also Biber et al. 1999: 305f; Quirk et al. 1985: 1282).[8] In line with Rosenbach (2003: 392) we can argue that newness increases the processing load and that this distribution might

---

[8] Givenness is operationalized as second-mention and definite expressions (*the girl, his father*) vs. first-mention and indefinite expressions (*a girl, some composer*). The occurrence of new information with the *of*-variant can also partly be adduced to positional preferences (cf. Hinrichs and Szmrecsanyi 2007: 452): With given information typically preceding new information, known possessors are placed first and encoded by the -*s*-genitive, while the possessed is placed last.

form another case of an explicit variant mitigating cognitive complexity, in this case triggered on the pragmatic level by information status.

13.4.3 *Analytic Support with abstract rather than concrete uses*

With Walker and Hulme (1999: 1258) we define concreteness "as an index of how directly the referent of a word can be experienced by the senses" (cf. also Mondorf 2009a: 91–3). Studies reveal considerable unanimity among subjects who were asked to rate words as concrete or abstract. While *ball* and *ship* are clearly assigned to the concrete category, *logic* and *conscience* have been classified as abstract (cf. Gilhooly and Logie 1980).

For semantic complexity we are in the lucky position of having ample independent psycholinguistic evidence showing that abstract words are harder to process than concrete words. First, Moss and Gaskell (1999) report shorter reaction times for concrete than for abstract words. Second, EEG measurements (cf. Weiss and Rappelsberger 1996: 17f) show that concrete words are easier to memorize and retrieve. This processing difference is attributed to the fact that concrete nouns refer to objects that can be perceived via highly diverse channels (seeing, hearing, feeling, smelling, or tasting). Third, neurophysiological studies report the simultaneous activation of more and more widely spread sensory-based features when using concrete rather than abstract nouns. And finally, serial recall of concrete nouns is more accurate than that of abstract nouns.

concrete words benefit from a stronger semantic representation than do abstract words and...the quality or strength of a word's semantic representation contributes directly to how well it can be recalled. (Walker and Hulme 1999: 1261)

In accordance with these findings, empirical analyses in Mondorf (2007: 219) have revealed that semantic complexity triggers higher ratios of Analytic Support, as illustrated by the following examples.

(5)   the beer is bitter**er** (*Daily Telegraph* 1994)   concrete
        the **more** bitter takeover battles of the past (*Daily Telegraph* 1991)   abstract

For this study, seven adjectives were selected, because they were equal in length and sufficiently numerous in matching concrete and abstract uses. Given the scarcity of comparatives in general and of semantic contrasts in highly specific matching contexts in particular, even megacorpora comprising more than 900 million words fell short of qualifying as a useful database, which is why retrieval by means of Google was chosen. The vast quantity of resultant entries (with over 22,000 entries for *a dark colo(u)r*) meant that the general procedure of manually editing each entry had to be abandoned for the sheer reason of economy. Instead, waste entries were minimized by searching for exact strings, for example "*a more round face*" and "*a rounder face*" using the quotation mark option in Google. Another problem with using web data is that search strings can occasionally render crucially different constructions ("a cleaner room" provides instances of the genitive "a cleaner's room" in Google), a problem that did, however, not occur with the noun combinations analyzed in the present study. What remains is the general messiness of web data, which includes doublets and errors. In order to restrict the amount of non-native data wherever possible, the search was restricted to English language domains. When evaluating the results in Figure 13.4, it is important to bear in mind that according to the vast majority of grammar books the *more*-variant should not occur at all with these monosyllabic adjectives. The vertical axis provides the percentages for the *more*-variant. The ratio for, for example, *more round* is higher with abstract uses of the adjective *round* than with concrete uses. Thus, *a more round number* scores 24% (leaving only 76% for the synthetic variant *a rounder number*) but *a more round face* is used in 4% of the cases (leaving 96% for the synthetic variant *a rounder face*).

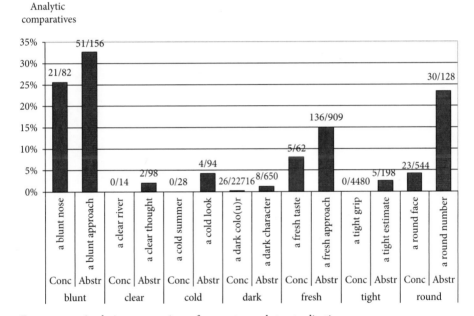

FIGURE 13.4 Analytic comparatives of concrete vs. abstract adjectives

Note: Number~Analytic~ = 311. Based on retrieval of English language texts by means of Google (August 9, 2004 and October 12, 2004). Apart from the figures for *blunt* and *clear*, the differences are statistically significant.

Source: Taken from Mondorf (2007: 219).

Confirmatory findings on these semantic complexity effects are also reported in a very sophisticated psycholinguistic follow-up study by Boyd (2007: 77).

The distribution indicates that for all seven adjectives the use of the *more*-variant is higher with abstract than with concrete concepts. Semantic complexity can thus be shown to trigger Analytic Support.

13.4.4 *Analytic Support with negated rather than affirmative contexts*

Another determinant that has been shown to condition the choice between synthetic vs. analytic variants in both Spanish and English is negation. Independent psycholinguistic evidence has largely confirmed that negation is cognitively more complex than affirmation, leading to delayed statement verification (cf. Wason 1961) and delayed picture verification (cf. Gough 1965; Slobin 1966; MacDonald and Just 1989: 641). This processing difference has repercussions for grammatical variation.[9]

For Mexican Spanish, Lastra and Butragueño (2010) report a statistically significant increase of the analytic variant (*voy a comer*) from 91% in affirmative to 96% in negated sentences.

(6) Comeré.   affirmative context
     No **voy a** comer   negated context

For English mood alternation, language users can express irrealis by choosing the synthetic variant (i.e. the subjunctive is marked by a zero-inflected verb form as exemplified in *have-Ø* in (7)) or the analytic form, which uses a periphrastic modal instead (e.g. *would have*). The analytic subjunctive is reported to be favored in negated contexts in Schlüter (2009: 300)—a fact that might at least be partly attributed to the proclivity to analytic variants in negated contexts.[10]

(7) (…) on the condition that he have-Ø in-home aides …   affirmative
     context … on the condition that he **would** not have to work … (COCA)
                                                          negated context

The increased processing effort associated with negated contexts appears to be mitigated by the choice of analytic variants in both Spanish and English.

As regards the distribution of *will* and *BE going to*, the categorization into synthetic vs. analytic is less straightforward, as Table 13.1 and the discussion in Section 13.4.1 have indicated. On the basis of the number of lexemes involved and the degree of cliticization *will* is considered the synthetic variant, while *BE going to* is rated as more analytic, since it includes several portmanteau morphemes, which increase its morpheme to word ratio. As regards the factors determining the choice between both future variants, negation is one of at least three cognitively complex environments that have been shown to trigger higher ratios of the analytic *BE going to*. Negated contexts generally increase the ratio of the *BE going to*-variant as opposed to the synthetic *will*-future (cf. Szmrecsanyi 2003: 316).[11]

---

[9] For English, syntactic variation phenomena involving the choice between a marked *to*-infinitive vs. a zero-variant also show that negated contexts trigger higher ratios for the explicit variants than affirmative contexts (cf. Horn 1978: 191–205; Rohdenburg 2008). The percentage for *help to* in negative contexts amounted to 87% (34 cases) in negated contexts, while in general its share was merely 43% in British newspaper data.

(a) She helped me Ø make a hash of things.   affirmative contexts
(b) She helped me not **to** make a hash of things.   negated contexts
     (based on Rohdenburg 2008).

[10] A possibly related aspect contributing to the preference of modal periphrasis according to Schlüter (2009: 299) is the *Embedded Negation Constraint* by Horn (1978: 191), according to which "[t]he less the dependent clause looks and acts like a sentence … the less negation is admitted without corresponding discomfort, if it is admitted at all."

[11] The other two contexts are dependent rather than independent clauses and longer rather than shorter sentences (cf. Szmrecsanyi 2003: 316).

(8)   ...if you**'ll** provide the contact information, I**'ll** check his story out.
affirmative context

(9)   If she's <u>not</u> **gonna** provide the information he wants, this is <u>not</u> **going to** make a prosecutor happy...(COCA)
negated context[12]

All findings concur that—in line with the Complexity Principle and more specifically with the Principle of *Analytic Support*—the more explicit/analytic variant (*BE going to*) is favored in negated, that is, cognitively complex, environments.

13.4.5 *Analytic Support with low frequency rather than high frequency words*

In German the periphrastic perfect (*Sie hat gebraucht...*) has increasingly replaced the preterite (*Sie brauchte...*). One of the few environments in which the decrease of the synthetic preterite is delayed is extremely frequent verbs, that is, well-entrenched verbs that exert a lower processing load than rare verbs (cf. Jäger 1971). Similar frequency effects have also been observed for English comparatives, where the analytic *more*-variant is chosen more often with extremely rare adjectives than with highly frequent ones (cf. Mondorf 2009a: 40–3).

13.4.6 *Analytic Support with complements rather than adjuncts*

Given the high degree of dependency between an adjective and its complement(s), it has been argued in Mondorf (2009a: 57–79) that the presence of complements triggers a higher share of analytic comparatives than its absence.

(10)   Never have I felt **more** proud <u>to be a conservative</u>.   + infinitival complement
       (*Guardian* 1994)
       I'd be even proud**er** if John Cleese were in it   – infinitival complement
       somewhere.
       (*Guardian* 1992)

Figure 13.5 summarizes corpus-based findings which reveal that all adjectives increase their use of the analytic variant in the presence of a complement. This has been attributed to the higher processing demands effected by the strong dependency relations between an adjective and its complement in Mondorf (2002). Follow-up studies using judgment tasks as well as reaction-time experiments have found that comparatives plus infinitival complements produce shorter reaction times if the comparative is formed analytically than if it is formed synthetically (cf. Boyd 2007: 27–32).

At a Symposium on Determinants of Grammatical Variation, Jack Hawkins (p.c.) raised the following question: It would be interesting to see if complements but not adjuncts raise the use of the *more*-variant. If the strength of dependency relations between an adjective and its complement are responsible for Analytic Support,

---

[12] Note that an example using the contracted forms (the clitic '*ll* and *gonna*) would be even better suited to illustrate the synthetic–analytic contrast.

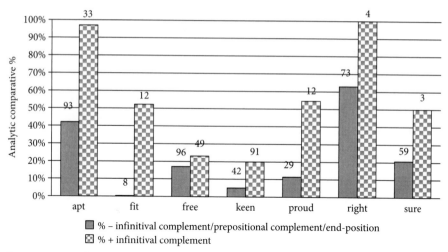

FIGURE 13.5 Analytic comparatives of monosyllabic adjectives in non-attributive position +/− infinitival complement

Note: Number$_{Analytic}$ = 1047.

Source: Based on Mondorf (2009a: 65).

adjuncts should not trigger Analytic Support to the same extent as complements, since obligatory complements express necessary information complementing the adjectives' meaning, while adjuncts merely convey additional optional information. Consequently, the presence of complements should increase the processing load, but the presence of adjuncts should not. We are now able to answer this question by taking a closer look at *than*-phrases.

Quirk et al. (1985: 462) list *than*-phrases exemplified in (11) among adjectival complements rather than adjuncts:

(11)   Delays are the worst in a decade and planes are **more full** than ever. (COCA)

However, several aspects cast considerable doubt on their complement status: First, generative approaches portray *than*-phrases as licensed by the degree marker rather than the adjective (cf. Haumann 2004), an analysis which would imply that they are not part of the adjective phrase. Consequently, we would not expect *than*-phrases to trigger *more*-support, because they are semantically and syntactically less dependent on the adjective. What is more, corpus findings presented in Mondorf (2006: 593) show that Quirk et al.'s (1985: 462) claim that monosyllabic adjectives take the analytic form "more easily when they are predicative and are followed by a *than*-clause" must be attributed to their predicative use alone. And indeed, there is ample corpus evidence showing that *than*-phrases do not significantly affect comparative alternation (cf. Leech and Culpeper 1997: 367; Lindquist 2000: 129; Mondorf 2002: 74, 2009a: 123–6; Hilpert 2008: 407). They do not behave like complements, simply because they are adjuncts; and in line with these findings we can now answer Hawkins' question in the positive: The strength of semantic and/or syntactic dependency relations determines whether Analytic Support does or does not take place. While complements trigger Analytic Support, adjuncts (in our case *than*-phrases) do not.

13.5 The historical development

English has often been cited as a language that has developed from synthetic to analytic, so we could expect that the degree of competition between both variants is declining. Others have claimed that as regards comparatives, this typological tendency appears to have been reversed in English (cf. Kytö and Romaine 1997: 344).

While it is a truism that no language can be described as completely synthetic or analytic, even for individual structures, this question can be less clear-cut than expected (e.g. the *going to* vs. *will* future). But even duly assuming that syntheticity and analyticity are a matter of degree, we are faced with problems in operationalizing these highly pervasive concepts.[13] Any meaningful account of syntheticity needs to move beyond the Greenbergian parameters in order to account for the number and diversity of dependencies that exist on the syntagmatic and the paradigmatic levels, etc.

While the situation appears to be more straightforward for English with its highly isolating features—at least at first sight—the treatment of morphosyntactic alternation patterns indicates that we are merely looking at the tip of the iceberg. When zooming in on the actual distribution of synthetic vs. analytic comparatives throughout the history of English, any claims stating that the English language or English comparative formation has developed from synthetic > analytic or vice versa turn out far too coarse to grasp the systematic variation that has evolved throughout the last four centuries.

13.5.1 *Less frequent adjectives have come to require Analytic Support*

A corpus-based study of the diachronic development of Analytic Support with comparatives has revealed that monosyllabic adjectives and disyllabic ones in <-y> (*heavy, lucky,* etc.) have increased their ratios for the synthetic variant since around 1600 up to Present-day English. Fifteen other groups of formally defined adjectives (e.g. those ending in *-ful, -ure, -ous, -ward, -some,* etc.) have increased their share of analytic variants in the past four centuries. This development has culminated in a situation in which most morphological groups of disyllabic adjective types are knock-out contexts for the synthetic comparative variant (cf. Mondorf 2009a: 128f). The only two groups of adjectives that have decreased their share of the *more*-variant over time are monosyllabic adjectives and disyllabic ones in <-y>. What these have in common is that they are also the most frequent groups, as Figure 13.6 indicates.

---

[13] An in-depth treatment of the pitfalls in defining these concepts in German is found in Nübling (2010: 1), who comes to the conclusion that once we take the measurement of syntheticity seriously, there is "not much evidence that German has become a more analytic language."

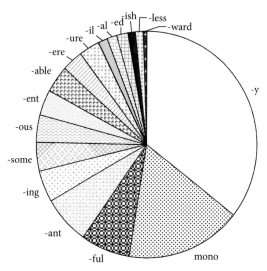

FIGURE 13.6 Token frequency of comparatives (both synthetic plus analytic) with different groups of adjectives

Note: Number = 12166.

Source: Based on Mondorf (2009a: 131).

Being short and highly frequent, it is argued in Mondorf (2009a: 130), the two adjective groups do not require Analytic Support to the same extent as rarer adjectives. These data also indicate that lumping all adjectives together conceals a systematic division of labour in which short and highly frequent adjective types have come to favor the synthetic comparative, while other adjective groups have become 100% analytic.

13.5.2 *Analytic Support with syntactically complex comparatives emerged after the nineteenth century*

In addition, the diachronic analysis presented in Mondorf (2009a: 161–4) has revealed that the preference of the *more*-variant for syntactically complex environments has not always been around in the English language. It is only after the eighteenth century that the analytic variant increases in the presence of complements. Figure 13.7 provides the ratio of analytic comparatives in the absence of complementation (solid line) in contrast to the presence of complementation (dashed line) for eight adjectives.[14] It is only in the eighteenth century that the division of labor emerges and analytic variants come to be preferred in syntactically complex environments.[15]

---

[14] The curves are additionally labeled with the absolute numbers of occurrences in order to indicate whether the numbers are large enough to permit the deduction of meaningful claims.

[15] For a more detailed account of the historical development of comparative alternation, cf. Mondorf (2009a: 117–70).

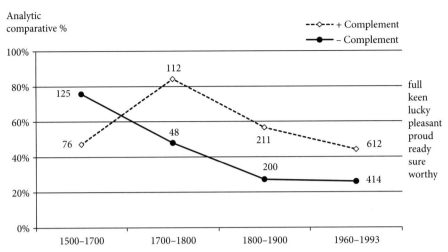

FIGURE 13.7 Diachronic development of analytic comparatives according to the presence/absence of complements

Note: Number$_{\text{Synthetic + Analytic}}$ = 5987.

Source: Based on Mondorf (2009a: 160).

13.6 Competing motivations or division of labour?

By drawing on descriptive variation linguistics and approaches based on typological and psycholinguistic principles, we arrive at a processing-based explanation for the systematic similarities within a range of six morphosyntactic alternations from three languages, that is, English comparative alternation, English mood alternation, English genitive alternation, English and Spanish future alternation, and German mood alternation. The Principle of Analytic Support provides the common denominator for a series of individual—at first glance unrelated—variation phenomena that are affected by processing demands exerted by syntactic, semantic, or pragmatic complexity.

By linking Hawkins' (1994) processing theory, typological syntheticity measures, and Rohdenburg's (1996) Complexity Principle, the cline shown in Figure 13.8 for Analytic Support can be postulated.

FIGURE 13.8 Cline for Analytic Support

Research on morphosyntactic variation reveals that what appears to be competing motivations at first glance turns out to be part of an intricately systematic adaptation to processing demands resulting in a division of labor between both variants. Syntheticity is favored in comparatively easy-to-process contexts. Analyticity is resorted to in cognitively more demanding contexts, thereby mitigating processing effort. This division of labor must have developed some time after the eighteenth century in English.

The historical development of morphosyntactic alternation patterns observed for six synthetic–analytic contrasts raises the question of why, for instance, the English language has not long ago settled the conflict between synthetic and analytic variants by promoting one variant to the detriment of the other. After all, in other areas, the system has established purely analytic rather than synthetic marking, as, for instance, in case marking (with the exception of the genitive). Why did this stream-lining not take place in the area of English comparatives, genitives, or subjunctives?

My suggestion is that the English language has, in fact, settled the conflict—in the form of an emergent division of labor. The outcome, that is, that the analytic variant is required in harder to process environments is hardly surprising if we assume that analytic structures are able to mitigate the processing load. It appears to be the case that languages retain morphosyntactic alternations in order to optimally exploit the system.

14

Formal vs. functional motivations for the structure of self-repair in German

MARTIN PFEIFFER

14.1 Spoken language, self-repair, and competing motivations

This study focuses on the syntactic analysis of self-repair in German.[1] Self-repair is a highly frequent phenomenon and is often considered one of the prime examples of the characteristics of spoken language: The traces of speech planning that become manifest in self-repair illustrate its linear progression in time. According to Auer (2009: 2), "the temporality of spoken language can be viewed as both cognitive and interactive, and from at least three perspectives." The first characteristic of spoken language is its transitory nature, which arises due to the limited working memory capacity of the language users. The second is the synchronization of the streams of consciousness of the speaker and the listener: The production and reception processes occur at (almost) the same time in face-to-face conversation. The third aspect, and for the subject of this chapter arguably the most important, is the irreversibility of spoken language: It is impossible to undo what has been said.

In order to cope with the characteristics of language use in real-time, spoken interaction relies on "basic operations of on-line syntax" (Auer 2009: 4). One of these operations is called retraction. Retractions "refer back in time to already existing syntactic structures which [speakers] reactivate and change" (Auer 2009: 7). The importance of this operation for the organization of spoken language becomes particularly apparent in instances of self-repair, which treat problems in already produced parts of the utterance under way. Self-repairs are defined as repetitions, substitutions, insertions, or deletions of a part of the emerging utterance by the speaker. These basic repair operations, each comprising several sub-operations

[1] I am grateful to all of the participants of the "Conference on Competing Motivations," November 23–25, 2010, at the Max Planck Institute for Evolutionary Anthropology, Leipzig, for their comments and suggestions. I would like to thank Peter Auer, Theodoros Papantoniou, Kobin Kendrick, and three reviewers for helpful comments on earlier versions of this chapter.

which cannot be detailed here (but see Pfeiffer 2014), are the four ways in which the syntactic structure of an utterance can be manipulated.[2] In this chapter, the focus will be narrowed to substitutions, in other words, the replacement of one part of the emerging syntactic gestalt by another in order to address some problem in the already produced part of the utterance. Figure 14.1 shows a typical instance of substitution:

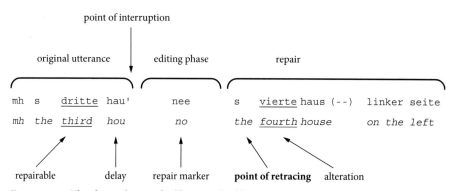

FIGURE 14.1 The three phases of self-initiated self-repair
Source: Illustration and terminology (slightly modified) are taken from Levelt (1983: 45).

This chapter focuses on the third phase, specifically the point of retracing, which is the structural feature of self-repair that is directly linked to "retraction" as one of the basic operations of online syntax. Speakers usually have options when choosing the point of retracing. In Figure 14.1, for instance, the speaker could have retraced directly to the repairable, the adjective *dritte* ('third'), in order to replace it immediately. However, she selects (the reduced form of) the definite article *s* ('the') as the starting point for the repair operation. This observation prompts the research question of the present study: How does the speaker choose the point of retracing? What are the motivations that influence this selection process?

In this chapter, it will be argued that the formation of the language system underlies both formal (internal) and functional (external) motivations, and that the interplay between these two types of motivations plays a crucial role in selecting the point of retracing. This point of view is based on the competing motivations model developed by Du Bois (1985), which argues that grammars should be seen as "adaptive systems, i.e., both partially autonomous (hence systems) and partially responsive to system-external pressures (hence adaptive)" (Du Bois 1985: 344). On the one hand, the structure of language is organized by formal regularities internal to the language system. On the other hand, language use underlies various functional constraints that in turn influence the language system as well. This influence of external functional motivations is reflected in, for example, the process of grammaticization. The aphorism "grammars code best what speakers do most" coined by

---

[2] As the focus of this chapter will be on the process of retraction, mere pauses and hesitation markers that are seen as instances of self-repair in Conversation Analysis (cf. Schegloff et al. 1977) will not be considered here.

Du Bois (1985: 363) expresses this view and assumes an important relationship between the functions of language use and the form of the language system.

Let us now approach self-repair from this perspective. Self-repair is both part of the organization of spoken language and partly organizes spoken language itself. If there are competing formal and functional motivations at work that shape the language system, we can assume that this is not restricted to "grammar" in its traditional sense, but also concerns the phenomenon of self-repair as a part of the structure of spoken language. If we adopt the competing motivations model in our analysis of self-repair, the constraints imposed on the repair system by the language-specific grammar can be seen as formal motivations. On the other hand, the interactional and cognitive constraints self-repair is subject to must be adapted to in order for it to function for the speaker (e.g. quick error correction) and the recipient (e.g. easy processability); these can be seen as functional motivations.

The main objective of this study is to apply the competing motivations model (Du Bois 1985) in order to explain the organization of retractions in self-repair. It would go beyond the scope of the present paper to develop a model that includes all the formal and functional motivations that play a role in structuring self-repair in German; therefore, this chapter will develop a model that will focus on one formal and one functional motivation within one syntactic constituent, namely the prepositional phrase. An exhaustive treatment of competing motivations in self-repair will be a project for further empirical research (cf. Pfeiffer 2014).

The following section will first give a theoretical overview of different strands of research on self-repair in general and on studies on the syntax of self-repair in German more specifically.[3] This will be followed by an analysis of several instances of substitutions in German prepositional phrases and a subsequent discussion of the competing formal and functional motivations that shape their syntactic structure. Finally, the last section will emphasize the importance of a competing motivations model for explaining the structure of self-repair.

14.2 Research on the syntax of self-repair

In the study of repair in spoken language, there are three main strands of research. In Conversation Analysis, repair is perceived as a functional resource for dealing with problems in speaking, hearing, and understanding (cf. Schegloff et al. 1977; Schegloff 1979). In psycholinguistic research, in contrast, the main interest is directed not towards the functions repair fulfills, but towards the cognitive processes it reveals. From this point of view, self-repair tells us something about, for example, monitoring processes (e.g. Levelt 1983; Postma 2000) and the influence of frequency effects on the point of interruption (cf. Kapatsinski 2010). The third strand of research, Interactional Linguistics, shares with Conversation Analysis a common interest in interaction. However, interactional linguists have a stronger interest in the explanation of linguistic structure as a resource for the accomplishment of interac-

---

[3] Research on the prosody of self-repair will not be considered in this overview. For an analysis of intonational aspects in German, cf. Pfeiffer (2012).

tional tasks (cf. Selting and Couper-Kuhlen 2000; Couper-Kuhlen and Selting 2001). Adopting such a point of view, recent comparative studies have shown that the syntactic organization of self-repair is shaped by the different morphosyntactic structures characteristic of different languages (cf. Fox et al. 1996; Fox et al. 2009; Birkner et al. 2010, 2012), for example morphological complexity, word order, strength of bonds between constituents, and extent of grammatical marking.

The first studies on syntactic aspects of self-repair in German were carried out by Uhmann (1997a, 1997b, 2001, 2006). Uhmann's (2001) "Extended Head Rule" claims that the structure of self-repair in German is determined by a purely syntactic property, namely the functional head immediately c-commanding the repairable. To simplify somewhat, Uhmann's basic assumption is that speakers who carry out self-repair in German start, depending on the respective phrase, with the determiner, preposition, or finite verb directly preceding the repairable. However, Pfeiffer (2010) shows that the Extended Head Rule encounters several theoretical and empirical problems. It seems that, in order to explain the structural diversity in self-repair, we must consider not only syntactic, but also functional, motivations.

However, it is yet largely unknown to what extent functional (interactional and cognitive) motivations compete with the formal (grammatical) motivations mentioned above in determining the syntax of self-repair in a specific language. This question will be addressed in the empirical part of this chapter (Sections 14.4 and 14.5).

14.3 Data

This chapter attempts to explain how selection of the point of retracing works in a particular syntactic domain, namely the prepositional phrase in German. This syntactic constituent was chosen for this study because it exhibits considerable grammatical marking. On the one hand, the preposition determines the case of the nominal phrase. On the other hand, the nominal phrase is marked according to number, gender, and definiteness. Syntactic constituents that are grammatically "heavy" (i.e. those that are marked by several grammatical categories) are particularly likely to exert a syntactic influence on the point of retracing in self-repair and, therefore, to make visible the role of formal motivations (cf. Birkner et al. 2010, 2012).

This study is based on a self-repair corpus comprising a total of 2,574 instances that were collected from audio-recorded everyday conversation, informal interviews, and psychotherapeutic interaction in German.[4] For the present study, only substitutions of the noun within prepositional phrases were included, amounting to a collection of eighty instances. Other types of substitution within the prepositional phrase, for instance, substitutions of the determiner which occur very frequently

[4] For a syntactic and functional analysis of the entire corpus, see Pfeiffer (2014). I would like to thank Peter Auer and Margret Selting (principal investigators) as well as Peter Gilles and Jörg Peters (team members) for giving me permission to use their informal interview data from the DFG-funded research project "Dialektintonation" which was carried out at the Universities of Freiburg and Potsdam from 1998 to 2005. I am also grateful to Karin Birkner and Fabian Overlach for kindly providing me with psychotherapeutic conversations and interview data.

within German prepositional phrases (cf. Birkner et al. 2012: 1428f.), were excluded. The reason for this restricted focus is that an additional option for retracing in substitutions of the noun does exist. While substitutions of determiners within prepositional phrases include only two possible points of retracing (i.e. the determiner and the preposition), substitutions of the noun in prepositional phrases have more heterogeneity regarding the point of retracing, as there is the additional option of going back directly to the noun to replace it immediately.[5] In turn, more structural variety may help isolate the formal and functional motivations that influence the selection of the point of retracing within a certain syntactic constituent. Thus, substitutions of the noun within prepositional phrases were chosen for the present study, although this group is among the rarer types of repair within the corpus. Due to this rarity, I do not claim representativity for the quantitative distributions presented here. Nevertheless, preliminary suggestions for modeling the interplay of competing motivations in self-repair will be made and can be verified and extended by future research based on more data from various syntactic domains.

14.4 Data analysis

Analysis is divided into two main sections. The group of semantic repair, which comprises the three subgroups semantic elaboration, semantic error repair, and unclear semantic repair, will be analyzed first, followed by examples of phonological repair. Analysis will demonstrate a clear difference with regard to the retraction patterns between these two groups, while each group, taken alone, will be shown to be structurally homogeneous.

Before analysis of individual examples is shown, the quantitative distribution of the point of retracing in the different types of repair is presented (Table 14.1).

TABLE 14.1. **Distribution of the point of retracing in the different types of repair**

	Semantic elaborations	Semantic error repair	Unclear semantic repair	Phonological repair
P	22 (71%)	20 (100%)	8 (80%)	1 (5%)
Det	3 (10%)	0 (0%)	0 (0%)	0 (0%)
Noun	4 (13%)	0 (0%)	2 (20%)	18 (95%)
Conj	2 (6%)	0 (0%)	0 (0%)	0 (0%)
Total	31 (100%)	20 (100%)	10 (100%)	19 (100%)

[5] Also, as the adjective occurs before the noun in German, there is the additional possibility of retracing to the adjective before substituting the noun. However, as adjectives occur rarely in the corpus, this theoretical possibility is neglected here. Moreover, in all types of substitutions, there is the theoretical option of retracing to an earlier syntactic constituent before the prepositional phrase, which occurs rarely as well.

When substituting the noun in a prepositional phrase, speakers retrace back to different points within the emerging syntactic structure. In my data, the constituents used as points of retracing are prepositions (P), determiners (Det), nouns, and conjunctions or subjunctions (Conj). Theoretically, while the adjective position is a possible destination of retracing as well, speakers in my collection did not use it as such. As can be seen, there is a strong tendency in the three subgroups of semantic repair to retrace to the preposition, in other words, to repeat the preposition (and the determiner) before carrying out the substitution of the noun. In these examples, the noun is not a frequent destination of retracing. Conversely, in the group of phonological repair, there is a strong preference for retracing directly to the noun in order to replace it immediately. In contrast to the group of semantic repair, the preposition is not a frequent point of retracing in this data. The difference between phonological repair and semantic repair with respect to the point of retracing is highly significant ($\chi^2(1) = 46.03$; $p < 0.01$; phi $= 0.78$), whereas the difference between the three different types of semantic repair is not significant with regard to the point of retracing. These initial observations will be illustrated with several examples in the following sections.

14.4.1 *Semantic repair*

The group of semantic repair includes all examples in which the originally produced noun is substituted by a noun with a different meaning ($n = 61$; 76%). This category comprises three subgroups: semantic elaborations, semantic error repair, and unclear semantic repair. The group of semantic elaborations treats problems of lexical or terminological inappropriateness or problems of referential imprecision. This type of self-repair differs from semantic error repair, which treats "real" lexical errors.[6] The examples in the corpus were categorized as semantic elaborations when both the replaced and the replacing expression could be interpreted as "true" in the specific context of the utterance. This means that both the original and the repaired version of the noun can be used and make sense in the respective semantic context (but the substituting noun is more exact). When the repairable is not a correct alternative in the respective context, the example was categorized as an instance of semantic error repair. At times, primarily due to early interruption of the repairable, it was unclear whether an alteration of the noun was a semantic elaboration or a semantic error repair. These examples were categorized as unclear semantic repair.

14.4.1.1 *Semantic elaborations*   The group of semantic elaborations represented by examples (1)–(4) is the largest subgroup of the collection ($n = 31$; 39% of the collection). In most examples, speakers retrace to the preposition when elaborating on the noun ($n = 22$; 71%; see Table 4.1).

---

[6] The distinction between semantic elaborations and semantic error repair in the present chapter is similar to the terminology introduced by Levelt (1983: 52–4). According to Levelt's terminology, the examples in Section 14.4.1.1 would be categorized as instances of appropriateness-repair (A-repair). He differentiates this type of repair that aims at, for example, ambiguity reduction, or at appropriate and coherent terminology from instances of error-repair (E-repair) that correct errors, such as semantic or phonological errors.

In the conversation just before extract (1), fro3a complains about the undisciplined behavior of certain people in public and identifies foreigners and their children as one of the main causes of this problem. In l. 04, the wife of fro3a, fro3b, initiates and carries out self-repair (transcription follows GAT 2, cf. Selting et al. 2009, an asterisk marks the point of interruption; interlinear glosses are provided only for the lines that contain the self-repair):

(1)

```
01 fro3b:    =des het aber noch ganz Andere (.) äh:
                                  [ gründe und URsachen;
             but there are other reasons and causes as well
02 fro3a:                         [ ha jo des ach och GOTT
             <<dim> da könnscht ja noch.>]
             oh for sure that oh my god of course there are
03 fro3b:    und kann_ma au jetz nit uff_s]
             AUSland,*
             and you can' t PTCL PTCL    on    the.N.SG
             foreign.countries.N.SG
             and you can't (put the blame) on foreign countries*
->04         äh:    oder    uff    die      AUSländer-
             uh     or      on     the.PL   foreigners.M.PL
             uh or on foreigners
05 fro3a:    jaja aber die (.) die lErne doch des von UNsere;
             sure but they learn it from our (kids)
```

Starting at l. 01, the wife disagrees with fro3a's point of view and argues for a more comprehensive consideration of the problem. From l. 05 on, fro3a tries to mitigate the rigor of his earlier xenophobic remark.

In l. 04, fro3b initiates self-repair after the noun *AUSland* ('foreign countries'). This repair initiation becomes perceivable for the recipient by the use of the repair markers *äh:* ('uh') and *oder* ('or'). She retraces to the (dialectal form of the) preposition *uff* ('on'), repeats the preposition, and substitutes the original noun with the new noun *AUSländer* ('foreigners'). As the new noun differs from the repairable in number and gender, the determiner, which carries the grammatical marking of nominal phrases in German, must be substituted as well (*s* 'the.N.SG'→ *die* 'the.PL'). Thus, the retraction must go back at least to the determiner. However, the speaker does not select this minimal span of retracing, but instead uses the preposition as a starting point for carrying out self-repair. In the substitution in l. 04, fro3b elaborates on who exactly cannot or should not exclusively be blamed for the observed problematic behavior. Both nouns, the original one and the new one, seem adequate in this context, but fro3b decides to talk about persons (*AUSländer* 'foreigners') instead of using the broader and more abstract concept of *AUSland* ('foreign countries'). Therefore, this example can be categorized as an instance of semantic repair, more specifically as a semantic elaboration.

While, in the first example, the noun was completed prior to repair initiation, the speaker sometimes interrupts the repairable in semantic elaborations, as in the following example. In extract (2), P84 talks about his professional skills:

(2)
```
01 P84:   wobei i sag beWUSST,=
          I deliberately say
```
```
->02      =i bin in meinem   gschä'*  in meinem   JOB,(--)
          I   am  in my.N.DAT busine.N in my.M.DAT job.M
          I am in my busine* in my job
```
```
03        äh (-) i bin DURCHschnitt,=
          uh I am average
```

In l. 02, P84 initiates self-repair by interrupting the noun, most probably the noun *gschäft* 'business,' with a glottal stop. The speaker retraces to the beginning of the prepositional phrase, repeats the preposition and the determiner (*in meinem* 'in my'), and substitutes the interrupted noun *gschä'* ('busine') with *JOB* ('job'). In this example, the form of the determiner does not change (because the masculine dative and the neuter dative form of the definite article are homomorphous in German). Interestingly, just as in example (1), the speaker does not select the more economic option of retracing directly to the repairable. As this instance of self-repair shows, an interruption of the repairable in semantic elaborations is generally also accompanied by a retraction to the preposition (see Section 14.5.2 for a more detailed discussion of the point of interruption).

In example (3), the speaker selects the minimal span of retracing and goes back directly to the noun. This point of retracing is quite rare in semantic elaborations ($n = 4$; 13%; see Table 14.1). In this extract, k07 talks about a citizen's movement that provides flood protection:

(3)
```
01 k07:   un:d ähm: (-) die haben ne broSCHÜre rausgegeben;
          and uh they have published a leaflet
```
```
->02      bei welchem wAsser* (.) hOchwasserstand sie ihr auto
          wo HINsetzen können,
          at which   water       high-water level you your car
          where park can
          on where you can park your car, at which water* high-water level
```

In l. 02, k07 interrupts her utterance after the first part of a compound noun, retraces to the noun slot, substitutes the first part of the compound noun *wasser* ('water') with the more precise noun *hOchwasser* ('high-water'), and then continues with the last part of the compound noun *stand* ('level'). In two of four cases of retraction to the noun, the speaker elaborates on the repairable by adding a specifying first component to it, thereby producing a compound. In these instances of self-repair, the syntactic form of the nominal phrase does not change, as it is determined by the last part of the compound noun. Although the last part of the compound noun (*stand* 'level') is not delivered phonetically before the speaker initiates repair, it is already projected by the original utterance, as the simple noun *wasser* would not be possible in this context. Apparently, in these particular instances of specification, the speaker can use the more economic option of retracing directly to the noun instead of going back all the way to the preposition.

14.4.1.2 *Semantic error repair*   The second type of semantic repair is the group of semantic error repairs (*n* = 20; 25% of the collection). In this type of self-repair, we find only retractions to the preposition (see Table 14.1.):

(4)

```
01 i-fro1:   wann isch_en_s   kirchenpatrozinium        in her' *
             when is PTCL  the church's patron saint day in her
             in ZÄHringen,
             in zähringen
             when is the church's patron saint day in Her* in Zähringen
```

In this example, i-fro1 starts producing the noun *her'* (most likely the beginning of *herdern*, a part of the city of Freiburg). After having interrupted the noun, the speaker retraces to the preposition, repeats it, and replaces the repairable with the noun *ZÄHringen*, a name that refers to another neighborhood of Freiburg. Note that in this example, too, the speaker selects the preposition as a point of retracing, though she could have retraced to the noun instead. This structure corresponds to the general preference for retraction to the preposition observed in semantic elaborations.

In the following extract, k10a describes the location of a building in *hohenLIND*, a neighborhood of Cologne. In ll. 02 and 03 he refers to a landmark that the recipients can use as a starting point for his description:

(5)

```
01 k10a :   von    von    von        hohenLIND?
            from from from hohenlind
02          von   der    pfarREI',*
            from the.F parish.F
            starting from the parish*
->03        äh    von:   unserm      KRANkenhaus aus-
            uh    from   our.N       hospital.N  PREP
            uh from our hospital
```

Apparently, the first referent in l. 02 (*pfarREI* 'parish') is not accurate and needs correction. After initiating repair with a glottal stop, the speaker retraces to the beginning of the prepositional phrase and replaces the original nominal phrase *der pfarREI* ('the parish') with *unserm KRANkenhaus* ('our hospital'). In addition to the semantic difference between the substituted and the substituting noun, the new nominal phrase contains a possessive article and is altered in gender. In this example, just as in examples (1) and (2), a retraction to the determiner would be possible, but is ignored in favor of a retraction to the preposition.

14.4.1.3 *Unclear semantic repair*   While most examples could be clearly identified as instances of either semantic elaboration or semantic error repair, some cannot be clearly identified due to the speaker breaking off the noun early (*n* = 10; 12%).

In example (6), ko7 talks about immigrants who arrived in Cologne in the 1970s
and the possibilities they had to learn German:

(6)

```
  01 ko7:  die    ham    nie   gele:rnt äh: die: SPRAche.
           they have never learned uh the language
->02        (ja    dann) die   jingen nich in die ro'* in die
           (PTCL then) they went    not  to the ro  to the
           Abendschule,
           evening school
           they didn't go to the ro* to the evening school
```

In l. 02, ko7 interrupts the noun after the first two phonemes *ro*, repeats the preposition and the determiner, and substitutes the repairable with *Abendschule* ('evening
school'). It is unclear whether *ro* is the beginning of, for example, an evening school's
name, which would mean that this self-repair is a semantic elaboration, or the
beginning of an erroneous lexical item, which would mean that the example should
be classified as semantic error repair. However, the group of unclear semantic repair
does not differ from the other two categories with respect to the point of retracing—
it includes predominantly retractions to the preposition ($n = 8$; 80%).

14.4.1.4 *Summary: Semantic repair*   Within the group of semantic repair, the vast
majority of examples ($n = 50$; 82 %) exhibit a retraction to the preposition before
carrying out the replacement. This result confirms earlier studies (Uhmann 2001,
2006; Pfeiffer 2010; Fox et al. 2009; Birkner et al. 2010, 2012) that have revealed a
strong tendency for retracing to the preposition when carrying out self-repair within
the prepositional phrase in German. This finding can, in line with the studies
mentioned above, be ascribed primarily to two grammatical features of the
prepositional phrase:

1. The preposition in German—which always requires a complement phrase,
   usually a nominal phrase—governs the complement noun phrase by determining its case (genitive, dative, or accusative) (Gallmann 2006: 848); and
2. The tendency of the preposition and the determiner in German to cliticize (e.g.
   bei dem 'at the' → *beim* 'at.the').

Both features, but in particular the process of cliticization, make evident the strong
bond between the preposition and its complement in German. This bond partly
explains why there is a strong preference for speakers of German to begin with the
repetition of the preposition when carrying out self-repair in prepositional phrases.
When selecting the point of retracing, speakers regularly ignore the determiner as a
possible starting point (cf. Uhmann 2001, 2006), respecting the bond between the
preposition and the nominal phrase. This is in contrast to other languages, such as
English, in which retraction to the determiner within the prepositional phrase seems
more common (cf. Fox and Jasperson 1995: 102–3), while speakers tend not to retrace
to the preposition (cf. Fox et al. 2009: 285). The weaker bond between the preposition
and its complement in English also becomes obvious in preposition stranding,
namely the occurrence of "stranded" prepositions separated from their complements

(e.g. *what are you looking at?*). This phenomenon does not occur in German (Takami 1992: 252). As the analysis in this section suggests, speakers ignore not only the determiner, but also the noun as a possible point of retracing in semantic repair in prepositional phrases. This shows the strong formal motivation for maintaining the syntactic unity of the prepositional phrase when selecting the point of retracing.

As shown, there are examples of semantic repair in which the speaker does not retrace to the preposition, but to other constituents within the emerging syntactic structure. This illustrates that other motivations play a role in determining the point of retracing, for instance the motivation for minimizing the span of retracing in certain types of specification (see example (3)), which are outside the scope of this chapter.

14.4.2 *Phonological repair*

In this section, some examples of phonological repair ($n = 19$; 24%) will be analyzed. In this type of repair, the repairable usually contains a slip of the tongue, in other words, a phonological error. When initiating repair, speakers usually break-off the noun that contains the phonological error. Thus, with respect to the point of interruption, phonological repairs are similar to examples of unclear semantic repair. However, these two categories can be distinguished quite easily, as the phonological contrast between the repairable and substituting noun is much stronger (i.e. they consist of different phonemes) in instances of unclear semantic repair.

When speakers carry out phonological repair, they usually retrace directly to the word that contains the error (cf. Uhmann 2006; Pfeiffer 2010, 2014). This general tendency also holds true for retractions in phonological repairs of nouns in prepositional phrases. Consider the following extract (7), in which Sbr tells a story about her ex-boyfriend who did not want to remove his shoes and clothes at the beach because he did not like sand.[7]

(7)
```
  01 Sbr:   Angezogen,=ne,
            completely dressed
  02        weil ja SAND[war;=ne, ]
            because there was sand
->03 Jrg:     [<<f, all> aber doch nich]  mit    der   bul'*
            BUNDfaltenhose;>
                       but   PTCL not    with   the   plean
            pleat-front trousers
            but not with the plean* pleat-front trousers
```

In l. 03, Jrg's astonished exclamation contains an instance of phonological repair. He initiates repair by cutting off the repairable *bul'* ('plean'), retraces to the beginning of the word, and substitutes the erroneous beginning of the compound noun with its phonologically correct form *BUNDfaltenhose* ('pleat-front trousers').

---

[7] It is quite difficult to "translate" repairables containing phonological errors into another language. In order to reflect the phonological characteristics of the error in the object language, I tried to replicate the anticipation of phonemes in the English translation.

In the following example, the instance of phonological repair has a similar syntactic structure. In this extract, hho4 talks about some of his former classmates who had come to Hamburg with refugee treks during the Second World War:

(8)

```
01 hho4:  äh es waren auch schon VIEle aus- (-)
          uh there were also quite a lot from
02        die also NICH aus hamburch kamen-
          who did not come from Hamburg
->03      die also durch   die FLÜCKlich'* (-) FLÜCHTlingstrecks
          °h nach hamburch gekommen sind.
          who PTCL through the reku         refugee      treks
          to hamburg have come
          who have come to Hamburg with reku* refugee treks
```

In l. 03, he cuts off the repairable that contains two phonological errors (*FLÜCKlich'* 'reku'), retraces to the beginning of the noun, and replaces the repairable with the correct form of the noun (*FLÜCHTlingstrecks* 'refugee treks').

The next example, in which ddo1a recounts how they lost touch with a Polish exchange student, is the only one in my collection in which the speaker retraces to the preposition when carrying out phonological repair:

(9)

```
01 ddo1a:  der is aber nIscht wieder ge[KOMmen;]
           but he did not come back
02 i-ddo1:                             [mhm,]
                                        PTCL
->03 ddo1a: [desis::] °h im   fa'* äh im   SANde verloofn;=  ne,
            it  COP   into ra  uh into sand run.off.PTCP PTCL
            it ran off into fa* into sand / we lost touch
04 i-ddo1: [mhm:],
            PTCL
```

In l. 03, ddo1a initiates repair by interrupting the phonologically incorrect form of the noun *fa*, repeats the cliticized form of the preposition and the determiner *im* ('into'), and substitutes the incorrect form of the noun with the correct one (*SANde* 'sand'). The point of retracing in this example, which deviates from all other phonological repairs in my collection, can be explained by the fact that *im Sande verlaufen* ('to lose touch') is a fixed collocation. Thus, a specific motivation may be at work here: Speakers seem to respect the bond between parts of a collocation when carrying out retractions in self-repair.

However, in the vast majority of phonological repairs in my corpus ($n = 18$; 95%), the point of retraction is the repairable, that is, the noun that contains the slip of the tongue. This is quite surprising, given the strong motivation for retracing to the preposition in semantic repair. How can these retractions to the noun be explained? The findings suggest that there is a functional motivation that is responsible for this retraction pattern. In phonological repair, the substituting noun and the substituted noun have the same syntactic form. In semantic repair, however, the new noun often does not correspond to the repairable in gender, number, and/or definiteness, and changing these syntactic categories can affect the form of the determiner. Consequently, as the syntactic categories of the noun are not altered in phonological repair, there is no need to go back to the beginning of the nominal or prepositional phrase. Instead, given that the syntactic form of the nominal phrase is already clearly established in the mind of the speaker, there is a strong motivation to retrace directly to the noun, selecting the minimum span of retracing and aiming for maximum efficiency. This functional motivation has an interactional basis: It helps the speaker convey an utterance in the desired form as quickly as possible to the recipient.

14.5 Discussion

In the first part of the discussion, the main findings of the data analysis will be integrated into a competing motivations model for the structure of self-repair within prepositional phrases in German. With these theoretical implications in mind, the second part will critically discuss an alternative hypothesis.

14.5.1 *Formal vs. functional motivations*

Following Du Bois (1985), this chapter argues that an adequate explanatory model for the syntactic structure of self-repair cannot be based on purely language-internal features, but must recognize the interaction of competing formal (grammatical) and functional (cognitive and interactional) motivations. In his influential paper on competing motivations, Du Bois (1985: 347) states: "No theory of discourse and grammar will ultimately be adequate, I believe, without an explicit theory of the competition and systematic reconciliation of external and internal motivations." To show that this assumption holds true for the domain of self-repair as well, the following three questions must be answered:

1. What are the external and internal motivations in self-repair?
2. What do they compete for?
3. How are they reconciled?

First, as was explained above, two competing motivations have been identified thus far. The external (functional) motivation has to do with efficiency: Speakers tend to resolve trouble in their utterance as quickly as possible. The functional motivation "carry out self-repair as quickly as possible" has an interactional and a cognitive facet. On the one hand, it works toward quickly resolving conversational trouble and adhering to the social norm of errorless pronunciation. On the other hand, in order to achieve this interactional task, the speaker relies on monitoring processes that enable a quick detection and treatment of the problem. The internal (formal) motivation has to do with the grammatical characteristics of the prepositional phrase in German, that is, the strong bond between the preposition and its complement. It is reflected in the tendency to retrace to the preposition and can be paraphrased as "respect the syntactic unit prepositional phrase." As was indicated earlier, these motivations are only two of the numerous motivations that potentially influence the point of retracing in German. In the model outlined here, both the functional and formal motivation (and all the other motivations that potentially influence the structure of self-repair) are thought to operate simultaneously, with varying strengths, whenever the need for self-repair arises.

Second, the motivations compete for the point of retracing, which is a "limited good" in Du Bois' (1985: 354) sense: There can be only one point of retracing for each retraction carried out. When the functional motivation outweighs the formal motivation, the speaker retraces directly to the repairable. When the formal motivation is stronger than the functional motivation, the retraction goes back to the preposition.

Third, it is the type of repair that resolves the conflict between the competing motivations. This means that the strength of each motivation varies according to the type of problem that needs repair: The functional motivation is stronger for the treatment of phonological repairables, and the formal motivation is stronger for resolving semantic trouble. In phonological repair, the syntactic categories of the nominal phrase are not affected during the self-repair operation. Therefore, the speaker can retrace directly to the repairable to carry out self-repair with maximum efficiency, and need not go back to an earlier point within the syntactic structure. In this type of repair, the preponderance of the functional motivation causes the speaker to retrace to the repairable in nearly all cases.

In semantic repair, by contrast, the formal motivation is stronger, which leads to a retraction to the preposition. This enables the speaker to embed the repair operation within the larger syntactic constituent, which may help the listener process the replacement of an element within the emerging utterance. Some instances of semantic repair involve an alteration of cliticization of the preposition and the determiner, which forces the speaker to retrace to the preposition ($n = 8$; 13%). In other cases, the replacement of the noun causes an alteration of the syntactic categories of the nominal phrase (number, gender, or definiteness, without involving an alteration of cliticization), which affects the form of the determiner. In these examples ($n = 9$; 15%; see example (1)), the speaker must retrace at least to the determiner in order to substitute the whole nominal phrase, but need not go back all the way to the preposition. However, the strong bond between the preposition and the determiner leads to a retraction to the preposition in eight out of nine cases. In the examples of semantic repair in which no grammatical category is altered ($n = 44$; 72 %), even a retraction directly to the noun would be possible. However, despite this possibility, speakers retrace to the preposition in 77% of these instances as well (compared to 82% for all the instances of semantic repair).

So why do speakers—against the motivation of carrying out repair as quickly as possible—go back to the preposition in most of these cases as well? Obviously, factors other than the two motivations presented above must be involved. Two explanations would be compatible with each other and with the competing motivations model discussed thus far. First, we have observed that a high percentage of retractions to the preposition (77%) occur in instances of semantic repair in which the syntax of the self-repair does not force the speaker to go back further than the repairable. This suggests that the mere *possibility* of changing either the (de)cliticization of the preposition and the determiner or the syntactic form of the determiner (or both) implicated in semantic repair leads to the self-repair structure that involves a retraction to the preposition. This retraction pattern is analogous to "obligatory" cases in which speakers are forced to go back to the beginning of the prepositional phrase. Second, an additional functional motivation may be at work here. It might be that speakers generally need more time in semantic repair compared to phonological repair due to the planning processes involved in retrieving the correct semantic concept to be conveyed. The larger span of retracing, then, would provide the speaker with additional planning time. However, this functional (cognitive) motivation would not imply that formal motivations are to be excluded from the model. Only formal motivations can explain why it is exactly the preposition (and not, for example, the determiner or a constituent preceding the preposition) that speakers select when retracing to an earlier point within the emerging syntactic gestalt.

14.5.2 *Alternative hypothesis: The point of interruption*

As the examples in Section 14.4.2 indicate, speakers interrupt the repairable in 16 out of 19 instances of phonological repair (84%). This gives rise to an alternative hypothesis that runs counter to the competing motivations model presented above, namely that it is the point of interruption (and not an interplay of competing motivations) that determines the point of retracing. Tables 14.2 and 14.3 show the distribution of the point of interruption across the different types of repair.

TABLE 14.2. **Distribution of the point of interruption in the different types of repair**

	Semantic elaborations	Semantic error repair	Unclear semantic repair	Phonological repair
In repairable	12 (39%)	9 (45%)	10 (100%)	16 (84%)
After repairable	14 (45%)	8 (40%)	0 (0%)	3 (16%)
In delayed word	0 (0%)	2 (10%)	0 (0%)	0 (0%)
After delayed word	5 (16%)	1 (5%)	0 (0%)	0 (0%)
Total	31 (100%)	20 (100%)	10 (100%)	19 (100%)

TABLE 14.3. **Distribution of the point of interruption in semantic and phonological repair**

	Semantic repair	Phonological repair
In repairable	31 (51%)	16 (84%)
After repairable	22 (36%)	3 (16%)
In delayed word	2 (3%)	0 (0%)
After delayed word	6 (10%)	0 (0%)
Total	61 (100%)	19 (100%)

Speakers can break-off the utterance at different points in the emerging structure: within/after the repairable or within/after a *delayed word*, which is defined as a word that is produced after the repairable and before the point of interruption (see Figure 14.1).

When carrying out self-repair, speakers might adhere to the following simple rule: If a word is interrupted, retrace to the nearest constituent boundary. Or, from a different angle, it might be self-interruption that marks an error. This corresponds to Levelt's (1983: 63) pragmatic hypothesis for the interruption of error repairables: "it is all right to interrupt a word which needs total replacement because it is erroneous, but it is not good practice to interrupt a correct word which only needs further specification." In Levelt's data, error repairables (i.e. lexically and phonologically incorrect words) tend to be interrupted more frequently (23%) than inappropriate words (7%). However, Table 14.2 shows not only that phonologically erroneous words are often interrupted (84%), but also that the speaker interrupts the noun in 39% of cases of semantic elaboration. Additionally, there is no significant difference between semantic elaborations and semantic error repairs (39% vs. 45%) with regard to the point of interruption. Moreover, 15 out of 16 (94%) phonological repairs that interrupt the repairable retrace directly to the noun, but only 5 out of 31 (16%) semantic repairs that interrupt the repairable involve a retraction to the noun. All these findings, which indicate that it is indeed the type of repair (and not the interruption of the repairable) that has a crucial influence on the point of retracing, support the competing motivations hypothesis.

Nevertheless, there is a significant difference between phonological repair and semantic repair with respect to the point of interruption ($\chi^2(1) = 6.85$; $p < 0.01$; phi = -0.33). The tendency to interrupt the repairable is stronger for phonological repair than for semantic repair (84% vs. 51%, Table 14.3). Conversely, in only 16% of phonological repairs is the noun completed prior to repair initiation, whereas this is the case for 49% of semantic repairs. A significant difference is also shown to exist between semantic error repair and phonological repair ($\chi^2(1) = 4.13$; $p < 0.05$; phi = -0.34). On the cognitive level, speakers seem to detect phonological errors more quickly than semantic errors, which is indicated by a higher number of interruptions of the repairable in phonological repair compared to semantic error repair (84% vs. 45%, see Table 14.2). This suggests that the speaker's monitor (cf. Levelt 1983, 1989; Postma 2000) reacts to phonological errors in a special way: It detects them immediately and creates instructions for quick adjustment, that is, it aims to correct them as quickly as possible.

14.6 Concluding remarks

In this chapter it was argued that, contrary to Uhmann (2001, 2006), the structure of self-repair is not shaped by syntactic features alone, but also by functional motivations from interaction and cognition. Following Du Bois (1985), a competing motivations model was suggested to explain the point of retracing in substitutions of the noun in prepositional phrases in German. This model is preliminary, as it is based on a relatively small number of examples in only one syntactic context. However, the explanatory value of this model gives reason for confidence in its ability to explain the syntax of self-repair by integrating competing motivations from grammar, interaction, and language processing. On a more general level, this type of model can help shed light on the low-level organization of retractions as basic operations of online syntax (Auer 2009). In the long run, research in this area might also contribute to developing a theory of spoken language that takes into account the interrelation of grammar, interaction, and cognition (cf. Günthner 2007 on the need for a theory of spoken language, its possible value, and suggestions for its realization).

Overall, the findings in this chapter suggest that competing motivations, besides their importance for grammaticization in general (cf. Du Bois 1985), are also crucial to the formation of the repair system, which operates within and is constrained by a language-specific grammatical framework, but additionally adapts to the interactional and cognitive needs of participants engaged in self-repair.

14.7 Appendix

Transcription conventions (GAT 2, Selting et al. 2009)

[ ]	overlap and simultaneous talk
[ ]	
°h	inbreath of appr. 0.2–0.5 sec. duration
(.)	micro pause, estimated, up to 0.2 sec. duration appr.
(-) / (–)	estimated pauses of appr. 0.2–0.5 / 0.5–0.8 sec. duration
und_äh	assimilations within units
äh	hesitation marker
hehe	syllabic laughter
hm, mhm	continuers, monosyllabic tokens
hm_hm, aha	continuers, bi-syllabic tokens
(solche)	assumed wording
->	refers to a line of transcript relevant in the argument
=	fast, immediate continuation with a new turn or segment (latching)
: / ::	lengthening, by about 0.2–0.5 / 0.5–0.8 sec.
ʼ	cut-off by glottal closure
SYLlable	focus accent
sYllable	secondary accent
?	rising to high (final pitch movement of intonation phrase)
ʼ	rising to mid (final pitch movement of intonation phrase)
–	level (final pitch movement of intonation phrase)
;	falling to mid (final pitch movement of intonation phrase)
.	falling to low (final pitch movement of intonation phrase)
<<f>>	forte, loud (with scope)
<<all>>	allegro, fast (with scope)
<<dim>>	diminuendo, increasingly softer (with scope)

15

Six competing motives for repetition

JOHN HAIMAN

Ever since von der Gabelentz, the notion of competing motivations generally takes the point of view of the speaker, who may be impelled to utter *different* productions by a variety of contending needs: the need make himself clear, the need to impress, flatter, or intimidate his interlocutor, or the need to indulge his own laziness. But one could as well adopt the position of the hearer: given a *single* linguistic production, what meanings could lie behind it? This is the point of view I would like to adopt here. The medium of language is notoriously limited relative to the domain of thought, and so it comes about that many conceptual dimensions are forced to compete for expression in the same linguistic forms. In principle, given the sheer number of competing motivations which could lie behind any formal expression, it may be necessary to recognize that a given structure is therefore a priori entirely meaningless and arbitrary. Yet motivations exist, and we respond to them. How? This chapter is about one of the most semantically overburdened morphosyntactic devices available in language: that of simple repetition of a given form. In my discussion I will try to show that although repetition can have at least six different and hence competing motivations,[1] there are cues for distinguishing these in the grammar of at least one language where most of them occur. Here, first, are some motivations for grammatical repetition:

Within a text, repetition may be *iconically* motivated to express intensification, repetition, or conceptual symmetry; it may be *aesthetically* motivated by a love of symmetry for its own sake; it may be *histrionically* motivated, by the ham actor's compulsion to overdo his performance.

Intertextually, it may be motivated by the plagiarist's or language learner's desire to *pass* for his model; the sycophant's desire to voice *agreement* with his model; or the caricaturist's desire to *make fun of* his model. All of these kinds of repetition can

---

[1] This is not to say there may not be many more. But in what is held by some to be the most open-ended enumeration of the rhetorical functions of *repetitio*, Quintilian himself asserts only that words may be doubled for amplification (emphasis or clarification), pathos, or irony (2001: 116, 127, 131). Otherwise, he enumerates copious examples with punctilious formal characterizations, but without discussion of any meaning or pragmatic force they may have. Possibly repetition serves a purely decorative function in all of his unglossed examples.

be exemplified not only from language but also from non-verbal art and other varieties of human behavior as well. Nor should this list be considered as anywhere near complete—for example, one of the most fundamental and prosaic motives for repetition in conversation is to establish textual *coherence*, a subject which has been exhaustively dealt with by Halliday and Hassan (1976), Tannen (1985), among others, and which I will entirely ignore.

I will focus on the six that I have enumerated above, with special reference to mockery, because I think it is the least studied, and also because something like mockery may be implicated in the genesis of language. I will also try to show, with particular reference to one language, how these different kinds of repetition can be still at least to some extent distinguished. Partially this will occur through the use of lexical or morphosyntactic conventionalized "compensatory diacritics" which are presumably language-specific, and which are attached to the fundamental diagram of repetition (Haiman 1985b: 60–7). But partly it will occur in ways that are themselves partially motivated by the different conceptual dimensions that they express.

15.1 Iconic repetition

Reduplication, as everybody knows, almost universally expresses conceptual motions like iterativity, plurality, intensification, emphasis, duration, symmetry, and the like. Whether or not a language has institutionalized reduplication in its morphosyntax, the mere repetition of words will always be useable for the pregrammatical expression of duration and reiteration. That is, I believe there is no language in which it is impossible to repeat a verb, as in

(1) a. He climbed and he climbed and he climbed
     b. Bush lied and lied and lied

without meaning something like "he *kept on/continued* climbing" (thus, durative aspect), or "Bush lied *often* or *repeatedly*" (thus, iterative aspect).[2] (Note that the iconic representation of repetition persists even in language-specific non-verb lexicalizations like *on and on, over and over, time after time, again and again*.) I am almost as confident that there is no language in which it is impossible to say something like

(2) a. One went East, one went West
     b. The leap was quick, the return was quick
     c. The bigger they are, the harder they fall

without using the formal symmetry which results from repetition for the expression of something like conceptual symmetry. Formal symmetry, whether of the "alliterating" (ABAC) variety of (2a), the "rhyming" (ABCB) variety of (2b), or the "correlative" (parallel morphosyntactic structure for two mutually dependent clauses) variety of (2c), will always be a vehicle for the expression of conceptual

---

[2] This kind of iconicity is seldom given explicit recognition in most descriptive grammars. A welcome exception is Aikhenvald (2010b).

symmetry. Moving on down to less universally adopted structures, probably a significant minority of languages find some way of using repetition to express conceptual notions like distributivity (repetition here iconically signals repeated acts or states) and reciprocity (where repetition iconically signals symmetry). English, as we can see, has lexicalized both notions using the same word *each*, but many languages have not:

(3)   You can each take two pieces. (*each* signals distributivity)

(4)   They hit each other. (*each* signals reciprocity)

All of these can of course be grammaticalized in different languages to different degrees. Few languages are as exquisitely iconic in the representation of reciprocity as is Hua (Haiman 1985: 78–81), but very many do use repetition to convey the notion (Nedjalkov 2007b provides a survey). The same can be said for the encoding of distributivity: languages run the gamut from English (full lexicalization of the notion) to Cambodian (where it is expressed entirely by repetition, see Section 15.7.1).

Recurrent (crosslinguistic) formal symmetry may sometimes even serve as a heuristic for discovering unrecognized conceptual symmetry: for example, Haiman and Kuteva (2001) demonstrated that in a sample of nearly 200 languages, counterfactual conditionals exhibit a greater degree of formal parallelism in the protasis and apodosis than do the clauses of hypothetical and given conditionals. They argued that the hitherto unrecognized conceptual basis for this statistically significant finding is that counterfactual conditionals are more likely than hypotheticals or given conditionals to be biconditional.

Continuing on down, there will be a smaller number of languages which employ repetition for the expression of plurality and so on.

15.2 Decorative repetition

English has a small number of "twin forms" (Marchand 1960) like *helter-skelter*, *higgledy-piggledy, jibber jabber*, which seem to be iconically motivated in that they frequently express some notion of disordered iterativity (Waelchli 2005).[3] But not all twin forms seem to carry any such meaning, particularly in many of the languages of Southeast Asia. Rather, as many investigators have reported, formal repetition seems to have only a playful or artistic function. In Khmer, *lbej* means "famous," as does *lbej lba:nj*, whose second element is now a virtually meaningless *boriva: sap* "servant word,"[4] much like the *jibber* of *jibber jabber*. There are thousands of such twin forms in the language (Ourn and Haiman 2001; Haiman and Ourn 2009; Haiman 2010a, 2010b, 2011, to appear). It may be that many of the examples of rhetorical repetition which Quintilian 2001 enumerates with no reference to their semantic function belong here also.

---

[3] This disordered iterativity may also be the reason for the frequently observed pejorative connotations of such pairs, cf. Stolz (2008).

[4] Native grammarians have lavished considerable attention on the meanings and origins of such decorative expressions in Cambodian. For a partial survey, see Haiman (2011: ch. 4.5).

15.3 Histrionic repetition: The case of ideophones

The over-emoting of ham actors seems to be a matter of personal style rather than a topic for linguistic analysis. Yet it may be possible to speak of a grammaticalization of histrionic repetition as well. Ideophones, common in languages of Africa and Asia, have, since their formal recognition (Doke 1935), been considered a part of speech characterized by the fact that they do not describe, they somehow perform, what they denote (Kunene 2001). Speakers of European languages need to be advised that not all ideophones are onomatopoeic: they may be "performances" of sights, smells, textures, and facial or bodily attitudes, as well as of sounds. One of their almost definitional properties is that they tend to be accompanied by non-verbal gestures and facial expressions. With surprising frequency, ideophones are also reduplicating or repeated forms. Indeed it is often remarked about such words that the only kind of morphological alternation which they may undergo—and typically do undergo—is grammaticalized repetition, or reduplication.[5] In many cases, repetition is iconically motivated: ideophones reduplicate simply because they represent repeating actions, but this is not always true. (Even English has *tsk tsk*, an ideophone representing disapproval, or *unhunh*, an ideophone representing negation.[6]) In this connection, two recurrent facts are worthy of attention.

First: It is particularly notable that in some languages, the status of being an ideophone in the first place is conferred on an ordinary word simply and exclusively through the fact that it is repeated. In fact, reduplication alone has been elevated to quasi-definitional status for ideophones by Asher and Kumar, in their grammar of Malayalam (1997: 447). That is, while a given root may be a noun or a verb, or simply fail to occur at all as a simplex, when reduplicated, it functions ipso facto as an ideophone. This finding is replicated.

- In Khwe, *coe* is the name of the black-cheeked lovebird, but the reduplication of the name is an ideophone representing its call (Kilian-Hatz 2008: 246).
- In Udihe, *bugdu* means 'slippery', and is an adjective, but *bugdumce bugdumce*, also meaning 'slippery', is an ideophone (Nikolaeva and Tolskaja 2001: 383).
- In Semai, where "as a rule color terms and words for taste are ambivalently expressive and stative verbs," it is reduplication which separates the ideophonic sheep from the verbal goats : the root *cnga:l* 'red' is a case in point. Reduplicated, it is the ideophone *ci-cnga:l* 'appearance of a flickering red object,' as a verb, it yields the conventional series of derivations via other affixes, such as *c-r-nga:l* 'redden' (causative) Diffloth (1976: 255).

This suggests that in some languages at least repetition is not just an incidental but a definitional property of ideophones.

---

[5] I take it as self-evident that reduplication always originates as simple repetition, and is a conventionalized or grammaticalized form of it. For a clear exemplification, see David Gil's contribution to Hurch (2005).

[6] These are given in their conventional orthographic representation, one which obscures another frequent fact about ideophones—that they contain sounds (like clicks or nasal vowels, here) which are not phonemes in the host language.

Second: it is also notable that ideophones are characterized by a variety of more or less conventionalized formal devices which collectively can be characterized as "histrionic exaggeration." Thus Jaggar (2001: 690) and Wolff (1992: 453) point out that in Hausa, ideophones are frequently marked by exaggeration of both High and Low tones, as well as by extra lengthening of their vowel (if monosyllabic)—as well as by reduplication (Wolff 1992: 454, Jaggar 2001: 691). Egbokhane (2001: 88) notes that in Emai, reduplication or lengthening of the final vowel are equally characteristic of ideophones. In Urarina (an isolate) and in Udihe (Tungusic), where ideophones are not total reduplications, they are very typically marked by reduplication of the final syllable alone, thus Udihe *lebdelililili* 'fluttering,' *pesoso* 'sound made by a drinking female deer' (Nikoleva and Tolskaja 2001: 384), Urarina *tjwnenenene* 'sizzle' (Olawsky 2006: 283). Watters (2000: 196) notes simply that "ideophones commonly contain reduplicated syllables, or one of the vowels or consonants is extra long." Welmers (1973: 471) observes that ideophones are frequently performed in histrionic tones of voice, such as hushed or falsetto. In his grammar of Bininj-Guwok, Evans (2003a: 627) notes that "ideophones are accompanied by a reset of the intonational range, and often a change in voice quality, for example to a more nasalized production in the case of the ideophone representing the sound of the didgeridoo."

Of the eight fundamental properties of prototypical ideophones given by Childs in his grammar of Kisi (1995: 133), no fewer than FIVE can be characterized as histrionic. They include: raised or lowered registers relative to normal speech, rapid modulation or exaggerated range of registers, unusual phonation types such as breathy, creaky, or voiceless, exaggerated duration or abruptness, and a faster or slower rate of speech than normal. Dingemanse (2009a: 1) observes that in Siwu, ideophones are "morphologically special because they freely undergo various types of reduplication *and lengthening*" (my emphasis). Examples of the latter include:

(5) a. *kpoooo*   'serene'
     b. *kpiiiii*   'petrified'
     c. *kpɛtɛɛɛ*   'soaked'
     d. *saaaaa*   'cool tactile sensation'

He goes on to say (Dingemanse 2009b: 2) that ideophones are "performatively foregrounded, that is to say, they freely undergo various types of reduplication, lengthening, and expressive intonation"—as prototypically histrionic performances may also do.

Kita's observation (1997: 397) that Japanese mimetics are "the obligatory locus of the prosodic peak of the utterance" wherein they occur, may also be no more than a muted conventionalization of this widely attested "histrionic" flavor.

This range of observations suggests to me that the repetition of ideophones may be motivated by the same drive: the ideophone user's wish to put on some kind of theatrical performance (a fact most strongly emphasized by Kunene (2001), but repeated by virtually all other observers). Bearing in mind that the average performer is likely to overdo his performance, so that terms like "staginess" and "histrionics" at least in English are virtually synonyms for exaggeration, it is possible that repetition is conceptually akin to exaggerated duration, exaggerated amplitude, exaggerated intonation curves, fake (falsetto and creaky) voices, and the like.[7]

15.4 Intertextual conformity

A plagiarist is copying a brilliant student's responses on a final examination. On the last question, the brilliant student writes (6a), and the plagiarist disastrously writes (6b):

(6) a. I do not know the answer to this question.
     b. Neither do I.

To be a successful plagiarist, that is, to pass as the model imitated, is to copy the model exactly, without giving away that the plagiarist's production is a copy. One of the (clearly unintentional) metamessages conveyed in (6b) or in any anaphoric reduction like it, is of course that "this reduction is made possible only because it is a copy of a prior form." The plagiarist's motive is also the L2 learner's motive: both want to pass for the real thing, and not imperfect copies of it—hence (6a) is forced upon them.

15.5 Intertextual sycophancy

The failed plagiarist of (6b), on the other hand, is identical to the sycophantic ditto-head or yes-man, repeating his model with short-cuts that signal that agreement is all that he aspires to. The meta-message "this is a copy" is not only allowable, but strongly preferred in such "amen"-like productions.

15.6 The intertextual expression of contempt

There is an extremely close connection between respectful and disdainful imitation. It is reflected in the ambiguity of expressions like *mock* and *quote*. (There is nothing

---

[7] A literary example of hamming it up via repetition comes from Joseph Heller's *Catch-22*:

"Now, men, [we're going to synchronize our watches], " Colonel Korn began promptly in a sharp commanding manner, rolling his eyes flirtatiously in General Dreedle's direction. *"We're going to synchronize our watches* [one time] *and one time only,* and if it doesn't come off in that *one time,* General Dreedle and I are going to want to know why. Is that clear?" He fluttered his eyes toward General Dreedle to make sure his plug had registered. "Now set your watches for nine-eighteen." Colonel Korn synchronized their watches without a single hitch and moved forward with confidence. [He gave the men the colors of the day], and [reviewed the weather conditions] with an agile, flashy versatility, casting simpering looks at General Dreedle every few seconds to draw increased encouragement from the excellent impression he saw he was making. Preening and pruning himself effulgently and strutting vaingloriously about the platform as he picked up momentum, *he gave the men the colors of the day* again and shifted nimbly to a rousing pep talk on the importance of the bridge at Avignon to the war effort and the obligation of each man on the mission to place love of country above love of life. When his inspiring dissertation was finished, *he gave the men the colors of the day still one more time,* stressed the angle of approach, and *reviewed the weather conditions again.* (Heller 1972: 229)

inherently contemptuous in *mock duck*, yet the standard contempt-meaning of the word is patent in derivational forms like *mockery*. Nor is there anything inherently contemptuous in the nearly universal notion of quotation, a speech act which includes respectful allusion and citation, but the airquote gesture is a major signal of disdain in colloquial American.) Yet respectful and disdainful quotation are clearly very different. The profound distinction between "respectful imitation" (which may be born of either the conformist or sycophantic desire to conform to a model) and the "mocking imitation" which is born of contempt for it is neatly captured in a David Sipress cartoon which features an encounter between a bewildered woman wearing a crop-top and a bland man in suit and tie who is also wearing a crop-top. The woman wears the crop-top to conform with a fashion; the man wearing the same crop-top is mocking the fashion and the woman as well. His performance is ironic.

An example of the mocking use of repetition is offered in Riau Indonesian, a language where "they don't have (much) sarcasm." David Gil (my p.c. source for this observation) has observed that a speaker may correct her blunders by first repeating them sotto voce with extra length on the penultimate syllable, and then substitute what she meant to say:

(7)   I went to Jakarta—Jakaaaarta!—Penang.

Other speakers can mock the first speaker in the same way:

(8)   Speaker A: — I went to Jakarta
      Speaker B: — Jakaaaarta![8]

A stock example in English is *sure sure*, which parodies agreement. Many more examples are given in Haiman (1998). There is a small but growing literature in linguistics and in literary theory on the expression of irony and sarcasm, which focuses on mocking imitation. A major debate running through this literature is whether the sarcast/ironist is engaging in echoic *mention* (hence a kind of alienated repetition or imitation) (Sperber and Wilson 1981) or *pretence* (Clark and Gerrig 1984).

Both positions are clearly right in some way. Nevertheless, this distinction, it seems to me, is of limited usefulness for distinguishing conformity from contempt, and the resulting debate has increasingly focused on a non-issue and accordingly misses a number of conceptual points. First, pretence and imitation in general are not distinct, because, from child's play to hypocrisy, *all pretence is imitation, if not echoic mention*—nobody "pretends" to be something for which there is no model. Or if she does, we do not recognize it. Second, the notion of pretence alone does not give us any basis for distinguishing between the imitation born of the desire for conformity to a model and that born of the desire to mock that model. The plagiarist and the ironist are both pretending, after all.

Third, imitation alone also does not give us any basis for making this crucial distinction. The plagiarist, the sycophant, and the ironist are all imitating a model.

---

[8] Edith Moravcsik informs me that this strategy is also possible in Hungarian.

What crucially distinguishes plagiarism, agreement, and sycophancy from echoic mockery is that the latter comes with a metamessage explicitly advertising itself to be *only* an imitation or pretence: it is like Magritte's famous picture of a pipe with its caption "this is not a pipe."[9] While the formal devices whereby this metamessage is conveyed are of considerable interest and variety, the most important conceptual distinction is that this explicit metamessage *exists* for mockery, but not for sycophancy, conformity or for the trompe-l'oeil put-on (mockery disguised as conformity).

The same formal distinction is also crucial for the distinction between acts undertaken for themselves as means towards an end, and the pedagogical demonstrations of such acts[10] for an audience; and for the distinction between pragmatic acts and the theatrical representations of such acts in signs. Hence the distinction is important in the genesis of language in general, as noted by Rudi Keller. He points out (1994a: 49), If I want to surreptitiously signal to my wife that I am bored at an important meeting, I may yawn, but for my wife to get the message, she has to recognize that my yawn is

1. An imitation of a *yawn* (that is, the sign must be an icon)
2. [only] an *imitation* of a yawn (that is, the sign is just a sign, not the real thing).

How does the nonce-language creator manage this crucial second task and construct a "theatrical frame" around his yawn so that his interlocutor recognizes that it is indeed fake?

More generally, how are all the kinds of repetition enumerated so far kept distinct from one another, so that we can tell when a single speaker's production of AA signals iconic repetition, decoration, or staginess; or when a speaker's repetition of another speaker's A signals conformity, sycophancy, or contempt?

Sometimes, of course, it is difficult to perceive that distinction. One can be more catholic than the Pope with the intention of either emulating or mocking him: on the one hand, the sincere overimitation of a prestige model can be a generator of language change (Labov 1972), and on the other, there used to be a category of

---

[9] The explicit metalinguistic advertisement "this is only a sign" is a subcategory of what Sperber and Wilson (1981) call "mention," a much broader conceptual category which includes many non-ironic applications. In fact, "mention" includes the identification of signs as signs, that is, as grammatical language opposed to pragmatic action in the first place. This more general definition is suggested by an example from the Monty Python film *Life of Brian*, set in Biblical Judea. A rebel painting anti-Roman graffiti in bad Latin (*Romanes eunt domus*) on the walls is caught by a pedagogically minded Roman legionary who makes him write out the graffiti correctly, as *Romani ite domum* "Romans go home" a hundred times over, *as punishment*, on the same walls. If irony is echoic mention, then so too is the school-masterly pedantry about grammar parodied in this excerpt, and indeed any other kind of metalanguage, including the metamessage "this is a sign."

[10] Demonstrations may also be characterized by exaggeration. Here is Christophe Boesch (1993: 177) on a mother chimpanzee illustrating for her offspring the correct technique for using tools to crack nuts. "Ricci, *in a very deliberate manner*, slowly rotated the hammer into the best position for efficiently pounding the nut. *As if to emphasize the meaning of this movement, it took her a full minute to perform this simple rotation.* With Nina watching her, she then proceeded to use the hammer to crack ten nuts (of which Nina received six entire kernels and portions of the four others). Then Ricci left, and Nina resumed cracking."

offence in the Canadian army called "insolent subordination" where suspiciously slavish adherence to a model of saluting was recognized and punished (David Pentland, p.c.).

15.7 Compensatory diacritics to the rescue

Given that all of these conceptual dimensions are crowded around and competing for one possible means of expression, the question arises whether there are any means of nevertheless keeping them distinct. Khmer is a language in which almost all of these types of repetition occur, and are to some extent distinguished through language-particular means. The repetition diagram AA comes with compensatory diacritics, or additional labels.

15.7.1 *Iconic reduplication is effected in two ways*

First, by the *total repetition* of a noun (*strej strej* 'woman woman' = 'women') or an adjective to indicate plurality (*cah cah* 'old old' = 'old people') or of a measure phrase to indicate distributivity:

(9) a. *mkha:ng* *pi:* *neak*   *pi:*   *neak*
       one-side two person two person
       'two people on each side'

   b. *kmee:ng* *voat*   *mneak*   *mneak*
      youth   temple   one-person one-person
      'each temple boy . . .'
      Sot *tae* *mian* *lo:k* *kru:* *banghat* *mneak*   *muaj* *mneak*   *muaj*
      pure only have monk teacher train   one-person one   one-person one
      'had one monk apiece to train him'

(Note the repetition of "one," which appears both as a prefix *m-* and as a separate word *muaj* in the distributive expressions *mneak muaj* meaning 'one-to-one'.)

   c. *tev* *seuh* *riang* *riang* *kluan*
      to   pupil   form   form   self
      'each to his own pupil'

   d. *criang* *ni'muaj*   *ni'muaj*
      sing   each one   each one
      'each song'

(NB *ni'muaj* already means 'each one,' but distributivity in (9d) is emphasized by repetition of the Measure Phrase.)

   e. *daeu* *daoj ku:*   *daoj ku:*
      walk   by pair   by pair
      'walk two by two'

   f. *viphiak* *ta:m*   *piak* *muaj* *muaj*
      analyze   follow word   one   one
      'analyze word by word'

Second, there exists a (non-productive) reduplicating prefix to indicate intensity:

(10) a. *teuk* 'water'   → *ta-teuk* RED. + water 'thoroughly soaked'
      b. *tak top* 'not fluent' → *ta-tak ta-top* 'speak haltingly, disfluently, like a
                                   child'
      c. *tael taol* 'alone'   → *ta-tael ta-taol* 'completely alone'

15.7.2 *Decorative repetition*

In Khmer, purely ornamental repetition is sharply distinguished from iconic reduplication in two ways. First, it is signaled through the *partial rather than the total*
repetition of a root, by an alliterating *boriva: sap* 'servant word' root (*lbej lba:nj*
'famous + servant word' = 'famous').

The meaningless alliterating servant word may precede the meaningful root in
some cases:

(11) a. *don*   *da:p*   'deteriorate'
         —   deteriorate

      b. *hwc*   *haeu*   'fly'
         —   fly

      c. *banti:*   *bantoan*   'rush'
         —   rush

      d. *kni:*   *knia*   'companion; each other'
         —   companion

      e. *ranji:*   *ranjoa*   'shake'
         —   shake

      f. *jw:n*   *ju:*   'long time'
         —   long time

      g. *tranjee:ng*   *tranja:ng* 'jerky'
         —   jerky

      h. *samkeum*   *samkau:m*   'cadaverous'
         —   cadaverous

      i. *ejve:*   *ejva:n*   'baggage'
         —   baggage

      j. *roat*   *riaj*   'strew, scatter'
         —   strew

follow it in others:

(12) a. *sngiam*   *sngat*   'quiet'
         quiet   —

      b. *prajat*   *prajaeng*   'take care, pay attention'
         take care   —

      c. *mdec*   *mda:*   'how?'
         how   —

> d. *t'o:nj*   *t'ae*   'complain'
>   complain   —
>
> e. *tnguan*   *tngau:*   'heavy, serious, grave'
>   heavy   —
>
> f. *jap*   *jweun*   'complicated'
>   complicated   —
>
> g. *sneut*   *sna:l*   'intimate, close'
>   intimate   —
>
> h. *leak*   *liam*   'hide'
>   hide   —

or occur in either order with yet others:

(13) *srapo:n*   *srapoap*   'sad, melancholy'
      sad   almost dry (of clothes)[11]

Second, while iconic reduplication is subject to "iambic reduction" in the vernacular, so that the schema "AA" typically reduces to something like "aA,"[12] no such reduction affects decorative reduplication: "AA" either remains unaffected, or *both conjuncts are reduced to exactly the same degree* in what looks like a case of incipient non-referential agreement. For example, the decorative pair

(14) *damnae*   *damneung*   'information'
      —   information

May be "ground down," via iambic reduction, to either

(15) a. *tamnae*   *tamneung*   (via devoicing of the initial stop), OR
      b. *tanae*   *taneung*   (with both devoicing of the initial consonant and loss of the unstressed syllable coda [m])

But it is impossible for the conjuncts to differ in the degree of their reduction. Thus, consultants agree on the impossibility of the non-occurring:

      c. **damnae*   *tamneung/taneung*
      d. **tamnae*   *damneung/taneung*
      e. **tanae*   *damneung/tamneung*

(cf. Haiman 2011: chapter 4.3.1).

15.7.3 *Ideophones*

Histrionic reduplication is signaled again by total repetition of a root (e.g. *tu:h tu:h* = 'impression of slapping on make-up') and is therefore formally identical with iconic

---

[11] In this example (and many others), the servant word is not a totally meaningless string, but an existing word which has been "conscripted" to co-occur with the main verb (partly, largely, or entirely) on the basis of its sound. For English language analogs, consider pairs like *true-blue, loose-y goose-y*.

[12] It is likely that intensive C_iV-reduplication originated as a fuller form, and was reduced through this same process, which is both current and one of great antiquity in Khmer, cf. Haiman (2011: 69).

reduplication—except that no iambic reduction of ideophones occurs: the form "AA" remains "AA." A reduction to "aA," as in (16b), is unacceptable.

(16) a. *kda:m   via   keu:m keu:m   cenj   pi: ranthau: mau:k*
      crab   3   slowly   exit   from   hole   come
      'Slooooowly, the crab came out from the hole.'

      b. **kda:m kamkeu:m cenj pi: ranthau: mau:k*

15.7.4 Agreement with a respected other

Sycophantic conformity with a source is signaled by either a partial or a total repetition of the model. In addition to the usual possibility of elision and anaphora exemplified by structures like "neither do I," other possibilities for substitution exist. Consider the following snippet of "yes-man" behavior:

(17) Speaker A: —*kecka: jeu:ng   ba:n   samrac   awh   haeuj?*
                    matter   our   PAST   ready   exhaust   PERF
      'Is our business/plot completely ready?'

      Speaker B: —*ba:t   ruac   srac   awh   haeuj*
                    Yessir[13]   escape   ready   exhaust   PERF
      'Yessir, it is completely ready.'

Unlike the typical conformist, the sycophant is perfectly willing to broadcast the message that his performance is a copy. It seems that acceptable partial repetitions in slavishly respectful quotation can include dropping decorative infixation (Haiman 2011: ch. 3) so that a derived form is transformed into a root (*s-am-rac* 'ready' being reuttered as *srac* 'ready'), or by the substitution of synonyms for a given model (*ba:n*, one past tense auxiliary, being rather creatively[14] reuttered as *ruac*, another past tense auxiliary).

15.7.5 Disdainful quotation

Contempt for a source is indicated by the addition of a rhetorical or scornful negative *aena:* (literally "where") following the disdained word (*prak aena:* salary + where = 'you call this a salary?'). Unlike congeners such as English *my eye/foot/ass* or German *von wegen*, which typically co-occur with mocking repetitions of the disdained message, *aena:* seems to occur with the message stated only once. (I have not found bare repetition used for the expression of contempt in Khmer, and in fact the rhetorical negative has a somewhat wider range of meanings than just sarcastic '...not.'. See Haiman (2011: 230–1).)

Thus the morphosyntactic and lexical resources of Khmer are sufficient to distinguish five kinds of repetition: those which are used iconically, for decoration, for staginess, in conformity, and to express sycophantic agreement.

---

[13] *Ba:t* (from Pali *pada* 'foot') signals humble agreement for male speakers. So this is clearly a case of not just agreement, but conventionalized sycophancy.

[14] Via polysemy copying, cf. Heine and Kuteva (2005), Haiman (2011: ch. 10).

15.8 A possibly universal principle of modifying repetition

It seems clear that the ways that Khmer signals the differences between iconic, decorative, and histrionic repetition are language-specific and conventionalized. In a similar way as words such as *each, continue, again*, which have replaced the diagrammatic expression of distributivity, duration, and iteration, they can be regarded as compensatory diacritics that are appended to a diagram which is insufficiently explicit to convey its message alone. I am too timid to venture any general principles based on the distinctions from the data provided by this single language. The devices enumerated in Sections 15.7.1, 15.7.2, and 15.7.3 shall therefore be construed as arbitrary language-specific conventions. But there may be one universal principle for distinguishing anaphoric repetition (acceptable in the expression of sycophancy) from ironic repetition, and I will close with a statement of this principle.

Both anaphoric messages like *neither do I* and ironic messages like *thanks a whole bunch* are patently imitations of some model and advertise themselves to be so through an explicit metamessage. The partially unconscious and incidental metamessage of anaphora "I repeat" and the fully conscious and heavily stressed metamessage of irony "I repeat" are in principle exactly the same message, yet they are—I would hazard—always signaled distinctly. In particular, anaphoric reduction is always opposed to ironic elaboration.[15] There is no language known to me in which irony is signaled through reduction of the repeated model; likewise, there is no language in which anaphora is signaled through elaboration of this model. Could this have been predicted on a priori functional grounds?

Possibly. Unless, like emphatic/reflexive pronouns, they signal *surprising* coreference, the Ur-motivation for anaphoric expressions is a version of the principle of least effort: they are uttered to save time and energy. They must always therefore justify themselves as verbal short-cuts. Hence the near-ubiquity of zero anaphora in languages, the extreme unlikelihood of sesquipedalian pronouns, and so on.

The functional motivation for sarcastic expressions, on the other hand, is to establish one's separation from a model message from a clearly marked position of superiority. Assume that language is one-dimensional in that there are only three options one can exercise in transmitting a message: one can reduce the message, preserve it faithfully, or elaborate it in some way. (This still recognizes one more possibility than most theories of competing motivations in the literature, which

---

[15] Even contextually inappropriate non-reduction may sometimes be ironic. Failure to convert a noun phrase to an anaphoric pronoun when the referent is repeated, particularly when it occupies the same position in the same syntactic structure, seems somehow to make fun of the referent. An example is James Ellroy's obituary on Milo Speriglio, a private eye who won temporary fame for claiming that Marilyn Monroe had been murdered:

Milo proffered bulk weight as proof of credibility. Milo knew that large figures impress. Milo was a mousy little guy. Milo was a self-confessed publicity hound. Milo said "I only read books which have my name in them." Milo developed a crush on the Marilyn Monroe job. Milo wrote three books on her alleged murder. (Ellroy 2001)

And so on for three columns.

follow von der Gabelentz[16] in recognizing only the first two, cf. Haiman 2010b.) One cannot express one's disdain by reducing the model (because apparently this option is universally "taken" by the anaphoric strategy: *all* that one can signal by practical shortcuts is one's laziness and familiarity with the model[17]). Nor can one express contempt by exact repetition unless such repetition is contextually inappropriate. Recall the Sipress cartoon of the man in the crop-top. Possibly this is because perfect intertextual copying of an absent model is also to some extent "taken" by the strategy of the plagiarist. All that one can reliably do by slavish imitation is to pass for the model, unless such slavish imitation is contextually inappropriate. Hence what is left to express separation—or any other "added-value" meaning—is to provide some extra frame, flag, or artifice which calls attention to the performance as a performance.[18] That said, the variety of extra flags of the "sarcastive" which have the meaning "I disdainfully repeat" is itself sometimes highly motivated (Haiman 1998: ch. 4). It is not by accident that the flag of fakery is... *not!* in English, or the quotative/evidential perfect in Bulgarian, or some other marker that advertises artifice, such as added duration or a singsong intonation and so on.

Curiously, this requirement for some kind of elaboration is very similar to the requirement for signs in general. To be useable as an intentional sign, an action must

---

[16] Gabelentz and his successors are concerned with competing motivations for the reduced or expanded expression of a *single meaning*. This chapter is concerned of course with competing semantic motivations for the use of a *single form*. Either way, competing motivations are going to weaken an orderly isomorphic correspondence between form and meaning.

[17] One can, however, fake the symptoms of laziness to convey disdain. Two techniques which come close to using reduction as signals of sarcasm are themselves playful imitations of reduction rather than actual reduction. (That is, they are like Keller's signs of a yawn, rather than the yawn itself.) The first is the orthographic convention (in English, French, and German, at least) of rendering oft-repeated and thus risible clichés by means of dashes between the words.

Es war nicht Wir-gehen-jetzt-ins-Kino-und-hinterher-noch-was-essen-oder-ein-Bier-trinken, das übliche Program. ('It wasn't the now-we'll-go-to-the-movies-and-then-have-a-bite-to-eat-or-have-a-beer, the usual scenario'; Goosen 2003: 282)

La violence de la mer revenant-à-la-vitesse-du-galop-d'un-cheval sur les sables du Mont St. Michel ('The violence of the sea returning-at-the-speed-of-a-galloping-horse over the sands of Mt. St. Michel'; Daninos 1962: 13)

Moreover, when she loses at Mah Jongg, she takes it like a sport, not-like-the-others-whose-names-she-could-mention-but-she-won't-not-even-Tilly-Hochman-it's-just-too-petty-to-talk-about-let's-just-forget-she-ever-brought-it-up (Roth 1969: 12).

Wray (2002: 4) provides a definition of formulas which is relevant to this imitation of the abbreviation process: formulas are "word strings that are processed without recourse to their lowest level of composition." This is almost the same as a definition of words that consist of meaningless phonemes: formulas evince a kind of double articulation. Even when the banality of the formula is disparaged through this orthographic device, there is no formal reduction of the words themselves in the above representations of disdain.

The second is the artful affectation of affectlessness in cases like *Wow*. The lack of enthusiasm is orthographically signaled in the punctuation mark. But note that even in this clear case of what seems like disdain through (amplitude) reduction, the speaker's ironic intention is only plain if she makes it clear that she is not really exhausted, but only playacting exhaustion, very much in the spirit of Rudi Keller's mimed yawn: typically through faked exaggeration of its symptoms.

[18] "Too" faithful a copy of a *present* model draws attention to itself as possible mockery.

not only require some effort. This extra effort must also be emancipated from practicality—that is, it must be downright useless in practical terms, *and be seen to be so*. Barthes (1983) remarks that one may signal something arbitrary about oneself by fiddling around with some aspect of one's dress which has no useful practical consequences, such as wearing a kerchief on the left or the right, or by wearing a shirt with a logo, but not by wearing one's left shoe on one's right foot—too painful, usually, to be a viable signal.[19] To return to Keller's example, the yawn which signals "I am bored" may be advertised as a fake yawn most easily by being "stylized": that is, exaggerated beyond the requirements of usefulness, or decorated with some artificial flourish. Remarkably, the same exaggeration characterizes a great deal of ritualized animal communication (Tinbergen 1952; Wilson, 1975: ch. 10; Haiman 1998). A sign, like a mocking imitation, is an action which has been intensified in some way.

---

[19] Unless one explicitly wishes to advertise "I am a masochist," for example, in the pursuit of beauty. The frequently *concealed* hair-shirt behavior of self-flagellants and the modesty of almsgivers enjoined in the Sermon on the Mount may be seen as an attempt to avoid self-advertisement, and thus a recognition of Barthes' point that it, like all talk, is inherently cost-free, and hence in some way contemptible.

Part III

General Issues and the Extension of the Approach

16

Motivating competitions

JOHN W. DU BOIS

This chapter is about motivations, competitions, and resolutions: about the motivations that shape the organization of grammar, the competitions that arise between these motivations, and the resolution of these competitions by the systematic and systematizing processes of grammaticization.[1] Neither motivation nor competition can be understood in isolation; each must be viewed in relation to the other, and in relation to how speakers use language to achieve their communicative goals. It is in the real-time decision-making of verbalization and interpretation that competitions first arise, and ultimately must be resolved. Attending to the complex web of relationships between speakers, their interlocutors, their goals, their utterances, and the grammatical structures and functional strategies they deploy is key to understanding grammar in functional terms. Out of the dynamic flux of discourse, grammars emerge, each one offering a uniquely rich repertoire of means to organize the full scope and diversity of its speakers' communicative actions. From the perspective of functional linguistics, it is important to understand competition, motivation, and their interaction if we wish to answer the fundamental functional question: Why are grammars as they are? The functional program has been pursued with success by many key contributors (Givón 1979; Hopper and Thompson 1980; Comrie 1984; Chafe 1994; Goldberg 1995; Ariel 1999a, 2008b; Haspelmath 1999a; Croft 2000; Thompson 2002a; Clancy 2003; Hopper and Traugott 2003; Tomasello 2003a; Bybee 2007). But one key component of the functional enterprise seems ripe for reexamination. Competition between motivations has long been recognized to

[1] I thank the editors of this volume and three anonymous reviewers for a useful critique, which has improved this paper significantly. For their insightful comments on earlier versions of these ideas, I am indebted to audiences at the Conference on Competing Motivations (Max Planck Institute for Evolutionary Anthropology, Leipzig), the École Normale Supérieure, Paris, and the University of California, Santa Barbara. My understanding of functional linguistics has benefited greatly from extended discussions with Patricia Clancy and Sandra Thompson. Most of all, I have gained immeasurably from my many conversations about competing motivations, functional explanation, and all the rest with Mira Ariel.

At the conference he organized on iconicity in syntax (Haiman, 1985a), John Haiman introduced my talk, saying simply: It's about competing motivations. I immediately resolved to drop whatever title I had thought relevant and take the one he offered. Thanks, John.

play a critical role in the emergence of grammar (Du Bois 1985), and in recent years the issue has attracted increasing interest (Dressler 1997b; Heine 1997; Kirby 1997; Haspelmath 1999b; Browman and Goldstein 2000; Aissen 2003; Diessel 2005; Malchukov 2005; 2008a; Gast 2007; Jäger 2007; Fenk-Oczlon and Fenk 2008; Wedel 2009; Moravcsik 2010; Fischer 2010; Haiman 2010a); see also the chapters in this volume. Still, what competing motivations are and how they work remain little understood. There is much to be learned about how the perennial competition between alternative motivations unleashes forces that drive the continual adaptation and evolution of grammars.

To appreciate the explanatory power of competing motivations, two observations are in order. (1) In language, all motivations are competing motivations. (2) Competitions between motivations are actual, observable, and pervasive, embodied in the real-time dynamics of every effort by every speaker to use language to communicate. Taken together, these two observations are foundational for the present approach to competing motivations. There is no escaping competition. No motivation ever stands alone as the sole determinant of a sign, nor can it uniquely determine the linkage of form and function in any utterance. This holds true whether the utterance is seen as the product of one speaker's immediate expressive choices, or the engagement between several dialogic co-participants, or the dynamics of adaptive changes within a speech community, or the historical development of language change over generations. In each decision about what word or structure to use there is always another motivation, a second layer of strategy that must be simultaneously taken into account, as the speaker strives to select from among available options just those that are most likely to effectively realize the current communicative goal. In all but the simplest of messages, a multiplicity of functions brings multiple motivations into play. What drives the complexity of language in the first place is the speaker's need to express ever richer ideas, within the limited capacity afforded by the recipient's available attention. Once tempted by complexity, we are led into competition.

Competition is consequential for language, arising under all conditions of use and affecting all aspects of the system, including syntax, morphology, semantics, pragmatics, phonology, phonetics, and more. Most critical are the competitions between functional motivations, but competition remains relevant whether or not it involves motivation directly in an obvious way. For the language user, competitions are experienced as part of a decision-making process (Kahneman 2011; Cutler 2012), in which an act of choice is required between two or more alternatives. Each alternative is evaluated (Clark 1996) for the probability that it will contribute to the task at hand. A speaker of English who wishes to verbalize a three-participant event of transfer, for example, must decide whether to use the verb *give*, and whether to use the double object construction (*gave him his hat*) or the prepositional object construction (*gave it to the boy on the bicycle*). (I return to these constructions in Section 16.1). Neither the competition nor the decision that resolves it need be conscious; what matters is that the choice represents an actual cognitive process that takes time and resources, whose outcome is influenced by many factors (Gries 2003b; 2005; Bresnan et al. 2007b). On the other end of the communicative event, the recipient who hears the word *give* has to recognize it, choosing from among perceptually competing words (Cutler 2012), and must also decide which of its various senses is meant, whether to "transfer possession," "cause to experience," "fail to resist pressure"—to mention only a few of the dozen or more distinct senses of this versatile verb. Much of this competition plays out in milliseconds, outside the scope of awareness. But what, if anything, does competition achieve? The interplay of cognitive activation, competition, and suppression yields a single pragmatically viable winner (Gernsbacher and Faust 1991; Giora 2003; Cutler 2012). The global consequences of this local event are momentous. It amounts to a selective process that shapes the adaptive emergence of grammar (Du Bois 2003b; Steels 2012b).

To speak of motivation in the first place is to assume that language makes sense, in some sense. This is the fundamental premise of functional linguistics: The organization of grammar can be explained in terms of how it is used. Grammar adapts to serve the functional goals of its users while respecting and exploiting their capacities and limitations. Crucially, speakers' communicative goals typically require coordinating multiple strategies. Among these are: (1) the expression of distinctive and recognizable phonetic forms; (2) faithful pairing of form and function; (3) clarity and transparency in formulating salient meanings; (4) efficient management of limited cognitive resources; (5) identifying situated interpretations of uttered words and contextually relevant inferences; (6) coordinating verbal interaction between co-participants; and (7) adhering to linguistic norms and conventions.

No utterance can equally satisfy all these demands at once. Likewise in grammar, there can be no perfection of motivation in the evolved and evolving organization of the system, with its eternal residue of competitions not yet fully resolved. All one can say about a grammar, and all one needs to say, is that it is good enough: adequately adapted to meet the demands that are regularly placed on it by its users. While a competition that arises locally in a given communicative situation may be resolved for the specific case at hand, in global terms it is not likely to stay resolved for long. The contending forces remain in place, keeping competition alive and sustaining the tension between system and use. This tension in turn motivates the search for further innovations, keeping open the possibility of systemic change. Thus competition proves central to the processes of selection, adaptation, and emergence. For the linguist who accepts the challenge of explaining grammar, it is clear that the study of competitions is well motivated.

But we are getting ahead of ourselves. The remainder of this chapter proceeds as follows. Section 16.1 argues for the concrete reality of competition in language use, using the ditransitive *give* construction to illustrate competition between alternative ways of verbalizing three-participant events. Section 16.2 argues that competition arises between functionally motivated communicative strategies. Section 16.3 proposes a distinction between competing motivations and conflicting fitness criteria. Section 16.4 delves into the significance of the Functional Frequency Principle ("Grammars code best what speakers do most", Du Bois 1985), while Section 16.5 contemplates the recent historical context of the idea of competing motivations. Section 16.6 asks whether there can be motivation without competition. In conclusion, Section 16.7 presents ten key points that characterize competition and its role in shaping the adaptive motivation of grammar.

16.1 Real competition

Is competition in language something you can see, hear, or otherwise observe? Languages offer multiple alternative means of solving most communicative tasks. Consequently, speakers and hearers often face an embarrassment of riches, and may struggle—sometimes observably so—to choose a verbalization, or an interpretation. Each grammatical alternative offers distinct affordances (Gibson 1979; Greeno 1994; Marandin 2011), so speakers need to assess the benefits and tradeoffs involved. In effect the different grammatical options compete to offer users high utility at low cost.

But when and where does linguistic competition actually play out? Competition in language (Bates and MacWhinney 1987; MacWhinney, this volume) becomes real when communicative strategies are tied to real-time choices between functional units or patterns, such as words, structures, constructions, or rules. And such choices are actualized in the utterance arena (Du Bois in progress). In general, competition arises between functional units occupying the same functional niche,[2] understood as a micro-environment defined by the current communicative context, the goals of dialogic co-participants, and the grammatical alternatives available.

Evidence for the reality of the competition between motivations can be found in any domain of grammar, but for expository purposes I will focus on grammatical strategies for verbalizing three-participant events (Goldberg 1995; Gries 2005; Margetts and Austin 2007; Malchukov et al. 2010), especially those involving the verb *give* (Newman 1996, 2005; Haspelmath 2005a) and its competitors. Three-participant verbalizations are of particular interest because their expressive complexity can motivate the speaker's use of a relatively complex argument structure, for example ditransitive *he gives him his hat*, which is modestly more complex than a simple transitive or intransitive. Increased argument structure complexity calls for care in managing limited cognitive resources.

One way to monitor competition is to observe in real time the unfolding of the speaker's verbalization process (Chafe 1977, 1994). Contexts where competition becomes visible in verbalization include (1) disfluencies (Chafe 1979, 1994; Clark and Fox Tree 2002) and (2) variability between speakers in the linguistic strategies used to express the same (or similar) events.

Disfluency betrays indecision between competing alternatives. Two formulations compete, but just one completes. For example:

(1) (*Tastes Very Special* SBC031: 892.603–898.708)   (Du Bois et al. 2000–05)
    1   ROSEMARY;   .. So **they gave her some** —
    2   (H) He- —
    3   .. He or **she got** a- (0.4) **some pills for muscle spasms,**
    4   but it hasn't helped,

The speaker begins her utterance from one perspective, but soon abandons it. She truncates her projected clause (*they gave her some*—) halfway through the direct object noun phrase. After some false starts (*he-*) reflecting roughly the same

---

[2] For the niche concept in biology, see Odling-Smee et al. (2003); for linguistics, see Bickerton (2009).

perspective, she chooses an entirely different construction: *she got some pills*. Competing motivations enter the picture when two functional features that typically characterize the syntactic subject—agency and topicality—part company, and conflict in the attempted verbalization. Agency favors selection of the physician's assistant (*he*) as the subject, as the actor who acts to give the woman the pills. In contrast, topicality favors the female protagonist (*she*) as the overall discourse topic. She is mentioned sixteen times previously while he is mentioned only once in a completed clause (plus three times in false starts); she is named, while he remains nameless; she continues as discourse topic, while he is a local topic only, disappearing in the subsequent discourse. Agency is initially favored as the motivating criterion for subject selection (*they ... he ... he*), but topicality soon prevails, as the female protagonist (*she*) captures the subject slot (line 3). Once the topic/subject has been decided, a cascade of further consequences follow. The successful utterance selects for a complex functional unit linking the selected topic to a distinct choice of verb (*got*, replacing *gave*) and a less complex argument structure construction (transitive, replacing ditransitive).

What does the speaker's real-time experience of producing language tell us about competing motivations? Though a systematic analysis of many more such cases would be required before any general conclusions can be drawn, we can offer some initial observations. First, disfluencies can provide a valuable window on competition between alternative strategies in the utterance arena. Second, the event being described does not determine its own verbalization. Third, speakers have choices to make regarding perspectivization, viewpoint, and construal (Fillmore 1977; Langacker 1987; Chafe 1994). Fourth, the choice between functionally motivated strategies is consequential for the selection of grammar.

The second type of evidence for competition is more indirect, deriving from the variability of verbalizations of the same event by different speakers. Variation arises even when commonplace events are recounted with apparent objectivity. The following examples, intended to illustrate the range of grammatical options English affords for expressing three-participant events, come from speakers who were asked to tell what happened in a short film (the *Pear Film*, Chafe 1980; Du Bois 1980).[3] One highly salient moment in the film presents the following sequence of events: The Paddleball Boy finds the Bike Boy's hat lying in the road, whistles to the Bike Boy, runs to him, and gives him his hat. Even in a routine three-participant event like the transfer of a hat, there turns out to be enough expressive complexity to foster a surprisingly diverse array of solutions to the verbalization problem. In a sample of twenty speakers, at least a dozen distinct combinations of verb, particle, referential form, and argument structure were used to verbalize the hat transfer, exploiting constructions that differ in ways large and small. Different speakers say variously that the Paddleball Boy:

---

[3] The examples in this chapter are, with one exception, drawn from narrations by twenty speakers of American English (labeled S1, S2, etc.) of the events of the *Pear Film* (Chafe 1980). I have slightly simplified the transcriptions for clarity of exposition, omitting some details of prosody, and updating them in accordance with current "Discourse Transcription" (DT2) conventions (Du Bois 2013).

(2)   ... gave it to the boy on the bicycle   (S17)
(3)   ... gives him his hat   (S5)
(4)   ... gives him his hat back   (S3)
(5)   ... gives him back his hat   (S6)
(6)   ... gives him back the hat   (S18)

This set of verbalization strategies (there are more to come) reflects a choice between the prepositional object construction in (2), the simple double object construction in (3), and the double object-directional particle construction, with *back* inserted after either the theme (4) or the recipient (5)–(6).[4] But other verbs can be used as well, including *bring* and *take*:

(7)   ... brings the hat to the bicycle boy   (S12)
(8)   ... brings his hat to him   (S1)
(9)   ... goes and takes the hat to the kid   (S10)
(10)   ... takes the hat back, to him   (S13)

So far all these formulations have expressed the recipient overtly (*the boy on the bicycle, the kid, him*), whether in a prepositional object or indirect object slot. But even this is negotiable. Strategies exist to verbalize a transfer event without mentioning the recipient overtly. Here the speakers manage to convey the owner's receiving of the hat without using a noun phrase to refer directly to him (only to the hat, possessed or not):

(11)   ... for bringing back his hat   (S12)
(12)   ... brings the hat back   (S7)
(13)   ... bring the hat back   (S2)

This inferential strategy exploits a directional particle (*back*) to allow the hearer to infer the hat's recipient. Other constructional strategies for verbalizing a three-participant event while omitting the recipient include using a transitive (14) and even an intransitive verb (15):

(14)   ... returns his hat   (S1)
(15)   ... goes back with the hat   (S18)

These inferential strategies work for this specific event verbalization because the hat is being returned to its previous owner.

All of the constructional strategies in (2)–(15) represent effective alternatives for verbalizing the same event, though they differ in what is grammatically encoded vs. pragmatically inferred (Ariel 2008b). All compete for selection within the functional niche defined by the three-participant event verbalization task. These examples illustrate a critical but often overlooked factor in competitions between functional motivations: the pervasive role of inference as a supplement to grammatically coded

---

[4] For factors motivating particle placement, see Gries (2003a).

meanings. The fact that inference is part of virtually every utterance interpretation introduces an important variable into the continually renegotiable division of labor between pragmatics and grammar (Ariel 2008b), with major consequences for grammaticization.

What we can learn from observing discourse phenomena like disfluency (1) and variability (2–15) is that speakers' choices about how to represent an event carry consequences for grammatical selection. Making one key decision, for example about the perspectivization adopted, can shape the verbalization on multiple dimensions, triggering cascading effects on the choice of subject, verb, voice, transitivity, argument structure construction, word order, inference, and more. The variability of verbalization reflects the scope of competition between functional strategies, whether realized via code or inference. For any given event, the rich repertoire of available expressive options means that competition is inevitable. The conclusion is clear: To observe how competitive events shape the adaptive emergence of grammar, it will be critical to monitor discourse—especially spontaneous discourse.

16.2 Competing strategies

If we accept that competition is key to the adaptive processes that drive the emergence of grammar, there still remains the question: What is competing with what? The answer must reflect the fact that competition applies at several different levels in language. At one level, a linguistic sign (form–function combination) competes with its paradigmatic alternatives: Which of the alternative signs will be selected as the most useful for the present communicative goal? But on a deeper level, what competes is a functional strategy, as implemented in a specific functional unit (a sign, construction, collocation, rule, etc. that implements some function). As seen in the examples above, utterances have many parts, and involve multiple decisions. But the decisions are not made piecemeal. Compositionality brings together a set of mutually compatible functional units to form a functionally coherent grammatical entity. Crucially, the array of co-selected strategies should work well together to realize the goals of the utterance unit. Functional strategies compete to cooperate within the utterance.

To take an analogy from another domain of competition, consider a sailboat race. It is no use comparing a list of your sailboat's features to your opponent's list; what matters is the actual performance of the whole boat in the moment of use. The performance will be a function of the integration of components into a unified whole, creating a unit that interacts with its environment. This includes the unit's response to local environmental conditions, and to the implementation of strategies of use (in this case, sailing practices) that effectively exploit the capacities it offers. In the same way, competition in language is not about comparing idealized lists of linguistic features (*pace* Optimality Theory), but the selection of a coordinated set of functional elements and strategies to realize a complex but unified communicative intention. In the example of the sailing competition, what one is competing for seems obvious: the prize of a cup, some money, some prestige. Likewise, the competitors seem obvious: either this sailboat or that will reach the goal first. This we may call the external competition (or paradigmatic competition). But a closer look reveals another kind of competition going on. After the initial success has been savored, who or what will be given credit for it? Was it this aspect of the hull's water line, or that? Was it the coordination of hull design with sail design? What implications do the hull and sail designs have for strategic practices selected by the crew? The post-hoc assessments can get quite specific, evaluating a network of interconnected tradeoffs in design and strategy. And all of this will have consequences for what will be selected to be retained, and what will change, in the next generation of boats. Even the winner does not go unmodified, to keep up with future competitors. So it turns out that there is a second kind of competition going on, which we may call the internal competition. In internal competition, the competitors are different, as is their prize. Now it is strategies that compete, and what they compete for is control of the unit's functional design. There can only be one final design of the whole vehicle—the one that must enter the external competition—so any claims between competing strategies must be resolved internally. The result will be tested in a concrete, real-world event. The internal competition apportions credit to the components that have contributed to the success of the whole (Holland 1998), thus determining which design features, and which strategies, will outweigh the others, to be selected for transmission to the next generation. And the cycle begins again.

In language too, there is both external and internal competition. While differences abound (e.g. in how conscious the design process is, the amount of time available for a single design decision, etc.), some useful analogies may be drawn. On one level, competition in language arises between alternative utterance formulations (e.g. *gives him his hat* vs. *brings the hat back*), each serving as a holistic sign vehicle to realize some communicative goal. The paradigmatic competition between an utterance vehicle and its unrealized alternatives may be considered external competition. On another level, any complex utterance combines multiple strategic elements within it, leading to competition for credit between these strategies. This is internal competition, arising between functional units that are co-selected to cooperate in realizing an utterance. Internal competition continually redistributes the rewards of success in the game of language, due to the fact that inference, reanalysis, and grammaticization are always present and ready to challenge the status quo.

Competition in the functional niche is thus twofold: externally, over which available strategies will be selected to participate in realizing the utterance; and internally, over how those selected will be apportioned credit for their contributions to communicative success. Although external competition may be easier to observe and to apprehend, the more elusive internal competition is what ultimately holds the key to the emergence of functionally motivated grammars.

16.2.1 *From competition to emergence*

Competition plays an important role in the theory of evolution (Keller 1992), which contributes in turn to modern theories of emergence. For me the conception of emergence that proves most useful for linguistics comes from the study of complex adaptive systems (Kauffman 1993; Holland 1995, 1998, 2005; Steels 2012a), with origins in Darwinian evolutionary theory (Darwin 1859; Mayr 1982; Keller 1992;

Smith and Szathmáry 1995; Michod 2000). Applied to language, the idea of emergence extends naturally to the grammaticization of linguistic structure out of the patterning of language in use (Du Bois 2003b). In contrast, one conception of "emergent grammar" commonly cited in linguistics (Hopper 1998) takes a different tack, emphasizing the continual flux of ever-changing grammar, without committing to an account of what, if anything, eventually emerges from the flux. But if emergence is to be meaningful, something has to actually emerge. In language, what emerges is grammar. On this view the emerged grammar is largely stable, exhibiting great resources of self-organization to maintain its own systematicity, continuity, and discrete categoriality (Kirby 1997; Wedel 2002, 2009; Holland 2005; Givón 2009; Steels 2012a). But stability is not rigidity, and need not imply immunity from change. The systematicity of language is fully compatible with a capacity to adapt and evolve (Croft 2000; Givón 2009). Indeed, innovations arising through discourse plasticity (Du Bois, in progress) may start as deviations from the norm, but soon they compete with the norm. Such innovations spread via the population dynamics (Michod 2000; Nowak and Sigmund 2004; Lieberman et al. 2007) of structured utterance populations, with the potential to eventually reconfigure the structure of the linguistic system. Thus competition becomes key to defining grammaticization, understood as the adaptive emergence of new configurations of grammar by any means necessary.

16.3 Motivations and fitness criteria

To claim that a grammatical construction (say, the ditransitive construction in English) is functionally motivated is to hypothesize that there is a reason to associate this particular function with that particular form, in some respect. Motivation in this sense is local and parochial, tied to the specific linguistic particularities of the construction at hand and the larger grammatical context of the language in question (via relative motivation, Saussure 1916). But motivation can be contextualized from a global, language-independent perspective as well, linking it to more general and enduring factors such as expressivity and economy. For example, Steels and Loetzsch characterize "linguistic selection" as a process driven by at least four general evaluative criteria: "The strategies of the agents generate possible variants.... Which variants survive in the population should reflect expressive adequacy, minimal cognitive effort, learnability and social conformity" (Steels and Loetzsch, 2012: 57). Such global factors can be called, for lack of a better term, fitness criteria.[5] There are many such fitness criteria relevant to language; some are mutually compatible, some are not. Table 16.1 lists a number of fitness criteria which may be active in shaping language. The list is long and varied, which is to be expected given the range and complexity of factors

---

[5] Another alternative is to call them drives, adapting the terminology of Schuchardt (1885: 23) as revived by Haiman (2010b: 148). But the term drive seems to connote something psychological, internal to the individual. In contrast, what I wish to convey is the array of conflicting fitness criteria that control selection ("linguistic selection criteria" in the terms of Steels 2012b), which is more about the nature of the fitness landscape (Kauffman 1993; Michod 2000) that defines the environment for the "ecology of grammar" (Du Bois 1985).

that interact in the process of human decision-making. While some of the fitness criteria listed may turn out to represent mere nomenclatural variations, most capture something distinctive; here I have decided to err on the side of inclusion.[6] The fitness criteria are organized into five broad classes: meaning, cognition, sociality, aesthetics, and evolvability. The assignment to categories is mainly for convenience; many fitness criteria are multifaceted, with aspects that link them to more than one category. Conflicts between pairs of fitness criteria are especially likely to arise across categories, but may occur within them as well. While each fitness criterion would merit discussion in its own right, this is unfortunately beyond the scope of this chapter.

TABLE 16.1. **Conflicting fitness criteria drive competing motivations**

Meaning	Cognition
Clarity	Economy
Transparency	Simplicity
Iconicity	Ease
Analogy	Efficiency
Expressivity	Priming
Informativity	Memorability
Generalization	Distinctiveness
Individuation	Compositionality
Grounding/Indexicality	Reduction
Monosemy	Unification
Polysemy	Binding
Pith/Density	Arbitrariness/Opacity
Evolvability	**Sociality**
Transmissibility	Intersubjectivity
Fidelity/Heritability	Cooperation
Recognizance	Normativity
Learnability	Affiliation
Variability	Identity
Recombination	Power/Prestige
Viability	Autonomy
Plasticity	Evaluation
Adaptivity	
Weak linkage/Double articulation	**Aesthetics**
Fertility	Beauty
Population dynamics	Symmetry
Mindshare	Resonance
	Affect
	Creativity
	Extravagance
	Authority
	Ritual
	Play

[6] For the opposite strategy, recognizing a bare minimum of fitness criteria—framed as "competing drives"—see Haiman (2010b).

What is the relation between competing motivations and conflicting fitness criteria? To qualify as a competing motivation, the motivation must compete. If competitions are real (Section 16.1), they must be realized through the vehicle of an actual utterance. It is in the utterance arena that utterances succeed or fail, and with them the functional units that comprise them, along with their associated communicative strategies. In the ensuing internal competition, each participating unit is apportioned credit (Holland 1998). In contrast, the timeless factors that forever frame the terms of these competitions—like clarity and economy—remain unchanged, persisting long after the winners and losers have been evaluated. Fitness criteria define the enduring fitness landscape (Kauffman 1993; Michod 2000) within which functional units will continue to be evaluated and selected (Clark 1996; Steels 2012b). On this view, pairs of factors like clarity vs. economy, expressivity vs. simplicity, and informativity vs. resonance may turn out to be incompatible or conflicting fitness criteria, but they cannot be competing motivations as such. While attempts to satisfy clarity and economy often conflict, they remain simply incompatible fitness criteria, shaping the outcome of competitions but not themselves actually entering into competition as vehicles.

The distinction I introduce between competing motivations and conflicting fitness criteria is not widely recognized, and, it must be acknowledged, remains poorly understood. It is common to refer to the incompatibilities between pairs of factors (like some in Table 16.1) as competing motivations, speaking broadly. I see no problem with casual use of the term "competing motivations" as a conventional label for this phenomenon. Where the problem comes is if the phrase is taken literally, inviting a conception of competition as idealized, as if it occurs between two abstract concepts in a linguist's theory. Idealization and its companion essentialization are more widespread than might be thought. But idealized competition is not real competition (Section 16.1). It remains an interesting challenge for future research to clarify how the interaction between global fitness criteria, the fitness landscape, utterance vehicles, and local, language-specific motivations define the processes of evaluation and selection in the competition between functional strategies in language.

16.4 The Functional Frequency Principle

Two of the runaway successes of functional linguistics are corpora and frequency. Nowadays everyone wants a corpus, so they can measure the frequency of some linguistic phenomenon. But can one really gain insight into language just by counting the obvious (e.g. words or strings) and running the right statistics on them? Here I suggest that, before functional linguistics (or any linguistics) can make viable use of corpus frequency and quantification, it will first be necessary to problematize the nature of function itself.

Of the various proposals in the original *Competing Motivations* paper, the one that has gained the widest recognition is surely this: "Grammars code best what speakers do most"[7] (Du Bois 1985: 363). This principle, which I call the Functional

---

[7] These seven words have traveled far and wide, having been quoted in relation to a broad range of topics including: discourse and grammar (Thompson and Mulac 1991b; Hopper and Thompson 1993);

Frequency Principle, has been elaborated in later work (Du Bois 1987a, 1987b: 851, 2003a, 2003b: 49, 2006; Du Bois et al. 2003). The Functional Frequency Principle asserts that linguistic functions which are frequent in language use ("what speakers do most") will receive relatively economical encodings in linguistic structure ("grammars code best"). According to this conception, each grammar represents the outcome of a unique history of grammaticization. While linguists taking a functional perspective have mostly cited the Functional Frequency Principle with favor, those defending a formal perspective have been more critical (Newmeyer 1998: 62, 2003b).[8] Yet functional linguists too have raised questions, pointing to omissions and unclarities in the original formulation (Haspelmath 2004a). For example, Bybee questions what is meant by the word "best," while largely agreeing with the approach (Bybee 2007: 18). More critically, Haspelmath says:

> Du Bois (1987) observed that "grammars code best what speakers do most", but he did not explain how this marvelous fit of form to function comes about. If entrenchment, i.e. the establishment of patterns in speakers' mental grammars, is frequency-sensitive, we can actually explain such frequency-based generalizations. (Haspelmath, 1999b: 192)

What Haspelmath seems to overlook is that the "frequency-based generalizations" he would like to advocate are precisely what the "what speakers do most" clause of the Functional Frequency Principle is about. This is clear in the gloss provided in the original article, which specifically foregrounds the importance of frequency for explaining grammar:

> Unmarked grammar, we hypothesize, is distributed on the basis of "unmarked" (statistically most frequent) discourse. Grammars provide the most economical coding mechanisms (the highest "codability", the least marked forms) for those speech functions which speakers most often need to perform. More succinctly: Grammars code best what speakers do most. (Du Bois 1985: 362–3)

A more serious problem with Haspelmath's formulation is the attempt to locate grammaticization as a process interior to the individual mind—in "mental grammars." This overlooks the critical role of the utterance arena as the primary locus of real, non-idealized competitions, and of structured utterance populations as the locus of the population dynamics that drive historical processes of emergence and grammaticization.

Yet even with the 1985 gloss and further explication in subsequent work (Du Bois 1987b: 851, 2003a, 2003b), the precise meaning of the Functional Frequency Principle has remained elusive, even to its advocates—perhaps even to its author. The last four

---

frequency (García 1990: 3031; Bybee 2007: 18; Kuperman and Bresnan 2012: 588); grammaticization and functional explanation (Chafe 1994: 48; Durie 1995; Ariel 2000: 222, 2007: 265, 2008b: 183; Krug 2000; Goldberg 2004); typology (Dryer 1995; Croft 2003; Haspelmath 2004a; 2008b); sociocultural linguistics (Macaulay 1997: 169; Mori 1999: 3; Evans 2003b: 16; Ford 2004: 29); historical linguistics (Gast 2007; Fischer 2010); evolutionary linguistics (Haspelmath 1999b: 192; Evans 2003b); and others.

[8] The discussion of competing motivations by Newmeyer (this volume) contains much that I can agree with; for example, his critique of Direct Competition parallels my critique of transparent functionalism (Section 16.5 and Du Bois 1985).

words in particular conceal a special difficulty that is often overlooked. How are we to decide what speakers are *doing* when they are using language? At first blush the answer seems clear enough: Just take a corpus and count something—words, presumably. But why should we assume a priori that words are the appropriate unit of linguistic function? (And just substituting arbitrary sequences of words—n-grams—cannot in itself resolve the issue.) In fact it takes careful linguistic and functional analysis to determine which combinations of words and structures constitute the functional units that matter. The difficulty is present even at the level of describing the specific verbal actions of one speaker on one occasion. Among the ambiguities and complexities are those posed by higher-order categories like constructions (e.g. ditransitive *he gives the boy some pears*, S8), collocations (*gave it to*, S17; *gave him the*, S4), and idioms (*it looked like he was giving birth*, S14). It turns out to be surprisingly difficult to carve up an utterance into its components, in order to specify just what speakers *do* in ways that can be reliably linked to particular units of linguistic form. But for any meaningful quantification of linguistic function to be achieved, this problem needs to be resolved. One major challenge is "vertical competition," a type of internal competition where a complex functional unit competes for credit with its own component units. For example, is the verb *give* to be considered a functional unit in *giving birth* (S14) in the same way as in the evidently compositional ditransitive *gave him his hat* (S3)? While the answer in this case might seem obvious, vertical competition often poses a more significant analytical challenge. For example, is *back* to be considered an independent functional unit in *give back*, and if so, is this same configuration of functional units compositionally present in *bring back*? Judging by differences in its degree of optionality in each construction, *back* seems to play slightly different roles, even as it encodes the same event in ditransitive *gives him back his hat* (S6), monotransitive *brings the hat back* (S7), and intransitive *goes back with the hat* (S18). All of these argument structure constructions—with three, two, or even one core argument—can be used to express the same so-called three-participant event. Yet each draws on a different mix of coded meanings vs. inferential strategies (and core arguments vs. adjuncts) to communicate the same state of affairs, albeit with somewhat different perspectivizations. There is external competition between the alternative formulations. More elusive is the internal competition between vertically competing functional units and the strategies they embody. Because the internal competition is strategic, it is critical for linking competing motivations to grammaticization outcomes. While it is more difficult to isolate and quantify vertical and internal competition, the challenge must be addressed.

Despite the challenges in identifying functional units, identification clearly must precede counting. And quantification of some kind is indispensable if we hope to learn what speakers do *most*. While there is a statistical aspect to this question that has received sophisticated attention from corpus linguistics (Gries 2003a, 2009, 2010; Bresnan et al. 2007b; Baayen 2008), the problem I am raising here goes deeper, to the basic ontological question: What are the functionally relevant units of use, that is, those which are active for speakers as they make real-time verbalization choices? As a first approximation, construction models (Goldberg 1995, 2004, 2006; Haspelmath 2004a, 2008b; Gries 2005, 2010; Gast 2007;) and exemplar-based models (Bod 1998;

Wedel 2006) seem to hold considerable promise, offering analytical frameworks that can in principle be adapted to describe the kinds of functional units that operate (and compete) in the arena of language use. While there remain significant challenges to identify the right functional units, this will be indispensable to show the impact of functional frequency on the resolution of competitions between motivations.

While frequency and competing motivations have each received increasing attention in recent years, what has been missing is an understanding of the connection between them. The link is forged in the utterance arena where real competitions play out, leaving their myriad marks on vast utterance populations. To understand better how competing motivations shape grammar, it will be useful to step back and consider how the idea developed within the modern history of functional linguistics, and why it is so important to situate competing motivations in relation to grammaticization, discourse, and the evolution of language as a complex adaptive system.

16.5 Competing motivations revisited

The idea of competing motivations did not begin with the publication of *Competing Motivations* (Du Bois 1985). Earlier formulations of the idea had been advanced by a number of scholars under various labels, often with distinct goals, assumptions, and perspectives. Among the first to recognize the interaction of multiple explanatory factors were those steeped in the details of language change, such as Schuchardt and von der Gabelentz (cited in Haiman 2010b: 148). In this vein a key influence for me was Yakov Malkiel, who built on detailed and compelling evidence from Romance dialectal variation to provide a demonstration of "multiple causation" in language change, due to competing (and converging) morphological and phonological factors (Malkiel 1967). A specifically functional perspective on competing motivations was put forward by Haiman (1983, 1985b). Haiman identified iconicity as one of two key competing motivations, developing a theme that Behagel in the 1930s had dubbed his "highest law": "That which belongs closely together in the mind will also occur closely together" (Behagel 1932: 4), cited by Kathol (2000: 4). The upshot is that iconicity's only real competitor, according to Haiman, is economy.[9]

My original goal in writing *Competing Motivations* (Du Bois 1985) was to show how they could provide the driving force for grammaticization, understood as the process through which functionally motivated linguistic structure is crystallized out of patterns of language in use. Empirically this meant using the methods of discourse-functional linguistics to document the incipient patterning of grammar in populations of utterance tokens (a.k.a. the token aggregate), for example by demonstrating the skewed distribution of lexical noun phrases vs. pronouns within argument positions of the clause (Du Bois 1987b, 2003b). Theoretically, the goal was to

---

[9] Other early work in the modern era was done by Bates and MacWhinney (1987), Lass (1990), and others. For further historical discussion and references, see Haiman (1983: 814; 2010b) and, in this volume, the Introduction by Moravcsik and papers by MacWhinney and Haiman.

show how such functionally motivated patterns in discourse could in turn motivate the emergence of grammatical structures, for example by showing them to be responsive to the demands of a communicative function such as introducing new information (Du Bois 1985, 1987a, 1987b, 2003b). The study of competing motivations was to be part of a "metagrammatical" theoretical perspective "which treats grammars as adaptive systems" (Du Bois 1985: 344). To say that grammars are adaptive systems means they are "both partially autonomous (hence systems) and partially responsive to system-external pressures (hence adaptive)" (1985: 344). The complex adaptive systems approach to grammar would depend for its success, first, on recognizing the critical role of competing motivations, and second, on developing a theoretical framework capable of "describing and analyzing their interaction within specified contexts, and ultimately for predicting the resolution of their competition" (1985: 344). In recent years, interest in applying a complex adaptive systems approach to language has been accelerating rapidly (Gell-Mann 2005; Holland 2005; J. Blevins 2006; Oudeyer 2006, Steels et al. 2007; Beckner et al. 2009; Scott-Philips and Kirby 2010; Steels 2012a), though largely without recognition of the critical role played by competing motivations. The need for integrating competing motivations into complexity theory remains as great as ever, and cognitive-functional linguistics can play a significant role in clarifying how this works.

16.6 Are motivations competitive?

Up to now this chapter has focused primarily on competition, exploring its role in the selectional processes that drive the emergence of functionally motivated linguistic structure. But what about motivation itself? How does it figure in the processes of competition and grammaticization, if indeed it does? Here I address two related issues: First, I ask whether there can be a motivation that is immune from competition. Second, I consider where motivation fits into the picture of competition and grammaticization.

16.6.1 *Is there motivation without competition?*

Evidence from numerous studies (Du Bois 1987b, 2003b; Dressler 1997b; Heine 1997; Haspelmath 1999b; Diessel 2005; Malchukov 2005, 2008a; Gast 2007; Jäger 2007; Wedel 2009; Fischer 2010) suggests that competing motivations affect the evolution of every part of grammar, in all languages at all times. On a narrower time scale, competition is evident in the utterance arena as well, where it acts to shape the processes of linguistic production, perception, and reproduction (Bates and Mac-Whinney 1987). The question naturally arises, whether there can be any linguistic motivation that remains untouched by competition.

It is remarkable that as late as 2011 an entire volume of studies devoted to linguistic motivation (Panther and Radden 2011) could appear without a single index entry referring to competing motivations, nor to competition of any kind. (It is no accident that in this volume, empirical evidence of language use in the form of attested discourse data is scarce as well.) What appears instead are multiple claims, accompanied by icon-laden diagrams, of the supposed motivation for a given grammatical structure, without any clear indication of whether the putative motivation (e.g. a conceptual image) has been subjected to competition. But a motivation that does not have to compete in the utterance arena is effectively exempted from the adaptive process of selection. This is a problem. Bypassing competition short-circuits the very forces that drive the emergence of grammar. Taken to its logical conclusion, the non-competitive approach to motivation leads to an optimistic, Panglossian conception of linguistic function, as each structure attains a pinnacle of apparently "optimal" design without being tested by competition in the utterance arena. But such an idealization of the relation between structure and function misreads the nature of adaptation (Gould and Lewontin 1979; Mayr 1982; Smith and Szathmáry 1995), and overlooks two key facts about language. First, it treats language as an entity not subject to established principles of evolutionary change. Motivation without competition is untested motivation, missing out on the effects of selection and adaptation. Second, it fails to account for the systematic presence of typological diversity in the world's languages. Typology is important because it documents the diversity of solutions to the same ecological demands. Taken together, these oversights lead to a failure to come to terms with the fact that every structure in every language is the product of processes of culture-historical evolution (Cristofaro, this volume; Fischer 2010). It is to be expected that processes so powerful and pervasive as competition and selection will leave their mark on the functionally motivated system of grammar.

16.6.2 *How do motivations enter into competition?*

The focus so far has been on competition between utterance formulations (external competition) and between communicative strategies (internal competition). But where does motivation come into the picture? Motivation surely plays a role in competing motivations, but it is not easy to say what it is (once we let go of the idea that factors like clarity and economy are themselves competing motivations; see Section 16.3). Before we can hope to answer the question, it is necessary to clarify what factors are involved in an actual competition. There are at least four major players that need to be recognized: (1) the whole utterance, representing the communicative "vehicle" which succeeds or fails in the utterance arena; (2) the functional units (words, morphemes, and constructions) that cooperate to make up the utterance; (3) the communicative strategies linked to these functional units, which cooperate to bring about the success of the whole utterance, and (4) the fitness criteria that define the fitness landscape for language, determining what counts as success in the utterance arena. Where is motivation in all this? One could call an utterance motivated if its design leads to achieving the immediate communicative goal. But linguists generally aspire to a broader level of generalization, applying motivation to components of the system of language. Thus motivation (as opposed to arbitrariness) is ascribed to certain linguistic signs, constructions, paradigms, rules or, potentially, any fact, structure, or property of language.

But what, after all, is motivation? Motivation brings together two things, a problem and a strategy for solving it. To call a linguistic structure motivated is to assert that the solution fits the problem, the means suits the end, the form supports the function. A motivated strategy works to solve the problem *as if* by design, displaying an efficient linkage of mechanism to goal, of structure to function. Note that the strategy need not be designed by anyone; from the perspective of evolutionary theory, it can arise as an adaptive response to selection. Thus motivation becomes a key bridging concept linking form and function, and system and use.

This conception of the role of motivation in language, sketched out all too briefly here, merits an in-depth treatment in its own right; this remains an essential task for future research.

16.7 Conclusions

In seeking to motivate competition as a fundamental issue for linguistics, I have argued that it must play an integral role in any explanation for why grammars are as they are. Competition arises between different strategies for achieving a given communicative goal, and impacts grammar through processes of selection, adaptation, and grammaticization. But functional strategies must be embodied in functional units (tied to forms such as words or constructions) before they can enter into actual competition. It is in the utterance arena that competition plays out as a real, embodied practice. In the dialogic moment of verbalization and interpretation, the speaker and hearer are each faced with multiple competitors: the paradigm of alternative functional units, each with its own strategic motivation, that constitute the set of more or less viable alternatives in a given functional niche. These compete over a limited set of outcomes: at the lowest level, the precise phrasing (or situated interpretation) of a single utterance; at the highest level, the enduring organization of grammar. Why is there always more than one competitor? Because there is more than one way to solve the problems that language users face. Grammars afford discourse plasticity, which provides language users with the liberty to solve problems, sometimes in new ways. The terms of the competition are framed by an array of functional fitness criteria, some conflicting and some converging, which together define a complex fitness landscape that grounds the evaluation and selection of utterances and the strategies they embody. But no solution to the verbalization problem can equally satisfy all the conflicting demands. This compels us all to continually renew the processes of competition and selection. In doing what we must, we give new impetus to the forces of grammaticization that drive the endless adaptation and evolution of grammar.

I have argued that competition between motivations is motivated, representing an essential aspect of the adaptive processes that drive the emergence of grammar. But how can we characterize the phenomenon of competition, as it applies to language? Ten points are key:

1. *Competition is real.* Competitions between motivations are real for speakers and hearers in the moment of verbalization and interpretation, making demands on their online decision-making capacity to choose between functionally motivated alternatives.

2. *Competition is strategic.* Competition pits one functional motivation against another, as one communicative strategy tied to a functional unit is selected over its competitors.

3. *Competition is pervasive.* In language, all motivations are competing motivations. Wherever one motivation is found, another is sure to be near at hand— competing with the first. Competitions arise between motivations in all but the simplest of utterances, affecting all aspects of the utterance and all components of the linguistic system.

4. *Competition is situated.* Competitions play out in the utterance arena, within the specific setting of the functional niche. In the utterance arena a particular array of strategies linked to functional units is brought together to form the current utterance. The functional niche defines a detailed environment within which specific grammatical constructions regularly compete, and become adaptive over time.

5. *Competition is complex.* Competitions are motivated by the speaker's drive to express ever more elaborated meanings and conceptualizations. The demands of expressive complexity are most effectively realized by building alliances among networks of strategies tied to functional units. Complexity pushes the limits of cognitive resources, setting up an environment that selects for strategies to manage resources efficiently.

6. *Competition is evaluated.* The communicative event does not end with verbalization and interpretation, but incorporates an assessment of the event's success or failure relative to its goals (Clark 1996), thus completing the dialogic circuit. The evaluation feeds into the internal competition, where credit is apportioned to the functional units that contributed to the successful utterance. It does not matter whether the evaluation is explicit or implicit, conscious or unconscious; what matters is that it creates a differential payoff to the competing strategies, thereby driving the process of selection.

7. *Competition is remembered.* The view put forward here is that language users retain not only a large body of experienced linguistic structures, along with their meanings, but also their evaluations as successful (or otherwise) acts of communication. This goes beyond the typical assumptions of exemplar-based grammar (Bod 1998) to emphasize that the structured populations of utterances must incorporate the consequences of evaluating competitive outcomes, if the cumulative force of selective adaptation is to be realized.

8. *Competition is resolved.* As important as it is, competition must at some point come to an end (if only for a time). If speakers are to get anything done, a resolution of competitions must be attained. Grammaticization achieves this by establishing a relatively stable norm that language users are more or less obliged to follow. In return, speakers are shielded from excessive demands for online decision-making. Grammaticization converts functional motivation into normative motivation. The resulting conventions relieve the speaker of the need to continually redesign the system in the moment of using it.

9. *Competition is inevitable.* The human mind is ingenious; presented with one way of accomplishing a task, it works to imagine a better way; presented with incompleteness (Deacon 2011), it seeks completion. Yet it is also parochial: the speaker's grasp of the system of language is limited and local (Ariel 2008b, ch. 5; Keller 1994a). Taken together, these two facts ensure that the introduction of local adaptations is likely to disrupt organization elsewhere in the grammar, viewed from a broader systemic perspective. The pattern of systemic disruption followed by regularizing analogy (Anttila 1977, 2003; Itkonen 2005; Blevins and Blevins 2009; Fischer 2010) drives an endless cycle of variation, competition, selection, and adaptation, continually renewing the evolutionary process.

10. *Competition is consequential.* The outcome of myriad local competitions impacts the dynamics of change in structured utterance populations, thus driving the processes of grammaticization that lead to the adaptive emergence of grammar.

Yet even after a functionally motivated system of grammar has emerged, its enduring norms and conventions are continually challenged by new competitions, renewing the cycle of grammaticization. Because competitions between motivations are not idealized but real, they must be studied where they actually occur, in vast populations of naturally occurring utterances. The picture I have presented necessarily remains incomplete, revealing a number of critical tasks that remain to be addressed: to identify the functional units that matter in language use; to assess their frequency in structured utterance populations; to clarify how functional motivations participate in competitions; and to document the population dynamics of utterance populations within which innovations spread, leading to the emergence of language as a complex adaptive system. Such an ambitious agenda calls for the combined efforts of discourse-functional linguists, cognitive linguists, corpus linguists, quantitative linguists, grammarians, typologists, and others. This convergence, though doubtless difficult to attain, will bring us closer to realizing the potential of competing motivations to explain why grammars are as they are.

17

Competing motivation models and diachrony: What evidence for what motivations?

SONIA CRISTOFARO

17.1 Introduction

The central assumption of competing motivation models is that the use of different constructions within the same grammatical domain (both crosslinguistically and within individual languages) reflects a competition between different functional principles. In classical competing motivation models proposed within the functional-typological approach (e.g. Du Bois 1985, 1987b, and this volume; Haiman 1985b; Croft 2003), this holds in the sense that different constructions originate from different principles that may become active on different occasions. In the one formal approach that incorporates the idea of competing motivations, Optimality Theory, the use of different constructions is assumed to originate from the fact that the corresponding principles are all simultaneously active in a speaker's mind, but they are ranked differently from one language to another (see, e.g., Aissen 2003 and de Hoop and Narasimhan 2005).

The various principles postulated in these models are usually defined on synchronic grounds. If the structural properties of some construction, as manifested at the synchronic level, can plausibly be related to some functional principle, then this principle is assumed to be responsible for the use of the construction, independently of the actual diachronic processes that lead to the development of the construction in individual languages. For example, as will be discussed in Section 17.2, one of several competing principles invoked to account for the existence of different alignment patterns is an economic principle whereby speakers use overt dedicated case marking only for the argument roles that are in need of disambiguation. This principle has been proposed based on the synchronic distribution of the relevant case markers, not any specific evidence about the processes that give rise to these markers in individual languages.

Over the past couple of decades, however, a number of linguists working within the functional-typological approach, particularly Aristar (1991), Bybee (1988, 2008), and Dryer (2006), have argued that, since the distributional patterns for particular constructions are a result of specific diachronic processes, the explanations proposed for individual patterns should refer to these processes, rather than the patterns in themselves (see also Newmeyer 1998, 2002, 2005, and this volume).

In this chapter, several diachronic processes will be discussed that lead to the development of patterns that have been accounted for, implicitly or explicitly, in terms of competing motivations, namely different alignment systems and the use of overt, as opposed to zero marking for singular and plural. These processes, it will be argued, provide no evidence for the competing motivations models that have been proposed for the relevant patterns on synchronic grounds, both in the sense that they do not provide evidence for the specific principles postulated in these models, and in the sense that they do not provide evidence for a competition between different principles pertaining to the encoding of a particular grammatical domain. Some real cases where the use of different constructions can be argued to originate from a competition between such principles will then be discussed.

17.2 The diachrony of alignment systems

17.2.1 *Competing motivation models for alignment systems*

As is well-known, the two arguments of transitive verbs and the only argument of intransitive verbs (henceforth, A, P, and S arguments) may or may not be encoded in the same way in the world's languages, yielding different alignment systems.

Many such systems conform to a general pattern whereby S arguments are encoded in the same way as either A or P arguments, while the latter two are distinguished, either by means of different markers, or by means of zero vs. overt marking, in which case zero marking is also used for S arguments. This has been argued to reflect an economic principle that leads speakers to distinguish between different argument roles only when they cannot avoid doing so, that is, when those roles could be confused. A and P arguments are encoded differently because they co-occur in transitive clauses, so they need to be disambiguated. S arguments occur in isolation, so they cannot be confused with other arguments. As a result, they do not need separate encoding, nor overt marking (Comrie 1978, 1989; Dixon 1979, 1994; see also, more recently, Song 2001: 156–7; de Hoop and Narasimhan 2005; Bickel 2011: 412).

Various principles have also been argued to exist that lead speakers to use the same constructions for different argument roles based on some shared property of these roles. For example, it has been claimed that S arguments may be encoded in the same way as A arguments because both of these roles typically correspond to agentive participants, topical participants, or, more generally, participants that represent a starting point in discourse. S arguments, however, may also be encoded in the same way as P arguments, because both of these roles typically correspond to participants introduced for the first time in discourse, because certain types of S arguments correspond to nonagentive participants, or, in some analyses, because the participants most immediately involved in the state of affairs being described occur in S or P role (Moravcsik 1978; Dixon 1979, 1994; DeLancey 1981; Du Bois 1985, 1987; Mithun 1991; Mithun and Chafe 1999; Givón 2001; Song 2001; among several others).

These principles, as detailed by Du Bois (1985, 1987b), compete with each other to the extent that they imply that individual argument roles may be encoded in different ways. However, they are also inherently in competition with the tendency to encode some roles through zero marking. If particular roles are associated based on some property that they share, for example topicality, then it is to be expected that the constructions used to encode these roles may be ones that explicitly encode the relevant property, at least originally. This may lead to the use of overt, as opposed to zero marking for some roles. This appears to be the case, for example, in a number of languages where an overt marker used for A and S arguments developed from a topic marker (see, e.g., König (2008) and references therein on a number of African languages, particularly an ongoing such development in !Xun).

In principle, the alignment systems attested crosslinguistically are exhaustively accounted for by the idea that they are a combined result of the tendency to use different constructions for the roles that need to be disambiguated and various principles leading to the use of the same construction for roles perceived as similar. Many of the diachronic processes that lead to the development of individual systems, however, do not actually provide evidence for these mechanisms, and hence for a competition between them.

17.2.2 *Alignment systems arising through grammaticalization*

A major source for the development of new alignment systems is the grammaticalization of markers for particular argument roles from elements originally used in other functions. For example, new markers for P arguments can develop from "take" verbs in constructions of the type "take X and Verb (X)." The taking event is accessory to the event described by the other verb, and the "take" verb is reinterpreted as merely indicating the P role that the entity being taken plays both in the taking event and in the event described by the other verb. This process has been described, for example, for Mandarin Chinese (Li and Thompson 1981, among others) and several West African languages (Lord 1993), illustrated in (1) from Twi.

(1) Twi (Niger-Congo)
  a. ɔkɔm   **de**   *me*
     hunger   take   me
     'Hunger takes me'   (Lord 1993: 70) [from an earlier description of the
                                                             language]

  b. *o-***de**   *afoa*   *ce*   *boha-m*
     he-OBJ   sword   put   scabbard-inside
     'He put the sword into the scabbard'   (Lord 1993: 66)

  c. *aivu̠a*   **de**   *kannea*   *ni*   *ahuhuru*   *ma*   *asase*
     sun   OBJ   light   and   warmth   give   earth
     'The sun gives light and warmth to the earth'   (Lord 1993: 66)

In some languages, the markers used for A arguments can transparently be related to indexical elements, that is, demonstratives and (third-person) pronouns. This is illustrated in example (2) for the Australian language Bagandji. McGregor (2008) accounts for this pattern by assuming that indexicals are initially used in apposition to nouns occurring in A function to emphasize that these nouns (exceptionally) encode new information. As a result, they are reanalyzed as marking the A role.

(2)   Bagandji (Australian)
      *yaḍu-**duru***   *gāndi-d-uru-ana*
      wind-DEM/ERG   carry-FUT-3SG.SUBJ-3SG.OBJ
      '**This wind** will carry it along / The wind will carry it along'   (Hercus 1982: 63)

Another path to the development of A markers has been described by Rude (1991, 1997a) for Sahaptian languages. In these languages, a Proto-Sahaptian suffix **-ɨm* (possibly derived from a verb 'come' in a serial verb construction) gave rise to a directional marker used on both verbs and nouns to indicate motion of an entity towards the speaker or the hearer, as illustrated in (3a). When attached to the A argument of a transitive clause, as in (3b), the suffix was reinterpreted as a marker of the A role.

(3)   Sahaptin (Sahaptian)
      a. *áw*   *i-qʼínum-**im**-a*   *wínš*
           now   3NOM-see/look-CSL-PAST   man
           'Now the man looked *this way*'   (Rude 1991: 41)

      b. *áw-naš*   *x̣wɨsaat-**nim*** *i-twána-**m**-aš*
           now-1SG   old.man-ERG   3NOM-follow-CSL-IPFV
           'Now the old man is following me'   (Rude 1991: 41)

The grammaticalization of new markers for particular argument roles often takes place in languages where all roles are initially encoded in the same way (the majority of the languages taken into account in the crosslinguistic survey of case marking of full NPs presented in Comrie (2008). In this case, depending on whether the new marker is used for A or for P, the process may yield systems where S and P are undifferentiated and A is encoded differently (as, e.g., in Bagandji), or patterns where A and S are undifferentiated and P is encoded differently (as, e.g., in Twi), that is, ergative or nominative systems.

    These processes are independent of the various principles that have been postulated to account for alignment systems on synchronic grounds, such as the need to distinguish between different argument roles or the fact that different roles may be associated based on some property that they share. Rather, the grammaticalization of new markers for particular roles reflects a mechanism whereby some components of the meaning of a complex expression (the description of a taking event, the signaling of new information, or that of directionality) are bleached over time, and the forms originally encoding these components are reinterpreted as indicating an associated argument role. As all roles were encoded in the same way in the original system, the roles that are not involved in this process remain undifferentiated in the resulting system (for similar considerations, see Dixon 1981: 72, 130).

17.2.3 *Alignment systems originating from reanalysis of argument structure*

New alignment systems also arise through the reanalysis of the argument structure of particular constructions. For example, ergative systems have been argued to sometimes arise from intransitive constructions of the type "X is done by Y" as these become functionally equivalent to transitive ones, "Y has done X." In the resulting transitive constructions, X, the P argument, is marked in the same way as S arguments, because it originates from the S argument of the source construction, while Y, the A argument, has dedicated marking, because it maintains the oblique marking of the agent of the source construction, from which it originates. This process has been postulated, for instance, for the Hindi perfective construction in (4), whose presumed Sanskrit antecedent is reported in (5) (see Verbeke and De Cuypere 2009; Stroński 2011; Verbeke 2013 for recent comprehensive reviews of the issues involved).

(4) Hindi (Indo-European)
     *laṛk-e = **ne**   bacch-e = ko   mār-a   hai*
     boy-OBL-ERG   child-OBL-ACC   hit-PRF.M.SG   be.AUX
     'The boy has hit the child'   (Verbeke and De Cuypere 2009: 5)

(5) Sanskrit (Indo-European)
     *devadatt-**ena**   kaṭa-ḥ   kṛ-taḥ*
     Devadatta-INSTR   mat-NOM   make-NOM.PST.PTCPL
     'The mat is made by Devadatta'   (Verbeke and De Cuypere 2009: 3)

Gildea (1998) provides a detailed description of similar processes of reanalysis in Cariban languages. In this case, the process starts from complex sentences involving nominalized verb forms, which may give rise to either nominative or ergative systems as they are reinterpreted as monoclausal structures. For example, Gildea argues, the Wayana progressive construction in (6) originated from constructions of the type "X is occupied with Verbing," or "X is occupied with the Verbing of Y," which were reinterpreted as intransitive or transitive monoclausal structures, that is, "X is Verbing," "X is Verbing Y." This yielded a nominative system, in that, in the resulting constructions, A and S arguments are encoded in the same way because they both originate from the S argument of the main clause in the source construction, while P arguments are encoded differently because they originate from the possessor argument. The Cariña future construction in (7) originated from constructions such as "It will be X's Verbing," or "To Y will be Y's Verbing," in which the nominalized verb was possessed by its notional P or S argument, and its notional A argument was encoded as a recipient and had dative marking. These too were reinterpreted as monoclausal structures, that is, "X will Verb" or "X will Verb Y." This yielded an ergative pattern, in that, in the resulting constructions, S and P arguments originate from the possessor argument of the nominalized verb, so they both maintain possessor marking, while A arguments are encoded differently because they maintain the marking of the dative NP from which they originate.

(6) Wayana (Carib)
     i-pakoro-n   iri-Ø   pɔk   wai
     1-house-POSS   make-NOMLZ   occupied.with   1.be
     'I'm (occupied with) making my house (lit. 'my house's making')
                                                    (Gildea 1998: 201)

(7)   Carinã (Carib)
    a. **i**-*woona-ri-ma*
       1-cultivate-NMLZ-3.be
       'I will cultivate'   (Gildea 1998: 169)

    b. **i**-*aaro-ri-ma*
       1-take-NMLZ-3.be
       '(Somebody) will take me'   (Gildea 1998: 169)

    c. *a-eena-ri-ma*   *i-*'**wa**
       2-have-NMLZ-3.be   1-DAT
       'I will have you'   (Gildea 1998: 170)

Reanalysis of argument structure has also been argued to be the source of active systems (see, e.g., Harris 1985; Malchukov 2008b; Mithun 2008). For example, transitive constructions with unexpressed third-person A arguments, such as "(It) burned me," can be reinterpreted as intransitive ones, such as "I am burned," where the verb describes the state resulting from the action described by the transitive clause. The P argument of the transitive verb becomes the S argument of the intransitive one, so that the two come to be encoded in the same way. This process has been postulated for several language families by Malchukov (2008b) and Mithun (2008), and some languages provide direct diachronic evidence for it. For example, Holton (2008) shows that, in Galela, the formal identity between the S argument of stative intransitive verbs and the P arguments of transitive verbs, illustrated in (8a), originated from the fact that intransitive clauses with stative verbs were originally transitive clauses with a third-person nonhuman A argument cross-referenced by a verbal prefix *i-*. In the late nineteenth century, as can be seen from (8b)–(8c), this prefix became optional and eventually disappeared, which led to the reinterpretation of the transitive clause as a corresponding intransitive one.

(8)   Galela (Austronesian)
    a. *ni-kiolo*
       2SG.U-asleep
       'You are asleep'   (Modern Galela: Holton 2008: 261)

    b. **i**-*mi-tosa*
       3SG.A.NONHUM-3F.SG.U-angry
       'She is angry'   (19th century Galela: Holton 2008: 272)

    c. *mi-pereki*
       3F.SG.U-old
       'She is old'   (19th century Galela: Holton 2008: 272)

The various processes of reanalysis imply that the way in which individual arguments are encoded in the resulting alignment systems depends on how the corresponding NPs were encoded in the source construction. What gives rise to the various systems are whatever factors motivate the reinterpretation of the source construction, for example the conceptual connections between certain types of transitive and intransitive clauses, or those between certain types of complex sentences and the corresponding monoclausal structures.[1] In this respect, just like alignment systems arising from grammaticalization, these particular cases provide no evidence that the various patterns are related to the need to disambiguate particular argument roles, or to some perceived similarity between different roles in themselves.[2]

To the extent that grammaticalization and reanalysis of argument structure do not provide evidence for individual principles pertaining to the encoding of argument roles, they do not provide evidence for a competition between these principles either. These processes, however, also pose a more general challenge for existing competing motivation models. These models assume that there are different principles pertaining to the encoding of the same grammatical domain, which lead speakers to create different constructions for that domain. When alignment systems originate from the reinterpretation of pre-existing constructions, however, they are not motivated by any principle pertaining to the encoding of argument roles in themselves. Rather, they are a result of the fact that particular constructions lend themselves to different interpretations and can be reanalyzed as encoding particular argument roles, as well as the fact that all roles were initially zero marked and this pattern can be maintained for the roles not involved in the reinterpretation process. In this respect, there is no competition between different principles specifically pertaining to some grammatical domain (in this case, the encoding of particular argument roles), only a relatively generic competition between the tendency to maintain the conventional interpretation of particular constructions (Newmeyer 2002, this volume), and the principles leading to the reinterpretation of these constructions.

17.3 The diachrony of singular and plural marking

17.3.1 *Competing motivation models for singular and plural marking*

One of the best-known typological generalizations, first proposed by Greenberg (1966a), pertains to the use of overt marking for singular and plural. Overt marking tends to be used for plural rather than for singular, that is, languages usually have either zero marking for singular and overt marking for plural, or overt marking for both (Corbett 2000; Croft 2003; Haspelmath 2005c). The use of zero marking for singular and overt marking for plural is considered a textbook case of economy. Since plural is less frequent in discourse, it is more difficult to identify, so it needs to be indicated overtly. On the other hand, speakers do not use overt marking for singular because they do not need to do so, in that singular is more frequent

---

[1] This raises the question of what motivates the alignment pattern of the source constructions in the first place. As far as nominalizations are concerned, it has been observed that the use of possessor marking for both notional S and notional P arguments might originate from the fact that these are usually the only overt arguments in a nominalization, and they independently receive possessor marking in analogy with non-derived NPs (Koptjevskaja-Tamm 1993: 260; Gildea 1998: 122–3).

[2] Contrary to traditional explanations, this analysis does not address the issue of why the alignment systems attested crosslinguistically do not usually display dedicated marking for S arguments. If alignment systems originate from the reinterpretation of pre-existing constructions, however, this can be accounted for by assuming that there are no constructions that are usually reinterpreted as encoding argument roles and are restricted to S arguments.

in discourse and therefore it is easier to identify (Greenberg 1966a; Croft 2003; Haspelmath 2006, and 2008b).

The economy analysis does not account for the fact that some languages do use overt marking for singular. However, there is a long tradition according to which overt coding of the various meaning components involved in a particular expression should be favored anyway, because it responds to a general iconic principle of transparency and isomorphism (see, e.g., Haiman 1985b; Dressler 1987; Croft 2003). This principle contrasts with the economic tendency to leave more frequent meanings unmarked, so the competition between the two, as is argued by Croft (2003), can account for the fact that singular may or may not be overtly marked from one language to another.

In what follows, it will be argued that, just as in the case of alignment systems, several diachronic processes that lead to the development of overt markers for singular and plural pose a number of challenges to this view, both in the sense that they do not actually provide direct evidence for the particular economic or iconic principles postulated in the analysis, and in the sense that they do not provide evidence for a competition between different principles pertaining to the encoding of singular and plural in themselves.

17.3.2 *Some possible sources for singular and plural markers*

In languages where overt marking is used for both singular and plural, the markers often also encode gender. As has been shown by Greenberg (1978) and others, gender markers often originate from demonstratives and personal pronouns. For example, Heine (1982) argues that this has been the case in Kxoe, where gender markers, as can be seen from Table 17.1, are similar in form to third-person pronouns.

TABLE 17.1. **Gender/number markers and third-person pronouns in Kxoe**

		SG	PL	
Nouns	M	/õá̰-mà	/õá̰-//uˤa	'boy'
	F	/õá̰-hὲ	/õá̰-djì	'girl
	C	/õá̰-('à), /õá̰-djì	õá̰-nà	'child'
Pronouns	M	xà-má, á-mà, i-mà	xà-//uá, á-//uá, í-//uá	'he'
	F	xà-hὲ, á-hὲ, i-hὲ	xà-djí, á-djí, í-djí	'she'
	C	(xa-'à)	xà-nà, á-nà, í-nà	'it'

Source: Khoisan (Heine 1982: 211)

As demonstratives and personal pronouns often have distinct singular and plural forms, the result of the grammaticalization process may be a system where gender markers also function as markers for singular and plural. What gives rise to these systems are whatever factors motivate the grammaticalization of the relevant demonstrative or pronominal forms into gender markers, rather than the need to give overt expression to particular number values (either because these values are less frequent, as is argued for plural, or because they should be expressed anyway, as is argued for singular).[3]

Overt markers for either singular or plural can also originate from morphemes that are originally used for other functions, but co-occur with expressions that imply the notions of singular or plural, such as indefinite pronouns, expressions of multitude, or numerals. Over time, these expressions are dropped, and the meanings of singular or plural that they convey may be transferred on a co-occurring morpheme. In Imonda (Seiler 1985: 38–9), for example, the nonplural (singular and dual) marker ((9a)) evolved out of an oblique marker used in partititive constructions involving indefinite pronouns and numerals, that is, "one/two from among the group of X," as illustrated in (9b)–(9c). Likewise, the Bengali plural marker illustrated in (10a)–(10b) evolved from a genitive marker ((10c)), also used in partitive constructions involving expressions of multitude (e.g., 'many of us' and the like: Chatterji 1926: 734–5). In Assamese (Kakati 1962: 282–3), the plural marker illustrated in (11a) evolved from the former participle of 'be,' presumably when the latter was used in combination with numerals, as in (11b).

(9) Imonda (Border)
    a. *ka-**ianèi**   ainam   iaha-t*
       we-NONPL   quickly   die-CF
       'One of us would die quickly'   (Seiler 1985: 39)

    b. *po   me-**ianèi***
       water   hole-SRC
       'from underneath the water'   (Seiler 1985: 73)

    c. *agō-**ianèi**   sabla   ha-pia-ual-f*
       women-SRC   two   MO-come-DL-PRES
       'There are two women coming'   (Seiler 1985: 39)

(10) Bengali
    a. *āmhā-**rā***
       we-GEN
       'we'   (15th century: Chatterji 1926: 735)

    b. *chēlē-**rā***
       child-GEN
       'children'   (15th century: Chatterji 1926: 736)

    c. *āmhā-**rā***
       we-GEN
       'of us'   (14th century: Chatterji 1926: 735)

---

[3] A related issue is why demonstratives or personal pronouns have non-zero singular and plural forms in the first place. While the origins of demonstratives are in most cases obscure (Diessel 1999), it has been shown that different number forms of personal pronouns may be the result of the grammaticalization of different lexical items, for example "man" or "person" for third-person singular and "people" for third-person plural (Heine and Song 2011). These forms may also combine with demonstrative roots, yielding demonstrative forms overtly marked for number (see, e.g., Heine 1982: 215 on Kxoe).

(11)   Assamese (Indo-European)
   a.   *chātar*-**hāt**
        student-PL
        'Students'   (Modern Assamese: Kakati 1962: 295)

   b.   *dui*-**hanta**
        two-be.PTCPL
        'Both of you'   (Early Assamese: Kakati 1962: 282)

In this case too, the development of new singular and plural markers cannot obviously be related to the need to give overt expressions to these particular number values. In fact, the constructions that give rise to the relevant markers convey a meaning of singular or plural from the beginning. What happens is rather a process of metonymization (Traugott and Dasher 2005) whereby particular components of the meaning of a complex expression, such as plural or singular, are transfered from one formal component of that expression to another.

17.3.3 *Plural markers arising through grammaticalization*

A major source for the development of plural markers is also the grammaticalization of elements originally expressing other, related meanings, including for example distributive expressions, for example "snow here and there," "houses scattered here and there," or "their respective wives," and expressions such as "all," "several," "many," "a lot of," "people," "men," and the like. Examples (12)–(15) provide an illustration of the formal identity or similarity between these expressions and markers of plurality in different languages (for each of these languages, the process of grammaticalization is explicitly argued for in the source).

(12)   Southern Paiute (Uto-Aztecan)
   a.   *qaʼnɪ*   /   **qaŋqaʼnɪ**
        house   /   house.DISTR
        'house, houses'   (Sapir 1930–31: 258)

   b.   *piŋwa-*   /   **piviʼŋwa.mï**
        wife   /   wife.DISTR.their
        'wife / their (vis.) wives'   (Sapir 1930–31: 257)

   c.   *tɔtsɪˈʼait.ï*   /   **tɔˈtɔʼtsʼait.imï**
        headless   /   headless.DISTR
        'headless / each having no head, headless people'   (Sapir 1930–31: 257)

(13)   Kpelle (Niger-Congo)
   a.   *pɛ̀rɛ-**ŋa***
        house-DISTR
        'houses here and there, some scattered house out of the total group'
                                                (Welmers 1969: 77)

   b.   *nûu*   /   *nûa*
        person   people
        'person / people'   (Welmers 1969: 77)

(14)   Bhojpuri (Indo-European)
    a. *ghar*   **sahb**
       house   all
       'houses'   (Grierson 1883–87: 7)

    b. *mali*   **log**
       gardener   people
       'gardeners'   (Grierson 1883–87: 7)

(15)   Tlingit (Na-Dene)
    a. *yuyā*   *LAn*-**q!**
       big   whale-COLL
       'a big whale'   (Swanton 1911: 169)

    b. *lîngît* / *lîngît′*-**q!**
       man   /   man-COLL
       'man or men / many man together'   (Swanton 1921–22: 169)

    c. *gux* / *gux*-**q!**
       slave / slave-COLL
       'slave / slaves'   (Swanton 1921–22: 169)

    d. *hît*   / *hî′*-**q!î**
       house   house-COLL
       'house / houses'   (Swanton 1921–22: 169)

The grammaticalization of these expressions into plural markers is presumably based on the fact that they are typically used in contexts that involve plurality. Distributives in themselves do not imply plurality, as witnessed by expressions such as "snow here and there" or the like. However, as has been pointed out by Sapir (1930–31: 257) and Mithun (1999: 90–1), when distributives are applied to humans and animates in general, the notion of distribution is practically equivalent to that of plurality. Humans and animates are typically conceived as inherently individuated, so, if distributives are applied to these entities, this implies that there is a plurality of them; conversely, a plurality of individuated entities must be distributed over space, so the terms for these entities will carry distributive markers every time more than one is mentioned. Over time, then, the overlap between distribution and plurality may trigger the reinterpretation of distributive markers as plural markers.

Similar observations apply to expressions such as "all," "several," "a few," "a lot of," "people," and the like. These too are associated with the notion of plurality in all or many of their contexts of occurrence, and in many cases the meaning components that they contribute in addition to plurality, while relevant to the situation being described, are communicatively peripheral. For example, sentences such as "mark where all the windows are" (as opposed, e.g., to "all the windows are shuttered and most are double-glazed"), or "several/a few/a lot of people do that, but I don't" (as opposed to "I blocked several people and they continue to have access to my discussions," "a few people can get a lot done," "a view shared by a lot of people") are normally used as equivalents of their unquantified counterparts, "mark where the windows are" and "people do that, but I don't." In this case, the notions of quantification associated with "all," "several," "a few," or "a lot of" are not particularly prominent vis-à-vis that of membership within a set (windows, people) consisting of a plurality of elements. Likewise, the meaning component "human" contributed by expressions such as "people" is redundant when these expressions, as is often the case, are used in combination with terms referring to humans (e.g. "the British people" "the wizard people"). It is then possible that the reduced contextual prominence of their other meaning components triggers the reinterpretation of individual expressions as encoding plurality.

The mechanism underlying these processes is one which is sometimes referred to as generalization (Bybee et al. 1994: 81–7, 289–93), and has been argued to be involved in several cases of grammaticalization, including for example the development from motion verbs to futures, from locative expressions to progressives, and from body parts to spatial expressions (Heine et al. 1991; Bybee et al. 1994; Hopper and Traugott 2003; Eckardt 2006, among others). Individual expressions come to encode particular notions, in this case plurality, because they are associated with these notions in specific contexts, and other meaning components that they contribute may be less prominent and are eventually obliterated. This mechanism is based on the fact that different meaning components may have different prominence in different contexts, so it cannot obviously be related to the lower discourse frequency of the notions that come to be expressed, for example plurality.[4]

The various diachronic processes leading to the development of overt marking for singular and plural have similar implications as those discussed in the previous section with regard to alignment patterns. In some cases, the fact that singular and plural are marked overtly is a by-product of processes which are independent of the expression of number in itself, but involve elements originally marked for number. In other cases, singular and plural markers presumably originate from processes of context-induced reinterpretation, that is, particular forms take on a singular or plural meaning that is present in the context (and is sometimes specifically contributed by a co-occurring element). If either singular or plural are zero marked, then, this may be because none of these processes has taken place in the language,

---

[4] An alternative possibility would be that the evolution of plural markers out of expressions such as "all," "people," distributives and the like takes place because the language has no grammatical means to encode the meaning of plural and speakers recurrently use these expressions in order to specifically convey this meaning. In this case, the low discourse frequency of plural and the related need to disambiguate this notion could still be the ultimate explanation for the process. No evidence of this has, however, been provided in the literature, nor is there any evidence that there actually is a significant number of contexts in which speakers really need to disambiguate plural from singular (contexts in which this information is communicatively relevant and cannot be retrieved, that is). In fact, the grammaticalization of plural markers often takes place in languages that already have such markers (see, e.g., Jhā 1958: 291 on Maghadan languages). More generally, no assumption is usually made in the literature that particular processes of grammaticalization are triggered by the fact that the source construction is used in order to express a less frequent notion.

rather than because of specific principles that lead speakers to use zero marking for those particular number values.[5]

These facts are independent both of the principles postulated to account for the distribution of zero vs. overt marking for singular and plural on synchronic grounds, such as economy and isomorphism, and of any principle pertaining to the encoding of singular and plural in themselves. In this respect, there is no evidence either for a competition between economy and isomorphism in the expression of singular, or for a competition between different principles specifically pertaining to this domain. All there is evidence about are, once again, the contextual factors that lead speakers to reinterpret particular constructions, and a competition between these factors and the tendency to maintain the conventional interpretation of the constructions.

17.4 Some "true" cases of competing motivations

In the previous sections, it was shown that in many cases the development of different constructions within the same grammatical domain is a direct or indirect result of processes of context-induced reinterpretation of pre-existing constructions, independently of any competition between principles pertaining to that particular domain in itself. A different scenario will now be considered, one in which this development can indeed be regarded as evidence for such a competition.

In a number of cases, various constructions used within the same domain appear to directly reflect different meaning components of that domain, pointing to a competition between different possible construals of the same situation.

This is illustrated by several constructions used to encode the same relationship between states of affairs in complex sentences (see Cristofaro 2003 for further discussion). For instance, examples (16)–(18) illustrate some constructions that are commonly used crosslinguistically in sentences expressing commands or suggestions, such as "He told/ordered/commanded them to leave." The Abun construction in (16) is representative of a type where a "say" verb, or a complementizer derived from such a verb (in this case, the complementizer *do*), are used to introduce the clause that expresses the object of the command or suggestion, that is, "X commanded Y, saying, Y should do Z." This can be related to the fact that a command or a suggestion is usually expressed verbally, so it can be construed as an indirect report. Retuarã, as can be seen from (17), uses the same verb form as in purpose clauses, so the construction has a structure of the type "X commanded Y, so that Y would do Z." This can be related to the fact that commands or suggestions are expressed with the goal of obtaining the realization of some state of affairs. Finally, the Old Akkadian example in (18) involves two sequential clauses, that is,

---

[5] This analysis does not account for the fact that overt markers for plural appear to be more common than overt markers for singular, in the sense that singular markers are usually only found when the language also has a plural marker, while many languages have just plural markers. In principle, this could be due to the greater need to disambiguate plural, as claimed in traditional explanations. To the extent that singular and plural markers originate from processes of context-induced reinterpretation of pre-existing constructions, however, this issue should be addressed by looking at what source constructions could give rise to individual markers, and how these are actually used in discourse, not the synchronic distribution of the markers in itself.

"X commanded Y, and Y should do Z." This can be related to the fact that the object of a command or suggestion may be construed as a possible consequence of the command or suggestion itself.

(16) Abun (Austronesian)
    An *syugat*   *men-ka-we* **do**   *men-ka-we* *ki*   *suk-du*
    3SG   command 1PL-CL-two COMP 1PL-CL-two say NOM-speak
    ré *o*   *nde*
    this again NEG
    'He commanded the two of us not to tell this story again' (Lit. 'He commanded the two of us saying not to tell this story again')
                                    (Berry and Berry 1999: 166)

(17) Retuarã (Tucanoan)
    wiʔi-baĩpi   *dã-re*   *hãʔbẽ-eʔka-ki*   *dã-po-ri-ẽrã*
    house-owner 3PL-TERM order-PST-M.SG 3PL-leave-EP-PURP
    'The house owner ordered them to leave'   (Strom 1992: 159)

(18) Old Akkadian (Afro-Asiatic)
    qibi-š   *sum-ma*   *nār-ī*   *litter-a*
    say.IMP-to him-PTCL canal-my he.should.return-to-me
    'Tell him to return my canal to me' (Lit. 'Speak to him and he should return my canal to me')   (Deutscher 2000: 125)

A similar situation is found in sentences that describe a process of sensory perception of an ongoing state of affairs, such as "The woman saw him go out," or "He heard children playing." Sometimes, as illustrated by the Bininj Gun-Wok constructions in (19a), these involve constructions of the type "X saw it, Y did Z." In other cases, the construction has a structure of the type "X saw Y, Y was doing Z," as in (19b), or "X saw Y (who was) doing Z," as in (20) and (21). In this latter case, the perceived state of affairs is encoded through modifying expressions usually used to attribute a property to a particular referent, for example relative pronouns or participial verb forms. This alternance can be related to the fact that a process of sensory perception applies both to the perceived state of affairs as a whole and to the individual entities involved in it, so either of the two can be construed as an object of perception. Also, the fact that a perceived entity is involved in some state of affairs can be construed as a property of that entity, which accounts for the use of modifying expressions, or as additional information conveyed by a separate independent clause, which accounts for structures such as the one in (19b).

(19) Bininj Gun-Wok (Australian)
    a. *Na-bene* *maihh* *a-na-ng*   *ga-m-golu-rr-en*   *gaddu-be*
       M-DEM   bird   1/3-see-PP 3-hither-descend-RR-NPST up-ABL
       djohboi
       poor.thing
       'I've seen those birds coming down (to the waterhole) from higher up, dear little things' (Lit. 'I saw it, birds were coming down')   (Evans 2003: 634)

b. ŏ-na-ng   kabene-h-barndi   kore   kadum,
   3/3PAST-see-PP   UAUG-IMM-be.high.NP   LOC   high
   bene-h-ngu-ni   man-ekke   man-karralarlhmanj
   3UAUG.PST-IMM-eat-PL   VE-DEM   III-bush.cashew
   bene-h-darllke-yi
   3UAUG.PST-IMM-crack-PL
   'He saw the two of them up in the tree eating bush cashew fruit' (Lit. 'They
   saw the two of them, they were up in the tree, they were eating bush cashew
   fruit')   (Evans 2003a: 636)

(20)   French
       J'   ai   vu   Jean   qui   fumait
       I   AUX.1SG   see.PST.PTCPL   Jean   who   smoke:IMPF:3SG
       'I saw Jean smoking' (Lit. 'I saw Jean who was smoking')
                                                    (van der Auwera 1985: 219)

(21)   Ancient Greek
       kaí   hē̄   gunḕ   eporaî   min
       and   the   woman   see:PRES.IND.3G   3SG.ACC
       exiónta
       go.out:PRES.PTCPL:ACC.M.SG
       'And the woman saw him go out' (Lit. 'The woman sees him (who was) going
       out')   (Herodotus, 1.10.6)

These facts suggest a scenario whereby different constructions come to be used in a
complex sentence because they are a standard way in which the language expresses
particular meaning components of that sentence, rather than as an effect of the
reinterpretation of pre-existing constructions.

   To the extent that this is the correct explanation for the origin of individual
constructions, these really are cases where there is competition between different
mechanisms pertaining to the same grammatical domain, in this case several
possible construals of the same situation, where different meaning components are
given different prominence. This scenario applies, presumably, to several domains
besides complex sentences, so this is a general pattern that is captured by existing
competing motivation models. A very similar scenario is in fact depicted in Du Bois'
chapter in this volume. Grammaticalization and processes of context-induced reinterpretation in general, however, are pervasive crosslinguistically, and in many cases
the origin of individual constructions is unknown, so it cannot be ruled out that their
use in a particular domain actually originates from these processes. This means that
the competing motivation scenario may be rarer than is usually assumed, and
whether or not it applies to particular cases should always be established based on
specific hypotheses about how the relevant constructions may have originated in
individual languages.

17.5 Concluding remarks

Competing motivations models, and functionally oriented explanations in general, are routinely proposed on synchronic grounds. Yet, the diachronic processes that give rise to the relevant constructions often pose several challenges for the explanatory hypotheses that can be proposed based on the synchronic distributional patterns for these constructions.

The most straightforward sense in which this holds is that individual constructions may originate from mechanisms other than those that can be postulated on synchronic grounds, and these mechanisms may not be the same from one instance of the construction to another (for example, in different languages, overt markers for plural or for particular argument roles may be the result of the reinterpretation of different source constructions). This implies that any model of the principles that lead to the use of particular constructions, including competing motivation models, should take into account the diachronic development of these constructions, rather than just their synchronic distribution.

In theory, this does not affect the core idea of competing motivation models, in that, even if the principles that give rise to individual constructions are not those that can be postulated on synchronic grounds, different principles may still be in competition within some grammatical domain, leading to the use of different constructions for that domain. This is, for example, a plausible explanation for the use of different constructions in some types of complex sentences.

Often, however, the use of individual constructions for some particular domain is best accounted for in terms independent of that domain in itself. In some cases, this is because this use originates from processes of context-driven reinterpretation of constructions originally used for other domains, possibly due to the varying contextual prominence of different aspects of the meaning of these constructions, or the fact that particular elements within these constructions take on a meaning originally associated with a co-occurring element. In other cases, the fact that some domain is encoded by a particular construction is a by-product of a restriction in the original contexts of use of that construction due to the development of some other construction. This is the case, for example, when zero marking becomes restricted to particular argument roles or number values as a result of the grammaticalization of overt markers for other roles or values originally also encoded through zero marking.

These processes have long been described in grammaticalization studies and studies of language change in general, but their implications for competing motivation models and synchronically oriented explanations have generally failed to be fully appreciated. The notion of competing motivations implies that each of the constructions used within some grammatical domain should be accounted for in terms of a distinct principle specifically pertaining to that domain, in the sense of principles that are somehow part of a speaker's mental representation and lead speakers to use precisely those constructions for precisely that domain. This has, in fact, often been described as an inherent problem of competing motivation models, in that there may be a proliferation of explanatory principles for which no independent evidence is available (Newmeyer 1998: 145–53, among others). In many cases, however, there is no need to postulate such principles, because the distribution of individual constructions is simply a result of what source constructions are initially available in the language, and how these can be reinterpreted. More generally, these cases do not involve any competition between different principles, except in the sense of a competition between the context-induced factors that determine the reinterpretation of a source construction and the tendency to maintain the conventional interpretation of that construction.

The necessity to adopt a diachronic perspective does not imply that the motivations for individual distributional patterns should be investigated exclusively on diachronic grounds. While diachronic processes point to principles that lead speakers to create novel constructions, a speaker's acquisition and use of the existing constructions of their language may be driven by distinct principles, and it is possible that such principles are in competition within particular grammatical domains, as assumed in several chapters in this volume. Also, the idea that individual distributional patterns are a result of the reinterpretation of particular source constructions does not account for why precisely those constructions are selected for reinterpretation from one language to another, so this issue should be investigated independently of the reinterpretation process in itself.

However, in order to conclude that a particular principle leads speakers to create novel constructions, we need evidence about how those constructions originated, and in order to conclude that particular principles govern a speaker's acquisition or use of existing constructions, we need psychological evidence about how these constructions are represented in a speaker's mental grammar. In neither of these cases, then, can the role of individual principles be assessed based on synchronic distributional evidence alone.

18

Where do motivations compete?

FREDERICK J. NEWMEYER

18.1 Introduction

This chapter explores two approaches to competing motivations within grammatical theory.[1] Section 18.2 introduces the two approaches, which I call "Direct Competition" and "Indirect Competition." Section 18.3 is an extended discussion of why I believe Indirect Competition to be the superior of the two. Section 18.4 is a brief conclusion.

18.2 Two approaches to competing motivations

The primary background assumption in this chapter is that important properties of natural language syntax have been shaped by external functional considerations. Leaving aside economy and the influence of frequency, which in a sense are orthogonal to other types of functional explanation, there are three major classes of external explanations for grammatical structure:

(1) *Processing-based explanations*: There is pressure for structure to be organized so as to allow the rapid and efficient recovery of meaning. (EXAMPLE: in VO languages, VP constituents tend to increase in structural complexity from left-to right: [$_{VP}$ V NP PP CP]; *[led] [my students] [to the realization] [that all grammars leak]*; Hawkins 1994, 2004.)

(2) Structure-concept iconicity-based explanations: *There is pressure for structure and meaning to be in alignment. (EXAMPLE: In general, semantic constituents match up with syntactic constituents.)*

(3) *Structure-discourse iconicity-based explanations*: There is pressure for the "flow" of structure to iconically reflect the flow of information in discourse. (EXAMPLE: Praguean "Communicative Dynamism": Old information tends to precede new information, so the passage of structure iconically reflects the passage of time; Firbas 1965.)

[1] I am greatly indebted to Brian MacWhinney, Edith Moravcsik, and three anonymous referees for their penetrating comments. While space limitations did not allow me to explore every suggestion that they made, I hope to have responded adequately to those that they considered to be the most important.

It is an interesting question whether (2) and (3) can be reduced to (1), as is argued in Newmeyer (1998). However, that question will not be pursued here.

Another background assumption is that motivations can and do compete with each other. That is, they can pull on language in different directions. Since the existence of competing motivations is the theme of this collection of chapters, I hardly need to dwell on the point. But to provide one short example of motivations in competition, consider the fact that there can be pressure from the parser to postpose the proper subpart of some semantic unit, thereby resulting in a loss of structure-concept iconicity. An example is provided by (4a)–(4b):

(4)   a.   [Many objections to the new work rules] were raised.
       b.   [Many objections] were raised [to the new work rules].

Extrapositions like (4b) are responses to pressure to postpose heavy constituents. The greater the ratio of the extraposed material to the predicate, the more likely extraposition will occur in discourse. The smaller the ratio, the less likely extraposition will take place (see Francis and Michaelis, this volume). Hence, the price paid for the extraposition is the breaking up of the semantic unit *many objections to the new work rules.*

The question to be addressed here is where this competition is played out, so to speak. That is, what is the relationship between the mental grammar and the motivations, often in competition with each other, that are responsible for the properties of the grammar? Another way of putting the question is to ask in what arena the competing factors are resolved. Broadly speaking, there have been three types of answers to these questions, two of which are types of what I call "Direct Competition" and one of which is "Indirect Competition":

(5)   Direct Competition. There is direct linkage between properties of particular grammars and the competing functional motivations that account for those properties, ...

       a.   ... to the point that grammars themselves are ill-defined objects. (Extreme Direct Competition)

       b.   ... so that subparts of grammars can be "tagged" with the functional motivations responsible for the diachronic development and synchronic maintenance of that subpart. (Moderate Direct Competition)

(6)   Indirect Competition. There is no direct linkage between competing external functions and grammatical properties. The influence of the former on the latter is played out in language use and acquisition and (therefore) language change and manifests itself in the crosslinguistic distribution of grammatical elements.

I have little to say about Extreme Direct Competition here, since I feel that it is an indefensible position. This approach to syntax is probably best known from the writings of Paul Hopper and Sandra Thompson, where it is given the name "Emergent Grammar" (see Hopper 1988: 120–1). In this approach, put only slightly metaphorically, the motivations shaping grammatical structure are fighting each other as we speak, to the point where grammar as such "emerges" with one particular speech act, ebbs, and then "reemerges" with the next. The basic assumption underlying Emergent Grammar seems to be that a formal structural system (as in the mainstream view of grammar) is by definition unable to interact with or be affected by external forces. Hence one must abandon the very idea of such a system. But as I have argued in a number of publications (see especially Newmeyer 1998), such an assumption is unwarranted.

The remainder of this chapter will hence focus on Moderate Direct Competition, which I refer to simply as Direct Competition (DC) in what follows, and Indirect Competition (IC).

The roots of DC go back at least to the 1970s. For example, Langacker (1974) and Creider (1979) hypothesized that each transformational rule could be identified as having some particular functional motivation. So a fronting rule might be attributed to the functional need of creating a topic, a deletion rule to the function of abetting economy, and so on. To give another example, Dik (1989) called attention to cross-linguistic variation in the indirect object construction. The orderings depicted in (7a) and (7b) are both well attested crosslinguistically (English of course has both orders):

(7) a. Direct Object—Indirect Object
     b. Indirect Object—Direct Object

Dik links the first order to the function of iconicity, since it reflects the movement of the object from the donor to the recipient. The second order is said to have a functional linkage as well, since it places the "more prominent" indirect object before the "less prominent" direct object. So in some languages the former motivation prevails and in others the latter prevails. Likewise, any approach that attributes a degree of prototypicality to a grammatical property is an example of DC, given the standard functionalist position that prototypicality facts are motivated externally (Croft 1990, 1991). To give one example, in George Lakoff's (1987) version of Cognitive Linguistics, members of grammatical categories can be assigned a degree of prototypicality within that category, which is itself determined by external functional and cognitive considerations. The claim is that the more prototypical a category member is, the more it exhibits the characteristic grammatical behavior of members of its class.

The most worked out approaches to DC have their roots in Optimality Theory (OT), in particular the version of OT developed for syntax by Judith Aissen and Joan Bresnan, where each constraint is paired with a functional motivation (Bresnan 1997; Aissen 2003). In this approach, the competition among motivations is played out in terms of constraint rankings. The motivation that "wins," so to speak, is the constraint that is higher ranked than the loser. For example, Aissen develops her approach to Differential Object Marking in terms of the competition between the two functionally-motivated constraints in (8):

(8) Two constraints at work in the analysis of Differential Object Marking (Aissen 2003):
     a. $*\emptyset_C$ "Star Zero": Penalizes the absence of a value for the feature CASE. (MOTIVATION: a hearer-based need for clarity.)

b. *STRUC_C: Penalizes a value for the morphological category CASE. (MOTI-VATION: economy-based, since it reduces the amount of structure that needs to be processed.)

This approach to DC within OT has been developed in the most detail in recent years by a series of papers by Andrej Malchukov. Malchukov, unlike Aissen, puts into competition functionally-motivated constraints with those that are *structurally-based*. Two examples are provided below:

(9)   (Malchukov 2006a) The morphosyntactic properties of nominalizations are constrained by the competitive interaction of:
   a. Functionally motivated constraints on deverbalization and substantivization.

   b. Structural conditions on output–output correspondences between morphological structure of nominalizations with that of the finite verbs, on the one hand, and nonderived nouns, on the other hand.

(10) (Malchukov 2006b) Transitivity alternations are constrained by the competitive interaction of:
   a. An iconically-motivated principle (Relevance), which states that a transitivity parameter should be preferably encoded on the "relevant" constituent (i.e. the constituent to which this parameter pertains).

   b. A structural principle (Primary Actant Immunity), which prohibits case marking of the primary actant without a concomitant diathetic shift.

Language change is an ideal testing ground for the relative adequacy of DC and IC and will therefore occupy a central position in the discussion that follows. Changes—at least those that are attested or reconstructed with a high degree of certainty—are more concrete and easier to study than more abstract properties of grammars. It is far easier, for example, to answer question (11a) than question (11b):

(11) a. What was the functional motivation (if any) for the appearance of "supportive *do*" in the history of English syntax?

   b. What is the functional motivation (if any) for the presence of "supportive *do*" in the syntax of Modern English?

Also, an understanding of (11a) helps to shed light on (11b) in a way that an understanding of (11b) is not necessarily helpful to an understanding of (11a).

Now, it seems that DC rather strongly implies a particular view of language change. If grammars are collections of properties that have functional motivations, then any *change* in a grammar is necessarily a change in the degree of functionality of one or more of those properties. Clearly, such a view embodies a default assumption about the nature of language change. It will, at least in the typical case, be in the direction of maximizing the functionality *of* those properties. If that were not the case, it is difficult to see what content DC could possibly have. Indeed, it is difficult to see what interest it could possibly have. It would be an odd theory that demanded a functional motivation for each, say, grammatical rule, but disavowed the necessity for rule changes to be consequences of the maximization of function. Likewise, if some new property is added to the grammar, it will, all other things being equal, have to be functionally motivated. Such a conclusion follows automatically from the hypothesis that grammatical properties are linked to functional motivations.

As it turns out, a number of scholars have taken the strongest possible position along these lines, namely, that individual instances of language change must be functionally motivated:

Saying that a certain feature of linguistic design or change cannot be functionally explained is tantamount to saying that we have not yet been able to find a functional explanation for that feature. (Dik 1986: 22)

Others have taken a somewhat weaker approach to the grammar–function linkage, in that they recognize that synchronic grammars are filled with rules of dubious functional utility, but they nevertheless still uphold the idea that each instance of language change is functionally motivated. Such a view embodies a position along the following lines:[2]

What I will argue here is that, in each instance, a *crazy* synchronic state of the grammar has arisen via diachronic changes that are highly *natural* and presumably motivated independently by various communicative [i.e. "functional"—FJN] factors. (Givón 1979: 235, emphasis in original)

If the weaker version of DC fails at the diachronic level, then the stronger version could hardly be correct at the synchronic level. The remainder of the chapter will therefore put the spotlight on language change as a testing ground for DC versus IC. It will conclude that there is little diachronic support for DC.

18.3 Indirect Competition is better motivated than Direct Competition

The remainder of this chapter is devoted to arguing that IC is better motivated than DC. The former will be fleshed out in more detail as the presentation proceeds. I offer four (to a certain degree, overlapping) arguments in favor of IC: Section 18.3.1, DC underplays or ignores the role of conventionality as an explanatory factor; Section 18.3.2, DC exaggerates the function-drivenness of language change; Section 18.3.3, DC is forced to downplay the (nonfunctional, in the ordinary use of the term) structural-systematic pressures on grammars; Section 18.3.4, DC has difficulty dealing with the incidentally dysfunctional consequences of an otherwise functionally-motivated change.

---

[2] For an updated and better worked out account of how languages develop rare "crazy" rules, see Malchukov (2010). Malchukov gives examples of such rules developing as a result of a conflict between a grammaticalization path and a functional constraint, as a result of the co-occurrence of several conditions from different domains, and from incomplete grammaticalization cycles.

18.3.1 *DC underplays or ignores the role of conventionality as an explanatory factor*

Let us raise some very simple questions about English grammar. For example, "Why does it place subjects before objects?" or "Why doesn't it permit null subjects?" One might be tempted to provide very functionalist-sounding answers to these questions, such as "Subjects precede objects because they have cognitive prominence over objects and cognitive prominence is iconically represented" and "There are no null subjects because agreement too weak to license them." But those are the wrong answers. Synchronic English grammar has those properties because they were in the grammars of the previous generation of English speakers. The factor that best explains why a person's grammar has the properties that it has is *conventionality* (see especially Croft 2000: 7). The desire to conform to the conventions of one's speech community is certainly functionally motivated, though it is not the sort of functional motivation that can be stated as a synchronic constraint in an OT-style grammar. The basic problem is that the forces (functional or otherwise) that bring a construction into a language are not necessarily the same ones that keep it there. To give one example in support of such an idea, in Modern English, the genitive can either precede or follow the noun it modifies:

(12)   a. GEN-N: Mary's mother's uncle's lawyer
        b. N-GEN: the leg of the table

The GEN-N ordering is unexpected, since English is otherwise almost wholly a right-branching language. The question, then, is why English-speaking children acquire the GEN-N ordering. The short, and completely correct answer, is "conventionality." They learn that ordering because they detect it in their speech community. But the long answer is very interesting, and drives home the great divide between the functional explanation of the rise of a rule in a particular grammar and the complex array of factors that lead to the preservation of that rule. The Old English of 1000 years ago was largely left-branching. The dominant orderings at that time were OV and GEN-N, the correlation predicted by parsing efficiency. The shift to VO order in Middle English went along with a shift to N-GEN order, as might be expected. But the shift started to reverse itself in Early Modern English, with the percentage of GEN-N orders starting to increase. The reason for this reversal appears to be that the two genitive orderings began to be differentiated functionally. In particular, GEN-N began to be favored for animate genitives and N-GEN began to be favored for inanimate genitives (Kroch 1994; Rosenbach and Vezzosi 2000). Such a differentiation in function should not be surprising, given the tendency for animates to occur earlier and inanimates later (see Tomlin 1986). But it needs to be pointed out that as far as the English genitive is concerned, the differentiation is only a general tendency, not a hard and fast rule. So inanimates do occur in the GEN-N construction (13a) and animates do occur in the N-GEN construction (13b):

(13)   a. the table's leg
        b. the treachery of the enemy

Now then, what is the relation between the rules and principles that license these two orders and the various motivations, functional or otherwise, that gave rise to them? The answer is too complex to allow any simplistic account in terms of DC. At least three pressures are at work in maintaining the two genitive orders in Modern English:

(14) a. The pressure of conventionality.
      b. The pressure to order animate arguments before nonanimate arguments.
      c. Purely structural pressure, caused by the existence of noun phrases with the structure [NP's N] and [N of NP] where there is no semantic possession at all:
         i. Tuesday's lecture
         ii. the proof of the theorem

In other words, it would be at worst impossible and at best wholly unrevealing to decompose the grammar of English genitives into rules or constraints, each one of which is provided with a functional motivation.[3]

18.3.2 *DC exaggerates the function-drivenness of language change*

DC would certainly receive support if grammars could be reduced to the competition between externally-motivated constraints of the type illustrated in (1)–(3) and broad structural principles that themselves might ultimately be shown to admit to external motivation. But that is not possible for a number of reasons, the most fundamental of which is the fact that the maximization of communicative efficiency, which is the idea underlying (1)–(3), is only one of many types of forces involved in the shaping of language structure. Most importantly, a longstanding tradition holds that the primary function of language consists in the establishment of social and personal ties within communities of speakers. As noted in Van Valin (1981b: 59) (see also Seuren 2009: ch. 4):

> . . . language is used to establish, reinforce, maintain, and express social relationships, rather than convey information. In the literature of the ethnography of communication there are numerous case studies of verbal interactions in which the exchange of information is minimal but the social aspect is maximal (see Bird and Shopen 1979; Keenan and Ochs 1979; Haviland 1980).

The literature is replete with examples of speech communities preserving or even creating communicatively dysfunctional structural properties as a means for manifesting group solidarity and pride in their distinctiveness relative to neighboring communities.[4] Peter Trudgill, in particular, has stressed that small tight-knit communities

---

[3] See Rosenbach (2010) for an account of English genitives that is broadly compatible with the one presented here. Rosenbach discusses the functional factors that over time have helped to shape the modern English construction, but she does not attempt to break down the current construction into a set of formal rules, each with its own functional motivation.

[4] An anonymous referee remarks that she or he does not "see any useful boundary between processing function and social function." But surely the latter are arbitrary in a way that the former are not. Some societies might value "*r*-dropping" and others *r*-retention. But we would be quite surprised to find a speech community where structurally simple clauses were more likely to be extraposed than structurally complex ones.

are more likely than larger open ones to preserve a high number of irregular forms and to undergo "less natural" phonological changes (see especially Trudgill 1992). As far as the preservation of irregularity is concerned, Seuren and Hamans (2010) note that Dutch aristocrats (or would-be aristocrats) go out of their way to use non-standard highly irregular verbal forms "to emphasize that they are so far above the norm that they can afford borrowing from below it" (2010: 137). They also call attention to the loss of plural marking for English nouns denoting certain species of animals (*fish*, *deer*, etc.), which started in the hunting jargon of the elite and spread first to farmers and then to the general population. And as far as "unnatural" phonological changes are concerned, Andersen (1988) points to the (functionally bizarre) development of parasitic consonants out of diphthongs in a number of isolated far-flung dialects spoken in Europe. For example, the German dialect of Waldeck in Hesse has *biksen* (cf. *beißen*) 'to bite'; *fukst* (cf. *Faust*) 'fist'; and *tsikt* (cf. *Zeit*) 'time.'

On a related point, a number of linguists have claimed that at least some of the changes associated with grammaticalization are literally *dysfunctional*. So consider the historical development of Latin *casa* 'house' to French *chez* 'at (somebody's place)' (Svorou 1994; Longobardi 2001). Was this change functionally motivated? That depends on what one means by 'functional'. According to Haspelmath (1999c), it had its origins in what he calls "speaker extravagance." Language users made unusually explicit formulations in order to attract attention. The first Old French speakers to say *casa* (which ultimately developed into *chez*) instead of simply *a*, were not making anything "more functional" either for themselves or their addressees, at least not if "functional" has something to do with maximizing economy of effort, being more semantically transparent, and so on. Just the opposite was the case: They were adding an unnecessary complication to the grammar for the sake of, basically, showing off.

Prescriptive norms as well play a role in maintaining aspects of grammars, even when those aspects appear dysfunctional from the point of view of communicative efficiency. For example, forms like (15a) are part of the usage of most English speakers:

(15)   a. He and I left. (prestige usage)
       b. Him and me left. (nonstandard, but widespread, usage)

Emonds (1986) argues, convincingly in my opinion, that (15a) would have died out centuries ago in favor of (15b) if the latter had not been censured by prescriptive grammarians. Indeed, there are a number of points that suggest that forms like (15a) are wholly unnatural in the context of modern English grammar: College and business writing handbooks have to devote entire sections on subject pronouns; there is widespread overcorrection of usage (e.g. *Did you see he and I?*), suggesting that "correct" usage has not been internalized; the handbooks often resort to an "avoid the construction" strategy for conjoined subject pronouns; and even middle-class children go through a stage of producing *Him and me left*.[5] Along similar lines,

---

[5] Emonds argues that the prestige use is much more complex grammatically than the nonstandard usage, though space limitations prevent me from developing his argument here.

von Polenz (1972: 99–100) points out that the Standard German nominal case endings, which threatened to fade away centuries ago, were kept alive through the efforts of the educational establishment.

One need not dwell on the problems posed for the DC model by aspects of grammatical structure whose origins and maintenance can be understood only in terms of the social context of speech. It is not far-fetched (albeit it would be a gross oversimplification) to "link" the English process extraposing relative clauses to the function of aiding sentential processing. But what would be the synchronic internal-grammatical linking to the process generating nonstandard verb forms in one dialect of Dutch, to the odd English plurals, to the parasitic consonants in Waldeck German, to the initial appearance of the odd features of French described above, or to the preservation of moribund forms? "Speaker extravagance" is not the sort of motivation that one would want to reduce to an OT-style constraint, even if one could do so. It does not say much for DC if grammars are full of words, constructions, and rules that entered the language for, essentially, anti-functional reasons. The social context forms a backdrop to a holistic view of grammatical innovation, use, and change, and is not an entity that can atomistically be linked to a particular feature of a particular grammar.

Even ignoring the social context, not all innovations make things easier for language users, in any obvious sense of the term "easier." Historical linguists with a functionalist bent tend to stress the common tendency to rule generalization in language change, where an existing rule tends to broaden its scope to maximize the transparency of the link between form and meaning. But the reverse is also attested, namely the *shrinking* of the applicability of a rule, sometimes with consequences chaotic for any iconic relationship between form and meaning. For example, Old English, like most modern Germanic languages, was a V2 language, with a productive process moving verbs from V to I to C, as in (16):

(16)

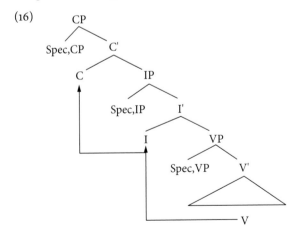

For reasons that have been debated extensively, the I-to-C component of the movement has become restricted to tensed auxiliaries, as (17a)–(17b) shows:

(17)   a.   Have you been working hard?
       b.   *Worked you hard yesterday?

But bafflingly, some phrasal elements in Spec, CP still trigger this inversion and some do not:

(18)   a.   Under no circumstances will I take a day off.
       b.   *Given any possibility will I take a day off.

(19)   a.   So tall is Mary, she can see into second story windows.
       b.   *Solved the puzzle has Mary, so she can be proud of herself.

In fact, the situation is still more complex, since some inversion triggers were historically late innovations, presumably introduced by analogy to the existing inverted forms, even while the majority of fronted phrases ceased to function as triggers. Whatever motivations were responsible for the current state of affairs are lost in the mists of time, rather than playing out in the grammar of Modern English.

   We find analogous examples in morphological change. For example, as is well-known, a huge number of irregular verbal forms have been regularized in the past thousand years of English. Yet at least one originally regular form, the past tense of *dive*, became the irregular *dove* in some dialects of English, presumably by analogy with forms such as *strive–strove*, *weave–wove*, and so on. Bidirectional analogy has been much more extensive in Dutch (Seuren and Hamans 2010), where we have many regulars that were originally irregular and many irregulars that were originally regular.

   Analogical change is "functional," in the sense that the leveling of paradigms tends to increase the transparency of the form–meaning interface. That is, it increases iconicity. But the fact that analogical change can work in opposite directions in the same language and in the same time period vitiates the idea that the model of DC can have any explanatory content. If there exists an explanation of why *healp* became *helped* while *dived* became *dove*, it clearly involves more than saying that both were analogical changes, triggered by the function of iconicity. If (counterfactually) *rād* ('rode') had developed into *rided* and *dēmde* ('deemed') into *dempt*, we could have pointed to analogy as well! It would seem that the characterization and explanation of the developments here is beyond the available resources of the DC model.

   One might suggest (as did an anonymous referee) that analogical change (including the bidirectional variety) can be modeled/predicted if one takes frequency information into account as an explanatory functional factor. I am skeptical that such is generally the case. For example, *dive* is much less frequent than *arrive* and much more frequent that *skive* ('to cut into thin layers'), yet it was *dive* rather than the other two verbs that developed an analogical irregular past form. To provide another example, according to K. Aaron Smith (2001), in the history of English, frequency drove the replacement of *be* by *have* as the auxiliary used with participles. In his view, since *have* was always more frequent than *be* in this respect, over time the former drove out the latter. So we now say *The messenger has come* and not *The messenger is come*. But the frequency-based explanation has no account for why in German the exact opposite has happened. According to Piebsch and Collinson in their book *The German Language*, some verbs—for example *folgen*—that used to take *haben*, now take *sein*. Another curiosity of German (and Low German) is the use of the auxiliary *sein* with the verb *sein* itself. This differs from the other Northwest Germanic languages like English and the Scandinavian languages, which use the auxiliary *have*. There are some interesting differences in usage between German dialects of the north vs. those of the south. In dialects of the north (including Standard German), stative verbs like *stehen* 'stand' and *sitzen* 'sit,' but not *sein* itself, take the auxiliary *haben*. In the south they take *sein*. Since we have no reason to believe that verbs translating as 'follow,' 'stand,' 'sit,' and so on would be used more in one part of the Germanic-speaking world than another, is it clear that the frequency of use of a particular form is only one of a number of factors driving language change. A final example that warns us of an overreliance on frequency as an explanation is from Brinton and Traugott (2005: 17–18). Citing Haspelmath (2002), they note that the suffix *-ment* is extremely common in Modern English, but is not being extended to new forms. It would appear that in this case some structural factors predominate over frequency-based ones.

So far, the discussion has revolved around the innovation of "internal" changes, that is, those that do not seem to have been triggered by language contact. But a sizeable amount of grammatical change is contact-induced. Here, the kinds of factors at the root of a DC approach are even more remote. Borrowed forms are often counter-functional, in the sense that they are the source of numerous disharmonies, say in terms of word order correlations (for an overview, see Harris and Campbell 1995). For example, Amharic, which was originally VO, like most Semitic languages, borrowed OV and genitive-noun order from neighboring Cushitic languages, but retained prepositions; Ahom (Thai) borrowed modifier-head order from Assamese (Indo-European) or some Tibeto-Burman language; several Munda languages borrowed Modifier-head order from Dravidian; and Pipil, Xinca, and Copainalá Zoque borrowed VOS from neighboring Mayan languages. All of these cases led to disharmonies, thereby decreasing parsing efficiency, without any obvious gain in functionality in some other respect.

18.3.3 DC is forced to downplay the (nonfunctional, in the ordinary use of the term) structural-systematic pressures on grammars

I illustrate my point here by reference to the history of preposition-stranding in English, that is, sentences like the following:

(20) a. Who did you talk to?
      b. Mary was talked to.

Preposition-stranding is one of the rarest of grammatical phenomena, being attested only in Germanic (but not in German and only marginally in Dutch), marginally in French, and possibly in the Niger-Congo languages Vata and Gbadi. Why is it so rare? I know of only one functional explanation, that presented in Hawkins (2004). Hawkins argues that its existence leads to the potential of assigning *wh*-fillers to the wrong gaps in on-line processing. The following example illustrates the problem:

(21)   Who did you ask *[____] John about ___?

On-line, the filler would be incorrectly assigned to the first gap, rather than the second. Be that as it may, stranding has existed since Old English. But interestingly, its domain of application has changed over the years and, for the most part, has expanded:

(22)   Chronology of preposition-stranding in English (Allen 1980; van Kemenade 1987)
    a. Old English period (it could apply with all *wh*-movement type operations without an overt *wh*-pronoun; topicalization)
    b. Early Middle English (with overt *wh*-movement)
    c. Later Middle English (with passives)
    d. Modern English (over a direct object; e.g. *Who did they take advantage of?*; *Mary was taken advantage of.*)

So what is going on here? What we have is a classic case of an existing grammatical process expanding its domain. Speakers have the pattern and seem to love it and to use it in more and more contexts. Possibly one could model the process in OT by positing that the constraint licensing P-stranding became more and more dominant over the centuries (or perhaps by positing that some other constraint became less dominant). But that seems like the wrong way to look at things. Such an OT account would boil down to no more than saying that at time x P-stranding worked one way and that at time y P-stranding worked a different way. What one wants is at least the beginnings of an explanation of *why* throughout the history of English, speakers have felt no hesitation in expanding the domain of what at first glance appears to be a dysfunctional grammatical process. I would speculate that what is behind the story is the existence, from very early stages of English, of other sentence types with P-like final elements:

(23)   a. Phrasal verbs with postposed particles:
        i.   I looked the answer up.
        ii. Let's check it out.
    b. Final P-like directional particles
        i.   I found this lying around.
        ii. She's coming up (e.g. the stairs)

In other words, P-stranding has been reinforced by the existence of similar, but analytically independent, constructions in the language. But once one talks about existing patterns exerting pressure on a particular construction, one has necessarily moved away from the constraint-motivation isomorphism of DC.

18.3.4 *DC has difficulty dealing with the incidentally dysfunctional consequences of an otherwise functionally-motivated change*

Lightfoot (1999) has given a compelling example of how difficult it can be to tease out the relative roles of different explanatory factors in a particular situation, with its resultant difficulty for the DC model. In a nutshell, Lightfoot demonstrates that a formal constraint, whose ultimate explanation is most likely functional, can nevertheless have *dysfunctional* consequences, leading grammars to resort to formal means (but different means for different languages) to overcome these consequences. Consider the principle of Lexical Government (24), a key element of the theory of Chomsky (1981):

(24)   Lexical Government: Traces of movement must be lexically governed.

This condition does a lot of work. For example, it accounts for the grammaticality distinction between (25a) and (25b):

(25)   a.   Who$_i$ was it apparent [e$_i$ that [Kay saw e$_i$]]?
     b.   *Who$_i$ was it apparent yesterday [**e$_i$** that [Kay saw e$_i$]]?

In (25b) the word *yesterday* blocks government of the intermediate trace (in boldface) by the adjective *apparent*. Or consider phrase (26):

(26)   Jay's picture

Phrase (26) is at least 3-ways ambiguous: Jay could be the owner of the picture, the agent of the production of the picture, or the person portrayed (the object reading). The derivation of the object reading is depicted in (27):

(27)   [Jay$_i$'s [picture e$_i$]]

Notice that the trace is governed by the noun *picture*. Now consider phrase (28):

(28)   the picture of Jay's

Phrase (28) has the owner and agent reading, but not the object reading, That is, Jay cannot be the person depicted. The derivation, schematically illustrated in (29), explains why:

(29)   *the picture of [Jay$_i$'s [e e$_i$]]

The trace of *Jay's* is not lexically governed; rather it is governed by another empty element, understood as "picture."
    Lightfoot is quite open to the possibility that condition (24) might be functionally motivated:

...the general condition of movement traces...may well be functionally motivated, possibly by parsing considerations. In parsing utterances, one needs to analyze the positions from which displaced elements have moved, traces. The UG condition discussed restricts traces to certain well-defined positions, and that presumably facilitates parsing. (Lightfoot 1999: 249)

However, he goes on to show that this condition, functionally motivated though it may be, has dysfunctional consequences. The problem is that it blocks the straightforward extraction of subjects:

(30)   a.   *Who$_i$ do you think [e$_i$ that **e$_i$** saw Fay]?
     b.   *Who$_i$ do you wonder [**e$_i$** how [**e$_i$** solved the problem]]?

Sentences (30a)–(30b) are ungrammatical because the bold-faced subject traces are not lexically governed. Indeed, in the typical case, subjects will not be lexically governed. Nevertheless, it is safe to assume that it is in the interest of language users to questions subjects, just as much as objects or elements in any other syntactic position. In other words, the lexical government position is in part dysfunctional.

Interestingly, languages have devised various ways of getting around the negative effects of the condition. They are listed in (31a)–(31c):

(31) Strategies for undoing the damages of the lexical government condition:
    a. Adjust the complementizer to license the extraction.
    b. Use a resumptive pronoun in the extraction site.
    c. Move the subject first to a nonsubject position and then extract.

English uses strategy (31a):

(32) Who do you think saw Fay?

Swedish uses strategy (31b):

(33) Vilket   ord$_i$ visste   ingen   [hur   det/*e$_i$ stavas]?
     Which   word   knew   no-one   how   it/e   is spelled?
     'Which word did no one know how it is spelled?'

The resumptive pronoun *det* replaces the trace, so there is no unlexically governed trace to violate the lexical government condition. And Italian uses the third strategy (31c). In Italian, subjects can occur to the right of the verb and this is the position from which they are extracted (as in 34):

(34) Chi$_i$ credi   [che   abbia   telefonato e$_i$]?
     who   do-you-think   that   has   telephoned?
     'Who do you think has telephoned?'

What we have here in other words are functionally-motivated formal patches for dysfunctional side-effects of a formal principle that is functionally motivated. I suspect that the sort of complex interplay between formal and functional modes of explanation is the norm, rather than the exception, in syntactic theory. I cannot see any coherent way to break down the explanatory mechanisms into atomistic constraints that compete with each other. What we need here, again, is the holistic approach of the Indirect Competition model.

Seuren and Hamans (2010) provide a different sort of example of a case where a functionally motivated innovation ended up having partly dysfunctional consequences. In the Middle Ages, German and Dutch innovated a verb clustering process, whereby originally bisentential structures containing a causative verb merged the two verbs into a single lexical unit. The result (represented in the modern forms of the language) is (35a)–(35b):

(35) a. sie den Mann gehen ließ. (German)
     b. zij de man gaan liet. (Dutch)
       'She let the man go'

This clustering was highly functional, in that it reduced the amount of processing required, as well as leading to more iconicity, given the intimate cognitive relationship between the words representing "let" and "go." But what happened was that as soon as the process caught hold, it burrowed its way through the grammar by affecting more and more complement-taking verbs. In others words, just as with P-stranding in English (see Section 18.3.3), structure trumped function, leading to a wealth of verb clusters that are next to impossible for a language user to parse. The following are structurally possible clauses in the two languages:

(36) a. ...daß Johann den Mann den Hund die Zeitung holen lassen sehen wollte
             ...that John the man the dog the paper fetch let see wanted
             '...that John wanted to see the man get the dog to fetch the paper'

      b. ...dat Jan de man de hond de krant wilde zien laten halen
             ...that John the man the dog the paper wanted to see let fetch
             '...that John wanted to see the man get the dog to fetch the paper'

Now of course, few speakers would ever actually produce such clauses. They would find some appropriate circumlocution to express the same idea. Nevertheless, their grammar provides such dysfunctional structures, which arose through a natural structural extension of a functionally motivated process.[6]

18.4 Conclusion

The essential message of this chapter is that languages are filled with constructions that arose in the course of history to respond to some functional pressure, but, as the language as a whole changed, the resultant elements of grammar ceased to be very good responses to that original pressure. Such facts seem challenging to any theory, like DC, in which grammatical processes are linked to their motivations. Put tersely, DC confounds what we know with how what we know got to be what we know. Parsing ease, desire for functional differentiation, pressure for an iconic relationship between form and meaning, and so on really are forces that shape grammars. Adult speakers, in their use of language, are influenced by such factors to produce variant forms reflecting the influences of these forces. Children, in the process of acquisition, hear these variant forms and grammaticalize them. In that way, over time, certain functional influences leave their mark on grammars. There is no place, indeed no *need*, for the factors accounting for morphosyntactic properties to match up in a one-to-one fashion with anything grammar-internal.

In a nutshell, then, to ask the question: "Is this rule or constraint (or whatever) motivated" is to ask the wrong question. No rule or constraint has a motivation in and of itself, but only within the total system in which it occurs, and crucially, in the history of that system. The root of the problem for the DC model is the fact that the interplay of explanatory factors is vastly too complex to allow individual motivations

---

[6] The Dutch structure is especially problematic from the point of view of language processing, in that it involves the sort of crossing dependencies that have been found only in a small handful of other languages.

to be attached to individual grammatical elements. Given the state of our knowledge about how the various competing factors affect form, we have no noncircular means for attributing a particular property of a particular language to a particular functional factor. The best we can do is to characterize the general, typological influence of function on form. But this is typical of explanation in general. Take cigarette smoking and colon cancer. We know that smoking is a risk factor in the development of colon cancer. We also know that a high-fiber diet helps to prevent it. But can we say with confidence that John Smith, a heavy smoker, has colon cancer *because* he smokes? Or can we say that Mary Jones, a nonsmoker and big consumer of high-fiber foods, does not have colon cancer *for that reason*? No, certainly not. Many individuals who smoke several packs a day will never develop colon cancer. Many nonsmoking individuals with a high-fiber diet, on the other hand, will develop the disease. To complicate things still further, many smokers also have high-fiber diets. In other words, both factors are exerting influence on them. The best we can do is talk about *populations*. The factors affecting language are much more poorly understood than those affecting health. Given our present state of knowledge about the full range of such factors and their interplay at the level of individual languages, it seems far too premature to attempt to link statements in particular grammars with particular motivations. But that still leaves the challenging research program of analyzing motivations as they compete in processing, usage, and acquisition, and understanding how this competition manifests itself in the crosslinguistic distribution of grammatical elements. Even this more modest research program is a crucial element of one of the central tasks facing theoretical linguistics today, namely understanding the relationship between grammatical form and those competing forces that help to shape that form.

19

Politeness distinctions in personal pronouns: A case study on competing motivations

JOHANNES HELMBRECHT

19.1 Introduction

Politeness distinctions in personal pronouns are paradigmatically encoded distinctions that express social aspects of the interpersonal relation between the speaker and the referent of the pronoun. These social aspects have to do with the relative position of the speaker vis-à-vis the referent with regard to social roles and social hierarchies that hold in the speaker community. These formally encoded distinctions—something like the opposition of French *tu/vous* (2SG.FAM/2SG.HON) or German *du/Sie* (2SG.FAM/2SG.HON)—are strong areal features. On a world-wide scale, there are roughly four large geographical areas with a significant density of politeness distinctions in personal pronouns. In addition, each of these areas shows a different type of politeness distinctions in second person pronouns.

As can be seen in Chapter 45, of the WALS Atlas (Figure 19.1; cf. Helmbrecht 2005b), the areas with this particular feature are South-East Asia (among others the black triangles on the map), the Indic sub-continent (mostly black dots), parts of Mesoamerica, and Europe (mostly gray dots). On the other hand, there are large areas without any attested politeness distinctions in pronouns (marked by the white dots on the map); these are North America, South America, Papua New-Guinea, and Australia. The same holds for Africa, but there are a few exceptions.

The general question vis-à-vis these facts is: is it possible to explain—at least in part—the feature itself, its formal encoding, and its crosslinguistic distribution functionally by means of a competing motivations approach?

The general idea behind the competing motivations approach, which is widely shared among functionally oriented linguists,[1] is that the formal expression of

---

[1] In particular among those linguists who subscribe to the core assumptions of a usage-based approach, an utterance-based approach, or an evolutionary approach (cf. Du Bois 1985; Langacker 1987, 1991; Hopper 1998; Croft 2000; Barlow and Kemmer 2002; and many others).

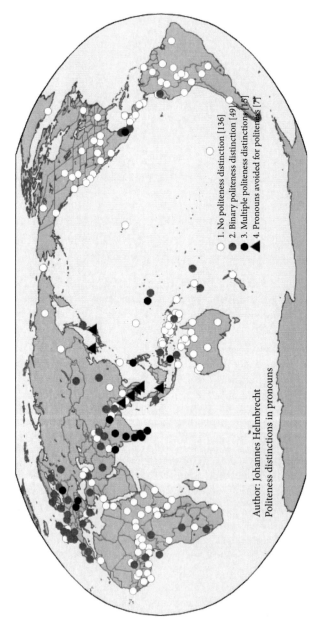

1. No politeness distinction [136]
2. Binary politeness distinction [49]
3. Multiple politeness distinction [15]
4. Pronouns avoided for politeness [7]

Author: Johannes Helmbrecht
Politeness distinctions in pronouns

FIGURE 19.1 The *World Atlas of Language Structures*: 'Politeness distinctions in pronouns'
Source: Helmbrecht (2005b: 186–90).

grammatical categories and constructions can be explained as compromise solutions between different functional motivations (cf. Du Bois 1985).

The application of such an approach therefore requires identifying all internal and external motivations that are relevant for a specific phonological or grammatical feature in an individual language or crosslinguistically, and calculating the relative strength of each motivation. The relative strength of each motivation in such an explanatory scenario varies according to the linguistic contexts in which the feature appears.

The competing motivations approach is tightly bound to usage-based, utterance-based, and evolutionary approaches in linguistics. They have in common that the language user is thought of as a rational agent who has the capability to choose from his or her repertoire the form or linguistic expression that fits his or her communicative and social purposes best. The individual language user is the locus where internal and external motivations interact.

The challenges of a competing motivations explanation are to (a) develop criteria that allow identifying all relevant motivations, and (b) to develop a model or mechanism that allows describing the target form or expression as an outcome of the interaction of the participating motivations in the history of language use. In what follows I will try to develop a competing motivations explanation of the emergence and diffusion of the 2SG.HON pronouns among the languages of Europe that derive etymologically from a 2PL pronoun.

First (Section 19.2), I will summarize the relevant historical facts of the emergence and diffusion of the 2PL as a 2SG.HON pronoun in Europe. Then, social and functional motivations that can be hypothesized to be important in this historical process will be discussed and applied to these particular instances of language change (Section 19.3). Finally, I will offer an evaluation of the presented analysis and some conclusions (Section 19.4).

19.2 The emergence and diffusion of polite pronouns in Europe

Most standard languages in Europe have at least one binary politeness distinction in their paradigms of personal pronouns, and it is always the second person that is involved. From a European perspective, it seems quite natural that politeness distinctions almost exclusively appear in second-person pronouns. However, such distinctions can frequently also be found in third-person pronouns and even first-person pronouns crosslinguistically at least in languages that have them also in the second person. There is probably a Politeness Hierarchy in personal pronouns, as illustrated in (1):

(1)   Hierarchy of politeness distinctions in personal pronouns: 2 < 3 < 1
      (cf. Brown and Levinson 1987; Croft 2003: 160f; Helmbrecht 2004: 292–5)

such that this distinction will appear in the second person first, then in the third person and lastly in the first person. In rather synchronic terms this hierarchy says that if a language has this distinction in the first person then it has it in all others too.

The presence of binary politeness distinctions means that there is only one politeness distinction formally encoded as can be illustrated with the *tu/vous* distinction in French. The T pronoun (*tu*) is used to refer to familiar and intimate individuals such as family members, friends, colleagues, and so forth. The V pronoun (*vous*) is used to address all others, in particular strangers (cf. the T/V terminology from Brown and Gilman 1960). Second-person pronouns that distinguish more than two levels of politeness are rare in the languages of Europe (it is reported, however, from e.g. Rumanian (cf. Braun 1984) and Lithuanian (cf. Mathiassen 1996; Ambrazas 1997)).

Binary politeness distinctions are synchronically the dominant type in Europe (see the gray dots in Figure 19.1), but this has not always been so historically. German and other European languages developed at one period in their history an even more elaborate system of politeness distinctions in the second person, which eventually collapsed during the nineteenth and twentieth centuries to a simple binary system (Table 19.1).

TABLE 19.1. **Politeness distinctions in German 2SG pronouns**

Politeness value	Old High German/Middle High German	17th century	18th century	Early 19th century	Contemporary standard German
More formal	*ir* (<2PL)	*er* (<3SG.M) *sie* (<3SG.F) *ihr* (<2PL)	*Sie* (<3PL) *er* (<3SG.M) *sie* (<3SG.F) *ihr* (<2PL)	*Sie* (<3PL) *ihr* (<2PL) *er* (<3SG. M) *sie* (<3SG.F)	*Sie* (<3PL) *du*
	du	*du*	*du*	*du*	
Less formal			*du*	*du*	

Source: Adapted from Simon (1997).

The first attestation of the use of 2PL pronouns as a polite form of 2SG address can be found in the Old High German (OHG) period around the ninth century. This use became more and more regular in the Middle High German (MHG) period. At this time, the use of the two 2SG pronouns was largely asymmetrical, that is, the socially superior received the polite pronoun *ir* (2SG.HON), but gave the familiar pronoun *du* (2SG.FAM). The use of the polite pronouns in the subsequent centuries remained asymmetrical until the nineteenth century. It then became more and more symmetrical, no longer reflecting different social status. The asymmetrical use of polite forms of address is determined by the differing social status of the speech act participants, the symmetrical use of address forms reflects solidarity or social closeness (Brown and Gilman 1960; Brown and Levinson 1987: 74–84).

As Table 19.1 shows, this originally binary system expanded to a ternary system in the seventeenth century by introducing a super polite second-person pronoun into the paradigm. This super polite form derived etymologically from the 3SG pronoun which also remained to be used as such.

Around the eighteenth century, the paradigm of personal pronouns became even more complex by distinguishing four levels of politeness. Speakers of German began to use the 3PL pronoun as a super polite form of address (2SG. HHON) which led to a slight degradation of the other forms with regard to the degree of respect they assign to the Hearer. This system underwent some changes before it began to collapse by the middle of the nineteenth century. For instance, the degree of respect expressed by *er/sie* (<3SG.M/F) diminished. Therefore, these forms appear somewhat lower with regard to the formality scale in Table 19.1. The result is the contemporary binary opposition between *du* (2SG.FAM) vs. *Sie* (2SG. HON). This is a very simplified picture of the history of the pronominal paradigm, but gives an idea of the ways in which politeness distinctions in personal pronouns emerged and changed during previous centuries in German and some other languages of Europe.

The etymological source of the polite pronouns in German and most other European languages are personal pronouns that already existed in the respective paradigms, but acquired an additional meaning as second-person polite forms. Sometimes these pronouns lost the original meaning; at other times they retained it (as is the case in German). However, etymological sources other than personal pronouns do exist, too (see Helmbrecht 2005a for details).

There are at least three important peculiarities with regard to the emergence and diffusion of the politeness distinctions in personal pronouns in the European linguistic area:

The first peculiarity is that almost all languages that acquired a second-person polite pronoun at some point in their history began with a 2PL pronoun used as a polite 2SG.HON form. One notable exception is Hungarian.

The second peculiarity is that the areal spread of this distinction was not random. There is a diffusion of the use of the 2PL as a 2SG.HON pronoun from the center of the European linguistic area up to the fringes of Europe. The center of this area which is also called the Charlemagne *Sprachbund* comprises today's Germany and France; compare the summary of the first attestation of this use of 2PL pronouns in some standard languages of Europe in Table 19.2. The x-axis of Table 19.2 represents the historical time line beginning from late antiquity in the third century up to our times. The y-axis lists the historical language varieties for which a 2PL as 2SG.HON use is first attested. For German, the first attestation of this use stems from the ninth century and was found in Old High German texts. The shaded cells indicate the persistence of this use as a 2SG.HON in the history of the individual language. Many languages gave up the use of the 2PL as 2SG.HON some centuries after its adoption in favor of alternative polite pronouns of address (cf. the example of German in Table 19.1).

TABLE 19.2.   **First attestation of a 2PL > 2SG.HON use in some languages of Europe**

Century	3.–5.	9.	11.	12.	13.	14.	15.	16.	17.	18.	19.	20.
languages												
Latin (Late-)	X											
German (OHG)		X										
French (Old)			X									
Spanish (Old)				X								
Dutch (Middle)					X							
English (Middle)					X							
Norwegian (Old)						X						
Italian						X						
Danish (Old)						X						
Czech							X					
Polish								X				
Icelandic									X			
Russian										X		
Serbian											X	
Bulgarian											X	

Source: Adapted from Helmbrecht (2010).

Some comments on the facts summarized in Table 19.2 are due:

1. The use of a 2PL as 2SG.HON form of address is probably an innovation in Late Latin; there are letters dating back to the third to fifth centuries written in Latin by different Bishops in southern France (cf. Chatelain 1880).

2. It is likely that the real diffusion started in medieval times among the royal courts and higher nobility in France. The French court was certainly the trend setter in medieval times for all royal courts in Europe with regard to fashion, life style, art, literature, and architecture. This was the time when the culture of knighthood emerged.

3. It can also be assumed that there was close contact among the courts of that time and that the customs and manners of the French court and nobility were adopted by the other European courts and nobles to various degrees.

4. A closer look into the history of the politeness distinctions in pronouns suggests that there are at least two directions of diffusion: first of all, there is diffusion from top to bottom in the individual speech communities. This means, the custom to use polite pronouns was probably adopted first among the members of the royal court and the nobility before it was also adopted in the upper middle class and then descending the social scale later on. Secondly, as Table 19.2 shows, there is diffusion from a geographical center (today's France/Germany) to the fringes of Europe. Languages geographically more distant from the center adopted the 2SG.HON later. This can best be seen with regard to the Scandinavian languages and the Slavic languages.

5. The diffusion of the use of the 2PL as a 2SG.HON pronoun can be thought of as following a gradual, step-by-step model. The languages that were directly adjacent to the center adopted this trend quickly almost at the same time. From these languages, this fashion spread slowly to the next neighboring language, step-by-step until it reached the periphery of Europe in the East. For instance, there is some evidence that the use of the 2PL as the polite form of address in Czech was borrowed from German in the fifteenth century. So this spread was no longer directly influenced and triggered by the prestigious French model. The eastward spread of this feature hence followed a step-by-step model.

6. Some cautionary remarks are also due: Table 19.2 summarizes the findings with regard to the first attestation. This first attestation, however, does not reveal anything about the historical appearance of this feature. It may be the case that it was used much earlier, but we have no written records of it. In addition, this first attestation does not really tell us to what extent the speaker population adopted this feature. In addition we do not know much about the specific rules of use of the borrowed polite pronominal forms: who gives 2SG.HON to whom and what does he or she receive in turn? The contemporary languages of Europe that have a polite distinction in the second person do not have identical rules of use and it is plausible to assume that this was also the case some centuries ago. What is known from studies of Old French (Foulet 1918–19; Lebsanft 1987; Mason 1990) or Old High German texts (Ehrismann 1902, 1903; Simon 2003) is that the use of the 2SG.HON was neither stable nor obligatory at that time, but allowed for some freedom of choice—probably pragmatic factors were effective.

The third peculiarity has to do with the type of borrowing. There is not a single case of borrowing in the narrow sense of *matter replication* (Matras 2009) involved here; that is, it was never the pronominal form that was borrowed among the SAE languages. It is always the kind of use of a form, for example the use of the 2PL as 2SG.HON which was borrowed. This means with regard to polite pronouns that what we find eventually could be exclusively subsumed under the rubric pattern replication.

Pattern replication—other terms are calques or pattern transfer—means that it is not words or other linguistic material of the donor language that are borrowed, but constructions in a wide sense. Important subtypes of pattern replication are contact-induced grammaticalization and polysemy copying (Heine and Kuteva 2005:100–3, 2006). Pattern replication has to be considered as a kind of compromise strategy on the part of the bilingual speaker. On the one hand, the bilingual speaker needs to flag language loyalty by avoiding matter replication. On the other hand, the bilingual speaker strives for the reduction of the processing load by allowing patterns to converge. Hence, according to Matras (2009: 234–7), pattern replication seems to be the outcome of competing motivations. On the one hand, there is a social or conventional need to stick to the language of the actual speech situation or context, that's language loyalty; on the other hand the processing load is reduced by assimilation of the constructional patterns of the repertoire languages of the bilingual speaker.

The diffusion of the 2PL as 2SG.HON use in the languages of Europe could be considered as a third subtype of pattern replication which could be termed "pragmatic replication." What is borrowed is a pragmatic strategy to avoid direct reference to the addressee in specific speech act contexts, namely those contexts in which there exists a high risk for the speaker to violate the face wants of the addressee. The attempt to avoid or to redress a face threatening act is seen in politeness strategies in linguistic behavior. This politeness strategy (see Section 19.3.2) can be hypothesized to be one of the motivations for the diffusion of the use of 2PL as 2SG.HON pronouns.

It is intuitively clear that this motivation contradicts the economy motivation and the motivation to be efficient with respect to processing costs. The politeness strategy leads to more complex expressions of addressee reference. Efficiency and economy are hence weak motivations for the diffusion of the 2PL as 2SG.HON use in Europe, but may constrain the development of paradigmatic complexity.

A third motivation instantly comes to mind: prestige. It can be hypothesized that the direction of the diffusion is strongly determined by prestige—the use of a 2PL as a 2SG.HON is adopted from the speech community with high prestige by speech communities of lower prestige. This holds for both directions of the spread, the center–periphery diffusion and diffusion down the social scale within societies.

All three hypothetical external motivations for the spread of the politeness distinction in pronouns, economy, politeness, and prestige will be discussed in turn in more detail including their possible interaction with internal motivations.

19.3 The competing motivations analysis

The challenge of a competing motivations explanation for a specific language change is to identify all relevant external and internal motivations and to describe their interaction in a non-ad-hoc way. This means that for all motivations that are relevant in a specific historical process, their effects in isolation and the criteria for how to identify them have to be specified. The methodological starting point is the natural language user and his/her linguistic behavior in specific contexts under the influence of these motivations. The interaction of the different motivations and the relative strength of each will change depending on the context. Principled explanations for the varying strength of the individual motivations have to be sought.

19.3.1 *Economy*

Second-person pronouns with or without politeness distinctions belong to the large group of referential expressions, and more specifically, to the functional domain of person reference. The formal or syntactic domain—at least in our case—is roughly identical with the NP (or DP). What does economy as a motivation in the linguistic behavior of the language user mean?

The speaker tries to communicate what he or she has to say in the least costly way. This holds in turn also for referring expressions. The shorter the referential expression the less costly it is. The lower threshold of this correlation is the ability to identify the referent by H. The ability to identify the referent of an NP depends on the amount and kind of background knowledge H has. This background knowledge is part of the wider context of the communicative situation or speech act, respectively. S knows or has an idea about the background knowledge of H at each point in the conversation.

If the referent is a speech act participant or already given in discourse, its identification is easier for H than the other way round. Newly introduced referents have to be marked linguistically in various ways, for instance by additional information given by nominal modifiers. Hence topical and given information may be presented to H by shorter expressions than new and non-topical information. This is just one functional motivation for the almost universal distinction between personal pronouns and nouns. Compared to nouns, personal pronouns are shorter or unmarked in various ways: they represent a full NP and combine minimally the categories definiteness/givenness, and various person and number values. Nouns, on the other hand, need to be specified for these categories morphosyntactically. The unmarkedness of personal pronouns vis-à-vis nouns within referential expressions (NPs) can be shown by applying the well-known markedness criteria established in typology such as structural coding, inflectional potential, distributional potential, and typological and textual frequency (cf. Greenberg 1966a; Croft 1990, 2003). If one just takes the last of these criteria, the textual frequency criterion, the markedness relation between nouns and pronouns can easily be shown by means of simple text counts (Table 19.3).

TABLE 19.3. **Distribution of NP-Types in different text genres**

NP-type	Oral genres	Written genres
1SG	209 (18%)	3 (0,3%)
2SG	92 (8%)	1 (0,1%)
3SG	96 (8%)	72 (6%)
1PL	55 (5%)	17 (1%)
2PL	23 (2%)	0 (0%)
3PL	16 (1%)	15 (1%)
Personal pronouns total	491 (43%)	91 (9,1%)
Demonstratives and other definite pro-forms	202 (18%)	74 (6%)
Indefinite pronouns	65 (6%)	36 (3%)
Lexical NPs (nouns)	374 (33%)	962 (82%)
(All NPs) total	1132 (100%)	1180 (100%)

Source: Helmbrecht (2006).

The text counts are based on a small balanced corpus of texts that were taken from the online corpus of the IDS (Institut für Deutsche Sprache, Mannheim). The corpus contains two sub-corpora, one with oral texts and the other one with written texts. The oral texts (6,266 words) comprise class-room conversations, private family conversation, and a biographical interview; the written texts (6,326 words) are basically newspaper articles from different sources. The number of words in both text corpora is approximately identical, and surprisingly, the number of referential expressions (NPs) is almost identical in both corpora as well. However, the distribution of the principal NP types varies greatly between the two text types. Oral texts show a clear asymmetry in the frequency of personal pronouns (43%) vs. lexical NPs (33%), that is, NPs that contain a noun as head. Not surprisingly, this is not the case in written texts, where personal pronouns comprise only (9.1%) of all kinds of NPs vis-à-vis (82%) of lexical NPs.

Furthermore, looking at the relative frequencies among the different person–number values of personal pronouns, it is obvious that there are very different (functionally motivated) hierarchies. The lower frequencies of personal pronouns in written texts (with the exception of the third persons) have to do with the lack of common or shared speech act situations which constitute face-to-face communications. In addition, written texts almost exclusively contain statements; questions and commands are rarely found (see Table 19.4). If singular and plural values are conflated, oral texts show a person hierarchy 1 < 2 < 3 which is reminiscent of the empathy hierarchy. Again, not surprisingly, the written texts show a clear dominance of the third person 3 < 1 < 2 (see also Table 19.5).

What does this mean with respect to politeness distinctions in second-person pronouns? Second-person pronouns refer to a speech act participant who is given in the speech situation. They compete with other address terms such as titles, proper names, and combinations of these for this purpose. The difference is that they presuppose a shared speech situation and that their referent can be identified only with respect to the actual speaker. Increasing the number of category values such as the distinction between familiar vs. polite and/or the pronominal forms such as an additional second-person honorific pronoun in the paradigm, as has happened in most of the languages of Europe, is certainly not economic. This increase in paradigmatic complexity does not increase the functionality of personal pronouns as referential means. From a functional point of view, a pronoun does not need politeness distinctions, the combination of person value plus number value is functionally sufficient for the identification of the referent, since the referents of personal pronouns are always topical or given pragmatically. Thus, the economy motivation cannot explain the emergence and spread of 2SG.HON pronouns from 2PL pronouns.

19.3.2 *Politeness*

Brown and Levinson (1987) define politeness as a linguistic behavior that tries to diminish or to reduce the face threatening potential of speech acts. Face is a psychological notion. It is defined as the "public self-image that every member wants to claim for himself" (Brown and Levinson 1987: 61). It has two related aspects, the negative face and the positive face. Negative face is defined as the "basic claim to territories, personal preserves, rights to non-distraction—i.e. to freedom of action and freedom from imposition" (Brown and Levinson 1987: 61); positive face is defined as the "positive consistent self-image or 'personality' (crucially including the desire that this self-image be appreciated and approved of) claimed by interactants" (Brown and Levinson 1987: 61). Face threatening acts can be thought of as speech acts that threaten the positive or negative face desires of the language user.

There are numerous linguistic strategies language users employ to diminish or to redress the face threatening potential of speech acts. They are systematically described by Brown and Levinson. There are strategies that redress the negative face wants of the language user, that is, the so called negative politeness, and the same holds for the positive face desires of the language user, that is, the so called positive politeness.

In the present context, it seems that the following two negative politeness strategies ((2a)–(2b)) are particularly relevant to explain the politeness distinctions in pronouns (cf. Brown and Levinson 1987: 131); they are effective in the functional domain of person reference.

(2) Negative politeness strategies that minimize face threats.
  a. Minimize face threats by giving explicit deference (cf. Brown and Levinson 1987: 178ff)
  b. Dissociate S and H from the particular infringement: avoid direct reference to the S and the H either by impersonalizing S and H or by avoiding the personal pronouns "I" and "you" (cf. Brown and Levinson 1987: 190–206).

Negative politeness strategy (2a) is the source for the development and usage of titles that explicitly express the social relation between S and H in a way that the socially superior H receives an explicit indication of his social superiority vis-à-vis the inferior S; for instance, a title such as "Your Highness" explicitly assigns H a high position on a social scale. This strategy is universally applicable: it can be hypothesized that honorific titles no matter their origin (kinship terms, social role, social status, prestigious function, etc.) exist in each language and society.

In terms of markedness theory (cf. Greenberg 1966a; Croft 1990, 2003), this strategy leads to expressions that are more marked than the expressions for the same referential function without politeness meanings. For instance, *Mrs. Smith* is more marked than *Sally* if both expressions refer to the same person. The effects of this strategy are completely opposed to the effects of the economic motivation discussed in Section 19.3.1.

Strategy (2a) involves, among other things, the use of titles in combination with personal names. This combination can be analyzed syntactically either as a modification or as an apposition—this choice may vary crosslinguistically. Personal pronouns in general do not allow restrictive modification and apposition except in very limited ways. Therefore, there are internal grammatical reasons that prevent strategy (2a) being applied to personal pronouns.

Negative politeness strategy (2b) is certainly responsible for the polite extension of the meaning of second-person plural and third-person pronouns. The use of 2PL pronouns as 2SG.HON is a kind of impersonalization of the H within the crowd of multiple addressees. The same holds for the use of third-person pronouns as 2SG.

HON pronouns, since the H is symbolically treated as a non-speech act participant, that is, as being absent from the speech act situation.

The strategy to impersonalize S and H and to avoid direct reference by means of avoiding personal pronouns of the first and second person singular leads to more complex pronominal paradigms simply by increasing the number of category values that are expressed by the same members of the paradigm.

There is one problem that arises with strategy (2b) It affects the 1SG and the 2SG in similar ways. How can the politeness hierarchy 2 < 3 < 1 cited in example (1) be explained? Or more precisely: why do politeness distinctions first appear in second-person pronouns? There may be two related answers to this question.

First, it can be safely assumed that face threatening acts mostly threaten the positive and negative face wants of the H. Thus, second-person pronouns are the prime targets of strategies such as impersonalization and explicit assignment of deference.

Politeness distinctions in first-person pronouns can be found in many language of the South East Asian area such as Burmese, Thai, Japanese, Korean, Indonesian, Vietnamese, and so forth. These polite first-person pronouns are so-called humbling forms, since they are used if H is considered socially superior or higher on the social status scale than S. Using these humbling first-person pronouns, S depicts himself as socially low and inferior in order to raise H symbolically on the social scale. The reason why these first-person honorific pronouns ("humbling forms") are much rarer crosslinguistically than politeness distinctions in second-person pronouns can be explained by the fact that on the one hand these forms redress the face threatening potential for H, but at the same time they are threatening the face desires of S himself. To depict oneself as socially inferior is itself face threatening for S and thus less favored universally than the avoidance of direct H reference.[2]

The second explanation has to do with the grammatical properties of face threatening speech acts. Among the speech acts that most typically threaten the negative face desires of H are orders and requests, that is, speech acts with the illocutionary force "question" and "command." In clauses with these illocutionary forces, the second person is way ahead in terms of frequency than the other persons (Table 19.4). Therefore, in these contexts, it is the second person that is the prime target for the two politeness strategies mentioned in example (2).

---

[2] A functional explanation for the middle position of polite third-person pronouns in the politeness hierarchy has still to be sought. My guess is that the choice of a polite reference of a third person may depend on the social relation between S and referent and/or the relation between H and the referent. Thus there is some ambiguity possible, if either S is on T terms with the referent, and H on V terms with the referent, or the other way round. Observations of third-person reference in discourse support this idea. It can often be observed that S displays uncertainties with regard to the choice of the referential expression in third-person references. For instance, if S is on T terms with the third-person referent he or she might use a nick name or some expression of social intimacy. If, however, S knows that H is on V terms with the referent, it can be the case (and often is) that S decides to use a more formal expression such as a combination of title and last name (e.g. *Mr. Smith*). This ambiguity with regard to the S or H perspective could be the reason for the relative rarity of politeness distinctions in third-person pronouns. However, more research is necessary to decide this question.

Table 19.4 summarizes the text count with regard to the correlation of different NP-types in subject function and the illocutionary force of the clauses; Table 19.5 presents the results in form of person hierarchies. The text corpus is the same as for Table 19.3. Tables 19.4 and 19.5 both clearly show that in questions and commands, the second person is the most important NP type in subject function. This dominance holds only for oral texts.

TABLE 19.4. Correlation of NP-Type in subject function and illocutionary force

NP-Type	Statements		Questions		Commands	
	Oral	Written	Oral	Written	Oral	Written
1SG	136 (28%)	1	9 (11%)	0	0	0
2SG	**21 (4%)**	0	**43 (51%)**	0	**16 (89%)**	0
3SG	60 (12%)	47 (12%)	9 (11%)	0	0	0
1PL	38 (8%)	12 (3%)	2	0	1 (5,5%)	0
2PL	**7 (1%)**	0	**3 (4%)**	0	**1 (5,5%)**	0
3PL	8 (2%)	4 (1%)	1	0	0	0
Total personal pronouns	270 (56%)	64 (22%)	67 (79%)	0	18 (100%)	0
Demonstratives and other definite pro-forms	94 (20%)	9 (2%)	9 (11%)	1	0	0
Indefinite pronouns	26 (5%)	19 (5%)	2	0	0	0
Lexical NPs (nouns)	64 (13%)	290 (76%)	7 (8%)	3	0	0
Total	480 (100%)	382 (100%)	85 (100%)	4 (100%)	18 (100%)	0

Source: Helmbrecht (2006).

TABLE 19.5. Person hierarchies with regard to clause type (illocutionary function)

Statements		Questions		Commands	
Dialogic	Written	Dialogic	Written	Dialogic	Written
1 > 3 > 2	3 > 1 > 2	**2 > 1 > 3**	0	**2SG > 2PL/1INCL.PL**	0

Source: Helmbrecht (2006).

So far we have discussed two different motivations and the way they operate in the context of person reference: economy and politeness. Economy is the prime motivation to present given and topical information by shorter expressions than new or non-topical information. Speech act participants and third-person referents are given (in different ways) and tend to be topics. Personal pronouns are the grammatical forms that present given and topical referents *par excellence*. These referents are identified almost solely by their speech act role. For third persons things are a bit different. Formally, personal pronouns are unmarked compared to nouns with regard to their referential function.

Politeness is hypothesized to be a universal of linguistic behavior. In the context of face threatening speech acts, language users try to reduce the face threatening potential of certain speech acts by utilizing politeness strategies. In the functional domain of person reference, such strategies comprise the impersonalization of speech act participants and the explicit expression of deference. Since questions and commands are speech acts that tend to be inherently face threatening for H, it is quite natural that both strategies operate first on the terms of second-person address, that is, proper names and second-person pronouns. The interaction of the two motivations rightly predicts that politeness distinctions appear first in the second person and last in the first person with the third person somewhere in the middle of the hierarchy. In addition, from a diachronic point of view, the hypothesis may be deduced from what has been said above that politeness distinctions may arise historically first in specific speech acts, namely questions and commands. Both hypotheses need further research and clear historical evidence which cannot be provided yet.

It seems that both motivations discussed so far, economy and politeness, are capable of explaining the politeness hierarchy in (1) which is a synchronic general-ization over crosslinguistic facts. But how can economy and politeness explain the areal distribution and the historical diffusion of the 2PL as 2SG.HON use in Europe? A potential answer could be found in the social structure of European societies that developed in medieval times. These societies were highly stratified caste- or class-based societies. Social status became a highly important property of the individual. In such a socially stratified society, the face threatening potential of speech acts such as questions and commands might rise significantly, to the extent that speakers in cross-class or cross-caste communication have a strong motivation to apply negative politeness strategies. Such a social feature of language use may perhaps be more easily borrowed if the receiving language belongs to a society with similar social structures. Under this condition, politeness may also be a strong motivation for borrowing such pragmatic strategies. In the next section a further functional moti-vation will be discussed, namely prestige. It is hypothesized that prestige was a strong factor in the spread of the 2PL as a 2SG.HON use in European languages.

19.3.3 *Prestige*

There are generally three important motivations for borrowing: gaps, language processing, and prestige (cf. Matras 2009: 149–153).

1. *Gaps*: words or more complex expressions are borrowed because they fill gaps in the recipient language. This is an instance of matter replication by Matras (2009: 149f). The gap-filling motivation for borrowing could be interpreted as an instance of the broader economy or efficiency motivation. The bilingual language user uses a word or an expression from the donor language in certain discourse contexts of the recipient language, because he or she has no adequate word or expression in his or her repertoire of the recipient language. The choice of the foreign word or expres-sion, however, violates the constraint to keep the two languages separate, that is, to not use the one language in a context when the other is required.

The gap-filling motivation for the adoption of politeness distinctions in pronouns is not a very likely explanation. One reason is that there are no real gaps in the recipient languages: all affected European languages had second-person pronouns before they borrowed the 2SG.HON use of a 2PL pronoun. What was missing was a polite second-person pronoun, but such a form is not really essential for the referential functions of the language. However, it could be imagined that a second-person pronoun could be borrowed precisely for this additional politeness meaning; but since personal pronouns strongly resist borrowing crosslinguistically (for somewhat vague reasons), this may also hold for polite pronouns.[3]

2. *Language processing*: bilinguals have to select context-appropriate structures from one language within their repertoire and to suppress inappropriate structures from the other language; in order to simplify this selection process, the separation of the two subsets (the two languages) are lowered in certain contexts allowing the two languages to converge. This is always an instance of pattern replication. The deeper reason for the lowering of the separation between the two languages is that the bilingual language user looks for the most efficient category or construction no matter which language it is drawn from. Since a certain discourse context requires sticking to one language, that is, to obey language loyalty, only the most efficient pattern is transferred to the recipient language. As was suggested in Section 19.3.2, politeness is a counter-economic motivation, so there are no processing motivations for the language user to borrow such patterns.

3. *Prestige is a sociological notion* that describes the appreciation and high esteem for an individual or for a group of individuals by members of the same or another group. Prestige is often associated with the social status or the social class of the individual. In highly stratified societies, prestige is usually attributed to members of the nobility or the upper classes.

Prestige can also be attributed to languages and language varieties. The high prestige of an individual language or language variety derives from the social prestige the speakers of this language or variety have. High prestige languages or language varieties are often dominant or majority languages vis-à-vis minority languages, or they are varieties that are spoken by high prestige groups in a society. Prestige-driven borrowing can be explained by the following linguistic behavior: bilingual speakers "imitate elements of the speech of a socially more powerful, dominant community in order to gain approval and social status" (this is mainly seen as an instance of matter replication by Matras (2009: 150)).

What are the criteria for the identification of prestige as the dominant motivation for the borrowing and diffusion of linguistic features?

---

[3] Pronouns are not likely candidates for borrowing for the following reasons: they are not a label for a unique referent but have a very general meaning; they are not associated with certain activity domains, but again are very general in their usage; personal pronouns do not have a specific clash potential between S's intention and H's expectation, and they have no discourse managing function; (cf. Matras 2009: 208). With nominal address terms and titles (e.g. *Madame* < French), this may be another story; however, the examples given by Matras are not as convincing as he thought they were.

1. assignment of social attributes to other speakers and speaker groups;
2. language attitudes with regard to other languages and language varieties;
3. if a language, language variety, or register has a certain prestige for a recipient group, it is likely that not just one feature will be borrowed, but also others; one has to look for bundles of borrowings in one direction;
4. a good indicator of prestige as a motivating factor is if the direction of borrowing between two languages is always the same;
5. prestige-driven borrowing leads to synonymy, since forms and patterns are not borrowed to fill gaps in the recipient language; so there are forms and patterns for the same function already there;
6. There may also be extra-linguistic evidence, if there are cultural features that are—at the same time—adopted in the same direction as the linguistic features.

More specifically in the case of the 2PL as 2SG.HON use, there are probably two directions of borrowing:

1. The first direction is from the prestigious French royal courts and nobility to the comparable elite groups in the neighboring languages. This hypothesis is plausible, because of the role the French court and the French nobility played in Europe over many centuries. However, more linguistic and perhaps extra-linguistic evidence is needed for this hypothesis. (A good example is perhaps the Russian case).
2. The second direction is from the elite groups (royal court, nobility) down the social scale to lower social classes within a speaker community; middle and lower classes adopt the conventions of the higher classes such as the nobility in order to be like them; this can be considered an act of identification. However, much more research is needed to verify this hypothesis.

It is obvious that both directions of diffusion are interwoven and they happen simultaneously. I believe that prestige is a particularly important motivation for the downward spread of polite pronouns, while politeness itself may be the stronger motivation for the center–periphery spread of this feature. These are speculations that need much more research in order to be confirmed. Perhaps there is close cooperation of both factors in this historical process.

The three external motivations discussed: economy, politeness, and prestige, along with internal factors such as paradigmatic and syntagmatic properties are able to explain the emergence and historical spread of the 2PL as a 2SG.HON use in Europe (see Table 19.6). They seem also to be able to explain the typological facts—the politeness hierarchy—with regard to politeness distinctions in personal pronouns. The question remains however: can these motivations also explain the non-occurrence of this feature in so many large areas in the world? The general answer has to be yes, although there is no possibility to investigate this question empirically. The reasons for the non-occurrence of this linguistic feature have to be sought in the social structure of the societies and the interplay of politeness, prestige, and economy. The linguistic areas in which 2SG.HON pronouns do not occur are North and South America, Papua New Guinea, Australia, and to some extent Africa. Most of the languages in these areas

TABLE 19.6. **Summary of the relevant motivations**

	Economy	Politeness	Prestige
Effect on the linguistic behavior of the language user	Forms/expressions are formed as short as possible (restricted by the comprehensibility of H)	(a) avoidance of first-person and second-person direct reference; (b) expressing explicit deference (within the context of face-threatening acts)	Using linguistic forms or patterns from the prestige language/variety in order to gain social status (in contexts where only the recipient language is appropriate)
Criteria for identification	Forms/expressions show properties of the unmarked value with respect to (a) structural coding, (b) inflectional and distributional potential, and (c) textual and typological frequency	(a) impersonalization of person reference by non-prototypical uses of deviant pronouns (b) development of titles and title/ proper name constructions	(a) language attitudes of the low prestige towards the high prestige group (b) borrowing of several features in only one direction (c) in the case of matter replication, frequent synonymous pairs (from the prestige language and the recipient language expressing the same concept)

were originally spoken by small ethnic groups. These small-scale and mostly egali-
tarian cultures do not have the same kind of social hierarchies as the societies of
Europe, India, and South East Asia. It seems that socially complex large-scale class
and caste societies tend to develop this linguistic feature. In addition, it can be
speculated that this feature is adopted or borrowed only in languages with a similar
social structure. If there were hunter and gatherer societies in the middle of Europe
can it be speculated that they would not have borrowed this feature?

19.4 Conclusions

The analysis presented for the emergence and spread of the 2PL for 2SG.HON use in
the languages of Europe demonstrates that with regard to areal typology or, more
specifically, with linguistic areas, social motivations are indispensible for a competing motivations analysis. Recent research in historical linguistics and in the fields of
language contact and linguistic borrowing contains frequent reference to the idea
that innovation is exclusively functionally motivated (cf. e.g. Croft 2000; Matras
2009), and that propagation is exclusively socially motivated (Weinreich et al. 1968;
Labov 1994a, 1994b; Croft 2000). Both ideas have turned out to be wrong. Seiler
(2006) has shown that propagation may also be functionally motivated in the sense
that the functionally more efficient form or construction has a greater chance of
being adopted and to diffuse. The present examination of the diffusion of the use of
2PL pronouns as 2SG.HON pronouns has demonstrated that innovation may be
almost purely socially motivated.

20

Or constructions: Monosemy vs. polysemy

MIRA ARIEL

20.1 Introduction

Most research on competing motivations focuses on marking grammatical functions.[1]
Does the language go accusative, or does it go ergative, for example (Du Bois 1985,
1987b, and onwards)? Given a limited good grammar, languages tend to mark only
one of these functions, so the two compete over grammatical coding. Under a
different type of competition, a semantic one, given that more than one function
is to be conveyed by language, the question is whether to devote one or more than
one linguistic code to these functions. In other words, does the language go monosemous, where each form is associated with one function? Or does it go polysemous,
where each form is used to convey more than one function (regardless of the
question whether these functions are semantically specified for the form or pragmatically derived via inference)? This was the competition noted by Zipf (1949).

Should natural language opt for unification, where few forms serve a multitude of
meanings? Or should languages aim for one-to-one form/function associations,
where each form is dedicated to a single function? Obviously, no natural language
opts for any exclusive application of either one of these two competing principles.
Rather, in some (but not other) cases some (but not other) languages opt for
polysemy, while in other cases the same languages may very well prefer monosemies.
Moreover, polysemies and monosemies are not static. Through semanticization and/
or grammaticization, monosemies can turn polysemous, and polysemies can turn
monosemous.

Applied to constructions (in the sense of Construction Grammar), the competition arises between a single (super-)construction associated with multiple meanings

[1] Funding for this research was received from THE ISRAEL SCIENCE FOUNDATION, grant # 161–09.
I am grateful to Elsi Kaiser for taking the time to provide me with the Finnish examples. The comments
from my two anonymous referees, as well as from my no-longer-anonymous referee, Andrej Malchukov,
were quite challenging and I'm very happy to have had them.

(construction polysemy, accompanied by heavy inferencing) and multiple sub-constructions, each with its own dedicated meaning (monosemy, or near monosemy, accompanied by minimal inferencing) (see Lakoff 1987; Goldberg 1995).[2] And constructions too are dynamic entities (Israel 1996). Discourse use tends to increase construction polysemy (and inferencing), since we mobilize current constructions for expressing additional messages (relying on addressees' inferential abilities). At the same time, such extensions naturally trigger the evolution of new independent sub-constructions, where the form of the original construction has been constrained or slightly modified (Thompson 2002b). These newly created sub-constructions counter the polysemy development of the (super)-construction. In fact, they increase monosemy (and decrease inferencing). So the general picture is that constructions simultaneously develop into more as well as into less polysemous structures. The goal of this chapter is to exemplify the variation between construction polysemy accompanied by heavy inferencing (unification) and construction monosemy (diversification), which requires only minimal inferencing. The semantic domain I examine is disjunctive constructions.

It is not so obvious how the disjunctive relationship should be defined for natural language. Logical disjunctions are defined as constructions combining two or more propositions, at least one of which is guaranteed to be true. I have argued against this definition as the minimal semantics for disjunctions, and proposed to define a disjunction as a set of alternatives the speaker raises, none of which is guaranteed to be true and/or intended by the speaker (Ariel 2008a). In other words, my definition is more minimal than the logical definition, and allows for the possibility of disjunctions such as (1), where the speaker is not even committed to one of the alternatives being true (see also Jennings 1994; Zimmermann 2000; Geurts 2005):

(1)   ... Part of the shares were transferred to the children ... **or** they were returned and divided up **or** partly returned **I don't remember** ... (Originally Hebrew, Lotan 1990: 12).

Note that the speaker's "I don't remember" means that he's not committed to any one of the alternatives mentioned in his disjunction (a third alternative, not mentioned by him could very well be the case). While I propose that the speaker raises alternatives for which she undertakes no commitment,[3] this does not mean that all, or even most disjunctions are in fact interpreted in this minimal way. Quite the contrary. Pragmatic inferences commonly enrich this very bare semantic meaning into a variety of disjunctive interpretations which we examine in this chapter. This is why I consider the basic construction to be polysemous.

There is one additional constraint on disjunctive alternatives that we must mention, though. Speakers do not simply lump together two options which they are not sure about. There has to be some relevant relationship between the disjuncts, which is tighter than the relation between two adjacent "maybe" utterances (which is why

---

[2] Goldberg refers to the tension between Maximized Economy, which constrains the number of constructions, and Maximized Expressive Power, which promotes a multitude of constructions.

[3] This analysis is also in agreement with Mauri's (2008) typological findings about disjunctions.

not every such pair is paraphrasable by *or*). I suggest that the most general way to characterize this relevant relationship is that each of the disjuncts must be construable as a member of a single higher-level category which is discourse-relevant.

If I am right, then disjunctions such as "X *or* Y" are semantically (not necessarily pragmatically) not too different from "maybe X, maybe Y." Indeed, here is a nongrammaticized disjunction from English, which is substitutable by *or* alone, most likely because the two alternatives explicitly mentioned are the only possible options, which are, moreover, mutually exclusive:

(2) a. ... Practices of abortion of, **perhaps**, pre-partum, **perhaps** postpartum (LSAC).

  b. ~ ... Practices of abortion of, pre-partum, **or** postpartum.

By far, the most minimal means with which to express a disjunction is to not use any grammaticized form for that purpose (Haspelmath 2004b; Mauri 2008). This is an extreme application of the unification strategy, and one which depends on addressee's inferential work to derive a disjunctive interpretation (Section 20.2). In Section 20.3 I present some of the variety of uses speakers make of the basic [X *or* Y] construction in English. I briefly present a few cases of the opposite, diversification strategy, where multiple sub-constructions are used to convey mostly specialized disjunctive sub-interpretations in Section 20.4. Section 20.5 demonstrates the co-existence of diversification and unification strategies: The specialized sub-functions are not obligatorily expressed by the specialized sub-constructions. Rather, they can still be expressed via the basic, highly polysemous disjunctive super-construction. In other words, the tradeoff between monosemic codes involving minimal inferencing and polysemic codes necessitating inferencing is not only resolved at the language system level. Rather, very often, speakers have to make online choices between maximal (specific) and minimal (general) coding.

20.2 Doing without dedicated disjunction forms

The most minimal strategy speakers can use to convey a disjunctive interpretation actually lacks any grammatical form, of whatever function. The addressee must then reach the disjunctive interpretation purely by inference. Here are a two such cases. The strings interpreted as disjuncts are marked in bold:[4]

(3) a. **You come, you don't come**, it doesn't matter to me (Originally Hebrew) ('**Whether** you come **or** not ...') (angeles-il.com, spotted April 6, 2011).

  b. After I give birth to **child two** of my own, of course (originally Hebrew) ('... a child **or** two ...'). (cafe.themarker.com/topic/1934261, spotted April 3, 2011)

The examples in (3) are interpreted as disjunctions, and indeed, *or* can be added without changing their meaning. Mauri (2008) has argued that zero form disjunctions are

---

[4] I thank Jack Du Bois (p.c.) for drawing my attention to the existence of zero-marked clausal constructions as in (3a).

unattested in the many languages she examined. Indeed, it seems that the truly zero strategy exemplified in (3) is heavily restricted.[5] So it is quite possible that this very minimal strategy does not ever become a full-fledged grammatical strategy (except for the numbers and a [X *not* X, *it doesn't matter*] form, perhaps, which are partially marked).

More often, in the absence of a dedicated disjunctive form, speakers mobilize for this purpose a form not specialized for disjunctions. The forms here chosen must convey at least part of the meaning of disjunctions. In this way, they can lead relatively easily to a disjunctive interpretation via an inferential process which starts off from the conventional meaning of the marker chosen. According to Mauri's (2008) typological examination of disjunctive constructions (see also Haspelmath, 2004b, 2007b), disjunctions are routinely expressed by irrealis markers (occurring in both clauses), some of which may undergo grammaticization into full-fledged disjunctive constructions. Wari, for example, can express the disjunctive idea with a [perhaps X perhaps Y] pattern, or with an [if X, if Y] pattern, both markers of irrealis, but routinely recruited for a disjunction interpretation. In Nànáfwɛ the counterpart of 'if not' has grammaticized into a disjunction connective. Hakha Lai can use its question particle to create a disjunctive construction [Question particle X? Question particle Y?]. Questions, argues Mauri, naturally imply irrealis for their propositional content. To get the feel for how a nongrammaticized disjunction can be so interpreted, consider the following, originally Hebrew, example (and see again (2a)):[6]

(4)   You need to get more focused, and think what you want. Do you want to be an instructor? Do you want to engage in sports activities? Do you want to be in an office? Do you want to be on a military base at all? (sf.tapuz.co.il/shirshur-339-111587572.htm)

Given the discourse topic, choices among military jobs, where one is expected to be assigned one and only one military job, it is not difficult to infer a disjunctive relationship here ('do you want X *or* do you want Y *or*...?').

Note that the examples in Section 20.2 manifest an obvious tradeoff between form minimality and context maximality. Although we get no marking (in (3)) or no dedicated marking (in (2a), (4)) for disjunction (in principle, these are cases of high polysemy of use), the addressee is not as heavily burdened as one might think. Other, contextual cues supporting a disjunctive interpretation are in place, thus paving the way for a relatively easy process of inferencing. It looks like cases where the alternatives form a tight set (consecutive ascending numbers) and/or are in an either/or relationship (so-called exclusive disjunctions, (see (2a)) are the ones more easily identified as disjunctions even in the absence of disjunctive marking.

---

[5] The extra-constructional "it doesn't matter to me" supports the disjunctive interpretation in (3a). Consecutive ascending numbers often allow zero marked disjunctions as well (e.g., *five, six* = 'five or six').

[6] Incidentally, while Hebrew does have a question particle, most Hebrew questions are not so marked. Intonation serves as a question indicator in spoken discourse, and ? signals a question in writing, as is the case in the questions above.

So, extra-constructional contextual bias for a disjunctive reading plays a crucial role in speakers' successful use of a polysemous form.

20.3 The basic polysemous disjunctive construction: X *or* Y

Most of the languages we are familiar with only occasionally revert to a totally indirect (inferential) strategy for expressing the disjunctive idea. More commonly, these languages use a dedicated disjunctive connective, which creates the counterpart of English [X *or* Y] construction. Here are a few typical examples for the basic disjunction construction in English, [X *or* Y]:

(5) a. ALINA: Ed's the one that'll come in,
           . . . (TSK) and he'll go ahead and say,
           . . (H) this is what needs to be done.
           . . . Okay,
           and h- –
           or he'll look at you,
           and he'll go,
           that was a stupid thing to do (SBC: 008)

   b. A: Would you like tea **or** coffee?
      B: Neither. I'll have that juice (LSAC).

   c. MONTOYO: . . The Greeks were . . major contributors to this political
                 process of development,
                 . . of concepts.
                 Demos . . . cratos.
                 People . . . govern,
                 or people rule. (SBC: 012)

   d. MARY: . . Hand me that ashtray.
             . . . **Or** your light,
             I mean.

   e. ALICE: when Ron gets home from work,
           . . . I wanna spend time with #Ron,
           because Ron,
           . . . usually doesn't get home till **nine or ten**. (SBC: 007)

The interpretation of 5(a) supports the so-called inclusive semantic meaning of *or* assumed by practically all semanticists and pragmatists, following Horn (1972 and later work). Most likely, Alina does not only think that just one of the alternatives she mentions about Ed's behavior is true, quite possibly both alternatives might be true. This inclusive reading of X *or* Y is one possible interpretation of the basic construction. Example (5b) involves what is usually called the exclusive reading disjunction, where the speaker does not know whether X is the case nor whether Y is the case, but she assumes that one of them, and only one of them is true, or intended. Following Horn (1972) most linguists, whether neo-Gricean like Horn (Levinson 2000) or not (Chierchia and McConnell-Ginet 1990; Gamut 1991), assume that this exclusive reading is the unmarked, prevalent, reading that natural language disjunctions receive.

Example (5c) exemplifies an Equivalence disjunction, where the alternatives mentioned do not stand for different states of affairs, but rather, for different linguistic formulations of one and the same state of affairs. Example (5d) differs from (5c), in that Mary is not leaving the choice between "that ashtray" and "your light" to the addressee. She is actually asking for the lighter only. The second disjunct here is a repair on the first one, which is then not to be seen as endorsed by the speaker. Finally, in (5e) Alice does not necessarily intend any one of the alternatives explicitly mentioned ("nine," "ten"). Instead she intends her addressee to construct an ad hoc higher-level category of something like "a late time of the day in which Ron gets home from work." I have argued that this is the most prevalent use speakers make of disjunctions (Ariel 2008a).

How do addressees know how to interpret the [X *or* Y] construction, which is obviously so highly polysemic in use? Heavy inferencing is involved, taking into account contextual assumptions about the nature of the world, as well as speakers' reasonable intentions within the specific context. In 5(a) Alina is describing Ed's outrageous behavior. The alternatives mentioned add up to a picture of an aggressive man, and there is no reason to think that only one of the options could be true according to Alina. Rather, Alina provides the addressee with two examples of Ed's behavior (on different occasions presumably) so that the addressee can form the generalization about Ed's conduct by herself. This is not the case in 5(b). Based on general knowledge, the addressee realizes that the alternatives in (5b) are mutually exclusive. This is why the disjunction is interpreted as an exclusive disjunction.

Montoya in (5c) lists two alternatives which are semantic paraphrases of each other. Since they denote the same state of affairs, they cannot possibly constitute two truly independent alternatives (in the sense that one can choose between the real-world options). Example (5d) is recognizable as a repair, whereby the first disjunct is to be simply canceled in fact, with the help of multiple cues. First, content-wise, it is not very plausible that Mary would leave it up to her addressee to decide whether she wanted the ashtray, the lighter, or possibly both. Second, the afterthought intonation gives away that the disjunction is asymmetric, the second disjunct replacing the first one (note that *or* in (5d) follows a final, falling intonation contour). Third, *I mean* is a conventional marker of repair. Example (5e) is probably the most interesting case, where, although Alice linguistically specifies two clear alternatives, she is actually committed to neither. Rather, *nine or ten* is used to evoke a single ad hoc higher-level category, "a late time for Ron to come home from work," which has infinitely many possible instantiations. The inference here is based on the addressee reasoning that people do not stay late at work up to precisely a round hour, and the exact time does not really matter. A very useful way to get people to access an abstract category is to provide them with some of its category members as concrete examples. This is especially true when the members (the disjuncts) constitute highly accessible, basic-level categories (such as "nine" and "ten").

The examples in (5) by no means exhaust the uses of the basic [X *or* Y] construction in natural discourse (see Ariel and Mauri (2014) for at least fourteen discourse functions for *or* constructions). However, they are enough to demonstrate how polysemous a construction can be. We have seen five different readings for [X *or* Y] in example (5): Inclusive (5a), exclusive (5b), equivalence (5c), repair (5d), and the creation of an ad hoc higher-level category (5e). In order to determine the precise reading intended by the speaker, addressees must revert to inferencing, based on relevant contextual assumptions. It is only to be expected that when the construction is polysemous, a heavy dose of inferencing will be necessary. Now, we have seen that the inferential work is also guided by helpful cues from the speaker. But importantly, the cues we have noted are not grammatical codes for the said interpretation. They are optional, they are not uniform per interpretation, and they do not force the relevant reading, although they do help the addressee adopt it. In the next section we examine cases where the speaker does not just cue the addressee as to her intended interpretation, she actually encodes it.

20.4 Some specialized disjunction sub-constructions

So far we have seen that various disjunctive interpretations can be conveyed without any (dedicated) codes and via the basic disjunction construction [X *or* Y]. We now see how disjunctive interpretations can be conveyed by a number of specialized disjunctive sub-constructions, each allowing a much narrower range of interpretations.

I have stated that the polysemy and monosemy of forms is a dynamic matter in Section 20.1. Indeed, a construction which is clearly polysemous in its discourse use can evolve into a set of monosemous sub-constructions, and this is probably what happened to the basic [X *or* Y] construction. Although highly polysemous constructions such as [X *or* Y] depend on heavy inferencing, speakers routinely help their addressees out by throwing in contextual cues pointing in the right (disjunction) direction. The inferencing called for by the examples in Sections 20.2 and 20.3 was therefore facilitated. But crucially, speakers also minimize addressees' inferential processing by carefully choosing the material they insert into the open slots of the construction (X and Y here). The theoretically polysemous basic construction is not as polysemous in practice when combined with certain linguistic expressions which guide the addressee towards the specific disjunctive interpretation intended. The point is that if these choices are made consistently enough in discourse they may bring about the grammaticization of a new disjunctive sub-construction which is far less polysemous, sometimes even monosemous.

Now, it is no trivial matter to identify at what point in time some discourse pattern has grammaticized into a new (sub-)construction. For a clear grammaticization to have taken place we would preferably see both a formal and a semantic change from the basic construction: Restrictions may be imposed on the form and/ or content of one or both of the disjuncts and/or the relation between them and/or on the disjunctive connective. Thus, the relevant form may no longer be just the basic [X *or* Y] construction, but rather, a somewhat modified, more specific form. For example, the second disjunct may be restricted to *something* ((6)), or both disjuncts may be infinitivals which carry opposite polarity values ((7)). The connective too may be restricted, for example, to *or else* or to *either . . . or* (not here discussed). In the most obvious cases, a semantic change accompanies the new sub-construction. For example, as we see below, the *something* in [X *or something*] no longer has to introduce a viable alternative. It can function instead as a hedge on the first disjunct.

Other cases are less clear-cut, and may only constitute an easily accessible (even automatic) route to a certain interpretation which the addressee could have in principle reached by relying on the basic construction and by drawing further inferences based on the utterance in the given context. Repeatedly used chunks are most likely to be stored as such, despite the fact that they maintain full compositionality (Bybee 2002). Chunking can explain why speakers tend to repeatedly insert specific lexical material into the basic construction, when they could have easily chosen a synonymous expression (see the discussion of the difference between [X *or something like that*] and [X *or something like this*] in the following paragraph. Differential acceptability judgments for seemingly identical constructions in different languages also testify to the grammatical or near-grammatical status of such emerging sub-constructions. In fact, the existence of intermediate cases is just what we would expect if grammaticization is a gradual process that takes place in real-time. We examine a few sub-constructions of the basic [X *or* Y] construction below. Some of them are more clearly evolved as distinct constructions than others.

Consider (6):

(6)   a. RICKIE: . . . So is he in like jail **or something**? (SBC: 001)
      b. CINDY: . . . What was it?
                      ((1 line omitted))
         ANDREW: Helen Steiner Rice.
         CINDY: Yeah.
                      ((3 lines omitted))
         CINDY: (H) Helen Steiner Rice,
                      ((1 line omitted))
                      or [something like that].
         DARLENE: [Helen] . . Keller Rice.
         CINDY: . . . **Or something like that**, (SBC: 052)

Example (6a) exemplifies the very frequent [X *or something*] construction, no doubt a later development of the [X *or something like that*] construction, exemplified in (6b). This *or* construction is recent enough that its evolution is transparent. Example (6b) can easily be analyzed as an instantiation of the super-construction [X *or* Y]. Cindy explicitly mentions two alternatives, "the name Helen Steiner Rice" or "a name similar to that, i.e., to Helen Steiner Rice." Indeed, there is nothing opaque about [X *or something like that*], which would justify the assumption of an independent sub-construction. It is just a case where the speaker chose *something like that* as her Y constituent. This is why, while Russian lacks the [X *or something*] construction, it can use [X *or something like that*], as an instantiation of the general construction.[7] Still, out of thirty cases in the SBC where Y is *something* + some modifier, twenty-three are specifically *something like that*. More specifically, out of twenty-four nontruncated *or something like*..., twenty-three are *or something like that* (rather than *this*, for example, which occurs only once).[8] So, it looks like [X *or something like that*] is a highly salient instantiation of the [X *or* Y] construction. If so, we can explain the shortening of the disjunction into [X *or something*], as in (6a). Note that the latter is indeed interpreted as "X or something like X" (Ball and Ariel 1978, based on questionnaire results). But what counts as similar or not is not necessarily based on the semantics of the disjuncts. Rather, it is very much context-dependent. In one of the most intriguing cases examined by Ball and Ariel, subjects determined that "going to a movie next door" could count as the "something" disjunct in *we'll go for a walk or something*. This occurred when the promise to *go for a walk or something* was to serve the goal of entertaining a partner, who has been bored at home all day.

Constructions have a life of their own. While the compositional meaning of [X *or something like that*] involves two distinct (even if similar) alternatives, the constructional meaning of [X *or something*] no longer necessarily involves two (or more) similar alternatives. Rather, what we often get is a single, hedged alternative as in 6(a).

Next, consider (7):

(7)   FOSTER: ... We have clear passages of Scripture,
         (H) which seem to indicate that man .. has a free will,
         .. and that he can exercise that will,
         .. **to follow,**
         or not to follow.
         (H) **To respond or not to respond.** (SBC: 025)

Just like the disjunctions in (6b), those in (7) seem perfectly compositional. We have two very distinct alternatives, opposites in fact. But of course, there is more to these disjunctions. Following the original source resonated by it ("to be or not to be"), the [*to* Verb *or not to* Verb] construction is restricted to cases of dilemma. This is not the case for all X *or not* X cases, as (8) shows:

(8)   KATHY: I don't know,
         if that's how you **do it or not.** (SBC: 009)

The latter are reserved for cases where people do not know whether X is or is not the case (as well as the "it doesn't matter" reading—see example (3a)). Further support for the constructional status of [*to* V *or not to* V] comes from the subtle difference between (7) and (9):

(9)   ~ he can exercise that will **to follow or not**

---

[7] I owe this observation to Andrej Malchukov.
[8] There were two truncated utterances, where the missing NP could very well have been *that* in fact.

The resonance with Hamlet is here lost as is the sense of a very difficult and important decision. So [*to* Verb *or not to* Verb] must be a sub-construction with its own noncompositional dilemma meaning.

Additional evidence for the conventionality of sub-constructions is the fact that different languages do not necessarily have the same disjunctive sub-constructions, even though they have the basic [X *or* Y] construction. Consider the translation of A in (10a) into Finnish (10b), courtesy of Elsi Kaiser (p.c.):[9]

(10)   a. A: Would you like cake or something?
           B: Yes, please.

       b. Haluaisitko   kakkua
           Want-COND-2nd-SG-QUESTION PARTICLE   cake-PART
           tai   jotain   muuta   pientä?
           or   something   else   small?
           'Would you like cake **or something else small**'?

It seems that Finnish lacks an [X *or something*] construction, as does Russian. Kaiser also doubted very much that Finnish had a counterpart disjunction for the [X *or* X] construction exemplified in (11):

(11)   Am I right or am I right?

There are many productive *or* sub-constructions that we cannot here discuss (e.g. *either* X *or* Y).[10] Quite a few *or* sub-(and sub-sub-)constructions are idiomatic uses of [X *or* Y], such as *do or die, more or less, ready or not*. My main point is that beside the super [X *or* Y] construction, English has evolved numerous specialized sub-constructions (as have a number of other languages), such as the ones exemplified in Section 20.4. These inherit some of the features associated with the basic [X *or* Y] construction, but add (as well as cancel) other specific meaning aspects. The sub-constructions are quite monosemous, especially in comparison to the super-construction. Their interpretations are then virtually guaranteed, no inferencing required.

20.5 On constructions and sub-constructions

Does the rich variety of specialized disjunctive sub-constructions affect the basic [X *or* Y] construction? Do these sub-constructions eliminate the ability of the basic

---

[9] I thank Elsi Kaiser for thoughtfully translating my English disjunctions into the best Finnish counterparts she could come up with. Interestingly, these did nt all end up as disjunctions in Finnish.

[10] We have focused on choices between polysemous vs. monosemous expressions of the disjunctive interpretation, pretending that there is no limit on how monosemous constructions can be. But we should note that languages may also impose limits on "diversification." Some languages, for example, make the disjunctive marker optional in questions (Japanese, see Mauri 2008). English has a ban against *either* X *or* Y in alternative questions (Moravcsik 1971). Since questions, especially ones where a choice between alternatives is requested from the addressee, are naturally interpreted as disjunctions, marking here may seem redundant to speakers.

construction to convey certain contents, in effect taking its place for those specific functions? Or, do they compete with it for those functions? Based on the examples which follow it looks like the sub-constructions can co-exist with the basic super-construction. For the most part, what the sub-constructions achieve in a one form/ one function manner (monosemously), the basic construction can achieve with the help of pragmatic inferencing. In other words, the polysemous construction can be contextually enriched to convey the messages more directly expressed by the sub-constructions.[11] Its use does not necessarily get restricted to functions not servable by the sub-constructions.[12] But if so, the sub-constructions compete with the basic construction. How is this competition resolved?

Let us first establish that [X *or* Y] can convey the messages conveyed by the sub-constructions analyzed above. Indeed, as compared with the [X *or something like that*] construction, consider the basic construction, realized as "X *or something like X*" in (12a), "X *or something like this*" in (12b), and "X *or something along that line*" in (12c):

(12) a. Is it like Generation X type thing, **or** something Like Generation X? (LSAC)

   b. ANDREW: you wouldn't wanna know.
         Mine is called uh uh=,
         Seven Habits of Effective People **or something like this?**
      DARLENE: Oh.
      ANDREW: (H) bullshit stuff (SBC: 052).

   c. KRISTIN: A couple tortillas,
         or maybe a sandwich,
         or something along that line (SBC: 041).

There is no reason to assume that *Generation X type thing,* **or** *something Like Generation X* is differently interpreted than *Generation X type thing or something like that* would have been interpreted. The same applies to the examples in (12b) and (12c). Next, the basic construction realized as *thoracic surgeon or some horse manure* in (13) is not too different from [X *or something*] in (6b) above (*jail or something*), where the second disjunct merely signals a loosening of the meaning of the first disjunct, no similar additional alternatives really being entertained (see Ariel, in preparation for the loosening use):[13]

(13) ALINA: . . He's a [thoracic surgeon,
      LENORE: [@@@@@]
      ALINA: **or some**] . . **horse manure,** (SBC: 006)

---

[11] Of course, there always is a difference between conventionally and directly expressing some message (by the sub-constructions) and conveying that same message indirectly (via inference).

[12] Andrej Malchukov quite sensibly proposes that the more frequently some sub-construction is used for its evolved function, the more likely it is that that function will be blocked for the basic construction. Unfortunately, I cannot as yet provide empirical evidence for this proposal.

[13] The two examples are not identical, though. Alina's second disjunct in addition expresses contempt, but that is because of its content. Such differences are orthogonal to the claim at hand, namely that both [X *or something*] and [X *or* Y] can convey a message whereby the second disjunct hedges the first one without offering any viable alternative.

In fact, [X *or* Y] can be used to convey most of the interpretations that the dedicated sub-constructions convey. This then is a case of rather heavy polysemy. But further research is needed before we can conclude that the basic [X *or* Y] construction is not affected by the availability of the sub-constructions. It may very well be that the very frequent use of the basic construction to convey a single ad hoc higher level category, rather than two (or more) distinct alternatives (see again (5e)) may be the result of relegating so many of the other discourse functions to the dedicated sub-constructions that have evolved.

Now, the way I have presented the facts so far, some *X or Y* string either is or is not a construction, and the competition has been between a variety of dedicated (virtually monosemous) disjunctive sub-constructions and a basic polysemous [X *or* Y] construction. The latter, I have assumed, can be pragmatically enriched by adding on contextual assumptions, so that when the compositional meaning of the construction is augmented by these inferences the total conveyed meaning is equivalent to the meaning expressed by the dedicated sub-constructions. Indeed, we saw that the discourse functions encoded for the sub-constructions can be conveyed by the basic [X *or* Y] construction, provided enough contextualization is available to enrich the basic disjunction into the special reading.

However, making this absolutely reasonable assumption we encounter a few puzzles. Surprisingly, not only do the conventionalized sub-constructions not cross easily from one language to another, as we have seen in Section 20.4; my attempts to get [X *or* Y] translations for some of the English [X *or* Y] constructions were not successful either. For example, when asked to translate into Finnish the [X *or* Y] in (14a), Elsi Kaiser (p.c.) chose to either add the Finnish counterpart of "otherwise" (14b) or to turn the construction into a negative conditional construction (14c):

(14) a. Let's eat **or** I'll starve to death.

  b. syödään   nyt,   tai   muuten   minä   kuolen   nälkään
     Let's-eat   now   **or** **otherwise**   I   die   hunger-ILLATIVE
     'Let's eat now or otherwise I will die of hunger.'

  c. ellei   me   syödä   pian   niin   minä   kuolen   nälkään.
     If-not we   eat   soon   **then** I   die   hunger-ILLATIVE.
     'If we don't eat soon I will die of hunger.'

If inferencing is a universal mechanism, which it has to be, given similar contextual assumptions, the inferred interpretations should be quite similar crosslinguistically. Specifically, it stands to reason that just as speakers of English consider "I'll starve to death" an obviously dispreferred alternative, so do Finnish speakers. If so, all they need to do when faced with a literal translation of the English (14a) is to integrate into their basic disjunction meaning the fact that disjunct Y is ruled out. If they did that, they should quite straightforwardly get a reading where the speaker very strongly endorses the X disjunct. But my informant did not think that [X *or* Y] was an acceptable translation here. It seems that Finnish opts for different strategies for conveying such dispreferred Y disjunctions, with additional compositional material specifying more explicitly that the Y disjunct is a "second best".

Similarly, with respect to (15), Kaiser noted that "I really prefer this with 'ja' (and)" ('life **and** death'), although she thought an "or" was possible:

(15)   It's a matter of life **or** death.

The same is true for Hebrew, and Andrej Malchukov has the same intuition about Russian. Interestingly, while the counterpart of *X, or I am a pope* sounds acceptable to him in Russian, he could not find any textual examples for its use.

Finally, my native Hebrew-speaking students refused to accept the Hebrew translation of (16), even though I replaced the English-specific *I'm a monkey's uncle* with a Hebrew idiomatic equivalent expression for an impossible state of affairs ("I'm a jar"):[14]

(16)   ~??ze   xayav   li-hiyot   ha-albom   porec   ha-derex,
         This   has.got   to-be   the-album   breaking the-way,
         o   she-ani   cincenet.
         or   that-I   jar.
         'This has got to be the breakthrough album, or I'm a jar.'

No doubt, these sub-constructions are language-specific, despite the fact that their evolution from the basic polysemic construction seems extremely transparent, and should have been enabled in all languages with the help of contextually driven inferences. Since speakers mobilize current forms for innovative meanings, which may then become conventional means for the innovative interpretation, it is not necessarily the case that all languages would choose the same construction for conveying the new message (although, no doubt, the choice is heavily restricted). Now, once a particular language recruited a particular construction for the novel message, it would tend to not also convey the same message by mobilizing yet another construction. It is possible that since Hebrew uses a counterfactual negative conditional to express the message intended in (16) ("If this will not be the... I'm a jar"), it preempts the use of a counterfactual disjunction for this purpose.

There obviously is much more conventionality to language use than pragmatists like to admit. The radical pragmatics position that anything that *can* be left to inference should be assumed to be pragmatically triggered online, rather than linguistically encoded, is a radical exaggeration. While ad hoc inferences are no doubt an inherent feature of linguistic communication, not all potentially inferable interpretations are in fact inferred in real time. Many inferences undergo at least some conventionalization, even when they remain completely transparent and compositional (e.g. [X or *something like that*]). The concept of Generalized Conversational Implicatures captures a similar phenomenon.

More recently I have argued that discourse is rife with extragrammatical conventions, which guide interlocutors' interpretations, although they involve neither grammar nor inference (Ariel 2010: 9.5). There is a rather large set of regularities of "how we, speakers of language X, do things" in order to convey our messages. This

---

[14]   Elsi Kaiser did accept an X *or* Y disjunction here, where she replaced the English-specific proposition with the Finnish counterpart of "I'll eat my hat."

mobilization of certain constructions in the service of further discourse functions, although transparent, and although dependent on inferencing in the initial stages, is conventionalized, at least to some extent, in that it is highly accessible to speakers. This is why in the absence of a salient discourse pattern whereby some specific construction is (also) used to perform some additional function, interlocutors have a hard time using and interpreting such cases, which is what we saw for Hebrew and Finnish (examples (1), (14)). This also explains why repair *ors* are quite frequent in English (close to 20% of the *ors* in SBC), but quite marginal in Hebrew (about 4%, Kuperschmidt 2012).

Of course, such innovative uses, accompanied by inferencing, do occasionally occur, which is how innovations are initiated, such as the ones which led to the evolution of the [X *or something like that*], [X *or something*], [X *or* X] constructions, etc. But such innovations depend on a very supportive context. The seemingly transparent (sub-)constructions here discussed are ones which no longer require such a rich context. They are already represented as salient discourse patterns for speakers, despite the fact that they can plausibly be triggered by pragmatic inferencing. In other words, some constructions are fully grammaticized, and can be quite opaque (noncompositional), others may be conventional although they are in principle transparent. Languages which lack, say an [X *or* Y] equivalent, do lack that grammatical construction. But they may still have a nongrammaticized *conventional* means (strategy) to express disjunctive relations, for example by mobilizing the [*perhaps* X, *perhaps* Y] discourse pattern.

20.6 Conclusions: Polysemy, monosemy, and context

Disjunctive constructions minimally introduce multiple alternatives, which must be construable as distinct instances of some higher-level discourse-relevant category (e.g. "hot drinks" for (5c)). I have proposed that such constructions can be used to profile quite a variety of discourse functions, which are conveyed either by the basic [X *or* Y] construction or by specific disjunctive sub-constructions. I have emphasized that the basic disjunctive construction, and to some extent, even some of the sub-constructions are polysemous, requiring contextual inferencing. For example, in order to decide that a repair disjunctive interpretation is intended, the addressee must rely on contextual cues. The same is true for the decision whether *or something* points to other similar alternatives, or merely serves to hedge the first alternative.

Based on the typological literature (most notably Mauri 2008), some languages opt for heavy polysemy accompanied by inferencing and/or heavy reliance on salient discourse patterns associating forms with functions they do not grammatically encode. Interestingly perhaps, no language demonstrates exclusive monosemy (eliminating all inferencing). English seems to combine polysemy ([X *or* Y]) with a set of sub-constructions which are monosemic, or virtually so. The competition between polysemy and monosemy is then not restricted to the language system. It constitutes a real-time competition in that speakers must choose between these options. For example, why did the speaker in (2a) choose a [*perhaps* X *perhaps* Y] nongrammaticized pattern, rather than the [X *or* Y] construction? I must leave this intriguing question to future research, but I expect there to be an inverse relationship between contextual cues and degree of monosemy. The more contextual cues there are, the more accessible the specific disjunctive interpretation is and the more minimal (polysemous) the form can be.

At the same time, I have pointed out that contextual inferencing is not as freely employed as pragmatists commonly assume (See Ariel 1999b; Ariel 2010: 9.4 on "ugly facts").[15] Often enough, quite a bit of conventionality is actually involved in a speaker's choice to mobilize a particular construction for conveying a noncanonical interpretation. This is certainly the case in the use speakers make of the basic [X *or* Y] construction to profile a variety of disjunctive interpretations. We can perhaps say that for the most part (innovations excluded) [X *or* Y] exhibits a limited polysemy of use, such that the addressee relies on inferences to choose the specific interpretation intended by the speaker, out of a number of interpretations potentially conveyed by the construction. He probably does not need to derive the interpretation "from scratch." Once again, more conventionality entails less inferencing.

According to Zipf, it is the speaker's job to balance between her own interest in "least effort," realized by unification (polysemy), and the addressee's interest in "least effort," realized by diversification (monosemy). We have seen that languages do not have to choose one or the other option when disjunctive interpretations are involved. They may make available both a basic polysemous construction, as well as a variety of nearly monosemic constructions. Where the grammar allows for minimalist (polysemous) versus maximalist (monosemous) options, speakers must juggle these options in real-time interactions, balancing their choices of whose "least effort" they prefer, based on how facilitating the context is for the disjunctive reading they intend, but other pragmatic motivations may be involved. One such motivation may be that speakers sometimes wish to vary the means by which they convey certain meanings (Keller 1994a). This could motivate the mobilization of the highly polysemous X *or* Y to convey repairs, conditional threats (*Your money or you life*), etc.

---

[15] "Ugly facts" are linguistic facts that seem to be transparently derivable so there should be no need to specify them in the grammar or lexicon, but they turn out to be conventional after all. One such example is the different rendering of the same concept expressed in English by *clothes line* and in Hebrew by the equivalent of "laundry line." Only conventionality can account for the different choice in the two languages.

Sentence grammar vs. thetical grammar: Two competing domains?

GUNTHER KALTENBÖCK AND BERND HEINE

21.1 Introduction

That language structure is shaped at least to some extent by competing motivations is a hypothesis that has given rise to quite some discussion ever since it was proposed as a theoretical concept (Haiman 1983; Du Bois 1985). At the same time, it has been discussed controversially (e.g., Cristofaro n.d.; Newmeyer 1998, 2003a), but it has also found some wider applications in recent works on linguistic analysis (see Moravcsik and Malchukov, this volume). It would seem that there are three kinds of phenomena that have been at the center of attention in the analysis of motivating forces, namely the following:

(a) the goals of speakers and hearers,
(b) features of language structures, and
(c) metalinguistic tools that are used to describe and/or explain language structure.

All three phenomena have been studied by linguists interested in competing motivations: (a) surfaces as the implicit or explicit objective in many works, but much of the research on the typology of language structures has focused on (b). In more recent work, the main focus of attention has been on (c), which relates to the structure of metalanguages, that is, the conceptual apparatus employed by linguists in describing and understanding languages (Moravcsik 2010; see also the introductory chapter to this volume). Our interest here is primarily with (a), that is, with what in the wording of Hawkins (this volume) concerns performance selections between competing forms of language structure, but we also need to draw heavily on (b) to reconstruct (a), and on (c) to understand (b).

The chapter proposes a distinction made in the organization of discourse that has so far received little attention. In a view of grammar as an adaptive domain, as proposed by Du Bois (1985; cf. also Gell-Mann 1992; Givón 2009), grammar is shaped by essentially two different forces: internal motivations, arising from within the language domain, and external motivations, pertaining to the domain of functional discourse requirements (cf. Du Bois 1985: e.g., 344). As the term "adaptive system" already suggests, grammar can be described both as a conventionalized *system* in which grammatical categories are stored for reuse in "a more or less frozen or reified form," and an *adaptive* activity in the sense that "it responds to the pressures from the external 'environment'" (Du Bois 1985: 362). In language use these two forces, persistence of the system and responsiveness to the discourse situation, constantly interact and compete with each other and need to find some kind of cost-efficient reconciliation.

Grammar, in other words, has to take care of two potentially conflicting aims. On the one hand, it has to be sufficiently fixed and constrained in order to work as a system, on the other it has to preserve sufficient flexibility to be able to respond to the requirements of the immediate discourse situation. One obvious constraint of language is that of cohesive linear flow, that is, the need to string words together—one at a time—while observing certain word order restrictions and conventions. This constraint is of particular relevance in spoken online production, which takes place in real time (Biber et al. 1999: 1048) and involves a considerable degree of planning. At the same time the linear flow of verbal communication and its concomitant degree of planning may be in conflict with external discourse requirements especially in spoken production, where the complexity of the discourse situation may require attending to simultaneously occurring events, and to do so with a certain degree of spontaneity.

Sometimes pressures of the immediate discourse requirements may be deemed more important by the speaker than the need to conform to the system constraints of linear flow and adjacency. This can be illustrated by the following examples of spoken English,[1] where the interpolated elements (in bold print) temporarily disrupt the structure of another construction and in this way add an extra plane of communication which in some form relates to the immediate discourse situation.[2]

(1)   And what we found <,> was uhm <,> **could you turn the slide projector off please** uhm very substantial mortality difference within the population (ICE-GB: s2a-047-110)

(2)   Walker gets a hand on it but the ball in fact runs out to long-on where Andy Roberts who is by the way the smallest first-class cricketer **we checked it up earlier on** does the fielding and that's the end of Worcestershire's innings (ICE-GB: s2a-013-137)

(3)   What I've done here **I hope you don't entirely disapprove** is try and limit the time taken on this item by putting it in writing (ICE-GB: s1b-075-180)

Interpolated elements such as these are hard to reconcile with rules or conventions characterizing the "system," yet they tend to be accepted by interlocutors as not breaking any rules. They are commonly referred to as parentheticals but will be

---

[1] The examples in (1)–(3) are from the British component of the *International Corpus of English* (ICE-GB). The mark-up symbol <,> indicates a short pause, <,,> indicates a long pause.

[2] Throughout the chapter, items printed in bold are theticals.

referred to here by the term *theticals*, which subsumes a wider class of elements (see Section 21.2). What these examples illustrate is, first, that there is a strategy of "opting out," that is, of temporarily stepping out of the linear confines of online production. This creates an extra communicative dimension, a parallel space, which allows the speaker to respond to immediate requirements arising from the situation of discourse.

And, second, examples (1)–(3) also show that theticals differ greatly in the way and the extent to which they contribute to the information content of an utterance. For example, the thetical in (1) can be described as being in some sense "text-irrelevant."[3] That in (3) on the other hand contributes more directly to the content of the utterance; note that the latter, but not the former, can be linked to the preceding discourse by means of *and*.

Building on Kaltenböck et al. (2011), the present chapter describes the characteristic properties of such thetical elements and how they are used in discourse (Section 21.2). On the basis of the distinctive properties of these elements, it further argues that theticals constitute a separate domain of grammar, one that we will call Thetical Grammar (TG) (Section 21.3). We will argue that Thetical Grammar not only complements but also competes with what is referred to as Sentence Grammar (SG) (Section 21.4). Section 21.5 provides some conclusions and an outlook for further research. The data presented in the chapter are taken from English, mostly from the British component of the *International Corpus of English* (ICE-GB) (cf. Nelson 2002).

21.2 The class of theticals

As noted above, the external discourse requirements of a particular speech situation may sometimes be considered more pressing than the need to stick to the linear conventions of Sentence Grammar. In such a case, a speaker may choose to temporarily step out of the linear confines of syntax and create an extra plane of communication which caters for the immediate demands of the discourse situation. The linguistic elements involved in this communicative strategy include what is commonly referred to as parentheticals, parenthetic adjuncts (Corum 1975), disjuncts (Espinal 1991), interpolations, extra-clausal constituents (Dik 1997), inserts, syntactic non-clausal units (Biber et al. 1999: 1082, 1099), supplements (Huddleston and Pullum 2002), or epistemic adverbial phrases[4] (Thompson and Mulac 1991a, 1991b; Thompson 2002a: 143), etc., but most authors converge on calling them parentheticals.

Our decision to break with this tradition by replacing the term parenthetical by the reduced form thetical[5] is that not all instances of this category are in fact

---

[3] We are grateful to an anonymous reviewer for drawing our attention to this fact.

[4] Thompson (2002: 143) also uses the term "parenthetical" but in a more restricted sense, e.g., for frequent complement-taking predicate phrases that become epistemic adverbial phrases, such as *I guess, I think*.

[5] The term thetical must not be confused with that of "thetic" statement (Kuroda 1972; Lambrecht 1994; Sasse 1987; 2006); see Heine et al. (2013).

parenthetical in the sense that they are interpolated in or require a host utterance.[6] Rather, theticals may be added at the periphery of an utterance, or they may even form utterances of their own. It is for this reason that we follow Dik (1997: 379) in distinguishing parentheticals, which "interrupt a clause," from other kinds of theticals which can stand on their own, or precede or follow a clause.[7] These other kinds of theticals are called by Dik extra-clausal constituents (ECCs), a term that he also uses as a hypernym for both. Our reason for not adopting this term and instead using "thetical" generally for both his parenthetical and ECC is that the latter term implies that the clause, or more generally SG, enjoys a privileged status vis-à-vis theticals. As we will argue in Section 21.4, such a claim is debatable; rather the two are assumed to belong to separate domains of what we call Discourse Grammar. We will return to this issue in Section 21.

What unites the category of theticals are certain shared formal characteristics (as discussed in Section 21.2.1; see also Heine et al. 2013) and a very general common functional motivation, which is that of presenting information as being outside the current plane of communication. As such, theticals are particularly suited for the expression of information that is seen as immediately relevant to the discourse situation (see Section 21.2.2 for details). It is only natural, therefore, that theticals should be used more frequently in spoken language, which is more responsive to the situational context and, because of its online production, more exposed to the pressures of linear flow than written texts.

21.2.1 *Formal characteristics*

Although generally quite short,[8] theticals may consist of anything from a single word (e.g., English *like, say, what*; Dehé and Kavalova 2007b: 1–2; Dehé 2007: 263), as in (4) below, a phrase, a clause, or even a chunk that does not form a syntactic constituent to more complex structures involving clause combining, as in example (5) (for survey discussions, see, e.g., Corum 1975; Espinal 1991; Dik 1997; Biber et al. 1999: 1082; Wichmann 2001; Grenoble 2004; Kaltenböck 2007; Brinton 2008: 7–14; Kaltenböck et al. 2011; Heine et al. 2013 as well as the contributions in Dehé and Kavalova 2007a).

(4)   I'd be far more upset if somebody **say** scratched one of my records than tore one of my books. (ICE-GB; Dehé and Kavalova 2007b: 2)

(5)   Peter I think the important thing **I think this is understood by people in Britain in a way which I think perhaps the rampant jingoism which I see expressed in some portions of the British press do not understand** is that the people of Britain do know are not in jingoistic mood for war. (ICE-GB: s1b-027-37)

---

[6] In view of the extreme syntactic independence of some of the categories, Biber et al. (1999: 1082) propose a type of nonclausal unit that they call inserts for English units such as *sorry, oh, thanks,* or *well*.

[7] Note that Thompson (2002: 143) restricts the term parenthetical to frequently used "epistemic adverbial phrases" occurring in medial or final position of their host clause.

[8] Biber et al. (1999: 1070–2), for instance, note a shorter length for their category of nonclausal units as opposed to clausal units (4.95 vs. 7.52 words per unit).

What sets theticals apart from elements of Sentence Grammar (SG) are the properties listed in (6). These properties have to be taken as prototypical rather than obligatory (see Kaltenböck et al. 2011, 2.6.).

(6)   Formal properties of theticals
    a. They are syntactically independent of their environment.
    b. They are prosodically set off from the rest of the utterance by a separate intonation contour and pauses.
    c. They have non-restrictive meaning.
    d. They tend to be positionally mobile.
    e. Their internal structure is built on principles of SG but can be elliptic.

Let us briefly look at these properties in turn (cf. also Kaltenböck et al. 2011).

Property (6a) strictly concerns the *external* syntax of theticals: They are not an argument of any kind of their host utterance, and they do not form constituents with units of SG. Most studies agree that theticals have no syntagmatic (i.e., paratactic or hypotactic) link to their host clauses (cf., e.g., Kaltenböck 2007). They have consequently been described as disjunct constituents (Grenoble 2004: 1972; Quirk et al. 1985; Espinal 1991), syntactically "independent" in the sense of McCawley (1982), or as optional expressions that are syntactically unintegrated or detached from the host (or anchor) clause or any SG structure (e.g., Quirk et al. 1985: 853; Biber et al. 1999: 1067; Peterson 1999; Huddleston and Pullum 2002: 1350). Thus, in the following example, deletion of a verb phrase (VP) is not affected by the thetical *of course*—that is, VP deletion operates as if the thetical were not there:

(7)   John talked, **of course,** about politics and Mary did too. (= Mary talked about politics ≠ Mary talked too ≠ Mary talked, **of course,** about politics too). (McCawley 1982: 96)

Some theticals may share properties with subordinate constructions, adjuncts (Jackendoff 1972), or matrix clauses (Pittner 1995; de Vries 2007: 203–5). However, they are not arguments of any kind of their host utterance and all attempts to relate theticals in a principled way to SG have failed so far. Some theticals can also stand alone, that is, they can form utterances of their own (e.g., *You know?*).

Property (6b) can be taken as the prosodic reflection of the syntactic independence noted in (6a). Although the prosodic features identified for theticals may vary, most studies agree that theticals are prosodically set off in some form from the rest of the utterance. In English this is typically achieved by a separate tone unit, which may be offset by pauses. This pattern is often referred to as "comma-intonation'" (see the next paragraph), or appositional intonation (Dixon 2005: 233) and represents a break in the intonation curve of the base sentence. Other possible prosodic correlates are lowered or raised pitch, rising-type tones, narrower pitch range, diminished loudness, increased tempo, and the blocking of sandhi rules (see, e.g., Kutik, Cooper and Boyce 1983; Ziv 1985: 181–2 Nespor and Vogel 1986; Safir 1986: 672; Haegeman 1988: 250; Bolinger 1989; Hoffmann 1998: 300; Rouchota 1998: 105; Wichmann 2004; D'Avis 2005; Dehé and Kavalova 2007b: 13; Dehé 2007: 262; Kaltenböck 2008, 2009; Dehé and Wichmann 2010; for more details).

Prosodic non-integration is generally taken to be a primary, defining characteristic of theticals. Burton-Roberts (2005: 180), for instance, maintains that all theticals
have in common, observationally, "that they are marked off from their hosts by
some form of punctuation in writing or special intonation contour in speech". Potts
(2003) even proposes a syntactic feature COMMA for theticals with "comma-
intonation" to signal that these units do not contribute to assertive content (see
Rouchota 1998: 105; Blakemore 2006: 1673). Prosodic separation from the rest of the
utterance by "breaks or pause-like inflections in the prosodic contour" also constitutes one of the defining features of the extra-clausal constituents proposed by Dik
(1997: 381). Similar views on the central status of prosody for the definition of
theticals have been expressed by Pittner (1995) and Grenoble (2004: 1972).

In written language the prosodic breaks are typically signaled by orthographic
means such as commas, full stops, dashes, and parentheses. In the following example, for instance, the left boundary is marked by a full stop and the right boundary by
a comma:[9]

(8)   It is not possible to give a definitive set of rules in this paper. **Instead,** two examples
      are given showing how the mapping is achieved. (ICE-GB: w2a-038-092)

Despite the importance accorded to prosody by most authors, it is not as reliable a
criterion for identification as it might seem. In fact, a number of studies have shown
that not all theticals are prosodically set off from their host and that they do not
necessarily form a single, prosodically defined class (e.g., Astruc 2005; Bolinger 1989:
186; Dehé 2007; Dehé and Kavalova 2007b: 14; Espinal 1991: 734; Kaltenböck 2007: 3;
Reinhart 1983: 178–9; Wichmann 2001: 186). A main reason for the lack of prosodic
cues of some theticals is their gradual integration into the SG of their hosts owing to
frequent use, and also to grammaticalization (see Kaltenböck et al. 2011: sect. 2.6.). As
a consequence of this process, theticals may lose in prosodic distinctiveness, to the
extent that (6b) may no longer be a distinguishing property. We therefore take (6b)
not as a necessary but—in conjunction with the other criteria of (6)—as a sufficient
criterion. In other words, the presence of a separate intonation contour and/or
pauses is indicative of the presence of a thetical while absence does not mean that
the relevant unit is not a thetical. Property (6c) concerns the meaning of theticals.
Rather than being restricted to and determined by the syntax of the sentence, that
meaning relates to and essentially has scope over the situation of discourse.[10] Thus,
the item *really* in (9a) is an adverb that is restrictive in the sense that it determines
the meaning of the predicate. In (9b) and (9c), by contrast, it is non-restrictive in
that it is not semantically part of the clause *Bob is a poet* but rather concerns and has
scope over the situation of discourse—in this case more specifically the nature of

---

[9]   The unit *instead* occurs both as an SG item (e.g., in the preposition *instead of*) and as a thetical. That
it is a thetical in the present example is suggested most of all by the fact that it is set off prosodically (and
by punctuation marks) from the rest of the discourse unit.

[10]   The term "non-restrictive meaning" is taken from and used largely in the sense of Huddleston and
Pullum (2002: 1350–62).

speaker–hearer interaction. As we will see in Section 21.2.2, the situation of discourse is composed of a network of interlocking components The difference between restrictive and non-restrictive meaning is fairly obvious when components such as speaker–hearer interaction are concerned, as in (9b)–(9c), while it is minimal when the component concerned is text organization.

(9)   a. Bob is really a poet.
      b. Bob is a poet, **really.**
      c. **Really,** Bob is a poet.

Property (6d), positional mobility, can be seen as a direct result of the syntactic independence of theticals. As pointed out in various studies (e.g., Urmson 1952; Corum 1975: 137; Ziv 1985: 182; Peterson 1999: 237; Wichmann 2001: 179; Brinton 2008: 18), many theticals are not tied to a specific position in the host construction but may occur in several locations. In fact, many can occur virtually anywhere within an utterance, or as utterances of their own. Still, there are some constraints on placement, most of all relating to their discourse-specific functions (see Emonds 1973: 338, Grenoble 2004: 1966–7, and Brinton 2008: 8 for a discussion of English comment clauses), and certain theticals are restricted to specific positions of an utterance (Kaltenböck et al. 2011: sect. 2.4).

Property (6e) concerns the *internal* structure of theticals, which can take the form of a fully-fledged clause in accordance with the rules of SG, as in examples (1)–(3) above, but it may also be elliptic in a way that is at variance with the requirements of SG (cf., e.g., Biber et al. 1999: 1099). A paradigm example is provided by comment clauses and reporting clauses, that is, two theticals that are characterized by the ellipsis of the complement, cf. (10a).[11] Corresponding SG units such as (10b), by contrast, require a complement clause. Accordingly, an SG utterance such as (10c) without a complement would not appear to be well-formed.

(10) a. *Mary—**I just learned from her daughter**—is coming over to visit.*
      b. *I just learned from her daughter that Mary is coming over to visit.*
      c. *?I just learned from her daughter.*

Further examples of such reduced, non-clausal theticals are given in (11), where (11a) contains a verbless clause, (11b) an adjective phrase, and (11c) a clause (*you know*) lacking a complement, like (10a).

(11) a. *The visitors, **most of them students**, were rather surprised.*
      b. *The chairman, **angry at the delay**, demanded a full report.*
      c. *John lives in London, **you know**.*

Note, however, that with the example of a comment clause like *you know* in (11c) the situation is less clear if it occurs in clause-initial position, especially with an omitted *that*-complementizer, as in (12a). Here *you know* can be interpreted as a matrix

---

[11] Even if one were to argue, as some have in fact done (see Kaltenböck et al. 2011 for discussion), that the complement in (10a) is provided by the host utterance *Mary is coming over to visit*, the fact remains that the thetical in (10a) has the appearance of a reduced clause.

clause taking the following clause as its complement, or as a thetical and therefore as syntactically independent from the second clause. Cases such as these have been discussed controversially in the literature (cf., e.g., Brinton 2008: 10–14 for an overview), but it seems that prosody plays a decisive role: prosodic separation from the following clause will normally confer thetical status to the initial clause; cf. example (12b) and the discussion in Kaltenböck (2009, 2011) and Dehé and Wichmann (2010).

(12)   a. *You know John lives in London.*
       b. **You know**, *John lives in London.*

Lack of a constituent that would be required by the rules of SG can thus be a good indication that a particular unit is in fact a thetical. On the other hand, absence of ellipsis cannot automatically be equated with absence of thetical status. As noted above, theticals may also have non-elliptical, clausal structure. This raises the question of how to distinguish a clausal thetical from an independent SG clause, which also fulfills the criterion of syntactic independence (cf. 6a).[12] In the case of interpolation, such as example (13a), this question is easy to answer. With juxtaposed clauses such as (13b), on the other hand, the status is less clear and requires still further research. Conceivably, prosodic realization, which can be assumed to be similar to the one in (13a) in terms of reduced pitch (and possibly loudness), plays an important role in marking a juxtaposed clause as thetical.[13]

(13)   a. *She called John—**he is one of my best friends**—to find out what had happened.*
       b. *She called John. He is one of my best friends. They talked about what had happened.*

21.2.2 *Functional characteristics*

Theticals are notoriously difficult to define in terms of their meaning. Although a number of different semantic generalizations have been proposed (e.g., Rouchota 1998; Grenoble 2004; Blakemore 2006), these seem to apply only to particular types of theticals rather than the class as a whole (see, e.g., Ifantidou-Troki 1993; Ifantidou 2001; Blakemore 2006: 1684; Dehé and Kavalova 2007b: 9–10). Theticals clearly fulfill a number of different functions which are hard to subsume under a common heading. This multifunctionality (cf. Dik 1997: 383) seems to stem to a large extent from their unconstrained nature in terms of syntactic use, as we saw above. By presenting an element as independent from its surrounding syntactic structure (i.e., as a thetical) its meaning is no longer defined with regard to its syntactic function. Instead, it is now free to relate to the "larger" environment, which is that of the

---

[12] Cf., e.g., Peterson (1999: 241–2) on the non-syntagmatic link between juxtaposed clauses.
[13] Cf. also Mazeland (2007: 1819), who notes that inserts between "turn constructional units" in a multi-unit turn can be analyzed as parentheticals because "[t]he activity implemented in the turn as a whole—a story telling—is not yet possibly complete at this point". But an anonymous reviewer, drawing attention to Ariel (2010), argues that she or he would strongly oppose a position that the backgrounded, but syntactically independent matrix sentence (*he is one of . . .*) in (13b) should be taken as a thetical as well. It would seem that in the absence of more empirical data, both positions can be defended.

situation of discourse. Theticals are thus responsive to the particulars of the immediate discourse situation. In that sense they can be seen as "anchored," either in a host construction or in the discourse situation as a whole. And it is this close link to the immediate situational context or verbal cotext that shapes the meaning of a specific thetical and accounts for the multifunctionality of the class as a whole. To determine the communicative function of theticals it is therefore necessary to take into account the entire situation of discourse, which is best thought of as consisting of a network of interrelated components, as outlined in (14). Some illustrative examples of each are given in (15) to (20) (for a more detailed discussion see Kaltenböck et al. 2011: 861–4).

(14) Components determining the situation of discourse
       A. Text organization
       B. Source of information
       C. Attitudes of the speaker
       D. Speaker–hearer interaction
       E. Discourse setting
       F. World knowledge

(15) Text organization
       a. *The warning—**that prices should be lowered**—was ignored.*
       b. *But I think there is a problem that the English **I u use the word English advisedly** do start out with low aspirations when it comes to education and training.* (ICE-GB: s2a-037-38)

(16) Source of information
       a. *And in the end they don't uh because **as you say** the priests in Jerusalem in service in Jerusalem hang on to their jobs.* (ICE-GB: s1b-001-107)
       b. *Last night ITN showed these pictures of a school clinic in a town sixty miles from Baghdad which **Iraqi officials said** had been hit by allied bombing.* (ICE-GB: s2b-001-64)

(17) Attitudes of the speaker
       a. *You could **I suppose** commission some prints of you yourself.* (ICE-GB: s1a-015-037)
       b. ***Sadly**, the soil fails disastrously after a few years and is then fit to support only worthless scrub.* (ICE-GB: w2b-028-058)

(18) Speaker–hearer interaction
       a. *Very short skirt on **if you don't mind me saying**.* (ICE-GB: s1a-040-089)
       b. *Mary—**I hate to tell you this**—is coming over to visit.* (Kaltenböck 2007: 39)

(19) Discourse setting
       a. *So what we can do in fact **I'll just turn it off** <,> is to use that signal to train people's ability to perceive voicing.* (ICE-GB: s2a-056-87)

b. *He designed a torsion apparatus to measure the friction <,> **excuse me** <,> and found some most surprising results.* (ICE-GB: s2a-041-1)

(20) World knowledge

a. *Jake asserted—**this is how all moralists speak**—that the young are spoiled.* (de Vries n.d.)

b. *And it wasn't till the end of the year uh that it was quite clear **I don't think that this is disputed** <,> that he wasn't going to <,> uh get them…* (ICE-GB: s2a-063-71)

The components distinguished in (14) are not to be understood as mutually exclusive but as overlapping categories. A number of examples can, in fact, be analyzed with reference to more than one component. What matters is that theticals have the entire pragmatic environment of linguistic communication in their scope. Of course, the same can be said of SG. The difference is that theticals underscore their discourse relevance by their special formal features (as discussed in Section 21.2.1), which set them apart from SG and thereby mark their contribution as immediately relevant.

21.2.3 *A catalog of theticals*

Based on the discussion of formal characteristics in Section 21.2.1 we can now give a brief overview of the main categories of theticals. To do so, it is useful to make a distinction between three different structural types, namely instantaneous, constructional, and formulaic theticals. *Instantaneous theticals* can be formed freely any time and anywhere, as illustrated by the examples in (1)–(3). They frequently take the form of a main clause as in (21a), or clause fragment as in (21b), but, being largely free combinations in terms of content and morphosyntactic form, they exhibit few constraints in their structure and meaning.

(21) a. *And of course during the nineteenth century **we can't hide the fact** Egypt became very much a hunting ground for agents on behalf of museums in Europe.* (ICE-GB: s2a-052-81)

b. *The main point—**why not have a seat?**—is outlined in the middle paragraph.* (Burton-Roberts 2005: 180)

But quite often, theticals take the form of "prefabs," that is, of combinations of words that are likely to co-occur (Erman and Warren 2000). And some of them may undergo constructionalization (Evans 2007: 370). The latter can be classified as *constructional theticals*, that is, recurrent patterns, or constructions of theticals having a schematic format and function. Paradigm examples are provided in Table 21.1 (see also Kaltenböck et al. 2011).

TABLE 21.1. **Some constructional theticals of English**

Type of constructional thetical	Example
A. Comment clauses	*So I'll just have to wait **I guess*** (ICE-GB: w1b-003-162)
B. Reporting clauses	*Britain **he said** could compete and win* (ICE-GB: s2b-005-129)
C. Tag questions	*In fact we had a horror **didn't we** on the way* (ICE-GB: s1a-021-036)
D. Left-detached topics	***Now your parents** are they alive and well* (ICE-GB: s1a-051-305)
E. Right-dislocations	*They've got a pet rabbit <,> **Laura and her boyfriend Simon*** (ICE-GB: s1a-017-128)
F. Afterthoughts (repairs)	*Their mufti **I mean their weekend clothes** <,> uh is a bit restrictive* (ICE-GB: s1a-054-157)
G. Phrasal appositives	*William Colby, **CIA chief of the day**, claimed recently that his agency had spent nearly $100 million 'supporting politicians'* (ICE-GB: w2c-010-028)
H. Appositive (or non-restrictive) relative clauses	*He's gone a bit sort of quiet <,> **which is unusual for Moses*** (ICE-GB: s1a-040-023)
I. *And*-clauses	*And during the last five years **and I take the figures quite arbitrarily** the gross national product has gone up by forty per cent in that period eighty-five to eighty-nine* (ICE-GB: s2b-036-101)

Formulaic theticals are essentially invariable, that is, morphosyntactically unanalyzable information units that are short, and most of them are positionally variable; Table 21.2 provides a few examples.

TABLE 21.2. **Some formulaic theticals of English**

Category	Examples
Conceptual theticals	*as it were, for example, if you will*
FSEs	*good morning, hello, please, thank you*
Vocatives	*Sir!, Waiter!*
Imperatives	*Come on!, Piss off!*
Interjections	*boy, damn, fuck, hell*

21.3 Competing grammatical domains?

The main claims made in the present chapter are the following:[14]

(22) a. Theticals are different enough from SG units to justify their analysis as not belonging to the same domain as SG.

      b. Theticals are similar enough to each other to justify their analysis as a domain of their own.

      c. In order to communicate successfully, speakers have the option to choose between the two domains in organizing their texts.

While (22a) is based on our definition of theticals in (6), the other two claims are more difficult to substantiate. The claim in (22b) rests most of all on the observations made in Section 21.2.2: The meaning of theticals is determined by the situation of discourse rather than by the syntax of a sentence. Finally, in Section 21.5, we will return to (22c).

As was outlined in the introduction, speakers are constantly confronted with a general problem in communication, namely how to handle the dichotomy between the linear flow of verbal communication and the immediate communicative and cognitive needs arising from the discourse situation. To deal with this problem, we argue, they dispose of two contrasting domains for organizing their linguistic discourse: Sentence Grammar (SG) and Thetical Grammar (TG). Each operates on its own principles for organizing discourse. The major dimension of SG is syntactic hierarchy, which is the central concern of most mainstream schools of contemporary linguistics. TG, on the other hand, is largely free from this constraint, being characterized by syntactic independence and positional mobility (see Section 21.2.1). It is therefore optimally suited to attend to the immediate communicative needs of the discourse situation (see Section 21.2.2). TG thus adds an extra dimension, described by Espinal (1991) in terms of a three-dimensional syntactic model, which allows the speaker to temporarily escape the narrow confines of linearity. SG and TG can therefore be thought of as two different cognitive domains (see Kaltenböck et al. 2011), which are presumably computed in separate intensional domains (Espinal 1991: 730)[15] and which together constitute *Discourse Grammar*.

Discourse Grammar consists of all the linguistic resources that are available for constructing spoken, written, or signed texts. In the framework used here, expounded in Heine et al. (2013; see also Kaltenböck et al. 2011), it is composed of the two domains discussed above (see Figure 21.1) plus the conventions used to integrate these domains for designing and organizing texts.

---

[14] We are grateful to an anonymous reviewer of this chapter for valuable suggestions on this issue.

[15] Espinal (1991: 730) uses the term *disjunct*, which largely corresponds to, but is less inclusive than our term thetical.

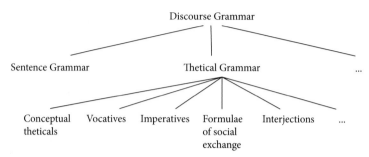

FIGURE 21.1 Domains of Discourse Grammar

SG is organized in terms of constituent types such as clauses, phrases, words, and morphemes plus the syntactic and morphological machinery to relate these constituents to one another. We assume that the nucleus of the clause is the verb and its argument structure, optionally extended by peripheral participants (or adjuncts).[16] With its rich repertoire of form–meaning units and its diversified structure of relating these units to one another, SG allows the speaker to encode virtually any conceptual information in a coherent and a consistent way. In doing so it has the potential to create its own textual world, one which can be fairly independent from the immediate situational context.

TG, by comparison, is syntactically more independent, allowing insertion almost anywhere in an utterance, but this comes at the price of greater contextual/situational dependence. This means that for their appropriate interpretation, theticals need to be associated with a specific situation of discourse. As argued by Haegeman (1991) in what she calls the radical orphanage approach, a speaker has to establish the relevance of a thetical by an inferential process (as outlined, e.g., by Relevance Theory) which takes into account the immediate context of the utterance. Take the utterance in (23), conveniently classified as an insubordinate clause (Evans 2007), which can only be successfully interpreted against the backdrop of a particular situation of discourse, such as a speaker moving past neighbors in a crowded cinema to take his/her seat (cf. Haegeman 1991: 246).[17]

(23)   *If you don't mind.*

It is this pragmatic bond with a specific context that frees the thetical from the convention of syntactic links and the linear constraints of SG. This flexibility, in turn, is essential for theticals to be able to fulfill their functional purpose as spontaneous reactions to the discourse situation. Rather than being restricted to the information coded in the text, theticals have the entire environment of discourse in their scope: the speaker, the hearer, their relation to one another, to the text, and to the situation in which discourse takes place (see Section 21.2.2), allowing the

---

[16] The notion of SG that we propose here is a narrow one compared to that of most other linguistic models, which tend to treat theticals as more or less marginal appendages of SG.

[17] That (23) is a thetical is suggested in particular by its specific elliptic structure, consisting of a subordinate clause but lacking a main clause (cf. (6e)).

speaker to present different "worlds" of experience in a concise and cost-effective way within one and the same utterance.

21.4 Relationship between the two domains

The observations made in this chapter are restricted to two domains of grammar that are suggestive of a competitive relationship. While the two domains are conceptually distinguished by both speakers and hearers, they interact with one another in a number of ways and to the extent that the resulting linguistic structures are not neatly separated from one another but rather have the appearance of a continuum.

Acknowledging the distinction between two different domains of grammar raises a number of questions, in particular the following two that are central to the discussions of this volume:

(a) What is relationship between the two domains: Is one of them dominant or more prominent?
(b) Are the two in competition?

With regard to question (a) it would seem that there are a number of reasons for assigning SG a central role. First, it provides a syntactic frame for structuring texts. Second, it accounts for most of the conceptual information and linguistic material to be found in texts. Third, it also provides a conceptual host for many, even if not for all categories of TG. And fourth, it provides the etymological source for theticals, in that the latter are invariably coopted from units of SG.

Nevertheless, there are reasons for not according SG any privileged status vis-à-vis TG. The main reason is that, like SG units, many instances of TG categories can form utterances of their own. Another reason is that, at least in spoken discourse, TG units may play a crucial role in structuring linguistic interaction, being at times more central to the communicative goals of speakers than SG units.

It is probably best to think of SG and TG as two complementary domains each of which is disposed to take care of different communicative roles. SG is ideally suited for presenting propositional information in a linear format (cf. the ideational function of Halliday 2004), relying on mechanisms such as clause structure, phrase structure, coordination, subordination, etc. As such, it is responsible for the linear development of ideas and the progression of communication with a view to some larger communicative goal (e.g., reporting an event, telling a story, arguing a case, etc.), all of which involve a certain amount of planning. TG, on the other hand, pursues more short term, instant communicative goals, typically in the form of a spontaneous reaction to the immediate situation of discourse. In that sense it can be seen as more interactional (Mazeland 2007: 1843ff.).

Depending on the type of communication, either SG or TG can be expected to play a more central role. Highly interactive conversation, for instance, can be expected to make greater use of TG than a written text. Irrespective of the text medium, however, most communicative events will show a certain tension between the need to develop the communication further on the propositional level while at the same time attending to the particulars of the immediate speech situation. SG and

TG can therefore be seen as competing domains in the sense that they will be activated to different degrees and for different purposes to respond to the changing discourse needs in an ongoing communicative event.

Question (b), whether the two domains compete with one another, raises a number of theoretical issues that we are not able to deal with satisfactorily in this chapter. If one assumes, as we in fact do, that the main goal of linguistic discourse is to communicate successfully, then a central concern of interlocutors is to search for an optimal solution for structuring their discourse presentations. In this search, the two domains provide an important alternative. SG is ideal for presenting conceptual-propositional information while TG lends itself particularly well to expressing speaker attitude and relating to the social interaction or the situation in which discourse takes place (see Section 2.2). But there are also communicative contents where the interlocutor can draw on information units from either domain—in other words, where there can be said to be direct competition between the two domains as, for example, in (13).

Instantaneous theticals can be seen as efficient in the sense that the communicative benefit derived from their use will outweigh the extra processing cost arising from the temporary suspension of the linear flow of SG. The extra processing effort required allows the speaker to respond flexibly and spontaneously to immediate discourse requirements. It can also be assumed that the processing cost for inserting a thetical will in most cases be less than the one required for packaging the same information into SG, which presumably involves more planning and may result in greater syntactic complexity. Rather than increasing the syntactic complexity of SG, theticals make demands on processing memory for the temporary interruption of the linear flow of communication. The use of a thetical—provided it is not too long and syntactically complex—is therefore likely to represent a more cost-effective option for the communicative returns it yields.

With formulaic theticals (see Section 21.2.3) the principle of economy is even more obvious. As units which are prefabs (Erman and Warren 2000) or fixed in structure, they are highly cost-effective and user-optimal in that they do not have to be assembled online and thereby reduce processing costs for the speaker. This is particularly important for spoken language, where the retrieval of fixed phrases frees up time needed for SG planning. More importantly, however, holistically stored phrases can be accessed quickly, which is necessary for spontaneous responses to the immediate situation of discourse.

21.5 Conclusion

In Section 21.1 we noted that our concern in this chapter is essentially with two main options that speakers have in deciding between competing forms of language structure. The chapter has tried to show that linguistic discourse organization operates on more than just a single plane and involves at least two different domains, namely that of Sentence Grammar and that of Thetical Grammar. Furthermore, we argue that one of the main goals of language use is to communicate successfully. Accordingly, a central concern of interlocutors is to search for an optimal solution for structuring their discourse presentations. In this search, the two domains distinguished provide an important alternative. Sentence Grammar is an almost ideal tool for presenting conceptual-propositional information. Thetical Grammar on the other hand has the entire situation of discourse in its scope; it is best suited to finding expressions for speaker attitudes, social interaction, or for information relating to the situation in which discourse takes place.

Competition comes in when the interlocutor has the option of drawing on information units from either domain for a given purpose. This appears to be the case, for example, when reporting an event can be encoded alternatively by means of an SG unit, that is, a main clause–complement construction as in (24a), or of a thetical comment clause, as in (24b).

(24)　a. He said that Britons could compete and win.
　　　b. Britons, **he said,** could compete and win. (ICE-GB; Kaltenböck 2007: 41)

With each of the two domains specializing in different communicative functions—SG being particularly apt for the linear development of propositional information and TG being especially suited for responses to immediate discourse needs—activation of each domain will depend on the specific type of communicative event. Most speech events, however, can be expected to involve both functions, that is, a close interplay between SG and TG. Using only TG would result in a deficit of conceptual-propositional expression. Using only SG, by contrast, would pose a serious problem to social interaction, and in some societies would come close to a collapse of linguistic communication. It seems safe to assume that the cognitive principle underlying the alternate activation of the two domains is that of cost-efficiency or economy (cf., e.g., Hawkins 2004). That there are contrasting cognitive-neural correlates associated with the distinction between the two domains has been argued by Heine et al. (2013), but this is an area that needs much further research.

Theticals play an important role not only on the level of language use, where they contribute significantly to discourse organization and effective communication, but also on the level of the grammatical system. From the point of view of grammar as an adaptive system (as briefly outlined in Section 21.1), theticals can be seen as an effective way of making grammar more flexible and adaptive to immediate discourse needs. As such, they are an important means that contributes to the overall "fitness" (Gell-Mann 1992) of Discourse Grammar.

Acknowledgments

We wish to express our gratitude to a number of colleagues who have been of help in writing this chapter, in particular to Brian MacWhinney, Andrej Malchukov, Edith Moravcsik, T. Givón, Martin Haspelmath, Jack Hawkins, Christa König, Tania Kuteva, Haiping Long, Heiko Narrog, Seongha Rhee, as well as to three anonymous referees of this chapter. The second-named author also wishes to thank the Korean Ministry of Education, Science and Technology for generously having sponsored the research leading to this chapter within its World Class University program.

22

Conclusions: Competition across time

BRIAN MACWHINNEY

Research on competing motivations has proceeded along two separate branches. The first, with an older academic pedigree, focuses on language change and typology. This branch has emphasized general motivations (often indicated by capitalization) such as Easiness, Faithfulness, Bias, or Harmony. The second branch has developed within psycholinguistics, where the focus has been on competition between specific linguistic forms in real time. Although these two branches may seem unrelated, they are in fact closely intertwined. This relation is articulated most clearly by the theory of usage-based linguistics which views the general motivations as background pressures biasing the specific online competitions. The current volume has been devoted to the exploration and integration of both of these two branches. In this chapter, I will argue that, in order to understand the relations between these two types of competition, we need to elaborate the theory of timeframe integration. We need to understand how processes organized on very different timeframes compete and cooperate to determine language processing in the present moment and its long-term cognitive and social consequences.

22.1 Competition and Systems Theory

Competition is fundamental to biological processes. Darwin (1859) showed how the evolution of the species emerges from the competition between organisms for survival and reproduction. The three basic principles underlying evolution are proliferation, competition, and selection. Proliferation generates organismic variation through mutation and sexual recombination. Organisms then compete for resources or rewards such as food, shelter, and the opportunity to reproduce. Finally, selection involves the ways in which strong and successful organisms produce offspring that also survive and reproduce.

In order to achieve proliferation, systems rely on the recombination of smaller parts. For biological evolution, the parts are the genes. For the brain, the parts are neuronal structures working in competition. In his seminal article on the architecture of complexity, Simon (1962) emphasized the idea that cognitive processes were partially decomposable into elementary information processes or modules. Minsky (1985) pursued this idea by characterizing the mind as a society of interacting smaller processes. Both Simon and Minsky believed that people could solve large problems by combining smaller pieces in various ways. For Simon, creativity arose from the proliferation of these combinations and the subsequent imposition of mental selection of the best outcomes. Current models of cognition such as ACT-R continue on the pathway outlined by Simon and Minsky, but with increasing emphasis on links between cognition and the brain (Anderson 2007).

Aware of the limits of reductionism, Simon (1962) emphasized that complex systems were only partially decomposable. Dressler, Libben, and Korecky-Kröll (this volume) raise this same concern regarding reductionism in their discussion of competing motivations. Indeed, work in the physical, biological, and social sciences has underscored the limits of reductionism and the importance of emergent patterns of organization on higher levels (Kontopoulos 1993). The basic principles here can be nicely illustrated by considering the four levels of emergent structure during protein folding (MacWhinney 2010). The primary structure of the protein is determined by the sequence of amino acids generated by copying sequences from RNA; the secondary structure involves coils and folds created by hydrogen bonding across the amino acid chain; the tertiary structure emerges from hydrophobic reactions and disulfide bridges across secondary structures; and the quaternary structure derives from the aggregation of polypeptide subunits based on the ternary structures. In this partially decomposable emergent system, each level involves a configuration of components from lower levels, but the biochemical constraints operative on each level are unique to that level and only operate once that level has emerged during the process of folding. I will argue that these principles of partial decomposability and level-specific constraints apply with even greater force to the study of language, where the interactions between levels and timeframes are so intense. Reduction of language to simple composition of single building blocks is clearly impossible. Instead, we need to understand how complex levels such as syntax or discourse build upon lower-level structures, while still responding to level-internal pressures and constraints. In the terms of Dressler et al. (this volume), the issue for language study is figuring out how much weight preferences from higher levels have upon choices at lower levels. In the end, this is a matter of measuring the strength of competing motivations and the ways in which they mesh.

Functionalist accounts such as the Competition Model (MacWhinney 2012) view forms as competing for the expression of communicative functions or motivations. Across time, variation within both individuals and speech communities creates a proliferation of forms, and selection then determines which of these forms should survive in which communicative niches. As MacWhinney, Bates, and Kliegl (1984) noted, "the forms of natural languages are created, governed, constrained, acquired and used in the service of communicative functions." Bates and MacWhinney (1982) dissected this position into three separate claims. The first is that language change across generations is controlled by communicative function; the second is that language acquisition in the child is shaped by communicative function; and the third is that language form in real-time conversations is controlled by communicative function. Back in 1982, it was not clear how to test or elaborate these claims and their interactions. However, ongoing advances in our understanding of the neural and social underpinnings of language now allow us to trace these interconnections in much finer detail.

To understand the linkages between processing, acquisition, and language change, we need to supplement current functionalist theories in two ways. First, we need theories that describe the mechanics of competition within individual timeframes in detail. Second, we need to understand how motivations arising from contrasting timeframes interact to impact these competitions.

22.2 The mechanics of competition

Linguistic theories often stop short of specifying the actual way in which forms compete. For example, Halliday's (2004) Systemic Function Grammar (SFG) describes in admirable detail an array of communicative options, but fails to take the additional step of showing how those options cooperate and compete during processing. Sociolinguistic accounts (Maling 2006) based on Variable Rule Analysis (Kay 1978), as well as Optimality Theory (Kager 1999) take the analyses a step further by quantifying or ranking the strengths of specific competitive processes. Psycho-linguistic models such as Parallel Distributed Processing (1986) or the Unified Competition Model (MacWhinney 2012) advance the discussion still further by proposing specific mechanisms of competition that align with what we know about processing on the neuronal level (Pulvermüller 2003; Rosenbaum, 2014).

Competing forms express underlying communicative motivations in differential ways, linked to alternative timeframes. Consider the example of German pronouns for referring to the hearer (Helmbrecht, this volume). In Middle High German, the 2PL pronoun *ihr* was used as an honorific when referring to a hearer of higher social status. In the seventeenth century the 3SG pronouns *er* and *sie* entered as more marked honorifics. In the eighteenth century, yet a fourth level of politeness was added by using 3PL pronouns for the honored hearers. Each of these shifts was motivated by a complex set of motives, including the basic need to express deference (Brown and Levinson 1987), emulation of the French court by other royal courts, influences from bilingual speakers, and imitation of the royal courts by other segments of society. Contravening these pressures for differential marking were pressures for economy of reference that eventually led to the collapse of the earlier four-level system to the two-level system of modern German. Across these centuries, fundamental social changes in Europe led to marked modulations in the strengths of the underlying motives. Apart from the social changes, there were processing motives linked to the complexity of multiple honorific levels and perceived changes in the fashionableness of new markings, once they had become widely diffused outside the court.

Other formal competitions may be responsive to very different motives. For example, relative clause extraposition (RCE) is influenced by processing motives such as clause length and intervening material length, as well as communicative motives such as definiteness, restrictiveness, previous mention, and presentational focus (Francis and Michaelis, this volume; Hawkins, this volume; Strunk, this volume). The forms of language arise from the complex interaction of these underlying motives, as discussed in every chapter in the current volume. In much of this literature, there is an emphasis on a basic competition between the motivations of Easiness and Faithfulness. It is true that many competitions can be viewed through this bipolar lens. However, there are other major motivation groups such as Politeness, Prestige, Social Solidarity, Paradigmatic Harmony, Bias, Retrievability, and Identifiability that have impacts throughout language. Moreover, these general motives are further expressed in complex and nuanced ways throughout language and communication. In fact, the competing motivations underlying language are as complex and varied as human life itself.

The handmaiden of competition is cooperation. As Du Bois (this volume) and Bates and MacWhinney (1982) have pointed out, humans have a great many ideas that they would love to express all at once. But language only allows us to say one thing at a time. One way in which language addresses this problem is by allowing motives to form coalitions. For Bates and MacWhinney (1982) the possible solutions to competition were: (1) peaceful coexistence, (2) divide-the-spoils, and (3) winner-take-all. We can illustrate these solutions by looking at subject marking in English. In the unmarked active transitive clause, the subject expresses a coalition of motives including agency, perspective, givenness, and topicality. This construction represents a *peaceful coexistence* or coalition between the motives, because they all point in the same direction. Peaceful coexistence arises from natural patterns of cooccurence in the real world. For example, the properties of solidity, boundary, and firmness tend to cooccur for objects. Animals tend to have cooccuring features of agency, movement, warmth, directed attention, and so on. The category of definiteness involves a peaceful coexistence based on uniqueness determined by relations such as class membership (*the first door*), unique geographical feature (*the Sahara*), object owned (*the University of Colorado*), and so on.

When speakers of a language choose to emphasize one of the features in a peaceful coalition over others, the coalition can break down, creating a *divide-the-spoils* solution. For example, English uses the passive construction as a way of dividing the spoils between the topic/perspective that wins the main prizes of subject position and agreement and the agent that is awarded the "consolation prize" of placement in a by-clause. An alternative to the divide-the-spoils approach is the *winner-take-all* solution. For English transitive verbs, this solution gives rise to the truncated passive. In that solution, the agent is not expressed at all. Moravcsik refers to the winner-take-all strategy as involving *override*, because one motivation overrides others. In addition, she and Malchukov (this volume) note that competition can be resolved through the strategy of *blocking* in which both motives fail to achieve mapping to surface forms. The Competition Model work has never considered the effects of *blocking*, because it is difficult to use as stimuli forms that do not occur.

22.3 Timeframes and meshing

We can illustrate the meshing of timeframes by looking at the great astronomical clocks or *horologs* in the Gothic city hall clock towers of Europe such as Lund, Prague, and Strasbourg. These clocks display the time in minutes, hours, days, and months, while also displaying the positions of the sun, moon, and the stars of the zodiac. Coordination of these displays is controlled by a central periodic oscillation that produces changes in the long-term positioning of the various dials through wheels that mesh in complex, but accurate ratios.

Timeframe meshing in human language is more complicated and more flexible than meshing in clocks. In language, meshing involves four different major systems: dynamic neural processing, memory storage, social interaction, and environmental changes. Within each of these major systems there are scores of additional timeframes that must all be coordinated to have their effects at the moment of speaking. Let us now take a closer look at each of these four major systems.

22.3.1 *Processing wheels*

Like the heart, the brain has central timekeepers or rhythms produced by neural assemblies sensitive to hormonal control (Buzsaki 2006). Such timekeepers can then control the iterative loops (Feldman 2006) involved in walking, breathing, or speaking. In speech, the basic iterative rhythm involves the repetitive production of syllables lasting about 150 ms each (Massaro 1975). The output of this basic wheel is modified by inputs from other wheels. For example, there is a wheel grounded in the lexicon that imposes syllabic stress. This second wheel operates not at the timeframe of the syllable, but at the slightly longer timeframe of the metrical foot. It must coordinate with syllabic rhythm in order to properly impact motor output. In this case, one wheel meshes with another, not because they are both driven by gears, but because the slower wheel becomes dynamically entrained across development by the faster wheel (Iverson and Thelen 1999). As in the rhythms controlling the beating of the heart, there are neural feedback mechanisms that can modify rhythms to respond to stress, relaxation, or sleep.

22.3.2 *Memory wheels*

Linkage across timeframes also depends on memory. In order to understand how this works, it will help to take a detour into the simpler world of the honeybee. Menzel (1999) explains how honeybee cognition relies on five memory phases, each involving different cellular processes, different timeframes, and different environmental challenges. The first phase is early short-term memory (eSTM). When foraging within a single patch of flowers of the same type, bees are able to maintain attention on a pollen source through activity within an activated neural ensemble (Edelman 1987; Pulvermüller 2003) without consolidation. In the second phase of late short-term memory (lSTM), synthesis of the PKA protein kinase begins to solidify the active circuit. The third phase of middle-term memory (MTM) spans a timeframe of hours and involves the formation of covalent modifications in the synapses between neurons. During these first three timeframes, bees have not yet returned to the hive, but are still processing flowers encountered during a single foraging bout. The fourth phase of memory consolidation relies on the formation of early long-term memories (eLTM) through the action of NO and PKC1. This type of consolidation is important, because it allows the bee to return to remembered pollen sources even after a trip back to the hive. The fifth phase of consolidation in late long-term memory (lLTM) operates across a timeframe of over three days, using PKC2 protein synthesis for even more permanent memories. Thus, each of the five phases of memory consolidation is responsive to the nature of the memory that must be retained to allow the bee to continue successful foraging.

This linkage of memory to ecological tasks is not unique to bees. We find the same five memory mechanisms operating across these timeframes in humans. For humans, there are additional mechanisms that support even more complex consolidation into cortical structures over longer timeframes for increasingly complex memories (Koechlin and Summerfield 2007). Many of these additional mechanisms rely on links between the hippocampus and the cortex (McClelland et al. 1995; Wittenberg et al. 2002), including episodic storage in the medial temporal lobes (Daselaar et al. 2004). Links between the hippocampus and auditory cortex also support our ability to pick up sequential and distributional statistical patterns (Thiessen and Erickson 2014).

Patterns that reveal themselves more slowly across longer timeframes, such as words, constructions, or social rules require more comparison across input exemplars (Ellis et al. 2014). Once a basic set of patterns has been stored in memory, new higher-level patterns can emerge through processes of generalization and association. Understanding how generalizations arise across multiple domains and timeframes is a fundamental task for the theory of child language development (MacWhinney 2014).

22.3.3 *Social wheels*

Bees also engage in communication to locate pollen sources (von Frisch 1962). However, what the bee finally encodes is not the information conveyed in these dances, but the actual nature and location of the pollen source. For humans, the details of the many spatiotemporal processes driving communicative interactions are of great importance in themselves. Children learn to be responsive to syllables, words, collocations, gestures, turn-taking patterns, proxemics, and other patterns during conversation. The long-term memories incorporating these patterns can be viewed as collections of social memes (Mesoudi et al. 2006). For these patterns, the Darwinian processes of proliferation, competition, and selection operate across spatiotemporal frames involving specific social interactions, which must then be further synchronized with the requirements of memory and processing.

22.3.4 *Environmental wheels*

Because so many aspects of our environment are shaped by human structures and interactions, it is often difficult to see how the long-term changes in the natural environment produce impacts on language. In the extreme, forces such as glaciation, global warming, desertification, hurricanes, epidemics, or famine can lead to extinctions of whole language groups. However, the power of these natural forces is no greater than that of the forces of war, genocide, migration, and slavery brought about by man upon man.

22.4 Why study timeframes

The reader may ask whether it is really important for linguists to understand the meshing of timeframes. There are three answers to this question. The first is that failure to appreciate timeframe meshing can lead to the generation of unproductive debates. This problem is particularly acute for the theory of Competing Motivations, because the global motivations impacting output are not unitary pressures, but rather complex interactions across many wheels for processing, memory, and social interaction. Without understanding how motivations impact wheels across timeframes, we cannot understand how global motivations like Faithfulness and Easiness get cashed out in detail. The second answer is that the audio and video data we record from language production arise from the meshing of all these wheels. In order to detect the effects of these processing, memory, and social forces, we need to pull them apart statistically and analytically by detecting patterns in their combined effects on the output. This is the empirical approach of the Competition Model and variationist analysis (Poplack and Cacoullos 2014), as well as the major lesson to be derived from the chapters in this book. The third reason for wanting to understand the meshing of timeframes is to advance the scientific content of interactions across Linguistics, Biology, Psychology, and Sociology. In this chapter, my goals for timeframe analysis are more modest. Here, I will simply focus on considering how the findings presented in this volume can be interpreted in terms of the theory of timeframe meshing.

Online meshing takes in motives or pressures from across at least ten major functional domains of competition or *arenas*. These ten arenas include: word production, word comprehension, sentence production, sentence comprehension, language acquisition, diachronic change, interactional maintenance, encounter structure, group membership, and phylogenetic change. We will focus our attention here on the first six of these arenas, saying only a little about the next three, and nothing about phylogenetic change (but see MacWhinney 2008a).

22.5 Word production

Word production is the first functional arena we will examine. We have already described the 150 ms timeframe during which single syllables are articulated and the way in which wheels operating on other timeframes mesh into this syllabic backbone. This involves the meshing of word-level patterns into a sequence of motor commands being formulated in motor cortex. There are even more rapid timeframes at the output end of speech production that involve the tuning of articulatory gestures by the cerebellum and basal ganglia.

Those timeframes are important for understanding the competition between Faithfulness and Easiness. Faithfulness requires a close match between the output and the target form in long-term memory. On the level of specific articulatory gestures, as modulated by the cerebellum, Faithfulness attempts to hit articulatory targets (MacNeilage 1998) or end points as accurately as possible. To implement Faithfulness across the board, the speaker must increase attentional control and monitoring at both the lexical and articulatory levels (Roelofs 2011). However, attention is a limited good. So, increased Faithfulness to one aspect of communication, such as articulation, could come at the expense of reduced attention to some other aspect of behavior, such as monitoring for appropriate conversational sequencing or paying attention to where one is walking. Competing with Faithfulness is the motivation of Easiness that seeks to minimize effort in production. Easiness leads to all manners of assimilations and deletions, both within and between words. During speech, it can be implemented in a general manner by reducing attention. These reductions in attention can then impact individual wheels operating on lexical selection, tongue position, and so on. However, similar effects may arise instead from the long-term storage of reduced forms for frequent collocations, rather than from online processing at the moment (Bybee and Beckner 2014). The application of Easiness is facilitated by the fact that speech is so redundant that the listener can still extract the message despite omissions and assimilations. In this sense, the shape of language represents a long-term memetic adaptation to the competing demands of Easiness and Faithfulness during language usage (Regier et al. 2014).

Direct competitions arise not from the global motivations, but from specific forms that compete tightly for similar ecological niches. Consider the case of the production of *flaste* as a blend between *flavor* and *taste* (Stemberger 1985). Here, the speaker is trying to describe the flavor and taste of a type of ice cream. Both lexical items become activated at the same time, in part because they reside in the same area of the lexical map. Normal lexical processing works in a winner-take-all fashion to choose a single best matching item. However, in this particular case, the competition is not resolved in time and both elements manage to activate gestures in the output articulatory buffer, resulting in *flaste* as a blend error. In this way, various speech error phenomena, including exchanges, anticipations, perseverations, and omissions arise from failures to control lexical competition and activation. For example, Pouplier and Goldstein (2010) showed how competition operates up to the last minute in the production of consonantal anticipations. Pfeiffer (this volume) shows that corrections are sensitive to the shape of the construction in which they are embedded. In German, prepositions are tightly linked to their nouns through case and gender. Therefore, prepositional phrases constitute a unit of production. When the nouns in these prepositional phrases are corrected for semantic reasons, then the whole prepositional phrase must be retraced. English repairs, on the other hand, are far less likely to require retracing of the preposition. Through fine-grained analyses of this type, we can see how lexical competition shines a flashlight on the structures involved during the speech production process.

Current theories view lexical items as structured into *gangs* based on semantic similarity (Armstrong and Plaut 2008) and *cohorts* based on phonological similarity

(Norris 1994). The theory of self-organizing feature maps (SOFM) (Kohonen 2001) links these gangs to specific neighborhoods in the local neural topography. Analogy arises from the extension of local patterns to neighboring items and competition arises between similar items in the neighborhood. There is evidence that the brain uses this system of topological organization across all types of cortical areas, ranging from tonotopic organization in auditory cortex (Wessinger et al. 1997) to the detailed somatotopic body maps located in motor cortex (Hauk et al. 2004).

As in the case of articulatory processing, there are neuronal events at very quick timeframes that shape the overall outcome of lexical access. The basic speed of neuronal firing is in the order of 2–7 ms. If we consider that it takes perhaps 150 ms to activate a lexical item, then at least a dozen connections could be firing during this period. Some of these firings will be incomplete, some will require summation, and some will involve connections from distant cortical areas that will take somewhat longer to transmit impulses, but there is clearly time for a rich variety of interactions between items and patterns, particularly within tightly organized lexical areas. Much of the competition occurring within lexical fields involves inhibition. Inhibitory processes operate not only within gangs, but also between larger areas. Inhibition plays a major role in controlling language selection in bilinguals (Prior and MacWhinney 2010) and there are also fundamental processes of competition, cooperation, and inhibition that operate between the two cerebral cortices (Gazzaniga 1970).

Another major source of competition during production involves the coordination of gesture and speech. Just as prosody must integrate itself temporally into the 150 ms wheel of syllable production, gesture must integrate itself into the peaks and valleys of prosody. Some gestures are planned to coincide with lexical stresses; others are intended to align with pauses. McNeill (2005) and others believe that this synchronization between language and gesture occurs because both forms of expression arise from shared "growing points" within the fundamental system of embodied cognition (MacWhinney 2008b).

Production involves far more than lexical access and articulation. To produce complex words and sentences, we must figure out how to combine lexical items. Dual-route models of morphological processing of the type formulated by Mac-Whinney (1978) or Pinker (1999) are based on a competition between rote and combination. To study this competition, Stemberger and MacWhinney (1986) used resistance to induced speech errors to show that high frequency regulars such as *wanted* are more often produced by rote than lower frequency regulars like *spliced*. Because both rote and combination produce the same outcome, we cannot know which pathway is operative in a given case. It is possible that advances in neuroimaging such as MEG, ECoG, or NIRS may eventually allow us to trace these effects, but we already know that both routes are possible and that speakers rely on one route for some trials and the other route for other trials, depending on additional factors, such as previous lexical priming. Psychologists refer to competitions of this type as "horse races" in which two or more processes are operating in parallel and the faster one wins (Ratcliff et al. 1999). These basic facts regarding alternative brain pathways, horse races, and the cooperative and competitive nature of language processing are incompatible with grammatical formulations that view language processing as algorithmic, deterministic, and strictly modular. It is this underlying processing indeterminacy that gives rise to the conclusion (Sapir 1921) that "all grammars leak."

The competition between rote and combination is reflected historically in the forces that determine the order of derivational and inflectional morphemes. As Dressler et al. (this volume) note, affix order is governed by a principle of relatedness: Derivational markers are closer to the stem than inflectional markers both positionally and conceptually. This tendency can be seen as a consequence of the tendency for derived forms to be encoded by rote (lexicalization) rather than combination. Forms that are retrieved by rote can then be treated as units for further inflectional processing, whereas trying to insert inflectional markings into already unitized rote forms would be difficult. In terms of processing and memory, derivational forms can be retrieved as wholes, because their shape is seldom altered by syntactic combination. Because derivational forms are stored by rote, they are then exposed to memetic forces for phonological changes and semantic drift.

Mondorf's analysis (this volume) of the competition between the synthetic comparative (e.g. *fuller*) and the analytic comparative (e.g. *more full*) in English provides detailed evidence regarding the competition between rote and combination. Synthetic forms are more likely to be stored and produced by rote, whereas analytic forms are most likely to be produced by combination. Mondorf (2009a) shows how competition between these two form types is influenced by twenty-six factors or motives. In general, there is a preference for the synthetic form when the stem is short and there are few additional factors complicating processing. This preference could reflect the fact that, in the race against combination, rote retrieval will win as long as the target form is high in frequency. If processing is slowed down by additional factors, then there will be more time for the analytic comparative to win out in the competition.

Mondorf notes that the analytic operator *more* can also function as a quantifier and the synthetic suffix *-er* can also function as an agentive suffix. She suggests that these ambiguities should diminish the validity of these cues, as analyzed by the Competition Model. A similar point was raised by Pelham (2011) in regard to the difficulties that ambiguities cause to children learning English pronouns. However, ambiguity will only have this effect if alternative readings arise in actual sentence processing. In the case of the comparative, the theory of item-based processing (MacWhinney 1975a) holds that the comparative reading is only activated if the head is an adjective. During processing, there can be a brief moment of uncertainty regarding the identity of the head in processing of sequences such as *more heavy armour*, but once attachment is resolved, the cue itself is completely reliable.

Haspelmath (this volume) considers another consequence of the horse race between rote and combination. This is the competition between marking and zero marking. Typically, zero marking applies to highly frequent unmarked categories such as Singular or Subject. It also arises in patterns such as differential object marking (DOM) (Malchukov 2008a). In all of these cases, zero marking expresses Easiness without sacrificing Faithfulness, as long as the contrasting cases are marked.

Haspelmath (this volume) notes that the preference of zero marking for high frequency items can occasionally be reversed under the pressure of analogy, which is the motive that Malchukov calls *Harmony*. To derive a fuller understanding of the competition between Easiness, Faithfulness, and Harmony, we will need to dig more deeply into the psycholinguistics of lexical competition. Specifically, we need to contrast analytic lexical combination (*more happy*), inflectional combination (*runs*), compositional compounding (*cherry pie*), non-compositional compounding (*blackboard*), derivational combination (*happier, feathers*), morphological rote with analogical or minor rule support (*bend-bent, send-sent*), and full rote (*went*). These various levels of analyticity involve not just the competition between rote, analogy, and combination (MacWhinney 1975b), but also the contrast between combinations of free and bound morphemes, transparent and opaque semantics (Plaut and Gonnerman 2000). We can better understand the full range of competitions by linking each of these pressures to the neurological mechanisms that support real-time production.

Pursuing his examination of the role of systematicity and analogy, Haspelmath notes that lexical classes are grounded on semantic and syntactic contrasts, rather than frequency information. He says that there is something "very natural" about these divisions, but that "we do not know what it is." Let me suggest that this pervasive feature of human language arises from the way in which the lexicon is structured in the cortex during development. For example, the DevLex model of the child's lexical acquisition (Li et al. 2007) shows how lexical groups emerge in self-organizing maps (Kohonen 2001) by detecting correlated regularities (Burgess and Lund 1997) in syntactic combination and semantic features. This form of organization is important because it allows distant connections from frontal areas to connect accurately to the correct part of speech and grammatical class areas in lexical space. Essentially, the brain provides mechanisms for the support of lexical field organization that function in parallel for both semantic classes and grammatical classes.

22.6 Word recognition

Word recognition relies on a basic auditory wheel that is synchronized to the same 150 ms timeframe as the articulatory wheels that produce chains of syllables (Massaro 1987). As in word production, lexical items compete during recognition in terms of gangs and cohorts. However, during perception, there is no requirement for lexical items to trigger events in the motor cortex. Instead, the impact of word recognition and sentence comprehension is to trigger interpretations in mental model space. During this process, comprehension involves motivations that are analogous to Faithfulness and Easiness in production. In recognition, the basic competition is between the Faithfulness achieved by focusing on bottom-up activation and the constructive Easiness achieved by relying on top-down information. Speed-readers rely on top-down information and minimize reliance on bottom-up information. If they use this balance carefully and strategically, they can still achieve good comprehension in less time than those who focus on the bottom-up information provided by individual words. Sentence processing shows similar effects.

Beginning second language learners find that they spend so much time focusing on individual lexical items that they sometimes miss the overall message of a sentence. As they learn to integrate top-down processes with bottom-up information, their processing improves (Presson et al. 2013).

Word recognition is fundamentally easier than word production. This difference reflects the fact that recognition is easier than recall. In the case of recognition, there are usually enough intersecting cues in the input to determine a unique winning word. Exceptions occur under conditions of noise. In production, we often fail to recall names or words that we would easily recognize. This is because recall involves the smooth generation and utilization of cues to separate out a winning word from its competitors.

22.7 Sentence comprehension

Sentence comprehension for spoken language operates within a timeframe of a few seconds. Although there is no fixed rhythmicity within this timeframe, there is a default framework for organizing comprehension in terms of the unit of the clause. Within this frame, comprehension is subject to the same competing pressures of Faithfulness, Easiness, and Harmony that we find at other timescales. Research in the Competition Model framework (<http://psyling.talkbank.org/UCM>) has analyzed sentence comprehension and production in terms of the competition between functions and forms. In production, functions compete for mapping to forms. In comprehension, forms compete for mapping to functions. Although these two processes work in opposite directions, they rely on a common set of form–function mappings and cue strengths. Because it is easier to control stimuli in comprehension experiments, there is more Competition Model work on sentence comprehension than on sentence production, although the model has been articulated for both processes. As in word recognition, sentence comprehension involves a competition between top-down processes that maximize Easiness and bottom-up processes that maximize Faithfulness. These motivations operate both cooperatively and competitively. Faithfulness works to link together lexical items into grammatical relations, based on item-based frames and higher-order constructions (MacWhinney 1975a, 1982, 1987, 2012). This is done on the basis of cues to attachment relations found in word order, morphological markers, and lexical semantics. For example, in the English sentence *the girl ate the apple*, the choice of *girl* as the agent is favored by the preverbal positioning cue, as well as the animacy cue. Listeners use these various cues to determine attachment, assign grammatical roles, and process anaphoric links between referents. Easiness or top-down processing can work to speed up bottom-up processing by forming biases and anticipations (Elman 1990) that may occasionally be contradicted by bottom-up information. When this happens, comprehension can involve slowdowns for ambiguity resolution or recovery from garden pathing.

In a given sentence, cues often yield alternative possible attachments and interpretations. To resolve these competitions, listeners rely on cue strength. In accord with Darwinian theory, the model holds that the strongest cues are the ones that have proven themselves most reliable in previous comprehension efforts. The

Competition Model views both first and second language acquisition as a process of learning these cues and setting their proper relative strengths. The timeframe of this learning extends over years, but the strengthening of individual cues occurs each time a sentence is processed. When the cues function correctly, each usage leads to a modest growth in strength, eventually producing proceduralization, fluency, and entrenchment (MacWhinney 2012). When the use of a cue leads to error, its strength is diminished and there can be a search for additional cues to resolve the competition. In this way, the fast moving timeframe of sentence comprehension meshes with the much slower process of setting cue strengths.

The principles of the Competition Model have been incorporated into a variety of other accounts, with additional mechanistic (MacDonald et al. 1994; Elman et al. 2005; O'Grady 2005) and neurolinguistic (Bornkessel-Schlesewsky and Schlesewsky, this volume) detail. In order to provide ways of comparing first and second language acquisition, the basic principles of the model have been reformulated in the Unified Competition Model (MacWhinney 2012). Nearly all of the chapters in this volume explore issues of relevance to the Competition Model. What is exciting is the way in which all this new data allows us to deepen our understanding of the linkage of competing motivations across divergent cue types and timeframes.

22.7.1 *Cues and biases*

The primary empirical claim in the Competition Model is that cue strength (as measured in sentence processing experiments) is a direct function of cue reliability (as measured from corpora). To achieve high cue strength, it is not enough for a cue to be merely frequent, rather it is more important that it be reliable and always point to the correct interpretation when it is present. Although a basic level of frequency is necessary for cue learning, the model holds that it is reliability and not frequency that is the determinant of strength or entrenchment. There are several additional factors that modify this basic relation between cue strength and reliability.

The most important limitations to the force of reliability stem from processing or *cue cost* factors, including ambiguity. When listeners are allowed to assign grammatical relations after the end of the sentence, we find an optimal pattern of cue integration based on reliability. However, when competition is measured online using ERP, crossmodal priming, joystick motions, or picture choice, a different pattern emerges. In this case, listeners depend on the most dominant cue in the language and attempt to assign that cue to one of the items in the clause.

A second major limitation relates to the Bias motivation triggered by perspective taking. In all languages studied so far, the first nominal functions as the default starting point or perspective for sentence interpretation (Bornkessel-Schlesewsky and Schlesewsky, this volume; MacWhinney, 1977, 2010; Gernsbacher 1990). The timeframe for perspective maintenance derives from higher-level top-down processes of discourse interpretation and integration, but it meshes with sentence level cues on the quicker timeframe needed to determine role assignment.

For sentence comprehension, Bornkessel-Schlesewsky and Schlesewsky (this volume) demonstrate the pervasiveness of the preference for assignment of an initial nominal to the actor role. The Perspective Hypothesis (MacWhinney 1977) links this bias to the fact that people use the "starting points" of sentences to construct actions from their own human perspective. In a series of comprehension studies, Gernsbacher (1990) showed how pervasive this bias is in English. McDonald and MacWhinney (1995) were able to show that the establishment of a perspectival bias in a sentence persists across a longer timeframe than do more punctate cues such as implicit causality and pronominal coreference. MacWhinney and Pleh (1988) showed that perspective is temporally dominant, even in a language like Hungarian that makes strong use of case-marking and topic-marking. As long as we are dealing with SVO, SOV, and VSO languages, the application of the Perspective Hypothesis is fairly straightforward. Although VOS languages like Malagasy or Tagalog would seem to defy the linkage of perspective to the first nominal, we do not yet have published work evaluating how topic, perspective, and agency operate in processing terms in these languages.

The Competition Model analyzed the subject category as a coalition of the motives of agency, givenness, topic, and perspective. Bornkessel-Schlesewsky and Schlesewsky (this volume) show how such coalitions can be understood in terms of the theory of attractor networks. They then consider the important issue of the timeframe of the components of this coalition. The component with the most enduring timeframe is that of the human perspective. Consider the sentence, *the ball hit the boy*. The viewpoint of a boy is always more basically human than the viewpoint of a ball. However, if the previous discourse has been discussing its motions then *the ball* may be more topical. The most fast-moving timeframe is the one that determines agentive action. In this case, the action of hitting promotes the candidacy of *the ball* for subject. Well-constructed texts maintain a single topic as the perspective throughout, contradicting agency as necessary to trigger constructions such as the passive, the inverse, object fronting, or clefting. The Perspective Hypothesis views these shifts as causing increased processing load, and Bornkessel-Schlesewsky and Schlesewsky cite ERP studies by Hung and Schumacher (2012) confirming this claim. Bornkessel-Schlesewsky and Schlesewsky then proceed to argue that processing of the subject coalition utilizes the dorsal neural processing stream. This claim is in accord with the analysis of MacWhinney (2009), as well as that of Koechlin and Summerfield (2007). It is clear that agency is more local and initial than topic and perspective. However the details of the temporal, neural, and conceptual relation between topicality and perspective may require further analysis.

22.7.2 *Competition and the acquisition of grammar*

The Competition Model has also been used to account for the learning of grammatical patterns in various languages. Some of the most creative and convincing work in this area has come from workers in Leipzig, Manchester, and Liverpool. This group has emphasized the role of usage-based inputs to the child and the role of item-based constructions and formulas (Tomasello 2003a). Within this framework, Krajewski and Lieven (this volume) provide a clear summary of the Competition Model approach to grammatical development. They review a set of recent studies using sentences with novel verbs in transitive sentences. Unlike earlier Competition Model studies, these new studies allow us to separate learning based on individual verbs from learning of more general constructions. This method tends to focus more on later stages of development, rather than the earlier development of the control of grammatical marking on the basis of item-based patterns. For example, Dabrowska and Tomasello (2008) taught Polish children a new verb that took an object in the instrumental case in one gender. They found that even 2-and-a-half-year olds were then able to mark new objects in another gender with the instrumental. But this learning is based on the single new verb that was taught and hence is only item-based, rather than construction-based. It is important to remember that individual verbs continue to behave in unique item-based ways even in adult sentence processing (Corrigan 1986; Trueswell and Tanenhaus 1994). From the viewpoint of the theory of timeframes, what is important about all of this work is the way in which it provides us with additional understanding of the quick acquisition of item-based patterns and the much slower acquisition of generalized constructions that are being abstracted in memory from collections of item-based patterns.

Rowland, Noble, and Chan (this volume) provide further detail on this issue by examining the competition for object and recipient roles in dative constructions in English, Welsh, and Cantonese. MacWhinney (in press) shows how constructions operate in terms of a hierarchy with item-based patterns at the lowest level, functional constructions at the mid-level, and global patterns at the highest level of generality. These three levels correspond naturally to three developmental timeframes with item-based patterns being acquired quickly and more general constructions being slower to form. There is little dispute about the existence of these contrasting levels of generalization (Goldberg, 2006; Kemp et al. 2007). However, the details of these developments are not yet well quantified. The studies by Rowland et al. (this volume) are quite important in that regard. They show how competition between constructions slows initial acquisition in English and Cantonese. In Welsh, where there is no such competition, datives are acquired earlier. These findings are in accord with the Competition Model analysis, as well as Slobin's (1973) one-form/one-function principle which holds that acquisition is facilitated when the child can map a form directly and simply to a single function, but delayed when the mapping is more complex and ambiguous. In terms of the theory of timeframe meshing, this suggests that delays in acquisition will arise as the child strives to acquire additional cues to sort out and control the details of the competition.

22.8 Sentence production

For sentence production, the speaker relies on the same system of cues and weights that support comprehension. This insures that the speaker marks functions in a way that can be accurately decoded by the listener. To achieve this linkage, comprehension and performance must refer to a core representational format for phonology (Hickok 2009), lexicon (Li et al., 2007), syntax (Kempen 2014), and pragmatics (Haiman, this volume). Unlike the competence component of generative theory (Chomsky 1975), the Competition Model views this shared format as composed of a relatively simple set of linked form–function mappings or constructions (Goldberg 2006). The fundamental difference between production and comprehension is that production maps functions to forms, whereas comprehension maps forms to functions. Thus, sentence production involves recall, whereas sentence comprehension involves recognition. Just as word production is more difficult than word recognition, sentence production is more difficult that sentence comprehension. In production, one must make a series of careful choices regarding conjugation, declension, and complex sentence patterns. Some of these decisions must be made well in advance, even when the speaker has not fully formulated (Levelt 1989) the complete form of the utterance. Because of this, the motivation of Easiness plays a greater role in sentence production than sentence comprehension.

Three chapters in this volume explore ways in which forms compete during production. These chapters focus specifically on how competing motivations determine the positioning of relative clauses. Looking at 1,300 sentences from the Tübingen Treebank of Written German, Strunk (this volume) finds that relative clause extraposition (RCE) to the end of the sentence is favored by four factors: long relative clauses, absence of any intervening DP, minimal amounts of intervening material, and indefiniteness of the head. In an acceptability judgment study, Strunk finds that the presence of a demonstrative modifier, such as *derjenige* 'that one' on the head can increase the acceptability of clauses that have been extraposed across long distances.

In a second chapter on this topic, Francis and Michaelis (this volume) also find that RCE increases when extraposed clauses are longer, when the subject noun is indefinite, when the predicate is presentational or passive, and when the predicate is accessible from prior discourse context. This patterning indicates that RCE is functioning very much like a presentational construction. Using stepwise logistic regression, Francis and Michaelis show that each of these four factors makes an independent contribution. Moreover, the model based on a complete integration of the factors is nearly a perfect fit to the data. Interestingly, there are times when this smooth cue integration breaks down. Francis and Michaelis note that one of the instances that violated the cue prediction model was this marginally acceptable spoken production: *The best singer is this Olaf Bergh that I've seen.* Here, the RCE of *that I've seen* seems to be functioning more as a real afterthought, than as a presentational construction.

This type of complete cue integration described by Francis and Michaelis is comparable numerically to the high levels of model fit reported from Competition Model studies of cue integration (McDonald and MacWhinney 1989) for case role assignment. Such clear and stable results emphasize the extent to which the language processor is able to integrate patterns from contrasting timeframes online. Although these cues derive from somewhat different timeframes, they must all be available at the time when the head noun is produced, so that the speaker can produce either RCE or non-RCE at the transition between the subject and the predicate. In effect, production models must be structured to allow for online cue integration from these contrasting timeframes.

In a third chapter dealing with competition in production, Hawkins (this volume) shows how a wide range of typological patterns can be understood in terms of competing motivations. The fundamental constructs of this analysis align very closely with those from the Competition Model, while extending that analysis in important ways to typological data. Like O'Grady (2005) and MacWhinney (1987), Hawkins argues that the processor attempts to minimize cue cost by forming phrasal attachments as soon as possible. This principle accounts for the preference for short intervening domains in RCE observed by Strunk, Francis and Michaelis, and Hawkins (1994). It also explains how competing prepositional phrases are ordered in relation to the main verb, why languages attempt to place prepositions close to the verb and nouns to which they relate, what forms of center embedding are most generally tolerated, and the competition of direct objects and oblique arguments for positioning near the verb. However, the process of minimizing domains is not the only motivation in sentence production. Hawkins also considers the preference for placing fillers before gaps, showing that this motivation is stronger than the motivation for minimizing domains, when the two are in competition. This results in a preference for placing the relative clause after the head noun in OV languages like Hungarian or Persian. Further exploring the relative strength of competing motivations, Hawkins shows how a semantically based principle of placing the Agent before the Patient can compete with the motivation of consistency of case marking. Following Primus (1999), he shows how languages that have been described as OVS or OSV are really functioning not to prepose Patient before Agent, but to prepose Absolutive before Ergative, because this reduces the load on working memory. Despite this advantage for ordering Absolutive first, the fact that most ergative languages place the Ergative first indicates that the Bias motivation for marking the thematic role of agency is inherently stronger than the Harmony motivation for marking case (Malchukov, this volume), in accord with the analyses of Bornkessel-Schlesewsky and Schlesewsky (this volume) and MacWhinney (1977).

Optimality Theory—as represented in this volume by chapters from Malchukov and Lamers and De Hoop—provides another framework for analyzing preferences and competition. Lamers and De Hoop find a relatively higher level of object fronting in the elicited production of sentences with unaccusative psych verbs in Dutch such as *bevallen* 'to please' as opposed to causative psych verbs such as *overtuigen* 'to convince.' In order to produce utterances that begin with animate nouns as their starting point (MacWhinney 1977), Dutch speakers can either use passives or OVS word order. However, passivization is not possible for the unaccusatives. This means that, instead of using the consolation prize of the passive, Dutch speakers must resort to the consolation prize of OVS ordering for the unaccusatives. As a result, the strengths of OVS and passivization are reversed for the unaccusative psych verbs compared to the causative psych verbs. This leaves open the question of why the unaccusatives do not allow passivization. To account for this, Lamers and De Hoop note that the subjects of causative psych verbs such as *overtuigen* 'to convince' are more agent-like than the subjects of unaccusative psych verbs such as *bevallen* 'to please.' This effect seems to be centered in the implicit causality relations (McDonald and MacWhinney 1995) of the verb. With a verb such as *convince*, there is an animate object that undergoes a psychological change of state or knowledge, whereas with a verb such as *please*, the animate object barely changes psychological state. It is the activity of this change of mental state that qualifies the object of the causative psych verb for passivization. This analysis shows how case role and word order cue configurations are determined first by the semantics of individual verbs, and then by the semantics of larger verb groups (MacWhinney, in press).

22.8.1 *Production, typology, and language change*

When we move from synchronic studies of sentence production to studies of typology and language change, we cross a major divide in our thinking about competing motivations. Synchronic studies can observe competition in progress at the moment, whereas diachronic studies must assume that changes emerge from the variation inherent in synchronic competitions. It is at the moment of sentence production that a speaker will drop an ending, level a paradigm, or forge a new construction. However, we can use our understanding of forces operative in the moment to illuminate the past. There is nothing radical about this assumption—it is the same assumption upon which Evolutionary Biology (Darwin 1859), Astronomy, and Geology (Hutton 1788) are based. Evolutionary Biologists, such as Darwin, are confronted with a pattern of distribution of species at a given moment in geological time and space and must reason back from this pattern to an understanding of the forces governing this distribution. Astronomers can access historical depth by comparing images derived from alternative distances in the cosmos. They can reason back from these snapshots across time to an understanding of the forces and patterns generating these images and changes. Geologists have access to present patterns of deposition, erosion, and orogeny, as well as the relatively complete record of the past available from rock exposures and drill cores. By considering detailed records of the moment of speaking across time, language scientists have access to similar data. Like astronomers, geologists, and evolutionary biologists, they must use these data to figure out how diverse processes mesh across time.

The emergence of differential object marking (DOM) (Malchukov 2008a) can be viewed as an illustration of the meshing of online pressures into the slower diachronic timeframe. For example, languages like Turkish and Hebrew may mark the direct object when it is highly prominent in terms of its definiteness. Over time, this marking can extend to other types of prominent objects, as in Spanish. In these developments, Harmony comes to dominate over Easiness. Eventually, the marking can extend to all objects and become no longer differential, as in Hungarian.

Hughes and Allen's (this volume) study of subject omission in child language provides an useful window on how synchronic pressures can lead to diachronic changes. They show that young English-speaking children tend to omit subjects when these are highly accessible (MacWhinney and Bates 1978). Hyams (2011), Ariel (1990) and others have noted similar effects of accessibility in adult pro-drop languages such as Italian or Chinese. In effect, the same pressures for dropping subjects that operate in adult Italian can be seen in both child English and highly informal conversational English. More generally, across languages and constructions, we can often first see the effects of pressures for Easiness in child language and informal adult conversation.

Malchukov (this volume) argues that variations in alignment preferences across constructions may arise from the competition between the motivations of Bias and Harmony. Malchukov's Bias motivation includes a cluster of motivations impacting alignments between role relationships across constructions. In particular, he notes that imperatives tend to prefer accusative alignment, whereas nominalizations show a preference for ergative alignment. Malchukov argues that Harmony modifies this construction-specific biases. Like Cristofaro (this volume) and Newmeyer (this volume), he stresses the extent to which alternative resolutions of these Bias pressures arise from complex interactions of constructional types in a language at a given point in its historical development. For ergative languages, one solution to the competition between Bias and Harmony is to ignore ergative Harmony and to shift entirely to accusative marking for imperatives. Another is to retain absolutive agreement in imperatives, while losing ergative agreement. Yet another solution prohibits expression of the ergative A in an imperative, while allowing expression of the absolutive A. Malchukov's analyses show how the competition between Bias and Harmony is filtered out into finer detail against a backdrop of other features of the language such as case marking and agreement details.

Harmony can also exert a pressure toward reinterpretation of "peaceful coexistence" relations. Cristofaro (this volume) notes how the topic marker in !Xun is being reinterpreted as a subject marker. As Bates and MacWhinney (1982) and many others have noted, the high correlation between topic, givenness, perspective, and agency produces systems in which markings express all of these functions at once, but with differential emphasis in alternative competing constructions. As Dressler et al. (this volume) note, systems of interdependent motivations of this type are "the most problematic ones to identify and classify." They are also the most likely targets for reinterpretation across generations. Over time, a marking that is narrowly identified with one of these functions in the interlocking system can be reinterpreted as marking another motivation in the set (MacWhinney 1989). These readjustments are the linguistic equivalents of changes in Evolutionary Biology in which new forms arise to interpret old forms and new functions are first interpreted by old forms.

In another illustration of this process of reinterpretation, Cristofaro shows how markers of O(bject) can arise from the reinterpretation of verbs like *take*, whereas markers of A(gent) arise from the reinterpretation of deictics. For both alignment systems and number marking, Cristofaro shows how changes in the grammar can arise from the reinterpretation and grammaticalization of particular morphemes. This position is further supported by Newmeyer's (this volume) analysis of competing patterns for preposition-stranding and aux-inversion in English. In such cases of reinterpretation, it often happens that only parts of a construction move to the new configuration, leaving other parts in the old state. In general, such cases of reinterpretation to maximize Harmony provide good illustrations of the operations of competition and selection (MacWhinney 1989).

Competing motivations operating across diverse timeframes also impact the selection of more lexically limited grammatical constructions. Ariel (this volume) examines the competitions of lexicalized forms for marking disjunction. The choice between the marking of disjunction with *or* as opposed to more specific constructions such as *or else, or something like that*, and *perhaps* depends on the extent to which the speaker wants to favor Faithfulness over Easiness. An even more extreme case of favoring Easiness over Faithfulness arises in cases where the conjunction is omitted altogether, leaving it to the listener to infer a disjunction. As Ariel points out, the development of these systems over time is governed by both Faithfulness and Easiness. The use of old forms for new functions initially supports Easiness over Faithfulness. However, over time, these new functions for old forms give rise to their own new forms, eventually increasing Faithfulness. A good example of a change of this type that may be in progress involves the reduction in English of the phrase *or something like that* to merely *or something*.

22.9 Interactional pressures

When people engage in conversations, they find themselves subjected to a wide variety of interactional pressures. They are supposed to be relevant, brief, and helpful (Grice 1975); they should follow rules of conversational sequencing (Schegloff 2007); they should take their listeners perspective by implementing recipient design (Garfinkel 1967); they should follow and appreciate the communications of the other person; and they should maintain topic flow and relevance (Halliday and Hasan 1976). As Augustine (1952) put it, they should "delight, inform, and persuade." To keep all of these balls in the air, speakers make use of a wide variety of conversational devices such as tempo change, prosodic variation, overlap, pausing, gesture, and proxemics, as well as linguistic devices for perspective shifting (MacWhinney 2008b), politeness, sarcasm (Haiman, this volume), denial, and agreement. These various interactional pressures and motives can arise from either long-term influences, such as years of experience with a marriage partner, or short-term experiences, such as coming to realize that a new acquaintance stutters or likes Jazz (Goodwin 1994).

As Bates and MacWhinney (1982) noted, these multidimensional motives must be packaged into the single linear stream of speech. Kaltenböck and Heine (this volume) have explored ways in which these conversational pressures for linearization (Levelt 1981) lead people to include (paren)thetical material within utterances. These insertions constitute a separate domain of structure outside of the normal sentence grammar. The decision to resort to thetical insertion is motivated by attempts to express material that otherwise would not easily fit into sentence grammar. By providing sockets for such insertions in the form of structures such as tags, appositives, interjections, or dislocations, language is able to satisfy Faithfulness (or Expressivity) for multiple information streams.

Haiman (this volume) looks at the use of the device of repetition to express a wide variety of intentions, including intensification, symmetry, histrionics, plagiarism, agreement, and sarcasm. The forms Haiman discusses are not in direct competition, because they are formally distinct. The use of repetition to mark intensification involves simple lexical repetitions, such as *it was very very big* or *he climbed and climbed and climbed.* On the other hand, twin forms such as *helter-skelter*, Khmer servant words forms such as *banti: bantoan* 'rush,' or parallel constructions such as *one went East, one went West* do not involve simple repetition alone, but specialized lexical or morphological devices that mark particular, specific pragmatic motives or functions. In the case of histrionic reduplications such as *tsk-tsk* or *unh-unh*, the material being repeated is lexically quite distinct from repetitions of adjectives or verbs, even if they may originally derive from content words. Moreover, languages may load additional cues, such as falsetto or high pitch, onto repeated ideophones in order to further clarify their special status. Together these divergences and added cues help the listener understand when reduplication is used for histrionic effect rather than intensification, symmetry, or some other possible motive.

22.10 Social pressures

Conversational encounters also incur a wide variety of social pressures, deriving from competing role commitments operating across very different timeframes. For example, our membership in a given racial or gender group is essentially permanent, whereas our allegiance to a particular current popular fashion trend may not last more than a few months. In between these extremes are the timeframes of our allegiance to social class, clubs, regions, family, and friends. The meshing of allegiances and identities across all of these timeframes has an ongoing impact on language usage and form. Our choice of vocabulary, slang, topics, and even language is determined by the status of our social relations to the people we meet. We can select particular linguistic options to emphasize solidarity, impose our power, or seek favors. All of these motivations, options, and pressures operate across diverse timeframes whose operation must mesh during the moment of speaking.

Looking at 207 languages in the WALS Atlas, Helmbrecht (this volume) shows how the competing motivations of Easiness, Politeness, and Prestige impact the structure of systems of second person pronouns. As we noted earlier, these motivations operate on very different timeframes. Easiness works online to favor the choice of pronouns against proper names and titles that are more difficult to select and articulate. Politeness motivations operate in terms of longer-term power relations that encourage the speaker to use terms of deference for the addressee and terms of effacement for themselves. Within a still longer timeframe, the motivation of Prestige operates to diffuse forms of polite address conceived in high society and the court to broader social circles. Across a timeframe of centuries, forms that developed first in Old Latin and the court of Charlemagne then diffused to other countries in Europe. Helmbrecht argues that this spread was motivated by bilinguals seeking to obtain Prestige by identifying themselves with the cultural elite.

22.11 Direct competition and timeframes

Newmeyer (this volume) presents a critique of functionalist theories that subscribe to what he calls "direct competition," such as the Emergent Grammar approach of Hopper (1988). These approaches are in accord with the notion being developed here that what makes the whole system inherently adaptive and functional is the fact that motives from various timeframes must mesh at the moment of speaking. However, Hopper's account tends to minimize the role of consolidation in long-term memory. In that regard, Emergent Grammar differs fundamentally from the approach being developed here.

Newmeyer supports his critique of direct competition by citing several interesting problems in language change. The first is the competition between GEN-N (*Mary's book*) and N-GEN (*leg of the table*) forms of the possessive in English. Much like the choice between forms of the comparative (Mondorf, this volume), this competition is governed by a wide variety of cues. For example, GEN-N is used in *Riemann's Proof* with an animate possessor, but N-GEN is used in *the proof of the theorem* when the possessor is inanimate. Newmeyer believes that an analysis of the many cues and motives operative in the competition between these two constructions would be "unrevealing." On the contrary, it seems to me that it would be fascinating and instructive, as demonstrated by Mondorf's analysis of the competition for the comparative. This is not to deny the fact that many of these cues have become ossified and non-functional through the development of the language. Newmeyer's example of *Tuesday's lecture* is a good case in point. The use of GEN-N with this inanimate seems to be supported by a series of other constructions in the language such as *Tuesday's child is full of grace* or competition from *the lecture on Tuesday* as a non-possessive alternative.

Newmeyer presents another type of evidence regarding the operation of pressures from contrasting timeframes in his analysis of the loss of plural markings on forms such as *fish* and *deer*. These shortened forms originated in the hunting jargon of the elite which then spread to farmers and later to the general population. Newmeyer cites similarly "non-functional" developments in French, German, and Dutch. In all these developments, we see the operation of the slow timeframes of social diffusion for marking Prestige and other group membership motives. Newmeyer is convinced that these social motives should not be included in any reasonable grammatical analysis. However, if we view language as an adaptation situated within a widely divergent set of timeframes with their own unique motivations, then the whole system can be seen as coherent and functional.

Through his analysis of these complexities, Newmeyer reaches a conclusion that is very much in accord with the current analysis. He notes that the causation of cancer cannot be linked to some single overarching pressure. Smoking is certainly a high risk factor for cancer, but that risk can be further elevated through exposure to asbestos or radon or mitigated by consuming high-fiber foods. Exposure to asbestos can be a one-time event leading to long-term consequences, whereas exposure to radon is more likely to be an event occurring over years. Newmeyer warns against linking "statements in particular grammars with particular motivations." In the preceding pages, we have seen that simple one-to-one linkages in language are the exception, rather than the rule. Instead, what we have are remarkably complex linkages replete with reinterpretation of peaceful coexistence and divide the spoils solutions, always responsive to a menagerie of competing motivations operating across diverse timeframes. All of these pressures interact and mesh together in the moment of speaking, emphasizing the ways in which language adapts to competing motivations.

22.12 Conclusions

Given the centrality of proliferation, competition, and selection in biological systems, and the fact that language is one of these systems, it is difficult to imagine how a theory of human language could be constructed without assigning a central place to competition. Just as Dobzhansky (1973) has declared that "nothing in biology makes sense except in the light of evolution," we can say that nothing in language makes sense except in the light of competition. The chapters in this book have shown how competition is driven by competing motives. Because we use language as the basic glue for our social lives, these competing motivations are as diverse as the many facets of human life and thought. Moreover, they are organized into processes that operate across widely divergent timeframes, ranging from milliseconds to centuries. We can study how these motivations combine and mesh by dissecting spoken interactions, analyzing language structures, following children and adults learning language, and tracing usage through corpora. The results of these analyses will eventually be expressed through models linking all of these forces to online language processing in the brain.

References

Abbot-Smith, Kirsten and Heike Behrens (2006). How known constructions influence the acquisition of other constructions: The German passive and future constructions. *Cognitive Science* 30(6), 995–1026.

Ackema, Peter and Ad Neeleman (1998). Optimal questions. *Natural Language and Linguistic Theory* 16(3), 443–90.

Agresti, Alan (2002). *Categorical Data Analysis*. Hoboken, NJ: Wiley.

Aguado-Orea, J. J. (2004). The acquisition of morpho-syntax in Spanish: Implications for current theories of development. Unpublished PhD thesis: University of Nottingham.

Aikhenvald, Alexandra Y. (2010a). *Imperatives and Commands*. Oxford: Oxford University Press.

Aikhenvald, Alexandra Y. (2010b). *The Manambu Language of East Sepik, Papua New Guinea*. Oxford: Oxford University Press.

Aissen, Judith L. (1987). *Tzotzil Clause Structure* (Studies in Natural Language and Linguistic Theory, 7). Dordrecht: Reidel.

Aissen, Judith (2003). Differential object marking: Iconicity vs. economy. *Natural Language and Linguistic Theory* 21, 435–83.

Aitchison, Jean (2003). *Words in the Mind: An Introduction to the Mental Lexicon*. Oxford: Blackwell.

Akhtar, N. (1999). Acquiring basic word order: Evidence for data-driven learning of syntactic structure. *Journal of Child Language* 26(2), 339–56.

Akhtar, N. and M. Tomasello (1997). Young children's productivity with word order and verb morphology. *Developmental Psychology* 33(6), 952–65.

Alday, P., M. Schlesewsky, and I. Bornkessel-Schlesewsky (2014). Towards a computational model of actor-based language comprehension. *Neuroinformatics* 12, 143–79.

Allen, Cynthia L. (1980). *Topics in Diachronic English Syntax*. New York: Garland.

Allen, Shanley E. M. (2000). A discourse-pragmatic explanation for argument representation in child Inuktitut. *Linguistics* 38, 483–521.

Allen, Shanley E. M., Barbora Skarabela, and Mary E. Hughes (2008). Using corpora to examine discourse effects in syntax, in H. Behrens (ed.), *Corpora in Language Acquisition Research: History, Methods, Perspectives*. Amsterdam: Benjamins, 99–137.

Ambrazas, Vytautas (1997). *Lithuanian Grammar. Lietuvių kalbos gramatika*. Vilnius: Baltos Lankos.

Ambridge, B. (2010). Review of Insa Gülzow and Natalia Gagarina (eds.): *Frequency Effects in Language Acquisition: Defining the Limits of Frequency as an Explanatory Concept*. Berlin: Mouton de Gruyter. *Journal of Child Language* 37(2), 453–75.

Ambridge, Ben and Elena V. M. Lieven (2011). *Child Language Acquisition: Contrasting Theoretical Approaches*. Cambridge: Cambridge University Press.

Andersen, Henning (1988). Center and periphery: Adoption, diffusion, and spread, in J. Fisiak (ed.), *Historical Dialectology*. Berlin: Mouton de Gruyter, 39–83.

Anderson, John (2007). *How Can the Human Mind Occur in the Physical Universe?* New York: Oxford University Press.

Anderson, Stephen (1976). On the notion of subject in ergative languages, in C. Li (ed.), *Subject and Topic*. New York: Academic Press, 1–24.

Anderson, Stephen R. (1979). On the subsequent development of the "standard theory" of phonology, in Daniel A. Dinnsen (ed.), *Current Approaches to Phonological Theory*. Bloomington: Indiana University Press, 2–30.

Anttila, Raimo (1977). *Analogy*. Berlin: Mouton.

Anttila, Raimo (2003). Analogy: The warp and woof of cognition, in Brian D. Joseph and Richard D. Janda (eds), *The Handbook of Historical Linguistics*. Oxford: Blackwell, 423–40.

Ariel, Mira (1990). *Accessing Noun Phrase Antecedents*. London: Routledge.

Ariel, Mira (1999a). Cognitive universals and linguistic conventions: The case of resumptive pronouns. *Studies in Language* 23, 217–69.

Ariel, Mira (1999b). Mapping so-called "pragmatic" phenomena according to a "linguistic-extralinguistic" distinction: The case of propositions marked "accessible", in Michael Darnell, Edith A. Moravcsik, Frederick J. Newmeyer, Michael Noonan, and Kathleen M. Wheatley (eds), *Functionalism and Formalism in Linguistics*, vol. II: Case studies (Studies in Language Companion Series 41). Amsterdam: John Benjamins, 11–38.

Ariel, Mira (2000). The development of person agreement markers: From pronouns to higher accessibility markers, in Michael Barlow and Suzanne Kemmer (eds), *Usage-based Models of Language*. Palo Alto: Center for the Study of Language and Information, 197–260.

Ariel, Mira (2001). Accessibility Theory: An overview, in T. J. M. Sanders, J. Schilperoord, and W. Spooren (eds), *Text Representation*. Amsterdam: Benjamins, 29–87.

Ariel, Mira (2007). A grammar in every register? The case of definite descriptions, in Nancy Hedberg and Ron Zacharski (eds), *The Grammar–Pragmatics Interface: Essays in Honor of Jeanette K. Gundel*. Amsterdam: Benjamins, 265–92.

Ariel, Mira (2008a). *Or* constructions: Meaning and use. Paper presented at The Linguistics Colloquium, UC Santa Barbara, USA.

Ariel, Mira (2008b). *Pragmatics and Grammar*. Cambridge: Cambridge University Press.

Ariel, Mira (2010). *Defining Pragmatics*. Cambridge: Cambridge University Press.

Ariel, Mira and Caterina Mauri (2014). To exclude or include, or is that the question? Ms. Tel Aviv University and University of Pavia.

Aristar, A. R. (1991). On diachronic sources and synchronic patterns: An investigation into the origin of linguistic universals. *Language* 67, 1–33.

Armstrong, B. C. and D. C. Plaut (2008). Settling dynamics in distributed networks explain task differences in semantic ambiguity effects: Computational and behavioral evidence. Paper presented at the Proceedings of the 30th Annual Conference of the Cognitive Science Society.

Arnold, Jennifer E., Thomas Wasow, Anthony Losongc, and Ryan Ginstrom (2000). Heaviness vs. newness: The effects of structural complexity and discourse status on constituent ordering. *Language* 76, 28–55.

Arnon, I. (2011). Units of learning in language acquisition, in I. Arnon and E. V. Clark, *Experience, Variation and Generalization. Learning a First Language*. Berlin: John Benjamins, 1–13.

Arnon, I. and E. V. Clark (2011). Why "On your feet" is better than "feet"—Children's word production is facilitated in familiar sentence-frames. *Language Learning and Development* 7(2), 107–29.

Asher, R. and T. Kumar (1997). *Malayalam*. London: Routledge.

Astruc, Lluisa (2005). The Intonation of Extra-Sentential Elements in Catalan and English. PhD dissertation: University of Cambridge.

Atoyebi, Joseph, Martin Haspelmath, and Andrej Malchukov (2010). Ditransitive constructions in Yoruba, in Andrej L. Malchukov et al. (eds), *Studies in Ditransitive Constructions: A Comparative Handbook*. Berlin: Mouton de Gruyter, 145–66.

Auer, Peter (2009). On-line syntax: Thoughts on the temporality of spoken language. *Language Sciences* 31, 1–13.

Augustine, Saint. (1952). *The Confessions, Original 397 AD* (Volume 18). Chicago: Encyclopedia Britannica.

Austin, Jennifer (2010). Rich inflection and the production of finite verbs in child language. *Morphology* 20, 41–69.

Avelar, Juanito, Sonia Cyrino, and Charlotte Galves (2009). Locative inversion and agreement patterns: Parallelisms between Brazilian Portuguese and Bantu languages, in Margarida Petter and Ronald Beline Mendes (eds), *Proceedings of the Special World Congress of African Linguistics São Paulo 2008. Exploring the African Language Connection in the America.* São Paulo: Humanitas, 207–21.

Baayen, R. Harald (2008). *Analyzing Linguistics Data: A Practical Introduction to Statistics Using R.* Cambridge: Cambridge University Press.

Bader, M. and M. Meng (1999). Subject-object ambiguities in German embedded clauses: An across-the-board comparison. *Journal of Psycholinguistic Research* 28, 121–43.

Baicchi, Annalisa (2004). The cataphoric indexicality of titles, in Karin Aijmer and Anna-Brita Stenström (eds), *Discourse Patterns in Spoken and Written Corpora.* Amsterdam: Benjamins, 17–38.

Baković, Eric and Edward Keer (2001). Optionality and ineffability, in Géraldine Legendre, Sten Vikner, and Jane Grimshaw (eds), *Optionality-theoretic Syntax.* Cambridge, MA: MIT Press, 97–112.

Ball, Catherine N. and Mira Ariel (1978). *Or something*, etc. *Penn Review of Linguistics* 3, 35–45.

Baltin, Mark (1981). Strict bounding, in C. L. Baker and J. McCarthy (eds), *The Logical Problem of Language Acquisition.* Cambridge, MA: MIT Press, 257–95.

Baltin, Mark (2006). Extraposition, in M. Everaert and H. van Riemsdijk (eds), *The Blackwell Companion to Syntax, Volume 2.* Malden, MA: Blackwell Publishing, 237–71.

Bannard, C. and D. Matthews (2008). Stored word sequences in language learning—The effect of familiarity on children's repetition of four-word combinations. *Psychological Science* 19 (3), 241–8.

Bannard, C., E. V. Lieven, and M. Tomasello (2009). Modeling children's early grammatical knowledge. *Proceedings of the National Academy of Sciences* 106(41), 17284–9.

Barlow, Michael and Suzanne Kemmer (eds) (2002). *Usage-based Models of Language.* Stanford: CSLI Publications.

Barthes, R. (1983). *The Fashion System.* NY: Farrar, Straus, Giroux.

Bassène, Alain-Christian (2010). Ditransitive constructions in Jóola Banjal, in Andrej L. Malchukov et al. (eds), *Studies in Ditransitive Constructions: A Comparative Handbook.* Berlin: Mouton de Gruyter, 190–204.

Basten, Ulrike et al. (2010). How the brain integrates costs and benefits during decision making. *Proceedings of the National Academy of Science USA* 107, 21767–72.

Bates, Elizabeth and Brian MacWhinney (1982). Functionalist approaches to grammar, in E. Wanner and L. R. Gleitman (eds), *Language Acquisition: The State of the Art.* Cambridge: Cambridge University Press, 173–218.

Bates, Elizabeth and Brian MacWhinney (1987). Competition, variation, and language learning, in B. MacWhinney (ed.), *Mechanisms of Language Acquisition.* London: Lawrence Erlbaum, 157–93.

Bates, Elizabeth and Brian MacWhinney (1989). Functionalism and the competition model, in B. MacWhinney and E. Bates, *The Cross-linguistic Study of Sentence Processing.* New York: Cambridge University Press, 3–73.

Bates, Elizabeth et al. (1982). Functional constraints on sentence processing: A cross-linguistic study. *Cognition* 11, 245–99.

Bates, Elizabeth, A. Devescovi, and B. Wulfeck (2001). Psycholinguistics: A cross-language perspective. *Annual Review of Psychology* 52, 369–96.

Bates, Elizabeth, Brian MacWhinney, Christina Caselli, Antonella Devescovi, Francesco Natale, and Valeria Venza (1984). A cross-linguistic study of the development of sentence interpretation strategies. *Child Development* 55, 341–54.

Beckner, Clay, Richard Blythe, Joan Bybee, Morten H. Christiansen, William Croft, Nick C. Ellis, John H. Holland, Jinyun Ke, Diane Larsen-Freeman, and Tom Schoenemann (2009). Language is a complex adaptive system: Position paper. *Language Learning* 59(Supplement 1), 1–26.

Behaghel, Otto (1909). Beziehungen zwischen Umfang und Reihenfolge von Satzgliedern. *Indogermanische Forschungen* 25, 110–42.

Behaghel, Otto (1932). *Deutsche Syntax: Eine geschichtliche Darstellung* (Volume 4: *Wortstellung, Periodenbau*). Heidelberg: Carl Winters.

Belletti, Adriana and Luigi Rizzi (1988). Psych-verbs and Theta-theory, *Natural Language and Linguistic Theory* 6, 201–53.

Benveniste, Émile (1966). Structure de relations de personne dans le verbe, in É. Benveniste, *Problèmes de linguistique générale* I. Paris: Gallimard, 225–36.

Berry, K. and C. Berry (1999). *A Description of Abun: A West Papuan language of Irian Jaya*. Canberra: Australian National University.

Biber, Douglas, Stig Johansson, Geoffrey Leech, Susan Conrad, and Edward Finegan, (1999). *Longman Grammar of Spoken and Written English*. London: Longman.

Bickel, B. (2007). Typology in the 21st century: Major current developments. *Linguistic Typology* 11, 239–51.

Bickel, B. (2010). Absolute and statistical universals, in P. C. Hogan (ed.), *The Cambridge Encyclopedia of the Language Sciences*. Cambridge: Cambridge University Press, 77–9.

Bickel, Balthasar (2011). Grammatical relations typology, in Jae Jung Song (ed.), *The Oxford Handbook of Linguistic Typology*. Oxford: Oxford University Press, 399–444.

Bickerton, Derek (2009). *Adam's Tongue: How Humans Made Language, How Language Made Humans*. New York: Hill & Wang.

Bird, Charles and Timothy Shopen (1979). Maninka, in T. Shopen (ed.), *Languages and their Speakers*. Cambridge, MA: Winthrop, 59–111.

Birkner, Karin, Sofie Henricson, Camilla Lindholm, and Martin Pfeiffer (2010). Retraction patterns and self-repair in German and Swedish prepositional phrases., *InLiSt—Interaction and Linguistic Structure* 46, July, <http://www.inlist.uni-bayreuth.de/issues/46/htm>, accessed January 25, 2014.

Birkner, Karin, Sofie Henricson, Camilla Lindholm, and Martin Pfeiffer (2012). Grammar and self-repair: Retraction patterns in German and Swedish prepositional phrases. *Journal of Pragmatics* 44, 1413–33.

Bisang, W. (1996). Areal typology and grammaticalization: Processes of grammaticalization based on nouns and verbs in East and Mainland South East Asian languages. *Studies in Language* 20, 519–97.

Bittner, Dagmar and Klaus-Michael Köpcke (2001). Acquisition of the German plural markings: A case study in natural and cognitive morphology, in Chris Schaner-Wolles, John Rennison, and Friedrich Neubarth (eds), *Naturally: Linguistic Studies in Honour of Wolfgang Ulrich Dressler*. Torino: Rosenberg & Sellier, 47–58.

Bittner, Dagmar, Wolfgang U. Dressler, and Marianne Kilani-Schoch (eds) (2003). *Development of Verb Inflection in First Language Acquisition: A Cross-linguistic Perspective*. Berlin: de Gruyter.

Blakemore, Diane (2006). Divisions of labour: The analysis of parentheticals. *Lingua* 116, 1670–87.

Blansitt, Edward L. Jr. (1984). Dechticaetiative and dative, in Frans Plank (ed.), *Objects*. London: Academic Press, 127–50.

Blevins, James P. and Juliette Blevins (eds) (2009). *Analogy in Grammar: Form and Acquisition*. Oxford: Oxford University Press.

Blevins, Juliette (2004). *Evolutionary Phonology: The Emergence of Sound Patterns*. Cambridge: Cambridge University Press.

Blevins, Juliette (2006). A theoretical synopsis of Evolutionary Phonology. *Theoretical Linguistics* 32(2), 117–66.

Bloom, Lois (1970). *Language Development: Form and Function in Emerging Grammars*. Cambridge, MA: MIT Press.

Bloom, Paul (1990). Subjectless sentences in child language. *Linguistic Inquiry* 21, 491–504.

Blutner, Reinard, Helen de Hoop, and Petra Hendriks (2006). *Optimal Communication*. Stanford: CSLI Publications.

Bobaljik, Jonathan D. (2012). *Universals in Comparative Morphology: Suppletion, Superlatives, and the Structure of Words*. Cambridge, MA: MIT Press.

Bock, J. Kathryn and Richard K. Warren (1985). Conceptual accessibility and syntactic structure in sentence formulation. *Cognition* 21, 47–67.

Bock, J. Kathryn, Helga Loebell, and Randal Morey (1992). From conceptual roles to structural relations: Bridging the syntactic cleft. *Psychological Review* 99, 150–71.

Bod, Rens (1998). *Beyond Grammar: An Experience-based Theory of Language*. Stanford, CA: CSLI Publications.

Boesch, C. (1993). *Aspects of Transmission of Tool Use in Wild Chimpanzees*. Cambridge: Cambridge University Press.

Bolinger, Dwight (1989). *Intonation and its Uses: Melody in Grammar and Discourse*. London: Edward Arnold.

Bonin, Patrick, Christopher Barry, Alain Méot, and Marylène Chalard (2004). The influence of age of acquisition in word reading and other tasks: A never-ending story. *Journal of Memory and Language* 50, 456–76.

Bornkessel, Ina (2002). *The Argument Dependency Model: A Neurocognitive Approach to Incremental Interpretation*. Leipzig: MPI Series in Cognitive Neuroscience.

Bornkessel, Ina and Matthias Schlesewsky (2006). The Extended Argument Dependency Model: A neurocognitive approach to sentence comprehension across languages. *Psychological Review* 113, 787–821.

Bornkessel, Ina et al. (2004). Multi-dimensional contributions to garden path strength: Dissociating phrase structure from case marking. *Journal of Memory and Language* 51, 495–522.

Bornkessel, Ina et al. (2005). Who did what to whom? The neural basis of argument hierarchies during language comprehension. *NeuroImage* 26, 221–33.

Bornkessel-Schlesewsky, Ina and Matthias Schlesewsky (2008). An alternative perspective on "semantic P600" effects in language comprehension. *Brain Research Reviews* 59, 55–73.

Bornkessel-Schlesewsky, Ina and Matthias Schlesewsky (2008a). Unmarked transitivity: A processing constraint on linking, in R. D. Van Valin, Jr. (ed.), *Investigations of the Syntax–Semantics–Pragmatics Interface*. Amsterdam: John Benjamins, 413–34.

Bornkessel-Schlesewsky, Ina and Matthias Schlesewsky (2009a). *Processing Syntax and Morphology: A Neurocognitive Perspective* (Oxford Surveys in Syntax and Morphology 6). Oxford: Oxford University Press.

Bornkessel-Schlesewsky, Ina and Matthias Schlesewsky (2009b). The role of prominence information in the real time comprehension of transitive constructions: A cross-linguistic approach. *Language and Linguistics Compass* 3, 19–58.

Bornkessel-Schlesewsky, Ina and Matthias Schlesewsky (2009c). Minimality as vacuous distinctness: Evidence from cross-linguistic sentence comprehension. *Lingua* 119, 1541–59.

Bornkessel-Schlesewsky, Ina and Matthias Schlesewsky (2013a). Reconciling time, space and function: A new dorsal-ventral stream model of sentence comprehension. *Brain and Language* 125, 60–76.

Bornkessel-Schlesewsky, Ina and Matthias Schlesewsky (2013b). Neurotypology: Modelling cross-linguistic similarities and differences in the neurocognition of language comprehension, in M. Sanz, I. Laka, and M. K. Tanenhaus (eds), *The Cognitive and Biological Basis for Linguistic Structure: New Approaches and Enduring Themes*. Oxford: Oxford University Press, 241–52.

Bornkessel-Schlesewsky, Ina, T. Grewe, and Matthias Schlesewsky (2012). Prominence vs. aboutness in sequencing: A functional distinction within the left inferior frontal gyrus. *Brain and Language* 120, 96–107.

Bouma, Gerlof (2008). *Starting a Sentence in Dutch. A corpus study of subject- and object-fronting*. PhD dissertation: University of Groningen.

Bowerman, Melissa (1983). How do children avoid constructing an overly general grammar in the absence of feedback about what is not a sentence? *Papers and Reports on Child Language Development* 22, 23–35.

Bowerman, Melissa (1988). The "no negative evidence" problem: How do children avoid constructing an overly general grammar, in J. A. Hawkins (ed.), *Explaining Language Universals*. Oxford: Blackwell, 73–101.

Bowerman, M. and S. Choi (2001). Shaping meanings for language: Universal and language-specific in the acquisition of spatial semantic categories, in M. Bowerman and S. C. Levinson (eds), *Language Acquisition and Conceptual Development*. Cambridge: Cambridge University Press, 475–511.

Boyd, Jeremy (2007). *Comparatively Speaking: A psycholinguistic study of optionality in grammar*. Unpublished PhD dissertation: University of California, San Diego.

Branigan, Holly P., Martin J. Pickering, and Mikihiro Tanaka (2008). Contributions of animacy to grammatical function assignment and word order production. *Lingua* 118, 172–89.

Braun, Friederike (1984). Rumänische Anredeformen, in Werner Winter (ed.), *Anredeverhalten*. Tübingen: Narr, 151–89.

Braune, Wilhelm (1987). *Althochdeutsche Grammatik*. (14. Auflage, bearbeitet von Hans Eggers). Tübingen: Max Niemeyer.

Bresnan, Joan W. (1997). The emergence of the unmarked pronoun: Chichewa pronominals in optimality theory, in A. C. Bailey, K. E. Moore, and J. L. Moxley (eds), *Berkeley Linguistics Society 23: Special session on syntax and semantics of Africa*. Berkeley: Berkeley Linguistics Society, 26–46.

Bresnan, Joan and Judith Aissen (2002). Optimality and functionality: Objections and refutations. *Natural Language and Linguistic Theory* 20, 81–95.

Bresnan, Joan and Marilyn Ford (2010). Predicting syntax: Processing dative constructions in American and Australian varieties of English. *Language* 86, 186–213.

Bresnan, Joan and Tatiana Nikitina (2008). The gradience of the dative alternation, in L. Uyechi and L. H. Wee (eds), *Reality Exploration and Discovery: Pattern Interaction in Language and Life*. Stanford, CA: CSLI Publications, 161–84.

Bresnan, Joan, Ashwini Deo, and Devyani Sharma (2007a). Typology in variation: A probabilistic approach to *be* and *n't* in the Survey of English Dialects. *English Language and Linguistics* 11, 301–46.

Bresnan, Joan, Anna Cueni, Tatiana Nikitina, and R. Harald Baayen (2007b). Predicting the dative alternation, in G. Bouma, I. Kraemer, and J. Zwarts (eds), *Cognitive Foundations of Interpretation*. Amsterdam: Royal Netherlands Academy of Science, 69–94.

Brinton, Laurel J. (2008). *The Comment Clause in English: Syntactic Origins and Pragmatic Development* (Studies in English Language). Cambridge: Cambridge University Press.

Brinton, Laurel J. and Elizabeth C. Traugott (2005). *Lexicalization and Language Change*. Cambridge: Cambridge University Press.

Bromberg, Hilary S. and Kenneth Wexler (1995). Null subjects in child wh-questions, in C. T. Schütze, J. Ganger, and K. Broihier (eds), *Papers in Language Processing and Acquisition* (MIT Working Papers in Linguistics 26). Cambridge, MA: MIT Press, 221–47.

Brooks, P. J. and M. Tomasello (1999). Young children learn to produce passives with nonce verbs. *Developmental Psychology* 35(1), 29–44.

Browman, Catherine and Louis Goldstein (2000). Competing constraints on intergestural coordination and self organization of phonological structures. *Les Cahiers de l'ICP, Bulletin de la Communication Parlée* 5, 25–34.

Brown, Penelope and S. Levinson (1987). *Politeness: Some Universals in Language Usage*. Cambridge: Cambridge University Press.

Brown, Roger (1973). *A First Language: The Early Stages*. Cambridge, MA: Harvard University Press.

Brown, Roger and Albert Gilman (1960). The pronouns of solidarity and power, in Thomas Sebeok (ed.), *Style in Language*. Cambridge: MIT Press, 253–76.

Bruce, Les (1984). *The Alamblak Language of Papua New Guinea (East Sepik)*. Canberra: Australian National University.

Bugaeva, Anna (2010). Ainu applicatives in typological perspective. *Studies in Language* 34(4), 749–801.

Burgess, C. and K. Lund (1997). Modelling parsing constraints with high-dimension context space. *Language and Cognitive Processes* 12, 177–210.

Burton-Roberts, Noel (2005). Parentheticals, *Encyclopaedia of Language and Linguistics*. 2nd edn, Volume 9. Amsterdam: Elsevier, 179–82.

Buzsaki, G. (2006). *Rhythms of the Brain*. Oxford: Oxford University Press.

Bybee, Joan (1985). *Morphology: A Study of the Relation between Meaning and Form*. Amsterdam: Benjamins.

Bybee, J. (1988). The diachronic dimension in explanation, in J. A. Hawkins (ed.), *Explaining Language Universals*. Oxford: Basil Blackwell, 350–79.

Bybee, Joan L. (2001). *Phonology and Language Use*. Cambridge: Cambridge University Press.

Bybee, Joan L. (2002). Sequentiality as the basis of constituent structure, in Talmy Givón and Bertram F. Malle (eds), *The Evolution of Language out of Pre-language*. Amsterdam: John Benjamins, 109–34.

Bybee, Joan L. (2006). From usage to grammar: The mind's response to repetition. *Language* 82(4), 711–33.

Bybee, Joan (2007). *Frequency of Use and the Organization of Language*. Oxford: Oxford University Press.

Bybee, J. (2008). Formal universals as emergent phenomena: The origins of structure pre-servation, in J. Good (ed.), *Linguistic Universals and Language Change*. Oxford: Oxford University Press, 108–21.

Bybee, Joan (2010). *Language, Usage and Cognition*. Cambridge: Cambridge University Press.

Bybee, Joan and Clay Beckner (2014). Emergence at the crosslinguistic level: Attractor dynamics in language change, in B. MacWhinney and W. O'Grady (eds), *Handbook of Language Emergence*. New York: Wiley.

Bybee, Joan L. and Paul J. Hopper (eds) (2001). *Frequency and the Emergence of Linguistic Structure*. Amsterdam/Philadelphia: Benjamins.

Bybee, J., R. Perkins, and W. Pagliuca (1994). *The Evolution of Grammar*. Chicago and London: The University of Chicago Press.

Campbell, Aimee L. and Michael Tomasello (2001). The acquisition of English dative con-structions. *Applied Psycholinguistics* 22(2), 253–67.

Campbell, Aimee, Patricia Brooks, and Michael Tomasello (2000). Factors affecting young children's use of pronouns as referring expressions. *Journal of Speech, Language, and Hearing Research* 43(6), 1337–49.

Carlson, Gregory (1977). Reference to kinds in English. PhD thesis: University of Massachu-setts at Amherst.

Catani, Marco, D. K. Jones, and D. H. ffytche, (2005). Perisylvian language networks of the human brain. *Annals of Neurology* 57, 8–16.

Chafe, Wallace L. (1977). The recall and verbalization of past experience, in Roger W. Cole (ed.), *Current Issues in Linguistic Theory*. Bloomington: Indiana University Press, 215–46.

Chafe, Wallace L. (1979). The flow of thought and the flow of language, in Talmy Givón (ed.), *Discourse and Syntax*. New York: Academic Press, 159–81.

Chafe, Wallace L. (1980). *The Pear Stories: Cognitive, Cultural, and Linguistic Aspects of Narrative Production*. Norwood, NJ: Ablex.

Chafe, Wallace L. (1994). *Discourse, Consciousness, and Time: The Flow and Displacement of Conscious Experience in Speaking and Writing*. Chicago: University of Chicago Press.

Chambers, Jack K., Peter Trudgill, and Natalie Schilling-Estes (eds) (2003). *The Handbook of Variation and Change*. Oxford: Blackwell.

Chan, Angel (2010). The Cantonese double object construction with bei2 "give" in bilingual children: The role of input. *International Journal of Bilingualism* 14(1), 65–85.

Chan, Angel, Elena V. M. Lieven, and Michael Tomasello (2009). Children's understanding of the agent-patient relations in the transitive construction: Cross-linguistic comparisons between Cantonese, German, and English. *Cognitive Linguistics* 20(2), 267–300.

Chang, Franklin (2002). Symbolically speaking: A connectionist model of sentence produc-tion. *Cognitive Science* 26(5), 609–51.

Chang, Franklin, Gary S. Dell, and Kathryn Bock (2006). Becoming syntactic. *Psychological Review* 113(2), 234–72.

Chatelain, E. (1880). Du pluriel de respect en latin. *Revue de philologie* 4, 129–39.

Chatterji, S. K. (1926). *The Origin and Development of the Bengali Language*. Calcutta: Calcutta University Press.

Chierchia, Gennaro and Sally McConnell-Ginet (1990). *Meaning and Grammar: An Introduc-tion to Semantics*. Cambridge, MA: MIT Press.

Childers, Jane B. and Jae H. Paik (2009). Korean- and English-speaking children use cross-situational information to learn novel predicate terms. *Journal of Child Language* 36(1), 201–24.

Childs, T. (1995). *A Grammar of Kisi*. The Hague: Mouton.

Choi, S. (2006). Influence of language-specific input on spatial cognition: Categories of containment. *First Language* 26, 207–32.

Chomsky, Noam (1973). Conditions on transformations, in S. Anderson and P. Kiparsky (eds), *A Festschrift for Morris Halle*. New York: Holt Rinehart & Winston, 232–86.

Chomsky, Noam (1975). *Reflections on Language*. New York: Random House.

Chomsky, Noam (1981). *Lectures on Government and Binding*. Dordrecht: Foris.

Chomsky, Noam and Morris Halle (1968). *Sound Pattern of English*. New York: Harper and Row.

Choudhary, K. K. et al. (2010). An Actor-preference in a split-ergative language: Electrophysiological evidence from Hindi. Poster presented at the 23rd Annual Meeting of the CUNY Conference on Human Sentence Processing, San Diego, CA.

Christianson, Kiel and Fernanda Ferreira (2005). Conceptual accessibility and sentence production in a free word order language (Odawa). *Cognition* 98, 105–35.

Christofidou, Anastasia and Ioanna Kappa (1998). Pre- and protomorphological fillers in Greek language acquisition, in Steven Gillis (ed.), *Studies in the Acquisition of Number and Diminutive Marking* (Antwerp Papers in Linguistics 95), 193–214.

Clancy, Patricia M. (1993). Preferred argument structure in Korean acquisition, in E. V. Clark (ed.), *Proceedings of the 25th Annual Child Language Research Forum*. Stanford, CA: CSLI Publications, 307–14.

Clancy, Patricia M. (2003). The lexicon in interaction: Developmental origins of Preferred Argument Structure, in John W. Du Bois, Lorraine E. Kumpf, and William J. Ashby (eds), *Preferred Argument Structure: Grammar as Architecture for Function*. Amsterdam: Benjamins, 81–108.

Clark, H. and R. Gerrig (1984). On the pretense theory of irony. *Journal of Experimental Psychology: General* 113, 121–6.

Clark, Herbert H. (1996). *Using Language*. Cambridge: Cambridge University Press.

Clark, Herbert H. and J. E. Fox Tree (2002). Using *uh* and *um* in spontaneous speaking. *Cognition* 84, 73–111.

Cole, Peter, Wayne Harbert, Gabriella Hermon, and S. N. Sridhar (1980). The acquisition of subjecthood. *Language* 56, 719–43.

Comrie, Bernard (1976). The syntax of action nominals: A cross-linguistic study. *Lingua* 40, 177–201.

Comrie, Bernard (1978). Ergativity, in Winfred P. Lehmann (ed.), *Syntactic Typology: Studies in the Phenomenology of Language*. Austin: University of Texas Press, 329–94.

Comrie, Bernard (1981). *Language Universals and Linguistic Typology: Syntax and Morphology*. Chicago: University of Chicago Press.

Comrie, Bernard (1982). Grammatical relations in Huichol, in Paul J. Hopper and Sandra A. Thompson (eds), *Studies in Transitivity*. New York: Academic Press, 95–115.

Comrie, Bernard (1984). Subject and object control: Syntax, semantics, and pragmatics. *Berkeley Linguistics Society* 10, 450–64.

Comrie, Bernard (1989). *Linguistic Universals and Language Typology*, 2nd edn. Oxford: Blackwell (1st edn 1981).

Comrie, Bernard (2003). On explaining language universals, in Michael Tomasello (ed.), *The New Psychology of Language: Cognitive and Functional Approaches to Language Structure*, Volume 2. Mahwah, NJ: Erlbaum, 195–209.

Comrie, B. (2008). Alignment of case marking of full noun phrases, in M. Haspelmath, M. S. Dryer, D. Gil, and B. Comrie (eds), *The World Atlas of Language Structures Online*. Munich: Max Planck Digital Library, <http://wals.info/feature/98> accessed January 25, 2014.

Comrie, Bernard and Tanja Kuteva (2005). The evolution of grammatical structures and "functional need" explanations, in Maggie Tallermann (ed.), *Language Origins: Perspectives on Evolution*. Oxford: Oxford University Press, 185–207.

Comrie, Bernard, and Sandra Thompson (1985). Lexical nominalizations, in T. Shopen (ed.), *Language Typology and Syntactic Description*. Volume III. Cambridge: Cambridge University Press, 349–98.

Conwell, Erin and Katherine Demuth (2007). Early syntactic productivity: Evidence from dative shift. *Cognition* 103(2), 163–79.

Cook, V. (1976). A note on indirect objects. *Journal of Child Language* 3, 435–37.

Cooreman, Ann M. (1987). *Transitivity and Discourse Continuity in Chamorro Narratives*. Berlin: Mouton de Gruyter.

Corbett, G. G. (2000). *Number*. Cambridge: Cambridge University Press.

Corbett, Greville G. (2006). *Agreement*. Cambridge: Cambridge University Press.

Corbett, Greville G. (2007). Canonical typology, suppletion, and possible words. *Language* 83, 8–41.

Corbetta, M. and G. L. Shulman (2002). Control of goal-directed and stimulus-driven attention in the brain. *Nature Reviews Neuroscience* 3, 201–15.

Corrigan, Roberta (1986). The internal structure of English transitive sentences. *Memory and Cognition* 14, 420–31.

Corum, Claudia (1975). A pragmatic analysis of parenthetic adjuncts. *Chicago Linguistic Society* 11, 133–41.

Couper-Kuhlen, Elizabeth and Margret Selting (2001). Introducing Interactional Linguistics, in M. Selting and E. Couper-Kuhlen (eds), *Studies in Interactional Linguistics*. Amsterdam: John Benjamins, 1–22.

Crain, Stephen and Paul Pietroski (2002). Why language acquisition is a snap. *Linguistic Review* 19, 163–83.

Crain, Stephen and Rosalind Thornton (1998). *Investigations in Universal Grammar: A Guide to Experiments on the Acquisition of Syntax and Semantics*. Cambridge, MA: MIT Press.

Creider, Chet (1979). On the explanation of transformations, in T. Givón (ed.), *Syntax and Semantics, Volume 12: Discourse and Syntax*. New York: Academic Press, 3–22.

Creissels, Denis. (2009). *Le malinké de Kita: un parler mandingue de l'ouest du Mali*. Cologne: Köppe.

Cristofaro, S. (2003). *Subordination*. Oxford: Oxford University Press.

Cristofaro, Sonia (n.d.). Competing motivation models and diachrony: What evidence for what motivations? <http://www.eva.mpg.de/lingua/conference/10-CompetingMotivations/pdf/Konferenz_papers/Cristofaro.pdf> accessed January 25, 2014.

Crocker, M. W. (1994). On the nature of the principle-based sentence processor, in C. Clifton, Jr., L. Frazier, and K. Rayner (eds), *Perspectives on Sentence Processing*. Hillsdale, NJ: Erlbaum, 245–66.

Croft, William (1990). *Typology and Universals*. Cambridge: Cambridge University Press.

Croft, William (1991). *Syntactic Categories and Grammatical Relations: The Cognitive Organization of Information*. Chicago, London: The University of Chicago Press.

Croft, William (2000). *Explaining Language Change: An Evolutionary Approach*. London: Longman.

Croft, William (2001). *Radical Construction Grammar*. Oxford: Oxford University Press.

Croft, William (2003). *Typology and Universals*. 2nd edn. Cambridge, MA: Cambridge University Press.

Croft, William (2008). On iconicity of distance (comment on Haspelmath 2008a). *Cognitive Linguistics* 19(1), 49–57.

Culicover, Peter W. and Ray S. Jackendoff (2005). *Simpler Syntax*. Oxford: Oxford University Press.

Culicover, Peter W. and Michael S. Rochemont (1990). Extraposition and the complement principle. *Linguistic Inquiry* 21, 23–47.

Cutler, Anne (2012). *Native Listening: Language Experience and the Recognition of Spoken Words*. Cambridge, MA: MIT Press.

Cysouw, Michael (2010). Dealing with diversity: Towards an explanation of NP-internal word frequencies. *Linguistic Typology* 14, 253–86.

Dąbrowska, E. and M. Tomasello (2008). Rapid learning of an abstract language-specific category: Polish children's acquisition of the instrumental construction. *Journal of Child Language* 35(3), 533–58.

Dahl, Östen (2004). *The Growth and Maintenance of Linguistic Complexity*, Amsterdam: John Benjamins.

Dahl, Östen (2008). Animacy and egophoricity: Grammar, ontology and phylogeny. *Lingua* 118, 141–50.

Daninos, P. (1962). *Le jacassin*. Paris: Hachette.

Darwin, Charles R. (1859). *On the Origin of Species by Means of Natural Selection, or the Preservation of Favoured Races in the Struggle for Life*. London: Murray.

Daselaar, Sander, Dick Veltman, and Menno Witter (2004). Common pathway in the medial temporal lobe for storage and recovery of words as revealed by event-related functional MRI. *Hippocampus* 14, 163–9.

D'Avis, Franz Josef (2005). Über Parenthesen, in Franz Josef D'Avis (ed.), *Deutsche Syntax: Empirie und Theorie*. Göteborg: Acta Universitatis Gothoburgiensis, 259–79.

de Hoop, Helen and Monique J. A. Lamers (2006). Incremental distinguishability of subject and object, in L. Kulikov, A. L. Malchukov, and P. de Swart (eds), *Case, Valency, and Transitivity*. Amsterdam/Philadelphia: Benjamins, 269–87.

de Hoop, Helen and A. L. Malchukov (2008). Case-marking strategies. *Linguistic Inquiry* 39/4, 565–87.

de Hoop, Helen and B. Narasimhan (2005). Differential case-marking in Hindi, in M. Amberber and H. de Hoop (eds), *Competition and Variation in Natural Languages: The case for Case*. Oxford: Elsevier, 321–45.

de Swart, Peter J. F. (2007). Cross-linguistic variation in object marking. Dissertation: Radboud University Nijmegen.

de Vincenzi, M. (1991). *Syntactic Parsing Strategies in Italian*. Dordrecht: Kluwer.

de Vries, Mark (2007). Invisible constituents? Parentheses as B-merged adverbial phrases, in Nicole Dehée and Yordanka Kavalova (eds), *Parentheticals* (Linguistics Today, 106). Amsterdam and Philadelphia: Benjamins, 203–34.

de Vries, Mark (n.d.). The syntax of nonsubordination: Parenthesis, appositions and grafts, <http://odur.let.rug.nl/~dvries> accessed January 25, 2014.

Deacon, Terrence W. (2011). *Incomplete Nature: How Mind Emerged from Matter*. New York: Norton.

Deco, Gustavo, E. T. Rolls, and R. Romo (2009). Stochastic dynamics as a principle of brain function. *Progress in Neurobiology* 88, 1–16.

Deco, Gustavo et al. (2013). Brain mechanisms for perceptual and reward-related decision-making. *Progress in Neurobiology* 103, 194–213.

Dehé, Nicole (2007). The relation between syntactic and prosodic parenthesis, in Nicole Dehé and Yordanka Kavalova (eds), *Parentheticals* (Linguistics Today, 106). Amsterdam and Philadelphia: Benjamins, 261–85.

Dehé, Nicole and Yordanka Kavalova (2007a). *Parentheticals* (Linguistics Today, 106). Amsterdam and Philadelphia: Benjamins.

Dehé, Nicole and Yordanka Kavalova (2007b). Introduction, in Nicole Dehé and Yordanka Kavalova (eds), *Parentheticals* (Linguistics Today, 106). Amsterdam, Philadelphia: Benjamins, 1–22.

Dehé, Nicole and Anne Wichmann (2010). Sentence-initial *I think (that)* and *I believe (that)*: Prosodic evidence for use as main clause, comment clause and discourse marker, *Studies in Language* 34(1), 36–74.

DeLancey, S. (1981). An interpretation of split ergativity and related patterns. *Language* 57, 626–57.

Demiral, Ş. B. (2008). *Incremental Argument Interpretation in Turkish Sentence Comprehension*. Leipzig: Max Planck Series in Human Cognitive and Brain Sciences.

Demiral, Ş. B., M. Schlesewsky, and I. Bornkessel-Schlesewsky (2008). On the universality of language comprehension strategies: Evidence from Turkish. *Cognition* 106, 484–500.

Den Besten, Hans (1989). Studies in West-Germanic Syntax. Dissertation: University of Amsterdam.

Deutscher, G. (2000). *Syntactic Change in Akkadian: The Evolution of Sentential Complementation*. Oxford: Oxford University Press.

Diessel, H. (1999). *Demonstratives: Form, Function, and Grammaticalization*. Amsterdam and Philadelphia: John Benjamins.

Diessel, Holger (2005). Competing motivations for the ordering of main and adverbial clauses. *Linguistics* 43(3), 449–70.

Diessel, Holger (2008). Iconicity of sequence: A corpus-based analysis of the positioning of temporal adverbial clauses in English. *Cognitive Linguistics* 19, 465–90.

Diffloth, G. (1976). Expressives in Semai, in P. Jenner, S. Thompson, and S. Starosta (eds), *Austroasiatic Studies*. Honolulu: University Press of Hawaii, 1, 246–64.

Dik, Simon (1986). On the notion "functional explanation". *Belgian Journal of Linguistics* 1, 11–52.

Dik, Simon C. (1989). *The Theory of Functional Grammar; Part 1: The Structure of the Clause*. Dordrecht: Foris.

Dik, Simon C. (1997). *The Theory of Functional Grammar, Part 2: Complex and Derived Constructions* (Functional Grammar Series, 21). Berlin and New York: Mouton de Gruyter.

Dingemanse, M. (2009a). How to do things with ideophones: Observations on the use of vivid sensory language in Siwu. *SOAS Research Seminar*, June 3, 2009.

Dingemanse, M. (2009b). Ideophones in unexpected places. *Language Documentation and Linguistic Theory* 2.

Dittmar, M., K. Abbot-Smith, E. V. Lieven, and M. Tomasello (2008). German children's comprehension of word order and case marking in causative sentences. *Child Development* 79(4), 1152–67.

Dixon, Robert M. W. (1972). *The Dyirbal Language of North Queensland*. Cambridge. Cambridge University Press.

Dixon, Robert M. W. (1979). Ergativity. *Language* 55, 59–138.

Dixon, Robert (1981). Wargamay, in R. Dixon and B. Blake (eds), *Handbook of Australian Languages*. Volume 2. Amsterdam: John Benjamins, 1–144.

Dixon, Robert M. W. (1994). *Ergativity*. Cambridge: Cambridge University Press.

Dixon, Robert M. W. (2005). *A Semantic Approach to English Grammar*. Oxford: Oxford University Press.

Dobzhansky, Theodosius (1973). Nothing in biology makes sense except in the light of evolution. *American Biology Teacher* 35, 125–9.

Doke, C. (1935). *Bantu Linguistic Terminology*. London: Longmans, Green.

Donohue, Mark (1999). *A Grammar of Tukang Besi*. Berlin: Mouton de Gruyter.

Donohue, Mark (2008). Semantic alignment systems: What's what, and what's not, in M. Donohue, and S. Wichmann (eds), *Typology of Languages with Semantic Alignment*. Oxford: Oxford University Press, 24–75.

Dowty, David (1991). Thematic proto-roles and argument selection. *Language* 67, 547–619.

Dressler, Wolfgang U. (1984). Explaining Natural Phonology. *Phonology* 1, 29–51.

Dressler, Wolfgang U. (1985). *Morphonology*. Ann Arbor: Karoma Press.

Dressler, Wolfgang U. (1986). Explanation of Natural Morphology illustrated with comparative and agent-noun formation. *Linguistics* 24(3), 519–48.

Dressler, W. U. (1987). Naturalness in Word Formation. In W. U. Dressler, W. Mayerthaler, O. Panagl, and W. U. Wurzel (eds), *Leitmotifs in Natural Morphology*. Amsterdam and Philadelphia: John Benjamins, 99–125.

Dressler, Wolfgang U. (1988). Preferences vs. strict universals in morphology: Word-based rules, in Michael Hammond and Michael Noonan (eds), *Theoretical Morphology*. San Diego: Academic Press, 143–54.

Dressler, Wolfgang U. (1989). Prototypical differences between inflection and derivation. *Zeitschrift für Phonetik, Sprachwissenschaft und Kommunikationsforschung* 42, 3–10.

Dressler, Wolfgang U. (1995). Interactions between iconicity and other semiotic parameters in language, in Raffaele Simone (ed.), *Iconicity in Language*. Amsterdam and Philadelphia: Benjamins, 21–37.

Dressler, Wolfgang U. (1997a). On productivity and potentiality in inflectional morphology. *CLASNET Working Papers* 7.

Dressler, Wolfgang U. (1997b). "Scenario" as a concept for the functional explanation of language change, in Jadranka Gvozdanović (ed.), *Language Change and Functional Explanations*. Berlin: Mouton de Gruyter, 109–42.

Dressler, Wolfgang U. (2000). Textlinguistik und Semiotik, in Klaus Brinker, Gerd Antos, Wolfgang Heinemann, and Sven Frederik Sager (eds), *Text- und Gesprächslinguistik* I. Berlin: de Gruyter, 762–72.

Dressler, Wolfgang U. (2002). Naturalness and morphological change, in Brian D. Joseph and Richard D. Janda (eds), *The Handbook of Historical Linguistics*. Oxford: Blackwell, 461–71.

Dressler, Wolfgang U. (2003). Degrees of grammatical productivity in inflectional morphology. *Italian Journal of Linguistics* 15, 31–62.

Dressler, Wolfgang U. (ed.) (2006). Special issue: Natural Morphology. *Folia Linguistica* 40, 1–2.

Dressler, Wolfgang U. and Katarzyna Dziubalska-Kołaczyk (2006). Proposing morphonotactics. *Italian Journal of Linguistics* 18, 249–66.

Dressler, Wolfgang U. and Annemarie Karpf (1995). The theoretical relevance of pre- and protomorphology in language acquisition. *Yearbook of Morphology* 1994, 99–122.

Dressler, Wolfgang U. and Karlheinz Mörth (2012). Produktive und weniger produktive Komposition in ihrer Rolle im Text an Hand der Beziehungen zwischen Titel und Text, in Livio Gaeta and Barbara Schlücker (eds), *Das Deutsche als kompositionsfreudige Sprache*. Berlin: de Gruyter, 219–32.

Dressler, Wolfgang U., Willi Mayerthaler, Oswald Panagl, and Wolfgang U. Wurzel (1987). *Leitmotifs in Natural Morphology*. Amsterdam and Philadelphia: Benjamins.

Dressler, Wolfgang U., Gary Libben, Jacqueline Stark, Christiane Pons, and Gonia Jarema (2001). The processing of interfixed German compounds. *Yearbook of Morphology* 1999, 185–220.

Dressler, Wolfgang U., Laura E. Lettner, and Katharina Korecky-Kröll (2010). First language acquisition of compounds with special emphasis on early German child language, in Sergio Scalise and Irene Vogel (eds), *Cross-disciplinary Issues in Compounding*. Amsterdam: Benjamins, 323–44.

Dressler, Wolfgang U., Anastasia Christofidou, Natalia Gagarina, Laura E. Lettner, Katharina Korecky-Kröll, Marianne Kilani-Schoch, and Elena Tribushinina (2012). Morphological blind alley developments as a challenge to both usage-based and nativist acquisition models. In prep.

Dryer, Matthew (1986). Primary objects, secondary objects, and antidative., *Language* 62. 808–45.

Dryer, M. S. (1992). The Greenbergian word order correlations. *Language* 68, 81–138.

Dryer, Matthew S. (1995). Frequency and pragmatically unmarked word order. In Pamela A. Downing and Michael Noonan (eds), *Word Order in Discourse*. Amsterdam: Benjamins, 105–36.

Dryer, M. S. (1998). Why statistical universals are better than absolute universals. Papers from the 33rd Annual Meeting of the Chicago Linguistic Society, 123–45.

Dryer, M. S. (2005). Relationship between the order of object and verb and the order of relative clause and noun, in M. Haspelmath et al. (eds.), *The World Atlas of Language Structures Online*. Leipzig: Max Planck Institute for Evolutionary Anthropology, 390–3, <http://wals.info>, accessed January 25, 2014.

Dryer, M. S. with Gensler, O. D. (2005). Order of object, oblique, and verb, in M. Haspelmath et al. (eds), *The World Atlas of Language Structures Online*. Leipzig: Max Planck Institute for Evolutionary Anthropology, 342–5, <http://wals.info>, accessed January 25, 2014.

Dryer, M. (2006). Functionalism and the Metalanguage—Theory Confusion, in G. W. G. Libben, T. Priestly, R. Smyth, and S. Wang (eds), *Phonology, Morphology, and the Empirical Imperative: Papers in Honour of Bruce Derwing*. Taipei: The Crane Publishing Company, 27–59.

Dryer, Matthew (2007). Clause types, in Timothy Shopen (ed.), *Language Typology and Syntactic Description*, Volume II. 2nd edn. Cambridge: Cambridge University Press, 224–75.

Du Bois, John W. (1980). The search for a cultural niche: Showing the Pear Film in a Mayan community. In Wallace L. Chafe (ed.), *The Pear Stories: Cognitive, Cultural, and Linguistic Aspects of Narrative Production*. Norwood, NJ: Ablex, 1–7.

Du Bois, John W. (1985). Competing motivations, in John Haiman (ed.), *Iconicity in Syntax. Proceedings of a symposium on iconicity in syntax*. Amsterdam and Philadelphia: Benjamins, 343–65.

Du Bois, John W. (1987a). Absolute zero: Paradigm adaptivity in Sacapultec Maya. *Lingua* 71, 203–22.

Du Bois, John W. (1987b). The discourse basis of ergativity. *Language* 63, 805–55.

Du Bois, John W. (2003a). Argument structure: Grammar in use, in John W. Du Bois, Lorraine E. Kumpf, and William J. Ashby (eds), *Preferred Argument Structure: Grammar as Architecture for Function*. Amsterdam: Benjamins, 11–60.

Du Bois, John W. (2003b). Discourse and grammar, in Michael Tomasello (ed.), *The New Psychology of Language: Cognitive and Functional Approaches to Language Structure*, Volume 2. Mahwah, NJ: Erlbaum, 47–87.

Du Bois, John W. (2006). The Pear Story in Sakapultek Maya: A case study of information flow and Preferred Argument Structure. In Mercedes Sedano, Adriana Bolívar, and Martha Shiro (eds), *Haciendo lingüística: Homenaje a Paola Bentivoglio*. Caracas: Universidad Central de Venezuela, 189–220.

Du Bois, John W. (2013). Representing discourse. Linguistics Department, University of California, Santa Barbara.

Du Bois, John W. (in progress). Twelve principles of functional explanation. Linguistics Department, University of California, Santa Barbara.

Du Bois, John W., Wallace L. Chafe, Charles Meyer, Sandra A. Thompson, Robert Englebretson, and Nii Martey (2000–2005). *Santa Barbara Corpus of Spoken American English, Parts 1–4.* Philadelphia: Linguistic Data Consortium.

Du Bois, John W., Lorraine E. Kumpf, and William J. Ashby (eds) (2003). *Preferred Argument Structure: Grammar as Architecture for Function.* Amsterdam: Benjamins.

Dufter, Andreas, Jürg Fleischer, and Guido Seiler (eds) (2009). *Describing and Modeling Variation in Grammar* (Trends in Linguistics 204). Berlin and New York: Mouton de Gruyter.

Durie, Mark (1995). Towards an understanding of linguistic evolution and the notion "X has a function Y", in Werner Abraham, Talmy Givón, and Sandra A. Thompson (eds), *Discourse Grammar and Typology: Papers in Honor of John W.M. Verhaar.* Amsterdam: Benjamins, 275–308.

Dziubalska-Kołaczyk, Katarzyna (2009). NP extension: B&B phonotactics. *Poznan Studies in Contemporary Linguistics* 45, 55–73.

Dziubalska-Kołaczyk, Katarzyna and Jaroslaw Weckwerth (eds) (2002). *Future Challenges for Natural Linguistics.* München: Lincom.

Eckardt, R. (2006). *Meaning Change in Grammaticalization: An Enquiry into Semantic Reanalysis.* Oxford: Oxford University Press.

Eckardt, Regine, Gerhard Jäger, and Tonjes Veenstra (eds) (2008). *Variation, Selection, Development. Probing the Evolutionary Model of Language Change.* Berlin and New York: Mouton de Gruyter.

Edelman, Gerald (1987). *Neural Darwinism: The Theory of Neuronal Group Selection.* New York: Basic Books

Egbokhare, F. (2001). Phonetic correspondences in Emai attributive ideophones, in E. Voeltz and C. Kilian-Hatz (eds), *Ideophones.* Amsterdam: Benjamins, 87–96.

Ehrismann, Gustav (1902). Duzen und Ihrzen im Mittelalter [I]. *Zeitschrift für deutsche Wortforschung* 2, 118–59.

Ehrismann, Gustav (1903). Duzen und Ihrzen im Mittelalter [II]. *Zeitschrift für deutsche Wortforschung* 4, 210–48.

Eitelmann, Matthias (2012). Weighing end-weight as a determinant of linguistic variation and change. Paper presented at the 33rd ICAME conference, Leuven, 30 May–3 June.

Ellis, Nick, Matthew O'Donnell, and Ute Römer, (2014). Usage-based language learning. In B. MacWhinney and W. O'Grady (eds), *Handbook of Language Emergence.* New York: Wiley.

Ellroy, J. (2001). The stalking detective. *New York Times,* 7 January 2001.

Elman, J. L. (1990). Finding structure in time. *Cognitive Science* 14, 179–212.

Elman, J. L., M. Hare, and K. McRae (2005). Cues, constraints, and competition in sentence processing, in M. Tomasello and D. Slobin (eds), *Beyond Nature–Nurture: Essays in Honor of Elizabeth Bates.* Mahwah, NJ: Lawrence Erlbaum Associates.

Emonds, Joseph (1973). Parenthetical clauses, in C. Corum et al. (eds), *You take the high node and I'll take the low node.* Chicago: Linguistic Society, 333–47.

Emonds, Joseph E. (1986). Grammatically deviant prestige constructions, in M. Brame, H. Contreras, and F. J. Newmeyer (ed.), *A Festschrift for Sol Saporta.* Seattle: Noit Amrofer, 93–131.

Erguvanlı, E. E. (1984). *The Function of Word Order in Turkish Grammar.* Berkeley/Los Angeles/London: University of California Press.

Erman, Britt and Beatrice Warren (2000). The idiom principle and the open choice principle. *Text* 20, 29–62.

Espinal, M. Teresa (1991). The representation of disjunct constituents. *Language* 67, 726–62.

Evans, Nicholas (2003a). *Bininj Gun-wok: A Pan-dialectal Grammar of Mayali, Kun-winjku and Kune.* Canberra: Australian National University.

Evans, Nicholas (2003b). Context, culture, and structuration in the languages of Australia. *Annual Review of Anthropology* 32, 13–40.

Evans, Nicholas (2007). Insubordination and its uses, in Irina Nicolaeva (ed.), *Finiteness: Theoretical and Empirical Foundations.* Oxford: Oxford University Press, 366–431.

Evans, N. and S. Levinson (2009). The myth of language universals: Language diversity and its importance for cognitive science. *Behavioral and Brain Sciences* 32, 429–92.

Fausey, C. M. et al. (2010). Constructing agency: The role of language. *Frontiers in Psychology* 1, 1–11.

Feldman, Jerome (2006). *From Molecule to Metaphor: A Neural Theory of Language.* Cambridge, MA: MIT Press.

Felleman, D. J. and D. C. Van Essen (1991). Distributed hierarchical processing in the primate cerebral cortex. *Cerebral cortex* 1, 1–47.

Fenk-Oczlon, Gertraud and August Fenk (2008). Complexity trade-offs between the subsystems of language. In Matti Miestamo, Kaius Sinnemäki, and Fred Karlsson (eds), *Language Complexity: Typology, Contact, Change.* Amsterdam: Benjamins.

Ferreira, Fernanda (1994). Choice of passive voice is affected by verb type and animacy. *Journal of Memory and Language* 33, 715–36.

Field, Andy (2010). *Discovering Statistics using SPSS*, 3rd edn. London: Sage Publications Ltd.

Filipović, L. and J. A. Hawkins (2013). Multiple factors in second language acquisition: The CASP model. *Linguistics* 51(1), 145–76.

Fillmore, Charles J. (1977). Topics in lexical semantics. In R. Cole (ed.), *Current Issues in Linguistic Theory.* Bloomington: Indiana University Press, 76–138.

Fillmore, Charles J. (1999). Inversion and constructional inheritance, in G. Webelhuth, J.-P. Koenig, and A. Kathol (eds), *Lexical and Constructional Aspects of Linguistic Explanation.* Stanford, CA: CSLI Publications, 113–28.

Firbas, Jan (1965). A note on transition proper in functional sentence perspective. *Philologia Pragensia* 8, 170–6.

Fischer, Olga (2010). An analogical approach to grammaticalization, in Ekaterini Stathi, Elke Gehweiler, and Ekkehart König (eds), *Grammaticalization: Current Views and Issues.* Amsterdam: Benjamins, 181–219.

Fisher, C. (2002). Structural limits on verb mapping: The role of abstract structure in 2.5-year-olds' interpretations of novel verbs. *Developmental Science*, 5(1), 55–64.

Fodor, J. D. (1978). Parsing strategies and constraints on transformations. *Linguistic Inquiry* 8, 425–504.

Ford, Cecilia E. (2004). Contingency and units in interaction. *Discourse Studies* 6(1), 27–52.

Forrest, L. B. (1996). Discourse goals and attentional processes in sentence production: The dynamic construal of events, in A. E. Goldberg (ed.), *Conceptual Structure, Discourse and Language.* Stanford, CA: CSLI Publications, 149–62.

Fortescue, Michael D. (1984). *West Greenlandic.* London: Croom Helm.

Foulet, Lucien (1918–19). Le tutoiement en ancien français. *Romania* 45, 501–3.

Fox, Barbara A., and Robert Jasperson (1995). A syntactic exploration of repair in English conversation, in P. W. Davis (ed.), *Alternative Linguistics: Descriptive and Theoretical modes.* Amsterdam and Philadelphia: John Benjamins, 77–134.

Fox, Barbara A., Makoto Hayashi, and Robert Jasperson (1996). Resources and repair: A cross-linguistic study of syntax and repair, in E. Ochs, E. A. Schegloff, and S. A. Thompson (eds.), *Interaction and Grammar.* Cambridge: Cambridge University Press, 185–237.

Fox, Barbara A., Yael Maschler, and Susanne Uhmann (2009). Morpho-syntactic resources for the organization of same-turn self-repair: Cross-linguistic variation in English, German and Hebrew. *Gesprächsforschung—Online-Zeitschrift zur verbalen Interaktion* 10, 245–91. <http://www.gespraechsforschung-ozs.de/heft2009/ga-fox.pdf>, accessed January 25, 2014.

Fox, Danny, and Jon Nissenbaum (1999). Extraposition and scope: A case for overt QR, in S, Bird, A. Carnie, J. D. Haugen, and P. Norquest (eds), *Proceedings of the 18th West Coast Conference on Formal Linguistics,* 9–11 April 1999, Tucson. Somerville: Cascadilla Press, 132–144.

Franchetto, Bruna (1990). Ergativity and nominativity in Kuikúro and other Carib languages, in Doris Payne (ed.), *Amazonian Linguistics: Studies in Lowland South American Languages.* Austin: University of Texas Press, 407–27.

Francis, Elaine J. (2010). Grammatical weight and relative clause extraposition in English. *Cognitive Linguistics* 21(1), 35–74.

Francis, Elaine J. and Laura A. Michaelis (eds) (2003). *Mismatch. Form–function Incongruity and the Architecture of Grammar.* Stanford, CA: The Center for the Study of Language and Information.

Frazier, L. (1987). Syntactic processing: Evidence from Dutch. *Natural Language and Linguistic Theory* 5, 519–59.

Freudenthal, Daniel, Julian Pine, and Fernand Gobet (2007). Understanding the developmental dynamics of subject omission: The role of processing limitations in learning. *Journal of Child Language* 34, 83–110.

Friederici, A. D. (2009). Pathways to language: Fiber tracts in the human brain. *Trends in Cognitive Sciences* 13, 175–81.

Frisch, S. and M. Schlesewsky (2001). The N400 indicates problems of thematic hierarchizing. *Neuroreport* 12, 3391–94.

Frith, U. and C. D. Frith (2010). The social brain: Allowing humans to boldly go where no other species has been. *Philosophical Transactions of the Royal Society B* 365, 165–76.

Gabelentz, Georg von der (1901). *Die Sprachwissenschaft, ihre Aufgaben, Methoden und bisherigen Ergebnisse.* 2nd edn. Leipzig: C. H. Tauchnitz.

Gallmann, Peter (2006). Der Satz, in M. Wermke, K. Kunzel-Razum, and W. Scholze-Stubenrecht (eds), *Duden. Die Grammatik.* Mannheim: Dudenverlag, 773–1066.

Gamut, L. T. F. (1991). *Logic, Language, and Meaning,* Volume 1: Introduction to logic. Chicago: University of Chicago Press.

García, Erica C. (1990). A psycho-linguistic crossroads: Frequency of use. *Journal of Semantics* 7(3), 301–19.

Garfinkel, H. (1967). *Studies in Ethnomethodology.* Englewood Cliffs, NJ: Prentice Hall.

Gast, Volker (2007). *I gave it him:* On the motivation of the "alternative double object construction" in varieties of British English. *Functions of Language* 14(1), 31–56.

Gathercole, Virginia C. M., Nadine Laporte, and Enlli Thomas (2005). Differentiation, carry-over, and the distributed characteristic in bilinguals: Structural "mixing" of the two languages? in J. Cohen, K. T. McAlister, K. Rolstad, and J. MacSwan (eds), *Proceedings of the 4th International Symposium on Bilingualism.* Somerville, MA: Cascadilla Press, 838–51.

Gazzaniga, Michael S. (1970). *The Bisected Brain.* New York: Appleton-Century-Crofts.

Gell-Mann, Murray (1992). Complexity and complex adaptive domains, in John A. Hawkins and Murray Gell-Mann (eds), *The Evolution of Human Languages.* (SFI Studies in the Sciences of Complexity, Proceedings vol. XI) Redwood City: Addison-Wesley, 3–18.

Gell-Mann, Murray (2005). Language and complexity, in James W. Minett and William S.-Y. Wang (eds), *Language Acquisition, Change and Emergence: Essays in Evolutionary Linguistics*. Hong Kong: City University of Hong Kong, 389–410.

Gentner, Dedre (1983). Structure-mapping: A theoretical framework for analogy. *Cognitive Science* 7, 155–70.

Gentner, Dedre (1989). The mechanisms of analogical learning, in S. Vosniadou and A. Ortony (eds), *Similarity and Analogical Reasoning*. London: Cambridge University Press, 199–241). (Reprinted in *Knowledge Acquisition and Learning*, 1993, 673–94).

Gerdts, Donna (2010). Ditransitive constructions in Halkomelem Salish: A direct object/ oblique object language, in Andrej L. Malchukov et al. (eds.), *Studies in Ditransitive Constructions: A Comparative Handbook*. Berlin: Mouton De Gruyter, 563–611.

Gerken, LouAnn (1991). The metrical basis for children's subjectless sentences. *Journal of Memory and Language* 30, 431–51.

Gerken, L., R. Wilson, and W. Lewis (2005). Infants can use distributional cues to form syntactic categories. *Journal of Child Language* 32(2), 249–68.

Gernsbacher, Morton Ann (1990). *Language Comprehension as Structure Building*. Hillsdale, NJ: Lawrence Erlbaum.

Gernsbacher, Morton Ann and Mark E. Faust (1991). The mechanism of suppression: A component of general comprehension skill. *Journal of Experimental Psychology: Learning, Memory, and Cognition* 17(2), 245–62.

Gertner, Yael, Cynthia Fisher, and Julie Eisengart (2006). Learning words and rules: Abstract knowledge of word order in early sentence comprehension. *Psychological Science* 17(8), 684–91.

Geurts, Bart (2005). Entertaining alternatives: Disjunctions as modals. *Natural Language Semantics* 13, 383–410.

Gibson, E. (1998). Linguistic complexity: Locality of syntactic dependencies. *Cognition* 68, 1–76.

Gibson, Edward (2000). The dependency locality theory: A distance-based theory of linguistic complexity, in A. P. Marantz, Y. Miyashita, and W. O'Neil (eds), *Image, Language, Brain: Papers from the First Mind Articulation Project Symposium*. Cambridge, MA: MIT Press, 95–126.

Gibson, James J. (1979). *The Ecological Approach to Visual Perception*. Boston: Houghton Mifflin.

Gil, David (2005). From repetition to reduplication in Riau Indonesian, in B. Hurch (ed.), *Studies on Reduplication*. Berlin: Mouton de Gruyter, 34–56.

Gildea, S. (1998). *On Reconstructing Grammar: Comparative Cariban Morphosyntax*. Oxford: Oxford University Press.

Gildea, S. (2012). The referential hierarchy and attention. *Faits de langues* 38, 33–47.

Gilhooly, Ken J. and R. H. Logie (1980). Age of acquisition, imagery, concreteness, familiarity, and ambiguity measures for 1,944 words, *Behavior Research Methods, Instruments, and Computers* 12, 395–427.

Giora, Rachel (2003). *On our Mind: Salience, Context, and Figurative Language*. Oxford: Oxford University Press.

Givón, Talmy (1979). *On Understanding Grammar*. New York: Academic Press.

Givón, Talmy (ed.) (1983a). *Topic Continuity in Discourse: A Quantitative Cross-language Study*. Amsterdam: Benjamins.

Givón, Talmy (1983b). Topic continuity in discourse: An introduction, in T. Givón (ed.), *Topic Continuity in Discourse: A Quantitative Cross-language Study*, 1–41.

Givón, Talmy (1984). *Syntax: A Functional-Typological Introduction*, Volume I. Amsterdam: Benjamins.

Givón, Talmy (ed.) (1994a). *Voice and Inversion*. Amsterdam: John Benjamins.

Givón, Talmy (1994b). The pragmatics of de-transitive voice: Functional and typological aspects of inversion', in Givón, T. (ed.), *Voice and Inversion*. Amsterdam: Benjamins, 3–44.

Givón, Talmy (1995). *Functionalism and Grammar*. Amsterdam: Benjamins.

Givón, Talmy (2001). *Syntax: An introduction. Volume I*. Amsterdam and Philadelphia: John Benjamins.

Givón, Talmy (2009). *The Genesis of Syntactic Complexity: Diachrony, Ontogeny, Neuro-Cognition, Evolution*. Amsterdam and Philadelphia: Benjamins.

Glasser, M. F. and J. K. Rilling (2008). DTI tractography of the human brain's language pathways. *Cereb Cortex* 18, 2471–82.

Gleitman, L. et al. (2007). On the give-and-take between event apprehension and utterance formulation. *Journal of Memory and Language* 57, 544–69.

Goldberg, Adele E. (1995). *Constructions: A Construction Grammar Approach to Argument Structure*. Chicago: University of Chicago Press.

Goldberg, Adele E. (2004). Pragmatics and argument structure, in Laurence R. Horn and Gregory Ward (eds), *The Handbook of Pragmatics*. Oxford: Blackwell, 427–41.

Goldberg, Adele E. (2006). *Constructions at Work: The Nature of Generalization in Language*. Oxford: Oxford University Press.

Golob, E. J., H. Pratt, and A. Star (2002). Preparatory slow potentials and event-related potentials in an auditory cued attention task. *Clinical Neurophysiology* 113, 1544–57.

Goodwin, C. (1994). Professional vision. *American Anthropologist* 96, 606–33.

Goosen, F. (2003). *Liegen lernen*. Frankfurt am Main: W. Heyne.

Gordon, Peter C., Randall Hendrick, and Marcus Johnson (2001). Memory interference during language processing. *Journal of Experimental Psychology-Learning Memory and Cognition* 27(6), 1411–23.

Gough, Philip B. (1965). Grammatical transformations and speed of understanding. *Journal of Verbal Learning and Verbal Behavior* 4, 107–11.

Gould, Stephen J. and Richard C. Lewontin (1979). The spandrels of San Marcos and the Panglossian paradigm: A critique of the adaptationist programme. *Proceedings of the Royal Society of London* B 205, 581–98.

Graf, Eileen (2010). An experimental pragmatics approach to children's argument omissions. Unpublished doctoral dissertation: Max Planck Child Study Centre, University of Manchester, and Max Planck Institute for Evolutionary Anthropology, Leipzig.

Greenbaum, Sidney (ed.) (1996). *Comparing English Worldwide: The International Corpus of English*. Oxford: Clarendon Press.

Greenberg, Joseph H. (1954). A quantitative approach to the morphological typology of language. *International Journal of American Linguistics* 26, 178–94.

Greenberg, Joseph H. (1966a). *Language Universals, with Particular Reference to Feature Hierarchies*. The Hague: Mouton.

Greenberg, Joseph H. (1966b). Some universals of grammar with particular reference to the order of meaningful elements, in J. H. Greenberg (ed.), *Universals of Language*. Cambridge, MA: MIT Press, 73–113.

Greenberg, Joseph H. (1978). How does a language acquire gender markers? in J. H. Greenberg, C. H. Ferguson, and E. A. Moravcsik (eds), *Universals of Human Language. Volume 3*. Stanford: Stanford University Press, 47–82.

Greeno, James G. (1994). Gibson's affordances. *Psychological Review* 101(2), 336–42.

Gregory, Michelle L. and Laura A. Michaelis (2001). Topicalization and left dislocation: A functional opposition revisited, *Journal of Pragmatics* 33, 1665–706.

Grenoble, Lenore (2004). Parentheticals in Russian. *Journal of Pragmatics* 36(11), 1953–74.

Grewe, T. et al. (2005). The emergence of the unmarked: A new perspective on the language-specific function of Broca's area. *Human Brain Mapping* 26, 178–90.

Grewe, T. et al. (2006). Linguistic prominence and Broca's area: The influence of animacy as a linearization principle. *Neuroimage* 32, 1395–402.

Grice, H. (1975). Logic and conversation, in P. Cole and J. L. Morgan (eds), *Syntax and Semantics: Speech Acts* Volume 3. New York: Academic Press.

Grierson, G. A. (1883–1887). *Seven Grammars of the Dialects and Subdialects of the Bihárí language. Part III.* Calcutta: Bengal Secretariat.

Gries, Stefan (2003a). *Multifactorial Analysis in Corpus Linguistics: A Study of Particle Placement.* New York: Continuum Press.

Gries, Stefan T. (2003b). Towards a corpus-based identification of prototypical members of constructions. *Annual Review of Cognitive Linguistics* 1(1), 1–28.

Gries, Stefan T. (2005). Syntactic priming: A corpus-based approach. *Journal of Psycholinguistic Research* 34(4), 365–99.

Gries, Stefan T. (2009). *Quantitative Corpus Linguistics with R: A Practical Introduction.* London: Routledge.

Gries, Stefan T. (2010). *Statistics for Linguists Using R: A Practical Introduction.* Berlin: Mouton de Gruyter.

Gries, Stefan T., Beate Hampe, and Doris Schönefeld (2010). Converging evidence II: More on the association of verbs and constructions, in Sally Rice and John Newman (eds), *Empirical and Experimental Methods in Cognitive/Functional Research.* Stanford: CSLI Publications.

Grimshaw, Jane (1990). *Argument Structure. Linguistic Inquiry Monograph*, Volume 18. Cambridge, MA: MIT Press.

Grimshaw, Jane and Vieri Samek-Lodovici (1998). Optimal subjects and subject universals, in Pilar Barbosa et al. (eds), *Is the Best Good Enough? Optimality and Competition in Syntax.* Cambridge: MIT Press, 193–219.

Gropen, Jess, Steven Pinker, Michelle Hollander, Richard Goldberg, and Ronald Wilson (1989). The learnability and acquisition of the dative alternation in English. *Language* 65(2), 203–57.

Grünloh, T., E. V. Lieven, and M. Tomasello, (2011). German children use prosody to identify participant roles in transitive sentences. *Cognitive Linguistics* 22(2), 393–419.

Guasti, Maria Teresa (2002). *Language Acquisition: The Growth of Grammar.* Cambridge: MIT Press.

Guéron, Jacqueline and Robert May (1984). Extraposition and logical form. *Linguistic Inquiry* 15(1), 1–31.

Guerrero Medina, Pilar (ed.) (2011). *Morphosyntactic Alternations in English: Functional and Cognitive Perspectives.* London: Equinox.

Guerriero, Sonia, Yuriko Oshima-Takane, and Yoko Kuriyama (2006). The development of referential choice in English and Japanese: A discourse-pragmatic perspective. *Journal of Child Language* 33(4), 823–57.

Gülzow, Insa and Natalia Gagarina (eds) (2007). *Frequency Effects in Language Acquisition.* Berlin: De Gruyter.

Gundel, Jeanette K., Nancy Hedberg, and Ron Zacharski (1993). Cognitive status and the form of referring expressions in discourse. *Language* 69, 274–307.

Günthner, Susanne (2007). Brauchen wir eine Theorie der gesprochenen Sprache? Und: wie kann sie aussehen? Ein Plädoyer für eine praxisorientierte Grammatiktheorie. *gidi Arbeitspapierreihe* Nr. 6, <http://noam.uni-muenster.de/gidi/arbeitspapiere/arbeitspapier06.pdf>, accessed January 30, 2014.

Haegeman, Liliane (1988). Parenthetical adverbials: The radical orphanage approach, in S. Chiba, A. Shuki, A. Ogawa, Y. Fuiwara, N. Yamada, O. Koma, and T. Yagi (eds), *Aspects of Modern Linguistics: Papers Presented to Masatomo Ukaji on his 60th Birthday*. Tokyo: Kaitakushi, 232–54.

Haegeman, Liliane (1991). Parenthetical adverbials: The radical orphanage approach, in S. Chiba et al. (eds), *Aspects of Modern English Linguistics. Papers Presented to Masamoto Ukaji on his 60th Birthday*. Tokyo: Kaitakushi, 232–54.

Haggard, P. (2008). Human volition: Towards a neuroscience of will. *Nature Reviews Neuroscience* 9, 934–46.

Haiman, John (1980). The iconicity of grammar: Isomorphism and motivation. *Language* 56, 515–40.

Haiman, John (1983). Iconic and economic motivation. *Language* 59, 781–819.

Haiman, John (ed.) (1985a). *Iconicity in Syntax. Proceedings of a symposium on iconicity in syntax, Stanford*. Amsterdam/Philadelphia: Benjamins.

Haiman, John (1985b). *Natural Syntax: Iconicity and Erosion*. Cambridge: Cambridge University Press.

Haiman, John (1998). *Talk is Cheap*. Oxford: Oxford University Press.

Haiman, John (2010a). The creation of new words. *Linguistics* 48(3), 547–72.

Haiman, John (2010b). Competing motivations, in Jae Jung Song (ed.), *The Oxford Handbook of Linguistic Typology*. Oxford: Oxford University Press, 148–65.

Haiman, John (2011). *Cambodian: Khmer*. (LOALL 16). Amsterdam: Benjamins.

Haiman, John (forthcoming). *Ideophones and the Evolution of Language: From Gestures to Words*. Cambridge: Cambridge University Press.

Haiman, John and T. Kuteva (2001). The symmetry of counterfactuals. J. Bybee and M. Noonan (eds), *Complex Sentences in Grammar and Discourse*. Amsterdam: John Benjamins, 101–24.

Haiman, John and N. Ourn (2009). Decorative symmetry in ritual (and everyday) language. Roberta Corrigan et al. (eds), *Formulaic Language*, II: 567–87. Amsterdam: Benjamins.

Halliday, Michael A. K. and R. Hassan (1976). *Cohesion in English*. London: Longman.

Halliday, Michael A. K. (2004). *An Introduction to Functional Grammar*. 3rd edition. London: Arnold.

Halliday, Michael A. K. and C. Matthiessen (2004). *An Introduction to Functional Grammar*. 3rd revised edition. London: Hodder Arnold.

Hamann, Cornelia and Kim Plunkett (1998). Subjectless sentences in child Danish. *Cognition* 69, 35–72.

Harris, A. C. (1985). *Diachronic Syntax: The Kartvelian Case*. New York: Academic Press.

Harris, Alice C. and Lyle Campbell (1995). *Historical Syntax in Cross-linguistic Perspective*. Cambridge: Cambridge University Press.

Haspelmath, Martin (1999a). Explaining article-possessor complementarity: Economic motivation in noun phrase syntax. *Language* 75: 227–243.

Haspelmath, Martin (1999b). Optimality and diachronic adaptation. *Zeitschrift für Sprachwissenschaft* 18(2): 180–205.

Haspelmath, Martin (1999c). Why is grammaticalization irreversible? *Linguistics* 37, 1043–68.

Haspelmath, Martin (2001). Non-canonical marking of core arguments in European languages, in A. Aikhenvald et al. (eds.). *Non-canonical Marking of Subjects and Objects.* Amsterdam: Benjamins, 53–85.

Haspelmath, Martin (2002). *Understanding Morphology.* London: Arnold.

Haspelmath, Martin (2004a). Explaining the ditransitive person-role constraint: A usage-based approach. *Constructions* 2.

Haspelmath, Martin (2004b). Coordinating constructions: An overview, in Martin Haspelmath (ed.), *Coordinating Constructions.* Amsterdam: John Benjamins, 3–39.

Haspelmath, Martin (2005a). Ditransitive Constructions: The Verb 'Give', in Martin Haspelmath, Matthew S. Dryer, David Gil, and Bernard Comrie (eds), *The World Atlas of Language Structures.* Oxford: Oxford University Press, 426–429.

Haspelmath, Martin (2005b). Argument marking in ditransitive alignment types, *Linguistic Discovery* 3.1:1–21.

Haspelmath, Martin (2005c). Occurrence of nominal plurality, in B. Comrie, M. Dryer, D. Gil, and M. Haspelmath (eds), *The World Atlas of Language Structures.* Oxford: Oxford University Press, 142–5.

Haspelmath, Martin (2006). Against markedness (and what to replace it with). *Journal of Linguistics* 42, 25–70.

Haspelmath, Martin (2007a). Ditransitive alignment splits and inverse alignment. *Functions of Language* 14(1), 79–102.

Haspelmath, Martin (2007b). Coordination, in Timothy Shopen (ed.), *Language Typology and Syntactic Description, Volume II: Complex Constructions.* 2nd edn. Cambridge: Cambridge University Press, 1–51.

Haspelmath, Martin (2008a). Frequency vs. iconicity in explaining grammatical asymmetries. *Cognitive Linguistics* 19(1), 1–33.

Haspelmath, Martin (2008b). Creating economical morphosyntactic patterns in language change, in Jeff Good (ed.), *Language Universals and Language Change.* Oxford: Oxford University Press, 185–214.

Haspelmath, Martin (2008c). A frequentist explanation of some universals of reflexive marking. *Linguistic Discovery* 6(1), 40–63.

Haspelmath, Martin (2009). An empirical test of the agglutination hypothesis, in Sergio Scalise, Elisabetta Magni, and Antonietta Bisetto (eds), *Universals of Language Today* (Studies in Natural Language and Linguistic Theory, 76). Dordrecht: Springer, 13–29.

Haspelmath, Martin, Andreea Calude, Michael Spagnol, Heiko Narrog, and Elif Bamyacı (2014). Coding causal-noncausal verb alternations: A form-frequency correspondence explanation. *Journal of Linguistics*, to appear.

Haspelmath, Martin, M. S. Dryer, D. Gil, and B. Comrie (eds) (2005). *The World Atlas of Language Structures (WALS).* Oxford: Oxford University Press.

Hauk, Olaf, Ingrid Johnsrude, and Friedemann Pulvermuller (2004). Somatotopic representation of action words in human motor and premotor cortex. *Neuron* 41, 301–7.

Haumann, Dagmar (2004). Degree phrases versus quantifier phrases in prenominal and preverbal positions: A hybrid explanation for some distributional asymmetries, in Jennifer R. Austin, Stefan Engelberg, and Gisa Rauh (eds), *Adverbials. The interplay between Meaning, Context, and Syntactic Structure.* Amsterdam: Benjamins, 167–203.

Haupt, F. S. et al. (2008). The status of subject–object reanalyses in the language comprehension architecture. *Journal of Memory and Language* 59, 54–96.

Haviland, John (1980). Guugu Yimidhirr brother-in-law language. *Language and Society* 8, 365–93.

Hawkins, John A. (1983). *Word Order Universals.* New York: Academic Press.

Hawkins, John A. (ed.) (1988). *Explaining Language Universals*. Oxford: Blackwell.

Hawkins, John A. (1994). *A Performance Theory of Order and Constituency*. Cambridge: Cambridge University Press.

Hawkins, John A. (1999). Processing complexity and filler-gap dependencies. *Language* 75, 244–85.

Hawkins, John A. (2000). The relative order of prepositional phrases in English: Going beyond Manner-Place-Time., *Language Variation and Change* 11, 231–66.

Hawkins, John A. (2003). Why are zero-marked phrases close to their heads?, in Günter Rohdenburg and Britta Mondorf (eds), *Determinants of Grammatical Variation in English*, (Topics in English Linguistics 43) Berlin: Mouton de Gruyter, 175–204.

Hawkins, John A. (2004). *Efficiency and Complexity in Grammars*. Oxford: Oxford University Press.

Hawkins, John A. (2008). An asymmetry between VO and OV languages: The ordering of obliques, in G. Corbett and M. Noonan (eds), *Case and Grammatical Relations: Essays in Honour of Bernard Comrie*. Amsterdam: John Benjamins, 167–90.

Hawkins, John A. (2009a). Language universals and the performance–grammar correspondence hypothesis, in M. H. Christiansen, C. Collins, and S. Edelman (eds), *Language Universals*. Oxford: Oxford University Press, 54–78.

Hawkins, John A. (2009b). An efficiency theory of complexity and related phenomena, in Geoffrey Sampson, David Gil, and Peter Trudgill (eds), *Language Complexity as an Evolving Variable. Studies in the Evolution of Language*. Oxford: Oxford University Press, 252–68.

Hawkins, John A. (2011). Discontinuous dependencies in corpus selections: Particle verbs and their relevance for current issues in language processing, in E. M. Bender and J. E. Arnold (eds), *Language from a Cognitive Perspective: Grammar, Usage and Processing, Studies in Honor of Thomas Wasow*. Stanford: CSLI Publications, 269–90.

Hawkins, John A. (2014). *Cross-linguistic Variation and Efficiency*. Oxford: Oxford University Press.

Hawkins, John A. with P. Buttery (2009). Using learner language from corpora to profile levels of proficiency: Insights from the English Profile Programme, in L. Taylor and C. J. Weir (eds), *Language Testing Matters*. Cambridge: Cambridge University Press, 158–75.

Hawkins, John A. and P. Buttery (2010). Criterial features in learner corpora: Theory and illustrations. *English Profile Journal* 1, e5.

Hawkins, John A. and L. Filipović (2012). *Criterial Features in L2 English*. Cambridge: Cambridge University Press.

Hay, Jennifer (2001). Lexical frequency in morphology: Is everything relative? *Linguistics* 39(6), 1041–70.

Head, Brian F. (1978). Respect degrees in pronominal reference, in Joseph H. Greenberg (ed.), *Universals of Human Language*, Volume 3. Stanford: Stanford University Press, 151–211.

Heath, Jeffrey (1976). Ergative/accusative typologies in morphology and syntax, in R. M. W. Dixon (ed.), *Grammatical Categories in Australian Languages*. Canberra: Australian Institute of Aboriginal Studies, 599–611.

Heekeren, H. R. et al. (2004). A general mechanism for perceptual decision-making in the human brain. *Nature* 431, 859–62.

Heine, Bernd (1982). African noun class systems, in H. Seiler and C. Lehmann (eds), *Apprehension: das sprachliche Erfassen von Gegenständen*. Tübingen: Narr, 189–216.

Heine, Bernd (1997). *Cognitive Foundations of Grammar*. Oxford: Oxford University Press.

Heine, Bernd and Kuteva, Tania (2005). *Language Contact and Grammatical Change*. Cambridge: Cambridge University Press.

Heine, Bernd and Tania Kuteva (2006). *The Changing Languages of Europe*. Oxford: Oxford University Press.

Heine, Bernd and K.-A. Song (2011). On the grammaticalization of personal pronouns. *Journal of Linguistics* 47, 1–44.

Heine, Bernd, U. Claudi, and F. Hünnemeyer (1991). *Grammaticalization*. Chicago: University of Chicago Press.

Heine, Bernd, Gunther Kaltenböck, and Tania Kutevam (forthcoming). On reconstructing elements of early human language, in Claire Lefebvre (ed.), *Language Origins*. Cambridge: Cambridge University Press.

Heine, Bernd, Gunther Kaltenböck, Tania Kuteva, and Haiping Long (2013). An outline of Discourse Grammar, in Shannon Bischoff and Carmen Jeny (eds), *Reflections on Functionalism in Linguistics*. Berlin: Mouton de Gruyter, 155–206.

Heller, J. (1972). *Catch-22*. New York: Simon & Schuster.

Helmbrecht, Johannes (2004). Personal Pronouns—Form, Function, and Grammaticalization. (Habilitationsschrift). Ms: University of Erfurt.

Helmbrecht, Johannes (2005a). Typologie und Diffusion von Höflichkeitspronomina in Europa. *Folia Linguistica* XXXIX(3–4), 417–53.

Helmbrecht, Johannes (2005b). Politeness distinctions in pronouns, in Martin Haspelmath, Matthew S. Dryer, David Gil, and Bernard Comrie (eds), *The World Atlas of Language Structures*. Oxford: Oxford University Press. 186–190. (Available online at <http://wals.info/feature/45>, accessed March 25, 2011.)

Helmbrecht, Johannes (2006). Personal pronouns—a corpus analysis and its implications for language typology. Paper presented at the 39th annual meeting of the *Societas Linguistica Europaea* at the University of Bremen, August 30–September 2, 2006). Unpublished manuscript: University of Erfurt.

Helmbrecht, Johannes (2010). Höflichkeitspronomina in Europa—Synchronie und Diachronie eines arealtypologischen Merkmals, in Uwe Hinrichs (ed.), *Handbuch der Eurolinguistik*. (Slavistische Studienbücher). Wiesbaden: Harrassowitz, 691–711.

Hemforth, B., L. Konieczny, and G. Strube (1993). Incremental syntax processing and parsing strategies, *Proceedings of the 15th Annual Conference of the Cognitive Science Society*. Hillsdale, NJ: Erlbaum, 539–45.

Hercus, L. (1982). *The Bagandji Language*. Pacific Linguistics. Series B-67. Canberra: The Australian National University.

Hewitt, George B. (1979). *Abkhaz* (Lingua Descriptive Studies, 2). North Holland, Amsterdam.

Hickey, Raymond (2003). *Motives for Language Change*. Cambridge: Cambridge University Press.

Hickok, Gregory (2009). The functional neuroanatomy of language. *Physics of Life Reviews* 6, 121–43.

Hickok, Gregory and D. Poeppel (2004). Dorsal and ventral streams: A framework for understanding aspects of the functional neuroanatomy of language. *Cognition* 92, 67–99.

Hickok, Gregory and D. Poeppel (2007). The cortical organization of speech processing. *Nature Reviews Neuroscience* 8, 393–402.

Hilpert, Martin (2008). The English comparative—language structure and language use. *English Language and Linguistics* 12(3), 395–417.

Hinrichs, Lars and Benedikt Szmrecsanyi (2007). Recent changes in the function and frequency of standard English genitive constructions: A multivariate analysis of tagged corpora, *English Language and Linguistics* 11(3), 437–74.

Hirotani, M. et al. (2011). Who was the agent? The neural correlates of reanalysis processes during sentence comprehension. *Human Brain Mapping* 32: 1775–87.

Hoekstra, Teun (1984). *Transitivity: Grammatical Relations in Government-Binding Theory.* Dordrecht: Foris.

Hoekstra, Teun and Nina Hyams (1998). Aspects of root infinitives. *Lingua* 106, 91–112.

Hoffmann, Ludger (1998). Parenthesen. *Linguistische Berichte* 175, 299–328.

Holland, John H. (1995). *Hidden Order: How Adaptation Builds Complexity.* Boston, MA: Addison-Wesley.

Holland, John H. (1998). *Emergence: From Chaos to Order.* Oxford: Oxford University Press.

Holland, John H. (2005). Language acquisition as a Complex Adaptive System, in James W. Minett and William S.-Y. Wang (eds), *Language Acquisition, Change and Emergence: Essays in Evolutionary Linguistics.* Hong Kong: City University of Hong Kong Press. 411–36.

Holton, G. (2008). The rise and fall of semantic alignment in Northern Halmahera, Indonesia, in M. Donohue and S. Wichmann (eds), *The Typology of Semantic Alignment.* Oxford: Oxford University Press, 252–76.

Hopper, Paul J. (1988). Emergent grammar and the apriori grammar postulate, in D. Tannen (ed.), *Linguistics in Context: Connecting Observation and Understanding.* Norwood, NJ: Ablex, 117–34.

Hopper, Paul J. (1998). Emergent grammar, in Michael Tomasello (ed.), *The New Psychology of Language: Cognitive and Functional Approaches to Language Structure,* Volume 1. Mahwah, NJ: Erlbaum, 155–75.

Hopper, Paul J. and Sandra A. Thompson (1980). Transitivity in grammar and discourse. *Language* 56, 251–99.

Hopper, Paul J. and Sandra A. Thompson (1993). Language universals, discourse pragmatics, and semantics. *Language Sciences* 15(4), 357–76.

Hopper, Paul J. and Elizabeth C. Traugott (2003). *Grammaticalization.* 2nd edn. Cambridge: Cambridge University Press.

Horn, Laurence R. (1972). On the semantic properties of the logical operators in English. Mimeo, Indiana University Linguistics Club.

Horn, Laurence R. (1978). Some aspects of negation, in Joseph H. Greenberg (ed.), *Universals of Human Language,* Volume 4. Stanford: Stanford University Press, 127–210.

Horn, Laurence (1984). Toward a new taxonomy for pragmatic inference: Q-based and R-based implicature, in D. Schiffrin (ed.), *Meaning, Form and Use in Context.* Washington, DC: Georgetown University Press, 11–42.

Huck, Geoffrey J. and Na Younghee (1990). Extraposition and focus. *Language* 66, 51–77.

Huddleston, Rodney and Geoffrey K. Pullum (2002). *The Cambridge Grammar of the English Language.* Cambridge: Cambridge University Press.

Hudson, Richard (1980). *Sociolinguistics.* London: Cambridge University Press.

Hughes, Mary E. (2011). An analysis of discourse-pragmatic and grammatical constraints on the acquisition and development of referential choice in child English. Unpublished doctoral dissertation: Boston University, Boston, MA.

Hughes, Mary E. and Shanley E. M. Allen (2006). A discourse-pragmatic analysis of subject omission in child English, in D. Bamman, T. Magnitskaia, and C. Zaller (eds), *Proceedings of the 30th annual Boston University Conference on Language Development.* Somerville, MA: Cascadilla Press, 293–304.

Hughes, Mary E. and Shanley E. M. Allen (2013). The effect of individual discourse-pragmatic features on referential choice in child English, *Journal of Pragmatics,* 56, 15–30 <http://dx.doi.org/10.1016/j.pragma.2013.05.005>.

Hung, Y. C. and P. B. Schumacher (2012). Topicality matters: Position-specific demands on Chinese discourse processing. *Neuroscience Letters* 511, 59–64.

Hurch, Bernhard (ed.) (2005). *Studies on Reduplication.* Berlin: Mouton- de Gruyter.

Hutton, James (1788). Theory of the Earth; or an investigation of the laws observable in the composition, dissolution, and restoration of land upon the globe. *Transactions of the Royal Society of Edinburgh* 1, 209–304.

Hyams, Nina (1986). *Language Acquisition and the Theory of Parameters*. Dordrecht: Reidel.

Hyams, Nina (1996). The underspecification of functional categories in early grammar, in H. Clahsen (ed.), *Generative Perspectives on Language Acquisition*. Amsterdam: Benjamins, 91–127.

Hyams, Nina (2011). Missing subjects in early child language, in Jill De Villiers and T. Roeper (eds.), *Handbook of Generative Approaches to Language Acquisition*. Amsterdam: Springer, 13–52.

Hyams, Nina (2012). Eventivity effects in early grammar: The case of non-finite verbs. *First Language* 32, 239–69.

Hyams, Nina and Kenneth Wexler (1993). On the grammatical basis of null subjects in child language. *Linguistic Inquiry* 24, 421–59.

Ibbotson, P. and M. Tomasello (2009). Prototype constructions in early language acquisition. *Language and Cognition* 1(1), 59–85.

Ibbotson, P., A. L. Theakston, E. V. Lieven, and M. Tomasello (2010). The role of pronoun frames in early comprehension of transitive constructions in English. *Language Learning and Development* 7(1), 24–39.

Ifantidou, Elly (2001). *Evidentials as Relevance* (Pragmatics and Beyond, IV: 6). Amsterdam and Philadelphia: Benjamins.

Ifantidou-Trouki, Elly (1993). Sentential adverbs and relevance. *Lingua* 90(1–2), 69–90.

Israel, Michael (1996). The *way* constructions grow, in Adele E. Goldberg (ed.), *Conceptual Structure, Discourse and Language*. Stanford: CSLI, 217–30.

Itkonen, Esa (2005). *Analogy as Structure and Process*. Amsterdam: Benjamins.

Iverson, Jana and Esther Thelen (1999). Hand, mouth and brain. *Journal of Consciousness Studies* 6, 19–40.

Jackendoff, Ray (1972). *Semantic Interpretation in Generative Grammar*. Cambridge, MA: MIT Press.

Jäger, Gerhard (2007). Evolutionary game theory and typology: A case study. *Language* 83(1), 74–109.

Jäger, Siegfried (1971). *Der Konjunktiv in der deutschen Sprache der Gegenwart. Untersuchungen an ausgewählten Texten*. München: Hueber.

Jaggar, Philip (2001). *Hausa* (LOALL, 7). Amsterdam: Benjamins.

Jenner, P. L., S. Thompson, and S. Starosta (eds) (1976). *Austroasiatic Studies*. Honolulu: University Press of Hawaii.

Jennings, R. E. (1994). *The Genealogy of disjunction*. New York: Oxford University Press.

Jhā, S. (1958). *The Formation of the Maithili Language*. London: Luzon.

Jonides, J. et al. (2008). The mind and brain of short-term memory. *Annual Review of Psychology* 59, 193–224.

Jucker, Andreas H. (1995). *Historical Pragmatics: Pragmatic Developments in the History of English*. Amsterdam and Philadelphia: Benjamins.

Kager, R. (1999). *Optimality Theory*. New York: Cambridge University Press.

Kahneman, Daniel (2011). *Thinking, Fast and Slow*. New York: Farrar, Straus.

Kakati, B. (1962). *Assamese, its Formation and Development*. 2nd edn. Lawyer's Book Stall: Gauhati.

Kaltenböck, Gunther (2007). Spoken parenthetical clauses in English, in Nicole Dehé and Yordanka Kavalova, *Parentheticals* (Linguistics Today, 106.) Amsterdam and Philadelphia: Benjamins, 25–52.

Kaltenböck, Gunther (2008). Prosody and function of English comment clauses. *Folia Linguistica* 42(1), 83–134.

Kaltenböck, Gunther (2009). Initial *I think*: Main or comment clause? *Discourse and Interaction* 2(1), 49–70.

Kaltenböck, Gunther (2011). Linguistic structure and use: Explaining diverging evidence. The case of clause-initial *I think*, in Doris Schönefeld (ed.), *Converging Evidence: Methodological and Theoretical Issues for Linguistic Research*. Amsterdam and Philadelphia: Benjamins, 81–112.

Kaltenböck, Gunther, Bernd Heine, and Tania Kuteva (2011). On thetical grammar. *Studies in Language* 35(4), 848–93.

Kapatsinski, Vsevolod (2010). Frequency of use leads to automaticity of production: Evidence from repair in conversation. *Language and Speech* 53(1), 71–105.

Kathol, Andreas (2000). *Linear Syntax*. Oxford: Oxford University Press.

Kauffman, Stuart A. (1993). *The Origins of Order: Self-organization and Selection in Evolution*. Oxford: Oxford University Press.

Kay, P. (1978). Variable rules, community grammar, and linguistic change, in D. Sankoff (ed.), *Linguistic Variation: Models and Methods*. New York: Academic Press.

Kay, Paul and Ivan A. Sag (2012). Cleaning up the big mess: Discontinuous dependencies and complex determiners, in H. Boas and I. A. Sag (eds), *Sign-based Construction Grammar*. Stanford: CSLI Publications, 229–56.

Kayne, Richard (1994). *The Antisymmetry of Syntax*. Cambridge, MA: MIT Press.

Kazenin, Konstantin I. (1994). Split syntactic ergativity: Toward an implicational hierarchy. *Sprachtypologie und Universalienforschung* 47, 78–98.

Keenan, Edward L. (1984). Semantic correlates of the ergative/absolutive distinction. *Linguistics* 22, 197–223.

Keenan, Edward L. and Elinor Ochs (1979). Becoming a competent speaker of Malagasy, in T. Shopen (ed.), *Languages and their Speakers*. Cambridge, MA: Winthrop, 113–58.

Keller, Evelyn Fox (1992). Competition: Current usages, in Evelyn Fox Keller and Elisabeth A. Lloyd (eds), *Keywords in Evolutionary Biology*. Cambridge, MA: Harvard University Press, 68–73.

Keller, Rudi (1994a). *On Language Change: The Invisible Hand in Language*. London: Routledge.

Keller, Rudi (1994b). *Sprachwandel: Von der unsichtbaren Hand in der Sprache*. Tübingen, Basel: Francke.

Keller, Rudi (1999). Gibt es funktionale Erklärungen von Sprachwandel? in Siegfried Kanngießer and Petra M. Vogel (eds), *Elemente des Sprachwandels*. Opladen: Westdeutscher Verlag, 36–48.

Keller, Rudi (2005). Sprachwandel als Invisible-Hand-Phänomen, in Thomas Stehl (ed.), *Unsichtbare Hand und Sprecherwahl*. Tübingen: Narr, 27–42.

Kellerman, E. (1983). Now you see it, now you don't, in S. Gass and L. Selinker (eds), *Language Transfer in Language Learning*. Rowley, MA: Newbury House.

Kemp, C., A. Perfors, and J. B. Tenenbaum (2007). Learning overhypotheses with hierarchical Bayesian models. *Developmental Science* 10, 307–21.

Kempe, V. and B. MacWhinney (1998). The acquisition of case marking by adult learners of Russian and German. *Studies in Second Language Acquisition* 20(4), 543–87.

Kempen, Gerard (2014). Prolegomena to a neurocomputational architecture for human grammatical encoding and decoding. *Neuroinformatics* 12, 111–42.

Khalilova, Zaira (2009). A grammar of Khwarshi. PhD dissertation: University of Leiden.

Kibrik, Alexander E. (1985). Toward a typology of ergativity, in J. Nichols and A. Woodbury (eds), *Grammar Inside and Outside the Clause*. Cambridge: Cambridge University Press, 268–324.

Kilani-Schoch, Marianne and Wolfgang U. Dressler (2005). *Morphologie naturelle et flexion du verbe français*. Tübingen: Narr.

Kilian-Hatz, C. (2008). *A Grammar of Modern Khwe*. Köln: Rüdiger Köppe Verlag.

King, Gareth. (1993). *Modern Welsh: A Comprehensive Grammar*. London: Routledge.

Kirby, Simon (1997). Competing motivations and emergence: Explaining implicational hierarchies. *Linguistic Typology* 1(1), 5–31.

Kiss, Tibor (2005). Semantic constraints on relative clause extraposition. *Natural Language and Linguistic Theory* 23(2), 281–334.

Kita, S. (1997). Two-dimensional semantic analysis of Japanese mimetics. *Linguistics* 35/2, 379–415.

Kizach, J. (2010). The function of word order in Russian compared with Danish and English. PhD thesis: Department of English, University of Aarhus.

Koechlin, Etienne and Christopher Summerfield (2007). An information theoretical approach to prefrontal executive function. *Trends in Cognitive Sciences* 11, 229–35.

Kohonen, T. (2001). *Self-organizing Maps*. 3rd edn. Berlin: Springer.

Konieczny, Lars (2000). Locality and parsing complexity. *Journal of Psycholinguistic Research* 29(6), 627–45.

König, C. (2008). *Case in Africa*. Oxford: Oxford University Press.

Kontopoulos, Kyriakos (1993). *The Logics of Social Structure*. New York: Cambridge University Press.

Köpcke, Klaus-Michael (1998). The acquisition of plural marking in English and German revisited: Schemata versus rules. *Journal of Child Language* 25, 293–319.

Koptjevskaja-Tamm, Maria (1993). *Nominalizations*. London: Routledge.

Korecky-Kröll, Katharina, Gary Libben, Nicole Stempfer, Julia Wiesinger, Eva Reinisch, Johannes Bertl, and Wolfgang U. Dressler (2012). Helping a crocodile to learn German plurals: Children's online judgment of actual, potential and illegal plural forms. *Morphology* 22, 35–65.

Kortmann, Bernd, Edgar Schneider, Kate Burridge, Rajend Mesthrie, and Clive Upton (eds), (2004). *A Handbook of Varieties of English*, 2 Volumes. Berlin and New York: Mouton de Gruyter.

Koutsoudas, Andreas, Gerald A. Sanders, and Craig Noll (1974). On the application of phonological rules. *Language* 50(1), 1–50.

Krajewski, G. (2008). A constructivist investigation into the development of Polish noun inflections in children between two- and three-and-a-half years of age. Unpublished PhD thesis: University of Manchester.

Krajewski, G., A. L. Theakston, E. V. Lieven, and M. Tomasello (2011). How Polish children switch from one case to another when using novel nouns: Challenges for models of inflectional morphology. *Language and Cognitive Processes*, 26(4–6), 830–61.

Krajewski, G., Lieven, E. V., and Theakston, A. L. (2012). Productivity of a Polish child's inflectional noun morphology: A naturalistic study. *Morphology* 22(1), 9–34.

Krajewski, G., E. V. Lieven, and M. Tomasello (in prep.). The role of word order and case marking in Polish children's comprehension of transitives.

Kroch, Anthony S. (1994). Morphosyntactic variation, in K. Beals, J. Denot, R. Knippen, L. Melnar, H. Suzuki, and E. Zeinfeld (eds), *Papers from the 30th Regional meeting of the Chicago Linguistic Society, part 2: The parasession on variation in linguistic theory*. Chicago: Chicago Linguistic Society, 180–201.

Krug, Manfred G. (2000). *Emerging English Modals: A Corpus-based Study of Grammaticalization*. Berlin: Mouton de Gruyter.

Kunene, D. (2001). Speaking the act, in E. Voeltz and C. Kilian-Hatz (eds), *Ideophones*. Amsterdam: Benjamins, 183–91.

Kuno, Susumu and Ken-ichi Takami (2004). *Functional Constraints in Grammar: On the Unergative–Unaccusative Distinction*. Amsterdam: John Benjamins.

Kuperman, Victor and Bresnan, Joan (2012). The effects of construction probability on word durations during spontaneous incremental sentence production. *Journal of Memory and Language* 66(4), 588–611.

Kuperman, Victor, Robert Schreuder, Raymond Bertram, and Harald R. Baayen (2008). Reading Polymorphemic Dutch Compounds: Towards a multiple route model of lexical processing. Unpublished Manuscript. Max Planck Institut, Nijmegen.

Kuperschmidt, Itai. (2012). *Or* constructions in spoken Hebrew: A view from a methodological angle. Tel Aviv University.

Kuroda, S.-Y. (1972). The categorical and the thetic judgment. Evidence from Japanese syntax. *Foundations of Language* 9, 153–85.

Kutik, Elanah J., William E. Cooper, and Suzanne Boyce (1983). Declination of fundamental frequency in speakers' production of parenthetical and main clauses. *Journal of the Acoustical Society of America* 73(5), 1731–38.

Kytö, Merja and Suzanne Romaine (1997). Competing forms of adjective comparison in modern English: What could be quicker and easier and more effective? in Terttu Nevalainen and Leena Kahlas-Tarkka (eds), *To Explain the Present: Studies in the Changing English Language in Honour of Matti Rissanen*, (Mémoires de la Société Néophilologique de Helsinki 52). Helsinki: Société Néophilologique, 329–52.

Laaha, Sabine and Steven Gillis (eds) (2007). Typological perspectives on the acquisition of noun and verb morphology. *Antwerp Papers in Linguistics* 112.

Laaha, Sabine, Dorit Ravid, Katharina Korecky-Kröll, Gregor Laaha, and Wolfgang U. Dressler (2006). Early noun plurals in German: Regularity, productivity or default? *Journal of Child Language* 33, 271–302.

Labov, William (1966). *The Social Stratification of English in New York City*. Washington, DC: Center for Applied Linguistics.

Labov, W. (1972). *Sociolinguistic Patterns*. Philadelphia: University of Pennsylvania Press.

Labov, William (1994a). *Principles of Linguistic Change. Volume 1. Internal Factors*. Oxford: Blackwell.

Labov, William (1994b). *Principles of Linguistic Change. Volume 2. Social Factors*. Oxford: Blackwell.

Lakoff, George (1987). *Women, Fire, and Dangerous Things: What Categories Reveal about the Mind*. Chicago: University of Chicago Press.

Lambrecht, Knud (1994). *Information Structure and Sentence Form*. Cambridge: Cambridge University Press.

Lamers, Monique J. A. (2001). Sentence Processing: Using syntactic, semantic, and thematic information. GRODIL, 33. Dissertation, University of Groningen.

Lamers, Monique J. A. (2007). Verb type, animacy and definiteness in grammatical function disambiguation. *Linguistics in the Netherlands* 24, 125–37.

Lamers, Monique J. A. (2012). Argument linearization in Dutch: A multifactorial approach, in M. J. A. Lamers and P. de Swart (eds), *Case, Word Order, and Prominence: Psycholinguistic and Theoretical Approaches to Argument Structure*, Amsterdam: Springer, 121–44.

Lamers, Monique J. A. and Bob van Tiel (2012). Who or what we talk about: A comparative corpus study on the animacy structure of transitive sentences and sentence subjects. *Linguistic Evidence 2012*. Tübingen.

Langacker, Ronald W. (1974). Movement rules in functional perspective. *Language* 50, 630–64.

Langacker, Ronald W. (1977). Syntactic reanalysis, in Charles Li (eds), *Mechanisms of Syntactic Change*. Austin: University of Texas Press, 57–139.

Langacker, Ronald W. (1987). *Foundations of Cognitive Grammar. Volume 1*. Stanford: Stanford University Press.

Langacker, Ronald W. (1991). *Foundations of Cognitive Grammar. Volume 2*. Stanford: Stanford University Press.

Lass, Roger (1990). How to do things with junk: Exaptation in language evolution. *Journal of Linguistics* 26, 79–102.

Lastra, Yolanda and Pedro Martin Butragueño (2010). Futuro perifrástico y futuro morfológico en el Corpus Sociolingüístico de la ciudad de México. *Oralia* 13, 145–71.

Lazard, Gilbert (1998). *Actancy*. Berlin: Mouton de Gruyter.

Lebsanft, Franz (1987). Le problème du mélange du "tu" et "vous" en ancien français. *Romania* 108, 1–19.

Leech, Geoffrey and Jonathan Culpeper (1997). The comparison of adjectives in recent British English, in Terttu Nevalainen and Leena Kahlas-Tarkka (eds), *To Explain the Present: Studies in the Changing English Language in Honour of Matti Rissanen* (Mémoires de la Société Néophilologique de Helsinki). Helsinki: Société Néophilologique, 353–73.

Legate, J. A. and C. Yang (2007). Morphosyntactic learning and the development of tense. *Language Acquisition* 14(3), 315–44.

Lehmann, Christian (1974). Isomorphismus im sprachlichen Zeichen, in Hansjakob Seiler (ed.), *Linguistic Workshop II. Arbeiten des Kölner Universalienprojekts 1973/4*. München: Fink, 98–123.

Lehmann, Christian (1984). *Der Relativsatz. Typologie seiner Strukturen. Theorie seiner Funktionen. Kompendium seiner Grammatik*. Tübingen: Gunter Narr.

LePage, Robert B and Andrée Tabouret-Keller (1985). *Acts of Identity*. Cambridge: Cambridge University Press.

Leslie, A. M. (1995). A theory of agency, in D. Sperber, D. Premack, and A. J. Premack (eds), *Causal Cognition: A Multidisciplinary Debate*. Oxford: Clarendon Press, 121–41.

Levelt, Willem J. M. (1981). The speaker's linearization problem. *Philological Transactions of the Royal Society of London* 295, 305–15.

Levelt, Willem J. M. (1983). Monitoring and self-repair in speech. *Cognition* 14, 41–104.

Levelt, Willem J. M. (1989). *Speaking: From intention to Articulation*. Cambridge, MA: MIT Press.

Levin, Beth and Malka Rappaport Hovav (2005). *Argument Realization: Research Surveys in Linguistics Series*. Cambridge, MA: Cambridge University Press.

Levinson, Stephen C. (2000). *Presumptive Meanings: The Theory of Generalized Conversational Implicature*. Cambridge, MA: MIT Press.

Levy, Roger, Evelina Fedorenko, Mara Breen, and Edward Gibson (2012). The processing of extraposed structures in English. *Cognition* 122, 12–36.

Li, C. and S. A. Thompson (1981). *Mandarin Chinese: A Functional Reference Grammar*. Berkeley and Los Angeles: University of California Press.

Li, P., E. Bates, and B. MacWhinney (1993). Processing a language without inflections: A reaction time study of sentence interpretation in Chinese. *Journal of Memory and Language* 32, 169–92.

Li, P., X. Zhao, and Brian MacWhinney (2007). Dynamic self-organization and early lexical development in children. *Cognitive Science* 31, 581–612.

Libben, Gary, Gonia Jarema, Wolfgang U. Dressler, Jacqueline Stark, and Christiane Pons (2002). Triangulating the effects of interfixation in the processing of German compounds. *Folia Linguistica* 26, 23–43.

Lieberman, Erez, Jean-Baptiste Michel, Joe Jackson, Tina Tang, and Martin A. Nowak (2007). Quantifying the evolutionary dynamics of language. *Nature* 449, 713–16.

Lieven, E. V. (2008). Learning the English auxiliary: A Usage-based approach, in H. Behrens, *Corpora in Language Acquisition Research: Finding Structure in Data.* John Benjamins, 60–98.

Lieven, E. V. (2010). Input and first language acquisition: Evaluating the role of frequency. *Lingua* 120(11), 2546–56.

Lieven, E. V., H. Behrens, J. Speares, and M. Tomasello (2003). Early syntactic creativity: A usage-based approach. *Journal of Child Language* 30(2), 333–70.

Lieven, E. V., D. Salomo, and M. Tomasello (2009). Two-year-old children's production of multiword utterances: A usage-based analysis. *Cognitive Linguistics* 20(3), 481–507.

Lightfoot, David W. (1999). *The Development of Language: Acquisition, Change, and Evolution.* Oxford: Blackwell.

Lindquist, Hans (2000). Livelier or more lively? Syntactic and contextual factors influencing the comparison of disyllabic adjectives, in John M. Kirk (ed.), *Analyses and Techniques in Describing English: Papers from the nineteenth international conference on English language research on computerized corpora, ICAME 1998.* Amsterdam: Rodopi, 125–32.

Lohse, B., J. A. Hawkins, and T. Wasow (2004). Domain minimization in English verb-particle constructions. *Language* 80, 238–61.

Longobardi, Giuseppe (2001). Formal syntax, diachronic minimalism, and etymology: The history of French *chez. Linguistic Inquiry* 32, 275–302.

Lord, C. (1993). *Historical Change in Serial Verb Constructions.* Amsterdam and Philadelphia: John Benjamins.

Lotan, Saul (1990). A transcription of a conversation with a few income tax clerks (in Hebrew; unpublished).

Luck, S. J. and S. A. Hillyard (1994). Electrophysiological correlates of feature analysis during visual search. *Psychophysiology* 31, 291–308.

Lüdtke, Helmut (ed.) (1980). *Kommunikationstheoretische Grundlagen des Sprachwandels.* Berlin and New York: W. de Gruyter.

Macaulay, Ronald K. S. (1997). Standards and variation in urban speech: Examples from Lowland Scots. Amsterdam: John Benjamins.

McCawley, James (1982). Parentheticals and discontinuous constituent structure. *Linguistic Inquiry* 13, 91–106.

McClelland, J. L., B. L. McNaughton, and R. C. O'Reilly (1995). Why there are complementary learning systems in the hippocampus and neocortex: Insights from the successes and failures of connectionist models of learning and memory. *Psychological Review* 102, 419–57.

McDonald, J. L. (1987). Assigning linguistic roles: The influence of conflicting cues. *Journal of Memory and Language* 26(1), 100–17.

McDonald, J. L. (1989). The acquisition of cue-category mappings. In B. MacWhinney and E. Bates, *The Cross-linguistic Study of Sentence Processing.* New York: Cambridge University Press.

McDonald, J. L. and Brian MacWhinney (1989). Maximum likelihood models for sentence processing research. In B. MacWhinney and E. Bates (eds), *The Cross-linguistic Study of Sentence Processing.* New York: Cambridge University Press, 397–421.

McDonald, J. L. and Brian J. MacWhinney (1995). The time course of anaphor resolution: Effects of implicit verb causality and gender. *Journal of Memory and Language* 34, 543–66.

McDonald, Janet L., J. Kathryn Bock, and Michael H. Kelly, M. (1993). Word and world order: Semantic, phonological and metrical determinants of serial position. *Cognitive Psychology* 25, 188–230.

MacDonald, Maryellen C. and Marcel A. Just (1989). Changes in activation levels with negation. *Journal of Experimental Psychology: Learning, Memory, and Cognition* 15(4), 633–42.

MacDonald, Maryellen, N. J. Pearlmutter, and M. S. Seidenberg (1994). Lexical nature of syntactic ambiguity resolution. *Psychological Review* 101(4), 676–703.

McElree, B. (2006). Accessing recent events, in B. H. Ross (ed.), *The Psychology of Learning and Motivation* (46). San Diego CA: Academic Press, 155–200.

McGregor, W. B. (2008). Indexicals as sources of case markers in Australian languages, in F. Josephson and I. Söhrman (eds), *Interdependence of Diachronic and Synchronic Analyses*. Amsterdam: John Benjamins, 299–321.

MacNeilage, Peter (1998). The frame/content theory of evolution of speech production. *Behavioral and Brain Sciences* 21, 499–546.

McNeill, David (2005). *Gesture and Thought*. Chicago: Chicago University Press.

MacWhinney, Brian (1975a). Pragmatic patterns in child syntax. *Stanford Papers and Reports on Child Language Development* 10, 153–65.

MacWhinney, Brian (1975b). Rules, rote, and analogy in morphological formations by Hungarian children. *Journal of Child Language* 2, 65–77.

MacWhinney, Brian (1977). Starting points. *Language* 53, 152–68.

MacWhinney, Brian (1978). The acquisition of morphophonology. *Monographs of the Society for Research in Child Development* 43(1), 1–123.

MacWhinney, Brian (1982). Basic syntactic processes, in S. Kuczaj (ed.) *Language Acquisition: Volume 1. Syntax and semantics*. Hillsdale, NJ: Lawrence Erlbaum.

MacWhinney, Brian (1987). The competition model, in B. MacWhinney (ed.), *Mechanisms of Language Acquisition*. Hillsdale NJ: Erlbaum, 249–308.

MacWhinney, Brian (1989). Competition and lexical categorization, in R. Corrigan, F. Eckman, and M. Noonan (eds), *Linguistic Categorization*. Philadelphia: Benjamins, 195–242.

MacWhinney, Brian (1997). Second language acquisition and the Competition Model, in A. M. de Groot and J. F. Kroll, *Tutorials in Bilingualism*. Mahwah, NJ: Lawrence Erlbaum Associates, 113–142).

MacWhinney, Brian (2000). *The CHILDES project: Tools for analyzing talk*. Mahwah, NJ: Erlbaum.

MacWhinney, Brian (2004). A multiple process solution to the logical problem of language acquisition. *Journal of Child Language* 31(4), 883–914.

MacWhinney, Brian (2005). A unified model of language acquisition, in J. F. Kroll and A. M. B. de Groot (eds), *Handbook of Bilingualism: Psycholinguistic Approaches*. Oxford: Oxford University Press, 49–67.

MacWhinney, Brian (2008a). Cognitive precursors to language, in K. Oller and U. Griebel (eds.), *The Evolution of Communicative Flexibility*. Cambridge, MA: MIT Press, 193–214.

MacWhinney, Brian (2008b). How mental models encode embodied linguistic perspectives, in R. Klatzky, B. MacWhinney, and M. Behrmann (eds), *Embodiment, Ego-Space, and Action*. Mahwah: Lawrence Erlbaum, 369–410.

MacWhinney, Brian (2009). The emergence of linguistic complexity, in T. Givón and M. Shibatani (eds), *Linguistic Complexity*. New York: Benjamins, 405–32.

MacWhinney, Brian (2010). A tale of two paradigms, in Michele Kail and Maya Hickmann (eds), *Language Acquisition across Linguistic and Cognitive Systems*. New York: John Benjamins, 17–32.

MacWhinney, Brian (2012). The logic of the unified model, in S. Gass and A. Mackey (eds), *The Routledge Handbook of Second Language Acquisition*. New York: Routledge, 211–27.

MacWhinney, Brian (2014). Language development, in Lynn Liben and Ulrich Müller (eds), *Handbook of Child Language Development*. New York: Wiley.

MacWhinney, Brian (in progress). Competition across time, in Brian MacWhinney, Andrej L. Malchukov, and Edith Moravcsik (eds), *Competing Motivations in Grammar and Usage*. Oxford: Oxford University Press.

MacWhinney, Brian (in press). Item-based patterns in early syntactic development, in T. Herbst (ed.), *Valency Relations*. Berlin: Springer.

MacWhinney, Brian and Elizabeth Bates (1978). Sentential devices for conveying givenness and newness: A cross-cultural developmental study. *Journal of Verbal Learning and Verbal Behavior* 17, 539–58.

MacWhinney, Brian and Elizabeth Bates (1985). The development of sentence interpretation in Hungarian. *Cognitive Psychology* 17, 178–209.

MacWhinney, Brian and E. Bates (eds) (1989). *The Crosslinguistic Study of Sentence Processing*, New York: Cambridge University Press.

MacWhinney, Brian and Cs. Pléh (1988). The processing of restrictive relative clauses in Hungarian. *Cognition* 29, 95–141.

MacWhinney, Brian and C. Pléh (1997). Double agreement: Role identification in Hungarian. *Language and Cognitive Processes* 12, 67–102.

MacWhinney, Brian, E. Bates, and R. Kliegl (1984). Cue validity and sentence interpretation in English, German and Italian. *Journal of Verbal Learning and Verbal Behavior* 23, 127–50.

MacWhinney, Brian, Csaba Pléh, and Elizabeth Bates (1985). The development of sentence interpretation in Hungarian. *Cognitive Psychology* 17(2), 178–209.

Maguire, Warren and April McMahon (eds) (2011). *Analysing Variation in English*. Cambridge: Cambridge University Press.

Malchukov, Andrej (1995). *Even*. Munich: LINCOM.

Malchukov, Andrej (2004). *Nominalization/Verbalization: Constraining a Typology of Transcategorial Operations*. München: LINCOM.

Malchukov, Andrej L. (2005). Case pattern splits, verb types, and construction competition, in M. Amberber and Helen de Hoop (eds), *Competition and Variation in Natural Languages: The Case for Case*. Amsterdam: Elsevier, 73–117.

Malchukov, Andrej (2006a). Constraining nominalization: Form/function competition. *Linguistics* 44, 973–1009.

Malchukov, Andrej (2006b). Transitivity parameters and transitivity alternations: constraining co-variation, in L. Kulikov, A. L. Malchukov, and P. de Swart (eds), *Case, Valency, and Transitivity*. Amsterdam and Philadephia: John Benjamins, 329–59.

Malchukov, Andrej (2007). Reciprocal and sociative constructions in Even, in Vladimir P. Nedjalkov (ed.), *Typology of Reciprocal Constructions*. Amsterdam: Benjamins, 1643–75.

Malchukov, Andrej L. (2008a). Animacy and asymmetries in differential case marking. *Lingua* 118(2), 203–21.

Malchukov, A. (2008b). Split intransitives, experiencer objects and "transimpersonal" constructions: (re-)establishing the connection, in M. Donohue and S. Wichmann (eds), *The Typology of Semantic Alignment*. Oxford: Oxford University Press, 76–101.

Malchukov, Andrej (2009). Incompatible categories: Resolving the "present perfective paradox", in Lotte Hogeweg, Helen de Hoop, and Andrej Malchukov (eds), *Cross-linguistic Semantics of Tense, Aspect and Modality*. Amsterdam: Benjamins, 13–33.

Malchukov, A. (2010). "Quirky" case: Rare phenomena in case-marking and their implications for a theory of typological distributions, in J. Wohlgemuth and M. Cysouw (eds), *Rethink-*

ing Universals: How Rarities Affect Linguistic Theory. Berlin and New York: Walter de Gruyter, 139–67.

Malchukov, Andrej (2011). Interaction of verbal categories: Resolution of infelicitous grammeme combinations., *Linguistics* 49(1), 229–82.

Malchukov, Andrej and de Helen Hoop (2011). Tense, aspect, and mood based differential case marking. *Lingua* 121, 35–47.

Malchukov, Andrej L., Martin Haspelmath, and Bernard Comrie (2010). Ditransitive constructions: A typological overview, in Andrej L. Malchukov, Martin Haspelmath, and Bernard Comrie (eds), *Studies in Ditransitive Constructions: A Comparative Handbook*. Berlin: Mouton de Gruyter.

Maling, Joan (2006). From passive to active: Syntactic change in progress in Icelandic, in T. Solstad and B. Lyngfelt (eds), *Demoting the Agent: Passive, Middle and Other Voice Phenomena*. Philadelphia: John Benjamins.

Malkiel, Yakov (1967). Multiple vs. simple causation in linguistic change. *To honor Roman Jakobson, Volume 2*. The Hague: Mouton, 1228–46.

Malkiel, Yakov (1968). The inflectional paradigm as an occasional determinant of sound change. In Winfred P. Lehmann and Yakov Malkiel (eds), *Directions for Historical Linguistics*. Austin: University of Texas Press, 21–64.

Malouf, Robert (2003). Cooperating constructions, in E. J. Francis and L. A. Michaelis (eds), *Mismatch: Form—Function Incongruity and the Architecture of Grammar*. Stanford, CA: CSLI Publications, 403–24.

Manczak, Witold (1980). Frequenz und Sprachwandel, in Helmut Lüdtke (ed.), *Kommunikationstheoretische Grundlagen des Sprachwandels*. Berlin and New York: W. de Gruyter, 37–79.

Manning, Christopher D. (1996). *Ergativity: Argument Structure and Grammatical Relations*. Stanford: CSLI.

Manova, Stela (2011). A cognitive approach to SUFF1-SUFF2 combinations: A tribute to Carl Friedrich Gauss. *Word Structure* 4(2), 161–8.

Marandin, Jean-Marie (2011). Affordance and ability: How do participants replicate linguistic choices in the lab? *Belgian Journal of Linguistics* 25(1), 30–50.

Marblestone, K. L. (2007). Semantic and syntactic effects on double prepositional phrase ordering across the lifespan: PhD dissertation, University of Southern California.

Marchand, H. (1960). *The Categories and Types of English Word-formation*. Wiesbaden: Harrassowitz.

Margetts, Anna and Peter K. Austin (2007). Three participant events in the languages of the world: Towards a crosslinguistic typology. *Linguistics* 45(3), 393–451.

Markus, H. R. and S. Kitayama (1991). Culture and the self: Implications for cognition, emotion, and motivation. *Psychological Review* 98, 224–35.

Marshall, Chloë R. and Heather K. J. van der Lely (2006). A challenge to current models of past tense inflection. The impact of phonotactics. *Cognition* 100, 302–20.

Marshall, Chloë R., Theodoros Marinis, and Heather K. J. van der Lely (2007). Passive verb morphology: The effect of phonotactics on passive comprehension in typically developing and Grammatical-SLI children. *Lingua* 117, 1434–47.

Marslen-Wilson, W. (1973). Linguistic structure and speech shadowing at very short latencies. *Nature* 244, 522–33.

Mason, Patricia (1990). The pronouns of address in Middle French, in *Studia Neophilologica* 62, 95–100.

Massaro, D. (ed.) (1975). *Understanding Language: An Introduction-processing Analysis of Speech Perception, Reading, and Psycholinguistics*. New York: Academic Press.

Massaro, D. (1987). *Speech Perception by Ear and Eye*. Hillsdale, NJ: Lawrence Erlbaum.

Matessa, M. and J. R. Anderson (2000). Modelling focused learning in role assignment. *Language and Cognitive Processes* 15(3), 263–92.

Mathiassen, Terje (1996). *A Short Grammar of Lithuanian*. Columbus, OH: Slavica Publishers, Inc.

Matras, Yaron (2009). *Language Contact*. Cambridge: Cambridge University Press.

Matthews, D. and C. Bannard (2010). Children's production of unfamiliar word sequences is predicted by positional variability and latent classes in a large sample of child-directed speech. *Cognitive Science* 34(3), 465–88.

Matthews, Danielle, Elena V. M. Lieven, Anna Theakston, and Michael Tomasello (2006). The effect of perceptual availability and prior discourse on young children's use of referring expressions. *Applied Psycholinguistics* 27, 403–22.

Mauri, Caterina (2008). The irreality of alternatives: Towards a typology of disjunction. *Studies in Language* 32, 22–55.

Mayerthaler, Willi (1981). *Morphologische Natürlichkeit*. Wiesbaden: Athenaion [translated 1988. *Morphological Naturalness*. Ann Arbor: Karoma Press].

Mayr, Ernst (1982). *The Growth of Biological Thought: Diversity, Evolution and Inheritance*. Cambridge, MA: Harvard University Press.

Mazeland, Harrie (2007). Parenthetical sequences. *Journal of Pragmatics* 39, 1816–69.

Menzel, Randolf (1999). Memory dynamics in the honeybee. *Journal of Comparative Physiology A* 185, 323–40.

Merlini Barbaresi, Lavinia (2004). Alterazione, in M. Grossmann and F. Rainer (eds), *La formazione delle parole in italiano*. Tübingen: Niemeyer, 264–92.

Mesoudi, A., A. Whiten, and K. Laland (2006). Towards a unified science of cultural evolution. *Behavioral and Brain Sciences* 29, 329–83.

Michaelis, Laura A. and Hartwell S. Francis (2007). Lexical subjects and the conflation strategy, in N. Hedberg and R. Zacharski (eds), *The Grammar–Pragmatics Interface: Essays in Honor of Jeanette K. Gundel*. Amsterdam: John Benjamins, 19–48.

Michod, Richard E. (2000). *Darwinian Dynamics: Evolutionary Transitions in Fitness and Individuality*. Princeton: Princeton University Press.

Minsky, Marvin (1985). *The Society of Mind*. New York: Simon & Schuster.

Mishkin, M., L. G. Ungerleider, and Macko, K. A. (1983). Object vision and spatial vision: Two cortical pathways. *Trends in Neurosciences* 6, 414–17.

Mithun, Marianne (1984). The evolution of noun incorporation. *Language* 60(4), 847–94.

Mithun, Marianne (1991). Active/agentive case marking and its motivation. *Language* 67, 510–46.

Mithun, Marianne (1999). *The Languages of Native North America*. Cambridge: Cambridge University Press.

Mithun, Marianne (2005). Ergativity and language contact on the Oregon Coast: Alsea, Siuslaw, and Coos. *Proceedings of the Berkeley Linguistics Society*. Berkeley: University of California, 77–95.

Mithun, Marianne (2007). Integrating approaches to diversity: Argument structure on the Northwest Coast, in Yoshiko Matsumoto, David Oshima, Orrin Robinson, and Peter Sells (eds), *Diversity in Language*. Stanford: CSLI (Center for the Study of Language and Information), 9–36.

Mithun, Marianne (2008). The emergence of agentive systems in core argument marking, in M. Donohue and S. Wichmann (eds), *The Typology of Semantic Alignment*. Oxford: Oxford University Press, 297–333.

Mithun, Marianne and W. Chafe (1999). What are S, A, and O? *Studies in Language* 23(3), 569–96.

Mondorf, Britta (2002). The effect of prepositional complements on the choice of synthetic or analytic comparatives, in Hubert Cuyckens and Günter Radden (eds), *Perspectives on Prepositions*. Tübingen: Niemeyer, 65–78.

Mondorf, Britta (2003). Support for *More*-Support, in Günter Rohdenburg and Britta Mondorf (eds), *Determinants of Grammatical Variation in English* (Topics in English Linguistics 43). Berlin and New York: Mouton de Gruyter, 251–304.

Mondorf, Britta (2006). Rewriting English grammar books: Factors constraining the choice between synthetic and analytic comparative forms, in Christoph Houswitschka, Gabriele Knappe, and Anja Müller (eds), *Proceedings of the Anglistentag 2005, Bamberg* (Proceedings of the conference of the German association of university teachers of English). Trier: Wissenschaftlicher Verlag Trier, 587–607.

Mondorf, Britta (2007). Recalcitrant problems of comparative alternation and new insights emerging from internet data, in Marianne Hundt, Nadja Nesselhauf, and Carolin Biewer (eds), *Corpus Linguistics and the Web* (Language and Computers 59). Amsterdam/New York: Rodopi, 211–32.

Mondorf, Britta (2009a). *More Support for* More-Support: *The Role of Processing Constraints on the Choice between Synthetic and Analytic Comparative Forms* (Studies in Language Variation 4). Amsterdam and Philadelphia: Benjamins.

Mondorf, Britta (2009b). Synthetic and analytic comparatives, in Günter Rohdenburg and Julia Schlüter (eds), *One Language, Two Grammars? Differences between British and American English* (Studies in Language). Cambridge: Cambridge University Press, 86–107.

Mondorf, Britta (2010). Genre-effects in the replacement of reflexives by particles, in Heidrun Dorgeloh and Anja Wanner (eds), *Approaches to Syntactic Variation and Genre* (Topics in English Linguistics 70). Berlin and New York: Mouton de Gruyter, 219–45.

Moravcsik, Edith A. (1971). On disjunctive connectives. *Language Sciences* 15, 27–34.

Moravcsik, Edith (1978). On the distribution of ergative and accusative patterns. *Lingua* 45, 233–79.

Moravcsik, Edith (2010). Conflict resolution in syntactic theory. *Studies in Language* 34(3), 636–69.

Mori, Junko (1999). *Negotiating Agreement and Disagreement in Japanese: Connective Expressions and Turn Construction*. Amsterdam: Benjamins.

Morris, Charles W. (1971). *Writings on the General Theory of Signs*. The Hague: Mouton.

Morris, William C., Geoffrey W. Cottrell, and Jeffrey Elman (2000). A connectionist simulation of the empirical acquisition of grammatical relations. *Hybrid Neural Systems* 1778, 175–93.

Moss, Helen E. and M. Gareth Gaskell (1999). Lexical semantic processing during speech, in Simon Garrod and Martin J. Pickering (eds), *Language Processing*. Hove: Psychology Press, 59–100.

Mulder, Jean Gail (1994). *Ergativity in Coast Tsimshian (Sm'algyax)*. Berkeley: University of California Press.

Müller, Stefan (2004). Complex NPs, subjacency, and extraposition. *Snippets* 8, 10–11.

Muralikrishnan, R., M. Schlesewsky, and I. Bornkessel-Schlesewsky (2008). Universal and cross-linguistic influences on the processing of word order and animacy: Neurophysiological evidence from Tamil. Poster presented at the 21st Annual CUNY Conference on Human Sentence Processing.

Myachykov, A. and R. S. Tomlin (2008). Perceptual priming and structural choice in Russian sentence production. *Journal of Cognitive Science* 6, 31–48.

Myachykov, A. et al. (2011). Visual attention and structural choice in sentence production across languages. *Language and Linguistics Compass* 5: 95–107.

Næss, Å. (2007). *Prototypical Transitivity*. Amsterdam: John Benjamins.

Naigles, L. (1990). Children use syntax to learn verb meanings. *Journal of Child Language* 17(2), 357–74.

Nedjalkov, Vladimir P. (2007a). Overview of the research: Definitions of terms, framework, and related issues, in Vladimir P. Nedjalkov (ed.), *Reciprocal Constructions*, Volume 1. Amsterdam: Benjamins, 3–115.

Nedjalkov, Vladimir (2007b). Encoding of the reciprocal meaning, in Vladimir Nedjalkov (ed.), *Reciprocal Constructions*, Volume 1. Amsterdam: Benjamins, 147–207.

Nelson, Gerald, Sean Wallis, and Bas Aarts (2002). *Exploring Natural Language: Working with the British Component of the International Corpus of English*. Amsterdam and Philadelphia: Benjamins.

Nespor, Marina and Irene Vogel (1986). *Prosodic Phonology* (Studies in Generative Grammar, 28). Dordrecht: Foris.

Neter, John, William Wasserman, and Michael H. Kutner (1985). *Applied Linear Statistical Models: Regression, Analysis of Variance, and Experimental Designs*. Homewood, IL: Irwin.

New, J., L. Cosmides, and J. Tooby (2007). Category-specific attention for animals reflects ancestral priorities, not expertise. *Proceedings oft he National Academy of Science USA* 104, 16598–603.

Newman, John (1996). *Give: A Cognitive Linguistic Study*. Berlin: Mouton de Gruyter.

Newman, John (2005). Three-place predicates: A cognitive-linguistic perspective. *Language Sciences* 27(2), 145–63.

Newmeyer, Frederick J. (1998). *Language Form and Language Function*. Cambridge, MA: MIT Press.

Newmeyer, Frederick J. (2002). Optimality and Functionality: A Critique of Functionally-Based Optimality Theory. *Natural Language and Linguistic Theory* 20, 43–80.

Newmeyer, Frederick J. (2003a). Formal and functional motivation for language change, in Hickey, Raymond (ed.), *Motives for Language Change*. Cambridge: Cambridge University Press, 18–36.

Newmeyer, Frederick J. (2003b). Grammar is grammar and usage is usage. *Language* 79, 682–707.

Newmeyer, Frederick J. (2005). *Possible and Probable Languages: A Generative Perspective on Linguistic Typology*. Oxford: Oxford University Press.

Nikolaeva, I. and M. Tolskaja (2001). *A Grammar of Udihe*. Berlin: Mouton de Gruyter.

Norris, D. (1994). Shortlist: A connectionist model of continuous speech recognition. *Cognition* 52, 189–234.

Nowak, Martin A. and Karl Sigmund (2004). Evolutionary dynamics of biological games. *Science* 303, 793–9.

Nübling, Damaris (2010). Lässt sich ein Syntheseindex erstellen? Zur Problematisierung und Präzisierung eines (allzu) geläufigen Begriffs, in Dagmar Bittner and Livio Gaeta (eds), *Kodierungstechniken im Wandel: Das Zusammenspiel von Analytik und Synthese im Gegenwartsdeutschen*. Berlin and New York: Mouton de Gruyter, 1–22.

Nunberg Geoffrey, Ivan A. Sag, and Thomas Wasow (1994). Idioms. *Language* 70, 491–538.

Odling-Smee, F. J., K. N. Laland, and M. W. Feldman (2003). *Niche Construction: The Neglected Process in Evolution*. Princeton: Princeton University Press.

O'Grady, William. (2005). *Syntactic Carpentry*. Mahwah, NJ: Lawrence Erlbaum Associates.

Olawsky, K. (2006). *A Grammar of Urarina*. Berlin: Mouton de Gruyter.

Osgood, Charles E. and Annette M. Zehler (1981). Acquisition of bitransitive sentences: Prelinguistic determinants of language acquisition. *Journal of Child Language* 8, 367–84.

Oudeyer, Pierre-Yves (2006). *Self-organization in the Evolution of Speech*. Oxford: Oxford University Press.

Ourn, N. and J. Haiman (2001). Symmetrical compounds in Khmer. *Studies in Language*. 24(1), 483–514.

Pagel, M. and Q. D. Atkinson, and A. Meade (2007). Frequency of word-use predicts rates of lexical evolution throughout Indo-European history. *Nature* 449, 717–21.

Panther, Klaus-Uwe and Günter Radden (eds) (2011). *Motivation in Grammar and the Lexicon*. Amsterdam: Benjamins.

Peirce, Charles S. (1994). *Collected Papers*. Cambridge, MA: Harvard University Press.

Pelham, S. D. (2011). The input ambiguity hypothesis and case blindness: An account of cross-linguistic and intra-linguistic differences in case errors. *Journal of Child Language* 38(2), 235–72.

Penolazzi, B. et al. (2005). Processing of temporary syntactic ambiguity in Italian "who"-questions: A study with event-related potentials. *Neuroscience Letters* 377, 91–6.

Peters, A. M. (1985). Language segmentation: Operating principles for the perception and analysis of language, in D. I. Slobin, *The Crosslinguistic Study of Language Acquisition*, Volume 2. Hillsdale, NJ: Lawrence Erlbaum Associates.

Peters, A. M. (1997). Language typology, prosody, and the acquisition of grammatical morphemes. In D. I. Slobin, *The Crosslinguistic Study of Language Acquisition*, Volume 5. Mahwah, NJ: Lawrence Erlbaum Associates.

Peters, Pam, Peter Collins, and Adam Smith (eds) (2009). *Comparative Studies in Australian and New Zealand English: Grammar and Beyond* (Varieties of English around the World). Amsterdam and Philadelphia: Benjamins.

Petersen, S. E. and M. I. Posner (2012). The attention system of the human brain: 20 years after. *Annual Review of Neuroscience* 35, 73–89.

Peterson, Peter (1999). On the boundaries of syntax: Non-syntagmatic relations, in Peter Collins and David Lee (eds), *The Clause in English: In Honour of Rodney Huddleston*. Amsterdam and Philadelphia: John Benjamins, 229–50.

Pfeiffer, Martin (2010). Zur syntaktischen Struktur von Selbstreparaturen im Deutschen. *Gesprächsforschung—Online-Zeitschrift zur verbalen Interaktion* 11: 183–207, <http://www.gespraechsforschung-ozs.de/heft2010/ga-pfeiffer.pdf>, accessed January 30, 2014.

Pfeiffer, Martin (2012). What prosody reveals about the speaker's cognition: Self-repair in German prepositional phrases, in P. Bergmann, J. Brenning, M. Pfeiffer, and E. Reber (eds), *Prosody and Embodiment in Interactional Grammar* (Linguae & Litterae series). Berlin: de Gruyter, 40–72.

Pfeiffer, Martin (2014). Die syntaktische Struktur von Selbstreparaturen im Deutschen. unpublished doctoral dissertation: Albert-Ludwigs-Universität Freiburg.

Philipp, M. et al. (2008). The role of animacy in the real time comprehension of Mandarin Chinese: Evidence from auditory event-related brain potentials. *Brain and Language* 105, 112–33.

Pierrehumbert, Janet (2001). Exemplar dynamics: Word frequency, lenition and contrast, in Joan L. Bybee and Paul J. Hopper (eds), *Frequency and the Emergence of Linguistic Structure*. Amsterdam: Benjamins, 137–57.

Pine, Julian M., Elena V. M. Lieven, and Caroline F. Rowland (1998). Comparing different models of the development of the English verb category. *Linguistics* 36(4), 807–30.

Pinker, Steven (1989). *Learnability and Cognition: The Acquisition of Argument Structure*. Cambridge, MA: MIT Press.

Pinker, Steven (1999). *Words and Rules: The Ingredients of Language*. New York: Basic Books.

Pittner, Karin (1995). 'Zur Syntax von Parenthesen. *Linguistische Berichte* 156, 85–108.

Plag, Ingo (1999). *Morphological Productivity: Structural Constraints in English Derivation.* Berlin: Mouton de Gruyter.

Plag, Ingo (2003). *Word-formation in English* (Cambridge Textbooks in Linguistics.). Cambridge: Cambridge University Press.

Plaut, D. C. and L. M. Gonnerman (2000). Are non-semantic morphological effects incompatible with a distributed connectionist approach to lexical processing? *Language and Cognitive Processes* 15, 445–85.

Polinsky, Maria (1998). A non-syntactic account of some asymmetries in the double object construction, in J.-P. Koenig (ed.), *Conceptual Structure and Language: Bridging the Gap.* Stanford: CSLI, 403–23.

Polinsky, Maria (2005/2011). Antipassive constructions, in Matthew S. Dryer and Martin Haspelmath (eds), *The World Atlas of Language Structures online.* Munich: Max Planck Digital Library, chapter 108. Available online at <http://wals.info/chapter/109>, accessed January 30, 2014.

Poplack, Shana and Rena Cacoullos (2014). A variationist paradigm for linguistic emergence, in B. MacWhinney and W. O'Grady (eds), *Handbook of Language Emergence.* New York: Wiley.

Posner, M. I. and S. E. Petersen (1990). The attention system of the human brain. *Annual Review of Neuroscience* 13, 25–42.

Postma, Albert (2000). Detection of errors during speech production: A review of speech monitoring models. *Cognition* 77, 97–131.

Potts, Christopher (2003). Conventional implicatures: A distinguished class of meanings, in G. Ramchand and C. Reiss (eds), *The Oxford Handbook of Linguistic Interfaces.* Oxford: Oxford University Press, 475–502.

Pouplier, M. and L. Goldstein (2010). Intention in articulation: Articulatory timing in alternating consonant sequences and its implications for models of speech production. *Language and Cognitive Processes* 25, 616–49.

Prat-Sala, Merce and Holly P. Branigan (2000). Discourse constraints on syntactic processing in language production: A cross-linguistic study in English and Spanish. *Journal of Memory and Language* 42, 168–82.

Presson, Eleanor, Colleen Davy, and Brian MacWhinney (2013). Experimentalized CALL for adult second language learners, in J. Schwieter (ed.), *Innovative Research and Practices in Second Language Acquisition and Bilingualism.* Amsterdam: John Benjamins, 139–64.

Price, C. J. (2010). The anatomy of language: A review of 100 fMRI studies published in 2009. *Annals of the New York Academy of Sciences* 1191, 62–88.

Primus, Beatrice (1998). The relative order of recipient and patient in the languages of Europe, in A. Siewierska (ed.), *Consitituent Order in the Languages of Europe.* Berlin: de Gruyter, 421–73.

Primus, Beatrice (1999). *Cases and Thematic Roles—Ergative, Accusative and Active.* Tübingen: Niemeyer.

Primus, Beatrice (2006). Mismatches in semantic-role hierarchies and the dimensions of role semantics, in I. Bornkessel et al. (eds), *Semantic Role Universals and Argument Linking: Theoretical, Typological and Psycholinguistic Approaches.* Berlin: Mouton de Gruyter, 53–87.

Primus, Beatrice (2012). Animacy, generalized semantic roles, and differential object marking, in M. J. A. Lamers, and P. de Swart (eds), *Case, Word Order, and Prominence: Psycholinguistic and Theoretical Approaches to Argument Structure.* Amsterdam: Springer, 65–90.

Prince, Alan and Paul Smolensky (1993). *Optimality Theory. Constraint Interaction in Generative Grammar.* Technical Report 2, Rutgers University Center for Cognitive Science.

Prince, Alan and Paul Smolensky (2004a). Optimality Theory: Constraint interaction in generative grammar, in John J. McCarthy (ed.), *Optimality Theory in Phonology: A Reader*. Oxford: Blackwell.

Prince, Alan and Paul Smolensky (2004b). *Optimality Theory: Constraint Interaction in Generative Grammar*. Oxford: Blackwell.

Prior, A. and Brian MacWhinney (2010). Beyond inhibition: A bilingual advantage in task switching. *Bilingualism: Language and Cognition* 13, 253–62.

Pullum, Geoffrey K. and Barbara C. Scholz (2002). Empirical assessment of stimulus poverty arguments. *Linguistic Review* 19, 9–50.

Pulvermüller, F. (2003). *The Neuroscience of Language*. Cambridge: Cambridge University Press.

Quintilian. (2001). *The Orator's Education* Volume 4. (Loeb Classical Library 127). Translated by Donald A. Russell. Cambridge, MA: Harvard University Press.

Quirk, R., S. Greenbaum, G. Leech, and J. Svartvik (1985). *A Comprehensive Grammar of the English Language*. Harlow: Longman.

R Development Core Team (2013). *R: A language and environment for statistical computing*. Vienna: Foundation for Statistical Computing. <http://www.r-project.org>, accessed January 30, 2014.

Rappaport Hovav, Malka L. B. (2008). The English dative alternation: The case for verb sensitivity. *Journal of Linguistics* 44, 129–67.

Rasolofo, A. (2006). Malagasy transitive clause types and their functions. PhD dissertation: University of Oregon.

Ratcliff, Roger, Trisha Van Zandt, and Gail McKoon (1999). Connectionist and diffusion models of reaction time. *Psychological Review* 106, 261–300.

Rauschecker, J. P. (1998). Cortical processing of complex sounds. *Current Opinion in Neurobiology* 8, 516–21.

Rauschecker, J. P. and S. K. Scott (2009). Maps and streams in the auditory cortex: Nonhuman primates illuminate human speech processing. *Nature Neuroscience* 12, 718–24.

Ravid, Dorit, Wolfgang U. Dressler, Bracha Nir-Sagiv, Katharina Korecky-Kröll, Agnita Souman, Katja Rehfeldt, Sabine Laaha, Johannes Bertl, Hans Basbøll, and Steven Gillis (2008). Core morphology in child directed speech: Crosslinguistic corpus analyses of noun plurals, in Heike Behrens (ed.), *Corpora in Language Acquisition Research*. Amsterdam: Benjamins, 25–60.

Regier, Terry, Charles Kemp, and Paul Kay (2014). Word meanings across languages support efficient communication, in B. MacWhinney and W. O'Grady (eds), *Handbook of Language Emergence*. New York: Wiley.

Rehder, Bob (2001). Interference between cognitive skills. *Journal of Experimental Psychology: Learning, Memory, and Cognition* 27, 451–69.

Reinhart, Tanya (1983). Point of view in language—the use of parentheticals, in Gisa Rauh (ed.), *Essays on Deixis*. Tübingen: Narr, 169–94.

Rhodes, Richard A. (1990). Ojibwa secondary objects, in Katarzyna Dziwirek, Patrick Farrell, and Errapel Mejías Bikandi (eds), *Grammatical Relations: A Cross-theoretical Perspective*. Stanford: CSLI, 401–14.

Rhodes, Richard (2010). Ditransitive constructions in Ojibwe, in Andrej L. Malchukov et al. (eds.), *Studies in Ditransitive Constructions: A Comparative Handbook*. Berlin: Mouton De Gruyter, 626–51.

Rizzi, Luigi (1993/4). Some notes on linguistic theory and language development: The case of root infinitives. *Language Acquisition* 3(4), 371–93.

Rizzi, Luigi (2005). Grammatically-based target inconsistencies in child language, in *Proceedings of the Inaugural Conference of GALANA*. Cambridge, MA: UConn/MIT Working Papers in Linguistics.

Rochemont, Michael S. (1986). *Focus in Generative Grammar*. Amsterdam: John Benjamins.

Rochemont, Michael S. and Peter W. Culicover (1990). *English Focus Constructions and the Theory of Grammar*. Cambridge: Cambridge University Press.

Rochemont, Michael S. and Peter W. Culicover (1997). Deriving dependent right adjuncts in English, in D. Beerman, D. LeBlanc, and H. C. van Riemsdijk (eds), *Rightward Movement*. Amsterdam: John Benjamins, 279–300.

Roehm, D., M. Schlesewsky, I. Bornkessel, S. Frisch, and H. Haider (2004). Fractionating language comprehension via frequency characteristics of the human EEG. *Neuroreport* 15, 409–12.

Roelofs, Ardi (2011). Modeling the attentional control of vocal utterances: From Wernicke to WEAVER+, in J. Guendozi, F. Loncke, and M. Williams (eds), *The Handbook of Psycholinguistic and Cognitive Processes: Perspectives in Communication Disorders*. New York: Psychology Press, 189–208.

Roeper, Tom (2010). Interfaces, frequency, and the primary linguistic data problem. *Lingua* 120(11), 2538–45.

Roeper, Tom, Steven Lapointe, Janet Bing, and Susan Tavakolian (1981). A lexical approach to language acquisition, in S. Tavakolian (ed.), *Language Acquisition and Linguistic Theory*. Cambridge, MA: MIT Press, 35–58.

Rohdenburg, Günter (1996). Cognitive complexity and increased grammatical explicitness in English. *Cognitive Linguistics* 7(2), 149–82.

Rohdenburg, Günter (1999). Clausal complementation and cognitive complexity in English, in Fritz-Wilhelm Neumann and Sabine Schülting (eds), *Anglistentag Erfurt 1998*. Trier: Wissenschaftlicher Verlag, 101–12.

Rohdenburg, Günter (2003). Cognitive complexity and Horror Aequi as factors determining the use of interrogative clause linkers in English, in Günter Rohdenburg and Britta Mondorf (eds), *Determinants of Grammatical Variation in English* (Topics in English Linguistics 43). Berlin and New York: Mouton de Gruyter, 205–50.

Rohdenburg, Günter (2008). The effect of complement negation on the choice between more or less explicit sentential structures in English. Paper presented at the linguistics colloquium, 2 June 2008, Mainz University, Germany.

Rohdenburg, Günter (2009). Reflexive structures, in Günter Rohdenburg and Julia Schlüter (eds), *One Language, Two Grammars?: Differences between British and American English* (Studies in English Language). Cambridge: Cambridge University Press, 166–81.

Rohdenburg Günter and Britta Mondorf (eds) (2003). *Determinants of Grammatical Variation in English* (Topics in English Linguistics 43). Berlin and New York: Mouton de Gruyter.

Rohdenburg, Günter and Julia Schlüter (eds) (2009). *One Language, Two Grammars?: Differences between British and American English*. Cambridge: Cambridge University Press.

Rosenbach, Anette (2002). *Genitive Variation in English: Conceptual factors in synchronic and diachronic studies* (Topics in English Linguistics 42). Berlin: Mouton de Gruyter.

Rosenbach, Anette (2003). Aspects of iconicity and economy in the choice between the s-genitive and the of-genitive in English, in Günter Rohdenburg, and Britta Mondorf (eds), *Determinants of Grammatical Variation in English* (Topics in English Linguistics 43). Berlin: Mouton de Gruyter, 379–412.

Rosenbach, Anette (2005). Animacy versus weight as determinants of grammatical variation in English. *Language* 81, 613–44.

Rosenbach, Anette (2010). How synchronic gradience makes sense in the light of language change (and vice-versa), in E. C. Traugott and G. Trousdale (eds), *Gradience, Gradualness, and Grammaticalization.* Amsterdam: John Benjamins, 129–47.

Rosenbach, Anette and Letizia Vezzosi (2000). Genitive constructions in Early Modern English: New evidence from a corpus analysis, in R. Sornicola, E. Poppe, and A. Shisha-Halevy (eds), *Stability, Variation, and Change of Word Order over Time.* Amsterdam: John Benjamins, 285–307.

Rosenbaum, D. (2014). *It's a Jungle in There: How Competition and Cooperation in the Brain Shape the Mind.* New York: Oxford University Press.

Ross, John R. (1967). Constraints on variables in syntax. Ph.D. thesis: MIT, Cambridge, MA. (Published as Ross, John R. 1986 *Infinite Syntax!* Norwood: Ablex Publishing).

Roth, P. (1969). *Portnoy's Complaint.* New York: Random House.

Rouchota, Villy (1998). Procedural meaning and parenthetical discourse markers, in Andreas H. Jucker and Yael Ziv (eds), *Discourse Markers: Descriptions and Theory.* Amsterdam and Philadelphia: Benjamins, 97–126.

Rowland, Caroline F. (2007). Explaining errors in children's questions. *Cognition* 104(1), 106–34.

Rowland, Caroline F. and Claire H. Noble (2011). Knowledge of verb argument structure in early sentence comprehension: Evidence from the dative. *Language Learning and Development* 7(1), 55–75.

Rude, N. (1991). On the origin of the Nez Perce ergative NP suffix. *International Journal of American Linguistics* 57, 24–50.

Rude, N. (1997a). On the history of nominal case in Sahaptian. *International Journal of American Linguistics* 63, 113–43.

Rude, Noel (1997b). Dative shifting and double objects in Sahaptin, in Talmy Givón (ed.), *Grammatical Relations: A Functionalist perspective.* Amsterdam: Benjamins, 323–49.

Ruhland, Rick, Frank Winjnen, and Paul van Geert (1995). An exploration into the application of dynamic systems modelling to language acquisition, in M. Verrips and W. Wijnen (eds), *Amsterdam Series in Child Language Development: Volume 4. Approaches to Parameter Setting.* Amsterdam: University of Amsterdam, Intitute for General Linguistics.

Rumelhart, David and Jay McClelland (1986). *Parallel Distributed Processing.* Cambridge, MA: MIT Press.

Russell, James (2004). *What is Language Development? Rationalist, Empiricist, and Pragmatist Approaches to the Acquisition of Syntax.* Oxford: Oxford University Press.

Saffran, J. R., R. N. Aslin, and E. L. Newport (1996). Statistical learning by 8-month-old infants. *Science* 274, 1926–8.

Safir, Ken (1986). Relative clauses in a theory of binding and levels. *Linguistic Inquiry* 17(4), 663–9.

Sag, Ivan A. (2010). English filler-gap constructions. *Language* 86, 486–545.

Sano, Tetsuyo and Nina Hyams (1994). Agreement, finiteness, and the development of null arguments, in M. Gonzalez (ed.), *Proceedings of NELS 24.* Amherst, MA: Graduate Linguistics Student Association, University of Massachusetts, 543–58.

Sapir, E. (1921). *Language: An Introduction to the Study of Speech.* New York: Harcourt, Brace and Co.

Sapir, E. (1930–1931). *The Southern Paiute Language.* Boston: American Academy of Arts and Sciences.

Sasse, Hans-Jürgen (1987). The thetic/categorical distinction revisited. *Linguistics* 25, 511–80.

Sasse, Hans-Jürgen (2006). Theticity, in G. Bernini and M. L. Schwartz, *Pragmatic Organization of Discourse in the Languages of Europe.* Berlin and New York: Mouton de Gruyter, 255–308.

Saur, D. et al. (2008). Ventral and dorsal pathways for language. *Proceedings of the National Academy of Sciences* 105, 18035–40.

Saussure, Ferdinand de (1916). *Cours de linguistique générale.* Paris: Payot.

Savickienė, Ineta and Wolfgang U. Dressler (eds) (2007). *The Acquisition of Diminutives.* Amsterdam: Benjamins.

Schachter, Paul (1976). The subject in Philippine languages: Topic, actor, actor-topic, or none of the above, in Charles N. Li (ed.), *Subject and Topic.* New York: Academic Press, 491–518.

Schegloff, Emanuel A. (1979). The relevance of repair to syntax-for-conversation, in T. Givón (ed.), *Syntax and Semantics 12: Discourse and syntax.* New York: Academic Press, 261–86.

Schegloff, E. (2007). *Sequence Organization in Interaction: A Primer in Conversation Analysis.* New York: Cambridge University Press.

Schegloff, Emanuel A., Gail Jefferson, and Harvey Sacks (1977). The preference for self-correction in the organization of repair in conversation. *Language* 53, 361–82.

Schlesewsky, M. and I. Bornkessel (2004). On incremental interpretation: Degrees of meaning accessed during sentence comprehension. *Lingua* 114, 1213–34.

Schlesewsky, M. et al. (2000). The subject preference in the processing of locally ambiguous wh-questions in German, in B. Hemforth and L. Konieczny (eds), *German Sentence Processing.* Dordrecht: Kluwer, 65–93.

Schlüter, Julia (2005). *Rhythmic Grammar: The Influence of Rhythm on Grammatical Variation and Change in English* (Topics in English Linguistics 46). Berlin: Mouton de Gruyter.

Schlüter, Julia (2009). The conditional subjunctive, in Günter Rohdenburg and Julia Schlüter (eds), *One Language, Two Grammars?: Differences between British and American English* (Studies in English Language). Cambridge: Cambridge University Press, 277–305.

Schmidtke-Bode, Karsten (2009). *A Typology of Purpose Clauses.* Amsterdam: John Benjamins.

Schreuder, Robert and Harald R. Baayen (1997). How complex simplex words can be. *Journal of Memory and Language* 37, 118–39.

Schriefers, H., A. D. Friederici, and K. Kühn (1995). The processing of locally ambiguous relative clauses in German. *Journal of Memory and Language* 34, 499–520.

Schrott, Angela (ed.) (2005). *Historische Pragmatik und historische Varietätenlinguistik in den romanischen Sprachen.* Göttingen: Universitätsverlag Göttingen.

Schwegler, Armin (1990). *Analyticity and Syntheticity. A Diachronic Perspective with Special Reference to Romance Languages.* Berlin: de Gruyter.

Scott, S. K. and R. J. S. Wise (2004). The functional neuroanatomy of prelexical processing in speech perception. *Cognition* 92, 13–45.

Scott-Phillips, Thomas C. and Simon Kirby (2010). Language evolution in the laboratory. *Trends in Cognitive Sciences* 14: 411–17.

Seiler, Guido (2006). The role of functional factors in language change. An evolutionary approach, in Ole Nedergaard Thomsen (ed.), *Competing Models of Linguistic Change: Evolution and Beyond.* Amsterdam: Benjamins, 163–82.

Seiler, W. (1985). *Imonda, a Papuan language* (Pacific Linguistics, Series B-93). Canberra: The Australian National University.

Seiter, William J. (1980). *Studies in Niuean Syntax.* New York: Garland.

Selting, Margret and Elizabeth Couper-Kuhlen (2000). Argumente für die Entwicklung einer "interaktionalen Linguistik". *Gesprächsforschung—Online-Zeitschrift zur verbalen Interaktion* 1, 76–95.

Selting, Margret, Peter Auer, Dagmar Barth-Weingarten, Jörg Bergmann, Pia Bergmann, Karin Birkner, Elizabeth Couper-Kuhlen, Arnulf Deppermann, Peter Gilles, Susanne Günthner, Martin Hartung, Friederike Kern, Christine Mertzlufft, Christian Meyer, Miriam Morek, Frank Oberzaucher, Jörg Peters, Uta Quasthoff, Wilfried Schütte, Anja Stukenbrock, and Susanne Uhmann (2009). Gesprächsanalytisches Transkriptionssystem (GAT 2). *Gesprächsforschung —Online-Zeitschrift zur verbalen Interaktion* 10, 152–83.

Serratrice, Ludovica (2005). The role of discourse pragmatics in the acquisition of subjects in Italian. *Applied Psycholinguistics* 26, 437–62.

Serratrice, Ludovica and Antonella Sorace (2003). Overt and null subjects in monolingual and bilingual Italian acquisition, in B. Beachley, A. Brown, and F. Conlin (eds), *Proceedings of the 27th Annual Boston University Conference on Language Development*. Somerville, MA: Cascadilla Press, 739–50.

Serratrice, Ludovica, Antonella Sorace, and Sandra Paoli (2004). Crosslinguistic influence at the syntax–pragmatics interface: Subjects and objects in Italian-English bilingual and monolingual acquisition. *Bilingualism: Language and Cognition* 7, 183–205.

Seuren, Pieter A. M. (2009). *Language in Cognition*. Oxford: Oxford University Press.

Seuren, Pieter A. M. and Camiel Hamans (2010). Antifunctionality in language change, in *Folia Linguistica* 44(1), 127–62.

Shannon, Thomas F. (1992). Toward an adequate characterization of relative clause extraposition in modern German, in I. Rauch, G. F. Carr, and R. L. Kyes (eds), *On Germanic Linguistics: Issues and Methods*. Berlin: Mouton de Gruyter, 253–81.

Shimpi, Priya M., Perla B. Gamez, Janellen Huttenlocher, and Marina Vasilyeva (2007). Syntactic priming in 3- and 4-year-old children: Evidence for abstract representations of transitive and dative forms. *Developmental Psychology* 43(6), 1334–46.

Siewierska, Anna (1998). Languages with and without objects. *Languages in Contrast* 1(2), 173–90.

Siewierska, Anna (2004). *Person*. Cambridge: Cambridge University Press.

Siewierska, Anna (2005/2011). Passive Constructions, in Matthew Dryer and Martin Haspelmath (eds), *The World Atlas of Language Structures online*. Munich: Max Planck Digital Library, chapter 107. Available online at <http://wals.info/chapter/107>, accessed January 30, 2014.

Silverstein, Michael (1976). Hierarchy of features and ergativity, in R. M. W. Dixon (ed.), *Grammatical Categories in Australian Languages*. Canberra: Australian Institute of Aboriginal Studies, 112–71.

Simon, H. (1962). The architecture of complexity. *Proceedings of the American Philosophical Society* 106, 467–82.

Simon, Horst J. (1997). Die Diachronie der deutschen Anredepronomina aus der Sicht der Universalienforschung, in *Sprachtypologie und Universalienforschung* 50(3), 267–81.

Simon, Horst J. (2003). *Für eine grammatische Kategorie 'Respekt' im Deutschen. Synchronie, Diachronie und Typologie der deutschen Anredepronomina*. Tübingen: Max Niemeyer.

Skalička, V. (ed.) (1979). *Typologische Studien*. Braunschweig: Vieweg.

Skarabela, Barbora (2007). Signs of early social cognition in children's syntax: The case of joint attention in argument realization in child Inuktitut. *Lingua* 117, 1837–57.

Skarabela, Barbora and Shanley E. M. Allen (2002). The role of joint attention in argument realization in child Inuktitut, in B. Skarabela, S. A. Fish, and A. H.-J. Do (eds), *Proceedings of the 26th Annual Boston University Conference on Language Development*. Somerville, MA: Cascadilla Press, 620–30.

Skarabela, Barbora and Shanley E. M. Allen (2004). The context of non-affixal arguments in child Inuktitut: The role of joint attention, in A. Brugos, L. Micciulla, and C. Smith (eds), *Proceedings of the 28th Annual Boston University Conference on Language Development*. Somerville, MA: Cascadilla Press, 532–42.

Slobin, Dan I. (1966). Grammatical transformations and sentence comprehension in childhood and adulthood. *Journal of Verbal Learning and Verbal Behaviour* 5, 219–27.

Slobin, Dan I. (1973). Cognitive prerequisites for the development of grammar. In C. A. Ferguson and D. I. Slobin (eds), *Studies of Child Language Development*. New York: Holt, Rinehart and Winston.

Slobin, Dan I. (1982). Universal and particular in the acquisition of language. In L. R. Gleitman and E. Wanner, *Language Acquisition: The State of the Art*. Cambridge, UK: Cambridge University Press, 128–70.

Slobin, Dan I. and T. G. Bever (1982). Children use canonical sentence schemas: A crosslinguistic study of word order and inflections. *Cognition* 12(3), 229–65.

Smith, John Maynard and Eörs Szathmáry (1995). *The Major Transitions in Evolution*. Oxford: Oxford University Press.

Smith, K. Aaron (2001). The role of frequency in the specialization of the English anterior, in J. L. Bybee and P. Hopper (ed.), *Frequency and the Emergence of Linguistic Structure*. Amsterdam: John Benjamins, 361–82.

Smoczyńska, M. (1985). The acquisition of Polish, in D. I. Slobin, *The Crosslinguistic Study of Language Acquisition* Volume 1. Hillsdale, NJ: Lawrence Erlbaum Associates, 595–686.

Smolensky, Paul and Geraldine Legendre (2006). *The Harmonic Mind: From Neural Computation to Optimality-Theoretic Grammar*. Cambridge, MA: MIT Press.

Smolík, F. (2011). Comprehension of word order and case marking in Czech: Evidence from comprehension studies and structural priming. Poster presented at the conference Architecture and Mechanisms of Language Processing.

Snyder, William and Karin Stromswold (1997). The structure and acquisition of English dative constructions. *Linguistic Inquiry* 28(2), 281–317.

Sokolov, J. L. (1988). Cue validity in Hebrew sentence comprehension. *Journal of Child Language* 15(1), 129–55.

Song, Jae Jung (2001). *Linguistic Typology: Morphology and Syntax*. Harlow, Essex: Longman.

Sperber, D. and D. Wilson (1981). Irony and the use-mention distinction, in P. Cole (ed.), *Radical Pragmatics*. New York: Academic Press, 295–318.

Spina, Rossella and Wolfgang U. Dressler (2002). Variazione morfologica nella flessione verbale italoromanza, in Roland Bauer and Hans Goebl (eds), *Parallela* 9. Wilhelmsfeld: Egert, 389–408.

Stabler, E. (1994). The finite connectivity of linguistic structure, in C. Clifton, Jr., L. Frazier, and K. Rayner (eds), *Perspectives on Sentence Processing*. Hillsdale: Erlbaum, 303–36.

Stallings, Lynne M. and Maryellen C. MacDonald (2011). It's not just the "heavy NP": Relative phrase length modulates the production of heavy-NP shift. *Journal of Psycholinguistic Research* 40, 177–87.

Stallings, Lynne M., Maryellen C. MacDonald, and Pedraig G. O'Seaghdha (1998). Phrasal ordering constraints in sentence production: Phrase length and verb disposition in heavy-NP shift. *Journal of Memory and Language* 39, 392–417.

Steels, Luc (ed.) (2012a). *Experiments in Cultural Language Evolution*. Amsterdam: Benjamins.

Steels, Luc (2012b). Self-organization and selection in cultural language evolution, in Luc Steels (ed.), *Experiments in Cultural Language Evolution*. Amsterdam: Benjamins, 1–37.

Steels, Luc and Martin Loetzsch (2012). The grounded naming game, in Luc Steels (ed.), *Experiments in Cultural Language Evolution*. Amsterdam: Benjamins, 41–59.

Steels, Luc, R. van Trijp, and P. Wellens (2007). Multi-level selection in the emergence of language systematicity, in F. Almeida e Costa, L. M. Rocha, E. Costa, and I. Harvey (eds), *Proceedings of the Ninth European Conference on Artificial Life, LNAI 4648* Berlin: Springer-Verlag, 425–34.

Stemberger, Joseph (1985). *The Lexicon in a Model of Language Production*. New York: Garland.

Stemberger, Joseph and Brian MacWhinney (1986). Form-oriented inflection errors in language processing. *Cognitive Psychology* 18, 329–54.

Stephany, Ursula and Maria D. Voeikova (eds) (2009). *Development of Nominal Inflection in First Language Acquisition: A Cross-linguistic Perspective*. Berlin: Mouton de Gruyter.

Stolz, T. (2008). Total reduplication vs. echo-word formation in language contact situations, in P. Siemund and N. Kintana (eds), *Language Contact and Contact Languages*. Amsterdam: Benjamins, 107–32.

Strom, C. (1992). *Retuarã Syntax*. Summer Institute of Linguistics and the University of Texas at Arlington.

Stroński, K. (2011). *Synchronic and Diachronic Aspects of Ergativity in Indo-Aryan*. Poznań: Uniwersytet Adama Mickiewicza.

Strunk, Jan (2010). Enriching a treebank to investigate relative clause extraposition in German, in N. Calzolari, K. Choukri, B. Maegaard, J. Mariani, J. Odijk, S. Piperidis, M. Rosner, and D. Tapias (eds), *Proceedings of the Seventh Conference on International Language Resources and Evaluation (LREC'10)*, 19–21 May 2010, Valletta, Malta. Paris: European Language Resources Association, 1911–17.

Strunk, Jan (forthcoming). Relative clause extraposition in German. Ph.D. thesis: University of Cologne, Cologne.

Strunk, Jan and Neal Snider (2013). Subclausal locality constraints on relative clause extraposition, in G. Webelhuth, M. Sailer, and H. Walker (eds), *Rightward Movement in a Comparative Perspective*. Amsterdam: John Benjamins, 99–143.

Svorou, Soteria (1994). *The Grammar of Space*. Amsterdam: John Benjamins.

Swanton, J. (1911). Tlingit, in F. Boas (ed.), *Handbook of American Indian Languages. Volume 1*. Washington: Smithsonian Institution. Bureau of American Ethnology, 159–204.

Szmrecsanyi, Benedikt (2003). *Be going to* versus *will/shall*: Does syntax matter? *Journal of English Linguistics* 31, 295–323.

Szmrecsanyi, Benedikt (2005). Language users as creatures of habit: A corpus-based analysis of persistence in spoken English. *Corpus Linguistics and Linguistic Theory* 1(1), 113–50.

Szmrecsanyi, Benedikt (2009). Typological parameters of intralingual variability: Grammatical analyticity versus syntheticity in varieties of English. *Language Variation and Change* 21(3), 319–53.

Takami, Ken-ichi (1992). *Preposition Stranding: From Syntactic to Functional Analyses*. Berlin and New York: Mouton de Gruyter.

Takami, Ken-ichi (1999). A functional constraint on extraposition from NP, in A. Kamio and K. Takami (eds), *Function and Structure: In Honor of Susumu Kuno*. Amsterdam: John Benjamins, 23–56.

Tamura, Suzuki (2000). *The Ainu language*. Tokyo: Sanseido.

Tang, Sze-Wing (1998). On the "inverted" double object construction, in S. Matthews (ed.), *Studies in Cantonese Linguistics*. Hong Kong: Linguistic Society of Hong Kong, 35–52.

Tannen, D. (1985). *Talking Voices: Repetition, Dialog, and Imagery in Conversational Discourse*. Cambridge: Cambridge University Press.

Telljohann, Heike, Erhard W. Hinrichs, Sandra Kübler, and Heike Zinsmeister (2005). *Stylebook for the Tübingen Treebank of Written German (TüBa-D/Z)*. Tübingen: Seminar für Sprachwissenschaft, Universität Tübingen.

Theakston Anna, L. and Caroline F. Rowland (2009). The acquisition of auxiliary syntax: A longitudinal elicitation study. Part 1: Auxiliary BE. *Journal of Speech Language and Hearing Research* 52(6), 1449–70.

Theakston, A. L., E. V. Lieven, J. M. Pine, and C. F. Rowland (2005). The acquisition of auxiliary syntax: BE and HAVE. *Cognitive Linguistics* 16(1), 247–77.

Thiessen, Erik and Lucy Erickson (2014). Perceptual development and statistical learning, in B. MacWhinney and W. O'Grady (eds), *Handbook of Language Emergence*. New York: Wiley.

Thomas, Enlli M. and Virginia C. M. Gathercole (2007). Children's productive command of grammatical gender and mutation in Welsh: An alternative to rule-based learning. *First Language* 27, 251–78.

Thomason, Sarah G. (2001). *Language Contact. An Introduction*. Washington, DC: Georgetown University Press.

Thomason, Sarah G. and Terrence Kaufmann (1988). *Language Contact, Creolization, and Genetic Linguistics*. Berkeley: University of California Press.

Thompson, Chad L. (1994). Passives and inverse constructions, in T. Givón (ed.), *Voice and Inversion*. Amsterdam and Philadelphia: Benjamins, 47–63.

Thompson, Sandra A. (2002a). "Object complements" and conversation: Towards a realistic account. *Studies in Language* 26(1), 125–64.

Thompson, Sandra A. (2002b). Constructions and conversation. Unpublished MS: UC Santa Barbara.

Thompson, Sandra A. and Anthony Mulac (1991a). A quantitative perspective on the grammaticization of epistemic parentheticals in English, in Elizabeth C. Traugott and Bernd Heine (eds), *Approaches to Grammaticalization* Volume 1 (Typological Studies in Language, 19, 1.) Amsterdam and Philadelphia: Benjamins, 313–29.

Thompson, Sandra A. and Anthony Mulac (1991b). The discourse conditions for the use of the complementizer *that* in conversational English. *Journal of Pragmatics* 13, 237–51.

Thomsen, Ole Nedergaard (ed.) (2006). *Competing Models of Linguistic Change: Evolution and Beyond*. Amsterdam: Benjamins.

Thothathiri, Malathi and Jesse Snedeker (2008). Syntactic priming during language comprehension in three- and four-year-old children. *Journal of Memory and Language*, 58(2), 188–213.

Tiersma, Peter Meijes (1982). Local and general markedness. *Language* 58(4), 832–49.

Tinbergen, N. (1952). "Derived" acitivities. *Quarterly Review of Theoretical Biology* 27, 1–32.

Tomasello, Michael (1992). *First Verbs*. Cambridge: Cambridge University Press.

Tomasello, Michael (ed.) (1998). *The New Psychology of Language: Cognitive and Functional Approaches to Language Structure*, Volume 1. New Jersey: Erlbaum.

Tomasello, Michael (2000). Do young children have adult syntactic competence? *Cognition* 74(3), 209–53.

Tomasello, Michael (2003a). *Constructing a Language: A Usage-based Theory of Language Acquisition*, Cambridge, MA: Harvard University Press.

Tomasello, Michael (ed.) (2003b). *The New Psychology of Language: Cognitive and Functional Approaches to Language Structure*, Volume 2. New Jersey: Erlbaum.

Tomasello, Michael and P. J. Brooks (1998). Young children's earliest transitive and intransitive constructions. *Cognitive Linguistics* 9(4), 379–96.

Tomlin, Russell (1986). *Basic Word Order*. London: Croom Helm.

Tomlin, Russell S. (1995). Focal attention, voice, and word order, in P. Downing and M. Noonan (eds), *Word Order in Discourse*. Amsterdam: John Benjamins, 517–52.

Tomlin, Russell S. (1997). Mapping conceptual representations into linguistic representations: The role of attention in grammar, in J. Nuyts and E. Pederson (eds), *Language and Conceptualization*. Cambridge: Cambridge University Press, 162–89.

Traugott, Elizabeth C. and R. B. Dasher (2005). *Regularity in Semantic Change*. Cambridge: Cambridge University Press.

Trépos, Pierre (1957). *Le pluriel breton*. Brest: Emgleo Breiz.

Trudgill, Peter (1972). Sex, covert prestige, and linguistic change in urban English of Norwich. *Language in Society* 1, 179–96.

Trudgill, Peter (1992). Dialect typology and social structure, in E. H. Jahr (ed.), *Language Contact: Theoretical and Empirical studies*. New York: Mouton de Gruyter, 195–211.

Trueswell, J. C. and M. K. Tanenhaus (1994). Toward a lexicalist framework for constraint-based syntactic-ambiguity resolution, in J. C. Trueswell and M. K. Tanenhaus (eds), *Perspectives in Sentence Processing*. Hillsdale, NJ: Lawrence Erlbaum Associates, 155–79.

Ueno, T. et al. (2011). Lichtheim 2: Synthesizing aphasia and the neural basis of language in a neurocomputational model of the dual dorsal-ventral language pathways. *Neuron* 72, 385–96.

Uhmann, Susanne (1997a). Selbstreparaturen in Alltagsdialogen: Ein Fall für eine integrative Konversationstheorie, in P. Schlobinski (ed.), *Syntax des gesprochenen Deutsch*. Opladen: Westdeutscher Verlag, 157–80.

Uhmann, Susanne (1997b). *Grammatische Regeln und konversationelle Strategien. Fallstudien aus Syntax und Phonologie*. Tübingen: Max Niemeyer.

Uhmann, Susanne (2001). Some arguments for the relevance of syntax to same-sentence self-repair in everyday German conversation, in M. Selting and E. Couper-Kuhlen (eds), *Studies in Interactional Linguistics*. Amsterdam: John Benjamins, 373–404.

Uhmann, Susanne (2006). Grammatik und Interaktion: Form follows function? Function follows form?, in A. Deppermann, T. Spranz-Fogasy, and R. Fiehler (eds), *Grammatik und Interaktion*. Radolfzell: Verlag für Gesprächsforschung, 95–122.

Ungerleider, L. G. and M. Mishkin (1982). Two cortical visual streams, in D. J. Ingle, M. A. Goodale, and R. Mansfield (eds), *Analysis of Visual Behavior*. Cambridge, MA: MIT Press, 549–86.

Urmson, James O. (1952). Parenthetical verbs. *Mind* 61, 480–96.

Uszkoreit, Hans, Thorsten Brants, Denys Duchier, Brigitte Krenn, Lars Konieczny, Stephan Oepen, and Wojciech Skut (1998). Studien zur performanzorientierten Linguistik: Aspekte der Relativsatzextraposition im Deutschen. *Kognitionswissenschaft* 7(3), 129–133.

Valenzuela, Pilar (1997/2003). Basic verb types and argument structures in Shipibo-Conibo. PhD dissertation: University of Oregon.

Valian, Virginia (1991). Syntactic subjects in the early speech of American and Italian children. *Cognition* 40, 21–81.

Valian, Virginia (2009). Innateness and learnability, in E. Bavin (ed.), *The Cambridge Handbook of Child Language*. Cambridge: Cambridge University Press, 15–34.

Valian, Virginia and Zena Eisenberg (1996). The development of syntactic subjects in Portuguese-speaking children. *Journal of Child Language* 23, 103–28.

van Bergen, Geertje (2011). Who's first and what's next? Animacy and word order variation in Dutch language production. Dissertation: Radboud University Nijmegen.

van der Auwera, J. (1985). The predicative relatives of French perception verbs, in A. M. Bolkestein, C. de Groot, and J. L. Mackenzie (eds), *Predicates and Terms in Functional Grammar*. Dordrecht: Foris, 219–34.

van Kemenade, Ans (1987). *Syntactic and Morphological Case in the History of English*. Dordrecht: Foris.

van Tiel, Bob and M. J. A. Lamers (2007). Animacy in verschillende teksttypes. *Bulletin voor Taalwetenschap* 36, 19–38.

Van Valin, Robert D. Jr. (1981a). Grammatical relations in ergative languages. *Studies in Language* 5(3), 361–94.

Van Valin, Robert D. (1981b). Toward understanding grammar: Form, function, evolution (review of T. Givón, On understanding grammar). *Lingua* 54, 47–85.

Van Valin, Robert D. Jr. (2001). *An Introduction to Syntax*. Cambridge: Cambridge University Press.

Van Valin, Robert D. Jr. (2005). *Exploring the Syntax–Semantics Interface*. Cambridge: Cambridge University Press.

Verbeke, S. (2013). *Alignment and Ergativity in New Indo-Aryan Languages*. Berlin and New York: Mouton de Gruyter.

Verbeke, S. and De Cuypere, L. (2009). The rise of ergativity in Hindi: Assessing the role of grammaticalization. *Folia Linguistica Historica* 30, 1–24.

Verhoeven, Elisabeth (2007). *Experiential Constructions in Yucatec Maya: A Typologically Based Analysis of a Functional Domain in a Mayan Language*. Amsterdam: Benjamins.

Voeltz, E. and C. Kilian-Hatz (eds) (2001). *Ideophones*. Amsterdam: Benjamins.

von Frisch, K. (1962). Dialects in the language of the bees. *Scientific American* 207, 78–87.

von Polenz, Peter (1972). *Geschichte der deutschen Sprache*. Berlin: de Gruyter.

Vosberg, Uwe (2006). *Die Große Komplementverschiebung. Außersemantische Einflüsse auf die Variation satzwertiger Ergänzungen im Neuenglischen* (Language in Performance 34). Tübingen: Gunter Narr.

Waelchli, Bernhard (2005). *Co-compounds and Natural Coordination*. Oxford: Oxford University Press.

Walker, Ian and Charles Hulme (1999). Concrete words are easier to recall than abstract words: Evidence for a semantic contribution to short-term serial recall. *Journal of Experimental Psychology: Learning, Memory and Cognition* 25(5), 1256–71.

Wang, L. et al. (2009). Exploring the nature of the "subject"-preference: Evidence from the online comprehension of simple sentences in Mandarin Chinese. *Language and Cognitive Processes* 24, 1180–226.

Ward, Gregory and Betty Birner (1996). On the discourse function of rightward movement in English, in Adele Goldberg (ed.), *Conceptual Structure, Discourse and Language*, Volume 1. Stanford: CSLI Publications, 463–79.

Wason, Peter C. (1961). Response to affirmative and negative binary statements. *British Journal of Psychology* 52, 133–42.

Wasow, Thomas (2002). *Postverbal Behavior*. Stanford: CSLI Publications.

Wasow, Thomas and Jennifer Arnold (2003). Post-verbal constituent ordering in English, in G. Rohdenburg and B. Mondorf (eds), *Determinants of Grammatical Variation English*. The Hague: Mouton, 119–54.

Wasow, Thomas, T. Florian Jaeger, and David Orr (2011). Lexical variation in relativizer frequency, in H. J. Simon and H. Wiese (eds), *Expecting the Unexpected: Exceptions in Grammar*. Berlin: de Gruyter Mouton, 175–95.

Watters, John (2000). Syntax, in B. Heine and D. Nurse (eds), *African Languages*. Cambridge: Cambridge University Press, 194–230.

Weckerly, J. and M. Kutas (1999). An electrophysiological analysis of animacy effects in the processing of object relative sentences. *Psychophysiology* 36, 559–70.

Wedel, Andrew (2002). Self-organization and categorical behavior in phonology. *Berkeley Linguistics Society* 29, 611–22.

Wedel, Andrew (2006). Exemplar models, evolution and language change. *Linguistic Review* 23, 247–74.

Wedel, Andrew (2009). Resolving pattern conflict: Variation and selection in phonology and morphology, in James P. Blevins and Juliette Blevins (eds), *Analogy in Grammar: Form and Acquisition*. Oxford: Oxford University Press.

Wegener, Heide (2002). Aufbau von markierten Pluralklassen im Deutschen—eine Herausforderung für die Markiertheitstheorie. *Folia Linguistica* 36, 261–95.

Weinreich, Uriel, William Labov, and Marvin Herzog (1968). Empirical foundations for a theory of language change, in Winfried P. Lehmann and Yakov Malkiel (eds), *Directions for Historical Linguistics*. Austin: University of Texas Press, 95–188.

Weiss, Sabine and Peter Rappelsberger (1996). EEG coherence within the 13–18 Hz band as a correlate of a distinct lexical organisation of concrete and abstract nouns in humans. *Neuroscience Letters* 209, 17–20.

Weissenborn, Jürgen, and Barbara Höhle (eds) (2000). *Approaches to Bootstrapping: Phonological, Lexical, Syntactic and Neurophysiological Aspects of Early Language Acquisition*. Amsterdam: Benjamins.

Weist, R. M. (1983). The word order myth. *Journal of Child Language* 10(1), 97–106.

Welmers, W. E. (1969). The morphology of Kpelle nominals. *Journal of African Languages* 8, 73–101.

Welmers, W. (1973). *African Language Structures*. Berkeley: University of California Press.

Wessinger, C. Mark, Michael H. Buonocore, Clif L. Kussmaul, and George R. Mangun (1997). Tonotopy in human auditory cortex examined with functional magnetic resonance imaging. *Human Brain Mapping* 5, 18–25.

Wexler, Kenneth (1998). Very early parameter setting and the Unique Checking Constraint: A new explanation of the optional infinitive stage. *Lingua* 106, 23–79.

Wichmann, Anne (2001). Spoken parentheticals, in Karin Aijmer (ed.), *A Wealth of English: Studies in Honour of Goran Kjellmer*. Gothenburg: Gothenburg University Press, 171–93.

Wichmann, Anne (2004). The intonation of *please*-requests: A corpus-based study. *Journal of Pragmatics* 36(9), 1521–49.

Wiechmann, D. and A. Lohmann (2012). Domain minimization and beyond: Modeling PP ordering., *Language Variation and Change* 25, 65–88.

Wilson, E. O. (1975). *Sociobiology: The Abridged Edition*. Harvard: Belknap Press.

Winter, Werner (ed.) (1984). *Anredeverhalten*. Tübingen: Narr.

Wittek, A. and M. Tomasello (2005). German-speaking children's productivity with syntactic constructions and case morphology: Local cues act locally. *First Language* 25(1), 103–25.

Wittenberg, G., M. Sullivan, and J. Tsien (2002). Synaptic reentry reinforcement based network model for long-term memory consolidation. *Hippocampus* 12, 637–47.

Wolff, E. (1992). *Referenzgrammatik des Hausa*. München/Hamburg: Lit Verlag.

Wray, A. (2002). *Formulaic Language and the Lexicon*. Cambridge: Cambridge University Press.

Wurzel, Wolfgang U. (1984). *Flexionsmorphologie und Natürlichkeit*. Berlin: Akademie-Verlag [translated 1989. *Inflectional Morphology and Naturalness*. Dordrecht: Kluwer].

Wurzel, Wolfgang U. (1987). System-dependent morphological naturalness in inflection, in Wolfgang U. Dressler (ed.), *Leitmotifs in Natural Morphology*. Amsterdam: Benjamins, 59–96.

Wurzel, Wolfgang U. (1996). Morphologischer Strukturwandel: Typologische Entwicklungen im Deutschen, in Ewald Lang and Gisela Zifonun (eds), *Deutsch—typologisch. IDS Jahrbuch 1995*. Berlin: de Gruyter, 492–524.

Xanthos, Aris, Sabine Laaha, Steven Gillis, Ursula Stephany, Ayhan Aksu-Koç, Anastasia Christofidou, Natalia Gagarina, Gordana Hrzica, Nihan Ketrez, Marianne Kilani-Schoch, Katharina Korecky-Kröll, Melita Kovačević, Klaus Laalo, Marijan Palmović, Barbara Pfeiler, Maria D. Voeikova, and Wolfgang U. Dressler (2011). On the role of morphological richness in the early development of noun and verb inflection. *First Language* 31, 461–79.

Xrakovskij, Viktor S. (ed.) (2001). *Typology of Imperative Constructions*. Munich: Lincom.

Yokoyama, S. et al. (2006). Cortical activation in the processing of passive sentences in L1 and L2: an fMRI study. *Neuroimage* 30, 570–9.

Yokoyama, S. et al. (2007). Is Broca's area involved in the processing of passive sentences? An event-related fMRI study. *Neuropsychologia* 45, 989–96.

Zaenen, Annie (1993). Unaccusativity in Dutch: Integrating syntax and lexical semantics, in J. Pustejovski (ed.), *Semantics and the Lexicon*. Dordrecht: Kluwer, 129–61.

Zimmermann, Thomas Ede. (2000). Free choice disjunction and epistemic possibility. *Natural Language Semantics* 8, 255–90.

Zipf, George (1935). *The Psychobiology of Language. An Introduction to Dynamic Philology*. Cambridge, MA: MIT Press.

Zipf, George Kingsley (1949). *Human Behavior and the Principle of Least Effort*. Cambridge, MA: Addison-Wesley.

Ziv, Yael (1973). Why can't appositives be extraposed? *Research on Language and Social Interaction* 6(1), 243–54.

Ziv, Yael (1985). Parentheticals and Functional Grammar, in A. Machtelt Bolkestein et al. (eds), *Syntax and Pragmatics in Functional Grammar*. Dordrecht: Foris, 181–99.

Ziv, Yael and Peter Cole (1974). Relative extraposition and the scope of definite descriptions in Hebrew and English, in M. W. La Galy, R. A. Fox, and A. Bruck (eds), *Papers from the Tenth Regional Meeting of the Chicago Linguistic Society*, 19–21 April 1974, Chicago. Chicago: Chicago Linguistic Society, 772–86.

Zou, Kelly H., A. James O'Malley, and Laura Mauri (2007). Receiver-operating characteristic analysis for evaluating diagnostic tests and predictive models. *Circulation* 115, 654–7.

Zydorowicz, Paulina (2009). English and Polish morphonotactics in first language acquisition. PhD thesis: Adam Mickiewicz University Poznan.

Index